WORLD RELIGIONS

WESTERN TRADITIONS

EDITED BY
WILLARD G. OXTOBY

OXFORD UNIVERSITY PRESS
TORONTO NEW YORK OXFORD

Oxford University Press
70 Wynford Drive, Don Mills, Ontario M3C 1J9

Oxford New York
Athens Auckland Bangkok Bombay
Calcutta Cape Town Dar es Salaam Delhi
Florence Hong Kong Istanbul Karachi
Kuala Lumpur Madras Madrid Melbourne
Mexico City Nairobi Paris Singapore
Taipei Tokyo Toronto

and associated companies in
Berlin Ibadan

The acknowledgements on pp. 559–61 are a continuation of the copyright page

Canadian Cataloguing in Publication Data

Main entry under title:

World religions: western traditions

Includes bibliographical references and index.
ISBN 0-19-540751-2

1. Religions. I. Oxtoby, Willard G. (Willard
Gurdon), 1933– .

BL80.2.W672 1996 291 C95-933182-4

Editor: Valerie Ahwee

Designer: Brett Miller

Maps: Visutronx

5 6 — 00 99 98

This book is printed on permanent (acid-free) paper ∞

Printed in Canada

Contents

	List of Photographs	iv
	List of Figures	v
	A Personal Invitation	1
Chapter One	The Jewish Tradition Alan F. Segal	12
Chapter Two	The Zoroastrian Tradition Willard G. Oxtoby	152
Chapter Three	The Christian Tradition Willard G. Oxtoby	198
Chapter Four	The Islamic Tradition Mahmoud M. Ayoub	352
Chapter Five	Rivals, Survivals, Revivals Willard G. Oxtoby	492
Chapter Six	Traditions in Contact Willard G. Oxtoby	530
Appendix	Islamic Terms and Names From Arabic	557
	Acknowledgements	559
	Index	562

List of Photographs

A young boy at his Bar Mitzvah 14
Torah scrolls 71
An Ethiopian immigrant to Israel puts on the *tefillin* 83
A Yemenite rabbi 103
An Israeli soldier learns how to put on the *tefillin* 106
Interior of a Dublin synagogue 111
A spring harvest ritual in an Israeli *kibbutz* 112
Table setting for the Passover *seder* 116
A Passover meal 117
A *mohel* performs a circumcision 118
Ḥaredim pray at the Western Wall 142
Wedding in a Spanish-Portuguese synagogue 144
Shelters at the shrine of Pir-e Sabz 187
The Church of the Holy Sepulchre 227
Interior of St Paul's cathedral 228
Mosaic map of Jerusalem 241
Ukrainian Catholic church 245
St Peter's 248
Westminster Abbey 258
York Minister's Great East Window 260
Nave of Wells cathedral 261
York Minster 262
Canterbury 265
Dome of the Rock 393
Taj Mahal 445
Qairiwiyin Mosque 446
Muslims assemble for prayer 447
The Great Mosque 448
Glazed tiles on the Dome of the Rock 449
The Quṭb Minār 462
Entrance to the Great Mosque 463
Indian cliff dwellings of Mesa Verde 512
Totem poles 515

List of Figures

	Inside front cover: Religions of the World	
	Inside back cover: Time Line of Major Western Traditions	
1.1	Expulsion and Migration of Jews from European Cities and Regions, Eleventh to Fifteenth Centuries CE	94
2.1	Zoroastrianism: Major Spheres of Influence	171
3.1	Christianity: Major Spheres of Influence	284
4.1	Language and Culture in the Spread of Islam	450
5.1	Native Culture Groups and Missionary Activity in North America	516

A PERSONAL INVITATION

WILLARD G. OXTOBY

Once upon a time, many in the West regarded religion as a kind of cultural fossil. Aesthetically rich, anthropologically intriguing? Yes. But relevant to today's hard-nosed world of business and politics? Hardly at all. When I said that I studied religion, I used to be asked why I was wasting my life on something that had so little to do with where today's action is.

But nobody has asked me that question since 1979. In that year, the Shah of Iran was deposed in an Islamic revolution. A nation of 40 million people was apparently ready to make phenomenal sacrifices, putting people's lives and livelihoods on the line, to defend the values voiced by their religious leaders. Such values seemed utterly alien to those of development economists and politico-military strategists in the West. And not only in Iran but elsewhere, Muslims were saying no to the modern West. In increasing numbers, men from Algeria to Zanzibar started to wear turbans and grow beards, and more Muslim women on several continents began to wear head scarves.

To understand the modern world, we now realize, we need to take into account the meanings that its traditional religions have for their adherents.

Another breathtaking year was 1989, when the communist order of eastern Europe and the Soviet Union began to crumble. That year there were high hopes for democracy, peace, and progress. But experience soon showed that when the restraints of the socialist order were loosened, old passions and identities resurfaced—passions that one might have expected to die out. Feuds and divisions of populations in the Balkans, the Caucasus, and Central Asia erupted into bitter conflict. As often as not, these struggles had old religio-ethnic roots.

In the secular intellectual climate of the modern world, some philosophers and even theologians have asserted that God is dead. In the practical ethno-political climate of the modern world, however, religion is very much alive.

THE INVITATION

We invite you to share our fascination with religion. We do not see our mandate as making you either more religious or less religious. Rather, we want you to be better informed *about* religion—regardless of your own investment in any of its particular forms.

Evaluations of religion range all the way from enthusiastic praise to bitter condemnation. Religion has been considered by some as the loftiest, most profound expression of the human spirit. By others, it has been termed a blight on civilization, responsible for superstition, ignorance, hatred, repression, even genocide. There is a selection of evidence to support either extreme, since the history of religion displays a mix of spectacular success and abject failure.

Many who support a positive view of religion regard all or most of the religious traditions as having more or less equal value. Religions promote ideas of order and purpose in the universe, and motivations for order and benevolence in society. Some who hold a largely positive view of religion would go further and assert that the religious traditions are actually saying the same essential thing. If you find such a view tempting, we invite you to become more fully informed about the actual detail of the world's religious traditions, in their diversity and variety, so that you can advocate your position in a sophisticated rather than a naïve fashion.

Many in the modern world are disinclined to identify with any traditional religion. Some do so because they regard their own attitudes towards purpose and value in the universe as a private matter; they find no circle or group congenial for the expression of such an outlook in ritualized and traditional form. Others are appalled at the actions of human societies that consider themselves religious while perpetuating misery, plundering and butchering in the name of God.

The positive and the negative assessments of religion we have just sketched are both characteristically modern. Both types have come to the fore in Western civilization in the last 300 years. Both types take humanity as the common denominator of the various religions—as a measure of their achievement and sometimes also as an explanation of their nature and function.

But prior to the modern era, another kind of view was dominant in the West: one that differentiated between the positive and the negative in religion by distinguishing between one's own and others'. People over the centuries have seen their own way as truth and others' as error. A powerful influence of that type of view continues today, especially among religiously committed people. For very many, some aspects of religion, namely the faith and practice commanded by one's own tradition, are desirable, while the faith and practice of others is at best a waste of time and possibly downright damaging.

Comparisons are odious, we are told, and comparison of religions may be among the more odious of activities. Yet it is an irresistible human impulse to compare. Are there any guidelines?

One thing our observations may bear out is that evaluations of religions need to have a uniform standard. Achievements should be compared with achievements, and ideals compared with ideals. Religion's critics have concentrated on its poor achievement record. Its enthusiasts have often seen only its ideals. Apologists for particular religions have often praised their own tradition's ideals while denouncing others' poor achievement.

We tend to notice what we were looking for in the first place. Those who seek contentiousness in religion will find it in ample measure; and those who seek generosity of spirit may well for their part be pleasantly surprised at how much of it can be seen.

Insider and Outsider

One of the abiding issues in the academic study of religion is the conscious role of the observer. Being 'objective' is a value we are taught early in schools. Theorists today tell us, though, that objectivity as a goal is in principle impossible. Some even say that there is no such thing as objective truth; there are only people's status-related and class-determined interests.

We should recognize that every attempt at a historical account is a selection of material, and in that sense is an interpretation. Even if it were theoretically possible to describe something 'objectively', the choice to describe that thing and not something else can hardly be justified as objective.

The study of religion wrestles perpetually with the contrast of 'insider' and 'outsider' perspectives.

The religious participant can presumably speak from first-hand experience. One of the most famous formulations of a view of this type was stated by the German theologian and philosopher of religion Rudolf Otto, in the opening of his 1917 book known in English as *The Idea of the Holy*:

> The reader is invited to direct his mind to a moment of deeply-felt religious experience, as little as possible qualified by other forms of consciousness. Whoever cannot do this, whoever knows no such moments in his experience, is requested to read no farther; for it is not easy to discuss questions of religious psychology with one who can recollect the emotions of his adolescence, the discomforts of indigestion, or, say, social feelings, but cannot recall any intrinsically religious feelings (Otto 1923:8).

For more than two generations since Otto wrote those words, the argument has often been made that there is no substitute in religion for the faith of the adherent. Often, however, the discussion has confused information and analysis. Testimony is one thing, and cross-examination is another. A participant may, but also may not, be able to identify the assumptions on which a tradition rests, or the major transitions it has undergone. A participant may, but also may not, be able to describe fairly a variety of interpretations of the tradition offered by different sectors of the community.

At an opposite pole from Otto is the view that the only hope for scholarly credibility is to be found in the outsider's 'objective' detachment from religion and its claims. Stated in the extreme, one has lost that credibility if one even says a kind word about religion. Indeed, among scholars of religion are quite a few who have become profoundly alienated from the faith communities in which they were raised. And in the study of the major traditions of Asia, many significant findings have been achieved by outsiders—Westerners—some of whose pioneer figures did not even set foot in the lands about which they wrote. An outsider may not, but also may, have something important and useful to say about a religious tradition.

The insider-outsider question can be framed in terms of individual scholars' and students' attitudes, but we can also situate it in the context of institutional accountability. In the Middle Ages, theology was the 'queen of the sciences' in European universities, many of which had Christian church connections. In eighteenth- and nineteenth-century North America, a link with some ecclesiastical body continued to be characteristic of many colleges and universities.

The secularization of older institutions and the founding of new secular ones has meant an emerging distinction throughout the Western world between religiously sponsored and secularly sponsored efforts. Often what religious groups support in the study of their own traditions is now referred to as 'theological' activity, and the work of publicly funded institutions is termed 'scientific' study. But, in fact, there is a considerable overlap of scholarly findings among persons working in these two types of institutions, and scholars have worked in both types, sometimes simultaneously.

As a result, 'religious' versus 'secular' study of religion is a distinction that is much easier to draw when one compares institutions and their support than it is when one considers what individual authorities have to say. Many of us, particularly in historical studies, have become semispectators on our own traditions at the same time as we continue to identify with and participate in them. The contact of religions and the comparison of religions has resulted in our adopting a perspective of disciplined description—science?—towards our own tradition that is like what we use to handle others'. At the same time, we have come to extend towards the traditions of others some of the sympathy or empathy—theology?—that religiously committed people have classically claimed for their own.

In this text, our authors speak in some sense for their identities. Alan Segal is Jewish, Mahmoud Ayoub is Muslim, and I am Christian. The closest I can come to 'representing' Zoroastrianism is to have been made an honorary member of the Zoroastrian Society of Ontario. Some of the Mediterranean and Middle Eastern traditions we mention have no living adherents remaining to speak for them. But we hope that in all our descriptions we have been able to walk the tightrope of disciplined empathy without falling into the abyss—of advocacy on the one side, and of debunking on the other.

East and West

If one is to separate an Eastern group of religious traditions from a Western one, where and how does one draw the line? Borderlines, arbitrary or otherwise, produce borderline cases. To use the pigeonholes we create, we have to cut some birds in half.

Our list puts Islam with Christianity and Judaism as a 'Western' religion. The Hindu, Jain, Buddhist, Chinese, and Japanese traditions, by contrast, make up the 'Eastern' roster. This leaves the Sikhs (whom we treat in the Eastern volume) and the Zoroastrians (discussed in the Western) very appropriately perched as fence-sitters along our provisional cultural boundary.

As a concept, 'the East' makes sense at least to Europeans. Well into the twentieth century, the East was everything to the east of Europe. The Orient began where the Orient Express ran: Istanbul. For some purposes, it even included North Africa and began at Morocco.

A century ago, Islam was thought to be an Eastern religion, and Westerners who studied it were called orientalists. To us today, calling Islam Eastern seems misleading if not absurd. Islam shares its historical and theological roots with Judaism and Christianity, and developed virtually all its classic structures in the Mediterranean and Persian-speaking world. Scholars today regard Islam a religion of the West, even though the numerical majority of Muslims today live east of that world: in the Indian subcontinent, Malaysia, and Indonesia. When it comes to these lands, the boundary between East and West is blurred at best.

Some have contended that the Western religions are united by the notion of prophetic and scriptural revelation from their one God, while the Eastern religions share a focus on the achievement of reflective human insight by a wise teacher or sage.

Prophecy is a kind of religious communication where someone claims (or is claimed) to transmit a message from a divine source. The message is the word of God, whether dictated verbatim by the deity or formulated in language by the human prophet. The prophet proclaims, 'thus says the Lord'. This characterizes much of the most important insight in the religious traditions that have prevailed in our Western group.

Meanwhile, in the case of wisdom, insight is achieved by an individual through his or her own reflection. What is apprehended may be presented as an eternal or cosmic divine truth, but the sage's testimony is, 'I have meditated and reflected, and this insight has come to me.'

Such a classification has been used by a landmark work in the field. The Oxford scholar R.C. Zaehner (1913–74) employed it in 1959 when editing *The Concise Encyclopedia of Living Faiths*—actually not an alphabetically arranged reference work, as its title would suggest, but an advanced introductory survey. His two major divisions within the volume were 'Prophecy' and 'Wisdom'.

There are enough grains of truth in the prophecy-wisdom contrast to make it a useful topic for comparison and review *after* one has studied the individual traditions in the specific detail of their development and teachings, but it can be misleading if adopted beforehand and allowed to structure one's observations. For there are wisdom traditions in the West mixed in with the prophetic ones, and there are notions of revelation and scriptural authority here and there in the East.

We can speak in a fairly coherent fashion about the West and its role in the world. Since the end of the fifteenth century, European (subsequently Euro-American) civilization has achieved world dominance. This civilization's science and technology have spread worldwide, as have its political and philosophical traditions. Its dominant religion, Christianity, has been carried to the 'four corners' of the globe. And with Christianity's influence have gone particular notions of what 'religion' is in relation to other spheres of life such as the 'secular', notions not necessarily shared by the indigenous cultures of those lands.

But the East, for its part, is a hugely diverse region, with an inventory of cultural differences between southern and eastern Asia that could fill volumes. At the level of daily custom is the fact, for instance, that a billion people in China take their baths in the evening, while nearly a billion in India bathe in the morning. Or again, Japanese are Buddhists, but the Buddha as a historical individual who lived and taught in an Indian environment figures surprisingly little in their understanding and practice of Buddhism.

Does any common thread unify the East? We could even go so far as to suggest that 'the East' is a Western construct, existing as a coherent entity only in the mind of the West. The ancient Chinese, for instance, termed theirs the 'Middle' kingdom, not the Eastern one. In that, they were not unlike Westerners, who named a sea Mediterranean to imply that it was at the middle of their world.

For identifying the Eastern religions as a cohesive family, history and geography offer us a more useful foundation than do contrasts of outlook with the West. Buddhism is probably our best candidate for a common thread, in the following fashion. In India, the aggregate indigenous heritage, which we in modern times term Hinduism, was the milieu in which Buddhism arose and with which Buddhism shares some (but by no means all) of its own outlooks and practices. Carried then to East Asia, Buddhism interacted with the indigenous traditions there, which we identify in China as Confucianism and Taoism and in Japan as Shinto. With this perspective, a historical case can be made for seeing the principal Eastern religious traditions as a coherent package.

If we think that any contrast between East and West is overdrawn, we can point to challenges in life that human beings face worldwide. People sometimes quote the 1889 'Ballad of East and West' by Rudyard Kipling (1865–1936) to assert, or to excuse, Westerners' failure to understand Asia:

> Oh, East is East, and West is West,
>   and never the twain shall meet
> Till Earth and Sky stand presently
>   at God's great Judgment Seat.

But taking these lines out of context can reverse what Kipling had in mind. For Kipling continues:

> But there is neither East nor West,
>   border, nor breed, nor birth,
> When two strong men stand face to face,
>   tho' they come from the ends of the earth!
>   (Kipling 1892:75)

If Kipling were active today, he would doubtless call for a human common denominator in cross-cultural understanding. What distant traditions express in exotic vocabularies is often a universal appeal to human experience.

Some Practical Details

Frustration sets in when we encounter words and names in strange languages, as the biblical story of the Tower of Babel suggests. The rich fund of information about religions is expressed in texts and traditions in more languages than the average person can list, let alone speak. Translation equivalents can be chosen for some ideas, but one must soon deal with exotic names, as well as with key terms whose meanings are inevitably distorted in translation. Our authors have not shied away from presenting these.

Terms and names not written in our Latin alphabet have to be transliterated. Some writers in English avoid technical transliteration, either to ease the burden of effort for the reader or the burden of typesetting for the publisher.

Some books compromise by burying diacritical marks in indexes, glossaries, and notes, leaving them out of the main text. Non-technical spellings may offer an initial advantage, but they can hinder the reader wanting to move on to a more advanced level. We have therefore chosen to use standard transliterations throughout the text to help the reader become accustomed to their use.

There have been changes in fashion regarding which transliteration system to use, and there will doubtless continue to be changes. We can take as a current benchmark, however, the usage in the sixteen-volume *Encyclopedia of Religion* (Eliade 1987), one of the principal reference resources to which the reader may be inclined to turn. For the languages that are the principal sources of world religions terminology—Arabic, Sanskrit, Chinese, and Japanese—we use the same transliteration systems as the *Encyclopedia of Religion*.

Like the *Encyclopedia*, we have had to take sides on what is the most divisive current transliteration question affecting our material. It regards Chinese in particular. It is the choice between an earlier twentieth-century translation system, known after its originators as the Wade-Giles system, and another, introduced since mid-century, known as Pinyin. Pages illustrating the operation of each of these appear in the appendix to the other volume in this series.

With respect to the Jewish tradition, we have been less scrupulous. This is because Jewish writing in English reflects a variety of usages. These differ partly because of the source languages involved—Hebrew, Aramaic, Yiddish, or other—but also because a variety of non-technical renderings have become popularly established in English. Some authors writing in English render Hebrew with the sounds of the Ashkenazic pronunciation of central and eastern European Jewry, while others approximate the Sephardic pronunciation of Mediterranean Jews. Nor have biblical scholars, with strict but in some cases cumbersome proposals for transliterating biblical Hebrew, achieved full agreement in their own usage.

The Persian language, like English, has evolved through time and through the influence of language contact. For its pre-Islamic forms found in Zoroastrianism, we seek to simplify scholars' reconstructions while remaining faithful to their insights. For Farsi, the language of Islamic Iran, we attempt to follow the pronunciation of the language in preference to the script. Spoken Persian has the vowels *a–e–i–o–u*; but the Arabic system, in which Persian is written, strait-jackets the vowels into the *a–i–u* classes of standard Arabic. The poet who produced Iran's great national epic, for example, may be Firdausī to Arabists, but we give him his Persian pronunciation of Ferdowsī.

The reader will find diacritics on foreign terms, which are given as words in lower-case italics. Premodern foreign personal names and a few place names bear diacritics; since they are proper names, they are not italicized, nor are the proper names for holidays. If something is both italicized and capitalized, it is generally the title of a book.

Capitalization poses some problems in its own right. Remember that the distinction between capital and lower-case letters inheres in our alphabet, and not in the scripts of Arabic, Sanskrit, Chinese, or Japanese. Context in these languages may tell you whether something is a word or a name, but not necessarily and not always. Therefore, capitalization is a signal sent by the writer or editor in English, not by the material in a source language.

Italics (or their equivalent, underlining, if one is writing by hand or on equipment where italics are unavailable) make possible a conventional distinction, but one that in this work we have tried to dodge. That is the discrimination, long established in English usage, between scripture and other books. One uses italics, for instance, to give ordinary book titles, for instance, Homer's *Iliad*—but not the Bible nor, conventionally, any part of the Bible. Given this convention, to name a text in English is to be involved in every instance in a forced decision as to whether it is or is not scripture.

Confident that the scripture-versus-other-literature distinction could easily be generalized to the religious literatures of Asia, earlier writers in English have applied it wholesale. Do not the major Asian traditions themselves distinguish between more authoritative and less authoritative texts, between older works and later commentaries on them? Yes and no; the idea of a strictly limited canon hardly works for Taoism, for instance, and Shinto's narratives of Japanese origins are not agreed on as 'scripture' by everybody. And how helpful is it to decide that the Hindu Vedas are canonical, and therefore in roman type, while the *Bhagavad Gītā* is less so, and therefore to be written in italics? Hence, to avoid the arbitrariness of dividing the world's religious literature somewhere down the middle, we have elected to italicize the name of practically every scriptural text simply as a book, rather than privileging with roman type certain texts, including even the *Qur'ān* and individual biblical books.

We do not use the abbreviations BC and AD with calendar dates, however acceptable these may remain in fields outside religion. The expressions BC ('before Christ') and AD (Latin *anno Domini*, 'in the year of our Lord') are taken by some to imply special status and privilege for Christianity. Instead, writers on religion often use BCE and CE (referring to the 'common', not the 'Christian', era). The theological division of history around the birth of Jesus, it can be argued, is a move that belongs to the participant mode of religious discourse and not the mode of the observer.

Likewise problematical but less conventionalized is the handling of religious traditions' revelational, mythological, and hagiographical narratives. Christians assert that Jesus achieved miraculous things, and Buddhists report Śākyamuni's accomplishments—in both cases as historical events, in the past tense. Does the observer 'bracket' every faith-narrative with an expression like 'according to tradition' or 'some Hindus hold'? Scrupulous following of the observer's stance in this fashion can become both cumbersome and intrusive.

The solution we have tried to apply consistently is to use the present tense for reporting all faith-narratives. It is a convention often practised in describing the plot lines of imaginative literature; it is also commonly employed by philosophers to write about the views of particular authors and the structure of their arguments. In both cases, the present tense permits one to enter into the content and spirit of what is being reported without being so immediately distracted by questions of its historical verifiability. Our editorial experience is that present-tense usage renders traditional narratives vivid, and accessible simultaneously in the participant mode and the observer mode. We retain the past tense, on the other hand, to describe the changes over time within a tradition that any historian would describe as developments.

Of many other things, large and small, we could speak editorially, but more words of welcome will only delay the use of this book to which all are now invited. As we start, it remains only to render thanks—to the spiritual powers and devoted followers we are to meet, and also to the numerous colleagues and students whose responses and reactions have assisted in this work's preparation.

W.G.O.

Thanksgiving, 1995

REFERENCES

Eliade, M., ed. 1987. *The Encyclopedia of Religion*, 16 vols. New York: Macmillan.

Kipling, R. 1889. 'The Ballad of East and West'. In *Barrack-Room Ballads and Other Verses*, 75–83. London: Methuen.

Otto, R. 1923. *The Idea of the Holy*. London: Oxford University Press.

Key Dates

c. 1280 BCE	Moses leads the Exodus from Egypt
c. 1000 BCE	David takes Jerusalem, makes it his capital
922 BCE	Northern kingdom separates upon Solomon's death
722 BCE	Assyrians conquer northern kingdom, disperse its people
621 BCE	Josiah's reforms based on *Deuteronomy*
586 BCE	Babylonians conquer Jerusalem, deport its leaders
538 BCE	Persians conquer Babylon, permitting exiles' return
164 BCE	Rededication of temple after Maccabean uprising
70 CE	Roman siege of Jerusalem, destruction of temple
c. 200	The *Mishnah* of Rabbi Judah ha-Nasi
c. 500	Completion of the *Babylonian Talmud*
d. 942	Saadia, *gaon* in Babylonia
d. 1105	Rashi, commentator on Bible and *Talmud*
d. 1204	Moses Maimonides (*Guide for the Perplexed*)
d. 1305	Moses of León (*Zohar*)
1492	Expulsion of Jews from Spain
1520–3	Printed edition of the *Talmud* produced in Venice
1666	Sabbatai Zvi is promoted as the messiah
d. c. 1760	Israel ben Eliezer, the Baal Shem, in Poland
d. 1786	Moses Mendelssohn, pioneer of Reform in Germany
1881	Severe *pogrom* in Russia spurs Jewish emigration
1889	Conservative Judaism separates from Reform in the United States
1897	Theodor Herzl and the first Zionist Congress
1938	German synagogues vandalized, prelude to the Holocaust
1948	Israeli statehood

CHAPTER ONE

THE JEWISH TRADITION

ALAN F. SEGAL

Judaism is quintessentially a historical religion. It understands itself as founded by a divine revelation at Mount Sinai more than 3,200 years ago, given to the people Israel under the guidance of Moses. It sees the desires and demands of God in the events of history. The continuing moral and ritual obligations are expressed as a covenant, or agreement, with God, sealed at Mount Sinai.

A Ritual Initiation

One can see these obligations reaffirmed every Saturday, as thirteen-year-old Jewish children come of age in the Bar Mitzvah ceremony. Indeed, remarking on details of the Bar Mitzvah, we can sample some features of what Jews regard as significant in their tradition in general.

The Bar Mitzvah occurs as part of a congregation's weekly worship. Saturday for Jews is the day of rest, called the Sabbath. It is a day for prayer and public assembly in the synagogue, the Jewish house of worship and community meeting. In the Bar Mitzvah (Aramaic for 'son of the commandments') or Bat Mitzvah ('daughter of the commandments') ceremony, the teenager reads from a scroll of one of the five books of Moses, the first section of the Bible for Jews and also Christians, as well as an appropriate reading from the *Prophets*, a subsequent section of the Bible.

Marking the onset of adulthood at thirteen is based on an ancient concept of legal majority. The ceremony does not signify that the child has reached modern adult status; driving, voting, and independent financial decisions are for later. But it does publicly mark that the child has arrived at ritual and moral responsibility. His or her presence may be counted towards the *minyan*, the quorum of ten necessary to begin group prayer. The young person may be called to recite blessings over the readings from the *Law* and *Prophets*. Some congregations have

At his Bar Mitzvah, a thirteen-year-old boy wears the tallith *(a prayer shawl), and reads from the Torah scroll in the synagogue.*
(Michael Rumack)

young males wear a *tallith* prayer shawl for the first time, although other congregations postpone that honour until marriage.

For the first time, the child publicly reads from the scripture. Jews are expected to read and study their religious tradition over their entire lifetimes. In Jewish parlance, all the religious books, the Bible and its commentaries, are called Torah (i.e., religious law) and are viewed as the ultimate repository of religious truth. The celebrant of the Bar Mitzvah normally chants from the Torah scroll, having learned the traditional melodies and the special skills necessary to read the ancient calligraphy.

The child recites special blessings, which signal the rationale of the event. In them, one can see the community's values. First the community responds to the celebrant's blessings, reaffirming them. The celebrant then gives thanks for the scripture of *Law* and *Prophets*, which has served as a guide for the people Israel. Then Jerusalem and the dynasty of David are mentioned. Finally, the Sabbath itself is extolled for the beauty and quietude it brings. In the benediction the congregation notes that the only way in which Jews are different from anyone else is that they have been given the special responsibility of studying and keeping the Torah.

In other features Bar Mitzvah ceremonies differ significantly. Some synagogues conduct their services almost entirely in English or whatever is the local language. Others prefer a service largely, even wholly, in Hebrew. Some insist that the child learn only the traditional chants and melodies for reading from the ancient scrolls. Others substitute some combination of vernacular essays, programs of social action, and good works for some of the traditional Hebrew skills required of the children. Most North American synagogues today celebrate the occasion both for girls and boys, but the most traditional synagogues limit the ceremonies to boys. Many of those that reserve the ceremony to boys design another appropriate and equivalent ceremony for the girls.

The families of the celebrants normally host a luncheon or dinner for their relatives and friends after the ceremonies, where the child's success and the family's good fortune can be celebrated. Some are especially elaborate, with catered meals, and entertainment including dance orchestras. Others focus on the religious dimensions and are less elaborate.

Whatever the tradition of the individual congregation, the family itself spends much time and thought on the ways to prepare the child for the ceremony as well as exactly how to celebrate the event. The educational and celebratory aspects of the ceremony now normally practised in North America are hardly ancient at all. They have become characteristic of the Jewish community only in modern times, as Jews achieved legal rights and participated in the intellectual life of European society.

Moreover, the understanding of what Torah entails has undergone diverse interpretation and development. Varied applications of law have accumulated since the days reported in the first five books of the Hebrew Bible. Today, the community highlights the moral meaning of ritual obligation and subordinates older, outdated meanings, all the while maintaining that it is preserving them. We shall be illustrating such processes in the course of this chapter.

Overview: Diversity in Judaism

Judaism's present-day diversity can be best understood as the product of historical circumstance and development. In the process, Judaism has spawned two subsequent world religions, each enormously larger and more politically powerful than Judaism has been. The three religions—Judaism, Christianity, and Islam—trace their spiritual lineage to the biblical figure Abraham. Of them, Judaism is by far the smallest, at only 1 to 2 per cent of the size of the Christian and Muslim populations in the world. But its historical influence far outweighs its community's small size, for it was the Jewish people who brought the belief in one God to Christianity and Islam.

Christians and Muslims readily acknowledge a debt to ancient Judaism for religious ideas and practices. Each of the Abrahamic faiths sees itself as continuing and fulfilling the mission of ancient Israel. Each lays claim to the historical pedigree that the Hebrew Bible gives to its sense of divine guidance. But, concerned with their own interpretations of this heritage, Christians and Muslims often fail to appreciate the distinctive interpretations of the heritage that have developed in Judaism over the past two millennia. It will be our task in this chapter to sketch that development.

Is the Jewish heritage a religious heritage? The answer is both yes and no, depending on which Jews are asked. Yes, because many people do identify themselves as Jews on the basis of religious participation. One can join the Jewish community through conversion, and people frequently do convert to Judaism. But the tradition is far more commonly an inherited one, the identity of one's ancestors, so that Judaism is frequently considered an 'ethnic' religion.

Some Jews have said yes to their identity as ethnic while answering no to the question of Jewish religion. A substantial number of North Americans, Europeans, and Israelis identify themselves as Jews, but do not participate in the religious tradition. The people has a culture, with its literary and artistic traditions, its foods and folkways, and its roles in its social and historical milieu. Religion, to them, is a part of the culture, but not necessarily the defining part.

And neither is biological descent. The claim that the Jews are genetically a race, which has been a basis for twentieth-century persecution, simply cannot be substantiated. Ever since the ancient Hebrew kingdoms, people of diverse origins have converted or married into the community. Jews today exhibit a vast range of physical characteristics: eastern in eastern countries, African in Africa, European in Europe. Judaism can be identified as a religion, and the Jews have an identifiable culture, but identification on the basis of biological heredity is beset with error.

Jews number about 14 million worldwide today. Half of the Jews, more than 7 million, live in the Americas, mostly in the United States and Canada. A little fewer than a quarter, 3 million, live in Asia, mostly in Israel. And over a quarter, perhaps 4 million, remain in Europe, mainly in Russia and the other lands controlled until 1989 by the Soviet Union. The world population of Jews is down by almost one-third from what it was half a century earlier, in 1939. In that year the Second World War began, and by the time it was over in 1945, about 6 million Jews had been put to death by the Nazis, the political party that ruled Germany, in what is known as the Holocaust.

The cultural centres of Jewish life today are in the large eastern cities of North America, a few other cities, and in Israel. About half of all Jews remain unaffiliated with any synagogue. Those that do affiliate range across liberal and traditional categories. In the United States and Canada, the three major groupings are Reform, Conservative, and Orthodox. For understanding Judaism it is significant that its major divisions are based more on ritual and practice than on belief or doctrine. This contrasts with Christianity, where theology and creed are the crucial defining issues between denominations.

Jews understand that God expects fundamental moral conduct of everyone, revealed to all humanity in a covenant to Noah after the primeval flood and acccessible to the entire human race through reason.

In a subsequent covenant God promises, 'I shall be your God and you shall be my people.' The obligation to practise a number of special rules sets them apart from all other peoples and enforces upon them a system of holiness commanded by God. Jews think of themselves as God's special people, not in any racial sense but only in the sense that they are elected to a special responsibility, to serve as God's priests in the world.

THE BIBLICAL PERIOD

The Historical Development of Judaism

The Torah, whose recitation and observance is central, contains the history of Israel, but it is history written from a special perspective. It is the history of a people as they understand and follow a God who chooses them as his instrument. Some of that history is well known because the first stage of Hebrew religious literature, the Hebrew Bible, is scripture to Christians and Muslims also. Its interpretations differ not only *vis-à-vis* the other communities but within Judaism.

The liberal wing of Judaism accepts modern canons of history and reserves the right to question aspects of the accuracy and historicity of the biblical text, just as modern Christian and some Muslim scholars do. They distinguish among myth, legend, and history in the biblical text.

On the other hand, the traditional wing of Judaism believes every word in the text to be literally true, often in a historical sense. They take it to have been dictated to Moses and the various prophets by divine inspiration. The student must be sensitive and alert to a range of opposing perspectives on the same events.

In current historical knowledge, Israel first enters the secular historical record in the second millennium BCE. Jews often use the terminology BCE ('before the Common Era') and CE ('Common Era'), rather than the Christian designations BC ('before Christ') and AD (Latin *anno Domini*, 'in the year of our Lord'). This effort to avoid theologically endorsing a division of history around the life of Jesus has gained a measure of acceptance among scholars writing on other religious traditions as well.

There is a moment when from the standpoint of the modern historian, the narratives of ancient Israel come into focus. That is when we can begin to match Israelite narratives with people and events documented in the texts of other peoples, Israel's neighbours. Archaeology has recovered an Egyptian stela (monumental stone inscription) from about 1230 BCE with a hymn describing the victories of the Egyptian pharaoh Mer-ne-Ptah.

> Great joy has arisen in Egypt;
> Jubilation has gone forth in the towns of Egypt.
> They talk about the victories which Mer-ne-Ptah Hotep-hir-Maat
> made in Tehenu:
> 'How amiable is he, the victorious ruler!
> How exalted is the king among the gods!' ...
> The princes are prostrate, saying: 'Mercy!' ...
> Plundered is Canaan with every evil ...
> Israel is laid waste, his seed is not ...
> All lands together, they are pacified.
> (Wilson 1950:365–81)

The mention of Israel in the inscription uses an Egyptian hieroglyphic expression that seems to designate a people, rather than a nation with a land and fixed borders. Other texts, a century or so earlier, mention Hapiru ('Hebrews'?). So, whatever the historical value of the Hebrews' own legends, they clearly appear as a people identifiable by their neighbours by the end of the thirteenth century BCE. This, then, is our dividing line between biblical legend and biblical history.

It would be naïve to suggest that every subsequent detail in the Hebrew biblical narrative can be accepted as history without question. Historical inquiry becomes a puzzle of reasoning: figuring out what most likely happened, whatever the sources themselves may say. Of course, this enterprise yields an account that is relative and subject to revision, quite at odds with a traditional pious understanding of the Bible as factual in every detail.

Creation in *Genesis*

The first twelve chapters of *Genesis* describe the primeval history of the universe. In chapter 1, God creates heaven and earth. Interestingly, the text does not actually specify that the universe is created from nothing. It says, however, that God creates different things on each 'day' of creation, culminating with the creation of humanity, male and female, on the sixth day. On the seventh day, God rests, setting the pattern of a weekly Sabbath. The text describes the order of time to proceed from evening to morning, so Jews celebrate the Sabbath starting at sundown Friday night and ending at sundown on Saturday.

Chapter 2 of *Genesis* begins rather differently with God causing a mist to rise from the ground, out of which vegetation sprouts. He plants a garden in Eden and populates it with animals and the primal human couple.

Religious traditionalists studying the Bible worry about its seeming contradictions and try to rationalize them. Interpretation actually begins within the Bible. For instance, creation is the topic of what amount to comments by biblical writers. The author of chapter 45 of *Isaiah* explicitly says that God creates darkness, as well as light, which is hardly evident from the first chapter of *Genesis*:

> So that [people] from the rising and the setting sun
> may know that there is none but I:
> I am the LORD, there is no other;
> I make the light, I create darkness,
> author alike of prosperity and trouble.
> I, the LORD, do all these things (*Isaiah* 45:6–7).

The prophetic writer evidently needed to emphasize that God is the creator of good and evil, darkness and light, in contradistinction to the Zoroastrians, whose doctrines in his day may have been developing in the direction of two initial forces.

Modern biblical scholarship does not treat contradictory details in *Genesis* as a problem for human understanding of God's plan. Rather, it takes them as a clue to the composition of the text, identifying *Genesis* 1 as coming from one source and *Genesis* 2 from another. Their appearance together, it is held, comes from a compiler reluctant to make changes in either text. As we shall explain later, the first chapter is ascribed to a priestly writer commonly designated the P narrator; the second is considered an ancient Hebrew epic compiled by the king's court, and commonly designated JE.

Genesis 1 offers a hierarchical view of creation. Everything is arranged according to an order imposed by the days of the week. First is God, the creator, who creates by means of his word. Second is the Sabbath, the period of rest built right into the universe. And third is humanity, male and female, created at the last moment before the Sabbath in the image and likeness of God.

Another voice in the biblical narrative has Moses lecturing to the people,

> Take ye therefore good heed unto yourselves for ye saw no manner of likeness on the day that the LORD spoke unto you in Horeb out of the midst of the fire—lest ye deal corruptly, and make you a graven image … and lest you lift up your eyes unto the heavens, and when you see the sun and the moon and the stars, even all the host of the heavens, you be drawn away and wor-

> ship them and serve them, which the LORD your God has allotted unto all the people under all the heavens (*Deuteronomy* 4:15–19).

The Bible's view of creation story holds that humanity should never worship created objects like the sun, the moon, and the stars.

The Primal Couple

According to the Eden story, *Genesis* 2 ends with of God's creation of man and woman. 'Adam' is the Hebrew word for 'man' in the sense of humanity, but here appears also as the proper name of the individual created. Adam therefore has something like the same connotations as the term 'Everyman' in English. 'Eve', according to the biblical text and most interpreters, is derived from the word for 'living'.

In *Genesis* 2 theirs is a naïve innocence, as they stand in nakedness and without shame. *Genesis* 3 shows how this peace and harmony can be reversed. In a play on words, their nakedness (in Hebrew, *'arom*) is contrasted with the serpent's shrewdness (in Hebrew, *'arum*). The serpent presents the primal couple with a temptation to be like God, wise and immortal.

The characters are sketched with an economy of words. Adam is unwary and trusting. Eve, however, is quite verbal and evidently intelligent. The couple do not lack intelligence before they eat the forbidden fruit; rather, what they lack is moral sense—the tree is called the Tree of the Knowledge of Good and Evil. The story purports to tell us not how we got intelligence but how we learned to make moral distinctions.

Indeed, in the drama of the story, Eve's pre-existent intelligence appears to lead to her downfall. Easily enticed by the fruit (not specifically called an apple), the couple yield to temptation. While they are pictured as innocent babes in the woods, they clearly understand that they have disobeyed God. Afterwards they know something new: shame and guilt. This suggests that human beings develop from infants into creatures who have a moral capacity.

The Eden story explains the conditions of human life narratively, rather than in philosophical arguments. The pain and evil of human life have come about through human disobedience. Banished from God's immediate presence, people must live at a distance from God, though God still shows loving care even while expelling them. The narrative explains such varied things as why snakes crawl on the ground and bite human ankles, why women have pain in childbirth, why people have to work for a living, why we wear clothes, why the sexes are different, why people are ashamed when naked, why we die, and why men and women feel sexual attraction to one another. Some of these matters are natural, some are cultural, and others are ultimate issues of human existence. We call such stories 'etiological' because they offer explanations of origins for present circumstances.

According to later Jewish tradition, the story illustrates no original sin so great that it clouds human nature permanently, needing further atonement. That would put it in sharp disagreement with the dominant Christian interpretation of the scene, which insists on a deep and sinister relationship between sexuality, death, sin, and Satan, as the snake is often figured.

Although life is hard for humanity—we need to work for our livelihoods, and we are subject to venomous bites, childbirth, and death—there are also positive benefits implied in the story. Like God, humanity now has a moral capacity to choose the good and to keep God's laws. Making right choices is one of the Bible's major themes.

Myth and the Israelite Narratives

The first eleven chapters of *Genesis* comprise the Bible's primeval history. They offer a sequence of mostly bad examples illustrating why God had to choose a specific people to establish a covenant that would bring his ideas to the human race. Repeatedly, they show, humans do not excel at the task of governing themselves when left free to follow their own conscience. People so foul the earth with violence and corruption that God must find a way to destroy their evil society.

The story of the flood was a very well-known myth in the Ancient Near East. The Hebrews merely adopted a theme that was virtually universal among the peoples with whom they came in contact. Yet in the dominant Mesopotamian accounts, the gods cause the flood because they are disturbed by the din of human life, possibly suggesting overpopulation.

In the biblical version of the flood story, God acts out of moral motives to punish the obscene evil that humans and apparently even some rebellious angels (see *Genesis* 6:1–3) have perpetrated on each other and the earth. God floods the earth for a fresh start, allowing only Noah and the creatures on his ark to survive.

But even starting over does not stop human bad judgement. Immediately after the flood, the king of Babylon attempts to approach God's level by building a tower to heaven. God responds by confounding human language.

Not until the call of Abraham in *Genesis* 12 does the downward fall of humanity begin to find a positive solution. God chooses Abraham to be an example to humanity about how to live. Thus the primeval history is a prologue to the major action of the Hebrew Bible, which is the story of the people Israel in their relationship to God.

The word 'myth' has come to connote falsity, and many people today therefore do not use it of their own narratives. Israelite culture was based on the rejection of the nature and fertility mythology of the cultures around it, so for many

etiological

FLOOD story

years scholars and religious interpreters have been united in their judgement that Hebrew culture eschewed myth.

Israelite culture could be termed non-mythological to the extent that it demythologized nature, replacing the nature gods of the Ancient Near East with the bare objects of the physical universe. The heavens of Israelite culture, as we have said, were merely heavens, the earth merely earth: they were not gods. Throughout the Bible, the Israelites maintain that there is only one God, who controls the forces of nature.

Scholars writing on religion, however, speak of myth as a genre of narrative that attempts to express a specific culture's sense of the ultimate order of things. In such a connection, it is possible to think there are truths that myth attempts to assert.

In this latter sense, then, the Hebrew view of the relationship between God and the people Israel itself functions as myth. It expresses the ultimate meaning of life for Hebrew culture.

And it sees God as causing historical events. God's own name, Yahweh, as we shall assert below, may have originally meant 'he who causes to be'. If so, embedded in this etymology are far-reaching intuitions about the uniqueness of events. God causes history, not just the endless seasonal repetition that characterizes the concept of time in fertility cults.

Abraham

When we come to the narratives of the patriarchs, the tribal ancestors of the Hebrews, we see a transition from the imaginative paradigms of myth and allegory to the anecdotal detail of legend. While we have no evidence outside the Bible that Abraham, Isaac, Jacob, Joseph, or Moses existed, we can situate them plausibly in the culture of the Ancient Near East that is now documented in Mesopotamian, Egyptian, and other archaeological records.

These neighbouring cultures were known to the premodern West almost solely through the Bible's mention of them, but modern archaeological and textual research has brought to light many details of the patriarchs' world. We now have records of Ancient Near Eastern peoples, in the Mesopotamian plain of the Tigris and Euphrates rivers (today's Iraq) and in Egypt. Their history goes back 2,000 years before the Hebrews. Mesopotamian texts after 1800 BCE offer hints that within the fabric of the patriarchal stories there are strands of historically accurate material. For instance, the names of Abraham's ancestors resemble place names in records from northern Mesopotamia from the nineteenth to twelfth centuries BCE.

According to the biblical story, Abraham is told to leave his home in Ur of the Chaldees, in southern Mesopotamia. He is told to move to Haran, in northern Mesopotamia, and subsequently to the biblical land of Canaan, which is located mainly in the hill country known today either as the West Bank or alternatively as Judea and Samaria.

In *Genesis* 22 we find the well-known story in which God calls on Abraham to sacrifice his son Isaac as a burnt offering. Abraham prepares the fire and grasps his knife, when God's word comes at the last minute to spare Isaac and substitute an animal. The story of the forestalled sacrifice of Isaac emphasizes the divine opposition to human sacrifice in the religion of the Canaanites, while praising Abraham's obedience. And because 2 *Chronicles* 3:1 associates the summit of Moriah, the location of this event, with Jerusalem, the story also serves to explain why God wants animal sacrifices on Jerusalem's Temple Mount.

Though the patriarchs may appear on a remote historical threshold, the Hebrews themselves (and their descendants, the Israelites, Judeans, and Samaritans) did not consider themselves an ancient people. They saw themselves as a people newly born because of the specific command of their God. Subsequently, before the Bible was finished, the Jews achieved a long and eventful history, with the result that the Romans, for instance, could consider them an ancient people.

Covenant

'Covenant' (in Hebrew, *berith*) is the central organizing concept in Israelite religion. It is a theological term that means much the same thing that 'contract' does today. The purpose of life is defined by the special contractual relationship into which Abraham, Isaac, Jacob, and Moses enter with God. This covenant specifies exactly which human behaviours God wants and which he does not. It gives a divine mandate to their societal laws.

God is to oversee the destiny of the people descended from Abraham. All those who are party to the covenant become known as the people Israel, whether they later live in the southern kingdom of Judah or the northern kingdom, also called Israel.

God promises the land of Canaan to Abraham and his descendants. In their own narratives, the Hebrews are fully aware that the land was not originally theirs. Instead, they take it over from various groups of people already there whose behaviour they condemn as sinful. The Bible expresses a right to possession or repossession of the land as a promise from God. But the land is not a unilateral gift. Both sides must live according to specific obligations.

God ratifies this promise with a solemn, binding ceremony. In the narrative, God appears to Abraham during a vision, which for the narrator expresses the transcendence of the encounter and the awesomeness of the divinity. Yet the model for this covenant is a human ceremony, similar to formal legal agreements in ordinary human relationships such as treaty making. The central feature of the ceremony is a solemn oath.

> He said, 'O Lord God, how am I to know that I shall possess it?' He said to him, 'Bring me a heifer three years old, a she-goat three years old, a ram three years old, a turtledove, and a young pigeon.' And he brought him all these, cut them in two, and laid each half over against the other; but he did not cut the birds in two … When the sun had gone down and it was dark, behold, a smoking fire pot and a flaming torch passed between these pieces. On that day the Lord made a covenant with Abram, saying, 'To your descendants I give this land' (*Genesis* 15:8–10, 17–18).

The flaming torch, connoting the presence of God, passes between the pieces of the animals to signify that God has committed himself with a sworn oath. This strange ceremony has analogies with the treaty ceremonies of Ancient Near Eastern emperors, but it may also reflect less stylized agreements used by tribal chieftains. Apparently, the purpose of cutting up the animals is to invoke a curse upon any person who violates the oath.

This epic layer of the biblical tradition depicts a late Bronze Age practice of covenanting. God's providence is expressed as a treaty between two great though dissimilar chiefs—Abraham, the ancestor of all the people of Israel, and Yahweh, the God who promises to be faithful to those descendants, provided they behave fittingly.

To claim divine origin for law was in no way unusual. All the great Ancient Near Eastern cultures at the time of the Hebrews, as well as for centuries before them, thought of themselves as subject to laws given by the gods. For example, the Babylonian king Hammurabi (r. 1792–1750 BCE) was said to receive his law code from the god of wisdom, Shamash. However, Hammurabi's laws were also seen as his own great achievement of statecraft, embodying justice. The Israelites were distinctive in viewing their God as directly writing the law.

Ancient Near Eastern gods were almost always called upon to witness and protect the integrity of oaths. Practically every treaty between nations contained a list of gods who had witnessed and were responsible for protecting the sanctity of the oaths sworn by the two parties. But the Israelites were unique also in that they could depict no other gods than the one God as responsible for the enforcement of justice.

The Hebrews' legendary ancestors—Abraham, Isaac, Jacob, and Moses—are all pictured as making covenants with God. These legendary accounts parallel the ceremonial covenant making of such historical figures as the Hebrew kings David, Solomon, and Josiah, and the scribe Ezra. These great figures in biblical history each enacted in grand ceremonies the covenant between themselves, their people, and their God.

Biblical accounts of the patriarchal covenants express the perspectives and politics of the narrators. In the covenant with Abraham in *Genesis* 15, the following material is found in alternation with the portions quoted earlier.

> As the sun was going down, a deep sleep fell on Abram; and lo, a dread and great darkness fell upon him. Then the LORD said to Abram, 'Know of a surety that your descendants will be sojourners in a land that is not theirs, and will be slaves there, and they will be oppressed for four hundred years; but I will bring judgment on the nation which they serve, and afterward they shall come out with great possessions. As for yourself, you shall go to your fathers in peace; you shall be buried in a good old age.' …
>
> The LORD made a covenant with Abram, saying, 'To your descendants I give this land, from the river of Egypt to the great river, the river Euphrates, the land of the Kenites, the Kenizzites, the Kadmonites, the Hittites, the Perizzites, the Rephaim, the Amorites, the Canaanites, the Girgashites and the Jebusites' (*Genesis* 15:12–16, 18–20).

The important benefits of offspring and homeland will accrue to the descendants of Abraham as long as they keep faith with Yahweh's bond. Abraham himself, on account of his deep faith, is rewarded by being allowed to live to an old age and to be buried with his ancestors. The story omits any doctrine of reward after death. This society understands ultimate rewards concretely: an easy death after a long and comfortable life, with many descendants to carry on afterward. There is no interest in the final disposition of souls after death. Rather, one lives on in one's offspring. The story describes the benefits of the covenant to the people as the surviving heirs.

Historical events result from the direct intervention of God in response to the nation's behaviour. Over several centuries, Israelite groups and classes interpreted the events of their history in widely varying ways in terms of the covenant idea.

Moses and the Exodus

The narratives of the patriarchs as national ancestors in *Genesis* are followed by the dramatic role of Moses as leader and lawgiver in *Exodus*. Whereas the patriarchs represent a migration from Mesopotamia into the land of Canaan, the traditions regarding Moses place him in charge of a migration from the other centre of Ancient Near Eastern civilization, Egypt. These two migrations may have in fact overlapped a bit, some of the Hebrew ancestors coming from the direction of Egypt via the Sinai Peninsula and others from the east and north, in the direction of Mesopotamia.

In any event, the compilers of the biblical text have put the two in strict chronological and historical sequence, using the Joseph narratives of *Genesis* 37–50 to send the descendants of Abraham to Egypt, where they all become available to take part in the events of the Exodus under Moses. The editing emphasizes the linearity of Hebrew thought and its dogged historicism, with God viewed as the author of every consecutive event.

The Divine Name

Chapter 3 of *Exodus* relates an encounter Moses has with God during a visit to the wilderness prior to his people's escape from Egypt. In the account, Moses experiences a vision of God's presence as a flame in a bush that burns without being consumed. God then declares his identity as the God of the patriarchal lineage Abraham–Isaac–Jacob, and gives his personal name, represented in Hebrew by the four letters YHWH.

No one knows for sure how these letters are to be vocalized today, but the text of *Exodus* 3:14, 'I am who I am,' associates their meaning with the Hebrew verb *hayah*, 'to be'. Biblical scholars conventionally render the name 'Yahweh', partly because Hebrew personal names that incorporate it as a component often end in *-yahu*. Its original meaning may have been 'He who causes to be.' Thus what Yahweh tells Moses, 'I am who I am,' may mean 'I am the one who causes things to happen.'

Over the centuries, partly because of the commandment not to take God's name in vain, it became the practice not to pronounce the name at all. In traditional Judaism, to pronounce it was considered blasphemy—a theological four-letter word. However, traditional Judaism also forbade any tampering with the Hebrew scriptural text, which was written in consonants and where the sequence YHWH appeared in practically every column.

So without changing the Hebrew text, Jews would read aloud a Hebrew word resembling the title 'lord', *adonay*, where the four letters YHWH were written; or, if the written text said 'the Lord YHWH', they pronounced the Hebrew word for God, Elohim. Translations into English frequently render the divine name by printing the substitute term entirely in capital letters or small capitals as LORD or GOD.

Interestingly, the name 'Jehovah' came into use in Christian circles, through a literal reading of the four Hebrew consonants YHWH with their vowel diacritics signifying *adonay*. The usage 'Jehovah' gained currency especially as people in the Protestant Reformation turned to the Bible, in its original languages, for leverage against the institutional church but lacked mastery of the textual conventions in the Hebrew.

Jewish observance over the centuries has evolved other conventions, such as not even *writing* the four consonants and just writing double *y*, or *h* with an apostrophe. And in spoken usage, the Hebrew expression *ha-Shem*, 'the Name', is a frequent substitution. A further extension of piety found in Orthodox circles today is the avoidance in English of even writing the term 'God', substituting 'G–d' or 'L–rd'.

The Exodus

The Hebrews in the Exodus story are serving as work crews on Egyptian construction projects in the eastern part of the Nile Delta. The work amounts to slave labour, and God tells Moses to request their release from the Egyptian pharaoh. When Pharaoh refuses, God sends plagues on the Egyptians but spares the Hebrews, and they are able to escape Egypt. They cross the Yam Suf, supposed to be the Red Sea but literally the Reed Sea, which swamps Pharaoh's pursuers, and reach the barren Sinai Peninsula.

The entire Jewish people, whether they actually came from Egypt or only knew the story, subsequently identified with the Exodus. They took it as a metaphor of going from slavery to becoming a people with a destiny and a purpose. They expressed their participation in the event through the Passover festival.

During the forty years of nomadic life in the wilderness under Moses's leadership, the principal legal framework of Israelite society is laid out. Moses meets with God at Mount Sinai and receives the Ten Commandments as the core of Israel's law, written on stone tablets 'with the finger of God' (*Exodus* 31:18).

The Ten Commandments, found in *Exodus* 20:2–17 and yet again in *Deuteronomy* 5:6–21 (etymologically, the name 'Deuteronomy' means 'second law'), are stipulations of a covenant. In the ceremony, there is a communal oath taking: all the people, not just the patriarchal ancestor, swear to obey its terms.

The foundations of Israelite ritual life are also to be seen in the wilderness narratives. Moses's brother, Aaron, becomes the archetypal priest. Hebrew worship is instituted in an elaborate tent, the Tabernacle, serving as a temporary temple. Kept in it as the central cult object is a chest, the Ark of the Covenant, serving as the throne of God's invisible presence. No image of God is placed on this base, for God is not to be represented by any image, in sharp contrast to the image-rich usage of all of Israel's neighbours. Indeed, when Aaron capitulates to popular sentiment to set up a golden calf statue, Moses proclaims God's denunciation of the image as idolatry.

The Emergence of Israelite Kingship

The Israelites proceed from nomadic to settled life under Moses's successor, Joshua. The book of *Joshua* recounts some spectacular conquests as the Israelites enter the land of Canaan. But the following book, *Judges*, gives a rather more limited view of the initial Israelite effort at dispossessing the indigenous population. The Israelites, it indicates, are only able to gain a few positions in the hill country for themselves at first. The Canaanite peoples, far more civilized and culturally advanced, are already well established there, with heavily fortified cities and well-equipped armies.

The Israelites only gradually assert hegemony over the land. The largest threat to them is from the Philistines, people related in culture to the Mycenaean Greeks. The Philistines arrive on the coastal plain at about the same time as the Israelites emerge from the desert. The Philistines become coastland neighbours and rivals of the hill-country Hebrew tribes.

The name 'Palestine', used for the region in Roman times, recalls the Philistines. And although 'Philistine' now connotes a lack of culture, the biblical Philistines were at first more advanced technologically than the Hebrews. In particular, they had mastery of iron refining and smelting that was beyond the ken of the Israelite shepherds.

Though the Israelites with Yahweh as their God partially defeat the Canaanites, worshippers of Ba'al, they are tempted to emulate Canaanite religion. Yahweh finds the Canaanite religion abhorrent because of its practices of ritual prostitution and child sacrifice. Yahweh demands that the Israelites keep apart from the Canaanites and repudiate their practices, promising them progeny and long life if they obey his covenant.

The Israelites in this period had a loose tribal confederation. Informal chieftains, the *shofetim* (often translated as 'judges'), ruled the people. Their leadership was charismatic, meaning that it was entirely due to popular acceptance, there being no official process to elect or appoint them. Evidently there were local elders and priests too, but the people relied on the judges in moments of crisis. By modern historical standards, the judges are all legendary characters: Deborah, Samson, Shamgar, Jephthah, Ehud, and many more. In the eyes of the book of *Judges*, God chooses each of the judges to save the Israelites from a threat of foreign domination.

In the two generations coming shortly after 1000 BCE, Israelite society experienced a shift to a centralized monarchy. Kingship was a new institution, born to deal with the threats of the Canaanites and Philistines. According to the story narrated in *1* and *2 Samuel*, God picks first Saul, then David, and finally David's successors to be kings because the Israelites need relief from the Philistine menace. At first, God is reluctant to appoint a king, but both the people and the times seem to demand one. Ultimately God places the government squarely in the hands of a dynasty founded by the unlikely figure of David.

We first meet David as the youngest son of Jesse, young and inexperienced enough to be fit only to look after the sheep. But God strengthens his hand so that David, unifying the Israelite people, defeats the Philistines. The Bible leaves us with the impression that the Philistines disappear, although we know from the archaeology of the Philistine cities that they continued to exist, more or less powerful, throughout the entire period of Israelite settlement. David captures Jerusalem, hitherto not an Israelite but a Jebusite town, and makes it his capital.

David's successor, Solomon, his son by Bathsheba, his favourite wife, built a temple to Yahweh on the hill called Zion, the rock-outcrop ridge, a kind of acropolis, on the uphill side of Jerusalem. Solomon used lavish imported materials, such as cedar wood from Lebanon. He undertook other ambitious construction projects around the kingdom. His build-up of the central government, and his use of conscript labour, contributed to an alienation of the ten northern tribes.

On Solomon's death around 921 BCE, the kingdom broke up. The northern tribes, centring on Samaria, seceded and thereafter used the name 'Israel'. They continued for two centuries until overrun and dispersed by the Assyrian invasion in 722 BCE, after which they were referred to as the 'ten lost tribes'. The southern tribes, centring on Jerusalem, used the name Judah, and continued until the Babylonian invasion of 586 BCE.

Later, in the centuries following the demise of the Judean monarchy through the Babylonian conquest, the people elaborated a hope for a restoration of the Davidic kingship as a sign of God's continuing loyalty to his covenant people.

Editing the Five Books of Moses

In the northern and southern Israelite regions, the stories of Abraham and Jacob functioned to unify their populations, who shared a claim of descent from these patriarchs. The idea of a family relation to Jacob originated among the ten Hebrew tribes in the northern kingdom, and Jacob's alternative name, Israel, became the name of the people. Meanwhile, the idea of family relation to Abraham, who lived south of Jerusalem, solidified the remaining two Hebrew tribes in the southern kingdom of Judah. But stories of each region, north and south, were adopted by the other when the kingdom was unified under David.

The kingship as an institution was able to put its specific stamp and tone on many of the early traditions of Israel because it acted as the power that collected the stories. Later generations too looked back to the accomplishments of King David, followed by those of King Solomon, as manifestations of divine favour. As founder of the Judean dynasty, David is idealized for his military shrewdness. He is also depicted as faithful and as talented in music, so that the hymn collection of the Jerusalem temple, the contents of the book of *Psalms*, is attributed to him.

With the reign of Solomon, Israel's history writers see their little country as having at last achieved a world reputation. And indeed it did, although the immediate cause appears to be a short-lived power vacuum created by the decline of Egypt and the Mesopotamian empires simultaneously. Solomon enters into marriages with foreign princes, cementing political alliances, and hosts a visiting queen from Sheba, a region to the south in Arabia later fabled for its aromatic incense. Solomon is portrayed as the paragon of wisdom, and the biblical collection of *Proverbs* is attributed to him—though the burdens the Jerusalem government placed on the northern tribes, eventuating in their secession, hardly seem wise as a policy.

Besides those of the kingly groups in the society, we also have an enormous body of ancient traditions that were collected and transmitted by priestly circles. We see these traditions most clearly in the books of *Leviticus* and *Numbers*, centring around the priestly law code in *Leviticus* 18–26.

All the editorial voices so far mentioned—northern, southern, even priestly—put their individual stamps on the story of the giving of the law at Sinai. It is the crucial event defining the Israelite people and today still gives the Jewish religion its special character. To the Orthodox community this is the moment when the entire corpus of the five books of Moses was given, from the story of creation to the farewell address of Moses before he dies at the threshold of the promised land.

Various editors and transmitters of the text, from their own perspectives, clarified that the covenant between Israel and God entails a social contract. The Ten Commandments emphasize human social responsibilities, as does the Book of the Covenant, the extended law code that immediately follows the commandments. Similarly, the priestly narrators, interested in the liturgical aspects of the covenant ceremony, portray Moses as an intermediary between God and the people.

Critical study of the Bible in modern times has meant a major shift in questions asked of the first five books of the Bible. For centuries, tradition had ascribed their composition to Moses, acting under divine inspiration or dictation. Faced with a discrepancy or difficulty in the received text, a traditional commentator's approach would be to ask what God intended the text to mean. Modern study has tended to ask a different question: who would have chosen to make a particular statement, and why? Discrepancies become not a challenge to faith but a clue for investigation.

The Documentary Hypothesis

An early modern suggestion of the composite character of the *Pentateuch*, the five books of Moses, was offered by the French physician Jean Astruc (1684–1766), who called attention to differences in the name of God. He suggested that material by one author, who consistently referred to God as Yahweh, had been intermixed with that of another, who regularly referred to God as Elohim. Other investigators began to observe differences among literary forms within the text. By the second half of the nineteenth century, a theory of four major blocks of material in the *Pentateuch* was articulated by the German scholar Julius Wellhausen (1848–1918).

Wellhausen's theory, known as the Documentary Hypothesis, has been vehemently criticized by traditional Jews and Christians, who reject its humanizing assumptions. It has also been criticized by many liberal and radical scholars, who may share those assumptions but differ on details of composition and compilation. Still, the broad outlines identified in the Documentary Hypothesis continue to shape much contemporary scholarship and serve as a basis for refinement. In that sense, it stands as one of the great intellectual achievements of the nineteenth century.

The nineteenth-century Bible scholars imagined single people writing specific documents at specific times. Now we know that the sources represent the perspective of a group of different people writing under the auspices of a particular institution in the society—like the royal bureaucracy—and that their efforts continued, over several generations in each case.

The author or school using the name Yahweh is identified as the Yahwist. The material of this source is referred to as J. That is because the name Yahweh is spelled with J in German, the language of the scholars who first put forth the hypothesis. The Yahwist wrote in the southern kingdom of Judea, emphasizing southern localities and the role of Abraham, probably beginning before the division of the kingdoms late in the tenth century BCE.

The second source, E, is the work of the author or school termed the Elohist for its preference to refer to God as Elohim. E wrote in the northern kingdom after its separation, probably starting during the ninth century BCE, and emphasized northern local traditions. E's usage calls the sacred mountain Horeb, not Sinai; and Amorites, not Canaanites, are displaced in the settlement of the land. God is more awesome and remote for E than for J, and the covenant relationship is less nationalistic.

However, the two strands, J and E, were woven together in many places, yielding a great Hebrew JE epic, a strand of the text that can be recognized by its use of the term 'the Lord God' to speak of the divinity. The Garden of Eden story beginning in *Genesis* 2 is a good example of JE, while *Genesis* 1 represents a priestly prologue to the whole story.

During the reign of Josiah, in 621 BCE, a copy of the law was reportedly found during repairs to the Jerusalem temple, according to 2 *Kings* 22:8. On the authority of that book, Israelite altars elsewhere were suppressed and worship was centralized at the Jerusalem temple for the first time. Since *Deuteronomy* 12:13 restricts worship to one location only, and since there is little sign of complaint in earlier times about the worship of Yahweh at many sites, it is assumed that the book that was found was *Deuteronomy* and that it, the D source, was a new production.

Overtly, *Deuteronomy* is cast in the form of a sermon by Moses, which would place its setting 600 years earlier. But its vocabulary and concerns are those of Josiah's day, when the prophet Jeremiah was active. Indeed, Moses speaks of himself as a prophet in *Deuteronomy* 18:15 with the kind of role expectations that apply to the prophetic movement we know in the eighth and seventh centuries BCE but hardly earlier. Central to the D source is a rewards-and-punishments theology of national morality, not unlike that of the prophetical books.

In some ways the most striking aspect of the documentary hypothesis is its postulation of P, the priestly source, as a late contribution to the Pentateuchal corpus. It is thought to come from 586–539 BCE, the time of the Exile, when the Jerusalem temple had been destroyed and the Judean leadership deported by the Babylonians. It is replete with detailed descriptions and measurements of the temple and its furnishings. As long as the temple stood, these were hardly necessary, but with the temple in ruins, P offers a literary blueprint for its restoration.

Wellhausen's view of the P source as late, reflecting a kind of decline in Israelite religion, is in line with his general Protestant distrust of priestly roles in Christianity. But we now see that many of the P legal traditions clearly predate *Deuteronomy*. We have to distinguish between the time when the P document was edited and the times when the traditions within it originated. Though priestly materials can be very old, their voice in the document was the last one to be added. Priestly aficionados become the final editors of the *Pentateuch*. Indeed, Wellhausen used 'P' to designate the Pentateuchal writer, not the Priestly writer.

P ascribes the temple's features to the founding influence of Moses, describing the elaborate ritual apparatus of the tabernacle in the forty-year wilderness migration. In so doing, P seeks to lend authority to the cultus, even if reporting more gear than tent-dwelling fugitives could have carried around strains credibility. P's central concern for ritual is projected back to the account of creation itself, with the first chapter of *Genesis*, P material, building the Sabbath into the very formation of the world. With P's concern for law, four figures in Israel's primeval history emerge as recipients of divine law: Adam, Noah, Abraham, and Moses.

Israelite Society

We should like to know a great deal more about the ordinary details of life in the biblical period, but with such a complex history of tradition, a clear picture is difficult to gain. We would like to know, for instance, how the sexes interacted. With so much of the characterization of the patriarchs and matriarchs determined by typological and allegorical thinking of later generations, it is difficult to discover where authentic details lie or succeed at determining the period from which the data come.

We know rudimentary things, which seem stable over a great deal of time—for instance, that marriage was virtually universally practised among Hebrews, that men were allowed several wives if they could afford them, and that children were highly prized. Indeed, offspring are conventionally listed again and again as a reward of the covenant with Yahweh. On the whole, tilling the land and securing it from harm were men's occupations, while raising children and running the household were women's. This rather fixed notion of occupations would hardly suit most intelligent, highly mobile couples living in the urban centres of

THE TEN COMMANDMENTS, *EXODUS* 20:2–17

I am the LORD your God who brought you out of Egypt, out of the land of slavery.

You shall have no other god to set against me.

You shall not make a carved image for yourself nor the likeness of anything in the heavens above, or on the earth below, or in the waters under the earth. You shall not bow down to them or worship them; for I, the LORD your God, am a jealous god. I punish the children for the sins of the fathers to the third and fourth generations of those who hate me. But I keep faith with thousands, with those who love me and keep my commandments.

You shall not make wrong use of the name of the LORD your God: The LORD will not leave unpunished the man who misuses his name.

Remember to keep the sabbath day holy. You have six days to labour and do all your work. But the seventh day is a sabbath of the LORD your God; that day you shall not do any work, you, your son or your daughter, your slave or your slave-girl, your cattle or the alien within your gates; for in six days the LORD made heaven and earth, the sea, and all that is in them, and on the seventh day he rested. Therefore the LORD blessed the sabbath day and declared it holy.

Honour your father and mother, that you may live long in the land which the LORD your God is giving you.

You shall not commit murder.

You shall not commit adultery.

You shall not steal.

You shall not give false evidence against your neighbour.

You shall not covet your neighbour's house; you shall not covet your neighbour's wife, his slave, his slave-girl, his ox, his ass, or anything that belongs to him.

North America, but life was very different then, nor can we tell exactly how much equality existed within the household.

Abraham and Sarah, although they are pictured as a great prince and princess, seem to have a very informal relationship to the extent that Sarah is able to affect a great many decisions within the household. David is pictured as indulging his wives even in the highly charged political atmosphere of his old age, when the succession to his throne was paramount in everyone's mind. The power that women received was ascribed to them by their husbands, but it could be great. On the other hand, a woman without a father or a husband to act as her guardian and provide for her, such as a widow, was a true unfortunate whom Yahweh's laws sought to protect.

We note also that women appear frequently within the literary motifs of the narration. For example, the victory of the judge Deborah, like that of Ehud or

From the Prophetic Collections

It has been told you, mortal, what is good and what the LORD requires of you: only to act justly, to love mercy, and to walk humbly before your God (*Micah* 6:8).

He shall not judge by what his eyes see, or decide by what his ears hear; but with righteousness he shall judge the poor, and decide with equity for the meek of the earth; and he shall smite the earth with the rod of his mouth, and with the breath of his lips he shall slay the wicked (*Isaiah* 11:3–4).

In the days to come the mountain of the LORD's house shall be set over all other mountains, lifted high above the hills. All the nations shall come streaming to it, and many peoples shall come and say, 'Come, let us climb up on to the mountain of the LORD, to the house of the God of Jacob, that he may teach us his ways, and we may walk in his paths.' For [Torah] issues from Zion, and out of Jerusalem comes the word of the LORD; he will be judge between nations, arbiter among many peoples. They shall beat their swords into mattocks and their spears into pruning-knives; nation shall not lift sword against nation nor ever again be trained for war (*Isaiah* 2:2–4, also *Micah* 4:1–3).

Jephthah, or even the call of Abraham or David, is part of the motif of God's complete control over history. He chooses the least likely persons—women, left-handers, half-breeds, even youngest children fit to be shepherds like David—to show that it is he who brings victory and defeat. Deborah's feminine gender is thus as important as David's youth and weakness in showing God's power. Like the hardening of Pharaoh's heart, these themes function in the narrative to show the complete and unlimited control that God exercises. So the heroines of Israel—Deborah, Miriam, Jael—all attest to God's power, not their own, in the same way as do the deeds of the patriarchs or David.

God's complete control over history impinges on traditionally female roles in other ways as well. Many times when a special birth is to be announced, the mother is pictured as barren. The covenant is endangered, because the rewards of the covenant are many descendants. In many of these cases—Sarah's birth of Isaac, Rachel's birth of Joseph, Hannah's birth of Samuel, to name but a few—God is pictured as intervening directly. He prepares the womb for the special birth, which will benefit the people. Later, Greek notions of the birth of heroes, as the result of physical relations between gods and humans, apparently played a role in the New Testament and the doctrine of the virgin birth of Jesus. But the Hebrew Bible picks quite another way for a birth to be special or revelatory.

Although the personal lives of the Israelites are quite difficult to reconstruct, we have a bit more luck when comparing the legal system of the Hebrews

FROM THE *PSALMS* AND *DANIEL*

LORD, what is humanity that you are mindful of it,
Or mortals that you take notice of them?
Human life is but a breath of wind,
Their days are a shadow that passes away.
(*Psalm* 144:3–4)

Yahweh, hear my prayer,
listen to my cry for help,
do not stay deaf to my crying,
for I find shelter with you.
I am your guest, [but] only for a time,
a nomad like all my ancestors.
Look away, let me draw breath,
before I go away and am no more!
(*Psalm* 39:12–13)

And many of those who sleep in the dust of the earth shall awake, some to everlasting life, and some to shame and everlasting contempt. And those who are wise shall shine like the brightness of the firmament; and those who turn many to righteousness, like the stars for ever and ever (*Daniel* 12:2).

with those of their neighbours. The Hebrews appear on the whole to have sought out fairer rules than their more civilized neighbours. Incarceration as a punishment was virtually unknown, as opposed to other nations' practice. A large number of Hebrew laws allow for penalties of monetary restitution rather than bodily mutilation. Restitution is quite frequently substituted for crimes that in neighbouring countries were punished by death. By Greek and Roman times, the use of monetary compensations for loss was evidently universal.

On the other hand, in issues like murder or adultery, Hebrew society demands capital punishment universally, whereas other nations distinguished the rank of the perpetrator. In most Mesopotamian nations, an aristocrat could make restitution for the death of a commoner, but a commoner must suffer capital punishment for the same crime. Hebrew law makes no distinction in status of that sort. It does demand capital punishment in cases where the deity's dignity has been offended. Such cases include adultery: the husband is not the only aggrieved party because a marriage oath involving the divinity has been violated. The normal double standard of antiquity, where punishments for male infidelity are different than those for women, is exacerbated by the fact that men could marry more than one wife.

Of course, ancient society exhibited other social institutions that we find abhorrent. Slavery was alive and well throughout the ancient world. Hebrew slavery was rendered somewhat less offensive in a few important respects. The Bible forbids any Israelite from enslaving another for debt for more than a fixed term. In other words, if someone could not pay a debt, he could sell his and his family's labour as indentured servants. But at the end of the debt, at the puberty of a

THE *SHEMA*, *DEUTERONOMY* 6:4–9

[In Jewish liturgy this passage is called the Shema, *after its first word in the Hebrew. It is the watchword of Israel's faith, repeated morning and evening, as the text specifies.]*

Hear O Israel, the LORD our God, the LORD is One. You shall love the LORD your God with all your heart and with all your soul and with all your strength. These words which I command you this day are to be kept in your heart. You shall repeat them to your children, speaking of them indoors and outdoors, morning and night. You shall bind them as a sign upon your hand and wear them as signs upon your forehead; you shall write them on the doorposts of your houses and on your gates.

female slave, or at the next sabbatical year, the Hebrew slave must be given the opportunity to go free.

The Prophets

Alongside the priestly and legal interests in the Hebrew Bible, there is another and perhaps even more important voice: the prophets. Since both Christianity and Islam claim to be founded in prophetic insight as well, the prophetic movement may be said to have influenced more people than any other religious movement in human history.

The prophetic tradition appears to have grown out of Ancient Near Eastern spirit possession. Referring to the experience it cultivates, scholars use the term 'ecstasy' in a technical sense, meaning that the practitioner is displaced or transported outside of a normal pattern of awareness and conduct. We have evidence of various ecstatic prophets—such as Micaiah ben Imlah, as well as Elijah and Elisha perhaps—in the Bible from the time of the Hebrew settlement of the land, and during the early monarchy. This is before the rise of the prophets whose declarations are preserved in literary collections. Thereafter there are occasional indications that prophets continued to receive ecstatic visions.

Unfortunately, we have little evidence about the ways in which the literary prophets—those who have left us books in the Bible—received their messages. Regardless of the techniques they may have used to receive their prophecy, the entire institution of prophecy is ascribed only to the direct intervention of God. For the devout, it is God who grants visions or prevents them from being received. In prophetic writing the prophet communicates what he or she sees not as one's own words but as the message delivered directly by God through visions and inspiration.

The writings surviving from the prophets of the eighth to sixth centuries BCE or ascribed to them are notable for their rational clarity, their social criticism, and their poetic intensity. We have references to several women who served as prophets. For instance, the prophet Isaiah refers to his wife as a prophetess, and Moses's sister Miriam is a called a prophetess, as well as is the judge Deborah. But the prophets whose books appear in the Bible are males. The prophets appear in a variety of contexts both within the administration of the monarchy and as social critics outside of it. Wherever their social location, the message is always that the people are not living up to the expectations God has for them and that God will shortly exercise his powers as punisher if they continue in their ways.

The writings of the prophets communicate the concept of covenant not in the narrow technical language of treaties but in the broader language of metaphor. The prophet Amos delivers the words of Yahweh, 'You only have I known of all the families on earth. Therefore I will punish you for all your iniquities.' The word 'know' in this context has a technical ancient Hebrew meaning of recognizing a covenant obligation. Amos is not speaking the words of a divine despot. Rather, he represents Yahweh as publicly claiming a grievance. Yahweh seeks redress because Israel has defaulted on its sealed contract with him.

Marriage contracts are also covenants. The accusations of seduction and adultery in *Hosea* gain their force by describing the covenant between Israel and Yahweh as a troubled marriage. The prophet presents Israel as the wayward wife of Yahweh, who is to win her back and forgive her even for adultery with the Canaanite fertility gods:

> Therefore, behold, I will allure her, and bring her into the wilderness, and speak tenderly to her. And there I will give her her vineyards, and make the Valley of Achor a door of hope. And there she shall answer as in the days of her youth, as at the time when she came out of the land of Egypt. And in that day, says the LORD, you will call me, 'My husband', and no longer will you call me, 'My ba'al.' For I will remove the names of the ba'als from her mouth, and they shall be mentioned by name no more … And I will betroth you to me forever; I will betroth you to me in righteousness and in justice, in steadfast love, and in mercy. I will betroth you to me in faithfulness; and you shall know the LORD (*Hosea* 2:14–20).

If the people give up their sinful relationship with the Canaanites' goddesses and gods, including their sexual rituals of fertility and their abhorred child sacrifice, Yahweh will renew his covenant with them. The force of this prophetic writing depends on the prophet's effective use of the metaphors of love and betrothal for covenantal obligation. Since the name of the Canaanite god, Ba'al, also means 'husband', it, too, has become part of the extended metaphor of adultery. Through the ages, the Hebrew Bible's great sin of idolatry has continued to be identified with adultery.

The prophets criticized the nation as having failed in its covenant obligations. Despite their warnings, it drifted towards ruin. The literary prophets recorded the destruction of the northern and southern kingdoms. Some of the prophets had been antiestablishment; others belonged to it. But their stirring rhetoric, as well as their successful predictions of national destruction, convinced later Israelite society that they all spoke the word of Yahweh.

The Exile

The Judean kingdom fell to Babylonian invasion and deportation in 586 BCE. As much as any single event, the Exile marks the transition from the national cult of an ancient kingdom to the religious heritage of a widely dispersed people. From the sixth century BCE on, we speak of Jews and Judaism, rather than of Hebrews or Israelites and Hebrew or Israelite religion.

Solomon's temple was razed and lay in ruins for three generations. Leaders of Judean society were exiled to Babylonia. These catastrophes mark the disruption of many ancient Israelite institutions. As in the case of many historical transitions, not everything happened overnight, but the Exile gave focus and impetus to a number of significant social and religious changes.

The heritage was now more that of a subject or minority population than of a national state. Especially among Jews dispersed abroad, life was now more urban than agricultural, so that many of the old agriculturally based laws and rituals needed to be rethought. Even after the ruined temple was rebuilt, congregational life gained in emphasis over temple worship; at some time in the Exile, the institution known as the synagogue was born. The Aramaic language gradually replaced Hebrew as the vernacular, giving Hebrew a ritual and antiquarian role. Yearnings for the restoration of Yahweh's sovereignty came to envision a variety of forms, including a deliverer king (messianism) or an overhaul of the cosmos in battle and judgement at the end of the age (apocalyptic literature).

In each place where Jews sought to dwell, the meaning of the covenant would appear different:

> By the waters of Babylon, there we sat down and wept, when we
> remembered Zion. On the willows there we hung up our lyres.
> For there our captors required of us songs,
> and our tormentors, mirth, saying, 'Sing us one of the songs of Zion!'
> How shall we sing the LORD's song in a foreign land?
> If I forget you, O Jerusalem, let my right hand wither! Let my tongue
> cleave to the roof of my mouth, if I do not remember you, if I do not

set Jerusalem above my highest joy!
(*Psalm* 137:1–6)

The destruction of the temple brought on a crisis of confidence. It stemmed not from Yahweh's being viewed as a regional God only, for he was also lord of all creation, but from his having been worshipped in a single, principal location for so long. With that location destroyed, had Yahweh finally abandoned his people? The author of *Lamentations* 5:20–2 puts it:

> Why dost thou forget us for ever, why dost thou so long forsake us?
> Restore us to thyself, O LORD, that we may be restored! Renew our days as of old!
> Or hast thou utterly rejected us? Art thou exceedingly angry with us?

The nation needed a sign that God had not permanently rejected it. As if in response, the prophet Ezekiel describes a heavenly chariot driven by the glory of God. In Ezekiel's bizarre vision, Yahweh's heavenly chariot and the radiance of divine presence appear in a storm cloud, just as in the Canaanitelike imagery of *Psalm* 29. Abandoning the temple just before its destruction, God's presence approaches Babylonia. The concrete, mythological answer to *Psalm* 137's cry above about singing Yahweh's song in a foreign land is that one can because he came into exile with the people.

Thus, when Cyrus the Persian conquered Babylon in 538 BCE, he was seen by the Israelites living there as part of God's plan (see *Ezra* 1:1; *Isaiah* 41:2, 44:28, 45:1). Cyrus did not describe himself as the bringer of a new order to the world. He styled himself as the restorer of the ancient regimes destroyed by the Babylonians, and hence the champion of all the old gods. He allowed the traditional priesthood of Babylonia's god Marduk to practise their own religion. And he allowed the Jews to go back, as many as wanted, to Judea to set up their temple. When Ezra later describes the Persian permission to set up a new temple to Yahweh, he makes Cyrus sound like a worshipper of Yahweh:

> In the first year of Cyrus king of Persia, that the word of the LORD by the mouth of Jeremiah might be accomplished, the LORD stirred up the spirit of Cyrus king of Persia so that he made a proclamation throughout all his kingdom and also put it in writing: "Thus says Cyrus king of Persia: 'The LORD, the God of heaven, has given me all the kingdoms of the earth, and he has charged me to build him a house at Jerusalem, which is in Judah. Whoever is among you of all his people, may his God be with him, and let him go up to Jerusalem, which is in Judah, and rebuild the house of the LORD, the God of Israel—he is the God who is in Jerusalem' " (*Ezra* 1:1–3).

The covenant is being reformulated through the demand of circumstance. Now Yahweh must direct all of world history, not just the destiny of Judah. Cyrus was no exclusive worshipper of Yahweh. But the announcement of return was in keeping with his policy of patronizing the priesthoods and cults of the old order. The writer of *Isaiah* 45 is so impressed with Cyrus's rise to power that he calls him the 'messiah' (the anointed one), designated by Yahweh as his instrument to fulfil Israel's destiny.

The Second Commonwealth

Not all the Jews wanted to return to Judea under the new Persian policy. Many of the prospering artisans and aristocrats resisted persuasion and stayed. The Babylonian Jewish community, so influential in the writing of the *Talmud* in the second through seventh centuries, was founded at this time.

With prophetic rhetoric, a postexilic author of later chapters in *Isaiah* declares the theme of homecoming. He maintains that God is on the verge of repeating all his past deliverances.

> Comfort, comfort my people, says your God.
> Speak tenderly to Jerusalem, and cry to her
> that her warfare is ended, that her iniquity is pardoned,
> that she has received from the LORD's hand double for all her
> sins (*Isaiah* 40:1–2).

The exiles are to be drawn from the far corners of the earth. The new ingathering will be like a new Exodus, bringing the people of Israel across water and fire. *Isaiah* (43:15–19) says that, just as at the Red Sea (*Exodus* 15:3), Yahweh will appear as a warrior doing battle. New heavens and a new earth will be created. This new Israelite commonwealth will be a fresh start:

> Arise, shine; for your light has come, and the glory of the Lord has risen
> upon you.
> For behold, darkness shall cover the earth, and thick darkness
> the peoples;
> but the LORD will arise upon you, and his glory will be seen upon you.
> And nations shall come to your light, and kings to the brightness of
> your rising (*Isaiah* 60:1–3).

Isaiah's words are among the most stirring biblical passages. Unfortunately, the condition of the returning exiles was still poor. Archaeology suggests that the buildings were small and decayed quickly. In fact, the beginnings of the postexilic community, referred to as the 'second commonwealth', were so meagre that it is hard to reconstruct the actual events.

The fate of the succession of Judean kings is not known for certain. The Davidic king, who adopted the Babylonian name Sin-Ab-Usuru, or Sheshbezzar in Hebrew, arrived in Jerusalem shortly after the return began. Thereafter the descendants of David were called *nasi* ('prince') rather than *melekh* ('king'), perhaps in deference to the Persian Empire, which ruled the country from the east. Zerubbabel, another descendant of David's line, apparently arrived in Judea to succeed Sheshbazzar. The second temple was then completed in 515 BCE. After that, there is complete silence about Zerubbabel or the kingship.

The mysterious disappearance of the Davidic king stimulated legends about a future king. There developed an enormous amount of speculation about the meaning of 2 *Samuel* 7, which promised that the Davidic kingship would continue forever. Thus the idea was born that a king of David's line would return and bring with him a perfect order. Until this time, the term 'messiah' had always referred to the current anointed priest or king. Eventually, it grew to mean a future king, as there was no anointed, divinely sanctioned, king in the line of David on the throne, although the priestly line continued intact.

Ezra and Nehemiah, who established a firm government in Judea, came there as court officials of the Persian Empire. The date or order of their administrations is not certain, but the government that they set out was explicitly based upon the covenantal formula used in the first temple period. In describing the 'constitutional assembly' convened by Ezra, for instance, Nehemiah attempts to turn the Sukkoth ('Tabernacles') holiday into a covenant renewal ceremony, though he is aware that the crops are now promised to Persian overlords. Such a ceremony could not inaugurate independence. Instead, covenant renewal was a national day for the satellite region under Persian rule.

An inhabitant of this region, the former tribal territory of Judah, was known as a *yehudi*, a Judean. This is the source for the English word 'Jew'. But under the Persians and then the Greeks, *yehudi* usually meant simply 'Judean'. The term gained its modern sense of a member of the Jewish religion during the first and second centuries. The shift, just when the New Testament was being written, gave it a unique ambiguity then.

Endogamy, or marriage only within the group, is the most common marriage system in human society. But in the Hebrew case, it is also part of a larger symbolic system in which the holiness of the people is protected by concentric circles of exclusion, culminating in the purity of the high priest as he enters the inner sanctum of the temple on Yom Kippur, the Day of Atonement.

Avoiding foreign women had been a prohibition dominant in pre-exilic traditions. One reason apparently was the Canaanites' practice of child sacrifice, something that continued even into Roman times. Worship of Yahweh entailed marrying within Abraham's family; this guaranteed a national life through the gift of progeny, the very opposite of Canaanite child sacrifice.

Conversion into Judaism was the countervailing policy that allowed the program to work. The biblical book *Ruth* names a woman of the neighbouring

Moabites as an ancestor of King David. The story was edited as a polemical tract dramatizing the new change of status that would come to be called conversion. In this romance, the implicit metaphor is marriage into the family—rather than intermarriage, marriage out of the family. Even David's ancestors enter the family Israel from without, thus legitimizing the practice for later generations. The people of the covenant are defined ideologically, not just genealogically.

In the absence of a king, most of the affairs of state came under the purview of the priests. Use of the term 'theocracy' to refer to this system of government is etymologically imprecise, for God did not rule directly. Rather, the ruling priests claimed to be undertaking God's purposes. Some of the priests became political bureaucrats with priestly ordination.

A notable achievement of this period was the priestly aristocracy's editing of the first five books of the Bible. They were put together in a single work, consisting of five scrolls, during this period. The document came to be known as the Torah, a word originally signifying a priestly ordinance and reflecting the priestly editorial activity. But the priestly redactors did not basically alter the original epic stories in the document. Often they combined conflicting accounts of the same events and made a seeming whole out of the traditions in front of them. Gathering past traditions for posterity was characteristic of many countries in the Persian Empire and was, as in Israel, an attempt to preserve the traditions disrupted by the Assyrians and Babylonians.

The Torah became the foundation document of the nation in the second commonwealth period in somewhat the same way that the collected body of British law serves as Britain's constitution. However, the Hebrew constitution came complete with cosmogonic myth, epic, and narrative history because of the conventions in which covenants were written.

THE HELLENISTIC PERIOD

We call the age following Alexander's conquest of the Persian Empire in 331 BCE Hellenistic, in contrast to the preceding Hellenic age of the city-states in classical Greece. The word *hellenizō* in Greek means literally 'I speak Greek' or even 'I learn to speak Greek.' And Greek was adopted by many peoples of the eastern Mediterranean. It remained the major language of trade even after the Romans arrived.

But the common culture that evolved had little to do with the values of ancient Athens. It was a cosmopolitan imperial culture, largely oriental. It was emerging before Alexander's conquests, with Greek trade and cultural contact. Its outlook eroded the automatic assent of Judeans to the traditions of their forefathers. Judaism had to evolve new ways of understanding and explaining itself. This was true especially outside the ancient land of Israel, throughout the

Mediterranean and Mesopotamia, where the majority of Jews lived. They constituted the Diaspora (from Greek for 'sowing of seed', hence 'dispersal').

The Jewish community of Alexandria in Egypt adopted Greek styles of architecture and dress and Greek names. Most lost the ability to read Hebrew, so the Bible was translated into Greek in the early third century BCE. According to a legend in the *Letter of Aristeas*, the translation is the product of seventy scholars in Egypt who, working independently, by a miracle produce identical drafts for King Ptolemy II Philadelphos. The edition is thus called the *Septuagint* (abbreviated LXX; *septuaginta* means 'seventy' in Latin).

The story is only a fable, but it gives the *Septuagint* and the whole notion of translating the Bible into foreign languages a place of authority and respect. The miracle authenticates the translation to be as religiously authoritative as the original (contrast Islam, where the *Qur'ān* is explicitly in Arabic and a translation is held to be only an interpretation).

Translation brought the Bible into a whole new set of cultural expectations. Instead of reading it as the covenant charter of the Hebrew state, Jews in Alexandria treated their Greek Bible more as an object of literary study and of meditation. Thus the three divisions of Hebrew scripture, namely *Law*, *Prophets*, and *Writings*, were reshuffled into four: law, history, poetry, and prophecy. Essentially, the historical and poetical books that appeared in the *Prophets* and the *Writings* were sorted into new genre categories. It is thus that the books of *Kings*, which in Hebrew had been in the prophetic collection, and the priestly rewrite of them, *Chronicles*, from the *Writings*, came to be placed side by side, with their discrepancies the more evident through their juxtaposition.

The community still living in Judea may have kept more of its native ways, despite Hellenization even there. The very small district of Judea was not as big as the modern state of Israel. It was closer to the area of modern metropolitan Jerusalem. Surrounded by cities founded or settled on Greek models, it could hardly ignore Hellenistic culture. Hellenistic influence within Jerusalem is indicated by the amphitheatre and gymnasium constructed there in the second century BCE.

Hellenization progressed at different rates in different classes, accentuating separations and exacerbating conflicts among the social classes of Judea. Basically, those people who were interested in a life of leadership within the community and could afford the education sought out Greek educational institutions. They consisted mostly of the traditional rural aristocrats and the priests entrusted with running the country. A developing trades class also learned rudimentary Greek for use in international exchange. These Jews felt that Greek philosophy and culture did not interfere with their Jewishness.

There is some evidence of improvement in the status of women in the late Hellenistic world; Jewish women, especially the highly Hellenized ones, were able to take advantage of it. We find women listed as the leaders of Jewish congregations and as benefactors of various buildings, which suggests that they had the right to dispose of money and property.

The Greeks were initially impressed with Jewish traditions. Hecataeus of Abdera, for instance, who travelled and wrote in the fifth century BCE, prior to Alexander, lionizes Moses as one 'who did not make any kind of picture of gods, as he did not believe that God was in human form; rather the heaven which surrounds the earth was alone God and Lord of all.' Although Hecataeus did not get the details right, the tone of admiration is perceptible.

Theophrastus, writing in the fourth century BCE, calls the Jews a 'race of philosophers' because they 'discourse on the divine … observe the stars at night … and call to them in their prayers'. Many of the schools of Greek philosophy had evolved monistic or monotheistic teachings to explain the ancient myths and stories of the *Iliad* and *Odyssey* as allegories representing moral virtues. Thus it is not difficult to see why Hebrew monotheism was so impressive to them, even though they were dressing it up to suit their own romantic notions of the philosophical peoples of the east.

Not all pagan responses to Judaism were positive; some anti-Semitism does appear during the Hellenistic period. Most anti-Jewish comments by Greek and Roman writers merely express a general dislike of foreigners. But in the case of Apion in the first century, xenophobia crossed the line into anti-Semitism. According to the first-century Jewish historian Flavius Josephus in *Against Apion*,

> Within this sanctuary, Apion has the effrontery to assert that the Jews kept an ass's head, worshipping that animal and deeming it worthy of the deepest reverence; the fact was disclosed, he maintains, on the occasion of the spoliation of the temple by Antiochus Epiphanes, when the head, made of gold and worth a high price, was discovered (Thackeray 1927, 2:79–80).

The Maccabean Revolt and Ḥanukkah

Competition between two Greek dynasties descended from Alexander's generals, the Ptolemies of Egypt and the Seleucids of Syria, had an impact on the history of Judea. Antiochus III the Great, who came to the Seleucid throne in Antioch in 223 BCE, fought the Ptolemaic rulers of Egypt for more than two decades and won a decisive victory over Ptolemy V. As a result of his victory, the land of ancient Israel passed from the control of the Ptolemies into the empire of the Seleucids.

Antiochus III's son, Antiochus IV Epiphanes ('the God manifest'), is the Seleucid king whose villainy is recounted in the story of Ḥanukkah. The traditional version treats Antiochus as an insane and irrational tyrant, but what Antiochus did was more rational, even cynical. He installed his own candidate, Jason, for the Jewish high priesthood, over his rival and relative, Menelaus, and then changed his mind when Menelaus offered him more money. Antiochus cracked down on Jews who were rioting against his appointees for the priesthood. The temple was transformed into a cult place of Zeus, the supreme god of the Hellenized world, whom Greeks identified with Yahweh of the Hebrews. Antiochus could raid the temple for its riches, then declare martial law in Jerusalem and its environs by moving troops into the temple area, and suspend the local Torah constitution.

Antiochus apparently misunderstood the nature, depth, and extent of the religious sentiments of the Judeans, rather than desiring specifically to persecute the religion. His action may have been primarily economic and political. But since the community understood its identity as a subject population in terms of religion, from its own perspective threats to it logically amounted to attacks on religion.

A general revolt broke out in 166 BCE, led by a group of resistance fighters called the Maccabees ('hammer', the Hebrew nickname for their leader Judah). Though triggered by the external interference, it was partly an intra-Jewish civil war. A factor was the differential acculturation of classes in Judea to Hellenism. Issues between the Judean Hellenizers and the Maccabees were not wholly religious, but also political and economic. In *1 Maccabees* the most Hellenized faction is characterized as guilty of apostasy against the covenant, the Torah of Moses, and the holiness of the people. But there are hints that the charge of heresy was an exaggeration, that the reformers' motives were simply more political than the Maccabees':

> At that time there appeared in Israel a group of renegade Jews, who incited the people. 'Let us enter into a covenant with the gentiles round about,' they said, 'because disaster upon disaster has overtaken us since we segregated ourselves from them.' The people thought this a good argument, and some of them in their enthusiasm went to the king and received authority to introduce non-Jewish laws and customs. They built a sports stadium in the gentile style in Jerusalem. They removed their marks of circumcision and repudiated the holy covenant. They intermarried with gentiles, and abandoned themselves to evil ways (*1 Maccabees* 1:11–15).

The account imputes to these 'radical Hellenizers' an intent to repudiate the covenant with Yahweh in several ways. Loyalists considered intermarriage a sin. They saw non-Jewish customs being introduced into Jerusalem with a sports stadium. And the naked athletic competition of Greek culture reportedly prompted some Jewish males to conceal their circumcision, the mark of membership in the covenant community. This was a costly, vain, and painful operation, drawing the flesh of the penis forward over the glans. It is hard to imagine many Hellenized Jews actually undergoing it, but the text does suggest traditionalist alarm at the potential of assimilation.

The assimilationist reformers, changing worship and introducing the gymnasium onto sacred ground, probably thought they were advancing the political reputation of Jerusalem. But their changes were perceived in the less Hellenized rural areas as undermining the religious basis of Judean life, a violation of the Torah constitution. Worse yet, it was priests who were making these changes.

The Maccabean reaction prevailed. The rededication of the temple in 164 BCE, concerning which the populace could feel united, became the focus of the minor holiday called Ḥanukkah. The Maccabees enjoyed military successes, expanding the Jewish state to its pre-exilic boundaries. The rebels set themselves up as client kings. Called the Hasmoneans, their dynasty ruled in shaky and feverish independence for more than a century, from 165 BCE until Pompey's entrance into Jerusalem in 64 BCE brought Judea under Roman occupation. But the Hasmoneans were not anti-Hellenistic. Rather, they readily adopted Hellenistic culture.

Sectarian Strife

Samaritans

Descendants of the northern Israelite tribes and the peoples who were mixed with them during the Assyrian period, the Samaritans appear with a distinct identity in the Hellenistic and Roman era. They were sufficiently different from the Judeans to have quarrelled significantly with them. The old interregional rivalry between northern and southern kingdoms prior to the Exile doubtless fed into that quarrel.

In Hellenistic times, the Samaritans were in the process of becoming what they have remained, a separate group on the fringes of Judaism. They continue as a very small community in the West Bank, living mostly around the modern town of Nablus (from the Greek Neapolis), which is near the location of the ancient northern capital of Samaria.

Samaritans are distinguished from Jews in part by their corpus of scripture. They reject the *Prophets* and *Writings* in the Hebrew Bible, accepting only the first five books of Moses as canonical. Their *Pentateuch* differs from the one found today in the Hebrew Bible in that it contains several interesting additions about the prophet who is to be like Moses.

They are distinguished also by their continued practice of animal sacrifice. They slaughter and consume lambs at their annual spring Passover celebration on Mount Gerizim, near Nablus. By comparison, such sacrifice did not survive the first-century destruction of the temple in rabbinic Judaism. The religious leader of the Samaritans, who conducts the Passover sacrifice, continues to be a high priest.

There was apparently some spread of the Samaritan community in antiquity. We have evidence of synagogues of the Samaritans in Corinth, Greece, during the Roman period. There is thus an indication that the Jews were not the only people from the land of ancient Israel to have produced a diaspora. But the Samaritan diaspora has completely disappeared.

Dynamics of Hellenism

In Palestine, the sects of Hellenistic Judaism had a political dimension. In varying ways they sought to maintain Judaism under alien rule by specifying the features of the tradition they viewed as indispensable.

The Maccabean revolt was a watershed in the Hellenization process. Once Hellenization came into conflict with the traditional constitution, the Torah of Israel, it could no longer be tolerated.

But the converse was also true. A Greek custom, no matter how foreign, could be appropriated if a conflict with Torah could be avoided. Living in a foreign empire was acceptable if their political situation allowed for the Israelite constitution as well. Thus a second, subtler phase of Hellenization began, when Hellenistic ideas were adopted into Jewish culture after having been refashioned into uniquely Judean institutions.

Essenes

The cloistered group that produced the manuscript library discovered in 1947 near the Dead Sea at Qumran, the Dead Sea Scrolls, seems to match the description of the Essenes by the first-century writers Philo and Josephus. Apparently, the Essenes formed a separate group when a high priest not to their liking was appointed in Jerusalem. They had supported an alternate candidate who was more rigorously observant of the sect's understanding of the law, whom they called the Teacher of Righteousness or the Righteous Teacher.

With this teacher they retired to the desert to establish their own centre of priestly purity. The Essenes were found mostly in monastic retreats like the one excavated at Qumran, but they reportedly lived in cities as well.

Though they did not set up a temple in the desert, they interpreted their communal body as the temple of the Lord. The Essenes were distinguishable from other protest groups of their day by their priestly character. The especially prominent observance of priestly purity laws allowed the Qumran sect in its view to associate with the angels.

The community argued their ideas as interpretations of scripture. They produced *pesher*, a genre of commentary applying the text to the events of their own time. They read the past described in the Torah as the model of their future. They saw events as moving towards an apocalyptic climax: the angels would help them fight the battle against the children of darkness at the end of time.

The sect cherished a militant body of tradition. They thought of themselves as the children of Israel who, after spending a second forty years in the desert, would reconquer the promised land. They regarded the Hellenized Jews and gentiles as new Canaanites, who would have to be wiped out before a new community of redeemed Israelites could be formed. Like the children of Israel under Moses, they waited in the desert, poised like Joshua to retake the promised land from the sinners.

Sadducees

The sects can be correlated roughly to sociological groupings within Judean society. The Sadducees represented the upper stratum of Judean society, an upper-class political and occupational group. They were the party of the priestly establishment, intimately connected to temple life. The temple was the centre of their power, and they were in charge of its proper running. The Essenes, too, had some links with the upper stratum of society. With roots were in the priestly class, the Essenes shared some traditions with the aristocratic Sadducees, but in most sociological ways, the Essenes were quite different.

The Sadducees read the laws literally. In American constitutional parlance, they would be termed 'strict constructionists'. They also denied life after death. With the Pharisees, described below, they shared power in the Sanhedrin, a communal council with juridical functions, in the first century. The Sanhedrin became more and more a Pharisaic institution until it evolved into a rabbinic institution.

Pharisees

Another group, the Pharisees, are vilified in the New Testament as nit-picking hypocrites, interested in the outward forms of ritual more than the inward substance of righteousness, but this portrayal of the Pharisees by rivals is polemical and does not appreciate the heart of Pharisaism. By assigning priorities to the various commandments the law entails, and by focusing on the intention with which one performs them, the Pharisees sought to render the law humane and livable. In keeping with their spirit is this passage that appears later in the *Mishnah*:

> If one is on his way to slaughter his Passover offering, or to circumcise his son, or to partake of the betrothal feast at his father-in-law's house, and he remembers that he left leaven in his home, if he has time to go back and remove it, and then return to fulfill the precept, he should go back and remove the leaven; but if he has not time enough to fulfill both, he should annul the leaven in his heart. If he is on the way to rescue someone from an enemy troop, from a flood, from robbers, from a fire, or from a collapsing structure, he should annul it in his heart. But if it was to keep the [Passover] feast at a place of his own choice he must return at once (*Pesachim* 3:7).

The Pharisees were the most popular sect. From time to time they even achieved power in the temple, but they were more at home around the synagogues of Judea. They represented the middle classes. Some Pharisees were landowners. Others were skilled workers, in occupations like tent making, carpentry, and glass blowing. Scribal occupations, which many of them followed, were middle-class skilled professions, and they were able to serve clients of the aristocracy. Their later legal interpretations favour some kinds of commerce.

We do not know the Pharisees directly, since there is no Pharisaic document accurately datable to the first century. But the writings of the rabbinic movement a century later inherit Pharisaism, and there are the first-century reports of Josephus and Paul, who claim to have been Pharisees at different periods in their lives. Although Paul breaks with them, Josephus speaks of them with real respect:

> The Pharisees, who are considered the most accurate interpreters of the laws and hold the position of the leading sect, attribute everything to Fate and to God; they hold that to act rightly or otherwise rests, indeed, for the most part with men, but that in each action Fate cooperates. Every soul, they maintain, is imperishable, but the soul of the good alone passes into another body, while the souls of the wicked suffer eternal punishment (Thackeray 1927, 2:162–3).

> The Pharisees had passed on to the people certain regulations handed down by former generations and not recorded in the laws of Moses, for which reason they are rejected by the Sadducean group, who hold that only those regulations should be considered valid which were written down, and that those which had been handed down by former generations need not be observed. And concerning these matters that two parties came to have controversies and serious differences, the Sadducees having the confidence of the wealthy alone but no following among the populace, while the Pharisees have the support of the masses (Thackeray 1927, 13:297–8).

The Pharisees were disposed to interpret the scriptural text broadly. In contrast to the Sadducees, they could be termed 'loose constructionists' of the Torah. Unlike the allegorizers and the apocalyptic *pesher* writers, however, the Pharisees tried to lay down rules and procedures of exegesis by which the scripture could be understood. Rabbinic thought later, around 200, develops these principles.

Though the Pharisees were like an occupational group, they sometimes behaved more like a sect. They were especially punctilious about rules of purity and tithing that distinguished members in good standing from the general populace. Special groups called *havuroth* ('brotherhoods') that formed among them were even more strict about these issues. They preferred to live near their fellowship brothers within the general population. Far from acquiescing in the

Sadducees' establishment role, they disdained the priesthood as purely cultic functionaries and thought of themselves as the proper custodians of the law.

A Balance of Interests

In a society as dedicated to individualism and cosmopolitanism as was the Hellenistic world, sectarian life was functional. The culture encouraged different and opposing concepts of truth. Accommodating the variety of Hellenistic life was a practical method for achieving stability. Ignoring it in favour of a single orthodox interpretation would have produced wholesale defections from Judaic culture.

The complementary roles of Pharisees and Sadducees represent a sharing of power among occupational and class interests. The balance functioned similarly to that among today's major parties in the United States and (prior to 1993) Canadian political systems. All the other groups were in conflict with these parties and their hold on society.

Attitudes in the Diaspora

Philo was a first-century Alexandrian Jewish philosopher and a great intellectual of his day. His arguments reflect in sophisticated form views current among Hellenized Jews, not only in the Diaspora but including the Sadducees of Judea.

We see in Philo that in the Diaspora, too, Jews interpreted the Torah as part of their fundamental rule of life. But the most characteristic aspect of Diaspora thinking was its attempt to show that scripture and Greek philosophy were in complete harmony on essential issues. Since this agreement is not evident from a literal reading of scripture, Philo made systematic use of allegory, which the Greeks had developed to understand the Homeric epics and hymns.

For Philo, narratives like the Garden of Eden and the other creation stories symbolize the development of the soul's moral virtues. They are allegorically but not literally true. Although they show God creating the world of ideas before creating the material world and other parts of the cosmos, these events did not actually happen. In this respect, Philo's system of exegesis is quite modern. His insistence, though, that many of the laws in the Bible are to be carried out as they are written is one connection between Philo and the Sadducees.

Zealots

At an extreme on the political spectrum were those that refused to live under Roman authority under any circumstances. Most of the information about them comes from Josephus, who from his perspective describes as bandits people who appear to have had truly political motives. Foremost was an extended family in Galilee who constantly fomented trouble against Herod and the Roman rulers. Ezekias, Judas of Galilee, James and Simon, Menahem, and Eleazar—all members of this family—are mentioned by Josephus in ways that suggest they were revolutionaries.

The most famous of the revolutionary groups, called either the Fourth Philosophy or the Zealots, coalesced to make war against Rome. John of Gischala was an important figure in this movement, from the beginning of the revolt in Galilee in 66 until the final destruction of Jerusalem, in 70, when he was captured. Eleazar ben Yair, another Zealot, was the rebel leader, who oversaw the subsequent Jewish defence of the fortress Masada. In Josephus's narrative, he is given the stirring words recommending death over slavery that precede the garrison's mass suicide in 73:

> But since we had a generous hope that deluded us, as if we might perhaps have been able to avenge ourselves on our enemies ... let us make haste to die bravely. Let us pity ourselves, our children, and our wives, while it is in our own power to show pity to them; for we were born to die, as well as those were whom we have begotten ... But certainly our hands are still at liberty, and have a sword in them. Let them then be subservient to us in our glorious design; let us die before we become slaves of our enemies, and let us go out of the world, together with our children, and our wives, in a state of freedom (Whiston 1802:iii.471–2).

The Zealot movement upset the first-century Sadducee-Pharisee balance described above. The revolt against Rome left Jerusalem and the temple in ruins, and also destroyed Qumran. The rabbinic movement emerged from the ashes to carry on the traditions of Pharisaism.

The Concept of God

Jewish doctrine depends on the covenant idea. As spelled out by generations of commentators, the covenant assumes a single, all-powerful God who has for his own reasons chosen Israel to be his messenger to the world. God is seen as creator and revealer. Through the development of Jewish thought in historical contexts, the covenant relationship of Israel with its divinity remains central. The ups and downs that happen in Israelite and Jewish history are interpreted as the result of obedience or defiance of that covenant.

What God reveals is first of all laws for the moral governance of human action. There is evidence as early as *Deuteronomy* that the laws in *Exodus* were viewed by commentators on the Torah as being the fixed word of God. The prophets' role was to remind the people of their obligations to follow these laws.

The *Shema* (literally 'Hear!') of *Deuteronomy* 6:4 is the watchword or creed of Judaism: 'Hear, O Israel, the LORD is our God, the LORD is One.' God is affirmed as the unique and sole master of the universe, but there have been challenges during history. Throughout the biblical period, popular Israelite religion contained references to gods other than Yahweh. The prophets railed against Israelite worship of the agricultural deities of Canaan, for instance because of the sexual content of some of their rituals. Also biblical writers charged Canaanite religion with infant sacrifice, an assumption that seems to be confirmed by scholarship.

Further challenge to Judaism's claim of the uniqueness of God was to come through contact with Greek culture. Most philosophical Greeks had already given up the concept of a polytheistic universe. Greek philosophy viewed the universe as dependent on a single principle like love or beauty or the good, taking the traditional Greek gods as a kind of allegory of the virtues.

For Greeks, the highest good could not change, because change was conceived of as a kind of imperfection. Therefore the Greek ultimate good was not a creator, since that implied change. For the Greeks creation had to take place among the intermediary gods, with the so-called demiurge (a semidivine intermediary) rather than the divinity working for the benefit of people.

Hellenistic Jews tended to understand their Judaism in relation to the dominant cosmologies (theories of the universe) of the time. Under the influence of Greek thought, Jewish philosophers like Philo reasoned that there would have to be intermediaries who accounted for Yahweh's actions on this earth. They therefore were willing to posit certain principal mediators like the *logos*, a kind of instrumental divine intelligence.

The notion of intermediating connections was taken up by Christianity, which began as a movement within Judaism. It provided Christians with a way to present Jesus as having a double nature, divine and human at the same time, which altered the unitary nature of the divinity. With its positing of God's essence containing both a son and a father, Christianity presented Judaism with the strongest theological challenge of the Hellenistic period. Compared to Christianity, Persian Zoroastrianism, with its dualistic conceptions, was hardly a threat. The Persians, who ruled Palestine for two centuries but Babylonia for more than a thousand years, seem on the whole not to have sought to convert Jews to their religion.

Judaism puts the chosenness or election of Israel at the centre of its national history. It is not explicitly articulated as a doctrine in Judaism, but it is constantly assumed in the Hebrew Bible and in later commentaries on it. Chosenness involves responsibility as well as privilege. The prophets had especially warned that Yahweh was the Lord of all creation, including other peoples, and could easily abandon the Israelites, should they not live up to their covenantal obligations.

In the Hellenistic era, Jews did not expound unilateral chosenness as overtly as the Christians, who claimed to be heirs to the promises given to the Israelite nation without having to obey the specific ordinances of Jewish law. Jews, by contrast, saw themselves as the priests of the world, the only people so commissioned by Yahweh. Their role, to transmit to humanity the Torah received through Moses on Mount Sinai, is a special responsibility rather than a privilege.

Resurrection for the Righteous

We have to distinguish between Jewish projections of what might be the fate of the nation or the world at the end of this age on the one hand, and the destiny of the individual at the end of this existence on the other. Biblical literature abounds with examples of the first, but we come up practically empty-handed when looking for the second.

One's doctrine of the events at the end of the age is termed 'eschatology', from the Greek word signifying the study of the end. A genre of Jewish literature that developed in the later prophetic books and flourished in the Hellenistic era is termed 'apocalyptic', from the Greek word for unveiling (and the Latin equivalent is 'revelation'). Most apocalyptic literature is eschatological, but it has other characteristics too. The genre is visionary in its presentation; whereas the prophets had said 'thus says Yahweh', the apocalyptists more often wrote 'I saw, and behold.'

The visions offered a form of coded symbolic representation. A human figure can represent a divine one, a beast a dynasty, a horn on that beast one of its rulers. Sometimes the code is explained for the reader, as in the sequence of visions in the first six chapters of *Zechariah*. Other times, it is left undeciphered, offering a wide-open field for reinterpretation and innovative application in later centuries. By and large, the evident concern of these texts is the corporate fate of Israel, or of a particularly faithful subgroup.

Regarding the individual, the ancient Hebrews were hardly preoccupied with an existence after death. The original solution to the problem of where personality goes after death was Sheol, an underground place like the Greek Hades, where the person resides in greatly attenuated form. Sheol is certainly not equivalent to heaven or hell. It is a pit, a place of weakness and estrangement from God, to which all the dead go and from which the spirits of the dead issue on the rare occasions when they can be seen on the earth. Occasionally, the psalmists and prophets appear to think that the righteous live in God's presence, but exactly what they mean by this is unclear.

What mattered, rather than living on as a spirit, was living on in one's descendants. Progeny are important in the covenant promise to Abraham. And we can supplement this with negative instances: a curse in *Psalm* 109:13 is that the adversary's line be blotted out, and the blessing for eunuchs in *Isaiah* 56:5 is something better than sons and daughters.

Besides, there was no strict distinction between body and soul in ancient Hebrew thought, so there was less prominence for the idea that something separate from the body might survive death. The Hebrew word *nefesh*, which is often translated as 'soul', is better translated as 'person'. Adam is called a living soul, but a corpse is described as a dead soul, as in *Leviticus* 21:11 or *Numbers* 6:60.

What sustains creatures' life is their blood, which is not to be eaten: 'But you must not eat the flesh with the soul [i.e., life], which is the blood, still in it' (*Genesis* 9:4). Breath, hence spirit (i.e., 'wind') also departs at death. But there is no reward or desirability in the spirit's going out of the body; that is merely part of the mechanics of dying.

Nothing in Hebrew thought anticipates the postbiblical ideas of paradise or resurrection as a reward for a righteous life. When the possibility is raised as a direct issue, the answer seems to be no. Consider *Ecclesiastes* 3:19: 'For the fate of the sons of men and the fate of beasts is the same; as one dies, so dies the other. They all have the same breath, and man has no advantage over the beasts; for all is vanity.'

Another passage, though often read as a prediction of Job's resurrection, appears only to affirm that Job wants to be vindicated while still alive. Job seeks an advocate in a heavenly court, as the logical outcome of his challenge to the justice of God.

> For I know that my Redeemer (or Vindicator) lives, and at last he will stand upon the earth;
> and after my skin has been thus destroyed, then from my flesh I shall see God,
> whom I shall see on my side, and my eyes shall behold, and not another (*Job* 19:25–6).

Job, like *Ecclesiastes*, seems almost to argue explicitly against any simple pietistic belief in immortality, in direct contradiction to the way the book is usually understood today.

In the later prophetic books especially, the Canaanite mythological battle between Death and Ba'al is reused as a metaphor for the power of Yahweh. *Isaiah* 25:8 says, 'God will swallow up death forever.' *Isaiah* 26 and *Ezekiel* 37 speak of the restoration of the people as a resurrection of buried bones, but nothing in these verses implies the expectation of an individual resurrection. The metaphor of resurrection is explicitly interpreted as a description of a corporate renewal.

Judaism evidently developed the doctrine of resurrection in response to the problem of martyrdom. Martyrdom became an option only when one was asked to risk death specifically for one's religion, rather than for other interests, a development we locate in the Maccabean revolt.

And the first indubitable reference to resurrection in biblical literature comes from the visions of the book of *Daniel*, which date to the years of oppression in that revolt—not to the earlier Persian and Babylonian period, as the book purports. *Daniel* 12:2 states:

> And many of those who sleep in the dust of the earth shall awake, some to everlasting life, and some to shame and everlasting contempt. And those who are wise shall shine like the brightness of the firmament; and those who turn many to righteousness, like the stars for ever and ever.

Those who suffered and died in remaining true to God's Torah will be vindicated. The reference to the saved as 'sleepers in the dust' may be a reinterpretation of *Isaiah* 26:19. The expectation among the first-century Jewish followers of Jesus that he might survive death on the cross is understandable if they regarded him a martyr.

The doctrine of resurrection is this-worldly in orientation, imagining the next life to be comparable to the present one. But injustice is removed, with the next realm attending to unfinished business from the present one. Those who persecuted the righteous of Yahweh must be resurrected too, so that they can be punished.

The heavenly journey motif is important in *1 Enoch* and other apocalyptic literature. In most cases, a journey to heaven is assumed to take place at death, for paradise and hell were both thought to be located in one of the several heavens.

Great personages or mystics could undertake heavenly ascent during life by means of ecstatic trance or other out-of-body experiences. Mystical techniques appear in some Jewish apocalyptic literature. Once a credible prophet has reportedly visited heaven and seen the rewards there, the heavenly journey verifies the community's beliefs in compensation after death. No matter how the journey is made, the texts unanimously understand the power of the voyage as due to God's own desire for the adept to visit him.

Prior to the emergence of rabbinic Judaism and Christianity in the late first century, then, the idea of resurrection remained a novelty. It was, though, a topic of debate. The Sadducees rejected it entirely, as did the book of *Job,* and the *Wisdom of Ben Sira* 14:16–17. Pharisaism accepted the idea, as did Christianity.

The Messiah

Like the doctrine of resurrection, the hope for a messiah is an idea whose emergence and development we can locate historically within the experience of Israel. In Hellenistic times it came to mean an ideal expected king, who would lead Israel to victory, demonstrating God's power and vindicating God's reputation.

A doctrine of the end-time, seeing an end-purpose and plan to human life, appears in the biblical prophets, but the end of time did not necessarily entail a messiah. The earliest apocalypses—like the book of *Daniel*, for instance—did not specify a messiah at all, rather suggesting that an angel (a military-style 'messenger') would lead the final battle against the wicked nations that had scorned the laws of God.

'Messiah' comes from Hebrew *mashiah* ('anointed one'). Anointing was a characteristic Hebrew inauguration ritual for a divinely sanctioned official position. Mostly kings, but also prophets and sometimes priests, were appointed to office with oil poured over their heads.

This was a Hebrew custom, not a Greek one. When the word *mashiah* was translated into Greek, it became *christos* ('anointed'), which suggested little honour to a Greek. In the Greek tradition, kings and winning athletes were crowned with the branches of various shrubs and bushes, not anointed.

Until the sixth-century-BCE collapse of the Judean monarchy, the messiah *par excellence* was the currently reigning king. Of the relatively few instances of the word in the Hebrew Bible, most refer to the king's installation into office. Anointed status is mentioned for priests, patriarchs, and Saul's shield. Strikingly, the Persian king, Cyrus, is Yahweh's anointed in *Isaiah* 45. Clearly the concept begins as a recognition of divinely sanctioned special service.

Before the Exile, prophets in a few passages do expect that God will raise up a king who will rule with justice and righteousness. Experience with less than perfect kings, as well as with foreign influence, probably stimulated the belief in an ideal kingship. But as long as Hebrew kings reigned, they and not the ideal future kings were the anointed ones. The expected king is sometimes called the son of David (*Isaiah* 11; *Ezekiel* 34; *Micah* 5); or he is called the 'branch', ostensibly a 'new shoot of the Davidic family tree' (*Jeremiah* 23).

In the Persian period after the Exile, the idea of a future king was greatly augmented when the last heir to the Davidic throne disappeared without a historical trace. Since 2 *Samuel* 7 had promised that Israel should never fail to have a king of the Davidic line, there was a basis to hope for its restoration.

As the concept developed, the ideas associated with the expectation seemed to depend on the sect that promoted it, such as the Essene expectation of a priestly messiah. Meanwhile, in Alexandria, Philo also refers in a very veiled way to the messiah. He thinks of a future victory over evil and unjust rulers (*On Rewards* 115–19). Tactfully, he does not make explicit his criticism of the current political order or his hope for a pre-eminent role for the Jewish people in an anticipated revolution.

The expectation of a messiah tended to fit well with the expectation of divine vindication in the showdown scenarios of apocalyptic literature. Like other manifestations of divine overhaul of the existing order, the messiah would exemplify God's sovereign control of events and reward the piety of the faithful who had trusted in God.

At one place in apocalyptic literature a messiah's death is envisioned, but as a natural part of a sequence of eras. In 2 *Esdras* (or 4 *Ezra*) 7:28–30, God's kingdom is to be established by the messiah and his supporters, all of whom are to live 400 years. When all die at the end of this period, the world will return to chaos, followed by the general resurrection of the righteous.

Nowhere before the start of Christianity is there any evidence that the messiah will suffer, let alone die for humanity's sins. In fact, no matter who among the righteous is pictured as suffering, the messiah is the one expected finally to bring God's justice to the world. However supernatural his actions, the messiah was also a political figure.

The Bar Cochba revolt of 132–5, a century after Jesus, contained strong messianic overtones. When the revolt was quelled, the death of its messianic leader, as in Christianity, brought about the rise of a tradition that the messiah must suffer and die for the end to come, e.g., b. Suk. 52a. (This citation means *Babylonian Talmud*, tractate Sukkah, folio 52, side a. The standard edition of the *Talmud* was printed in Vilna, Lithuania, in 1880–6. The pagination was established by an earlier printed edition, produced in Venice in 1520–3.)

The disastrous wars against Rome and the spread of Christianity made the rabbinic community chary of messianic movements, as they exposed the community to Roman response. The rabbis cautioned never to give up faith that the messiah would come, but they warned that if one were ploughing a field and heard the report that the messiah had arrived, one should 'finish ploughing and then go to see whether the messiah has come.' Clearly, while one must not give up hope that the messiah will come, it would be foolhardy to give easy credence to anyone fomenting rebellion or heresy.

Messianism remained an ideal in Judaism through the centuries, its fire dimmed but not extinguished by failed attempts and questionable claimants. Significant as late as the career of Sabbatai Zvi in the seventeenth century or Jacob Frank in the eighteenth is the intense piety of a people eager for God to show his hand yet again in history, intervening to bring justice for the wicked and glory for the faithful.

Christianity

Christianity began as a sect within Judaism. Its uniqueness for Judaism is that it is the only Jewish sect of its day whose origins are well known. Thus we understand Christianity better by considering it as a first-century Jewish option, but we also understand the first-century Jewish options better by considering Christianity among them.

The message of Jesus that, with repentance, all are equal before God is typical of all sectarian apocalypticism of the time. The Christian practices of public repentance, baptism, and chaste communal living are likewise typical of the other contemporary apocalyptic groups. Yet the similarity only emphasizes the striking difference between Christianity and Essenism, for example. Essenism was priestly and largely interested in the cultic purity rules allowing priests to approach God's holy places.

Christianity, in spite of its many similarities with other apocalyptic groups, was almost hostile to purity rules. Its corresponding emphasis on converting the distressed or sinful began in the teaching of John the Baptist, became characteristically Christian, and probably reflected the strong charismatic influence of Jesus. Through John the Baptist, baptism became the Christian rite uniquely demonstrating repentance, though there is no good evidence that Jesus performed it.

Jesus does not stress a return to the old strict interpretations of the Torah, as did the other apocalyptic groups. Although Jesus accepts Jewish law, he occasionally indulges in symbolic actions to provoke questions about the purpose of the Torah, such as healing the chronically ill or picking grain on the Sabbath. These challenges to the Pharisees or other sectarian interpreters of the Torah do not necessarily imply that the Torah itself is invalid.

Although asceticism and perhaps monasticism were associated with the movement of John the Baptist, the majority of Jesus's early followers lived within the fabric of society. Like many other apocalyptic groups, Christians often lived together and shared possessions. Their communalism stressed chastity, not necessarily monasticism, though Jesus himself did not marry. The Jesus movement also contained the seeds of a radical criticism of private property. 'No man can serve two masters. You cannot serve God and mammon [i.e., money]' (*Luke* 16:13).

The Christians, like the other sects, posed a problem for the Romans and for cooperating upper-level Jewish administrators: their movement had a political as well as a religious orientation. The popular expectations it generated made the messiah a political figure. The anomaly of the situation is the pacifist goals that the strong, charismatic figure at its founding evidently had in mind.

RABBINIC JUDAISM

The Rabbinic Movement

The collapse of Jerusalem in 70 marks a major turning-point in the history of Judaism, comparable with the sixth-century-BCE Exile. For a second time, the temple was destroyed, and this time it was not rebuilt. Institutions and practices associated with temple worship—such as animal sacrifice—disappeared from Jewish life. As indicated, Israelite animal sacrifice remained only among the Samaritans.

It fell to the Pharisees to carry the responsibility, as the other principal first-century movements lost their base of power and their *raison d'être* in the disastrous failure of the war for independence in 70, and its sequel, the failed Bar Cochba revolt, which broke out in 132. For the Sadducees, the temple was no more. For the Essenes, the Qumran site was no more; it was razed by the Romans on their way to besiege the desert fortress of Masada after the sack of Jerusalem. And Rome would tolerate the Zealots no longer.

Pharisaic traditions, refurbished for a new national purpose, gave birth to the institutions of rabbinic Judaism. The chief custodians of the Jewish heritage were no longer the priests but the rabbis. Etymologically, the Hebrew term *rabbi* means 'great one', 'leader', or, as it appears to mean in the New Testament, 'master'. Later, it comes to have the implied sense of 'teacher', since the rabbis were legal specialists and teachers, not ministers.

Politically, the Pharisaic-rabbinic movement's status was soon resolved. A *modus vivendi* was worked out with the Romans. The rabbis conceded that the law of every host community was the law for the Jewish community. Palestinian Jewish community government was re-established, but with little political control. The Romans eventually granted limited local power to the patriarch, an officer in the rabbinic movement.

Tradition has it that while Jerusalem remained in ruins, Yochanan ben Zakkai received Roman permission to move a circle or academy of rabbinical study down to the town of Yavneh (in Latin, Jamnia) near the Mediterranean coast. Replacing earlier sectarianism with a more unified, less dissenting Jewish community was advantageous to the Romans. They desired a unified Jewish authority to prevent further rebellion and guarantee the collection of imposts and taxes.

Gradually during and after the second century, what had been a sect was transformed into a new kind of legal and religious establishment. The Pharisees had shared power with the Sadducees, but now the rabbis consciously tried to become national or 'catholic' rather than sectarian. The transition did take time; in the code of laws that developed, the earliest layers are concerned with sectarian issues.

Christianity was part of the sectarian life that preceded rabbinic Judaism, as Pharisaism was. Many consider Judaism an older religion than Christianity that stayed closer to the original culture. But rabbinic Judaism can be viewed as an unacknowledged new religion, a later offshoot of Israelite religion that formulated its principles after Christianity had already gone its own way. And rabbinic Judaism defined itself in conscious opposition to the sectarian battles and dogmatism that had characterized the time of that separation.

The rabbinic movement was not a hereditary priesthood. It handed the interpretation of law to an educated class open to anyone. Whoever sought out and received the requisite education could belong to it. One just went to the schoolhouse, later called a *yeshiva* ('sitting', 'session'). When finished with study to the satisfaction of the teachers, one was ordained a rabbi.

The rabbis directed attention to religious life, enforcing uniformity in areas of ritual and conduct. For reconstituting Jewish society, the national heritage had to be articulated in an exegetical and legal rationale. From now on, the covenant with God was viewed as performable largely through religious law under foreign overlords. Disputes over such issues as the right to decree a new month, based on sightings of a new moon, were far less severe than the earlier kinds of sectarian conflict between Sadducees, Essenes, and Pharisees.

Many Pharisees migrated to the cities of Galilee after the destruction of the temple, but there were many Jews whose interest in the rabbinic movement was sporadic. In the Diaspora, in Babylonia the rabbis had to share power with the exilarch, involving themselves in a continuous conflict. There is also evidence for the arrival of rabbinic Judaism in Egypt, but only after the more varied Hellenistic Egyptian Jewish community had been reduced by war, persecution, and attrition.

Religiously, restructuring required an innovative response: that though its loss was tragic, the temple is not absolutely necessary. There is another means of reconciliation between God and Israel, namely, doing good deeds or 'acts of lovingkindness'. In place of the temple's sacred space, the table of every Jew was made sacred through the elaboration of rules for purity. Other aspects of the temple service were transferred to the synagogue. If the community's traditions were to be perpetuated, they would have to be recorded in texts. The challenge paralleled what had faced the priestly writers in the time of the Exile. The earlier coping with the destruction of the first temple in the sixth century BCE provided ample precedents.

The Judaism that we know today is founded on the Judaism practised by the early rabbis in late antiquity. To the Jewish mind, everything in rabbinic Judaism is a natural development of the culture of the ancient Hebrews, accommodating the wider world, progressing organically in ritual and literature.

The Synagogue

The locus of public worship was no longer the temple but the synagogue (etymologically, the Greek means 'assembly' or 'gathering', in other words, the congregation, not the building). Jews continued to pray three times a day, as dictated by the Bible and the conventions of temple service, and to add special services in commemoration of the special services in the temple. But Jewish prayer never again revolved around a central temple, nor did it take place solely in synagogues thereafter. Jews who follow the traditional order of prayer do so in their homes or at work if no synagogue is available.

Synagogues may have first come into being as far back as the destruction of the first temple in 586 BCE. They had had a role to play in the Diaspora, in locales without access to the second temple. There, and for all Jews after 70, the synagogue served as a place of assembly, study, and prayer. Many of the temple's functions and much of the liturgy were transferred there and augmented by prayers, poems, and psalms written by rabbinic Jews.

During the first century, as ever afterwards, synagogues often met in the home of a wealthy patron or patroness, who might exercise considerable leadership and might even bequeath the house to the congregation after her death. This is how many of the earliest Christian congregations began as well. We have ruins of synagogue buildings beginning from the late first century. From before that, we have literary evidence that synagogues existed. There were, for instance, the myriad and monumental synagogues of Alexandria discussed by Philo, but they have left us no identifiable remains.

The early synagogue buildings were evidently of two kinds: the longhouse, a long rectangular room, or the basilica, modelled on popular Roman municipal architecture. There is some evidence that buildings designed for other purposes could be pressed into service as synagogues. This is how the council chamber at Masada, with its amphitheatre of descending rows of steps, appears to have been used by the Zealots when they captured the palace from Herod.

Synagogues initially had no provision for special seating for women. Perhaps their religious duties could be fulfilled at home, or perhaps the separation of sexes during worship had not yet taken hold. But Josephus describes a segregation in Essene worship in the first century. There is also evidence in dedicatory inscriptions that women were benefactors of synagogue buildings and held such titles as 'leader' or 'matriarch'. This tells us that women had the power to dispose of finances, but not the extent to which women were seen in the synagogue. Much must have varied with the culture, and wealthy Greco-Roman women normally kept themselves out of public view.

By the second and third centuries, synagogues began to evolve the specific architecture that now characterizes them. The congregation prayed facing Jerusalem, inclining all Jewish prayer towards the temple site. Cut or painted in the wall in front of them was a niche in which the Torah was placed during the service. Thus most synagogues in Western countries face east. For prayer at home, many Jews mark the direction with a plaque reading '*Mizrah*' ('east' in Hebrew).

At first the Torah scrolls, housed in other buildings for safe keeping and study, were brought to the synagogue for services. There is some evidence that at this time they were wheeled from place to place in a model of the ancient ark, now pictured as a four-wheeled cart with a model temple on top. The Hellenistic world pictured the ancient ark, too, as a cart rather than a box carried by poles; we can see this in the third- and fourth-century synagogue ruins at Kfar Nahum (Capernaum) in Galilee. This matches the Greek religious custom of periodically parading the sacred objects of a cult through the city in a model temple on wheels, called a *naiskos*.

SECTARIAN OPTIONS IN THE HELLENISTIC ERA

Now at this time there were three schools of thought (*haireseis*) among the Jews, which held different opinions concerning human affairs; the first being that of the Pharisees, the second that of the Sadducees, and the third that of the Essenes. As to the Pharisees, they say that certain events are the work of fate but not all; as to the other events, it depends upon ourselves whether they shall take place or not. The Essenes, however, declare that Fate is mistress of all things, and that nothing befalls men unless it be in accordance with her decree. But the Sadducees do away with Fate, holding that there is no such thing and that human actions are not achieved in accordance with her decree, but that all things lie within our power, so that we ourselves are responsible for our well-being, while we suffer misfortune through our own thoughtlessness (Josephus, in Stern 1927, 13:171–3, 288–98).

Eventually, the Torah niche became an elaborate and relatively stationary piece of furniture called the holy ark, permanently housing the Torah scrolls at the front of the synagogue. In later tradition, above the ark is a lamp, the *ner tamid* ('eternal lamp'), tended continuously in imitation of the lamps in the temple. Also part of synagogue architecture is the *bēma* (Greek for 'rostrum'), from which the Torah was read. When positioned in the centre of the congregation, this rostrum makes worship a kind of theatre in the round. When placed at the front with the the ark containing the Torah, it forms a kind of stage.

The seven-branched *menorah* ('candlestick' or 'lampstand') in both ancient and modern synagogues replicates an item of temple furniture. The Victory Arch of Titus in the Roman Forum depicts Roman soldiers carrying off a large seven-branched *menorah* as booty from the destruction of the Jerusalem temple. At that time the *menorah* became a symbol for Jewish culture and sovereignty. Today it is the official symbol of the state of Israel.

The six-pointed star, called the *Magen David* (Hebrew, 'the shield of David'), began to appear as a specifically Jewish symbol only in the Middle Ages. In the Hellenistic period it appeared as a decorative motif in synagogues. It probably became more popular in the Islamic period because Islamic culture, and Jews who were influenced by it, preferred geometric patterns to images of animals or people that might be taken as idolatry.

During the Hellenistic period, however, Jews seemed content to allow mosaics and frescoes in synagogues, generally shying away only from sculpture of the human form as offensive to their religious sensibilities. There is some evidence that when pious Jews used ordinary objects with depictions of human

ISRAEL'S ROLE AMONG THE NATIONS

Rabbi Eliezer said: 'All the nations will have no share in the world to come, even as it is said, "The wicked shall go into Sheol, and all the nations that forget God" [*Psalm* 9:17]. The wicked shall go into Sheol—these are the wicked among Israel.' Rabbi Joshua said to him: 'If the verse had said, "The wicked shall go into Sheol with all the nations," and had stopped there, I should have agreed with you, but as it goes on to say "who forget God," it means there are righteous men among the nations who have a share in the world to come' (*Tosefta Sanhedrin* 13:2).

Rabbi Jeremiah said: 'Whence can you know that the gentile that practices the law is equal to the high priest? Because it is said, "which, if a man do, he shall live through them" [*Leviticus* 18:5]. And it says, "This is the Torah of man" [2 *Samuel* 7:19]. It does not say, "the law of the priests, Levites, Israelites," but "This is the law of man, O Lord God." And it does not say, "Open the gates and let the priests and Levites and Israel enter," but it says: "Open the gates that the righteous may enter" [*Isaiah* 26:2]. And it says, "This is the gate of the Lord, the righteous shall enter it." It does not say, "The priests and the Levites and Israel shall enter it," but it says, "The righteous shall enter it" [*Psalm* 118:20]. And it does not say, "Rejoice ye, priests, Levites, and Israelites," but it says, "Rejoice ye righteous" [*Psalm* 33:1]. And it does not say, "Do good, O Lord, to the priests and the Levites and the Israelites," but it says, "Do good, O Lord, to the good" [*Psalm* 124:4]. So even a gentile, if he practises the Torah, is equal to the high priest (*Sifra* 86b; b. Baba Kamma 38a).

form, such as moulded figures frequently found on spoons or jars, they made a small symbolic cut on the object so that the figure would no longer be complete.

In antiquity, besides with the *menorah*, synagogues were decorated with depictions of the temple façade and rams' horns, but especially with flora of the holy land such as the palm, myrtle, willow, pomegranate, and other plants of the Sukkoth festival. Early synagogue buildings in Galilee have mosaic floors featuring the zodiac and seasons, with the sun in the centre, pictured as a young man standing in a *quadriga*, a Roman chariot with four horses. Evidently, the possibility of idolatry was avoided in flat representations of Greek gods, rather than the rounded, plastic statues that the pagans worshipped, and especially in depictions made to be walked upon.

The arts of the classical world could be put to use for Jewish decorative purposes in Roman and Byzantine synagogues. From the third-century synagogue at Dura-Europos in northeastern Syria come wall paintings (now preserved in the Damascus museum) depicting biblical stories. God is not portrayed directly, but his presence is symbolized by a hand appearing from the heavens.

The Essence of Religion

[Pirke Aboth *appears as a tractate in the Mishnah. The title is commonly translated* The Ethics of the Fathers, or The Sayings of the Fathers, *but a more accurate translation would be* The Chapters of the Ancestors.]

1:1. Moses received the Torah on Sinai and handed it down to Joshua, and Joshua to the elders, and the elders to the prophets, and the prophets handed it down to the men of the Great Assembly. They said three things: be deliberate in judgment, raise up many disciples, and make a fence around the Torah.

1:2. Simeon the Just was one of the last members of the Great Assembly. He used to say: 'Upon three things the world stands—on the Torah, on the Temple service, and on acts of kindness.'

1:12. Hillel and Shammai received Torah from them. Hillel says: 'Be one of Aaron's disciples, loving peace and pursuing it, loving mankind and bringing them near to the Torah.'

1:14. He used to say: 'If I am not for myself, who then will be for me? And if I am for myself alone, what am I? And if not now, when?'

1:18. Rabban Simeon ben Gamaliel says: 'On three things the world stands: on justice, on truth, and on peace, as it is written, "Execute the judgment of truth and peace in your gates" [*Zechariah* 8:16].'

2:8. Rabban Yochanan ben Zakkai received Torah from Hillel and Shammai. He used to say: 'If you have learned much Torah, do not take credit for yourself, for this was the purpose of your creation.'

Characters from Abraham through Ezekiel are depicted and dressed like the people of the Hellenistic world. The Torah niche is painted as a large sea shell.

Scripture and Commentary

The period after 70, when the rabbinic class was taking charge and formulating practices and institutions, marks the beginning of 'classical Judaism'. Its interpretation of the covenant's obligations has remained standard for Jews throughout the world to the present day. And, parallel to what had happened earlier in the sixth century BCE, the disruption of the temple's institutions left the surviving scriptural texts as a prominent source of authority.

The five scrolls of the *Law*, ascribed to Moses but completed by 400 BCE, were central. Another collection, which was probably stabilized by about 200 BCE, included the prophetical books. We can see that in the first century these two collections, the *Law* and the *Prophets* were scripture *par excellence* by looking at references that different groups made to them. The Christians, for instance, present

JUDAISM OUTLASTS THE JERUSALEM TEMPLE, DESTROYED IN 70

Once as Rabbi Yochanan ben Zakkai was coming from Jerusalem, Rabbi Joshua followed after him and saw the Temple in ruins.

'Woe unto us,' Rabbi Joshua cried, 'for the place where the iniquities of Israel were atoned is destroyed!'

'My son,' Rabbi Yochanan ben Zakkai said to him, 'do not grieve. We have another atonement as effective as this. And what is it? It is acts of lovingkindness, as it is said: "I desire mercy and not sacrifice"' [*Hosea* 6:6] (*The Fathers According to Rabbi Nathan* 6).

the golden rule (*Matthew* 7:12) or love of God and neighbour (*Matthew* 22:20) as summing them up. (The Jewish citation of the golden rule as summarizing the whole law is ascribed to Hillel, an influential scholar who lived a few decades before Jesus.)

But other religious literature was part of the scriptural heritage, too, as is evident from what was translated in the *Septuagint*. It included notably the book of *Psalms*, the temple hymn collection, but also 'wisdom' writings like *Job* and *Proverbs*, and a range of apocalyptic and historical texts. With the diversity of sectarian emphases, the number of writings that might be candidates for scriptural status was growing.

Tradition reports that the rabbis at Yavneh in about 90 put an end to the fluid situation in Jewish literature by deciding on the status of the third portion of the Hebrew canon, the sacred *Writings*. Books were supposed to be in Hebrew and pre-exilic. The second-century-BCE apocalypse *Daniel* made it by appearing outwardly to have these characteristics, whereas the more straightforward history of the same period in *Maccabees* was seen as ineligible.

For the rabbis, then, the Bible came to consist of three sections: the *Law* (Torah), the *Prophets* (in Hebrew, *Nevi'im*), and the sacred *Writings* (in Hebrew, *Ketuvim*). Jews often use the Hebrew acronym of these three sections, *Tanakh* (T–N–K), to denote this corpus of Hebrew scripture.

Midrash

After the biblical corpus became fixed or closed, in the early centuries CE, it remained the subject of considerable commentary. The rabbis collected and added to a growing body of Bible interpretation, known as *midrash* ('interpretation', i.e., commentary). Midrashic commentaries are mostly line-by-line interpretations following the sequence of the biblical text. They may be ordered also by the lectionary cycle (the schedule of biblical readings every week) traditionally used in the synagogue.

The early *midrashim* contain a great many legal discussions. In the first and second centuries, the Pharisees derived rulings about contemporary customs from the written text of the Bible by means of imaginative principles of exegesis. They then claimed that their interpretation was present from the very beginning.

These few books—the *Mekhilta* for *Exodus*, *Sifra* for *Leviticus*, *Sifre* for *Numbers* and *Deuteronomy*—contain a wealth of information about the context in which the legal discussions were held. The process of commenting continued for several centuries before the books were published separately, so it is not clear in individual cases without careful study which traditions can be dated early and which were late.

The rabbinic writers of *midrash* took it as their task not to write the Bible—for they considered its text unalterable—but rather to understand the significance of what the text contained. Often with remarkable ingenuity, they attempted to resolve contradictions implicit within particular biblical narratives or between one biblical passage and another.

There was much to interpret, for example, in the first chapters of the book of *Genesis*. Humanity is created male and female in chapter 1, yet we are introduced to Adam only in chapter 2. Only later does God create Eve. As well, the order of creation is different in the two chapters.

One strong traditional argument is that chapter 2 describes the events of the sixth day of chapter 1. Thus *midrash* discusses such possibilities as Eve's being Adam's second wife; the first, Lilith, who was the unsatisfactory wife mentioned in chapter 1, is eventually figured as a demon.

Another explanation the rabbis offer is borrowed from Plato's *Symposium*, in which the character Aristophanes suggests that human beings were originally born as double animals with two heads and four legs and arms. The Greeks used this amusing little story to justify the variety of sexual orientations in their society: after their separation, humans spend their lives looking for their other halves. The rabbis, however, use the story in quite a different way to explain how the text can refer to the creation of humanity, male and female in *Genesis* 1, yet narrate the story of Eve's creation in *Genesis* 2.

None of these explanatory stories is actually present in the text of the Bible at all, but they can all be considered part of Torah, in an extended sense. Jewish biblical interpretation is imaginative and sometimes far-fetched. Although rabbis invented rules of exegesis, biblical passages do not have a single authoritative interpretation. Jewish biblical commentary is a communal and composite literature, collecting all that various important rabbis said and gathering them under the category of the specific biblical verse.

In later *midrash*, the so-called homiletical *midrashim*, are a great many discussions apparently generated by rabbinic sermons. *Midrash* represents the effort over centuries of Jewish experience, still continuing today, to relate the Bible to the understanding and the concerns of the time.

The *Mishnah*

A major achievement in the rabbis' restructuring of the religion was their elaboration of the heritage of law. Forms that had been passed along orally in Pharisaism they now ordered and codified in writing. This basic literature of rabbinic Judaism consisted first of the *Mishnah* and then the *Talmud*.

As indicated above, rabbinic biblical commentary follows the sequence and structure of books already extant in the Hebrew canon at the end of the first century. By contrast, the *Mishnah* was a new production a century later, which had its own topically arranged structure. It is organized in six 'orders' or divisions: Seeds (agriculture), Festivals, Women, Damages, Holy Things (ritual), and Purifications. The *Mishnah* summarizes the application of the traditional law as the Pharisaic-rabbinic movement interpreted it. The oldest datable rabbinic document, it was produced shortly before 220 by Rabbi Judah, titled ha-Nasi ('the prince').

The operative concept by which the *Mishnah* was claimed to be authoritative was the notion of the 'oral law'—that is, that alongside the five books traditionally ascribed to Moses, there was another body of precedent and interpretation that had been passed down from Moses in a direct line of oral tradition. By this doctrine the rabbis could assert that their own interpretations were just as God-given as the doctrines written explicitly in the Torah constitution. But we cannot be sure whether the oral law was so called because originally it was forbidden to be written down or merely because it had started its existence in oral form.

The Pharisees claimed that only they, and not the priests or other Jewish parties, had received the tradition, and that only they were entitled to comment and decide upon its authoritative meaning. They claimed that though prophecy had ceased, their biblical exegesis was the true descendant of prophetic insight. This was the Pharisees' pretext for taking over the reins of government from the priests, whom they looked down on as mere practitioners, even though the priests had transmitted much ancient law and were responsible partners in the second temple government.

The development of Pharisaic traditions is reflected in two first-century schools of interpretation. One was led by Hillel, and the other by his contemporary, Shammai. The earliest stages may well have involved the codification of laws on the issues of most interest to the Pharisees—Sabbath law, purity, and tithing. Along with these, marriage and divorce were also of primary interest to the early rabbis, for rules of personal status defined membership in the Jewish community.

Enormous attention was given to the defunct sacrificial system in the temple, and purity issues that had depended upon the temple. Motivations for this effort included a desire to be closely associated with running the temple, should the temple be soon rebuilt; an antiquarian interest in preserving laws; and even an interest in reconstructing the legal system with the rabbis more firmly in control. The failure of the Bar Cochba revolt of 132–5 made it painfully clear that the temple would not soon be rebuilt, yet the rabbinic commentary on temple law continued, in preparation for the eventual messianic age.

By the second century it was taken for granted that the rabbinic movement had always been the majority movement in Judaism. The power and function of the competing first-century sects in a nation-state were forgotten. The rabbis' sense of control was projected backward onto traditions that had been laid down in totally different circumstances, some when Pharisaism was merely a sectarian movement in Judaism. Indeed, the original social function for the sects, to ensure that conflicting perspectives in the Hellenistic world were expressed in a healthy and functional way, was taken over by the rabbinic movement itself. Schools and factions within the rabbinic movement fought each other with clearly defined rules for scriptural exegesis.

Although the *Mishnah* of Rabbi Judah the Prince is highly honoured and quoted as authoritative, it is not the only repository of this earliest layer of Jewish tradition, produced by the first generations of the rabbis, who are often called the Tannaim (Aramaic for 'repeaters' or 'teachers'). Alternative Tannaitic traditions are also found in a book called the *Tosefta* (Aramaic for 'addition'), and they provide precedents of equal value in rabbinic discussions.

The *Talmud*

By about 200, the formerly open and growing body of interpretation that the Pharisees had rationalized as coming orally from Moses had, like the Bible, become a fixed, written text. And, like the Bible, the *Mishnah* of Rabbi Judah now became the subject of passage-by-passage commentary. The structure of the *Mishnah* in its six orders, subdivided into a total of sixty-three tractates, came to serve as the skeleton of this body of expansion, a large collection known as the *Talmud*.

There is one *Mishnah*. It is not longer than a desk dictionary. There are two different *Talmuds*, each commenting on the *Mishnah* and each closer to the size of a multivolume encyclopedia. Each *Talmud* consists of the Hebrew *Mishnah* of Rabbi Judah plus one of the two bodies of commentary, known as a *gemarah* (Hebrew *gemaroth*, 'completion').

One *gemarah* is from the Jewish community living in Palestine, the other from the Jewish community living in Babylonia. The *Mishnah* and the Palestinian *Gemarah* form the *Palestinian Talmud*; this material is also often referred to as the *Jerusalem Talmud*, though it was likely produced in the Galilee area of northern Palestine, not in Jerusalem. The same *Mishnah* and the other *Gemarah*, produced in Babylonia, form the *Babylonian Talmud*.

The *Mishnah* is in Hebrew, which was a language of past tradition and of liturgy and scholarly study, as church Latin became for Christians in the

European Middle Ages; both *gemarahs*, on the other hand, are in Aramaic, a vernacular language of the day, which is a Semitic language related to Hebrew.

Typically, the form of the text of the *Talmud* starts with a short passage from the *Mishnah* and then follows that with the text of the related *Gemarah*, which could be many times the length of the *Mishnah* text to which it was attached. In printed editions, such as the standard Vilna edition of 1880–6, the commentary nature of the tradition is graphically evident since the *Mishnah* and *gemarah* are printed in a small column in the centre of the page, while the columns on either side carry later additions, later commentaries, and various other study aids like cross-references.

The Palestinian or *Jerusalem Talmud* is an interesting source for history, lore, and tradition in Judaism. Those who produced it, however, suffered from a deteriorating situation. The economy was in decline, but worse for Jews was the Christianization of the Roman Empire. Emperors enacted discriminatory laws; about 425, the Christian emperor Theodosius II (r. 408–50) abolished the office of the patriarch, the head of the leading Palestinian academy.

Meanwhile in Babylonia, where the ruling Sasanian Persians were more tolerant to Jews, the Jewish community in Babylonia rose in importance to become the centre of Jewish life. The substantial and extensive *Babylonian Talmud* became the more authoritative one for the Jewish community, containing the more acute legal discussions. In the seventh century Muslims succeeded the Sasanians as rulers of the Mesopotamian or Babylonian region, which they called Iraq.

At first Palestine was in charge of the ritual calendar. Only Palestine could declare the arrival of a new month by direct observation of the moon. This was then communicated to other lands by a system of signal fires, runners, and rams' horns. When the calendar became mathematically calculated, the Babylonian community embarked upon an independent ritual life. This change formalized the primacy of the Babylonian Talmudic academies, which had been gaining in talent and prestige for generations.

The commentary of the *Gemarah* records discussions of over 2,000 sages, arguing over specific ways to resolve issues by reference to the text of the *Mishnah*. In contrast to the ordered discussion of the *Mishnah*, the discussions of the *Gemarah* are quite complex and far-ranging, indeed often free-associational. Even so, the text is written in a kind of Aramaic shorthand that signals through brief technical terms the formal characteristics of the specific arguments that are about to be mounted.

Since the text of the *Mishnah*, the core of the *Talmud*, is a document of law, a considerable amount of the *Gemarah* is strictly legal. Not all the legal discussion ends with a specific procedure that can be considered prescriptive for conduct. But where it does, Jews speak of such prescriptive discussion as *halakha* ('the way' or 'procedure', more specifically, the proper legal procedure for living life). Because of this, Jews can also speak loosely of any legal discussion as halakhic.

There is another style of expansion that is more anecdotal; it is referred to as *agada* ('narrative'). *Halakha* makes its directives by legal analysis and explicit statement; *agada* indicates a moral lesson by telling a story.

Jews conventionally make a kind of genre distinction between the topically arranged legal material of the *Talmud* as *halakha*, and the expansion on the narratives of the Bible in the *Midrash* as *agada*, because those works emphasize law and story respectively. Strictly speaking, however, there is both *halakha* (legal discussion) and *agada* (edifying stories) in each of the collections, *Talmud* and *Midrash*, though in vastly different proportions. As a result, Jews can use the terms *halakha* and *agada* in very wide and sometimes confusing ways. The words may refer to particular legal or folkloric techniques of analysing ancient text, or they can refer to specific books of the oral law in which these techniques are used.

The Status of Torah

The same elasticity of definition characterizes rabbinic and Jewish understandings of the term *torah*. In early first temple times, the word *torah* apparently meant only laws that governed priestly behaviour. But starting with the book of *Deuteronomy*, it was used to refer to a written book of law, then the whole *Pentateuch*, the first five books of the Bible, attributed to Moses.

In biblical times, books were written on scrolls. This form has been retained for the copy of the sacred text used in synagogue recitation. Called a *sefer Torah* ('book of the Torah'), it is written by hand on parchment and mounted on wooden rollers. For private study one would use a copy of the *Pentateuch* bound as a book (the form that replaced scrolls in late antiquity). That is called a *Ḥumash*, from the Hebrew word for 'five'.

In an extended sense, the Torah is the entire Hebrew Bible, the *Tanakh*. Further, even the books of the oral law, *Midrash*, *Mishnah*, and *Talmud*, can also be called by the term 'Torah'. That is because every discussion of holy law and procedure, whether it be moral, ritual, or ceremonial, was considered part of the same divine revelation, continuing unabated over the millennia. Thus 'Torah' can refer to any revelatory or canonical literature. In rabbinic parlance, the *Talmud* and the still later commentaries on the *Talmud*, produced in various lands and by various experts over the centuries, are part of Torah, although they are also called *Torah she ba'al peh*, 'oral Torah'.

The study of Torah continued unabated as the *Talmud* was completed. The two principal rabbinic academies in Babylonia were at the towns of Sura and Pumbeditha. They served as the intellectual centre of the Jewish world from the fourth to the ninth centuries and even after. There, the leader of the *yeshiva* or Talmudic academy, known by the honorific term *gaon* (meaning 'excellency'; plural, *geonim*), often had greater power and respect than the ostensible head of the Jewish community, the exilarch. This was because the *gaon* supervised the

The Torah scrolls flanking the ark in this synagogue in Cape Town have embroidered decorations representing the tablets of the Law with the Ten Commandments.
(Albert Beckman)

rabbinic enterprise of legal interpretation that was the principal locus of authority for most Jews.

The one major threat to the primacy of the *geonim* was the rebellion of the Karaites ('scripturalists'), a group of Jews who rejected the authority of the *Talmud* and its interpreters. The Karaites limited their canonical books to the Bible. The eighth-century founder of Karaism, Anan ben David, rejected wholesale not only the *Talmud*, but also the popular holiday of Ḥanukkah and other Jewish festivals that were not specifically mentioned in the Bible. His teachings, like Islam also, stressed a simplicity bordering on asceticism, as over against the elaborate and very intellectual accomplishments of the rabbis. Indeed, Karaism flourished in Muslim lands because of the culture's affinity for simple piety.

The Development of Jewish Law

With the *Talmud* compiled and undergoing no further addition, the ongoing development of Jewish law took three principal forms. One was the further passage-by-passage commentary on the Talmudic text that now included the *Gemarah* as well as the *Mishnah*. Jewish intellectuals over the world and across the centuries have written legal commentaries that concentrate on one or another aspect of the legal tradition, continuing until today.

Perhaps the most famous commentator on the *Talmud* was Rabbi Shlomo ben Yitzhak (1040–1105), who lived in Provence in France. As is common with rabbinic writers, he is known by the acronym of his title and name: Rashi (R–Sh–Y). His commentaries are invaluable for understanding the simple sense of difficult Talmudic passages. (Rashi wrote commentaries on biblical books as well, landmarks in the history of Jewish scriptural interpretation. Because he often translated difficult words into medieval French, Rashi is also consulted by scholars of French language and literature for his witness to the pronunciation of French in the eleventh century.)

Besides individual commentaries, great lights among the various rabbis commented on individual problems in the *Talmud*. A selection of these still later commentaries and elucidations appears on a printed *Talmud* page. These annotations are known as *Tosafot* (Hebrew for 'additions' or 'footnotes'). The term should not be confused with the *Tosefta* (Aramaic for 'the Addition'), which accompanies the *Mishnah* and is the early third-century collection of the sayings of the first rabbis, the Tannaim.

A second further development of legal tradition was the accumulation of a corpus of rulings made when individual communities wrote to the acknowledged expert rabbis of their generation, asking for advice on how to resolve specific issues. This *Teshuvah* ('return', i.e., response) literature, which was always a kind of public letter form rather than a purely private correspondence, is also known as *responsa* (Latin for 'answers'; singular, *responsum*) literature.

Actually, it is possible that this genre of literature is quite ancient, for the letters of Paul in the New Testament are a kind of *responsa*. They reflect Paul's answers to the questions that the early church communities were asking him. Although Paul is now part of Christian tradition, the process reflected in his writing displays the kinds of questions that Jews continued to ask in *responsa*. Orthodox rabbis today still issue *responsa*, and indeed are called on to extend Talmudic reasoning to situations newly raised by modern technology, such as birth control and modern medical procedures.

The third post-Talmudic development was the periodic compilation of the accumulating heritage into law codes. Essentially, a code does two things: (1) it is an attempt to sort out and classify legal material topically and logically; (2) it sorts through a great deal of interesting but theoretical discussion, trying to answer 'what we actually do in this situation'. Codes are simplifications of the complicated legal material. They are also interpretations, since the codifier must decide how the law is to be actually carried out. Thus, the codifier must be a very respected jurist for the work to have any acceptability. Rabbi Judah's *Mishnah*, the first rabbinic document, has many characteristics of a code except that it does not always give an answer to the practical question of what exactly to do.

In the medieval world further codes were formulated. Two influential medieval codes were the *Mishneh Torah* (A Copy of the Torah) of Moses

Maimonides (1135–1204) and the *Arba'a Turim* (Four Rows) of Jacob ben Asher (1269?–1340?). Following the outline of that work, Joseph Karo (1488–1575), a Spanish Jew who migrated to Safed in Palestine, brought diverse legal opinions together in a massive compilation titled *Bet Yosef* (House of Joseph). In 1565, Karo then produced a condensation of this work under the title *Shulhan Arukh* (Spread Table, an allusion to *Psalm* 23). The *Shulhan Arukh* continues even today to serve as a guide for Jews who want to know the practical procedures and behaviours that most simply carry out the Torah. It leaves aside the intricacies of legal discussion and various hypothetical solutions to possible contradictions in the law that one finds in the *Talmud* and commentaries.

Applying Legal Principles

Originally the civil law of the Israelites, the Torah became the religious law of rabbinic Judaism. Its provisions became the guide for moral conduct for Jews living millennia and thousands of miles from the ancient state. For such an ancient law to adapt and stay relevant to a people living in later ages, a healthy tradition of study and commentary had to develop.

Rabbinic Judaism emphasized the fatherhood of God and the brotherhood of Israel under God's revealed law. It gave enormous emphasis to proper ethical conduct. In detailing Jewish law, the rabbis were outlining an ethical program for Jews. The tradition called for numerous specific actions of both a ritual and a moral nature, but the basic ethical agenda was to analyse each situation to determine proper conduct. Since no two circumstances were fully identical, the study of the *Talmud* essentially trained the Jew in the principles of analysing every situation as minutely as possible and from every conceivable perspective.

'An eye for an eye, a tooth for a tooth', says the book of *Exodus*, implying a principle of compensation for damages. Stringent though this may sound today, it may have been humanitarian in the second millennium BCE. For in other cultures, a serf injuring a master might be put to death. The Bible suspends this, limiting penalties to the extent of the injury. But by the rabbinic period, this originally humane judgement came to seem harsh, a *lex talionis* ('law of retaliation'), as the Romans expressed it. The rabbis, after very little debate, concluded that the Bible means to limit compensation to paying a financial price for the victim's loss.

To a modern interpreter, a moral development over the ages is evident. In historical experience, the Israelite people decide which behaviours are moral and which can no longer be regarded as fair. Scholars can see the shift over time from physical to fiscal punishment, even though they cannot pin down its precise date from the available records.

Many Orthodox Jews, however, holding that scripture was given complete and verbatim by God at Sinai, maintain that such money compensation had been the intent of the verses all along. In this view, the text is inerrant but subject to interpretation, and the rabbis' interpretation was guided by the Holy Spirit.

Through a process of commentary, Jewish exegetes have applied the principles of Torah to their contemporary lives. An issue, for instance, is people's reluctance to lend money when the sabbatical year approaches, for fear that they would lose their capital. Even though the Torah does not speak specifically about this matter, the rabbis were confident that the answer to this problem could be found in scripture. In this case, to Hillel is attributed the suggestion of *takkanah* ('remediation'). It proposes that the court itself take over debts for the sabbatical year. Thus lenders can feel confident that they will recover their principal, and debtors can arrange the loans they need to meet their agricultural and mercantile needs.

Law is continually amplified in response to new situations. For guidance in dealing with them, people looked to the rabbis as a group of skilled professionals, an élite educated in precedent and tradition. And as with other legal development, it was hardly unanimous or monolithic. Currently, for example, Jewish law does not have a single answer on whether a woman may seek an abortion. The biblical precedent is found in *Exodus*, where a rule on accidental miscarriage is stated:

> When men fight, and one of them pushes a pregnant woman and a miscarriage results, but no other damage ensues, the one responsible shall be fined according as the woman's husband may exact from him, the payment to be based on reckoning. But if other damage ensues, the penalty shall be life for life, eye for eye, tooth for tooth, hand for hand, foot for foot, burn for burn, wound for wound, bruise for bruise (*Exodus* 21:22–5).

Rabbinic interpretation takes this to mean that the death of a foetus is a tort but is not in itself a capital crime. If the life of a mother is endangered, it is certainly permissible to destroy the life of the foetus. According to rabbinic law, a foetus is not a person, with the ability to own property and other personal rights, until it is born and shown to be viable. This is normally understood as surviving a month after birth.

Because of the nature of rabbinic law, however, whether or not to perform an abortion depends on subtle distinctions in rabbinic discourse. So as not to overstep the prohibitions, many Jews would only perform an abortion if there is an actual acute physical emergency in which the mother is endangered. Others, interpreting more broadly, might perform an abortion in any place where the mother reports that she is unable psychologically to deal with the resulting maternity. Still others, like the Reform movement, would say that it is important to consult the rabbinic opinions of the past, but their advice is not automatically binding on contemporary life. They might extend one principle or another discussed by the rabbis and come to a decision that is never actually attested by rabbinic opinion, justifying their decision on the basis of what a rabbi, operating under similar principles, might do today.

Purity and Community

When the rabbis turned their attention to some of the most arcane laws of the Torah constitution involving ritual purity, they were codifying a complex symbolic system. Purity laws have been viewed in modern times as a kind of primitive hygiene because societies tend to taboo harmful or noxious substances, such as corpses or human excreta. However, cultures often taboo completely harmless substances, while harmful ones are sometimes central to ritual events. Hebrew rules, similarly, do not always have obvious medical value.

Hebrew society, like many non-Western societies, had a series of food taboos. Of these the best known is the commandment not to eat the meat from pigs like ham or pork, nor even to touch it. Others included not eating blood, a kid seethed in its mother's milk, nor any of the birds and mammals that themselves violate these rules in their activity as predators.

A rabbinic ruling forbids eating meat and milk together, but this ruling is not biblical. The Bible says not to eat a young goat boiled in its mother's milk. It says nothing about keeping meat and milk strictly separate, but the rabbis developed this as a safeguard against violating the biblical rules. Implementing this separation, many Jews maintain two sets of dishes, silverware, and kitchen utensils, so as not to risk mixing traces of milk and meat products on one plate.

Nor does the Bible prohibit eating a fowl, which provides no milk for its young, at the same meal as cheese. Yet as the rules were interpreted, poultry was treated like meat and cheese was treated like milk, so that combining these too became illegal, at least for Jews in European countries. The Pharisaic-rabbinic expression of these rules illustrates what the rabbis called 'making a fence around the Torah', setting up rules that prevented inadvertent violations of Torah statutes.

The Pharisaic-rabbinic party extended the ritual of the temple to encompass the table of every Jew. The biblical rules that the slaughter of all kosher (ritually acceptable) animals be done in a humane way had an original application to sacrifice. The prohibition against eating blood, reflecting that only God had control over life, was now seen to emphasize separation and sanctity of every Jewish home. The rules required that only properly tithed produce be eaten, especially in countries other than Judea, where tithing obligations did not apply. Furthermore, there are special rules that pertain to the Passover holiday, such as not eating any bread with leavening in it at that time.

Another series of rules, rooted in the Bible, forbade contact with various polluting substances—like corpses, reptiles, menstrual blood, or semen. Touching these substances was not a sin in itself, unless it were done wilfully.

Indeed, persons were assumed to come into contact with these substances regularly and normally. The result of contact was uncleanness, which had to be removed by a visit to a *mikveh*, a ritual bathhouse, where a total-immersion baptism was regularly performed for the purpose of purification. These purity laws kept husband and wife from sexual intercourse for approximately the first two weeks of every menstrual cycle, and they entailed a ritual immersion after every meeting thereafter.

Purity laws were symbolic boundary markers, with social meanings. They separated the ritually pure from the less pious, and Jews from the host society, imposing a high degree of group coherence. As Pharisaism became rabbinism, the rules proliferated. Judaism did not forbid interaction with gentiles such as eating together, but the proliferation of dietary and purity laws certainly made it difficult. The rules marked off sexual relations with gentiles, who obviously did not practice the purity baptisms, as impure. Of course, if a gentile converted to Judaism, these objections were moot, since the gentile would begin to observe the purity rules.

The rules had the effect of idealizing the temple, which demanded the highest purity, at the same time as they recognized that it no longer existed and that sacrifice, the final stage in the purification process, was no longer possible. The rabbis built on the older Pharisaic rules, allowing many to fall into desuetude, to build up a new understanding of family purity that continues in Orthodox Judaism. Women and men still visit ritual baths to remove ritual impurities. But when the temple was destroyed, sacrifice as the ultimate way of removing impurity was destroyed with it.

In biblical society, the priests were a hereditary class, separated and maintaining a high degree of ritual purity. In one sense, with the temple gone, priesthood lapsed. In another sense, however, maintaining oneself ritually pure became an obligation of every Jew, whether descended from a priestly family or not. And rabbinic Judaism would think of the community as having a priestly role among the nations of the world.

Repentance

Besides the proper analysis and performance of each biblical law, the rabbis put great emphasis on the concept of forgiveness and repentance. Although the rabbis felt that righteousness and righteous deeds are what God wants, they did not design a 'scoreboard' religion in which good deeds could be totalled against bad. They constantly preached that repentance (Hebrew *teshuvah*, literally 'turning' or 'returning') is the purpose of, and is supremely able to transform, human life.

Everyone is asked to imagine his or her life as constantly balanced between good and evil deeds. Thus everyone constantly needs repentance in order to be received by God. The rabbis even suggested that there is no automatic atonement in the universe. Without repentance, all the various rites of atonement are merely attempts at magic. Although sacrifices were offered in the temple and the holiday of Yom Kippur grants atonement for communal sin, nothing is effected unless there is sincere repentance on the part of each person.

There are several stages to repentance. First, the person admits to having done wrong. The rabbis acknowledge that most sin is not committed by deliberately evil persons. Rather, it is done by people who know right from wrong and seek to do the right, but who have clever rationalizations that prevent them from seeing the evil of their ways. Thus the very first stage of repentance is to acknowledge openly the wrongness of one's ways. This confession is critical for everything that comes afterwards.

The next stage in repentance should be true and honest sorrow for the action. It does not follow automatically from the first stage. People may admit their sins without actually feeling sorry for having done them. Or they may rationalize their sins as necessary under the pressure of circumstances. True repentance means acknowledging all these thought patterns as traps.

One must promise never to repeat the sin, and take steps to follow through on that undertaking. But repentance does not merely mean feeling sad and promising to change one's behaviour. It also involves making the appropriate compensation to anyone injured by the sinner.

Some crimes, like murder, may require the death of the perpetrator as compensation, even though nothing can bring back the life of the murder victim. A person who truly repents and is willing to undergo this may enter God's presence as a forgiven sinner. In fact, the rabbis rarely had the authority to pronounce such a sentence on an offender. Since the Bible clearly pronounced capital sentences on offenders, they had to admit capital punishment as a possibility. But they imposed an immense number of legal strictures on their capital trials, so much so that one could practically never reach a clear-cut situation in which the capital penalty could be imposed.

If God's forgiveness accepts the sincere penitent, human forgiveness should imitate it. A person who has suffered damages from another could seek repentance and restitution, but thereafter is obliged to respond with forgiveness. One must seek the forgiveness of the person one has wronged, and if one is a sincere penitent who has accomplished all the stages of repentance, that victim must not unfairly withhold forgiveness. Only then may the sinner expect that God will provide repentance on Yom Kippur, the annual Day of Atonement.

Rabbinic Judaism has been characterized as a religion of works, but it nonetheless leaves an enormous place for divine grace. It emphasizes God's availability for forgiveness and the human need to achieve it. Indeed, besides Yom Kippur, marriage and death are also occasions that provide atonement for sin. In these observances, one sees the rabbinic decision to find other means for atonement than the temple sacrifices, which were tacitly acknowledged as no longer part of Jewish life.

The rabbis developed a very sophisticated notion of intention. In English common law, several stages of intention are important—for instance, in the definition of various degrees of murder. The rabbis similarly assumed that subtle differences in intention are important for understanding the significance of any action. Indeed, they usually assume a degree of intentionality that would be very difficult to ascertain in court under open testimony. This is because they automatically assume that God is a constant witness to the affairs of humans.

God knows the intentions of everyone and is present at any action. For the rabbis, this means that God assumes the burden of punishment and reward, even for actions not punishable at all. For instance, again in the issue of the death penalty, they assume that God will find an equitable solution. Even though human courts may be unable to punish a malefactor because of lack of evidence or rules of procedure, God will see that the correct punishments and rewards are administered. Thus, many of the death penalties in the Bible, usually those described with the phrase *kareth* ('cut off'), are assumed by the rabbis to be death at the hands of heaven. God will punish the person, and human courts have no business intervening.

This leads us to a subtle but important distinction. Rabbinic literature, we may say, outlines religious law, not a legalistic theology. Rabbinic law is actually ordinary law like other national law codes, covering civil and criminal situations, but distinctive in that God is seen as a constant participant in the process. We characterize it as a legal system in which God's actions are part of the law, not as a theology that is centred on and guided by legal action.

Commandments for Jews and Gentiles

Rabbinic thought had a clear notion of the Torah, both written and oral, as God's distinctive gift to the Jews. The next logical question for the rabbis to answer was what God intended for the gentile nations (in Hebrew, *goyim*). Did they have privileges and responsibilities in a divine plan, and what were the standards by which to judge their conduct?

In attempting to answer these questions, the rabbis began to articulate a theory of universalism. Of course, even the biblical writers had understood that God was Lord of the whole world, as well as of the people Israel. This is dramatically expressed in the Genesis creation story. In their day, various pre-exilic prophets had drawn the gentiles into their scenarios as instruments of punishment used by God to settle scores with a sinful Israel. Other prophets had pronounced against certain nations in God's name for overstepping the limits of the punitive roles assigned to them. Postexilic writings, including especially the apocalyptic genre, had envisioned a glorification of Israel and the subjugation of the gentile nations as a long-delayed demonstration of God's loyalty to his people. The longer such an intervention was delayed, the more dramatic it was expected to be eventually.

In the biblical account, Yahweh's transactions with Abraham and Moses establish specific privileges and responsibilities for the people of Israel. The Ten Commandments given to Moses are at the heart of the law, but in the classic rabbinic interpretation of Torah, the people Israel have to follow the 613 commandments, *mitzvoth*, given at Sinai. The number is conventional; the rabbis of the Middle Ages delighted in enumerating exactly 613 of them.

But before the covenant with Abraham and the formation of a distinct Israelite people, God makes a covenant with Noah, the survivor of the primeval flood, and seals it with the rainbow. The rabbis linked the salvation of the gentiles explicitly to this covenant, for in it God promises mercy and deliverance to all humanity. The rabbis see God as giving the non-Israelite nations specific commands, the so-called Noachic (or Noahide) commandments.

The number of the Noachic commandments varies from six to ten, depending on the rabbinic commentary on scripture that one consults, but they are conventionally called the seven Noachic commandments. They include prohibitions against blasphemy, idolatry, bloodshed, incest, and theft, together with eating flesh from living animals. Added to these is often the recognition of the true God.

The rabbis derived these ordinances from what they took to be scriptural revelation enabling the whole human race to know the meaning of righteousness. They interpreted various texts in *Genesis* in which God directs specific commands to the generations of Noah. But the Noachic commandments are consonant with universal human reason. They are universally recognizable moral imperatives, like 'natural' laws. Not only Jews but also pious pagans in the late Roman Empire could justify ethical monotheism philosophically.

In medieval Judaism, these Noachic commandments were utilized for a rabbinic treatment of the value in God's plan for the newer religions of Islam and Christianity—religions seemingly founded on biblical and Jewish principles but far greater in numbers and power.

The rabbis came to acknowledge Islam as consonant with the intent of the Noachic commandments. Islam had a strict monotheism and rejected the making of images. Sometimes the same was posited of Christianity. On the other hand, the rabbis sometimes balked at making theological room for Christianity, with its trinitarian doctrines and its rich Roman and Eastern traditions of devotion to *eikons* or 'images'.

Some rabbis, especially those living in Christian countries, pointed out that while Christianity is not strict monotheism because it associates a mortal and his image with God, which is *shittuf* ('associationism') or a 'two powers' heresy forbidden to Jews, righteous Christians could still count on eternal life, however, because the Noachic commandments do not specifically prohibit *shittuf* for gentiles. Other rabbis, often living in Muslim lands, judged Christianity as a violation of monotheism, as did the Muslims, by means of the Muslim rejection of associationism, the elevating of any thing or being to divine status alongside God.

Rabbinic Judaism drafted a universalism similar to current North American notions of cultural pluralism. Jewish intellectuals argued, in effect, that all worshippers of the one God, including the three Abrahamic faiths, should tolerate and respect one another. Both Islam and Christianity developed legal notions of the toleration of Jews—but as their own predecessors, rather than in the name of humanity. Obviously there are many examples of intolerance towards Jews in both Christian and Muslim lands, but these were illegal actions within the structures set up by both religious domains. Nor is it true that Jews always lived up to the rabbinic notion of the salvation of all righteous, whether Jewish or not.

Jews never explicitly eschewed conversion, and accept converts willingly today, when the political environment and the sincerity of the convert permit it. To some non-Jews, it may appear weak not to bear witness to one's faith by proselytizing, but the Jew feels that one does not need to convert a righteous gentile to assure his or her salvation. It is enough to preach that everyone should be righteous, which makes one the equal of a Jew in the eyes of God. Rather, conversion is reserved for those who want to join their fate with the people Israel.

MEDIEVAL JUDAISM

European and Eastern Judaism

A convention developed by which the Jews of the premodern world were divided geographically into two groups, the Sephardim and the Ashkenazim. The Sephardic Jews are those from around the Mediterranean, while the Jews termed Ashkenazic are descended from those who live in central and eastern Europe, away from the Mediterranean.

The names themselves arise from a reading of the biblical text: *Obadiah* verse 20 represents Sepharad as a place to which Jews migrated in the time of the Babylonian Exile, and Ashkenaz is in a series of names in *Jeremiah* 51:27. Identification of these biblical locations is speculative. One conjecture places both of them in what today is Turkey: the name Sepharad, subtracting the *ph*, could be Sardis, a coastal city on the Aegean, while Ashkenaz is believed to have been farther east, in the Anatolian interior near Mount Ararat and the Caucasus.

By the medieval period, Sepharad was identified with Spain. Sephardic Jewish intellectual history is dominated by Spain and Portugal. European Jewish settlement in the New World began with Sephardim from Spain, Portugal, and Italy, the pioneering lands of exploration and colonial empire building. In Italy and the Turkish Empire, there have been important Sephardic centres, and among the Sephardim one can include the Jews from Morocco to Iraq and the Yemen.

Ashkenaz was identified with Germany. The Ashkenazim include the Jews of Germany, Poland, Hungary, Romania, and Russia. Some settled in France and

England over the centuries prior to their descendants' migration to North America. The medieval experience of all Ashkenazim was as a minority under Christian domination that varied from ignorance and insensitivity at best to repression and persecution. There has been far more persecution of Jews in Christian lands than in Muslim lands. In medieval Europe there were burnings of the *Talmud*, and many Jews of western Europe were forced to migrate towards Poland and Russia.

After the middle of the nineteenth century, Ashkenazic Jews, so often uprooted in Europe, almost completely overpowered the earlier Sephardic settlement in the New World. North American Jews are today overwhelmingly Ashkenazic in style and culture. Jews from Muslim lands have not been a significant source of migration to North America, but larger numbers have migrated to Israel. Consequently, Israel today reflects more nearly equal numbers of Sephardim and Ashkenazim than do the United States and Canada.

Jewish cultural and intellectual life fared better in the medieval Islamic than the medieval Christian world. Islam's rapid early spread in the eastern Mediterranean in the seventh and eighth centuries brought freedom for Jews. Muḥammad had been deeply influenced by Jewish and to some extent Christian teachers before his experience of revelation. Though he grew impatient with the scepticism of both, particularly the Jews, Islam remained officially tolerant of both the Christian and Jewish communities. Although they were part of *dār al-ḥarb*, the world of struggle not under Islam, they were considered 'People of the Book' and entitled to certain legal rights, including the right to pursue their own religion.

Muslim rulers did not always live up to Islam's stated principles of tolerance. Jews were subjected to discriminatory legislation forcing them to pay special taxes, wear special garments, live in special quarters, stay off the roads when Muslims approached, and many other things. Nevertheless, Jews had considerable powers in Babylonia after the Muslim conquest. And they followed the Muslim conquest the whole length of the Mediterranean, to Spain. Wherever the Muslims conquered—from Spain in the eighth century to Anatolia in the fifteenth—they were welcomed by the Jewish community as liberators from Christian oppression.

Jews in Africa and Asia

Beyond the eastern Mediterranean world of the Arabs and their successors, the Turks, there lay regions in which Jews lived largely out of touch with the currents of either Sephardic or Ashkenazic Jewry. A small isolated community of Jews in Ethiopia survived in primitive village circumstances until modern times. They are derogatorily called Falashas ('exiles') by the Ethiopians. They likely reflect the presence of Judaism, and a Jewish emphasis in Christianity, to the east across the

Red Sea in southern Arabia in the centuries shortly before Islam. In their own tradition they consider themselves descendants of a retinue reputedly accompanying the Arabian queen of Sheba after her visit to the tenth-century-BCE king Solomon. In 1975, the Israeli rabbinate ruled that Falashas qualified as Jews for entry into Israel, to which most have migrated or been evacuated. They have experienced culture shock in Israel's modern secularity, but have also found familiar traditions there.

In Iran, one finds a historically and intellectually significant Jewish minority, whose presence dates back to early Islamic times; the ninth-century Karaite Benjamin of Nehavand, for instance, was an Iranian Jew. Since the establishment of modern Israel, the Iranian Jews have seen their status become politically sensitive, as suspected Israeli sympathizers. But this was not salient in 1948, when Iran considered the Israeli-Palestinian conflict a political matter *vis-à-vis* Arabs and maintained relations with Israel. Rather, Iranian suspicion of Jews has developed since the Israeli occupation of the Jerusalem shrine, the Dome of the Rock (contested because it stands on the site of the ancient Hebrew temple), in 1967, which galvanized the sentiment of non-Arab Muslims. An even more significant factor in Iran's change of opinion towards Jews has been the emergence of a theocratic and fundamentalist Islamic regime in Iran in 1979.

Let us look still farther east. There have been two historic communities of Jews in India: one on the southwestern or Malabar Coast, in Cochin, and the other on the western coast just south of Bombay. The origins of these Indian groups are uncertain, but both claim association with the ten legendary lost northern tribes of Israel, scattered by the Assyrian invasion and deportation of 722 BCE. The Jews of Cochin, already documented by medieval European and Arab travellers, were probably augmented by some migration from the Mediterranean at the end of the fifteenth century when Jews were expelled from Spain. They assimilated to Indian life, even exhibiting the rudiments of a caste structure in their own community. Soon after Indian and Israeli independence (1947, 1948), most of one subgroup in this community left for Israel, but the other remained in India as the Indian government would not allow them to take their financial assets out of the country.

In the region of Bombay, a Jewish community known as the Bene Israel ('children of Israel') were isolated from contact with other Jews until the eighteenth century, after which their somewhat sketchy acquaintance with Jewish tradition was renewed through contributions from three sources: Jews in Cochin, Jews in Baghdad, and Presbyterian missionaries from Scotland. The Bene Israel display considerable assimilation to the dominant Hindu environment, wearing Indian dress and making no great theological condemnation of polytheism. Until not long ago, they forbade the remarriage of widows and held that the eating of beef is prohibited in the Bible, these patterns evidently deriving from long immersion in Hindu culture.

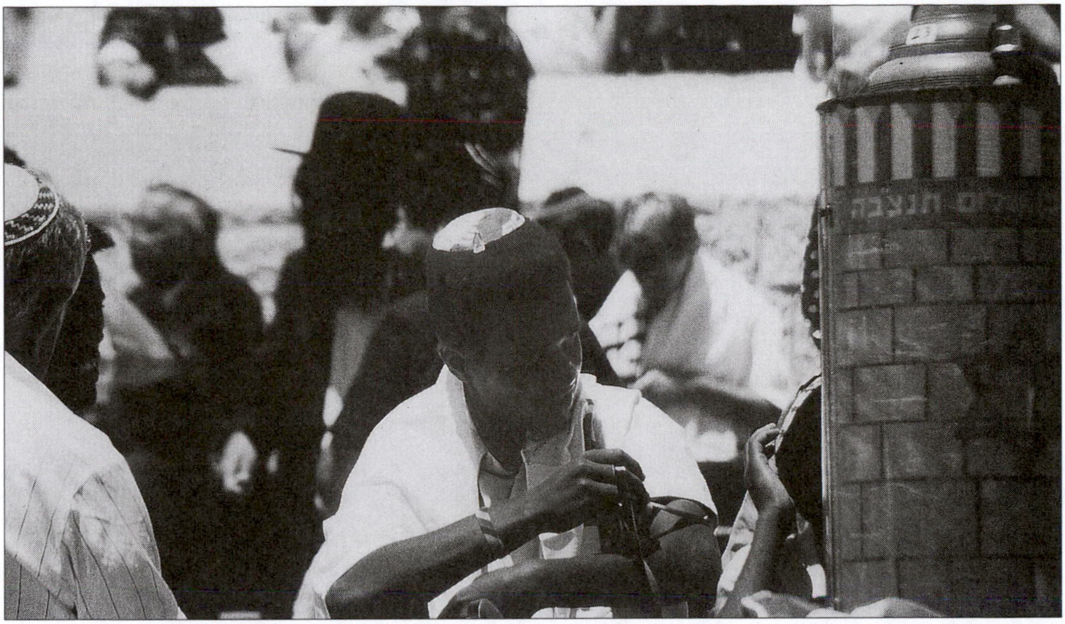

A Falasha (Ethiopian) immigrant to Israel binds to his arm the tefillin, *a small box containing words of scripture.*
(Albert Beckman)

Europeans, especially Christian missionaries who opened up contact with China in modern centuries, found surviving members of a community of Jews in the central Chinese city of Kaifeng. Chinese Jewish origins are attributed both to overseas and overland trade in the Middle Ages from the Yemen, Iraq, or Iran, around or across Asia. They settled in coastal cities, often in close association with the Muslims, many of whom also came to China as traders but in far greater numbers. The Chinese associated the two, but distinguished them in that the Jews characteristically wore blue turbans while the Muslims wore white. Both communities stood apart from the mainstream Chinese population because they avoided pork, a central item in China's diet.

Centuries ago, the Kaifeng community appears to have had Torah scrolls and some command of its religious heritage. But after the last rabbi died around 1800, decline accelerated, greatly augmented in the twentieth century by Marxist repression of religious beliefs and cultural differences. In China in 1981, the editor of this volume visited Kaifeng and met members of its surviving Jewish community. An estimated 200 families then had some recollection of Jewish ancestry. Their preservation of tradition was reported: 'In my grandfather's time we neither raised pigs nor ate pork. Today we eat pork, but we still do not raise pigs.' Recent contact with Jewish visitors who have brought them books about their Jewish heritage may restore some content to the religious life of the Chinese Jews.

RABBINIC EMPHASIS ON LOVE

Let not a man accustom himself to say, "Love the wise, and hate the disciples, love the disciples, but hate the ignoramus, but rather, "love all," and hate [only] the heretics, the apostates, and the informers," as David says, "Do I not hate them that hate thee?" "Thou shalt love thy neighbor as thyself, I am the Lord" (*Aboth de Rabbi Nathan* A, 16, 32b).

Medieval Jewish Social Custom

With Jews living in so many different places and cultures, it is no wonder that Jewish social customs differ radically. Law and custom (*minhag*) have had to adjust to these vast differences in time and place.

The role of women in Jewish society has followed changes in the cultures in which Jews reside. The ancient Israelites shared the practice of polygamy with their neighbours, although the *Genesis* story assumes a monogamous relationship between Adam and Eve. In eastern and especially Muslim lands, Jews continued to marry more than one wife, if they could afford such a complex household. The Muslim practice of limiting marriage to four wives probably was a Jewish custom that influenced Islamic legal discussion. The Jewish marriage contract, however, provides a number of safeguards for women that were not always available to women in the surrounding cultures.

Judaism also accepts divorce as a legal institution. It is mentioned several times in the Bible and treated explicitly in *Deuteronomy* 24:1–4. As in Islam, the grounds for divorce are theoretically quite wide but, again as in Muslim practice, the actual use of divorce as a remedy for a family crisis is strongly hemmed in by community opprobrium and is never undertaken lightly.

Even today, with the very considerable assimilation that has taken place in the Americas, the Jewish divorce rate is still considerably lower than that of the non-Jewish majority. This is particularly interesting when one considers that the rabbis allow divorce for virtually any reason. Divorces are instigated by the husband, though in a certain number of cases a court will enjoin a husband to divorce his wife, upon her request. No woman can be divorced against her will; therefore, mutual consent is required. The divorce, in Hebrew called a *get*, is presented to the wife by the husband. It regularly includes a financial settlement and the return of properties that rightfully belong to the wife.

Over the centuries, changes in marital customs and the status of women have occasioned the use of a rare but important rabbinic legal instrument, the *takkanah* ('remediation' in the sense of 'repeal'). The most famous *takkanah* on the subject of marriage is the repeal or ban (*herem*) of polygamy. This is often attrib-

The *Memoirs of Glueckl of Hamelin*

In my great grief and for my heart's ease I begin this book the year of creation 5451 [1690–1]—God soon rejoice us and send us His redeemer!

I began writing it, dear children, upon the death of your good father, in the hope of distracting my soul from the burdens laid upon it, and the bitter thought that we have lost our faithful shepherd. In this way, I have managed to live through many wakeful nights, and springing from my bed shortened the sleepless hours.

This, dear children, will be no book of morals. Such I could not write, and our sages have already written many. Moreover, we have our holy Torah, in which we may find and learn all that we need for our long journey through this world to the world to come. It is like a rope which the great and gracious God has thrown to us as we drown in the stormy sea of life, that we may seize hold of it and be saved.

The kernel of the Torah is 'Thou shalt love thy neighbor as thyself.' But in our days we seldom find it so, and few are they who love their fellowmen with all their heart—on the contrary, if a man can contrive to ruin his neighbor, nothing pleases him more.

The best thing for you, my children, is to serve God from your heart, without falsehood or sham, not giving out to people that you are one thing while, God forbid, in your heart you are another. Say your prayers with awe and devotion. During the time for prayers, do not stand about and talk of other things. While prayers are being offered to the Creator of the world, hold it a great sin to engage another person in talk about an entirely different matter—shall God Almighty be kept waiting until you have finished your business?

uted to Rabbenu Gershom (Gershom ben Judah Me'or Ha-Golah, c. 960–1028), to whom is also ascribed a *takkanah* preventing a woman from being divorced against her will.

Other traditions imply that banning polygamy was more or less a communitywide agreement, as in the end it would have to be. This *takkanah* essentially outlaws polygamy for Jews in Christian lands, though it obviously continues occasionally in Muslim lands even today. Some versions of the *takkanah* include a 1,000-year time limit, which would mean that Jews today are again free to marry polygamously. But no one has taken up this possibility; the *takkanah* is reaffirmed whenever it is discussed, as in the contemporary state of Israel, which partly bases its laws on rabbinic precedent.

Also, the biblical institution of levirate marriage (*yibum*), requiring a man to marry his childless deceased brother's wife, so as to produce heirs in his name,

A *Techina* (Devotional Prayer) for Women

This the woman says when she puts the Sabbath loaf into the oven:

Lord of all the world, in your hand is all blessing. I come now to revere your holiness, and I pray you to bestow your blessing on the baked goods. Send an angel to guard the baking, so that all will be well baked, will rise nicely, and will not burn, to honor the holy Sabbath (which you have chosen so that Israel your children may rest thereon) and over which one recites the holy blessing—as you blessed the dough of Sarah and Rebecca our mothers. My Lord God, listen to my voice; you are the God who hears the voices of those who call to you with the whole heart. May you be praised to eternity (Umansky and Ashton 1992:55).

falls into desuetude in rabbinic law. The correlative biblical procedure by which a woman is released from this legal arrangement (*ḥaliẓah* or 'unbinding') became the standard practice everywhere, even in polygamous cultures.

In areas and times when women were allowed rights, were educated, or could travel publicly, Jewish women also gained the benefits; but in areas where they could not, Jewish life sometimes followed that practice also. Through the ages affluent Jewish households often had highly educated Jewish women. Formerly, Jewish women were almost always literate enough to follow Hebrew synagogue services. Indeed, literacy in Hebrew was usually high in the traditional Jewish community.

The *Memoirs of Glueckl of Hamelin* give us an example of the place women could attain. Born in Hamburg, Germany, to a prominent family, Glueckl (1646–1724) married Hayyim of Hamelin at age fourteen. Soon after, she moved back to Hamburg with him and became his adviser in business, even while bearing twelve children. After his death in 1689, she carried on the business alone. At age forty-six, to conquer the grief of her husband's death and to educate her children in their family history, she set out to write her memoirs in Yiddish (a German dialect written in Hebrew characters). She continued the *Memoirs* when she had leisure, even after she married again, this time to Cerf Levy of Metz, a banker. Her writing shows her to be well educated, versed in traditional Jewish lore as well as having literary talent. Her work is a rare window into the private lives of seventeenth-century Jewry, including a valuable narrative of the arrival of Sabbatianism in Germany. (On Sabbatai Zvi's movement, see below.)

The differences among Jewish customs became an important issue in the modern state of Israel, as Jews from all over the world were reunited in one legal system. Bigamy was outlawed in Israel by the 1951 civil law protecting the equal

FROM BAḤYA IBN PAQUDA'S *DUTIES OF THE HEART*

You should know, O mortal, that the greatest enemy you have in the world is our evil inclination, which is woven into the powers of your soul and intertwined with the constitution of your spirit, sharing with you the direction of your bodily senses and mental faculties. He rules over the secrets of your soul, over the thoughts you keep hidden away in your mind. He is your counsellor in all your actions—seen and unseen—which you perform out of free choice. He lies in wait for your moments of inattention: you may be asleep to him, but he is always awake to you; you may be unaware of him, but he is never unaware of you. He dons for you the robe of friendship, and bedecks himself with the guise of love for you. He becomes one of your confidants and counsellors, one of the sincerest of your friends. He subtly deceives you, going along with what you want with outward signs and gestures of agreement, but all the while he is shooting at you his deadly arrows in order to destroy you, after the fashion of one of whom Scripture speaks: 'Like a madman shooting deadly darts and arrows, so is the man who deceives his fellow and then says, "I was only joking" [*Proverbs* 26:18–19]' (Alexander 1984:98–100).

rights of women, although immigrants to Israel with more than one wife, from countries where such unions were legal, were allowed to maintain that status. In 1950, the chief rabbinate of Israel unanimously decided that *ḥalizah* was preferred to levirate marriage, following the long-established rabbinic consensus.

Jewish Philosophy in the Middle Ages

Saadia

Medieval Jewish philosophy flourished primarily in Muslim lands, where Greek philosophy had deeply influenced the intellectual life of Islam. The earliest notable Jewish philosopher of the medieval period was Saadia (882–942), who became the *gaon* or principal of the major rabbinic academy of Sura in Babylonia. He translated the Hebrew Bible into Arabic and defended rabbinic Judaism against the popular following of the Karaites.

Philosophically, Saadia believed that there was no conflict between reason and revelation, a major theme in all of Jewish philosophical writings. Whenever biblical events or texts appear to contradict rational principles, the statements must be taken allegorically rather than literally. In this respect, Saadia was following a tradition that had begun with Philo in Alexandria in the first century. Saadia's major philosophical work was called *The Book of Beliefs and Opinions* (*Sefer Emunoth veDeoth*). In it, he maintains that Judaism alone is the divinely

FROM JUDAH HA-LEVI'S *KUZARI*

On fundamental principles, the philosophers hold opinions which are absurd to the intellect, and which the intellect treats with contempt. Such, for example, is their explanation of the revolution of the celestial sphere. They state that the sphere seeks for a perfection which it lacks, namely, to occupy all possible spatial positions. Since it cannot achieve such a state simultaneously in respect of each of its constituent parts, it attempts to achieve it by occupying each possible position in turn. Equally false is their opinion regarding the emanations which flow from the First Cause. They maintain that from an angel's knowledge of the First Cause there arises of necessity another angel, and from the angel's knowledge of itself there arises a sphere; and so the process of emanation advances step by step down through eleven stages will the emanations come to an end with the Active Intellect, from which arises neither an angel nor a sphere. And they hold other views like these, which are less convincing than those advanced in the *Sefer Yezirah*. All these opinions are highly dubious, and it is impossible to find any two philosophers agreeing on them. However, we should not blame the philosophers for this. Rather, they deserve our praise for what they managed to achieve simply through the force of rational argument. Their intentions were good, they established the laws of thought, and they rejected the pleasures of this world. They may, in any case, be granted superiority since they were not obliged to accept our opinions. We, however, are obliged to accept whatever we see with our own eyes, or any well-founded tradition, which is tantamount to seeing for oneself (Alexander 1984:14–19).

revealed truth. While human beings have the inherent power to derive truth by means of their rational faculty, revelation is a gift from God that enables people to shorten the amount of time needed to reason out a moral or cosmological problem. Thus, revelation and reason are in complete agreement.

Yehuda Ha-Levi

Yehuda Ha-Levi (1075–1141) was born in the city of Toledo in Spain shortly after that city fell under Christian control. Ha-Levi studied the *Talmud*, as did all Jewishly educated people of the time, but he is known for two other endeavours, his poetry and his philosophical book *The Kuzari*. Ha-Levi wrote Hebrew poetry that adapted the conventions current in Arabic poetry. His philosophical work, *The Kuzari*, is based on a famous legend that the Khazars, a Tatar people living near the Caspian Sea, had converted to Judaism sometime in the eighth century. These events were discussed by the Spanish Jew Hasdai ibn Shaprut (915?–975?), and his correspondent Joseph, the last Khazar king in the tenth century.

In Ha-Levi's version of the story, the conversion of the Khazars takes place after the monarch has a chance to listen to the wisdom of each of the three great religions—Islam, Judaism, and Christianity—through a religious leader representing each position. The rabbi cites the notion of *neẓaḥ Yisrael* ('the eternity of Israel'), Israel's survival against all odds throughout the many catastrophes of history, as an example of God's special interest in Israel. He also mentions the unbroken tradition of Judaism, much longer than Christian or Islamic tradition, together with the Jews' bravery in allowing themselves to be martyred for their faith.

Ha-Levi goes further, suggesting that both Islam and Christianity are appropriate preparatory faiths for naïve nations still on their way to accepting Judaism because they are not yet able to sustain the religious and philosophical analysis necessary to be Jews. When the nations of the world mature in their faith, they will be ready for Judaism. Of course, in the story that Ha-Levi tells, the Jewish advocate is the most persuasive, which is the reason that the Khazars embrace Judaism.

Maimonides

Moses Maimonides, or Moses ben Maimon (1135–1204), was born in Córdoba in Spain, lived in Egypt, and is by all accounts the most famous and most impressive of all Jewish philosophers. In religious texts he is usually known as 'Rambam': R–M–B–M, the acronym of 'Rabbi Moses ben Maimon'.

Maimonides was a refugee at age thirteen when the Almohads, a Muslim fundamentalist group from North Africa, took control in Spain. He fled to Morocco, then to Palestine, which was under the control of the Crusaders, and finally to Egypt, where he was able to find employment, and the freedom to practise his religion, as the court physician for the Muslim sultan Salāḥ al-Dīn (Saladin, r. 1169–93). In that connection, he wrote several important medical treatises.

Other medieval Jewish philosophers were polymaths, writing on scriptural, devotional, and scientific topics, but Maimonides's accomplishments were truly prodigious. Maimonides wrote the famous code of Jewish law, *Mishneh Torah*, in Hebrew. He also wrote a treatise on logic, and several *responsa* advising Jewish communities around the world on matters such as false conversions, the concept of resurrection, and the arrival of the messiah.

Seemingly to show his change of outlook from the technical works in Judaism to a wider concern with religious thought generally, Maimonides wrote his major philosophical treatise, *The Guide for the Perplexed*, in Arabic rather than Hebrew, although it was quickly rendered into Hebrew by his translator Ibn Tibbon. Written ostensibly as a letter of advice to a single student, the *Guide* was aimed at a considerable audience of acculturated Jews. Living in a cosmopolitan

MAIMONIDES'S TWELFTH FUNDAMENTAL PRINCIPLE OF FAITH

I believe in perfect faith that the Messiah will come, and we should not consider him as tardy: 'Should he tarry, wait for him' [*Habakkuk* 2:13]. No date may be fixed for his appearance, nor may the Scriptures be interpreted in such a way as to derive from them the time of his coming.

and philosophically sophisticated environment, that audience had begun to question the truth of their own religion.

Earlier medieval philosophers had drawn on Neoplatonism, a tradition extending back to the work of Plato that spoke of abstract ideas, an emanating universe, and mystical or intuitive apprehension of insight. Neoplatonism was characteristic of such Jewish philosophers as Saadia and Ha-Levi.

Maimonides had a deep knowledge of Aristotelianism, which put him at the forefront of the intellectual life of his day. The thought of the Greek philosopher Aristotle had been less widely known than Neoplatonism. It afforded more scope for analytic observation of physical phenomena and human behaviour. But it was comparatively suspect, because religious thinkers were only starting to assimilate it and because it gave the universe a more mechanistic explanation.

He accepts Aristotelian principles of physics provisionally for the purposes of proving the existence of God, even though Aristotle posited an eternal universe. Maimonides demonstrates that the world is God's free creation out of nothing, as he thinks the Bible maintains. He is opposed to Platonists' preference to see the world as an eternal and necessary emanation of God through the heavenly spheres. Maimonides suggests that when one believes the Bible, one needs no further proof, but he employs Greek philosophy to show that biblical religion is true anyway.

Rambam's greatest achievement is his effort to resolve the tensions between faith and knowledge. He sees absolutely no contradiction between reason and revelation. Like most Jewish philosophers before him, he suggests that the Bible speaks a special analogical and metaphoric language and is not to be taken literally where it appears to say something unflattering or untrue about God. The Bible's characterizations of the divine with human forms and feelings are meant to be systematically reunderstood as allegory.

Indeed, he tries to demonstrate that the revelation in the prophets is the perfection of both the intellectual and imaginative faculties, since the prophets received their truths as visions. The ordinances of Torah are all, in principle, reasonable. For Maimonides, the commandments are all rational, although we may not understand how. Regarding specific details of sacrifices and the like, reasons may ultimately be discovered for rules that until now seem beyond human ken.

The last part of *The Guide for the Perplexed* discusses the meaning of the commandments and also tackles difficult questions regarding God's providence.

The rabbis understood that, for the moral system they designed to be logical, not only must God be sovereign but that humanity must have free choice. Without free will the system of rewards and punishments that depends upon each individual's moral choices is merely some kind of absurd mechanistic game. The rabbis read the story of the Garden of Eden as the beginning of that power of choice.

But there is a dilemma. Whatever freedom is granted to individual humans appears to take away from God's perfect sovereignty. The rabbis were content to articulate the paradox in gnomic statements: 'All is foreseen yet free will is given', they said. Or they formulated: 'All is in the hands of heaven except for the fear of heaven', meaning that God controls everything except whether people respond to him. For the rabbis, this amounts to a statement of faith that God's powers are so great that they even overcome our formulation of the dilemma. But recognizing the problem to be a dilemma was no solution to the dilemma itself. It did not go away; Arab philosophers and intellectuals worried obsessively about whether human free will or God's sovereignty should take precedence in a description of the universe.

Maimonides contributes to this discussion by using Aristotle's cosmology to effect a compromise. He asks the question of divine providence in a traditional, scholastic way: 'How far does God's knowledge extend into our imperfect world?' Especially for philosophy drawing on the Platonic stream of ancient Greek tradition, such a question implies difficulties, since divinity was frequently seen as both perfect and changeless. If we suppose that God knows change, does this not compromise divine perfection?

Maimonides suggests that Arabic Aristotelian philosophy's description of God's knowledge as ending at the species level is correct for all species except humanity. For example, God does not know whether an individual swallow falls or hits a building. God's thinking extends to the species, but not to the individual. Because God thinks the notion of swallow, the species exists, but whether a particular swallow dies or survives is not part of God's general providence.

With the human capability of thought, however, humans also have the benefits of God's special providence. To the extent that humans use their rational facilities, God is able to perceive them as individuals and guide their actions. Prophets, who have perfected their rational and imaginative facilities, are therefore the model for human behaviour. The more we train and use our rational faculties, the more moral we become—because true morality is truly rational—and the more we are able to be guided by God's special providence.

This means, for Maimonides, that the truly rational person is the truly moral and good person, but it does not mean that the truly rational human will never experience sorrow or misfortune. It merely means that the moral person's misfortunes and setbacks are specifically known by God and somehow part of a divine plan, whereas for the ignoramus, the converse is true. The ignoramus is both intellectually and morally insensitive. Whether he flourishes or is cut down, indeed whatever happens to him, is accidental, in the same way that it is accidental whether a particular bird hits a building or flies free.

(By 'accidental' Maimonides means that the attribute is not part of the essence. A person may be tall or short; that is accidental. But in Aristotelian terms, human thought is a defining human characteristic; humans are rational essentially, by virtue of the essence of humanness.)

The universe for Maimonides is guided by rationality. It exists because God thinks it, and his thinking produces the emanations that form the heavenly orbs. This rationality is transferred from separated intelligence to separated intelligence (each is another name for the angelic ruler of each sphere) until it reaches the angel known as the Active Intellect. The Active Intellect is the separated intelligence (angel) in charge of the sublunar sphere. Humans can receive emanations from God through this angelic Active Intellect ruling the earth. Because of the action of this angel, we are able to form thoughts in our minds. We need the Active Intellect because our minds are perfect potentialities, passivities—in Latin scholastic parlance, *tabulae rasae* ('empty slates'). Through emanation, the Active Intellect confers God's active thinking to our minds.

We need to perfect our intellects through moral and intellectual schooling. To the extent that we do so, we are able to understand what the Active Intellect is emanating. The Active Intellect is also the angel of prophecy, which is the perfection of the intellectual and imaginative faculties. Thus revelation is merely the perfection of the rational principle.

God's emanations cannot be automatic because God must be free to give prophecy to whomever he wills. Of course God can withhold prophecy even from the perfectly trained human, but this would be exceptional. Prophetic powers are the acme and zenith of the intellectual life. The Torah, the perfect embodiment of prophecy, is a special gift to the Jewish people. All those who study and follow the law are, in fact, training to be prophets. We participate in prophecy to the extent to which we perfect our potentialities. The Greek philosophers, as well as the religions of Christianity and Islam, also and necessarily partake in this truth, but to a lesser degree because they have each fallen victim to error in one way or another. So for Maimonides, reason and revelation are identical processes, and they are both identical with the power by which God creates and preserves the universe.

Rambam's great accomplishment was to promote a thoroughly rational understanding of Judaism. A view of Judaism as rational had been present even during the disputes of the ancient rabbis over points of law, but the intellectual structure that Maimonides forged has characterized Jewish self-understanding to this day. It differs somewhat from orthodox Islam's prevalent view that reason should retreat before faith, and from Christian Aristotelianism, as exemplified by Thomas Aquinas (c. 1225–74), who suggested that faith must retreat before issues that are proven right or wrong by reason. For the Jew ever after, the formula was developed that sees all seeming contradictions between reason or science and faith as only apparent and ephemeral.

Science and religion, then, are in harmony for Maimonides, not in opposition. Maimonides wants to show that Judaism is perfectly in consonance with the particular world view, Aristotelian philosophy, that was maintained by the acculturated and affluent Jewish members of the enlightened Islamic society of his day. The guidance he hoped to provide the 'perplexed' among them was that accepting the principles of the world's 'science' (i.e., learning) should not bring their faith into question. He seeks to provide a religious dimension for the intellectuals of his day. A correct intellectual understanding of the world and of Jewish tradition is expected to yield perfect agreement between the two.

Nevertheless, it cannot be said that Jews universally admired or adopted Maimonides's system. Maimonides wrote for an élite among the Jews of his day in the Islamic world, speakers of Arabic who were in step with the Aristotelianism of medieval Islamic thought. The situation of Jews in Christian lands such as France was very different. There, his writing set off a century of fierce controversy within Judaism, which historians term the Maimonidean controversy. It was punctuated by book burnings and occasional edicts of ostracism by various rabbis opposed to Maimonides's enterprise.

On the whole, Maimonides's emphasis on reason has served the intellectual needs of the Jewish community well in times of peace and prosperity when an intellectual tradition could flourish. In times of trial and tribulation, mysticism seemed to provide better consolation than philosophy.

Jewish Mysticism

The toleration of Jews in Islamic Spain, which had allowed Maimonides's thought to flourish, was in decline. In the famous Reconquista, Ferdinand (r. 1479–1516) and Isabella (r. 1474–1504) brought Spain under Christian rule. Not long before they expelled the Moors from Spain (1502), they also expelled all the Jews (1492) with a cruel edict. Evidently they viewed the Jews as having been helpful in a culture shared with Arab Muslims, but once the Moors were largely gone, they saw no need for Jews in a Christian country. When Columbus set out on his celebrated voyage to the New World, he could not leave from the larger ports of Spain because the trade routes were clogged by Jews being expelled from their centuries-old Spanish home.

In their action, Ferdinand and Isabella followed other Christian monarchs of western Europe, who had expelled Jews previously. But the Iberian Peninsula

Figure 1.1

EXPULSION AND MIGRATION OF JEWS FROM EUROPEAN CITIES AND REGIONS, Eleventh to Fifteenth Centuries CE

Source: I.R. al Fārūqī and D.E. Sopher, *Historical Atlas of the Religions of the World* (New York: Macmillan, 1974):148–9.

contained an enormous number of Jews who had attained a very sophisticated and affluent culture. The result was devastating.

Those who stayed in a Christian world and remained Jews in secret were prosecuted by the Spanish Inquisition, an arm of the Church established in Spain in 1478, dedicated to rooting out Christian heresy. It specialized in discovering beliefs and observances among the *conversos* ('New Christians'), or Marranos ('pigs') as they were sometimes called derisively.

Most of the Jews who were expelled from Spain found their way to the Ottoman Turkish Empire, ruled from Istanbul, which was taken in 1453 by Sultan Mehmet II the Conqueror (r. 1451–81). One of his immediate successors,

Sultan Bayazid II (r. 1481–1512), on hearing of the Jewish expulsion from Spain, mocked the Spanish monarchs' lack of wisdom and suggested that Turkey would recover the squandered 'wealth' of Spain. He thereafter encouraged the dispossessed Jews to take shelter in his empire.

The spiritual crisis that the expulsion generated was not resolved particularly by further philosophical research. Rather, it was assuaged through the great impetus to mystical praxis and pietism.

Jewish mysticism has been claimed to be as old as the prophets themselves. There is evidence that the biblical prophets used group exercises or ascetic techniques to access God's word, and that some received visions in an ecstatic state. Hellenistic and medieval Jewish mystical writers, who claimed a privileged vision of God, argued for its accessibility through specialized techniques of scriptural interpretation. These writers based their descriptions on prophetic models. The most interesting biblical passages for these mystics are places where God deigns to show himself to his people in a human form. This form is called the *shekhinah*, 'presence', or the *kavod*, 'glory of God', and it subsequently was also interpreted as the principal messenger of God, the angel of the Lord.

In the apocalyptic tradition that followed prophecy, some visions involve God's human manifestations. Especially interesting is the so-called 'Son of Man', apparently a Hebrew idiom for 'manlike figure'. Probably an archangel such as Michael or Gabriel, he symbolizes the saints of the community in *Daniel* 7:13, a passage important to early Christianity as well as to Judaism. Furthermore, there is good evidence that Paul expressed his conversion to Christianity as a revelatory, mystical, and apocalyptic identification of Jesus as the messiah and the angel of the Lord. These early mystical traditions were impressive to many in the ancient world, but grew progressively more disturbing to the rabbis, who feared that mystical interpretation of texts would lead to the abrogation of the law.

The earliest and longest phase of Jewish mysticism is Merkabah ('chariot') mysticism. By this designation is loosely meant everything from the prophecy of *Ezekiel* and the apocalyptic visions in *Daniel* through the emergence of Kabbalah in the twelfth century. The central aspects of Merkabah mysticism are: (1) an interest in the human figure of God, even speculation on its size, as in the so-called Shiur Koma ('measurement of the body') literature, (2) heavenly ascents, (3) theurgic or magical spells and motifs, and (4) apocalyptic and revelatory writings.

The central experience was the ecstatic and theurgic (i.e., magical, spirit-inducing) journey of the adept to the heavenly throne room, there to see 'the king in his glory'. The texts relating such experience usually give an angelic name to the human figure on the throne, making it moot whether the adept actually sees God or his principal anthropomorphic manifestation. The texts, called the *Hekhaloth* ('Palaces') texts, were edited throughout the entire first millennium of Jewish mysticism. In the form in which we have them, they display many of the characteristic concerns of the Hasidei Ashkenaz, a group of medieval Jewish pietists who flourished in fourteenth-century Germany.

The development of the teaching called Kabbalah ('received tradition') is probably most responsible for the gradual diminution of Merkabah mysticism. A kind of Islamic mysticism, known as Sufism, probably also influenced the rise of Kabbalah and helped reduce interest in Merkabah. In medieval Jewish mysticism, the heavenly journey of the Merkabah mystics became spiritualized and allegorized until it symbolized, as well, a journey into the self.

In place of the heavenly palaces, Kabbalah developed a notion of ten *spherot* ('countings' or 'spheres'). These sometimes sound like the Greek notion of the heavenly spheres. Other times, they are not only aspects and emanations of God but also separable creatures, as well as objects of contemplation and manipulation through theurgic and meditative disciplines. By correctly aligning these *spherot* through rituals, pious deeds, and mystical meditations, the Kabbalist can affect the future course of events and participate in the divine plan for the universe.

The *Zohar*

The principal text of Kabbalah is known as the *Zohar*. It purports to be the work of Rabbi Simeon bar Yohai, a famous early third-century rabbi. Its real author was quite likely Moses ben Shemtov of León (1250–1305), a thirteenth-century kabbalist, who lived in Granada, Spain. The *Zohar* has a special mystical agenda. It describes God as an unlimited divine principle, En Sof ('without end'), who produces the universe indirectly as the series of emanations called the *spherot*.

Sometimes the *spherot* seem like the heavenly spheres of philosophical discourse; but other times they are more imaginative configurations of the different powers of God. They can be envisioned as forming a tree of life or even the primeval man, *adam ha-kadmon*. When they are arrayed as the primeval, cosmic man, they seem to be connected to the earlier notion of God's principal angelic mediator, who has gigantic size and somehow embodies the name of God. The correct unifications of the *spherot* will bring about the most harmonious balance of divine forces.

The *Zohar* reads this insight as implied in the biblical text. In form, then, it is a Midrashic exposition of scripture.

> He who desires to understand the wisdom of holy unity, let him contemplate the flame which rises from coal or from a candle for the flame rises only when it is attached to a material thing. Come and see: in the rising flame there are two lights, one a white shining light, and the other a dark bluish light that holds on directly to the candle … Come and see: there is no stimulus for the kindling of the blue light that it might provide the basis for the

> white light save through the people of Israel who … unite with it from below and continue in their endurance (*Zohar* III, 290a; Caplan and Ribalow 1952:161–2).

In this passage, the blue light is characteristically symbolic of the *spherah* known as Malkut ('kingship') or Shekhinah ('God's indwelling'), which is, in turn, identified with the spiritual presence of the people Israel. This particular *spherah*, or aspect of divinity, is not only grammatically feminine in Hebrew but has an explicitly feminine gender, and is viewed as taking part in sexual congress with the masculine aspects of God.

The white light conventionally symbolizes the higher spherah of *ḥesed*, God's aspect of 'lovingkindness'. The passage therefore says that even in a simple flame is a secret about how God and Israel interact. The existence and behaviour of Israel are deeply and integrally related to God's lovingkindness in the world. The purpose of these manipulations of God's various aspects in the world is for the correct flow of divine effulgence (*shefa*), which is normally viewed as best balanced when the upper *spherah* (normally Tiferet, 'beauty'), is properly related through *yesod* ('foundation') to the *spherah* Malkut or Shekhinah, the feminine aspect of God that signifies Israel.

This proper balance is often pictured as sexual intercourse, which could be affected by human behaviours, ritual and otherwise. When a kabbalistically sophisticated married couple had sexual relations with the proper intentions and motivations, with the proper meditations, the heavenly dimensions of God could also be similarly aligned. Thus, mystical Judaism often involved the behaviours of males and females in marriage together. But properly completed ritual actions like the blessing over wine (Kiddush, part of the grace before meals) could also have the same effect. In the following passage, the bride refers to the *spherah* Malkut or Shekhinah, while the husband is Tiferet, one of the higher *spherot*:

> Rabbi Simeon would sit and study Torah all night when the bride was about to be united with her husband. And we have learned that the companions of the household in the bride's palace are needed on that night when the bride is prepared for her meeting on the morrow with her husband under the bridal canopy. They need to be with her all that night and rejoice with her in the preparations with which she is adorned, studying Torah—progressing from the Pentateuch to the Prophets, and from the Prophets to the writings, and then to the midrashic and mystical interpretations of the verses, for these are her adornments and her finery (*Zohar* I, 8a).

This passage has many levels. First it is a simple description of the preparations that a bride and groom may make for their marriage. Secondly, it is a description of the *spherot* of Tiferet, a higher power of God, and Malkut or

Shekhinah, the feminine aspect of God. The *shekhinah*, in turn, takes up residence in the people Israel and helps direct it, so the story is allegorical for the role that Jewish learning plays in the 'love affair' between God and the world.

The system has seemed irrational, absurd, and even polytheistic to many of the deepest Jewish minds, influenced by the rational systems of the philosophers and legal specialists. Indeed, even ordinary Jews could see the threat that this system offered to monotheism. Nevertheless, it continued to appeal to a great number of people who were troubled by the distress that Jews had experienced and the continuing and enormous part that evil played in the world. Kabbalah always purported to explain continuous evil events as a misalignment of divine effulgence that needed human action to help the divinity in his progress towards the goal of cosmic perfection:

> The story of Jonah may be construed as an allegory of the course of a man's life in this world. Jonah descends into the ship: this is parallel to man's soul descending to enter into his body in this world. Why is the soul called Jonah [whose name literally means 'aggrieved']? For the reason that she becomes subject to all manner of vexation when once she enters into partnership with the body. Thus, a man in this world is as in a ship crossing the vast ocean and like to be broken, as it is written 'so that the ship was like to be broken' (*Zohar* on *Jonah* 1:4; Scholem 1949:103).

Each individual soul is put on earth with the vexation of the body for the purpose of making a journey towards perfection.

Luria and Sabbatai Zvi

Until Isaac Luria (1534–72), Kabbalah was largely a private, individual, contemplative discipline. Luria lived in the century after the expulsion from Spain and settled in the hilltop town of Safed in the Galilee region, making Safed a special place for mystics and eventually, in our times, artists and tourists.

Luria explains the tragedy of Jewish life in terms of a cosmic split in the Godhead. God starts the creation of the world by contracting himself (*tsimtsum*) to make room for it. This is a dangerous process, open to difficulty because, in contracting, God removes his perfection from the area that is to be the universe. For some reason when creation begins, the vessels that God designates to carry the divine sparks fracture, mixing up divine sparks within the gross and evil material of creation. The counterpart of this cosmic process is the exile (*galut*) of Israel.

The mystic then, in concert with God and a group of fellow mystics, seeks to help God return the divine sparks to their correct place. This *tikkun* ('rectification' or 'fixing') of the universe can be accomplished by human beings through a variety of processes, some of which are meditative or theurgic. Others are through pious acts, including ritual acts. The community that Isaac Luria founded in Safed practised acts of asceticism and observed the special rules of Judaism with special intensity, hoping that this would help God in the enterprise of redemption and hasten the coming of the messiah.

These mystical notions also quickened messianic expectations. In 1666, Sabbatai Zvi (1626–76) from Izmir (Smyrna), Turkey, an adept of Lurianic Kabbalah, was proclaimed the messiah by Nathan of Gaza and attracted a varied following of mystically oriented Jews. Influenced by the similar Christian quickening of millennialist expectations triggered by the date, the followers of the mystical messiah marched on the sultan in Istanbul. The sultan was not greatly worried at first. Gradually, however, he became aware of the potential danger of this rag-tag army camped outside the walls. He had Sabbatai Zvi imprisoned. When this did not completely stifle the messianic expectations of Sabbatai's followers, he offered Zvi a choice between conversion and death. Faced with a stark alternative, Zvi converted, and most of his followers gave up in despair.

Those who did not repudiate him saw in Zvi's actions a deeper meaning: that the commandments could be fulfilled by the messiah taking on the evil world directly and conquering it. This gave further impetus to the aspects of mysticism we term 'antinomian', that is, counter to rule or law. Many of the most devoted followed Sabbatai Zvi into Islam, where they became a group of crypto-Jews, continuing to practise their ancestral tradition in secret. There are still some members of this sect in modern Turkey, called in Turkish the Dönmeh ('returners').

From the point of view of Orthodox Judaism, the Sabbatians resemble the Christians because they are yet another mystical and antinomian messianic group whose teachings originally came from Judaism but who abandoned it over issues having to do with Jewish law. Another group of this type, in Podolia (western Ukraine), under the influence of a later Sabbatian, Jacob Frank (1726–91), became outwardly Christian.

Hasidism

Hasidism was inaugurated by Israel ben Eliezer (c. 1700–60), called the Baal Shem Tov ('master of the Good Name'), a title sometimes shortened to 'the Baal Shem' or abbreviated to 'the Besht'. He became an orphan and ward of the Jewish community shortly after his birth in Okup, in the eastern European region of Bukovina (now northern Romania and Moldavia). During his youth he eschewed scholarship and was known for his delight in telling stories to children and speaking to animals. He was many things—a Hebrew teacher, a lime quarrier, a small innkeeper, and a dabbler in Kabbalah.

But what seems to have impressed everyone who met him was his humility. He wandered from community to community in Podolia (western Ukraine) and Walachia (southern Romania), encountering people and making disciples. He appears to have received the title 'Baal Shem' as a result of being successful at curing and other actions that were supposed to be accomplished through use of God's name. Sometimes he organized impromptu retreats where he preached through informal conversations and humble lessons.

The Jews who were his principal audience knew enough Hebrew to say their prayers. But they were unable to attend the rigorous and élitist Talmudic academies of eastern Europe, which produced a leadership offering little relevance to the common folk. The Baal Shem Tov proclaimed a simple and accessible message: that the best way of communing with God is through humility, good deeds, prayer (ecstatic and otherwise), and joy. He preached the importance of mutual help, forbearance, and other virtues. He himself became the model for a Hasidic leader, a *tsaddik* ('righteous person'). He sought the presence of God in the events of everyday life.

Hasidic stories are like *agada*, seeking to show a moral lesson, often through the most mundane aspects of ordinary life. A famous Hasidic story ends with the moral that the student learns about the divine from watching the master tie his shoes. The stories of Hasidic masters often resemble strikingly the paradoxical exercise of a Zen *koan*.

The Besht's pietistic Judaism became very popular in eighteenth-century eastern Europe. Its adherents were called Ḥasidim ('pious ones'), recalling the virtue of *ḥesed*, steadfast loyalty or faithfulness owed to the other by each party to the biblical covenant relationship. (In the second century BCE, the designation 'Ḥasidim' had referred to Jewish loyalists in the Maccabean uprising, but that was a movement quite separate from the Ḥasidim in early modern eastern Europe.) After the death of the Baal Shem Tov, the movement of Hasidism was organized under the leadership of one of his primary disciples, Rabbi Ber of Mezeritz, known also as the Maggid ('preacher').

The theory of leadership under the *tsaddikim* ('righteous persons') was first articulated during the Maggid's life. According to this doctrine, all the subsequent leaders of Hasidism after the Baal Shem Tov were titled Tsaddik and became hereditary dynasties who could pass on their authority to their children. Thus a *tsaddik*, also called in Yiddish 'Rebbe', was both the holder of a hereditary office and a kind of intermediary between the people and God. The popular appeal of Hasidism provoked the opposition of the rabbinic community, who were characterized as Mitnagdim ('opponents') by the Ḥasidim.

When Hasidism spread to Latvia and Lithuania, the centre of rabbinic rationalism in eastern Europe, it changed character again. Talmudic training was quite common in these communities, and for Hasidism to spread there, it needed to gain a certain Talmudic expertise that it had not developed previously. Especially important in this transformation of Hasidism was Shneur Zalman

(1746–1812) of Lyadi, Belorussia. When he, a respected Talmudist, joined the movement, he signalled an attempt to synthesize Talmudic Judaism with Hasidic pietism. He wrote a philosophic tractate known as *Tania* (As It Is Taught).

His followers were known by an acronym, Habad (also transliterated Chabad, as it represents the three Hebrew letters Ḥ–B–D), representing the names of three *spherot*: Ḥokhma ('wisdom'), Bina ('insight'), and Da'at ('knowledge'). They are, however, more commonly known today by the name of the Belorussian town in which the movement centred—Lubavitch.

The followers of Shneur Zalman of Lyadi and of his descendants, the line of rabbis in the Schneerson family, are today commonly known as Lubavitcher Ḥasidim. Present in New York and its suburbs, they resemble strict Orthodox Jews, but technically they are not Orthodox in their beliefs and practices. Since 1994, when Rabbi Menachem Schneerson (1902–94) died without a male heir, the Lubavitcher have been without a leader. These and other Hasidic sects, founded by other early pupils of the Baal Shem Tov, have often been in sharp competition with one another and with the Orthodox majority. The Orthodox remain quite hostile to most of the Hasidic program.

JEWISH OBSERVANCES

Prayer

Prayer is a regular feature of rabbinic Judaism. Jews are enjoined to pray when they go to sleep and when they rise, after the passage in *Deuteronomy* 6:4–9, which commands Israel to love the Lord, to teach his laws diligently to the children, to keep them in the heart, and to speak of them morning and evening. The last of these instructions was taken to mean prayer.

Prayer continues to follow the order of the temple service, which was performed thrice daily. So Jews characteristically pray before retiring, after rising, and three times a day in a fixed order. Some of the prayers may be combined for convenience. First and last prayers every day tend to be private, as the others may be as well. But Jews try to find a *minyan*, a group of ten persons, usually in a synagogue, as a quorum for their daily prayers.

Although it is a commandment to attend synagogue, Jews may also address additional prayers to God at any time. One may pray virtually anywhere, as long as the place does not detract from the dignity of the prayer and as long as the proper *kavvanah* or spiritual intention can be achieved.

The Content of Prayer

One may recite God's praises, but prayers were strictly judged so as not to be idolatrous. For instance, no prayers to angels or intermediary beings were allowed.

Sabbath Blessings for Reading the Torah Scroll

[Before reading from the Torah]

Reader: Praised be the Lord, the source of blessing.

Congregation: Praised be the Lord, the source of blessing, throughout all time.

Reader: Praised are you, Lord our God, King of the Universe, who has chosen us from among all peoples by giving us His Torah. Praised are You, Lord who gives the Torah.

[After reading from the Torah]

Praised are You, Lord our God, King of the Universe, who has given us the Torah of Truth, planting within us eternal life. Praised are You, Lord who gives the Torah.

[Before reading from the Prophets*]*

Praised are You, Lord our God, King of the Universe, who has chosen the good prophets, and maintained them, whose utterances were truthful. Praised are You, Lord, who chose the Torah, Moses His servant, Israel His people and prophets of truth and righteousness.

[After reading from the Prophets*]*

Praised are you, Lord our God, King of the Universe, Rock of all ages, righteous in all generations, steadfast God, who speaks and the deed is accomplished, who decrees and fulfils, whose every word is truth and righteousness. Faithful are you, who is the Lord our God, and faithful are all Your words. None of your words will ever be found empty, for You are a faithful and merciful God and King. Praised are You, Lord, who are the faithful God in all your promises.

Show compassion for Zion, the habitation of our lives. And bring hope speedily in our days to the humbled soul. Praised are You, Lord who brings joy to Zion by her descendants.

Bring us joy, Lord our God, through Your prophet Elijah and the kingdom of the House of David Your anointed. May Elijah come soon, to gladden our hearts. May no usurper sit on David's throne, and may no other inherit his glory. For by Your holy name you have promised that his light shall never be extinguished. Praised are you, Lord shield of David.

For the Torah, for worship, for the prophets, and for this Sabbath day which you have given us for holiness and rest, for dignity and splendour—for everything—do we thank You and praise You. May Your name be praised continually for every living creature. Praised are You, Lord who sanctifies the Sabbath.

And indeed, we often find such prayers in documents like the *Sefer ha-Razzim* (Book of Mysteries), which contain clearly heretical magic. In a sense, the rabbis obviated the need to distinguish between magic and religion by declaring prayers to any intermediary to be a kind of idolatry.

A Yemenite rabbi. Jews from the Yemen immigrated to Israel after the middle of the twentieth century. (Albert Beckman)

FROM THE PASSOVER HAGGADAH LITURGY

This is the bread of affliction, the poor bread which our fathers ate in the land of Egypt. Let all who are hungry come and eat; let all who are in need come to our Passover *seder.* Now we are here; next year may we be in the land of Israel. Now we are slaves; next year may we be free!

The ethicization of prayer is in keeping with all other aspects of rabbinic Judaism, which concentrates on the ethical analysis of all acts. Rabbinic discussions of prayer assume that God hears prayer, but that humans should submit their prayer to the same ethical standards that govern the rest of behaviour. This notion may be seen even in the Bible, where the prayer of a thief is considered blasphemy (*Psalm* 10:3).

One may petition God's special favour, provided the advantage sought does not adversely affect anyone else. Jews are enjoined not to pray for things that might cause harm to others. Seeing a plume of smoke upon returning to one's city, Jews are not allowed to pray, 'Let it not be my house', because one implication of that prayer is hoping that the fire be in someone else's house. Jews are not allowed even to pray for the fall of one's enemies (*Avoth* 4:19). Instead, prayer for the benefit of others is constantly encouraged.

The rabbis took a very lively interest in the content of prayer, though they certainly allowed that Jews were free to pray in any language the heart might prompt. The very first tractate of the *Mishnah* and hence of the *Talmud* as well is *Berachoth* (Prayer). The rabbis' intention in putting this tractate first is seen in the fact that the first order of tractates was concerned with agricultural laws (*Zera'im*, 'Seeds'), but within that order the rabbis pre-empted the first tractate for prayer, even though there was an order devoted to Holy Things later on in the *Mishnah*. Thus, prayer is likely to be the very first subject a young Jew will encounter when beginning study of the texts.

The particular kinds of prayers offered and the specific texts of the prayers have developed over millennia of Jewish history. Traditionally prayer is said in Hebrew; even though prayer-books of Sephardic and Ashkenazic Jews (a distinction to be discussed later) differ somewhat, on the whole the order of Hebrew prayer is something that unites Jews the world over.

The Spirit of Prayer

Rabbinic law provides that prayer should be rightly intentioned towards God (b. Berachot 31a). This intention or *kavvanah* can be defined in a variety of ways and, indeed, should be appropriate for each action, not just prayer. Musical accompaniment is considered an aid in concentration. Thus, individual prayer may be chanted and synagogue services are always chanted, with different and appropriate cantillations for different parts of the service and different occasions. Jews have always sung songs as part of worship, not just in the context of religious life. One of the characteristics of the Hasidic movement is the special attention it pays to *kavvanah* in prayer and, indeed, to songs and the attainment of joy in prayer.

Items Worn in Prayer

When praying, Jewish men may choose to wear special clothes and articles derived from the dress specified in the Bible. Traditional Jews hold that the use of these garments and articles helps them attain the proper *kavvanah*.

Traditional Jews often pray in a *tallith*, a prayer shawl. This is a large rectangular piece of material that originated as an ordinary serapelike Hellenistic outer garment. The Jewish version contained the correct fringes at the corners, as specified by biblical law (*Numbers* 15:37–41). It is now worn when praying and at ceremonial functions.

Today, a *tallith* is a specially designed shawl, usually striped in blue and white, though other colours are also possible, and always featuring long fringes at the corners. Some Jews prefer very large ones that cover the shoulders as well as the neck, and drape amply over the back, as if they were a kind of cloak or robe. The ample *tallith* can be drawn over the head as a kind of hood, when concentrating in prayer. Other Jews prefer a *tallith* that is short, draped around the shoulders like a towel or a scarf.

Very Orthodox Jews wear the fringed *tallith*, enjoined by the Bible, at all times. They accomplish this by wearing a short *tallith*, called the *ḥatzi tallith* (half *tallith*), an undershirt that has the fringes of the longer garment, under their street clothes. At the other extreme, Reform Jews usually choose to do away entirely with the use of a prayer shawl, even while praying.

Jewish males cover their heads when praying, including on many occasions when prayers are offered, such as meals. In light of this practice, more traditional Jews simply wear a head covering all the time. Before the Middle Ages, the *tallith* itself served possibly as a head covering, being ample enough to be pulled up over the head when desired. In medieval and modern periods, a skullcap, called the *kippah* (Hebrew for 'cap') or *yarmulke* (the equivalent in Yiddish) has evolved. In the twentieth century, fashion has shrunk this cap to the dimensions of a beverage coaster, so that its wearers sometimes need to anchor the mini *kippah* with bobby-pins. Very Orthodox Jews try to wear a *kippah* all the time, even under ordinary hats.

In ancient days, no such head covering existed. Indeed, covering the head was often seen as a mark of sorrow. Perhaps the custom evolved from using the *tallith* to veil one's face and head when concentrating on prayer or in covering the face and eyes in the presence of the divinity. The specific history of the practice is lost. Reform Jews have characteristically decided that it is no longer necessary,

A proselytizer from the Lubavitcher Hasidic movement instructs an Israeli soldier in how to bind the tefillin *to his forearm and forehead.* (Albert Beckman)

even in prayer. But a fair number of modern Jewish males, particularly students, now often cover their heads all the time with a skullcap for the purpose of publicly stating their Jewish identity. And women, in the interest of equality, have begun to wear the *tallith* and *kippah* as well.

On weekdays, traditional Jews use *tefillin* in prayer. These are a pair of cubelike black boxes about 5 cm (2 in.) high, tied by leather thongs, one to the forehead and one to the upper arm. Inside the boxes are specific passages from scripture explaining their purpose and use. The usual name for these in English is 'phylacteries', a word derived from the Greek for 'protective charm'. But this is a false translation of the word *tefillin*, as the boxes have no 'guarding' or protective value.

The articles serve to fulfil literally the biblical commandment to bind the words of Torah 'upon the hand and as frontlets between the eyes'. This instruction appears in a passage in *Deuteronomy* 6, following the *Shema*, telling Jews how to love and worship God. (For the *Shema*, see the accompanying text selections.) Jews also put up scrolls called *mezuzoth* on their door-frames, in a cartridge the size of a lipstick. These scrolls contain the *Shema* and similar passages, in literal observance of this commandment.

Pious Jews put on *tefillin* each weekday morning. But putting them on is suspended on Saturday mornings, as it is considered work that would violate the Sabbath. One box is looped to the forehead by a thong. The second box is lashed to the arm, facing the heart. The leather thong is wrapped around the arm and around the fingers in a special pattern.

The custom is quite ancient. *Tefillin* have been found in the caves of Judea, dating to the time of the Bar Cochba revolt (132–5), so we know that they were already in use in Roman times. For Orthodox Jews these articles are used regularly as an aid to prayer, concentrating the mind and fulfilling the commandment. Reform Jews have suspended their use almost entirely.

Blessings

Jews also insist on blessing all the gifts that God provides. A formula for blessings was designed by the early rabbis. Like most Jewish blessings, it begins: 'Blessed art Thou, O Lord our God, King of the Universe [or king forever] …' and then continues with the appropriate words of thanks, specific to the occasion. Jews normally pronounce short blessings over wine and bread at every meal for which they are available. It seems likely that this blessing, as reinterpreted by Jesus, serves as the basis of the Christian Eucharist. After the meal, Jews normally recite a quite long doxology. If a sufficient number of people eat together, it is sung aloud communally.

The round of Jewish prayer is both greatly comforting and meant to express joy for God's creation. Even Reform Jews and Reconstructionists, who sometimes question whether God answers prayer, suggest that the constant round of Jewish prayer throughout the day, and even more the prayers for forgiveness as the high holidays approach, is beneficial in concentrating one's attention on the ethical goals of life.

The Weekly Sabbath

The Sabbath begins at sunset on Friday and continues to sunset Saturday. On Friday night Jews may attend synagogue services. Orthodox services tend to be short and close to sunset. Conservative and Reform Judaism currently favour a longer service, in the evening after the Sabbath dinner.

Even though it occurs every week, the Sabbath is surely the holiest day of the Jewish year. The prayers on that day consecrate it as a sacred time. Jews may attend synagogue for evening prayers, but cease all work at sundown. The observant Jew feels not the absence of ordinary work but rather the special quiet and rest of the Sabbath, given over to song, prayer, and quiet contemplation.

In the grand six-day creation story in *Genesis*, the Sabbath is built into the order of the universe. For the Jew today, it is also a remembrance of the Garden of Eden and an event that presages a return to Eden at the coming of the messiah. The Sabbath is also a primary sign of the endurance of the covenant with God:

> The Israelite people shall keep the sabbath, observing the sabbath throughout the ages as a covenant for all time: it shall be a sign for all time between Me and the people of Israel: For in six days the LORD made heaven and earth, and on the seventh day He ceased from work and was refreshed (*Exodus* 31:16–17; also Sabbath prayer-book).

Jews return home early on Friday afternoon so that they can prepare for the Sabbath by cleaning the house and themselves and preparing the special Sabbath meal. In the home, Jews light candles before the start of the Sabbath.

The meal itself contains customary graces or prayers over bread and wine, with special additions celebrating God's work of creation. Jews also use the dinner as an occasion for singing psalms, hymns, and special Sabbath songs. It is characteristic of the observance to have a specially fine family dinner, at which the best silver and china are used. Specially braided breads called *halloth*—so named after the showbread of the temple—are blessed together with the wine. In Jewish observance, besides the 'grace' over bread and wine before every meal, there is a longer doxology after the meal thanking God for the food. The meal is dedicated to celebrating rest and thanking God for the Sabbath.

But the Sabbath meal is really only an augmented form of an ordinary Jewish meal. Jews do not eat any meal without praising and thanking God. Virtually every action of the day that can be sanctified is sanctified by Jewish law. Every action is amenable to moral analysis and every religious rite is an object lesson in that point of view. The Jewish people, denied a country and great buildings, instead built up a system that sanctified the times of everyday occurrences and sought the presence of God in them.

Saturday morning, at least the men in the family normally go to synagogue, whose services last essentially the morning. They may return home for another special meal, using the afternoon for learning or quiet contemplation.

At the end of the Sabbath, many Jews return to synagogue to celebrate an evening boundary-marking observance called Havdalah. The Havdalah ('distinction' between the Sabbath and weekdays) service is performed with the use of wine, a braided candle, and a spice box, symbolizing the sweetness of the Sabbath. It also highlights the promise of the new week, blessing it until the next Sabbath. Songs wish everyone a good week. The service mentions the prophet Elijah, a messianic figure, presumably in the hope that he will come during the following week and mark the arrival of the messianic age.

Sabbath Restrictions

On the Sabbath, Orthodox Jews will do nothing at all defined as work, such as lighting fires or cooking foods. In strict observance, they may not even give a command on the Sabbath that work be done. Hence, in modern urban high-rises and hospitals, one encounters Sabbath elevators, programmed before the Sabbath to stop at every floor continually throughout that day. The Orthodox, who avoid driving on the Sabbath, seek to live within walking distance of the synagogue. They spend the Sabbath there, reading from the Torah and celebrating community events such as the Bar Mitzvah of the community's children. Reform and Conservative Jews spend time in their synagogues, but may also drive and do secular work—indeed, they may go out to the beach or enjoy a game of tennis or golf, Sabbath recreational activity not allowable in the Orthodox tradition.

Centuries ago, the ancient rabbis emphasized ritual behaviour for all Jews, not just for religious specialists, which had the effect of resisting acculturation in the Roman and Persian worlds. At the same time, they worked to make the rules more livable. One hardship in the rabbinic calendar arose whenever a holiday and the Sabbath fell on consecutive days, complicating the preparation of food. In such cases, a legal fiction called an *eruv* ('mixing', perhaps of the sacred with the profane) was instigated. The *eruv tavshilin* or 'cooking *eruv*' is an extension that moves the time frame of the Sabbath. It legitimizes cooking on the festival day preceding a Sabbath by symbolically starting the preparation of the Sabbath food before the festival. It is done with a conscious intent, a declaration, a prayer, and a symbolic act of food preparation. It can also be done on behalf of the entire community by the rabbi.

Similarly, the spatial frame of Sabbath activity can be extended. Ancient Sabbath laws forbid walking or carrying anything between 'private' and 'public' domains. Walking further than 2,000 cubits (.88 km or .55 mi) from one's house is also prohibited 'work'. An *eruv ḥatzerot* ('*eruv* of courtyards') allows various private areas to be linked together so that carrying and walking are unaffected by the rule. This can be accomplished in various ways, but today it is common for the Orthodox Jewish community to string a wire connecting the tops of a minimum of four poles at least ten handbreadths high. Existing telephone poles conveniently suffice. In New York, Toronto, and elsewhere in North America, many of the significant Jewish communities have erected *eruv*s around their entire cities or neighbourhoods. One in Washington, DC, incorporates the White House. As a result, observant Jews may walk further than the biblical Sabbath journey of 2,000 cubits while carrying items, strolling with their babies, or otherwise enjoying the peace of the Sabbath.

The Synagogue and Its Music

The chanting in the synagogue reaches a crescendo with the reading of the Torah scrolls, which traditionally happens on Mondays, Thursdays, the Sabbath, and special holidays. The synagogue service in antiquity, as now, was conducted by laypersons, not the rabbi, who is viewed as a jurist or even judge in various capacities.

The basic order of formal service in the synagogue follows the ancient temple service. It entailed song, musical accompaniment, and sacrifice. After the destruction of the temple in Jerusalem, all sacrificial service stopped, but the other aspects of the temple service—including music, when appropriate—were transferred to the synagogue and to individual piety.

The rabbis concentrated on moving rituals and prayers from the temple into the purview of the synagogue. One can see this activity already with the first rabbinic leader of the post-temple generation of 70, Yochanan ben Zakkai. His halakhic rulings mostly concern such things as the transfer of the blowing of the *shofar* from the temple to the synagogue. In this regard, the rabbis appointed the synagogue the successor to the temple as the place where the prayers of Jews were pre-eminently to be offered.

Before the publication of prayer-books, the order of the service was fluid within certain established limits. The rabbis specified the order of prayer and the specific formulations of each prayer, but they are unlikely to have innovated very much in this process. Probably they were just attempting to supervise and rule on what was already common practice in the community. People recited largely from memory and leaders could insert their own personal texts.

In time, services were graced by professional singers, known as *hazanin* or 'cantors', who continue to be part of Jewish worship. Today, they lead the congregation in prayers but not to sing them in unison; rather, by singing various lines from the prayer-books, they signal the congregation about the progress of the service. However, each person prays quietly but audibly at his or her own rate. The Reform movement at first opted for the decorum of a more European sense of unison recitation, but is now returning in a few ways to the more traditional style of Jewish prayer.

Of different styles of chant that have developed, the Yemenite system is by far the oldest. Jews in Yemen preserve the custom of chanting the *Targum* ('Translation' in Aramaic), an Aramaic translation of the Bible, after the Hebrew reading. This custom, formerly widespread in Judaism, must date back to a time when Aramaic was the vernacular and was better understood than Hebrew.

Chanting traditions influenced by German Jewry are at considerable variance from the Yemenite and differ also from the melodies cherished by former Spanish Jews. Different cantillations are used for the Torah and the *Prophets*, so that any knowledgeable person can immediately recognize what is being read from the sound of the chanting alone. Special systems to emphasize the solemnity of the occasion are used during the holidays of Rosh Hashanah and Yom Kippur.

Jewish music used in Western countries appears related to old Greek scales. Some of it must be of late Hellenistic origin, but it may incorporate still more ancient melodies. The written notation was introduced by the Masoretes, a group of scribes and scholars living in Tiberias, in the Galilee region, in the ninth and tenth centuries—the same group who developed the authoritative pronunciation for the biblical text and the various scribal procedures used to check that biblical manuscripts are copied correctly. Like their vowel diacritics, the musical *nekudot* or 'pointings' are written between, above, and below the consonants of the Hebrew text. These cantillation signs, called *trup* ('tropes'), are remarkably similar in form to the Byzantine musical signs.

A Bar Mitzvah in any denomination will normally involve some chanting. Bar Mitzvah celebrants are introduced to the cantillation marks, though since

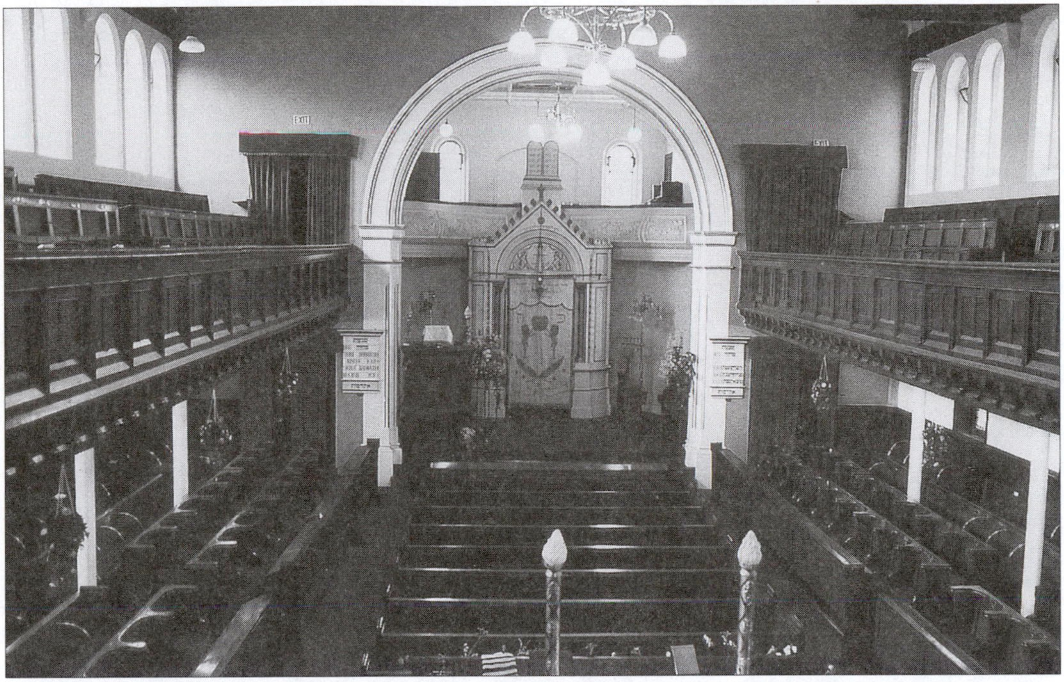

Like this building in Dublin, synagogues reflect the architectural styles of houses of worship in lands where Jews have settled.
(Albert Beckman)

cantors are specially trained in this art, few others keep it up. Initiates often memorize their parts rather than mastering the chanting; most North American Bar Mitzvah celebrants use a tape-recorded version to prepare their part.

Quite often synagogues had rooms to accommodate Jews visiting from other places. In North America, the homeless are often temporarily housed in synagogues, as in the neighbouring churches. Modern North American synagogues normally also contain a library and classroom wing to continue their traditional role as houses of study, as well as often a large social hall for the meals in celebration of weddings and Bar Mitzvahs. Only a few synagogues contain recreational and sports facilities, but those that have them are all the more noteworthy because they do.

The Annual Festival Cycle

The Jewish calendar is a lunar calendar. Each month starts with the new moon, a time for special prayers, and consequently the fourteenth of every month coincides with the full moon. Twelve lunar months add up to only 354 days, but the lunar calendar is kept in phase with the solar year through the addition of a leap

In an Israeli kibbutz, *a traditional spring harvest ritual is given the flavour of national pageantry as much as of religious observance.* (Albert Beckman)

month, Adar Sheni ('second Adar'), every few years. The rabbis used to base the calendar on direct observation, taking testimony from witnesses who had seen the new moon. It has been switched to astronomical calculation, with festival dates and leap months projected far in advance.

Years are now counted from the creation of the universe. The rabbis added up time spans mentioned in the biblical text to arrive at the conventional figure, in 2000 CE reaching 5761. Each year begins with a new moon around the fall equinox, marked by the celebration of Rosh Hashanah.

In preserving the ancient Hebrew festivals, biblical and rabbinic tradition interpreted them with new dimensions of symbolic meaning. There is clear evidence of agricultural and pastoral origins in their seasonal detail. Even in biblical times, they were given historical associations with events in the narrative of the people of Israel. Through rabbinic influence they also became spiritual holidays of contrition and contemplation.

New Year and the Day of Atonement

Rosh Hashanah (New Year) and Yom Kippur (the Day of Atonement) came at the autumn harvest, marked by the blowing of the ram's horn or *shofar*. In rabbinic observance, the *shofar* allegorically wakes up the congregation from its moral slumber with a reminder to consider carefully the deeds of the past year. This culminates on the Day of Atonement, the most solemn day of the year, when the imagery of sheep being counted by a shepherd or troops by a commander figures in the liturgy to describe the final judgement of people by God.

Sukkoth

At Sukkoth (booths or 'tabernacles'), concluding the autumn harvest, many Jews still build a *sukkah*, a small temporary shelter, outside the house and sleep in it for the eight-day festival or at least eat in it when possible. The agricultural origin of camping out in one's fields must have been to protect the ripening crop from creatures. In the Bible, the historical interpretation is to recall the Israelites' life in some temporary shelter during their migration from Egypt under Moses's leadership.

Ḥanukkah

Ḥanukkah is not an Israelite agricultural festival but a Hellenistic historical one, from the mid-second century BCE. It celebrates the victory of the Maccabean Jews over oppressors and the purification and rededication (*ḥanukkah*) of the temple, which had been profaned. The miraculous eight-day duration of one day's quantity of oil is symbolized by the Ḥanukkah *menorah*.

We can infer that the rabbis were not enthusiastic about observing the holiday from the lack of a tractate on it in the *Mishnah*. They sought to spiritualize it, turning it from the independence day of the Hasmonean dynasty into a celebration of God's deliverance by miracle. As a postbiblical holiday, Ḥanukkah was considered minor until modern times. In the twentieth century, North American Jews gave it increased emphasis because of its proximity to Christmas, when holiday activity preoccupies much of society. Modern Israelis also celebrate the holiday with gusto, finding in it the sense of a national liberation, and finding in the struggle with neighbouring Arabs as enemies some association with the ancient narratives of foreign oppression.

Purim

Purim, similarly a minor festival, usually falls in March. Its narrative, read from the book of *Esther*, recalls the deliverance of the Jews in Persia from destruction at the hands of Haman. Speculation as to antecedents behind the narrative points not to Israelite customs but to Babylonian and Persian names (the goddess Ishtar for Esther, the god Marduk for Mordechai, and the Persian month Farvardin for Purim). This holiday is celebrated rather like the North American Hallowe'en,

Rabbinic Humour and Wit

[Rabbinic humour was sharp and cogent. It was sometimes at the expense of ignoramuses, women, and gentiles. But often too, it was directed at the incongruity of the rabbis' own pretensions.]

Rabbah and R. Zera joined together in a Purim feast. They became drunk, and he cut R. Zerah's throat. On the next day, he prayed on his behalf and revived him. The following year he said, 'Will your honour come and we will have Purim together?' He replied, 'No. A miracle does not take place on every occasion' (b. Meg. 7b).

[Moses was taking dictation of the *Pentateuch* from God at Mount Sinai, and had reached *Genesis* 1:26: 'And God said, "Let us make man in our image, after our likeness."' Moses interrupted the dictation.] 'Sovereign of the Universe, why do you say "us" [in the plural] and leave an opening for the *minim* [Gnostics, Christians, and the like]?' The Almighty answered, 'Just you write, and he who wishes to err, let him err.'

'Teach us to number our days' [*Psalm* 90:12]. R. Joshua said: 'If we know exactly the number of our days, we could repent before we die.' R. Eliezer said: 'Repent one day before you die.' His disciples said: 'Who knows when he will die?' 'All the more, then, let him repent today, for perhaps he will die tomorrow. The result will be that all his life will be spent in repentance' (*Midrash Psalms* on *Psalm* 90:12 197a, section 16).

The Rabbis taught: The father has the following obligations towards his son: He must circumcise him, redeem him, teach him the Torah, take a wife unto him, and teach him a trade. Some say he must teach him to swim also. Rabbi Yehuda said: 'He that does not teach his son a trade, teaches him to rob.' Teaches him to rob? How is that?—we may say: as though he taught him to rob.

R. Eliezer used every argument to substantiate his opinion, but they [the other rabbis] would not accept them. He said, 'If the law is as I have argued, may this carob tree argue for me.' The carob tree uprooted itself and moved a hundred cubits from its place. Some say it moved four hundred cubits. They said, 'From a tree no proof can be brought.' Then he said, 'May the canal prove it.' The water of the canal flowed backwards. They said, 'From a canal no proof may be brought.' Then he said, 'May the walls of this House of Study prove it.' Then the walls of the house bent

with costume parties and merrymaking, even with gifts of candy. It can also be compared with Mardi Gras both in its late winter date and to some extent in its indulgent partying.

Passover

The important festival of Passover comes in the spring at the season of agricul-

inwards, as if they were about to fall. R. Joshua rebuked the walls and said to them, 'If the learned dispute about the law, what has that to do with you?' So, to honour R. Joshua, the walls did not fall down, but to honour R. Eliezer, they did not become straight again. Then R. Eliezer said, 'If I am right, may the heavens prove it.' Then a heavenly voice said, 'What have you against R. Eliezer? The law is always with him.' The R. Joshua got up and said, 'It is not in heaven' [*Deuteronomy* 30:12]. What did he mean by this? R. Jeremiah said, 'The Torah was given to us at Sinai. We do not attend to this heavenly voice. For it was already written in the Torah at Mt. Sinai that "By the majority you are to decide" [*Exodus* 23:2].' R. Nathan met Elijah and asked him what God did in that hour. Elijah replied, 'He laughed and said, "My children have defeated me"' (b. Baba Metzia 59b).

Why was man created on Friday? So that, if he becomes haughty, one can say to him, 'The gnat was created before you' (b. Sanhedrin 38a).

An idolater asked R. Yochanan b. Zakkai: 'These rites that you perform look like a kind of witchcraft. You bring a heifer, burn it, pound it, and take its ashes. If one of you is defiled by a dead body you sprinkle upon him two or three drops and you say to him: "You are clean!"' R. Yochanan asked him: 'Has a demon of madness ever possessed you?' 'No,' he replied. 'Have you ever seen a man possessed by this demon of madness?' 'Yes,' he said. 'And what do you do in such a case?' 'We bring roots,' he replied, 'and make them smoke under him. Then we sprinkle water upon the demon and it flees.' Said R. Yochanan to him, 'Let your ears hear what you utter with your mouth! Precisely so is this spirit a spirit of uncleanness, as it is written, "And also I will cause the prophets and the unclean spirits to pass out of the land" [*Zechariah* 13:2]. Water of purification is sprinkled upon the unclean and the spirit flees.' When the idolater had gone, R. Yochanan's disciples said to their master, 'Master, you have put off this man with a mere makeshift argument. But what explanation will you give to us?' Said he to them, 'By your life! It is not the dead that defiles nor the water that purifies. The Holy One, Blessed be He, merely says: "I have laid down a statute, I have issued a decree. You are not allowed to transgress my decree," as it is written, "This is the stature of the law" [*Numbers* 19:2]' (*Numbers Rabbah* 19:8).

tural rebirth and renewal. It ritually enacts 'spring cleaning' in the home. Kosher laws forbid all leavened foods, as defined by the rabbis; furthermore, all food that is eaten must be prepared on newly cleaned equipment. Various plants figure in the elaborate and symbolic Passover *seder* or ritual dinner, but the chief spiritual significance of Passover is one's sense of historical participation. The Passover liturgy, called the Haggadah ('narrative'), interprets the events. Unleavened bread,

The table setting for the Passover seder *includes the* matzoh, *a crackerlike square wafer of unleavened bread, here covered by a cloth with the Hebrew characters for* matzoh.
(Beverly Goldey)

for instance, is associated with haste in the departure of Moses and the Israelites from Egypt. The liturgy tells every Jew to look on himself or herself as having experienced the divine deliverance of the Exodus personally.

Shavuoth

Shavuoth ('weeks'), in late spring, was originally the barley harvest, and came to be observed with the eating of dairy foods. It is known to Christians as Pentecost (Greek, 'fiftieth') because it comes fifty days after Passover. Its historical interpretation in rabbinic Judaism is to celebrate the giving of the Torah on Mount Sinai.

The Ninth of Ab

Towards late summer, a fast-day is celebrated: the Ninth of Ab. This is taken as the historical anniversary of the destruction of the first and second temples. Fasting is from sunset to sunset, and includes the avoidance of all luxurious display—including wearing leather, which was considered a luxury item in rabbinic times. Hence where Orthodox observe this day, one can see congregations dressed in canvas tennis shoes.

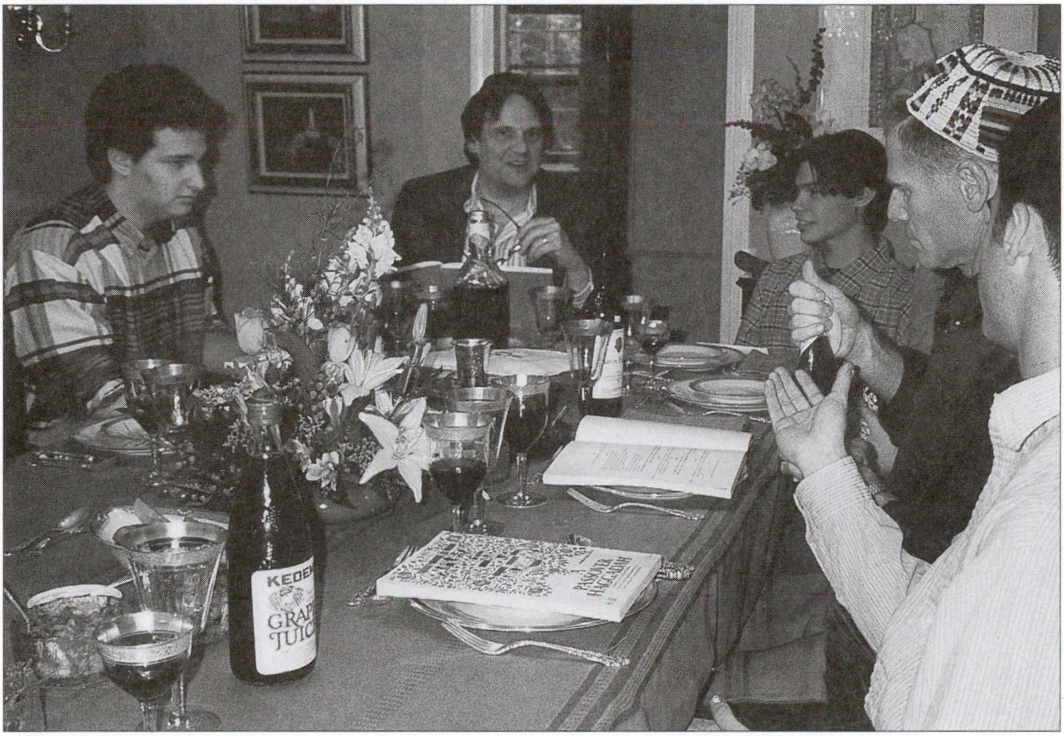

The seder *recalls the meal that the Israelites ate before fleeing Egypt.*
(Beverly Goldey)

Life-Cycle Rituals

Common to the world's religious traditions is the marking of certain transitional moments in a person's life. The Jewish tradition is no exception, with its 'rites of passage': for birth, coming of age, marriage, and death. In this chapter, we have mentioned the Bar Mitzvah or coming-of-age ceremony at our opening, and will return to the marriage ceremony when we conclude. Principal attention here will be given to the times of birth and death.

Birth

The most characteristic ritual concerned with birth is circumcision of the male foreskin. Jews only circumcise males. They do so, as a rule, on the eighth day of life, unless the health of the boy is endangered or some other necessity makes the operation undesirable. Normally, circumcision is done by a ritual circumciser called a *mohel*, hired for the occasion. These days, the *mohel* may also be trained as a local physician, but there are still many 'paramedical' people trained specially to do the operation according to the rabbinic procedure.

Circumcision usually takes place in the home. Normally a family will

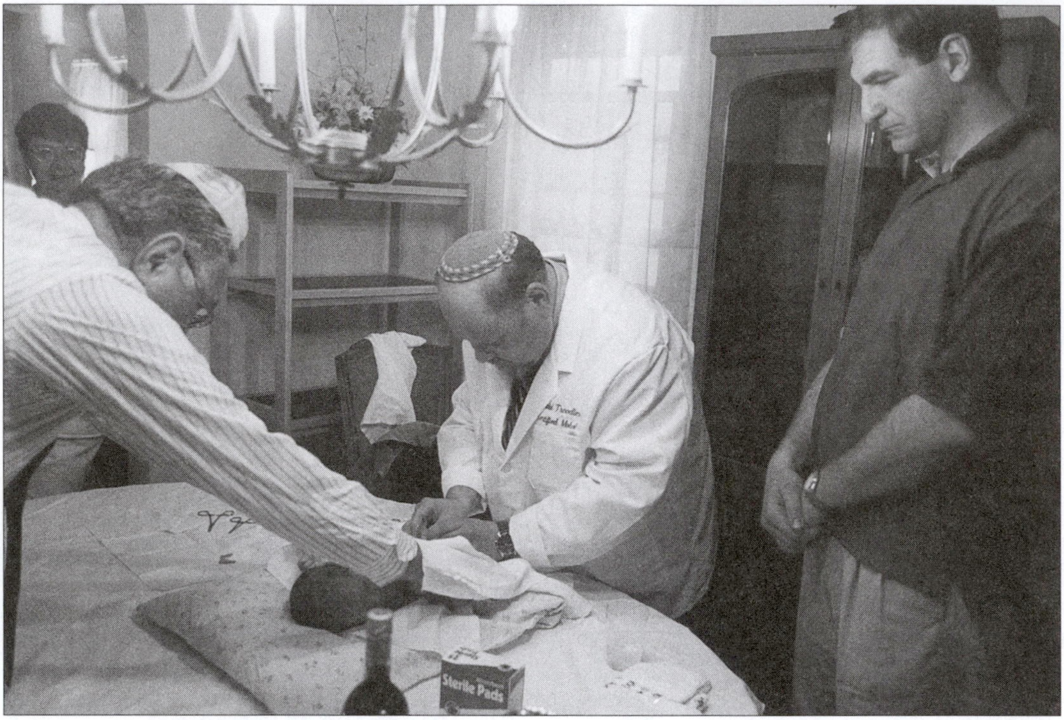

A mohel *performs the circumcision of a baby boy.*
(Albert Beckman)

gather together for it and to celebrate the birth. The liturgy of the occasion involves a commitment to give the child a Jewish education, stressing learning, the doing of good deeds, marriage, and a life within the community. Because the ritual is in the hands of the individual family, sometimes significant family traditions are included within it. In most of the home celebrations, a rabbi is unnecessary because the work is the *mohel*'s; a rabbi is traditionally a ritual and legal expert, not a leader of prayer or a circumciser. Many families insist, however, that a rabbi be present to make sure that the entire ceremony is legally acceptable.

After a Jew is born today, male or female, the family normally goes to synagogue and is awarded an *aliyah* ('going up'), one of the honours surrounding the reading of the Torah. After the parents recite the blessing over the passage of the Torah being read, the rabbi or the service leader will ask for special blessings on the child and announce the child's name. Since there are normally seven *aliyoth* each week, there is room for several baby namings and other important happy news for the community—engagements, prospective marriages, even prayers for the sick. In this way, the community learns of the important events in the life of each family as it attends the synagogue services. These customs, which were largely eliminated by Reform Judaism, are now being reinstated even there because the community so thoroughly enjoys hearing the happy news, the *nahath* (literally 'the pleasurable feelings', usually pronounced 'Nahas' in the Ashkenazic or Yiddish fashion).

Marriage

Marriage is universally lauded in Judaism. Though some great scholars are generally forgiven for not marrying, everyone is enjoined to do so, and to raise children. When it occurs within the sanctified borders of marriage, sexuality is encouraged both for procreation and for the pleasure it brings to the couple. Indeed, sexual pleasure and fulfilment is normally listed as a responsibility that a man owes his wife. Thus, Jewish marriages are great affairs of happiness in which the community normally is given to a modest degree of excess, but they are also governed by an air of religious seriousness and sanctity, as we shall see.

A marriage can be celebrated in a home as well as in a synagogue, hotel, or catering establishment. A rabbi is present more in a legal than a liturgical capacity; he makes sure that the marriage contract is properly prepared and also that the proper procedures are followed. Official witnesses to the legal proceedings must also be present. The same is true for a Jewish divorce. Only in a small number of cases in North America today are rabbinic specifications followed exactly; most citizens include also the national marriage and divorce customs of their countries.

Death

Jews believe that death should be faced resolutely and without illusion. There are a number of strange and interesting customs and not a few superstitions that accompany the bereavement process, but all is directed towards allowing the bereaved to come to terms with separation from their departed loved ones. Funeral activities can even be conducted in the home, though that is extremely rare in North America today.

The liturgy for the funeral is meant to console the grieving family members. It explicitly mentions that God will resurrect the righteous and that they will shine as the brightness of the firmament. They will be bound up into the bonds of life. But even at these moments, Judaism is relatively non-specific about how God will fulfil the prophecies that the dead will live again.

In traditional Judaism, the corpse was washed by a special society of laypersons. In the Hellenistic period, disposal of the body was accomplished using first sarcophagi (stone coffins kept above the floor in tombs) and then later interring the bones, as was normal for the period among gentiles as well. After the flesh had decomposed in the sarcophagus, the bones were ceremonially interred by the family.

In modern Judaism, burial is always in a plain coffin. No embalming is allowed. Hence interment is always done as quickly as is practical after the death,

THE KADDISH PRAYER

Reader:
Hallowed and enchanced may He be throughout the world of His own creation. May He cause His sovereignty soon to be accepted, during our life and the life of all Israel. And let us say: Amen.

Congregation and Reader:
May He be praised throughout all time.

Reader:
Glorified and celebrated, lauded and worshiped, acclaimed and honoured, extolled and exalted may the Holy One be, praised beyond all song and psalm, beyond all tributes that mortals can utter. And let us say: Amen.

May the prayers and praise of the whole House of Israel be accepted by our Father in Heaven. And let us say: Amen.

Let there be abundant peace from Heaven, with life's goodness for us and for all the people Israel. And let us say: Amen.

He who brings peace to His universe will bring peace to us and to all the people Israel. And let us say: Amen.

though no weddings or funerals are held on the Sabbath, that is, between Friday sundown and Saturday sundown.

When there is a death in a family, the community bands together to cook for the bereaved family, helping with logistics that would be difficult and freeing them from ordinary affairs for a time. The family announces hours for receiving visitors to the house for seven days after the burial, known as 'sitting Shiva' (from the Hebrew for 'seven'). Mirrors are covered. The family wear sombre colours and rip their clothing, often represented ritually by wearing a short black ribbon with a cut in it. All of these customs are meant to free the family from the ordinary and vain aspects of everyday life.

The children, by tradition especially the sons, honour the memory of the dead by reciting a special prayer, the Kaddish, for them daily for a year. Recitation of the Kaddish has been associated with grieving, but the prayer itself never mentions death or dying and only praises God for his many daily miracles. It is quite close to the Lord's Prayer of Christianity. The practice of saying this prayer for the dead in some contexts may have begun in Talmudic academies, where the death of a scholar could be marked in such a fashion by his students.

Religious Education

Children's religious education traditionally began around the age of five. There were often ceremonial parades displaying the new students to the community.

The education was confined to men, but the women were often literate in the vernacular. Young children began by learning the letters of the Hebrew alphabet, sometimes with the custom of cakes baked for them in the appropriate shapes. Bible was the first subject of study, during the grammar school years. After the text of the Bible, students studied the medieval Bible commentators Abraham ibn Ezra (c. 1090–1164) and Rashi.

Advanced education entailed *yeshiva* study. In it, the young men studied together with acknowledged Talmudic masters, trying to understand the refractory pages of the *Talmud* text. In between lessons, they prepared pages of the *Talmud* together in study groups. Young rabbinic sages also consulted a variety of commentaries. Primary among them were the *Tosafot* ('additions' in Hebrew), whose opinions appear in the margins of the Talmudic texts. Commentators were divided into the Rishonim (the earlier) and the Aharonim (the later). Some of their opinions were available in the printed texts, while others were published separately.

Most North American Jewish families believe that the children should be taught the literature, history, customs, and ceremonies, and often Hebrew. In more traditional Judaism, Jewish boys are taught at least the rudiments of Jewish law, including its sophisticated and complicated methods of reasoning as well as its content.

Today in even very conservative Jewish households, women are being educated in similar fashion. The proof of this is the popularity of the Bar Mitzvah or Bat Mitzvah ceremony. Families who belong to synagogues usually celebrate the ceremony as a kind of 'elementary school' religious graduation from the special training the child has undergone. Usually this first phase of Jewish education is accomplished by classes taken after school on three or even four days a week.

More and more Jewish parents are relying on parochial Jewish day schools because of the even more thorough religious training that the children receive. In these cases, the children normally spend about half the day studying Jewish subjects and the other half accomplishing the curriculum of modern North American primary and secondary schools.

Many Jewish children continue in education after the Bar Mitzvah ceremony. Reform Judaism has instituted a ceremony known as confirmation, usually at the completion of grade nine. Jewish confirmation is usually another graduation ceremony, accomplished at the late spring holiday of Shavuoth (Pentecost), convenient because it roughly coincides with the end of the school year in North America. Shavuoth is appropriate also because it has become the holiday associated with the giving of the Torah, in a sense bearing some parallels to the Christian association of Pentecost with the gift of the Holy Spirit.

But graduation is commencement, as educators in the United States are fond of reminding their audiences. These steps do not end a young Jew's obligation to learn, which is by rights lifelong. In Orthodox Jewish homes, the children are supposed to continue studying Jewish texts throughout life, doing so with their parents on holidays as well as with their peers during the week.

Members of other religious communities admire, indeed sometimes envy, the central role that study has in the Jewish tradition. It is pursued in the home; for example, it is not unusual for the leader of a Passover *seder* to open aspects of the ceremony up for debate and discussion, encouraging the various participants to bring all their acumen to bear on resolving wide-ranging issues suggested by the liturgy. It is pursued in the community; most North American synagogues sponsor high schools, where issues of Jewish life are discussed in a more informal way, usually a few times a week. Extensive programs in continuing and adult education cover elementary Hebrew, the prayer-book, the musical chant, philosophy, mysticism, and current books of Jewish interest. Perhaps the complexity of the rabbinic tradition is a blessing in disguise, providing as it does so much food for thought.

Conversion to Judaism

In the time of the Babylonian Exile, and as a direct consequence of it, the faith of Israel began to be maintained in scattered regions, among other populations. Whereas one generally had had to live in the Hebrew kingdoms to be considered an Israelite, one could now be a Jew while living elsewhere. Conversely, the possibility now arose that persons in various places, and of various origins, might wish to be considered Jews.

There were debates in the postexilic Judean community as to whether others could belong. The biblical book of *Ruth*, discussed already, opts for an inclusivist position. Likewise, the point to the book of *Jonah* is that God cares about the people of Nineveh in Assyria, however reluctant Jonah might be to preach to them. Scholars remain divided, however, concerning how much energy Jews actually devoted to proselytizing in the Persian, Greek, and Roman world.

Perhaps it was the need to live as a minority, as guests in foreign nations, that dampened Jewish proselytism. Seeking to convert the children of the host country would surely be seen as a very hostile and undesirable action. Indeed, proselytizing activity in medieval Christian and Islamic lands was punishable by death. In such a climate, active missionary work was necessarily curtailed; but passively, Jews since ancient times have been content to receive converts who truly desire to join the Jewish people.

Rabbinic Judaism came to specify three conditions for conversion: *milah* (circumcision, for men), *tevilah* (ritual immersion or baptism), and *kabbalat 'ol ha-mitzvoth* (accepting the yoke of the commandments). There are many stories of conversions in rabbinic literature. The rabbis sought to determine which candidates for conversion were sincere in their aspirations, for insincere converts endangered the community. They verified that converts were willing to cast their lot with this unfortunate and endangered people. With a yes answer, one was accepted. Usually conversions involved a period of training for the candidate to learn the extent of adult Jews' specific responsibilities.

When a male student is ready, the ceremony of circumcision is performed. Even an already circumcised man must undergo a symbolic shedding of blood for the conversion to be accepted. The difficulties surrounding this operation have always made conversion more popular among women than men.

The next requirement is ritual immersion, baptism. Jews baptize only by total bodily immersion. The Orthodox community, which still performs ritual immersions for a variety of purifying purposes, builds special facilities for bodily immersion, called *mikveh*s. Men and women visit these baths separately at specific times during the week. When a convert begins this life of ritual immersion, the first one is still noted as the purification from gentile life to Jewish life. The *mikveh* itself today is usually a pool like a swimming-pool but smaller. An important requirement it must meet is to contain a certain amount of 'living water' or free-flowing water from streams or rainfall.

The Christian rite of baptism is related to this Jewish rite, but it is unclear whether it originated as proselyte immersion or the more ordinary purification. John the Baptist, like the Essenes, appears to have used ordinary baptism for the purposes of signifying repentance to a purer life, in anticipation of the coming end of time. The Christian purification apparently arose from these notions.

Usually when a convert enters a *mikveh* a court of three rabbis, termed a *bet din*, is convened at the site. The rabbis examine the candidate, from behind a curtain if the convert is a woman. They ask about the convert's willingness to perform Jewish rites and responsibilities. They also allow the convert to demonstrate the knowledge he or she has learned from instruction. Then the candidate submerges completely in the *mikveh*, and upon coming up is a Jew in every respect. Converts are named as the son or daughter of Abraham so that they have complete Jewish names, indistinguishable from other Jews.

There is no way Jews can leave the people of Israel once entered by birth or conversion. One can apostatize; however, doing so does not remove one's Jewish identity but only changes one's status to that of a sinner.

THE MODERN WORLD

Judaism and Modernity

Both the Sabbatian movement and Hasidism, mentioned earlier, may be seen as reform movements within Judaism occurring in the early modern era. Another early move towards reform may be seen in the writings of Baruch Spinoza (1632–77). Living in the Netherlands, where Jews had achieved a relatively free and equal life under the tolerant Dutch regime, he challenged many of the traditional tenets of both Judaism and Christianity.

But a more far-reaching desire to reform Judaism came with closer contact with European life. For Jews, the real opportunity to join European life began with the conquests of Napoleon, who ruled France from 1799 to 1815. In these years, the ideals of the French Revolution spread in Europe: *fraternité, égalité, liberté*, or brotherhood, equality, and liberty.

Prior to this time, Jews had been living in various degrees of isolation. In various ages and places, Jews had lived in communities or quarters that were *de facto* concentrations, and frequently in Christian Europe this separation became legally sanctioned and enforced as a complete separation. From the sixteenth century such Jewish quarters were referred to as ghettos, after the local name of the Jews' district in Venice. Now, as the nineteenth century opened, Jews were swept into the political unrest brought upon Europe by the French Revolution. Such political and cultural participation was appreciably stronger in western Europe (from Germany westward) than in eastern Europe (from Poland eastward).

Reform

Reform Judaism arose in eighteenth-century Europe with the belief that Jewish life should parallel that of modern European society. Many Jews who left the ghetto simply disappeared into European life, often by converting to Christianity. Others, however, desired to reform Judaism in such a way that it could have a continuing part in modern European life. This movement reached its most significant form in Germany in the late eighteenth and early nineteenth centuries.

The first and most influential reformer, Moses Mendelssohn (1729–86), whose ideas preceded the French Revolution, may just as easily be seen as the father of modern Orthodoxy as of Reform, because his formula for the relationship between Jewish identity and European nationality became the basis for modern Jewish life almost everywhere. Mendelssohn was born in a ghetto in Dessau, Germany, and educated in traditional Judaism both at home and in Berlin. While in Berlin, however, he also studied German language and philosophy. With his unique skills he translated the *Pentateuch* and *Psalms*. He also attracted the attention and friendship of many prominent German intellectuals, including Gotthold Lessing (1729–81), whose character Nathan in the play *Nathan the Wise* is widely believed to be based on Mendelssohn.

In his treatise *Jerusalem*, Mendelssohn argues that the Jews of Germany should absorb as much as possible of German culture, enjoying the same kind of intellectual freedoms that other Germans have. This would in no way affect the essence of Judaism, which Mendelssohn argues is a religion of reason combined with a revealed law. Mendelssohn thus separated Jewishness from his personhood, making it an attribute, like any other affinity. In effect, he is arguing that

FROM AMERICAN REFORM PLATFORMS

Pittsburgh, 1885

We recognize in every religion an attempt to grasp the Infinite One, and in every mode, source or book of revelation held sacred in any religious system the consciousness of the indwelling of God in man. We hold that Judaism presents the highest conception of the God-idea as taught in our holy Scriptures and developed and spiritualized by the Jewish teachers in accordance with the moral and philosophical progress of their respective ages. We maintain that Judaism preserved and defended amid continual struggles and trials and under enforced isolation this God-idea as the central religious truth for the human race.

Columbus, 1937

In view of the changes that have taken place in the modern world and the consequent need of stating anew the teaching of Reform Judaism, the Central Conference of American Rabbis makes the following declaration of principles. It presents them not as a fixed creed but as a guide for the progressive elements of Jewry.

Judaism is the historical religious experience of the Jewish people [and] ... its message is universal, aiming at the union and perfection of mankind under the sovereignty of God. Reform Judaism recognizes ... progressive development in religion and consciously applies this principle to spiritual as well as to cultural and social life ...

Jews could be Germans in the same way that Protestants and Catholics could be German nationals too.)

The premise, of course, depends on the host country's acquiescence to these rational ideas. German toleration of Jews did not in any way follow immediately upon Mendelssohn's suggestions. Rather, German Jews endured a century of slow gains towards equal rights, sometimes helped and sometimes hindered by the lack of a single German political state itself. And in the twentieth century, Jewish nationality within Germany would be rescinded by Hitler, who would decide that German nationality should adhere to his pseudoracial definition.

But there was also a nagging question of whether Jews really wanted to give up their rights as a semiautonomous people within Europe. Napoleon assembled a 'Sanhedrin' in 1807 to determine whether Jews were truly interested in or committed to French citizenship. Indeed, a great many rabbis were suspicious of the opportunity, rightly seeing in Jewish emancipation a danger to Jewish survival. The delegates of the assembly answered Napoleon's questions in ways that suggested that they wished the privileges of French nationality. But, as feared, growing freedom brought with it not just a threat of dilution of Jewish life but soon also a growing number of defections to Christianity.

One response to the threat was through religious reform. Mendelssohn himself, in the previous generation, had remained a traditional Jew in all his household observances. But this formula did not attract many of those who had tasted German life. Indeed, Mendelssohn's son converted to Christianity, before the maturity of his grandson Felix Mendelssohn (1809–47), the famous pianist and composer.

The Reform movement, largely in Germany, sought to avoid the temptations of conversion by providing Jews with a religious life that was significant but also suited to the needs of the time. They renovated Jewish worship to resemble church services—including Western musical instruments, more vernacular prayer, and sermons in the vernacular. They abbreviated the services by cutting out numerous repetitions. Their original practice of following the holy day of the Christian majority and having Sunday Sabbath services, instead of the traditional Saturday Sabbath service, has largely fallen into disuse.

They also adopted Western dress and eschewed traditional dietary and purity observances. These features of Jewish life, treated as personal or congregational decisions, have largely disappeared in Reform Judaism or, as it is called in Britain, Liberal Judaism.

Taken to North America by German Jews who settled there, Reform continued to develop a sense of modernization and change, and imbibed the intellectual assumptions of the time. There was a philosophical preference for ethics over ritual, which made the Hebrew prophets heroes and valued the moral aspect of Moses's commandments ahead of the ritual. There was a tendency to see tradition as relative to its context in time, and not necessarily eternally valid. The following extracts from the platform of American Reform rabbis meeting at Pittsburgh in 1885 illustrate this.

- The Bible reflects primitive ideas of its own age, clothing conceptions of divine Providence in miraculous narratives.
- The laws regulating diet, priestly purity and dress do not conduce to holiness and obstruct modern spiritual elevation.
- We are no longer a nation but a spiritual community and therefore expect no return to Palestine.

Reform Jews often term their congregations 'temples', implying that the central place of worship is where they now live, and that no restoration of the first-century temple is contemplated or desired.

Conservative Judaism

Another attempt at reform was known as the *Jüdische Wissenschaft* ('science of Judaism') movement. This movement was founded in Germany in 1819 by

From S.R. Hirsch, *The Dangers of Updating Judaism*

But, above all, what kind of Judaism would that be, if we were allowed to bring it up to date? If the Jew were actually permitted at any given time to bring his Judaism up to date, then he would no longer have any need for it; it would no longer be worthwhile speaking of Judaism. We would take Judaism and throw it out among the other ancient products of delusion and absurdity, and say no more about Judaism and the Jewish religion!

If the Bible is to be for me the word of God, and Judaism and the Jewish law the revealed will of God, am I to be allowed to take my stand on the highway of the ages and the lands and ask every mortal pilgrim on earth for his opinions, born as they are between dream and waking, between error and truth, in order to submit the word of the living God to his approval, in order to mould it to suit his passing whim? And am I to say: 'See here modern, purified Judaism! Here we have the word of the living God, refined, approved and purified by men!'

Leopold Zunz (1794–1886) and enlisted scholars like Abraham Geiger (1810–74). It tended to look for historical justification before making an innovation. Zecharias Frankel (1801–75) was another reformer, who attended many of the meetings called by the reforming rabbis of Germany. Frankel, too, stopped short of the rational reforms offered by his colleagues, expressing instead that some rituals had legal and aesthetic justifications. Unlike some of his colleagues, he was not embarrassed by the ancient ritual and so preached its retention.

These scholars captained what has become Conservative Judaism in the United States and Canada. At first the Reform movements were separated only by taste and style. In the United States the reformers met together at a banquet in Cincinnati in 1889. The menu included seafood, specifically shrimp, which was biblically forbidden to Jews. This surpassed the reforming zeal of many of the invited guests. Those who stayed and ate became identified with the American Reform movement. Those who refused to eat coalesced into the American Conservative movement. Ideologically, those who felt that the biblical laws were valid tended to be those who respected the efforts of *Jüdische Wissenschaft*, the Science of Judaism school.

Conservative Judaism takes an intermediate position between Reform and Orthodoxy. The justification for change is usually historical precedent—not, as in Reform Judaism, rational procedure. If a particular custom can be shown to be fairly recent, such as dressing in black caftans, which began in fifteenth- to seventeenth-century Poland, then there is a precedent for changing one's dress. On the other hand, the order of prayers in the Jewish service is extremely old, going back to the temple service in the first century and earlier.

FROM SOLOMON SCHECHTER, *THE FAITH OF CATHOLIC ISRAEL*

Another consequence of this conception of Tradition is that it is neither Scripture nor primitive Judaism, but general custom which forms the real rule of practice. Holy Writ as well as history, Zunz tells us, teaches that the law of Moses was never fully and absolutely put into practice. Liberty was always given to the great teachers of every generation to make modifications and innovations in harmony with the spirit of existing institutions. Hence a return to Mosaism would be illegal, pernicious, and indeed impossible. The norm as well as the sanction of Judaism is the practice actually in vogue. Its consecration is the consecration of general use—or, in other words, of Catholic Israel. It was probably with a view to this communion that the later mystics introduced a short prayer to be said before the performance of any religious ceremony, in which, among other things, the speaker professes to act 'in the name of all Israel'.

So Conservative Jews, unlike Reform ones, have not tampered significantly with the traditional liturgy of Judaism. It is seen as firmly instituted by Jewish law, in the writings of the ancient rabbis. A Conservative synagogue will characteristically pray largely, but not entirely, in Hebrew and keep the traditional order of Jewish service intact.

Some aspects of the liturgy need to be changed because of modern ideological issues. For instance, many expressions that assume a patriarchal society have been changed or eliminated. Like the Reform movement, most Conservative Jews in the United States and Canada accept congregational seating of men and women together, allow women to participate in the services as freely as men, and now train women to lead worship as cantors and rabbis, as the Reform movement has been doing for many years. Most Conservative Jews resemble Reform Jews in their practice, while a very few have opted to live a life quite close to Orthodoxy.

Orthodoxy

In Orthodox Judaism, a great deal of traditional Jewish life remains, although many Orthodox Jews in North America have adopted modern styles of dress. Orthodox Jews conduct services in Hebrew and observe Sabbath obligations based on the ancient rules found in the Bible. They insist on kosher meals. And they have maintained traditional distinctions in gender roles, with the leadership in worship and ritual restricted to males.

The Orthodox have been uncomfortable with innovation, but have had to live in the modern world. While they have felt that reform programs such as *Jüdische Wissenschaft* were a betrayal of authentic Judaism, they have tried to find

FROM THEODOR HERZL, *THE IDEA OF THE JEWISH STATE*

The whole plan is basically quite simple, as it must be if it is to be comprehensible to all.

Let sovereignty be granted us over a portion of the globe adequate to meet our rightful national requirements; we ourselves will see to everything else.

To create a new sovereign state is neither ridiculous nor impossible. We have seen it happen in our own day, among people who were not largely middle-class as we are, but poorer, less educated, and hence weaker than ourselves. The governments of countries plagued by antisemitism will be keenly interested in obtaining this sovereignty for us ...

To sum up: *Ḥibbat Ziyyon* [love of Zion], no less than 'Zionism', wants a Jewish State and believes in the possibility of funding a Jewish State in the future. But while 'Zionism' looks to the Jewish State to provide a remedy for poverty, as well as complete tranquillity and national glory, *Ḥibbat Ziyyon* knows that our State will not give us these things until 'universal righteousness sits enthroned and holds sway in the life of nations and states'. *Ḥibbat Ziyyon* looks to a Jewish State to provide a 'secure refuge' for Judaism and a cultural bond to unite our nation. 'Zionism', therefore, begins its work with political propaganda; but *Ḥibbat Ziyyon* begins with the national culture, because only through that culture and for its sake can a Jewish State be established in a way that will be acceptable and beneficial to the spirit of the Jewish people.

a modern idiom for the preservation of traditional Judaism. Rabbi Samson Raphael Hirsch (1808–88) was among the most effective spokespersons for this perspective. He stopped merely condemning the reformers and outlined a positive program for modern Orthodoxy. He essentially gave credence to both the modern world and the traditional sources of Jewish identity, calling for both Torah (law, but here in the sense of 'Jewish religious truth') and *Derekh Eretz* (literally 'the way of the land', but here European life).

Living in a separate community in the German city of Frankfurt-am-Main, Hirsch maintained that although modern life brought many advantages that should be enjoyed, some separation of Jews from European life is salutary and citizenship a trial for Jewish survival. He suggested that the traditional rituals and observances are the best tried-and-true ways of training a person who is both a good person and a good Jew—a *Yisroel Mensch* ('a humane member of Israel'), as he expressed it. His balanced view of the role of tradition and modernity has in a general way set a pattern for the entire movement of modern Orthodoxy.

In Israel today official Judaism is Orthodox. This is mainly due to the influence of political parties in the life of the country. Israel has a bewildering number of political parties, the principal ones secular in their ideology, but some of the smaller ones very conservatively religious. No mainline party in the twentieth century has held power in Israel without the help of one or another of the traditionalist religious parties.

As a price for their votes, the religious parties demand that they be the only spokespersons for Judaism in Israel, and they make a number of religious demands on the national life of the country. Although Israel is a modern Western-style democracy, it continues to put marriage and divorce and other ceremonies of personal status in the society solely in the hands of the Orthodox religious communities resident there. This continues the practice of the Ottoman Turkish Empire, which ruled Jerusalem for four centuries from 1517 to 1917.

The differences among the main branches of North American Judaism are primarily differences in practice and ritual. Yet many individuals in the Reform and Conservative communities are virtually indistinguishable from one another in regard to their Jewish practice in everyday life. It is not doctrinal belief that distinguishes these branches, but rationale—of how accommodation to the host culture should take place. The most significant indicators of the orientation of a congregation in North America are usually the particular prayer-book and service that it designs for itself, and the particular national organization to which it sends its congregational dues.

Twentieth-Century Theology

Periods of Jewish acculturation and assimilation have stimulated Jewish theological and philosophical inquiry. In the twentieth century, as was true during the heyday of Arab-Jewish cooperation in Muslim Spain, Judaism has again entered a period of rich theological expression.

Franz Rosenzweig (1886–1929) is perhaps a good example of the kinds of forces that helped produced Jewish philosophical speculation in European and North American life. Rosenzweig was born into a cultured and affluent, assimilated, and not very religiously committed family that wanted him to become a physician.

He embarked on a career in philosophy and, at a key point in his life, decided that he could be the kind of Christian that Hegel had described in his philosophy. His path to Christianity, however, was changed by a conversation with a distant relative, Eugen Rosenstock-Huessy (1888–1973), who had already converted. Rosenzweig decided to convert 'not as a pagan but a Jew', continuing and deepening Jewish practice. After attending a Yom Kippur service in a small Orthodox synagogue in Berlin, he decided that Judaism is preferable to Christianity. Jews, he reasoned, are already with 'the Father' and therefore have no need to apply to 'the Son'.

Drafted into the German army in the First World War, he wrote his first and most systematic work, *Der Stern der Erlösung* (The Star of Redemption) on postcards that he mailed to his mother. In it he maintains an incipiently existentialist stance, declaring all truth to be subjective. Rosenzweig maintains that two religions are true in the subjective sense—Judaism and Christianity. In this he partially mirrors the universalism and cultural pluralism of the rabbinic tradition but, like Europeans of the early twentieth century, he generally leaves Islam out of his purview because the Ottoman Empire seemed too impotent a regime to be taken seriously. Instead, he sees the politically powerful countries of Christendom and considers that they are constantly projecting the purposes of God into the world, constantly helping to convert and transform it.

Jews, on the other hand, he characterizes as politically powerless but clear-sighted in their ritual and liturgical concerns. They are eternally with God, communicating with him through the eternally repeated holidays and rituals of Judaism. Although he did not start as a practising Jew, he maintained that one should leave oneself open to more and more contact with traditional Judaism. The Jew must open himself up to the possibility of contact with God through the *halakha*, the Jewish law.

For Rosenzweig, the Jew's covenant with God is eternal and timeless because all the mechanisms of Jewish life have insulated Jews from the vicissitudes of history and kept Judaism from diluting its spiritual power. Christianity, on the other hand, has had the job of extending out to bring the word of God to other nations and enjoys the benefits of political life, but in the process it risks the diminution and dilution that Judaism has avoided.

Tragically, Rosenzweig contracted amyotrophic lateral sclerosis ('Lou Gehrig's disease'), which left him completely paralyzed. A circle of admirers formed a prayer group around him. His personal courage and his understanding of the value of traditional Judaism from an equally strong position in liberal and secular thought gave him a following across the broad spectrum of modern Judaism. On the other hand, his concept of Judaism as outside of history, one with the Father eternally, can no longer be seriously maintained in a literal sense, because of the enormity of the events affecting Judaism in the twentieth century—everything from gaining political rights in Europe to the Holocaust and the modern state of Israel. Like it or not, Jews have now fully re-entered history.

Another person whose theological work has been significant to Judaism and to religious persons everywhere is Martin Buber (1878–1965), another religious existentialist. Buber was a student of Wilhelm Dilthey (1833–1911) and Georg Simmel (1858–1918), two important German intellectuals, but he also felt the influence of Hasidism through his family and especially his grandfather, Solomon Buber, who was a famous scholar of *midrash*. Buber and Rosenzweig were acquaintances, associates in Das jüdisches Lehrhaus ('The Jewish School') in Frankfurt, cotranslators of a German translation of the Bible, and close personal friends.

In 1923, Buber published his most famous work *Ich und Du* (translated into English as *I and Thou*), which a generation of religiously concerned thinkers within Judaism and without have studied, admired, scrutinized, and critiqued. The book is not so much a treatise as a poem suggesting that all human beings have moments of epiphany, I-Thou experiences, as Buber calls them, in which, properly understood, the divine presence and dialogue with God are felt. The rest of the time human beings observe the world functionally, in order to manipulate and control it. These are I-It experiences. Either kind of experience can be had with objects or persons; Buber is suggesting that there are two universal kinds of knowledge, not that we know people or things.

But, for Buber, behind every I-Thou experience is the presence of God, the Eternal Thou, yet no I-It experience can possibly condition, force, or occasion an I-Thou experience. Thus, the Bible is a record of I-Thou experiences, but it is itself merely an object. One can study the Bible carefully, but one is just as likely to have an I-Thou experience in looking at a piece of mica as in studying the prophet Micah. In this, Buber disagrees strongly with Rosenzweig, for whom the Bible and Jewish tradition are special sources of religious truth that bring the student closer to traditional Judaism. Buber's unwillingness to grant the Bible any special status as revelation has angered traditional Jews as much as it pleased other intellectuals and scholars of Western religion.

Buber lived far longer than Rosenzweig. He was forced to come to terms with the Holocaust, but because he was so close to the events, he did not wish to dwell on the horrors. Instead he claimed that God could sometimes hide his face—enter an eclipse, as he phrased it. Buber was an ardent Zionist and moved to Palestine in 1938. A proponent of a binational state for both Jews and Arabs equally, he seemed too idealistic to many of his colleagues. Buber was appointed to the Hebrew University until his retirement in 1951. But Buber was a professor of social philosophy and education, never holding a position in Jewish thought or philosophy, because there was too much opposition to his thinking in Jerusalem.

Yet Buber's mystical way of dialogue with God has had strong repercussions for religious thinking in the Christian, Muslim, Hindu, and Buddhist world. In non-Jewish circles, he has had many critics because he does not give adequate support for his notion that behind every peak experience is the voice of the Eternal Thou, seeking dialogue. His religious dialogue partners often conceive of mystical experience in quite different ways. But it can be said that Buber brought some of the impulses of Hasidic thinking—most notably, the intuition that the divine should be sought in the details of everyday life—into the mainstream of Judaism and Western thought.

Reconstructionism is a movement founded in the 1930s by Mordecai Kaplan (1881–1983), originally a Conservative rabbi. He attempted to define Judaism as a religious civilization or, in today's terms, a religious culture. He felt that belief in God was traditionally important to the people's self-understanding, but not in fact essential to the definition of the group. He thus translated references to the terms 'God' and 'Lord' with terminology like 'The Eternal'.

For many years, Reconstructionism was a kind of ideological position cutting across all North American Judaism, finding a considerable intellectual following among the Jews in the other movements. But in the 1960s, Reconstructionism became a separate entity by founding its own rabbinical seminary in Philadelphia. Today there are several Reconstructionist synagogues in North America, but it is still a very small segment of the community. Ideologically, many Jews who think of themselves as an ethnic group espouse Reconstructionist ideals, but remain within a Reform or Conservative synagogue.

Zionism

In the middle of the nineteenth century, nationalism became a powerful cultural and political force in Europe. In that climate, Jews explored the idea of returning from Europe to their ancient Near Eastern homeland. To be sure, medieval Jewish literature furnishes numerous references to the sense of absence from the land of Israel. Yehuda Ḥa-Levi wrote poetically of his sadness to be in the West (Spain), when his heart was in the East. The words of the Passover *seder*, 'next year in Jerusalem', attest an ongoing spiritual longing to go back, either now or in the messianic age. But the nineteenth century introduced several other currents that flowed together to give modern Zionism its impetus.

With the name Zion, the Bible refers to a ridge-top in Jerusalem as God's dwelling-place. What a tourist is shown today as Mount Zion is just outside the walls of the Old City of Jerusalem; Zion, the acropolis of the biblical city, is now called the Temple Mount. Even in antiquity the connotations of the name Zion extended to include the land with Jerusalem as its centre, and the people and their religio-political institutions. The modern movement to return to the ancient land of Israel, to found a nation there on the model of modern European nationalism, is called Zionism.

Significant among the forces that produced Zionism was the desire for a cultural revival of the Hebrew language as an important aspect of national identity. Momentum for unifying Italy and Germany, hitherto politically fragmented into various principalities, was derived from the fact that each of these peoples had a language in common.

By the same token, if the Jews were going to be a people in this age of emerging nation-states, they would have to have a common language. Many Ashkenazic Jews in central Europe spoke Yiddish, but it was not spoken by Jews everywhere and was not considered at the time to have a classical literature. Hebrew, still used extensively in prayer and for literary and intellectual purposes but otherwise rarely spoken, would better serve the purpose if it could be revived and its vocabulary updated.

One of the advocates of a Hebrew revival was the Lithuanian Peretz Smolenskin (1842–85), who settled in Vienna in 1868, but found himself out of step with the assimilationist spirit there. In *'Am 'Olam* (Eternal People), which he published in Hebrew in 1883, he claimed that to remain a people, the Jews would have to develop practical as well as spiritual ties to Palestine, and that the immediate practical step to be taken was to bind themselves to one another and to their tradition by speaking Hebrew. Eliezer Ben Yehudah (1858–1922) took upon himself the job of finding appropriate Hebrew vocabulary for the many new words of modern life. His seventeen-volume dictionary of modern Hebrew was completed posthumously in 1959.

Another nineteenth-century current was the desire for political experimentation. Moses Hess (1812–75), born in Bonn, Germany, was an early socialist thinker, whose ideas had an influence on the thought of Karl Marx. But his book *Rom und Jerusalem* (Rome and Jerusalem) in 1862 put forward the idea that the Jews as a people needed statehood and called on them to create a polity that could be a model of socialist principles and an example to the world. It is therefore no surprise that one of the hallmarks of Zionist settlement in Palestine in the first half of the twentieth century was the formation of collective agricultural settlements known as *kibbutzim*.

As the nineteenth century drew to a close, the desire for a haven from persecution grew. This was expressed often but perhaps no more dramatically than by Leo Pinsker (1821–91), who was 'converted' to that position by the tragedy of Jewish life in Europe. Pinsker was born in the Russian part of Poland. Working as a physician and living in the Ukraine's port of Odessa, he took an active role in Jewish cultural affairs; in the 1860s he strongly advocated the translation of the Bible and the Jewish prayers into Russian.

The *pogrom* (state-supported massacre of Jews) of 1871 challenged his ideas, but he retained his hopes for cultural assimilation. In 1881, however, another, more severe *pogrom* galvanized him into writing an anonymous pamphlet in German, *Auto-Emanzipation* (Self-Emancipation), addressed from his setting in Russia to Jews who lived to the west. Incisively, Pinsker contended that the Jews could not count on safety in the countries in which they lived as minorities. Cultural assimilation could not be trusted. The only safeguard for Jewish security and dignity would be a separate homeland.

The haven-from-persecution theme has been central to the modern Zionist movement. Theodor Herzl (1860–1904), a Viennese Jew, was the movement's principal founder figure. He became committed to the goal of Jewish statehood after covering the celebrated Dreyfus trial in France as a foreign correspondent. Alfred Dreyfus (1859–1935), a French army captain assigned to the war ministry, was charged in 1894 with selling secret information to the German military attaché. It was clear to all that Dreyfus was unfairly accused and convicted and that anti-Semitic thinking in the French armed forces had a controlling influence in the proceedings.

Although Herzl himself had grown up in an assimilated home, he came to believe that the only normal existence for Jews would be as a people in their own land, and that they would have to have a political state or something approximating it. His Zionistic ambitions were hence entirely secular and nationalistic in orientation. Indeed, Herzl and Pinsker flirted briefly with the notion that the Jewish national homeland could be elsewhere than the land of biblical Israel.

In the twentieth century, although the Zionist movement coalesced around Herzl's leadership, a diversity of themes remained. A number of intellectuals conceived of alternative ways to formulate Zionism. A Russian intellectual, born Asher Ginsberg (1856–1927), wrote under the *nom de plume* of Ahad Ha-'am ('one of the people'). He thought that a Jewish national homeland could be a spiritual centre for the development of the world and the Jewish people. For him, Jewish nationalism meant pride in the moral virtues that the Jewish people had always valorized. He pointedly defined his concept of Jewish life over against the concept of the *Übermensch* ('superior being') that the German philosopher Friedrich Nietzsche (1844–1900) had formulated. So even though Ahad Ha-'am was not religious in the traditional sense of the word, he was spiritually attached to the people Israel in a romantic, nationalistic sense.

Some Orthodox Jews have believed that human intervention in the return to Zion is a kind of sin. They refused to work for the creation of a modern state and, after it came into being in 1948, to acknowledge its existence. The only legitimate Jewish state, some of them said, would have to await the coming messianic age. Many settled in Israel anyway because it housed many of the important sites of Jewish history and was the only available asylum in the world after the Second World War. They continue to live as if the state did not exist, though they accept its subsidies for household life and education.

There has also been a religious Zionist movement, which accepts and supports the existence of a Jewish state. It is quite strong today. Indeed, most of the immigration to Israel from North America over the last two decades has been from religiously motivated Zionists. Several political parties in contemporary Israel are composed of religious Zionists.

But the notion of Jewish peoplehood also evokes loyalties other than religious ones. Jews who cherish no religious sentiments at all still seem ethnically or nationally attached to Israel and consider its present and continued existence to be important to their Jewish identity.

Furthermore, many Reform Jews, who earlier manifested some estrangement from Zionism because they felt completely at home in Germany or the United States or Canada, have come over the years to accept many Zionist premises. In recent decades following Israeli statehood in 1948, there have been palpable changes of position in the minds of North American Jews. Many supported Israel at the time of the Six-Day War in 1967, perceiving it surrounded by hostile nations led by Egypt. These perceptions were underscored in 1973 when it was attacked on Yom Kippur, the holiest day of the Jewish calendar. However, opinion was more divided concerning Israel's invasion of Lebanon in 1982 and its administrative and settlement policies in the West Bank and Gaza.

Jewish Migration to the Americas

The social process that accounts for the different approaches to Jewish identity in this century is assimilation or acculturation. One of the main differences between 'assimilation' and 'acculturation' is that assimilation assumes that during change or reform, there is a loss of previous identity. Acculturation, with its parallel movement often called modernization in anthropological literature, assumes many possible outcomes of the conflict between two cultures, including the eventual rejection of parts or all of the new culture by the native group.

Jews from different European countries have quite different understandings of their Jewish identities. The first wave of immigration to the Americas—mainly to South America, the Caribbean islands, and the United States—was of Spanish and Portuguese Jews in the eighteenth century. They account for the majority of the community of Jews in Curaçao and for the founding of several synagogues in the United States, including the famous Touro Synagogue in Newport, Rhode Island, and the Spanish-Portuguese Synagogue in Manhattan. Sephardim in North America include Jews of Spanish descent who had settled in England and Holland. A few Jews with Spanish names like Costas and Seixas still remain, but on the whole this wave has assimilated almost completely.

The German Jewish wave of immigration, which began in the 1840s after the failure of liberal political reforms in Germany, brought with it a group of people influenced by Reform who considered themselves Germans of the Mosaic persuasion—that is, German nationals who happened to be Jewish in religion. They settled mostly in the United States, often in the same areas where other German immigrants settled, namely the midwest. But they tended to be pedlars and shopkeepers rather than farmers.

Hence, the second wave of Jewish settlement in the Americas produced the German élite like the Bambergers, the Guggenheims, and the other successful mercantile families at the end of the nineteenth century. They arrived with many German customs, even including Christmas trees (called in German *Tannenbäume*, 'fir trees', a term with no explicitly Christian connotation). The seasonal customs were considered secular national customs because they were not specifically linked to church services in Europe but rather were based on earlier German pagan ceremonies.

The next and largest wave of Jewish immigration to America was from the *shtetlach* (singular, *shtetl*, Yiddish for 'little town') and the urban Jewish quarters of eastern Europe. The 3 million Jews living in areas controlled by Russia were not part of the same social forces that allowed for Jewish liberation in western Europe and the Americas. There was a cultural reform movement known as the

Haskalah ('Enlightenment'), which flourished during the relatively benign rule of Czar Alexander II (r. 1855–81). But thereafter, under Alexander III (r. 1881–94), the political and economic gains that Jews made were abruptly ended, while the intellectual currents of the Haskalah continued. This czar openly encouraged *pogroms*, massacres, and deportations of Jews.

His policies were directly responsible for the enormous wave of Jewish immigration that landed mostly on the eastern coast of the United States and in eastern Canada. At first most of the Jews came to New York. The German Jews, while they donated massively to help these indigent immigrants, were not particularly friendly towards these *Ostjuden* ('eastern Jews'), who were not literate in German or English and who quickly found jobs in the tobacco and clothing sweatshops of the lower East Side of Manhattan.

In Russia each ethnic group had been treated as a separate nationality. Even after the revolution in Russia, and until today, Jews find that their passports stamp them as 'Jews' as a nationality. Jews arriving from eastern Europe have tended to think of themselves as Jewish by nationality as well as by religion. Ironically, some thought they had sacrificed their religion in crossing the Atlantic, as Orthodox rabbis in Europe warned against the lands of North America as a place of non-kosher iniquity.

In 1922, new immigration quotas stopped the flow of Jewish immigration to the United States. Thereafter, Jews continued to arrive in Canada, Cuba, Mexico, and South America. Jews fleeing from Nazi oppression a decade later also headed for these climes, since the doors of the United States remained largely shut.

In Canada, Jews soon left the coasts, settling primarily in the large cities in Québec and Ontario, but also in Winnipeg. Francophone Jews from North Africa and French possessions tended to stay near Montréal because of its francophone environment, in spite of the considerable support that Montréal gave to Vichy France during the Second World War. Anglophone Jews settled in Montréal, too, but also tended to settle in Toronto and Canadian cities farther west.

Finally, the Jews who arrived in Canada and the United States after the Holocaust of the 1940s tended to be concentration-camp survivors. They had undergone enormous sacrifices to arrive in the New World, surviving horrifying deprivation and the near-extermination of their people. They had a much more urgent and intense feeling about the necessity for Jewish survival.

The European Holocaust

No event since the destruction of the second temple and the expulsion from Spain has so affected the Jewish people as the Holocaust in Europe. Adolf Hitler (1889–1945), whose National Socialists (of which name 'Nazis' is an abbreviation) came to power in 1933, was able to convince much of the German population that the Jews, and not the Allies of the First World War or the disastrous economic policies thereafter, had caused the economic woes of Germany in the 1930s.

The Nazis, fearing that the Jewish presence among them would sully their 'racial' superiority, and irrationally blaming Jews for the economic condition of post–First World War Germany, passed a series of laws that were ever more cruel to Jews. First they stripped Jews of German nationality. They looted Jewish stores and prevented Jews from practising their livelihoods. They sent Jews to concentration camps to work as slaves. Finally, they erected gas chambers and crematoria to kill the Jews, what the Nazis called *die Entlösung* ('the Final Solution' to the Jewish Problem).

Of course, Hitler could not have succeeded in this endeavour had not Europe supplied a tradition of two millennia vilifying the Jews. Indeed, the tradition has roots in the New Testament, which painted Jews in an extremely bad light for its own theological reasons. These images were available throughout the centuries to anyone who wished to exploit hatred against the Jews for his or her own purpose.

It is arguable that Hitler's war against the Jews was the most successful of all his endeavours. For whatever reasons, the Allies did not make a strong enough offensive against Hitler's war on the Jews, even when they clearly understood what he was doing. There were no Allied raids on the railroad tracks that daily took tens of thousands of Jews to their deaths. Worse still, in eastern Europe, especially in Poland, Hitler found some ready accomplices for his work.

Jews had lived and practised the virtues of non-violence and martyrdom, which were also so highly prized among their Christian neighbours. In the terrible nightmare of Nazi oppression, to help Jews meant almost certain death. Yet there were many individual Christians who risked death to help Jews escape, and many underwent the same fate as the Jews for helping them. The 6 million Jewish deaths in the Second World War amount to between one-third and one-quarter of the total death toll in Europe, sometimes estimated at 22 million. The Holocaust killed roughly a third of world Jewry—men, women, and children—in the space of a few years.

Jewry shuddered from the shock of the Holocaust, when the enormity of the crime became known. The Jews had always assumed that, although they might sin, the eternity of the people Israel was a sign of God's continuing favour. That Hitler came so close to exterminating a whole people, indeed that God could have allowed a deed so horrible as the wholesale killing of so many innocent and non-combatant men, women, and children, demanded a special answer. While the matter has not been satisfactorily answered, it is important to most Jews to continue to interpret historical events as an unfolding of God's design, in which their people have a special role.

It is interesting that the most significant responses have been literary, as the now world-famous stories of Elie Wiesel (b. 1928) have shown. Wiesel was a traditional *yeshiva* student in the town of Sighet in Romania when the Nazis arrived. His first novel, *Night*, is the chronicle of the murder of his family and his survival of the extermination camps. Since then, he has written movingly in fiction and non-fiction of the predicament of modern Jews. He has articulated an ambivalent and often tentative faith, but his mixture of doubt, together with a grudging affirmation of Jewish and human values in the face of the absurdity of existence, seems to speak to the complex feelings many Jews and gentiles have in contemplating the horrors of the modern world.

'Jews must continue to live so as not to grant to Hitler a posthumous victory,' says Emil Fackenheim (b. 1916), a German-born Toronto rabbi and professor who emigrated to Canada in 1938 and to Israel after 1981. In this regard, Fackenheim speaks for a wide spectrum of Jews who feel that Hitler's nearly successful program for the extermination of all Jews must be remembered and never allowed to happen again to anyone. The Holocaust has materially changed the language and importance of Jewish identity in the world. Jews are no longer permitted to undergo martyrdom (which had been judged as honourable starting in the Hellenistic era), no matter how good the reasons, because the people must survive. He feels a new commandment—a 614th that must be added to the traditional 613—has been spoken by God to the Jewish people. Many Jews, with Fackenheim, see the Holocaust as a warning that they must not allow themselves to be helpless anywhere again.

The foundation of the state of Israel is closely associated in the minds of most Jews with the terrible tragedy of the Holocaust. Although in no sense a compensation for the lives that were lost, the promise of Israel was of a place in the world where Jews might at last be safe. The Zionist campaign for a haven from persecution succeeded in enlisting not just Jewish support but that of non-Jewish leaders in the years following the Second World War. The United Nations voted to partition Palestine and thus create a Jewish as well as an Arab state there. It contributed greatly to resolving the problem of Jewish refugees in Europe, though the displacement of and conflict with the indigenous Palestinian Arab population for decades made for a reality that was bittersweet in comparison with the promise.

Peace and security are only beginning to become a reality for Jews and for Arabs in Israel. Israel is still surrounded by hostility and resentment among its neighbours, and for decades seemed unable to resolve some problems fundamental to accommodating an emerging Palestinian nationality. But breakthroughs in negotiation in the early 1990s gave new momentum to the hope that the problems could be managed and that Israelis and Palestinians, building their own distinct societies in the traditional land of Israel, could interact together in peace.

Assimilation

American culture has for many years assumed that assimilation is good for every ethnic group. Every group should blend together in the 'melting-pot'. Yet the American melting-pot has succeeded in blending together only some northern European immigrant groups. It has not yet really unified northern with other European immigrants, and it is moot whether it ever will. Blacks and Asians have remained distinct from the European communities.

One could argue that Jews have much to gain by ignoring the melting-pot idea. Indeed, for years Jewish leadership has railed against intermarriage involving the Jewish community. And for two generations, most Jews eschewed intermarriage; however, 55 per cent of all marriages involving Jews since 1985 have reportedly been with a non-Jewish partner. The survival of the Jewish community is not assured if most or all intermarriages signal the departure of the Jewish partner. It is unknown whether the numbers of converts to Judaism, especially in intermarriages, will help stabilize the Jewish community. Some projections envision the Jewish community as composed only of the most resistant to intermarriage, the Orthodox, in a few generations.

The situation in Canada is slightly different. Like the United States, Canada is a country built on immigration, but Canadians describe their society with the metaphor of a mosaic rather than of the melting-pot. Canadian nationality from earliest times assumed at least two different and somewhat unfriendly communities, the French and the English. The nation itself was formulated on the idea that the two different communities should comprise it with equal rights to carry on their differing lives. Every other immigrant group that came to Canada was theoretically incorporated into the French-English framework until the 1960s and 1970s, when 'multiculturalism', a type of cultural pluralism, evolved.

But Canada's formula does not necessarily imply any but the most casual cultural interactions and certainly has none of the implicit imperatives of the American melting-pot myth. In Canada, the concept of national identity and of groups' rights is different from that in the United States. Moreover, the Canadian Jewish community is younger, in the sense that it arrived in great numbers only after the doors of immigration were closed in the United States. For these reasons, the Jewish community is less assimilated in Canada than it is in the United States. But the cultural and social processes that affect Canada and the United States are so similar that one can easily envision a similar outcome for the Jewish communities in both countries.

Modernity: North America vs Israel

Modernity has transformed Judaism, allowing it to develop many different denominational groups, for the same reason that denominations developed in the Hellenistic period—to provide Jews with intelligent choices about how to live their lives Jewishly. The modern world, like the Hellenistic one, provides Jews with an assortment of lifestyles, which appeal to Jews in different ways and demand different ways of being Jewish. Creative Jewish minds therefore have found ways to accommodate these lifestyles with Judaism, formulating all the varieties of Judaism that are now available.

One contrast in Judaism that is often overlooked is the difference between North American Judaism and Israeli Judaism. North American Judaism is part of the democratic life of North America. Having been nurtured in adversity while working for equality, most North American Jews accept the notion that Jews should not only be good citizens of the state in which they reside, participating fully in its political and social life, but should also work for the continued cultural pluralism of North America.

Of course, there are exceptions to this rule in the more self-contained idea of community still found in the Orthodox and Hasidic communities. There is, further, a minority of Jews who have entirely given up on the idea of accommodation with modern life. These Jews, who call themselves *ḥaredim* ('tremblers') after a verse in *Isaiah* that describes the true worshippers of God in such terms, eschew all contact with the modern world. One can in a sense call them the fundamentalists of the Jewish tradition, in that they dislike the culture provided by modern life.

On the whole, however, North American Jews, while distressed by their growing intermarriage rate, are willing to risk the stress assimilation puts on Jewish survival because of the undeniable benefits of modern Western democratic life. North American Jews' identity is thus a blend of ethnicity and religion.

A different concept of Judaism has emerged in Israel. For Jews living in Israel, again with the exception of the *ḥaredim*, who represent a greater percentage of the population and have steadily been gaining political power under conservative governments, Judaism is a nationality. The majority of Israeli Jews observe the Sabbath because it is the national day of rest. They observe the Jewish holidays because they are national holidays.

But the majority of Israelis do not observe Sabbath regulations in the traditional sense. The beaches of Tel Aviv are just as busy on warm sunny Saturdays as are the beaches of Long Island in New York. Most modern Israelis, while they are willing to give to the Orthodox parties the powers necessary to rule properly, are unwilling to govern their lives by the same kinds of standards. Loyalty to Israel may be perceived as a religious duty by many Jews living in the Diaspora, but loyalty to Israel is a political and military matter for people actually living in the state.

So there is another kind of acculturation progressing in Israel. Most Israelis, while living in a state that is dominantly Jewish, are in the process of formulating an entirely new way to live Jewishly, a transformation just as sweeping as the one that is occurring among North American Jewry.

It is by no means clear that these different Jewish communities still really understand each other. Israelis see a threatening future for Jewry in American

Ultratraditionalist ḥaredim *pray at the Western Wall in Jerusalem. The lower courses of masonry date from Roman times when they stood as the enclosure of the temple precincts.*
(Albert Beckman)

street violence and anti-Semitism, while North American Jews see threats in Israel's ethnic polarization and confrontation. In the mid-1990s, despite moves towards peace with neighbouring Arab states, conflict between Jewish and Arab peoples within Israeli jurisdiction continued, and deep divisions among Jews were underscored by the 1995 assassination of Israeli prime minister Yitzhak Rabin (r. 1974–7, 1992–5). Though fragile, the peace process with the Palestine Liberation Organization made remarkable progress towards recognizing rights of both communities. Beyond formal agreements, its ultimate success would require two peoples, former bitter adversaries, to develop mutual trust over time.

Thus the prognosis for continued Jewish life is clouded, in spite of the affluence and achievements of the North American Jewish community and the fortitude and bravery of the Israelis. But if there is a Jewish people, it will be because a religious understanding of their history made it possible for them to survive as Jews.

Hope for the Future: A Jewish Wedding

A more optimistic note for the future of Judaism is the performance of a Jewish wedding, conducted when both the bride and the groom are Jewish, whether by birth or conversion. Weddings are performed in homes, in synagogues, and in hotels and catering halls. But, wherever they are performed, what they have in common is a bridal canopy, the *huppah*, which suggests a tent. The marriage ceremonies are conducted under it. Often the bride and groom are escorted to the *huppah* by their parents. But the bride may enter in a procession similar to Christian weddings. In Orthodox weddings, she will circle the groom seven times before the ceremony begins. The ceremony begins with the bride and groom drinking from a consecrated cup of wine.

The wedding is first of all a legal agreement in which the husband and wife pledge mutual support and aid. The husband declares, 'Be consecrated unto me as my wife according to the laws and traditions of Moses and Israel.' This in itself suffices as the groom's vow and is included in the marriage contract. But it is quite common in North America to add more obligations, possibly spoken and usually written into the contract: 'I will love, honour, and cherish you. I will protect and support you, and I will faithfully care for your needs, as prescribed by Jewish law and tradition.'

The bride, for her part, normally also makes a kind of declaration, which may be similar to the groom's vows: 'In accepting the wedding ring, I pledge you all my love and devotion, and I take upon myself the fulfilment of all the duties incumbent upon a Jewish wife.' One of the central aspects of the service is usually the bridegroom's giving a ring to the bride. The ring is conventional in the West, but the groom must give the bride a gift of sufficient worth to symbolize and formalize that a legal transaction, a *kinyan* ('acquisition'), is taking place.

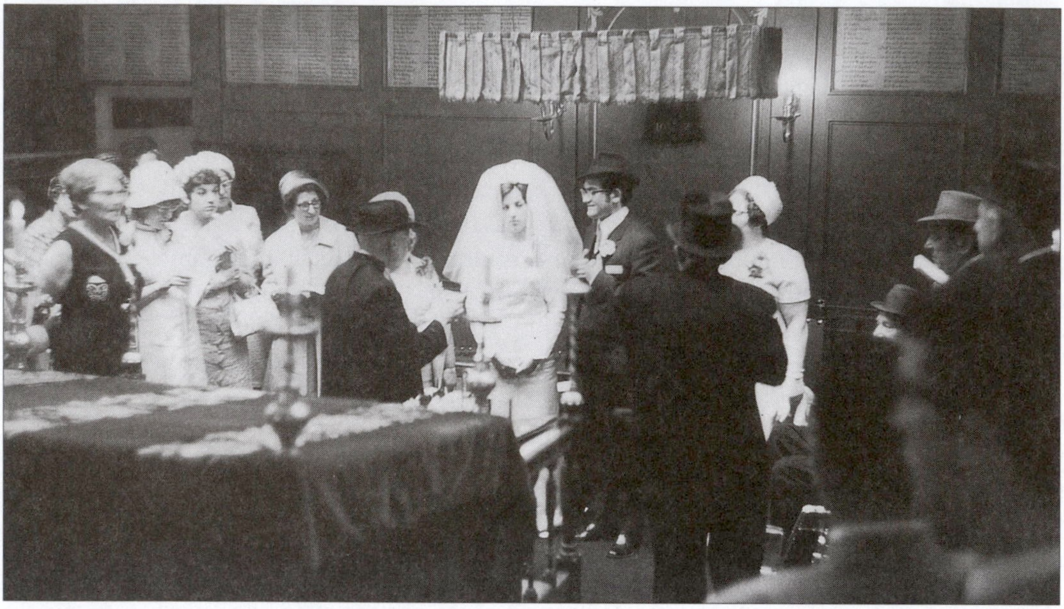

The bride and groom stand under the huppah *at a wedding in a Spanish-Portuguese (Sephardic) synagogue in Amsterdam.* (Albert Beckman)

After the legal formalities are concluded and the ring or rings exchanged, seven blessings are recited over a second cup of wine. The blessings sound notes of the creation, the creation of male and female, and the joy of ancient Judah in the celebration of marriages. In fulfilment of the last blessing, which prays for the sound of joy in Judah and Israel, the wedding usually continues with an enormous feast.

So lavishly and joyously celebrated that it appears often in films, the Jewish wedding provides perhaps the most fervent hope for Jewish survival. In consecrating the lives of two young Jews together, the community thanks God for creation and sustenance, remembers the past history of the community, pledges its responsibilities publicly, and prays for the continuation of the people. All of these themes are particularly poignant now with the future of the people Israel in doubt. One hopes that the blessings asked for in the wedding will continue to come to pass. Like a wedding, the covenant between God and Israel continues to mediate the sense of Jewish purpose in the world.

KEY TERMS

apocalyptic. Genre of literature with coded symbolic visions and their interpretation, often anticipating an imminent battle to end the unrighteousness of the present. Flourished in the Hellenistic era.

Ashkenazim. Jews of northern and eastern Europe as distinct from those of the Mediterranean.

Bar Mitzvah. Initiation of a thirteen-year-old boy into adult ritual responsibilities in the synagogue service. Some branches of Judaism parallel it with a Bat Mitzvah for girls.

berith. Hebrew term for covenant, the reciprocal relationship prescribing favour and loyalty between God and the Jewish people.

Diaspora. 'Dispersal', the Jewish world outside of the land of ancient Israel. It began with the Babylonian Exile, from which not all Jews returned.

Exile. The deportation of Jewish leadership from Jerusalem to Mesopotamia by the conquering Babylonians in 586 BCE. A rupture of local Israelite political, ritual, and agricultural institutions, it marks the transition from Israelite religion to Judaism.

Exodus. Migration of Hebrews from Egypt under the leadership of Moses, understood in later Hebrew thought as the birth of the Israelite nation.

gaon. Title of a senior rabbinical authority in Mesopotamia under Persian and Muslim rule.

Gemarah. The body of Aramaic commentary attaching to the Hebrew text of the *Mishnah*, which together with it makes up the *Talmud*, in both the *Jerusalem Talmud* and the *Babylonian Talmud*.

halakha. Material in the *Talmud* of a legal nature. By contrast, material in an anecdotal or narrative style is termed *agada*.

Ḥasidim. Term applied to two different groups of loyal or pious Jews: those who resisted Hellenism militarily in second-century-BCE Palestine, and the mystically inclined followers of the Baal Shem in eighteenth-century Poland.

ḥesed. Hebrew term for the loyal conduct, sometimes translated as 'mercy' or 'lovingkindness', incumbent on God and on humans as parties to the covenant relationship.

Ḥumash. The first five biblical books, the *Pentateuch*, when bound in book form for private study. In synagogue worship, the same text is read, but from a scroll.

Kabbalah. The medieval Jewish mystical tradition, given a classic expression as commentary on scripture in a text, the *Zohar*, compiled by Moses of León in the fourteenth century.

Karaites. 'Scripturalists', an eighth-century movement that rejected the *Talmud* and postbiblical festivals such as

Ḥanukkah, taking only the Bible as authoritative.

kosher. A designation of food as ritually acceptable, implying that all rabbinic regulations regarding animal slaughter and the like have been observed in its preparation.

Magen David. The six-pointed star or 'shield of David', a Jewish symbol since medieval times.

menorah. The seven-branched candlestick, a Jewish symbol since ancient times well before widespread adoption of the six-pointed star.

mezuzah. A small cartridge containing scriptural passages, placed at eye level on the outer door frame of a Jewish home.

midrash. Commentary on scripture.

minyan. The quorum of ten required for beginning a synagogue service of prayer.

Mishnah. The Hebrew text edited by Rabbi Judah ha-Nasi before 200, arranging topically the contents of the Oral Law inherited from Pharisaism and ascribed to Moses with an authority paralleling that of the written Torah.

Mishneh Torah. A topically arranged code of Jewish law written in the twelfth century by Moses Maimonides.

mitzvah. A commandment. In the Greek and Roman era, the Pharisaic-rabbinic movement identified exactly 613 specific commandments as contained within the Torah.

Passover. Major spring festival of agricultural rebirth and renewal, given a historical dimension by association with the hasty departure of Israelites from Egypt under Moses's leadership.

Patriarchs. Ancestor figures of the Israelite nation in the Hebrew Bible's narratives of origins.

Pentateuch. The first five books of the Hebrew Bible, ascribed by tradition to Moses, but regarded by modern scholarship as the result of several centuries of later literary activity.

rabbi. A teacher, specifically in Roman times an expert on interpretation of Torah. In two millennia since priestly sacrifices ceased with the destruction of the temple, the rabbi has been the scholarly and spiritual leader of a Jewish congregation, while the cantor is the liturgical specialist leading the musical chant in a synagogue service.

responsa. Accumulated correspondence by medieval and recent rabbinical authorities, consisting of rulings on issues of legal interpretation.

Rosh Hashanah. The new year festival, generally occurring in September.

Sabbath. The seventh day of the week, observed as a day of rest from ordinary activity by Jews since ancient times.

seder. 'Order'. The term is used for the ritual Passover supper celebrated in the home, whose liturgy is called the Haggadah. The six divisions of the *Mishnah* are also called orders or *seders*.

Sephardim. The Jews of the premodern

Mediterranean and Middle Eastern world as contrasted with those of northern and eastern Europe.

Septuagint. The Greek translation of the Hebrew scriptures, made in Alexandria in Hellenistic times.

shekhinah. The divine presence or 'dwelling', often described in visionary terms by ancient commentators on *Ezekiel* and by medieval mystics.

Shema. 'Hear', the first word of the statement in *Deuteronomy* 6 that God is one. That statement functions as the principal Jewish affirmation of faith.

sukkah. A temporary booth or shelter originally constructed in autumn to protect ripening crops and given a historical interpretation recalling the migration experience of the Exodus.

synagogue. The local place of assembly of Jews for congregational worship, which became central in the tradition upon the destruction of the Jerusalem temple.

tallith. A shawl worn for prayer, usually white with blue stripes and with fringes at the corners.

Tanakh. The three-part Hebrew scriptural collection, composed of Torah or law, *Nebi'im* or prophets, and *Ketuvim* or sacred writings, and named as an acronym of these three terms.

Tannaim. The rabbinic authorities whose opinions are recorded in the *Mishnah*. Distinguished from Amoraim, the rabbis whose opinions appear in the *gemarah* material of the *Talmud*.

Targum. An ancient translation of the Hebrew scriptures into Aramaic, a related language that supplanted Hebrew as the spoken language of many Jews by the time of Jesus.

tefillin. Small black leather boxes, also termed phylacteries, containing words of scripture, tied to the forehead and forearm by leather thongs.

Torah. A word meaning 'teaching' or 'instruction', whose application ranges in concentric circles from the Law of Moses to the entire scripture to the entire spiritual thrust of Jewish religion.

tsaddik. 'Righteous person', a title conveying the Hasidic ideal for a teacher or spiritual leader.

yarmulke. Yiddish word for the *kippah* or skullcap worn by Orthodox Jewish males.

yeshiva. A traditional school for the study of the scriptures and Jewish law.

Yiddish. The language spoken by many central and eastern European Jews in recent centuries. It is written in Hebrew characters and has some words derived from Hebrew, but it is essentially German in its basic structure and vocabulary.

Yom Kippur. The day of atonement, falling shortly after the autumn harvest new year or Rosh Hashanah. It is the day for the most solemn reflection and examination of one's conduct.

Zion. In biblical times, the hill in Jerusalem where the temple stood as God's dwelling-place. By extension, the land of the Israelites as the place of God's favour. In modern times a goal of Jewish migration and nation-state settlement.

FURTHER READING

Abrahams, I., ed. 1927. *The Legacy of Israel*. Oxford: Clarendon.

Agus, J.B. 1959. *The Evolution of Jewish Thought: From Biblical Times to the Opening of the Modern Era*. London: Abelard-Schuman.

Barnavi, E., ed. 1992. *A Historical Atlas of the Jewish People: From the Time of the Patriarchs to the Present*. New York: Schocken.

Ben-Sasson, H.H., ed. 1975. *A History of the Jewish People*. London: Weidenfeld and Nicolson.

Casper, B.M. 1960. *An Introduction to Jewish Bible Commentary*. London: Thomas Yoseloff.

Cohen, A.A. 1962. *The Natural and the Supernatural Jew: A Historical and Theological Introduction*. New York: Pantheon.

de Breffny, B. 1978. *The Synagogue*. New York: Macmillan.

Gaster, T.H. 1952. *The Festivals of the Jewish Year*. New York: William Sloane Associates.

Glazer, N. 1972. *American Judaism*, 2nd ed. Chicago: University of Chicago Press.

Hertzberg, A. 1972. *The Zionist Idea: A Historical Analysis and Reader*. New York: Atheneum.

Idelsohn, A.Z. 1932. *Jewish Liturgy and Its Development*. New York: Holt, Rinehart & Winston.

Kaniel, M. 1979. *Judaism*. Poole, Dorset: Blandford.

Kanoff, A. 1969. *Jewish Ceremonial Art and Religious Observances*. New York: Abrams.

Neusner, J. 1988. *The Way of Torah: An Introduction to Judaism*, 4th ed. Belmont, CA: Wadsworth.

Rabinowicz, H. 1960. *A Guide to Hasidism*. London: Thomas Yoseloff.

Scholem, G.G. 1974. *Kabbalah*. Jerusalem: Keter.

Schwarz, L.W., ed. 1956. *Great Ages and Ideas of the Jewish People*. New York: Random House.

Segal, A.F. 1986. *Rebecca's Children: Judaism and Christianity in the Roman World*. Cambridge, Mass.: Harvard University Press.

Simon, M. 1950. *Jewish Religious Conflicts*. London: Hutchinson.

Steinsaltz, A. 1989. *The Talmud, the Steinsaltz Edition: A Reference Guide*. New York: Random House.

Trattner, E.R. 1955. *Understanding the Talmud*. New York: Nelson.

Wilson, R.R. 1980. *Prophecy and Society in Ancient Israel*. Philadelphia: Fortress.

Yerushalmi, Y. 1982. *Zakhor: Jewish History and Jewish Memory*. Seattle: University of Washington Press.

REFERENCES

Alexander, P.S., ed. 1984. *Textual Sources for the Study of Judaism*. Manchester: Manchester University Press.

Ausubel, N. 1974. *The Book of Jewish Knowledge: An Encyclopedia*. New York: Crown.

Caplan, S., and H.U. Ribalow, eds. 1952. *The Great Jewish Books and Their Influence on History*. New York: Horizon.

Clarendon Press. 1913. *King James Bible*. Oxford: Clarendon Press.

Delegates of OUP and Syndics of CUP. 1970. *New English Bible*. New York: Oxford University Press and Cambridge University Press.

Encyclopedia Judaica. 1971–2. *Encyclopedia Judaica*, 16 vols. Jerusalem: Encyclopedia Judaica; New York: Macmillan.

Jewish Publication Society. 1985. *Tanakh*. Philadelphia: Jewish Publication Society.

Montefiore, C.G., and H. Loewe, eds. 1974. *A Rabbinic Anthology*. New York: Schocken.

National Council of Churches of Christ in the United States of America. 1946/52. *Revised Standard Version Bible*. New York: Thomas Nelson & Sons.

Newman, L.I., ed. 1934. *The Hasidic Anthology: Tales and Teachings of the Hasidim*. New York: Scribner.

Scholem, G.G. 1949. *Zohar: The Book of Splendor*. New York: Schocken.

Stern, M. 1974/80. *Greek and Latin Authors on Jews and Judaism*. Jerusalem: Israel Academy of Science and Humanities.

Thackeray, H. St J., trans. 1927. *Josephus in Nine Volumes*. Cambridge: Harvard University Press.

Umansky, E., and D. Ashton, eds. 1992. *Four Centuries of Jewish Women's Spirituality: A Sourcebook*. Translated by C. Weissler from the 1796 edition published in Horodno. Boston: Beacon Press.

Whiston, W. 1802. *The Genuine Works of Flavius Josephus*. Edinburgh: Thomas and John Turnbull, Canongate.

Wilson, J.A. 1950. 'Egyptian Hymns and Prayers'. In *Ancient Near Eastern Texts Relating to the Old Testament*, edited by J.B. Pritchard, 365–81. Princeton: Princeton University Press.

Key Dates

[?]	Zarathushtra: no consensus as to his date
538 BCE	Cyrus conquers Babylon, establishes Achaemenian Empire
331 BCE	Achaemenian Empire falls to conquest by Alexander
276 CE	State patronage for Kartēr; execution of Mani
528	Khosrow has Mazdak killed and his movement suppressed
632	First year of Yazdegerd III's reign and of AY calendar
642	Fall of Sasanian Empire to Arab Muslims in Battle of Nehavand
936	Possible date of Zoroastrian arrival in India
1010	Completion of the *Shāh Nāmeh* by Ferdowsī
1600	Composition of the *Qisseh-e Sanjan* by Bahman, son of Kaikobad
1759	Anquetil Duperron arrives in Surat, acquires *Avesta* manuscripts

CHAPTER TWO

THE ZOROASTRIAN TRADITION

WILLARD G. OXTOBY

Zoroastrianism developed in Iran for more than 1,000 years before Islam and became the state religion of the Sasanians, Iran's last great pre-Islamic empire. It is alive today in a small remnant community that preserved the tradition over the past fourteen centuries in India and Iran.

Zoroastrians call the supreme creator god Ahura Mazda, meaning 'Wise Lord'. Hence in ancient times they referred to themselves as Mazda worshippers, and also to their tradition as 'the Good Religion'. The name Zoroastrian was given later and refers to the tradition's priestly and prophetic teacher, Zarathushtra. His name came through Greek as Zoroaster, the form common in most of the West.

The Zoroastrian faith survives among only about 100,000 adherents. The statistics have an almost logarithmic proportion: in general order of magnitude, there are a hundred times as many Christians in the world (say 1.4 billion) as there are Jews (14 million), and there are in turn over a hundred times as many Jews as there are Zoroastrians (considerably fewer than 140,000). Yet we confidently reckon Zoroastrianism among the great religions, not for its present size but for the structure of its religious ideas and their contribution to the history of religion.

The picture of Zoroastrianism that we now sketch is one that will not resolve the outstanding issues, but may at least identify what the main issues are. In the process, we shall have to mention unfamiliar names, terms, and languages. For pre-Islamic Iran, we do this in a simplified form without the diacritical marks we would comfortably use for Sanskrit, Arabic, or later Persian items. That is because no one transliteration system commands a consensus among the specialists.

A Zoroastrian in or from Iran is called a Zartoshti in Farsi (the Persian language of Islamic Iran). The more generous population estimates for the community who have survived in Iran place their number at 25,000, and the more conservative estimates at half that. As a fraction of Iran's population, their present numbers represent one in a thousand. As a fraction of the Zoroastrian population worldwide, Zoroastrians in or recently from Iran are about one in every four.

Most Zoroastrians who consider western India, especially Bombay, their home, are known as Parsis ('Persians'). Within the vast population of India that community has dwindled to perhaps 75,000. With India's total population approaching a billion, their numbers represent less than one in 10,000, but as a fraction of Zoroastrians worldwide, those in or from India account for three out of every four.

It is useful to think of the Zoroastrian tradition as having existed in three main cultural eras across the long historical span of its development in India and Iran. First was an Indian context: at the dawn of their history, the Iranians shared a considerable repertory of their gods and rituals with a kindred people who entered India and contributed their hymns, the *Vedas*, to the Hindu tradition. Second was the context of Ancient Near Eastern cultures, when three successive Persian dynasties became masters of Mesopotamia (Iraq), inheriting its art and writing and becoming rivals successively of Greeks, Romans, and Byzantines over a period of eleven centuries. In the third phase, since the conquest of Iran by Islam, the Zoroastrians of Iran lived as a minority among Muslims while the Zoroastrians of India lived as a minority among Hindus, each influenced by the host environment.

Historical linkages with Judaism, Christianity, Islam, Hinduism, and Buddhism provide Zoroastrianism part of its significance to the world, a significance out of all proportion to the present worldwide numbers of the community, which is smaller than either Thunder Bay, Ontario, or Peoria, Illinois.

The religious thought of Zoroastrianism places it among the ten or so great religious traditions of human history. Certain of its features are of particular interest. One is ethics. Zoroastrians probably make morality as central as do the adherents of any religious tradition, past or present; morality is both an ideal and an achievement. Second, in eschatology, Zoroastrianism teaches in classic form the expectation of a world to come: both for the individual and for the world as a whole, this life will be overhauled and a utopian new age ushered in. Third, the Zoroastrian tradition offers a vivid example of the personification of evil. Though controlling most things, God faces a demonic antagonist, on account of whom he does not yet seem to control all. Fourth, Zoroastrian ritual includes the traditional disposal of dead bodies by exposure to birds of prey. And finally, there is the question of historical influence, of whether Zoroastrian ideas of eschatology or evil or the soul contributed to the development of comparable ideas in Judaism, Christianity, and Islam.

CLASSICAL ZOROASTRIAN HISTORY

There are few religious traditions whose historical development is as problematical as the Zoroastrian. There are gaps and contradictions in the record, and many of the texts are not reliably datable. Assumptions are therefore piled on assumptions, conjecture upon conjecture. Nowhere is this situation more acute than with the tradition's founder figure, Zarathushtra.

The Elusive Zarathushtra

The time, place, and details of Zoroaster's life are speculation, not consensus. Consensus credits him only with seventeen psalmlike compositions, called the *Gathas*, conventionally treated as five groups embedded in a larger collection of liturgical hymns called the *Yasna*, part of the Avestan scriptural collection. But beyond the *Gathas*' single-minded devotion to Ahura Mazda as lord, the strongly ethical and eschatological tenor of that devotion, and some slender references to a cattle-herding social context, little about Zarathushtra's life can be told except what comes from later legend.

It is partly because so little is conclusively known about Zoroaster that so many and such varied edifices of speculation can be constructed. From 1883 to 1891, the German philosopher Friedrich Nietzsche (1824–1900) set forth ideas about good, evil, and the human will in literary form as the oracular pronouncements of a prophet, *Also sprach Zarathustra* (Thus Zoroaster Spoke). Nietzsche had grown up with religion—his father and grandfather were Lutheran ministers—but in his alienation from it, he concentrated on an atheistic desire for the acquisition of power.

Of the ancient prophet Nietzsche used the name but little else. From him we find out not about Iranian religion millennia ago but some concerns of German philosophy a century ago. But Nietzsche, who studied and taught the Greek and Latin classics, lived at a time when the texts of ancient Iran and India were being studied and translated by European scholarship. That Nietzsche chose the figure of Zoroaster illustrates the prominence of the theme of good and evil in the Zoroastrian religious tradition, and in the modern West's perception of that tradition.

The one thing about Zoroaster that Zoroastrians and outsiders to the tradition alike have agreed upon is that the *Gathas* are his compositions. If they are not his, then nobody knows whose they are; and if they are not his, then the figure whose religious ideas we are really interested in is whoever else was responsible for the *Gathas*. The *Gathas* have been distinguished from the remainder of

FROM THE *GATHAS* OF ZARATHUSHTRA

[Zoroaster's rhetorical questions about Ahura Mazda's role as creator strike a note common in religious thought. Parallels to the Norse Edda *have been taken by some to imply a common Indo-European tradition, and parallels to* Isaiah 40 *have suggested Zoroastrian influence on the faith of Israel.]*

This I ask thee, speak to me truly, O Lord!
Who supports the earth below and (keeps) the heavens (above) from falling down? Who (supports) the waters and plants?
Who yokes the two steeds to the wind and clouds?
Who, O Mazdā, is the Creator of Good Mind?

This I ask thee, speak to me truly, O Lord!
What artificer created days and nights?
What artificer created sleep and wakefulness?
Who is it through whom dawn, midday, and evening (come to pass), reminding the religious (man) of his duty?
(*Yasna* 44:4–5; Malandra 1983:42–3)

[Zoroaster refers to the encounter of the two spirits, in a Gatha *passage that has become a mainstay for the subsequent development of doctrine about them. The passage also mentions in explicit series the combination of thought, word, and deed, which to many Zoroastrians is the essence of religion. The term 'drugwant' has connotations of both 'liar' and 'evildoer'.]*

Now, these are the two original Spirits who, as Twins, have been perceived (by me?) through a vision. In both thought and speech, (and) in deed, these two are what is good and evil. Between these two, the pious, not the impious, will choose rightly.

Furthermore, the two Spirits confronted each other; in the beginning (each) create(d) for himself life and nonlife, so

the *Yasna* text within which they are incorporated, and the distinction is easy enough to confirm, on two grounds.

One contrast is that the *Gathas* stand apart from the rest of the Avestan literature partly in the nature of their religious agenda. The remainder of the *Avesta* is primarily composed of ritual hymns recounting the achievements of the divine spirits in terms of animal or warrior strength, or in the fertility of nature, plus including a work on priestly purity regulations. By comparison, the rhetoric of the *Gathas* is a searching, hoping quest for confirmation that righteousness may triumph in the ultimate order of things. The devotion of the *Gathas* hopes that the Wise Lord will inspire his followers to the good thoughts, good words, and good deeds that will be reckoned as credits at the time of a final testing and retribution. The remainder of the *Avesta* invokes various deities and spirits directly, while the *Gathas* are addressed exclusively to Ahura Mazda, the Wise Lord. In

that (?) in the end there will be the worst existence for the Drugwants, but the best Mind for the Righteous.

Of these two Spirits, the deceitful (drugwant) chose the worst course of action, (while) the most beneficent Spirit who is clothed in the hardest stones (chose) Truth, (as) also (do) those who believingly propitiate Ahura Mazdā.

Between these two (Spirits) the daēwas did not choose rightly at all since, while they were taking council among themselves, delusion came upon them, so that they chose the worst Mind. Then, all together, they ran to Wrath with which they infect the life of man (*Yasna* 30:3–6; Malandra 1983:40).

[Zoroaster's piety in the Gathas *is frequently one that calls out to Ahura Mazda to confirm his faith and reassure him. Passages in this vein comprise a standard Zoroastrian prayer for protection, the* Kem na Mazda *prayer (titled by its first three words in Avestan), said when untying the* kusti.*]*

Whom, Mazda, hast Thou appointed protector for one like me, if the Wicked One shall dare to harm me? Whom but Thy Fire and Thy (Good) Purpose, by whose acts, Lord, Truth is nourished. Proclaim this teaching to my Inner Self!

Who will be victorious to protect through Thy teaching those who are the progeny in my house? As Healer of the world, promise to us a judge. Then let Hearkening come to him with Good Purpose, O Mazda—to him whomsoever Thou dost wish.

Protect us from the foe, O Mazda and Spenta Armaiti! Begone, daevic Drug! Begone the one of Daeva-origin, begone the one of Daeva-shaping, begone the one of Daeva-begetting! Begone, O Drug, crawl away, O Drug, disappear, O Drug! In the north shall you disappear. You shall not destroy the material world of Asha!

Reverence with which there is devotion and sacrifice (*Yasna* 46:7; 44:16; *Vendidad* 8:21; *Yasna* 49:10; Boyce 1984:42, 34, 58).

them, God's self-manifestation, rather than personifying natural forces, lends itself to interpretation as abstract qualities or semipersonified moral virtues.

To a historian, contrasts of this sort call to mind the step-by-step privileging of moral teachings in other religious traditions that started with ritual priesthoods. The Hebrew prophetical movement, at about 750 to 550 BCE, is one example. The career and concerns of Confucius and Mencius in China, from about 550 to 300 BCE, offer us other examples. With such parallels, Zoroaster is at least a prophet, if not also a sage, and it is tempting to view him as an ethical reformer of a previously ritual religion. On broad comparative grounds, it seems an open-and-shut matter. Thinking of Zoroaster as a prophet and hence as a reformer is made easier by usage in Islamic and modern times, when the term 'prophet' has been applied to Zoroaster's accomplishment, not only in Muslim, Jewish, and Christian discourse about Zoroaster but in the modern usage of Zoroastrians themselves. The connotations of prophet as messenger or reformer have adhered to Zoroaster despite the fact that in classical Zoroastrian tradition he is portrayed as an ideal priest, not as an opponent of priesthood.

However, a challenge to so easy a pigeonholing of Zoroaster arises when we consider the other principal contrast between the *Gathas* and the remainder of the *Avesta*. As it happens, the *Gathas* are in a dialect that is linguistically much more archaic than the rest of the *Avesta*, which linguists call the *Younger Avesta*. The observation was first made by the German scholar Martin Haug (1827–76). If we have just been thinking of the Avestan hymns to the various divinities as spiritually primitive and the *Gathas* as spiritually developed, we now have to reverse the sequence, thinking of the *Gathas* as linguistically primal and the other compositions as showing linguistic development.

In interpreting Zoroaster, then, one intellectually reaps as conclusions what one sows as assumptions. Scholars who work mainly with texts as linguistic objects tend more readily to see the prophet as a very archaic figure. Scholars who assume that religious traditions are profoundly conservative—and religion offers ample evidence for such a view—can read the *Gathas* as the faithful legacy of an oral tradition from a very early date, making him an ethical reformer centuries or millennia ahead of any others such as the Hebrew prophets or Confucius. (One objection one must meet if one is to defend such a view is to explain why so compelling an insight went unnoticed and unparalleled by anyone else for so long.) The archaic character of the *Gathas*' language also bolsters modern Zoroastrians' pride in their tradition, often expressed in the claim that Zoroaster was the world's first prophet.

Some attempts at dating rely not on Iranian but on Greek and Latin sources, in which there is hearsay evidence concerning the Persians. Pliny (23–79) quotes Hermippus (c. 250 BCE) as making Zoroaster the author of 2 million lines of verse and placing him 5,000 years before the Trojan War, that is, a round number of years before a semilegendary event. Such calculations result in a date 3,000 years before the invention of writing and therefore place on the text of the *Gathas* a massive burden of accuracy in oral transmission—albeit as poetry, whose structure is more stable than prose. In any case, Zoroastrians' pride in Zoroaster as the world's first prophet may have afforded Zoroastrians survival value over the past fourteen centuries in an Iranian society dominated by Islam, whose respect for Muḥammad is not as the world's first prophet but as the last in any series.

If one is to maintain as a historian that the ethical ideas of the *Gathas* developed later than the ritual content of the Avestan hymns, then one must service one's intellectual investment by accounting for the difference in dialect. Two lines of argument are often found for this. One is the suggestion that the *Gathas* and the rest of the *Avesta* may have come from two widely separated geographical regions where the forms of the language were different. To support the idea that archaic language might survive in an isolated locality while language changes elsewhere, scholars point to Elizabethan English spoken in tidewater Virginia and eighteenth-century French spoken in rural Québec.

Speculation often places the ritual *Avesta* in southwestern Iran because we know from inscriptions that kings who gave credit to Ahura Mazda came into conflict with priests to whom they referred as *magi*. That leaves northeastern Iran as a plausible homeland for Zoroaster, a location interpreters then seek to confirm from clues in the *Gatha*s that there was some struggle between nomads (may we suppose Central Asian nomads?) and the sedentary populations (may we assume a cattle-raising and agricultural community?) that Zoroaster seems to sympathize with.

The other line of linguistic defence of a late date for the *Gatha*s does not have to suppose a necessary geographical isolation. Instead, it operates from the observation that in many religious communities, archaic linguistic forms are cultivated as an active dialect for liturgical purposes. The speaker of English need look no further than usage in Protestant worship, where the use of the 1611 *King James* version of the Bible well into the twentieth century maintained its Elizabethan English as the dialect in which clergy talked when addressing God in ad-lib prayer. By this token, the *Gatha*s, like the biblical book *Deuteronomy*, could represent an introduction of ideas at a late date in a form purporting to be early.

On the surface, these issues may strike the beginner as highly technical, an edifice of scholarly theory rather than a description of Zoroastrian piety and devotion. Scholarly theory can indeed be pushed to extremes, as when Ernst Herzfeld (1879–1948) accompanied archaeologists excavating the ruins of the Achaemenian capital, Persepolis, in southwestern Iran in the 1930s. Herzfeld's historical imagination had Zoroaster walking over every stone of the ruins, at the same time as Sweden's Henrik S. Nyberg (1889–1974) assimilated the prophet to what was being found out about Siberian shamanism, well to the northeast of Iran. A third scholar, Walter B. Henning (1908–67), demonstrated in his *Zoroaster: Politician or Witch Doctor?* (1951) that neither of these extremes of reconstruction made much sense. However, historical reconstruction is practically always an attempt to fill in gaps by analogy with what one finds persuasive in some other context.

Zoroastrians themselves become quite excited about questions of the historical locale and contribution of Zoroaster. In the struggle for survival through the centuries, the Zoroastrian community did not have the luxury of a continuous, well-articulated premodern interpretive tradition comparable to the Sanskrit commentaries of Hindu *pandit*s or the Midrashic lore of Jewish *yeshiva* scholars. With the emergence of a large educated and professional element in the community today, whether in India, Iran, or overseas, the theories of scholars have been hotly debated, with the kind of energy that doctrinal controversies must have had in antiquity. Defending the prophet's life and his ethical contribution as historically early rather than historically late has become a kind of litmus test for faith, or at least orthodoxy. The issues are similar to what one encounters when discussing the date of the ideas in *Deuteronomy* or 'Second Isaiah' with conservative Jews or Christians.

Matters simmer down once one moves away from the religio-historical dating of the prophet and the *Gathas*. There is a sizeable body of legendary tradition in Persian literature about Zoroaster's life and accomplishments, but educated Zoroastrians quite readily recognize it as legendary. For instance, rather than crying, Zoroaster laughs when he is born. As an infant and youth, he is miraculously protected from wild beasts. As a young man, he performs miraculous cures, including reviving a horse that is near death. Reciting the prayer formulas, he fights off the spiritual forces of evil that tempt him. All such details are the material of legend, and rather affectionately cherished by most Zoroastrians as such. Educational materials for children devote particular emphasis to the childhood accomplishments of Zoroaster, making of him a hero figure for children, just as Christians have highlighted the twelve-year-old Jesus provocatively questioning the religio-legal authorities.

So, how do we sum up the historical Zoroaster? Reliance on some literary traditions can place him around 6300 BCE, while reliance on others can place him around 630 BCE. Reliance on hints of population conflict can place the prophet well to the northeast in Iran, while reliance on hints of involvement with named kings can place him well to the southwest. All that we can say with any assurance is that Zoroaster lived somewhere in Iran, probably at some time before the Achaemenians, that is, before the sixth century BCE.

The Aryans

Two migrations from some inner Asian region took place before the end of the second millennium BCE. One of these entered India from the northwest via what is now Afghanistan, and the other entered Iran, possibly by way of what is now northeastern Iran. We have no historical record of the parent population, but reconstruct their language and culture hypothetically from what the migrating groups had in common. Because one branch settled in India and the other in Iran, scholars refer to the people as Indo-Iranians. The people referred to themselves as Aryans.

We know the Indian branch of the Aryans as a formative element in the Hindu tradition and ancient Indian society. Their warriors subjugated the indigenous Dravidian population of India, and the Aryans became the ruling class. Hence in classical Indian literature, the Sanskrit term 'Aryan' comes to have a social-class connotation, meaning 'noble'.

Meanwhile, the other branch of the Aryans settled the Iranian plateau, becoming its principal population without leaving much literary evidence of having subjugated or displaced other population groups. As a consequence, the name Aryan there became the name of the region, not the name of a social class. 'The homeland of the Aryans' is the name that through centuries of linguistic erosion eventually became the name Iran.

The two Aryan branches had language in common. Similarities of both grammar and vocabulary are clearly recognizable between the language of the oldest Iranian texts (the Avestan scripture and the Old Persian imperial inscriptions) and the oldest Indian compositions (the Hindu *Vedas*). In fact, the grammar and vocabulary of Indian and Iranian languages match in more distant detail many features of Greek, Latin, German, English, and the Slavic languages, indicating a vast family relationship.

Theory moved beyond linguistic correspondence to two additional steps. The first of these was a biological theory. People who spoke related languages were thought to be descended from a common ancestry, so that one could speak of Aryan racial characteristics. Indeed, the name Aryan was associated in Hitler's Germany with pseudo-theories of racial purity that were promoted to exclude persons associated with other language groups, such as Hebrew, a Semitic and not an Indo-European language. Much unspeakable suffering was perpetrated. The second theoretical step moves on to the notion that people who speak the same language also have the same culture, including religious institutions and outlooks. A moment's reflection will demonstrate that in any age of migration or population contact, neither of these leaps based on language similarity necessarily follows. People of different biological heredity can learn the same language, and people can express different cultural outlooks in the same language.

The idea of a shared heritage may not therefore be valuable for predicting cultural development, where differentiation can take place, but it can be useful in retrospect for explaining cultural similarities, where differentiation is seen not to have happened. This is what we find when we look at the Hindu *Vedas* and compare them with the hymns in the Zoroastrian *Avesta*. Both sets of hymns appear to have been used as the texts of a sacrificial ritual, performed by a hereditary priesthood. In both cases the priests learned the hymns by rote memorization and recited them in a fixed linguistic form even as vernacular dialects shifted. In both cases the words of the hymns were thought to have a spell-like or charmlike quality, effective if properly pronounced, but powerless otherwise.

The gods addressed in the Vedic sacrifices and in the Avestan ritual are identified with tangible forces of nature, with the power of storm and flood, with the strength of ferocious animals or mighty warriors, and with the fertility of plants, animals, and humankind. Protection against demonic forces is provided by the gods, whose accomplishments and exploits are recalled in the hymns, presumably not so much to inform the deity of its power as to make the deity aware of the worshipper's acknowledgement of it. The aggregate of both the Vedic and the Avestan ritual is a polytheistic system: the gods have their domains and functions, their various portfolios. One prays to a deity for specific aid that that deity can provide. Some deities appear in the two pantheons with the same name: Mithra, for instance, is the overseer of contractual obligations and hence an enforcer of right conduct. The sacred intoxicant *haoma/soma* is also a shared feature, as is the performance of sacrifice in the presence of fire.

When so much is similar between the *Vedas* and the *Avesta*, one looks for contrasts and their significance. The word in India for a god, *deva*, matches the Iranian word for a demon, *daiva*. What was it that made one population's gods another population's demons? The opposing terms contrast as well: in India, an *asura* is a demon, whereas the term in Iran becomes part of the name Ahura Mazda, the Wise Lord. Hence it is persuasive to place Zoroaster and his devotion to the Wise Lord in Iran, at a point after the separation of Iran's Aryans from India's Aryans, but the shared patterns of the ritual religion at a time before the two branches separated.

The Avestan Scriptures

Since the introduction of writing in Iran, three principal script forms in succession have been used for writing down what was said in Persian languages. In the Achaemenian era (559–331 BCE), royal inscriptions were made in an alphabetical repertory of wedge-shaped signs inherited but simplified from Babylonian cuneiform writing. We call the language of the Achaemenian inscriptions Old Persian.

In the Parthian (c. 246 BCE–226 CE) and Sasanian (226–641) eras, a cursive (i.e., connected) form of the Aramaic alphabet, widely used in trade in Syria and Mesopotamia, was pressed into service to write the then current form of spoken Persian, which came to be called Pahlavi (meaning 'Parthian'). The Pahlavi script corresponded only poorly to the spoken sounds because it had been devised for a Semitic rather than an Iranian vocabulary, but people learned to cope and used it for centuries. After the Islamic conquest of Iran, the Arabic alphabet was adapted to write the newly developing form of Persian, commonly called Farsi, which also added a large inventory of Arabic words to its vocabulary. For at least two centuries after the Arab conquest, as Muslim Iranians were writing in Arabic and beginning to write in Farsi, Zoroastrians continued to produce religious literature in Pahlavi.

Because Zoroastrian literature was produced reflecting all three of these phases, one encounters alternate pronunciations and spellings of essentially the same name. The great God, for instance, was Ahura Mazda to the Achaemenians, but in Parthian and Sasanian times the same name became Ohrmazd. Likewise the evil spirit, Ahura Mazda's arch rival, was called Angra Mainyu in old Iranian, but Ahriman in Pahlavi. In the material that follows, we shall generally present Zoroastrian terminology in the older Iranian form.

The *Avesta*, the holiest body of Zoroastrian literature, is in the oldest form of the language, comparable in its phonetic system to the Achaemenians' inscriptions. There is a tradition that two master copies of a fuller version of it, written in gold letters on oxhides, were destroyed in 331 BCE when Alexander conquered the Achaemenian capital, Persepolis. Whether or not any such copy existed, such a tradition would be useful when people set about compiling the *Avesta* in Sasanian times. They could claim to be recovering it, rather than composing it.

Most likely, the ritual hymns of which the *Avesta* largely consists were transmitted orally among the priesthood, in a manner comparable with the *Veda*s of Hinduism, which for many centuries were not written down. For when the Sasanian *Avesta* was written, it was written in an alphabet adapted from the Pahlavi current at the time. Had the texts really been 'recovered' from a much earlier written tradition, such a recovery arguably would have included its form of writing. Religious traditions, after all, can be very conservative about the physical form of their texts. Consider, for example, that printed *Qur'āns* often have a flap around the outer edge of the pages that has disappeared from other Arabic printed books, or that copies of the Hebrew scriptures used in worship retain the scroll form that preceded the bound book.

The Avestan literature is in several sections. The principal extant parts are:

- The *Yasna* ('worship') contains seventy-two principal hymns recited daily. At the core of the *Yasna* is a body of seventeen hymns, in five groups arranged according to their poetic metre. As already indicated, these are known as the five *Gatha*s, generally agreed by both ancient tradition and modern scholarship to be from Zoroaster himself. These hymns are distinctive in ethical content from the rest of the *Avesta*, and in dialect also from practically all the rest of it as well. Reflecting a distinctively personal address to God, they focus on the demand for righteousness, on the reward of the righteous at the end of this age, and on the sovereignty of Ahura Mazda as God. Later theologians in the Zoroastrian tradition often based their thought on interpretations of the prophet's teaching as contained in the *Gathas*.
- The *Yashts* ('hymns') are linguistically less archaic but reflect practices that antedate the prophet's teaching. There are *yasht*s to deities known also from the Vedic hymns of India, and their tone is far more ritual than moral. Yet in much of the *Avesta* these hymns are presented as quotations from the prophet Zoroaster. One explanation of this attribution is that the old Indo-Iranian polytheistic tradition was later legitimated by being incorporated into the prophet's legacy after his teachings became influential.
- The *Videvdat* ('law against the demons'), known by the Pahlavi form of its name, *Vendidad,* is a collection of prose texts that counter the forces of evil through the detailed implementation of purity laws. Passages of the

AVESTAN HYMNS TO MITHRA, HAOMA, AND ABAN

[From the Avestan hymn to Mithra, which incorporates the worship of Mithra into the religion of Ahura Mazda by presenting the text as delivered by Ahura Mazda to Zoroaster.]

Ahura Mazdā said to Zarathushtra the Spitamid: When I created Mithra of wide pastures, I made him, O Spitamid, as worthy of worship and praise as myself, Ahura Mazdā ... Do not break a covenant, O Spitamid, neither (the one) which you might conclude with a drugwant nor (one) with an ashawan belonging to the Good Religion, for the contract applies to both of you, to drugwant and to ashawan.

Mithra of wide pastures gives possession of swift horses to those who are not false to a covenant. Fire (ātar), (the son) of Ahura Mazdā, gives the straightest path to those who are not false to a covenant. The good, strong, beneficent Frawashis of the Righteous give noble progeny to those who are not false to a covenant.

We worship Mithra ... who, overtaking (his) opponent(s), overcome by passion together with manly valor, strikes down (his) opponents with a toss (of his head) ... who cuts everything up; all at once he mixes together on the ground the bones, hair, brains, and blood of the men who are false to a covenant (*Yasht* 10:1–3, 70–2; Malandra 1983:59, 67).

[From the Avestan hymn to Haoma, the deity manifested in an intoxicating beverage prepared and consumed by the priests. Notice again the preface incorporating it into Zoroaster's religion.]

At the time of the pressing, Haoma approached Zarathushtra, who was putting the fire in proper order and reciting gathas. Zarathushtra asked him: Who, O man, are you, the most beautiful of the entire material world that I have seen ...? Then he, righteous Haoma who keeps death far away (?), answered: I, O Zarathushtra, am righteous Haoma who keep death far away. Seek me, O Spitamid; press me out for drinking; praise me for

Vendidad and the *Yasna* are repeated in a long, less frequently consulted section called the *Visparad* ('for all the lords').

- The *Khorda Avesta* ('shorter *Avesta*') is a collection of the most frequently used prayers. It is the portion of the *Avesta* most commonly circulated among Zoroastrians who are not practising priests.
- The *Sirozah* lists the deities governing the thirty days of the month.
- The *Hadhokht Nask* ('sayings'), is a description of the soul's fate after death.
- Short sections consist of the five *Nyaish* and five *gah* prayers.

Europeans were unaware of the *Avesta* until the seventeenth century when, with the growth of trade with India, manuscript copies began to reach Europe.

strength as the future Saoshyants will praise me …

Then Zarathushtra said: Reverence to Haoma! Good Haoma, well-created Haoma, properly created, good, created (?), curative, well-built, beneficent, victorious, yellow-colored, having tasty (?) stalks—so that (Haoma) is best for the drinker and the best provision for the soul. I call down, O yellow (Haoma), your intoxicating power, strength, victoriousness, (ability to grant) health, curativeness, prosperity, growth, force for the entire body, complete knowledge, (and) I call down this that I may go about among beings autonomous(ly), overcoming hostility, defeating the Lie (*Yasna* 9:1–2, 16–17; Malandra 1983:151–3).

[From the Avestan hymn to water (ābān), *personified as the heavenly river goddess Aredwī Sūrā Anāhitā.]*

Ahura Mazda said to Zarathushtra Spitama: On my account, worship her, O Zarathushtra Spitama, Aredwī Sūrā Anāhitā … who is a crop-increasing ashawan, a herd-increasing ashawan, an ashawan who makes the country prosper, who purifies the semen of all males, who purifies for conception the wombs of all females, who gives easy delivery to all females, who gives milk to all females regularly and at the proper time; (worship her), the vast, famed afar, who is as great as all these waters which flow forth upon the earth, who forcefully flows forth from Mount Hukairya to the Wouru.kasha sea …

Aredwī Sūrā Anāhitā said: O upright, righteous Spitamid, you should worship me with this prayer, sacrifice (to me) with this prayer from sunrise to sunset. You may drink this libation of mine (as well as?) the wise, skillful athrawans who have investigated the dictates and interpreted the teachings, who (are) tanu.māthra. Let not someone afflicted with …(?), nor a feverish person, nor a eunuch (?), nor a …(?), nor an impotent person (?), nor a woman, nor someone (who is) instructed (but) does not recite the Gāthās, nor a leper who has been isolated, consume this libation of mine (*Yasht* 5:1–3, 91–3; Malandra 1983:120, 127)!

The French scholar A.H. Anquetil du Perron (1731–1805) went to India, learned to read some Avestan from a Parsi priest in Surat, acquired manuscripts, and produced a translation. European study of the *Avesta* subsequently paralleled and drew support from study of the earliest Sanskrit literature, linguistically related. The name *Zend-Avesta*, used by nineteenth-century European writers, is a mistaken conflation of the name *Avesta*, 'basic text', with the term *zand*, 'commentary'.

The name Pazand refers to a technique of writing down prayers in middle Persian (Pahlavi) in the context of a liturgy in the older Avestan language. For this purpose, the Pahlavi-derived Avestan script, which was precise, was used in preference to the ambiguous everyday Pahlavi script. When priests encounter Pazand

The Achaemenians and Their God(s)

[In his lengthy cliffside inscription at Bisutun, the Achaemenian king Darius gives Ahura Mazda the credit for his success, but leaves open the possibility that other gods may matter too.]

Saith Darius the King: Within these countries, the man who was loyal, him I rewarded well; (him) who was evil, him I punished well; by the favor of Ahuramazda these countries showed respect for my law; as was said to them by me, thus was it done. Saith Darius the King: Ahuramazda bestowed the kingdom upon me; Ahuramazda bore me aid until I got possession of this kingdom; by the favor of Ahuramazda I hold this kingdom …

Saith Darius the King: Now let that which has been done by me convince thee; thus to the people impart, do not conceal it: if this record thou shalt not conceal, (but) tell it to the people, may Ahuramazda be a friend unto thee, and may family be unto thee in abundance, and may thou live long! Saith Darius the King: If this record thou shalt conceal, (and) not tell it to the people, may Ahuramazda be a smiter unto thee, and may family not be to thee!

Saith Darius the King: This which I did, in one and the same year by the favor of Ahuramazda I did; Ahuramazda bore me aid, and the other gods who are (Bisutun inscription, col. 1, lines 20–6; col. 4, lines 52–61; Kent 1953:119, 132).

[Xerxes, in an inscription at Persepolis, tells how he suppressed the worship of daivas.*]*

A great god is Ahuramazda, who created this earth, who created yonder sky, who created man, who created happiness for man, who made Xerxes king, one king of many, one lord of many …

Saith Xerxes the King: By the favor of Ahuramazda these are the countries of which I was king outside of Persia; I ruled over them; they bore tribute to me; what

passages in the middle of an Avestan ceremony, they mumble them rather than reciting them aloud.

The Achaemenian Era

Iran before Islam had a tradition of empire. In the twelve centuries from about 559 BCE to 642 CE, there were three great Persian empires, each of which is in its own way claimed as part of the Zoroastrian heritage. The first of these was the empire of the Achaemenian dynasty. It gathered strength shortly after 600 BCE and prevailed until overrun by Greek-speaking soldiers under Alexander the Great, of Macedonia, in 331 BCE. The Achaemenians' homeland was the province of Fars ('Persia') in southwestern Iran, where they had an administrative capital at Susa and a ceremonial capital at Persepolis. The Achaemenians were the great eastern

was said to them by me that they did; my law—that held them firm; Media, Elam, Arachosia, Armenia, Drangiana, Parthia, Aria, Bactria, Sogdiana, Chorasmia, Babylonia, Assyria, Sattagydia, Sardis, Egypt, Ionians, those who dwell by the sea and those who dwell across the sea, men of Maka, Arabia, Gandara, Sind, Cappadocia, Dahae, Amrygian Scythians, Pointed-Cap Scythians, Skudra, men of Akaufaka, Libyans, Carians, Ethiopians.

Saith Xerxes the King: When that I became king, there is among these countries which are inscribed above (one which) was in commotion. Afterwards Ahuramazda bore me aid; by the favor of Ahuramazda I smote that country and put it down in its place.

And among these countries there was (a place) where previously false gods were worshipped. Afterwards, by the favor of Ahuramazda, I destroyed that sanctuary of the demons, and I made proclamation, "The demons shall not be worshipped!" Where previously the demons were worshipped, there I worshipped Ahurmazda and Arta reverent(ly) …

Thou who (shalt be) hereafter, if thou shalt think, "Happy may I be when living, and when dead may I be blessed," have respect for that law which Ahuramazda has established; worship Ahuramazda and Arta reverent(ly) (Xerxes, Persepolis inscription H, 1–6, 13–41, 46–51; Kent 1953:138, 151–2).

[Artaxerxes II *invokes three gods by name in an inscription at Susa, and only Mithra in an inscription at Hamadan.]*

Saith Artaxerxes the King: By the favor of Ahuramazda this is the palace which I built in my lifetime as a pleasant retreat. May Ahuramazda, Anaitis, and Mithras protect me from all evil, and my building (Artaxerxes II Susa inscription D, 2–4; Kent 1953:155).

This palace, of stone in its column(s), Artaxerxes the Great King built, the son of Darius the King, an Achaemenian. May Mithras protect me … (Artaxerxes II Hamadan inscription B; Kent 1953:155).

rivals of classical Greek civilization. Stand-off military and naval battles, at Marathon in 490 BCE and Thermopylae and Salamis in 480 BCE, are famous in Greek history as major crisis points. Had the Persians won all of these, some historians speculate, the Achaemenian dynasty might have gone on to rule all of Europe, and Europe might have become Zoroastrian. However, that was not to be.

'A great god', inscriptions said, 'is Ahura Mazda, who made earth, made heaven, made mortals, made happiness for mortals, and made Darius king.' Under the Achaemenian rulers Cyrus (r. 559–530 BCE), Cambyses (r. 530–521 BCE), and Darius (521–485 BCE), Persian armies from southwestern Iran conquered much of the known world, assembling the largest empire that the world up until that time had ever seen. They and their successors held sway from what is today Pakistan and Tajikistan to Egypt and Turkey.

In their royal inscriptions the Achaemenian kings regularly name Ahura Mazda as their divine sponsor, so we suppose that whatever religious institutions they sponsored were of the religion of Ahura Mazda. In a lengthy inscription on the cliff face at Bisutun, just east of Kermanshah on the principal route through the mountains from Baghdad to Tehran, Darius reminds passers-by of how Ahura Mazda helped him consolidate power, but also mentions suppressing an uprising by one Gaumata, a 'Magian' or priest (*magu*).

Speculation therefore supposes that not all the priests in Iran were supportive of the Achaemenian kings, and that consolidating royal power meant coopting worshippers of deities other than Ahura Mazda. We know that when Cyrus conquered Babylon in 538 BCE, he was proclaimed a servant of Marduk, the Babylonian deity. We have hints that Achaemenian policy was to enlist the support of local populations through the sponsorship or preservation of their various religious allegiances; a Greek text preserves a letter from Darius to one of his provincial administrators to leave unmolested the trees in a garden sacred to Apollo. We also have an inscription from Xerxes (r. 485–465 BCE) in which he mentions suppressing the worship of *daivas*, false gods, so there must have been some limits to accommodation. Only with the later Achaemenian kings, such as Artaxerxes II (r. 404–358 BCE) do we find other deities than Ahura Mazda explicitly named in royal inscriptions.

The contrast we find in the Zoroastrian sacred texts between the *Gathas*' focus on Ahura Mazda and the *Yashts*' devotion to the Indo-Iranian pantheon could lead one to speculate about the literary materials as evidence of a political synthesis. The texts bring together the religion of Ahura Mazda and the polytheistic cult of the old Indo-Iranian deities as represented by the *magi*. In this line of reasoning, the *Gathas* reflect the faith of Zoroaster, while the *Yashts* reflect the religion of the Magians. A political synthesis between Ahura Mazda followers and Magians could have taken place, but we have no textual evidence whether such an event happened long before the Achaemenian kings or during the course of their reign, or centuries later during the compilation of the *Avesta*. We can only observe that eventually the hymns to the Indo-Iranian pantheon become incorporated in the *Avesta* as the direct gift or instruction of Ahura Mazda to Zoroaster. Editorial labels indicating this are manifestly additions to the material of earlier hymns. Such attribution to Zoroaster contributed to the premodern view of Zoroastrians that the entire *Avesta*, indeed the entire normative content of the Zoroastrian religion, was Zoroaster's own achievement, a view overturned only in the nineteenth century. Classical Zoroastrianism could have monotheistic tendencies and still retain multiple divinities; and the deities of the *Yashts* were termed *yazatas* ('worshipful beings') and seen as Ahura Mazda's host of heavenly deputies.

Before jumping to historical conclusions from undated literary materials—which is what the study of ancient Zoroastrianism inevitably entails sooner or later—we must note that there is no direct evidence that the Achaemenians spoke of Zoroaster. The kings do not name him in their inscriptions, nor during their reign do the Greek writers who give detailed descriptions of Persian custom based on travellers' accounts and military campaigns. One has to wait until the beginning of the Common Era (which is also when Matthew mentions *magi* as visitors to the infant Jesus) for mention of Zoroaster to appear in Greek or Latin writers. Whether the Achaemenians were 'Zoroastrians' is therefore a matter of definition. If being Zoroastrian means to worship Ahura Mazda as God, then the Achaemenians were such; if it involves also giving a prominent place to Zoroaster as the preacher of Ahura Mazda, then the jury is still out. In any event, later Zoroastrian tradition has claimed the Achaemenians as its patrons, using their architectural forms and their symbols widely in modern India and modern Iran.

Iran and the Faith of Israel

In the nineteenth century, scholars were theorizing about the development of Judaism as well as of Iranian religion. From Israel's theological outlook prevailing in the Hebrew kingdoms prior to 586 BCE, several discernible shifts took place in succeeding centuries, when the Achaemenians were the day's rulers of the world, the liberators of Hebrew exiles in Babylon and governors of the province containing Judea. The notion of Satan as God's rival, the notion of life after death, and the notions of a sequence of world ages and a final judgement and redemption are teachings that can be argued to have been elaborated in Israel's faith only after Achaemenians became rulers of the eastern Mediterranean. Yet apart from isolated suggestive words such as 'paradise' from the Iranian *pairidaeza*, 'pleasure garden', few specific details of transmission reward the investigator, and the general concepts are susceptible to explanation as developments from other sources internal and external to Israel. The evidence remains almost as fragmentary, and as circumstantial, but still as suggestive, as it was a century ago.

Some biblical scholars have suggested that Zoroaster's questions about the creation of the universe in *Yasna* 44 are strikingly similar to the rhetorical questions of 'Second Isaiah', the anonymous author of *Isaiah* 40. For biblical scholars, the temptation is to take Iranian religion as historically fixed at the time of Cyrus's conquest of Babylon, and suppose that it then impacted like a bombshell on the development of the faith of Israel. There is reason to entertain the idea seriously, for subsequent chapters in *Isaiah* have specific expectations of Cyrus, chapter 45 even making him Yahweh's servant, his anointed ruler or messiah, and declaring to Cyrus that Yahweh makes light and darkness, controlling good and evil.

Other biblical scholars dismiss the similarities by arguing that the Hebrews already had the ideas on their own; indeed, some conservative Jews and Christians have assumed that any influence proved by parallels is an influence of Israel on Iran, the other way around. Reasoning from parallels to influences is a treacherous business even in the best of times, but it is particularly risky when the parallels are universal features of human experience. The contrast of light and dark, or of good and evil, and even the association of the one with the other in an age before electricity, is as universal as counting by tens and presumably equally grounded in the structure of all our lives. It does not have to have been invented only once and ever thereafter spread by diffusion.

But if we dismissed these antiborrowing objections and supposed the *Gathas* to be a source for Second Isaiah, then we would have added dramatically to the edifice of historical speculation. We have not found Zoroaster's name in Achaemenian times, but we would have found the next best thing: traces of the texts that presumably were his very own creations, and forming so integral a part of the Achaemenian promotional effort that they could stir hope in a subjugated exile community of Jews even before the Achaemenians arrived as conquerors in Babylon.

The Parthian Era

After about a century of Greek rule, Iran was home for four-and-a-half centuries to the Parthian Empire (246 BCE–226 CE). We possess surprisingly little primary historical material from these centuries: from Iran itself, mainly coins, relief sculptures, and the archaeology of buildings. From the Roman Empire in its heyday, there are the accounts of Roman contact with and perception of their principal eastern rivals, the Parthians.

The Parthians' early homeland was the northeastern Iranian uplands, to the east of the Caspian Sea. Beginning about 246 BCE their dynastic founder, Arsaces I, established a kingdom in competition with the Greek-speaking successors of Alexander, who for two generations had been controlling everything from the Mediterranean to the frontiers of India. In the middle of the following century the Arsacid dynastic successor Mithridates I (r. c. 171–138 BCE) turned the Parthian kingdom into an empire that extended its control westward through Iran to Mesopotamia. The Parthian sphere of influence thus approached the eastern Mediterranean in the same period that the Romans were getting involved in the region, and for several centuries Rome and Parthia were to square off as imperial rivals, neither able to subdue the other permanently.

In picturing Iranian religion, we have so far presumed that the Achaemenians inherited or developed a synthesis of Ahura Mazda worship with the worship of the Indo-Iranian *yazata*s. If that was in place by the time of the Alexandrian conquest, then the next frame in the sequence shows Ahura Mazda receding into the background during the Parthian centuries. The Parthians devote principal attention to a deity Zoroastrianism handles as one of the *yazata*s, namely Mithra.

Mithra in Parthian times figures distinctly more importantly than does

Figure 2.1
ZOROASTRIANISM: Major Spheres of Influence

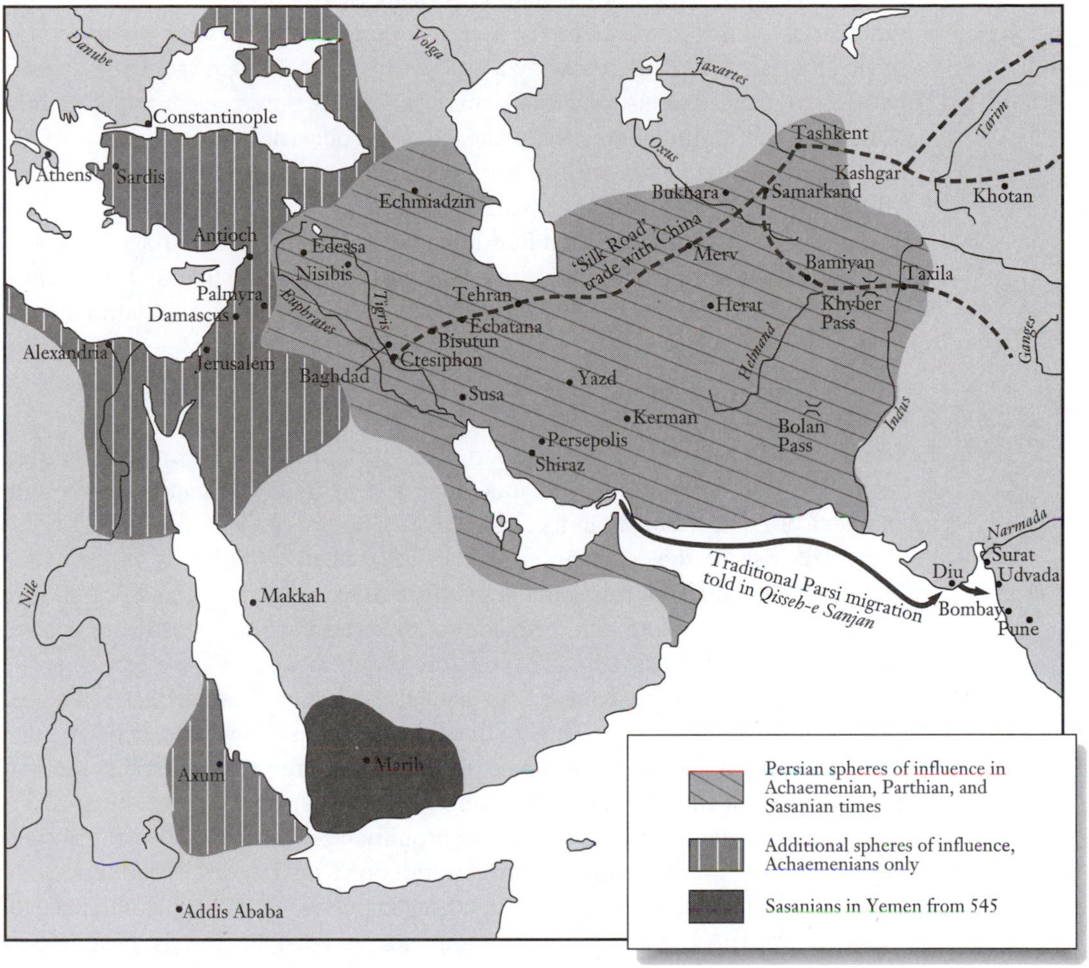

Ahura Mazda; Parthian kings' names included Mithridates, 'servant of Mithra'. Mithra is the chief figure, portrayed with the radiance of the sun, in sculptural reliefs such as the cliffside arch of Taq-e Bostan in Kermanshah, Iran. Mithra was not repudiated by later Zoroastrianism, and an important hymn to Mithra is among Zoroastrianism's ritual texts. So were the Parthians Zoroastrians? Though we hardly find them mentioning Zoroaster, the later tradition has been willing to consider them Zoroastrians.

Mithra had some influence outside Parthian territory, in the Roman empire. Mithra captured the imagination of Roman soldiers fighting the Parthians in the eastern Mediterranean. The figure of Mithra inspired an independent mystery cult. Roman Mithraism spread especially in the empire's port cities, trade routes, and the military garrisons of Britain and the northern Rhine–Danube frontier. It did not leave narrative textual traditions of its own, but we find in the Mithra sanctuaries of the Roman Empire a conventionalized representational portrait scene of a warriorlike figure slaying a bull, with shoots of grain springing up, and with astronomical or astrological symbolism. Some interpreters think Roman Mithraism was an initiation society like a lodge, concerned more with astronomical lore than with what we think of as religious salvation. Whatever Roman Mithraism was, it was hardly the worship of a *yazata* in Iranian form. Meanwhile, to the east of Parthia, Mahāyāna Buddhism was spreading from India to Central Asia and to China, and there are elusive suggestions that the figure of the *buddha* of a future age, Maitreya, might be related to Mithra, more than only in name.

The Sasanian Era

The Sasanian dynasty, third in the series of great pre-Islamic Iranian dynasties, ruled Iran from 226 until the Islamic conquest in 633–42. It marks the establishment of Zoroastrianism in its classic form.

The rise of the Sasanians began in 226 when Ardashir, a vassal of the Parthians who had been ruling in the province of Fars (Persia), seized power. Like the Achaemenians before him, he made southwestern Iran a dynastic home base. In many ways his dynasty sought to restore the traditions and the glories of the Achaemenians, their predecessors in Fars five centuries earlier. They claimed legitimacy as, in some sense, heirs of the Achaemenians. They used Achaemenian throne names; Ardashir, for instance, is the same name as Artaxerxes, sandpapered somewhat through language change over the centuries.

The Sasanians became a rich and prominent empire in the world of their day, controlling the trade routes between India or China and the Mediterranean. Central Asian Buddhist art, for instance, displays important influences of Sasanian forms and styles. Not least among these is a disk behind the head in portraits of Sasanian rulers, associating them with the radiant glory of the sun, which turns up as the halo in Buddhist as well as in Christian art. If we in the West have paid less attention than we should to the Sasanians, it is largely because Europe has been blocked from sympathetic access to them. Europe has identified with the Sasanians' ongoing imperial rivals, the Byzantine or eastern Roman Empire based in Constantinople.

The prophet Mani was born in 216 and was ten when the Sasanian dynasty came to power. He was apparently impressed by the new rulers, and was also profoundly convinced of an inclusive spiritual message. He had grown up in Christian Gnostic circles, and like the Gnostics saw Jesus as an emissary from the pure spiritual realm of Light whose message would redeem the souls of humans from bondage to matter in the mixed physical realm of Darkness. Mani promoted an ascetical discipline, giving spiritual privilege along with world-renouncing injunctions to the élite among his followers, consciously formed an organization, and had scriptures written and translated. He harmonized the teachings of Jesus with those of Zoroaster and the Buddha in a synthesizing amalgam. The dualism of Mani's religion, as contrasted with Zoroastrian teaching, is discussed in the concluding chapter of this volume.

The early Sasanian Empire was expanding rapidly. Shapur I (r. 240–71) took a Roman emperor, Valerian, captive in 259 (he died in captivity), and for a few years threatened to dislodge Rome from influence in the eastern Mediterranean until King Odenathus (r. 258–67) of Palmyra in Syria forced his retreat and chased him back all the way to Mesopotamia, besieging his capital, Ctesiphon, in 266. During the expansionist stage at around 245–50, when there were few limits to what might be thought possible, the Sasanians apparently experimented with Mani's new revelation as a candidate for a cross-cultural imperial ideology. Mani was a welcome figure at Shapur's court and wrote a treatise in praise of the king. But after the embarrassing defeat at the hands of the Palmyrenes, it appears, imperial ambitions had to be scaled down, and Mani eventually fell out of favour, to be replaced by an emphasis on indigenously Iranian rather than eclectic international religion.

Like the Byzantines, under whom Christianity became the state religion, the Sasanians established a state religion—a generation before Constantine. That established religion was Zoroastrianism, established partly through the efforts of a Zoroastrian high priest named Kartēr, who in his inscriptions brags about his achievements in promoting the religion under a succession of several Sasanian kings. By about 280, if we are to take Kartēr's word for things, rivals such as the Christians and the Manichaeans were curtailed, and the worship of Ahura Mazda became securely established in Sasanian Iran. Fire temples were expanded, and the Zoroastrian priesthood enjoyed patronage and privilege.

The Avestan scriptures were collected under the Sasanians. This activity may have taken time, but later literary traditions place it in the third century by mentioning a priest named Tansar as establishing the tradition through the recovery of the *Avesta*. Historians must sort out the sketchy details about Kartēr and Tansar and decide whether and how their institutional and textual efforts were related, but regarding the new status of Zoroastrianism as official, there is comparatively little dispute.

There was extensive activity, generating theological as well as secular literature, in Pahlavi, the Iranian language of the time. While the Avestan hymns were ritual invocations of divine figures, now their theological implications were spelled out in a growing Pahlavi literature: narratives of the creation and the expected final judgement, legal prescriptions, discussions of doctrine, and so on. Among the important texts is the *Bundahishn* (Original Creation), a narrative that structures the ages from creation through the present existence to the final judgement in four 3,000-year eras and rationalizes about the limitations of the evil spirit's power as a challenger of Ahura Mazda in the current era. Other important texts are the *Zand* or commentary on Avestan texts, the sagely advice contained in *Menok-e Khrat* (Heavenly Wisdom), and the *Shayast Ne-Shayast* (Do's and Don'ts), containing moral injunctions but also extensive purity regulations. The *Arda Viraf Namak* relates narcotic-induced visionary journeys of Viraf to the realms of the righteous and the wicked in the hereafter.

Zoroastrian religious authorities wrote in Pahlavi well into the ninth century, 200 years after the Islamic conquest, recording institutions now threatened by large-scale conversions to Islam. The *Denkart* (Acts of the Religion), an important encyclopedic collection, gathers together traditions of practice and interpretation. The priest Manushchihr gives opinions in his *Dadistan-e Dinik* (Religious Judgements). There was also material for a theological debate with the teachings of other religions. One of the ninth-century books is the *Shikand-Gumānīk-Vichār* (Decisive Resolution of Doubts), a work that combines a rationalizing defence of Zoroastrianism with a literalistic critique of the narrative details of Judaism's and Christianity's stories.

Zoroastrian usage preserved its identification with the Sasanian state in another way as well. Ancient dating in many places counted years from the enthronement of the currently reigning king. The last Sasanian king, Yazdegerd III, began his reign in 632, and while the decisive defeat by the Arabs ended his dynasty in 642 and Yazdegerd fled eastward, dying nine years later, the Zoroastrian religious calendar to this day still numbers the years from his accession in 632. In Western writing these dates are designated AY, from the Latin for 'year of Yazdegerd'.

In Zoroastrians' retrospect, the Sasanian era was a golden age because the religion was established and powerful. Like many ages that seem golden from a distance, the era had its share of controversy and conflict. A doctrinal controversy developed over a particular view about Zurvan (Time) whose advocates, since they did not prevail, were eventually viewed as heretics. The issue concerned how to view Ahura Mazda and Angra Mainyu as spirits in relation to each other, since it is desirable that Ahura Mazda have some advantage if there is to be hope for the world to turn out all right in the end and for a deity to be worth believing in. Yet the text of the *Gathas* in *Yasna* 30 refers to the two spirits as 'twins'. Therefore the Zurvanites speculated that they must have had a parent, and ascribed the paternity to a prior deity, to Zurvan or Time. Consequences of their position were a less distinct separation between good and evil, a demotion of Ahura Mazda to derivative status, and a fatalistic or deterministic compromising of the role of free choice; these tendencies may have led to Zurvanism's ultimate repudiation. The debate extended over a long period, and Sasanian royalty were apparently sympathetic to Zurvanism, but it was largely a theoretical and intellectual matter, rather than one affecting ritual or fragmenting the grass-roots public.

A crisis of a very different sort was the movement led by the social reformer

Mazdak. Restructuring was necessary during the time of his sovereign, Kavad (r. 488–531), since the Sasanians had been badly defeated by a people to the east, the Hephthalites, in 484. Mazdak had a dualistic teaching involving a hierarchy of powers and spirits and repudiating the material world as evil. It builds on Manichaean ideas, including Mani's asceticism. Like Mani two centuries earlier, the ruler gave him a hearing and imperial sponsorship. Mazdak's ideas were revolutionary; he wanted to abolish private property and the institution of the family, proposing that goods—and wives—be held in common. This was too much for the wealthy and for the priestly establishment, who backed Kavad's temporary overthrow by his brother Jamasp (r. c. 496–99). Kavad returned to power partly through Hephthalite support, but began to distance himself from the Mazdakites. He passed over his Mazdakite first son to favour as his successor his third son, Khosrow (r. 531–79), a staunch Zoroastrian, who instigated the murder of Mazdak and some of his followers at a banquet in 528. For clearing the way for a reinstitutionalization of Zoroastrianism, Khosrow is accorded the title Anoshirvan ('immortal soul') in Zoroastrian religious literature.

TEACHINGS AND OBSERVANCES

The Struggle with Evil

Zoroastrianism teaches a high standard of personal morality, incumbent on laity and priests alike. One's actions in this life form a basis for individual benefit or punishment in one's next existence, and the collective actions of human beings can help bring about the ultimate triumph of the forces of good against evil. Zoroastrians are in universal agreement that the essence of their religion is summed up in the motto: good thoughts, good words, and good deeds (*humata, hukhta, huvarshta*). Few traditions worldwide enjoy such unanimity, and few communities enjoy so much credit for a high moral standard.

In addition to the roster of the *yazatas* and Amesha Spentas, that is, the good spirits and entities, Zoroatrianism supposes corresponding evil spirits. From the creation through the present age to the final judgement and reordering of the universe, what goes on in the world is part of the overall contest between the powers of good and evil.

Zoroastrian attention to the role of an evil spirit, named Angra Mainyu in Avestan and shortened to Ahriman in Pahlavi, has led to characterization of the religion as dualistic. Indeed, the classical theology of the Sasanian and post-Sasanian era voiced dualistic doctrines. As narrated in the Pahlavi book *Bundahishn* (Original Creation), for the 12,000-year span of creation the lord Ahura Mazda is locked in conflict with his demonic adversary, Angra Mainyu. God enjoys a certain advantage over his foe from the beginning so that the ultimate victory of the good is ensured, but not without struggle. In modern times,

THE STRUGGLE WITH EVIL

[The Bundahishn, *a Pahlavi text, reflects the developed theology of the Sasanian era in its narrative of the conflict between Ahura Mazda (in Pahlavi, Ohrmazd) and the evil spirit Angra Mainyu (in Pahlavi, Ahriman).]*

Ohrmazd and the Space, Religion, and Time of Ohrmazd were and are and evermore shall be. Ahriman, slow in knowledge, whose will is to smite was deep down in the darkness: (he was) and is, yet will not be. The will to smite is his permanent disposition, and darkness is his place: some call it the Endless Darkness. Between them was the Void: some call it Vāy in which the two Spits mingle …

Ohrmazd, in his omniscience, knew that the Destructive Spirit existed, that he would attack and, since his will is envy … In ideal form he [Ohrmazd] fashioned forth such creation as was needful for his instrument. For three thousand years creation stayed in this ideal state, for it was without thought, without movement, without touch …

Because his [the Destructive Spirit's] will is to smite and his substance is envy, he made haste to destroy it. Seeing valour and supremacy superior to his own, he fled back to the darkness and fashioned many demons, a creation destructive and meet for battle. When Ohrmazd beheld the creation of the Destructive Spirit, it seemed not good to him,—a frightful, putrid, bad, and evil creation: and he revered it not … [the Destructive Spirit] uttered threats. And Ohrmazd said, "Thou canst not, O Destructive Spirit, accomplish all; for thou canst not destroy me, nor canst thou bring it about that my creation should not return to my possession."

Then Ohrmazd … knew that if he did not fix a time for battle against him, then Ahriman would do unto his creation even

when monotheism has been considered the highest form of religion by many in the English-speaking world, Zoroastrians have been emphatic in stressing the supreme lordship of Ahura Mazda and giving a monotheistic character to their faith.

The periodization in classical Zoroastrian theology moves from creation, whose hero is Gayamaretan (in Pahlavi, Gayomart), a kind of 'primal man', through the present age, whose spiritual guide is Zoroaster, and on to an expected renewal, when the saviour figure Saoshyant will reign. The final judgement will be a time of testing by fire, which Ahura Mazda controls, and the *Gathas* also allude to an ordeal where molten metal is poured onto people's bodies.

Purity and Pollution

Zoroastrian ethical teachings stress personal honesty and striving for harmony in

as he had threatened; and the struggle and the mixture would be everlasting; and Ahriman could settled in the mixed state of creation and take it to himself ... Ohrmazd said to the Destructive Spirit, "Fix a time so that by this pact we may extend the battle for nine thousand years." For he knew that by fixing a time in this wise the Destructive Spirit would be made powerless. Then the Destructive Spirit, not seeing the end, agreed to that treaty, just as two men who fight a duel fix a term (saying), "Let us on such a day do battle till night (falls)."

This too did Ohrmazd know in his omniscience, that within these nine thousand years three thousand would pass entirely according to the will of Ohrmazd, three thousand years in mixture would pass according to the will of both Ohrmazd and Ahriman, and that in the last battle the Destructive Spirit would be made powerless and that he himself would save creation from aggression.

Then Ohrmazd chanted the *Ahunavar*, that is he recited the twenty-one words of the *Yathā ahū vairyō*: and he showed to the Destructive Spirit his own final victory, the powerlessness of the Destructive Spirit, the destruction of the demons, the resurrection, the Final Body, and the freedom of creation from all aggression for ever and ever. When the Destructive Spirit beheld his own powerlessness and the destruction of the demons, he was laid low, swooned, and fell back into the darkness; even as it is said in the Religion, "When one third thereof is recited, the Destructive Spirit shudders for fear; when two thirds are recited, he falls on his knees; when the prayer is finished, he is powerless." Unable to do harm to the creatures of Ohrmazd, for three thousand years the Destructive Spirit lay crushed. While Ahriman lay crushed Ohrmazd created his creation (*Bundahishn* 1:1–15; Zaehner 1956:35–8).

society. Morally neutral in itself, the material world is the arena of right and wrong choices; in this Zoroastrianism contrasts sharply with the Gnostic- or Manichaean-type dualism that sees the world as estrangement from pure spirit and therefore to be rejected and overcome. Rather, the world is to be enjoyed, so asceticism finds little place in Zoroastrian tradition.

Zoroastrianism views the physical universe as God's good creation, attributing unpleasant aspects of it such as cold or drought to demonic counter-influences with a seemingly pre-ethical mythology. Since there is the danger of physical pollution within the world, elaborate steps are taken in Zoroastrian ritual and practice to maintain purity. The prime sources of pollution are dead or putrefying animal matter, including materials cast off from the human body. Elaborate ritual procedures, such as the premodern isolation of menstruating women in separate rooms, and the exposure of corpses to be consumed by vultures, serve to contain decay or to purify the individual.

The Amesha Spentas

Whatever the status of Ahura Mazda in Parthian times, during and since the Sasanian era he has reigned supreme. We have already seen how the *yazata*s, the 'worshipful beings' of the Indo-Iranian pantheon, became integrated under his supervision in the *Avesta*. In Zoroastrian theological thinking, possibly in Sasanian times, a second category of divine entities was elaborated, again functioning as assistants or subordinates of Ahura Mazda. These were the seven Amesha Spentas or 'holy immortals'. Whereas the *yazata*s incorporate narrative mythology and sacrificial ritual into the Zoroastrian system, the Amesha Spentas pursue a more abstract theological and ethical reflection.

The Amesha Spentas are personified qualities: Good Mind, Order, Dominion, Devotion, Wholeness, Immortality, and the Holy Spirit. They can be considered logically derivable from the moral and spiritual character of Ahura Mazda. They could relate theology to devotion when various religious traditions previously presented as narratives of myth were being fashioned anew as metaphysical systems. Christianity during the Sasanian era was working out a doctrine of the three persons of the Trinity and then the relationship of the divine and human natures in Christ. In the case of the Christian Trinity, the list of Father, Son, and Holy Spirit was not a recurring formula within the New Testament but rather a construct that was new in the 260s. Similarly with the Amesha Spentas: nowhere in Zoroaster's *Gatha*s does there appear a structured list of the seven. Instead, the Amesha Spentas are the work of exegetical theology, an attempt to gather attributes mentioned in passing in the *Gatha*s and to draw up a personified theological cast of characters.

The vocabulary of the Amesha Spentas is sprinkled through the *Gatha*s, not organized as a list. Since the Avestan script does not have capital letters, we cannot be fully sure whether the terms are qualities or names, but modern translators of the *Gatha*s into Western languages have quite confidently read the personification back into the text by capitalizing the translation equivalents wherever they appear. Curiously, one figure appearing as a personality within the text of the *Gatha*s, namely Sraosha ('obedience'), the lord who hears prayer and is a kind of angelic mediator for the devotee, does not become listed as one of the seven Amesha Spentas.

Why seven? There may be astrological reasons, such as the seven stars in the constellation of the Pleiades (Zoroastrianism does not really emphasize a seven-day week). Scholars have suggested an astronomical impetus for a Christian enumeration of seven deadly sins as well. In any case, the idea of seven carries over to the present, in a popular Iranian custom at Nowrūz, the spring-equinox new year. Iranians, most of whom are Muslim, set out in their homes dishes or small quantities of seven items whose Farsi names all begin with the letter *s*: sugar, an apple, honey, and so on. These seven, folklorists think, are a survival of devotion to the seven Amesha Spentas.

Prayer

The principal Zoroastrian prayer formulas are very old. They are in Avestan, and are repeated at various points throughout the *Avesta*. Their repetition reminds us that to make sense of the form and content of the text, we must appreciate the requirements of liturgical use. The amalgamating tendency of the tradition is particularly evident in a prayer recurring in litanies. Known by its first words in Avestan, it is called the *Yenhe Hatam*: 'Those beings, male and female, whom Lord Mazda knows the best for worship according to truth, we worship them all.'

There is evidence within the ancient texts that an incantationlike quality was attributed to prayers, for they report Ahura Mazda combatting evil spirits by reciting prayer formulas. The prayers are still repeated by rote by Zoroastrians, in Avestan, which is nobody's vernacular today. Though ritual in their function, they contain a strong ethical content. A key prayer, drawn from the *Gatha*s of Zoroaster, is named by its first words, *Yatha ahu vairyo*: 'As the Master is chosen, so is the Judge chosen in accord with truth. Establish the power of acts arising from a life lived with good purpose, for Mazda and for the lord [presumably Zoroaster] whom they made pastor for the poor.' Another prayer, which opens and closes many devotions, concentrates on Asha ('righteousness'). It is known by its first two words in Avestan, *Ashem vohu*: 'Righteousness is good, it is best. It is to be wished, for us it shall be wished. Righteousness belongs to Asha Vahishta [Best Righteousness].'

The standard benediction for many Zoroastrian ceremonies is a prayer for health, long life, and good fortune, called the *Tan Dorosti* ('Healthy Body'), which is not in the old Avestan but in the language of the Pahlavi stage. It reflects Sasanian religion in that it invokes divine benefit from two groups in the same breath: the *yazata*s and the Amesha Spentas. Zoroastrians also use the words *tan dorosti* as a conversational goodbye, like the expression 'be well', which is also what the medieval English *wassail* literally means.

The Role of Priests

Zoroastrian ceremonial obligations are carried out mainly by the priests, who more so than the laity are custodians of the ritual heritage. The priest says prayers on behalf of an individual whether or not the individual is present at the temple. A Zoroastrian fire temple is thus not characteristically a place for congregational worship at stated times but more like a shrine that the individual layperson may approach at any time.

Only males may be priests. Eligibility for priesthood is hereditary; priests marry, raise families, and pass on temple concessions to their heirs. To become a priest, a boy between seven and fifteen learns the Avestan prayers and services, generally by rote; he may also be instructed in their meaning, but the education can hardly be termed theological. There are three grades of priests, depending on apprenticeship and training: in ascending order, *mobed*, *ervad*, and *dastur*. Practising priests wear only white, symbolic of purity. (At feasts and other traditional functions, laymen wear black turbans and priests white.) Priests among the Parsis of India are not usually salaried but receive fees piecemeal from people for saying particular prayers on their behalf and for their relatives. Priests who have secular employment can serve part-time; demand for their services peaks at the year-end *muktad* ('departed souls') days in late August, when prayers are said for the dead.

Zoroastrian prayers are almost all in Avestan, which even in Sasanian times was an archaic language. They are therefore not understood by the average layperson, and even most Zoroastrian priests learn them by rote. This lack of comprehension is not so much a problem as one might think, however, for two reasons. First, many Zoroastrians assert that the prayers are effective acoustically when the priest has pronounced them. Correctly voiced, the prayers function as *manthra*, i.e., as chant formulas; both this term and the concept it names match Hindu understandings of the force of the Vedic prayers. Second, the priest's work is as an intermediary on behalf of the people. In this role it is considered more important that the priest be in the fire temple performing the proper rituals than that he be elsewhere, such as giving classes, delivering homilies, or engaging in bedside counselling.

Fire

The central symbol of divine presence is fire. It is no accident that Zoroastrians have been called 'fire worshippers' by their detractors. The typical Zoroastrian sanctuary is the fire temple, termed by the Parsis an *agiari*, 'fire place'. Within is a square chamber enclosed by grillwork and with vents in the roof that permit smoke to escape. On a stone platform in the chamber is a large metal urn. On a bed of sand or ash in the urn, the sacred fire burns continuously. It is maintained by the priest, who adds wood and says appropriate prayers in each of five *gahs* or periods during the day. We may consider the presence of texts for five *gahs* in the Sasanian *Avesta* evidence of a prototype for Islam's institution of that number of daily prayer times.

Congregational worship is not a regular feature of Zoroastrian ritual; rather, the individual layperson wishing prayers to be said on his or her own behalf, or for others, may at any time bring to the entrance of the inner enclosure an offering, especially of costly and sweet-smelling sandalwood, which the officiating priest adds to the fire. All continuously maintained Zoroastrian fires are in India, Pakistan, and Iran. Overseas Zoroastrian communities have generally not been able to afford to maintain fires around the clock. They can maintain a small oil-lamp or wood fire continuously in the home; such a fire is of the simplest grade, called *atesh dadgah*, 'fire of the appointed place [for ceremonies for the dead]'.

Priests can perform rituals to 'purify' fires. They do this by saying prayers as they hold a metal ladle of wood chips above a fire but not touching it, until the contents reach kindling temperature and burst into flame. Purifications produce Zoroastrian fires of two grades of sanctity higher than the *atesh dadgah*. The middle grade or *atesh adaran*, 'fire of fires', brings together from various sources four ceremonially ignited fires. The highest grade is the *atesh Behram*, 'fire of [the guardian] Varahran'. It requires combining fires from sixteen different sources, including various artisans' workshops, a (presumably non-Zoroastrian) funeral pyre, and, hardest to collect, a fire set by lightning. For the consecration, the entire *Yasna* and *Vendidad*, which require half a day each, must be recited by a pair of priests 1,128 times. That requires more than three years, unless multiple crews of priests divide the task and pray simultaneously. One can understand why there have not been new *atesh Behram* consecrations in recent decades.

The Zoroastrians of Iran have one *atesh Behram*, in the city of Yazd. The Parsis of India have eight such fires, four in Gujarat and four in Bombay. Of these, the fire in Udvada, on the Gujarat coast north of Bombay, is the most highly revered; it is said to have been kept burning continuously for over a thousand years. Zoroastrians in India make the fire in Udvada a goal of pilgrimage, and some perform a pilgrimage circuit of all eight of the Indian fires.

In India, access to the fire temples is restricted to members of the Zoroastrian ethnic community, the Parsis. Like other practices not shared with the Zoroastrians of Iran, this exclusion of outsiders appears as a development following Zoroastrian migration to India. It fits in with the boundaried, castelike nature of the Parsi community, which may have feared being engulfed by the vastly larger society that we call Hindu. However, religious rationales are offered, such as that foreigners might 'pollute' the fire.

Temporary fires can be kindled for thanksgiving services called *jashans* as well as for domestic worship outside the temple. The *jashan* ceremony requires at least a pair of priests, but may be performed anywhere. Besides the occasions of *gahambar* feasts, discussed later, a *jashan* may mark a special anniversary or such family matters as the move to a new home. In small communities and overseas, where a round-the-clock fire at an *agiari* would be prohibitive, the *jashan* is the principal community ritual. Seated cross-legged on a sheet with various flower and fruit offerings, the priests kindle a fire in a small metal urn and recite prayers for more than an hour. At the conclusion of the recitation, the congregation can file by, each person placing a pinch of sweet-smelling resin on the fire in a kind of participatory communion; then some nuts and raisins or other sweets are distributed.

The Zoroastrian Calendar

The Zoroastrian religious year follows an ancient solar calendar of twelve months of thirty days each, plus five remaining days that do not form part of any month as such but are a time of special ritual. They are called Gatha Days, being five in number. Parsis refer to them as *muktad* (Gujarati, 'released spirits') days, as they are a time of prayers for deceased ancestors.

There is a recurring pattern of devotion on a monthly cycle. Within each month, each day is named for a divinity or a divine manifestation. At least since Parthian and Sasanian times, the names of the months have been drawn from the same list. Consequently, about once a month the day and month names coincide, giving an occasion for special reverence. The ninth day of the month, sacred to fire, is favoured in any month for visits to the fire temple, but especially so in the ninth month, the month sacred to fire. The tenth day (water) of the eighth month (water) is a time when Zoroastrians stand at the edge of a body of water to offer individual prayers. Four days each month are dedicated to Ahura Mazda and to his creative manifestations, but they only roughly approximate weekly intervals; the outsider expecting a strict seven-day week in Zoroastrianism will look in vain for it.

The year-end *muktad* period, plus five other times of ritual observance through the year, are known in Pahlavi as *gahambars*, when Zoroastrians gather to pray and to feast. Related to the agricultural seasons in their origin, the *gahambars* were given a theological structure through association with the Amesha Spentas, the personified manifestations of divine qualities.

Because of discrepancies in separated communities over the past thousand years and the failure to adjust for leap years, there are now three Zoroastrian calendars and three New Year seasons: two in late summer and one, reflecting a return to the festival's Iranian origins, at the spring equinox. The typical overseas Zoroastrian community today bridges the discrepancy by having both a late August and a March equinox function.

Initiation and Marriage

Initiation, marriage, and death are the three principal stages of life marked by Zoroastrian rituals. The initiation, called *navjote* ('new birth'), is normally administered to a child aged seven, nine, or eleven. Following prayers in the fire temple, and the child's tasting a sip of bull's urine (which Zoroastrians hold to have purificatory properties), the priest invests the child with two items of clothing to be worn throughout life. One is the *kusti*, a tubular cord woven of wool, much like a pajama belt but about 3.5 m (11.5 ft) long. This is tied three times round the waist. It serves as a reminder for devotion as a Zoroastrian unties and reties the knots at the five times of prayer during the day, as well as when dressing or bathing. The other item is the *sudreh*, a loose-fitting undershirt with a very small pocket at the point of the V-neck. The initiate is told that the pocket is to be filled with one's good deeds. These two items mark observant Zoroastrians, especially in India, but there are concessions to life in a largely non-Zoroastrian society. For instance, a woman wearing a *sāri* might choose a mini-length *sudreh* not covering the waist. And in Iran, *kustis* are so frequently not worn under one's street clothing that at the entrance to a Zoroastrian temple or shrine, one finds a supply of *kustis* available on loan for use on the premises during prayer.

Zoroastrian marriage ceremonies in India are often performed in the courtyard adjoining a fire temple, where the guests assemble in the open air at sunset. During the ceremony, the couple is seated on a dais, while one or two priests recite the Avestan prayers, passing round and round the couple with a long roll of string and quite literally binding the couple together. The assembled guests, with little comprehension of the Avestan, carry on private conversations during the ceremony. Following the ritual, the Indian Parsis typically serve a banquet at long tables. Normally a modernizing and Westernizing people in India, Parsis revert to tradition in these banquets. The food is ladled out onto flat banana leaves, the rice and various curries (there should be meat, fish, and chicken courses) eaten with the fingers of the right hand. (In India, the left hand is reserved for personal hygiene.)

The Destiny of the Individual

Every mortal should choose the right, both so that one may individually achieve the reward of the righteous beyond death and so that good (*asha*) may triumph over the Lie (*drug* or *druj*) in the world. Each individual has a *fravashi* or angelic guardian spirit, as well as the *urvan* or soul that is lodged in the body during life. Upon death, the soul can be aided on its passage to the next existence. To pray for the soul, the family of the deceased conduct a three-day vigil after death. At the end of this period the soul is to make its way to a realm of reward or punishment depending on the record of its acts on earth. Zoroastrian literature has the motif of the Chinvat Bridge ('the Bridge of the Separator'), which widens when the righteous approach but narrows like a knife edge for the wicked so that they fall from it into the abyss of torment. In one Pahlavi narrative, the matter is personified graphically, if from a male bias. The soul of the righteous man encounters a beautiful maiden, asking, 'Who are you, fair maiden, fairer than any I ever saw during my life on earth?' She responds, 'I, O righteous man, am your good deeds, come to comfort you in this next life.' Meanwhile, the soul of the wicked man encounters another female creature, and asks 'Who are you, vile hag, uglier than whom I never met in my life on earth?'

The body left behind is subject to physical decay. Funeral practices involve ceremonially washing the corpse and putting the *sudreh* and *kusti* and a white sheet on it, before relatives and friends file by for last respects. In older centres in India, the corpse is then consigned to the open-air cylindrical 'tower of silence', the *dakhma*, for disposal.

For centuries, Zoroastrians in both Iran and India have exposed the bodies of the dead in round walled structures open to the air. The *dakhmas* permit vultures or other birds to make a meal of the flesh of the deceased, after which the sun-bleached bones can be shoved into a pit or well at the centre of the structure. When the pit is eventually filled, a new *dakhma* is constructed. Zoroastrians have justified their custom on the ground that it avoids polluting earth, air, fire, or water with decaying flesh, as would burial or cremation or throwing bodies or ashes into rivers. Advocates of the practice have also pointed out its egalitarianism; rich and poor are alike in death, placed in the tower without fanfare or possessions and covered only with a sheet that the corpse-bearers remove once inside. However, the families of the rich can still afford to have more prayers said for the departed.

In recent decades there has been increasing criticism of disposal by exposure. Modernizers have termed it no longer practical, claiming that the vulture population in crowded urban areas is no longer sufficient. They have also argued that it is misunderstood or found offensive by other communities or that it provokes a disrespectful curiosity. In Iran, exposure of the dead was dropped in 1971 in favour of burial, with the argument that *dakhma* use invited dangerous low-level overflights by pilots. There is debate as to how far back the practice of exposure can be traced, since in Achaemenian times, at least the kings were buried in above-ground or cliffside tombs. But 'sky burial' practised in Tibet—where the corpse is cut up and fed to the birds—suggests a long-standing reliance on exposure in inner Asia, particularly in regions of stony or seasonally frozen ground. In any case, for more than a century now, almost all new Zoroastrian communities established by migration outside of the premodern heartland of Iran and western India have used cemeteries rather than *dakhmas*.

Ceremonial Art and Architecture

We often use the term 'symbolism' to describe a religious tradition's associations of graphic forms that in some way stand for a religious figure or conception without explicitly depicting it. By the term 'iconography' we mean the conventional, often coded, details associated with direct pictorial representations of a tradition's figures.

Among Zoroastrianism's symbols, fire represents the divine presence, and a fire burning atop a waist-high urn or square altar is a frequent decorative device.

It appears particularly as an ornament on the roofs of fire temples, often with the flames sculpted in stone and gilded.

Another symbol, taken to represent Ahura Mazda, is the *farohar*, a disk with wings, a tail, a pair of antennae, and a male figure shown from the waist up in profile above it. The figure is bearded, wears a loose-sleeved robe, and holds a ring in his left hand. His beard and headgear are Achaemenian in style, which is no surprise because the *farohar* has been around for two and a half millennia. It appears, for instance, in relief accompanying the emperor Darius's inscription on the cliff face at Bisutun, near Kermanshah, Iran.

We have no ancient portraits of Zoroaster, but in recent centuries Parsis and Iranian Zartoshtis have developed an iconographic tradition depicting him. He has long, wavy hair cascading from under a small white turban. He has a full beard and is dressed entirely in white. He wears loose trousers beneath a loose knee-length robe, gathered by a sash at the waist. Over this robe he has a cape, and a scalloped hood with a small square tab in front covers his chest. There are the sun's rays or a halo behind his head, and he carries a staff in his right hand. The impetus for many of these details seems to have been the attire in Parthian representations of Mithra such as the Taq-e Bostan relief at Kermanshah.

The architectural essentials of an *agiari* or fire temple are few. Very simple premodern ones survive in rural villages in Gujarat, where they were rectangular one-roomed structures with tile roofs, with a vent at the apex of the roof for the smoke to escape. In a larger temple, there is an entrance vestibule, and within the main hall the urn that contains the fire is in an enclosure of metal grillwork the size of a small room. This enclosure is at the end of the building farthest from the entrance, and a gable in the roof for the smoke vents is located above it.

In the second half of the nineteenth century, growing Parsi prosperity in India coincided with the invention of photography and the circulation of photographs of the spectacular Achaemenian ruins at Persepolis. As a result, most *agiari*-building and renovation for the past hundred years has imitated Persepolis in decorative detail, particularly imitating the forms of its columns. Flanking the entrance, a favoured device is a pair of Persepolis-style sphinxlike, human-headed, winged bulls, a form the Achaemenians had acquired from the guardian motifs of earlier Mesopotamian art.

Zoroastrianism Since Antiquity

The Islamic Context in Iran

With the coming of Islam and the conversion of most Iranians to it, Zoroastrianism was reduced to minority status. Muslims handled the Zoroastrians theologically, like the Christians and Jews of Arabia, as pre-existing scriptural monotheists, 'People of the Book'. In effect, for all practical purposes, Ahura Mazda was equated with the God of Abraham and the *Avesta* was sufficiently scriptural to be placed in a category with the Torah and the Gospel, both of which are mentioned favourably in the *Qur'ān*. Moreover, Zoroaster came to be handled as a prophet. Since these developments were not inevitable, Zoroastrianism could have been proscribed.

Formal acceptance was one thing, but day-to-day coexistence was another. The Zoroastrians were mocked as fire worshippers and called by the derogatory term *gabars*, 'polytheists'. Persecution was at times severe. The Zoroastrians who remained in Iran retreated to remote villages in the region of Yazd and Kerman in south-central Iran. We glimpse the difficult situation facing the Iranian community in incidental remarks in the *revāyet* literature, an exchange of correspondence principally in Farsi on ritual matters from the late fifteenth to the mid-eighteenth century, when Zoroastrians in India sought rulings and opinions from the community in Iran. The Zoroastrians' lot began to improve only in the nineteenth century, when Manekji Limji Hataria, a Parsi from India, reported on conditions among his Iranian coreligionists and campaigned to improve them, organizing modern schools and achieving the repeal of the Islamic *jizyah* or poll tax on non-Muslims in 1882. Zoroastrians began to participate in the modern development of the country, and during the twentieth century many moved to the capital, Tehran.

Alongside the social history affecting Iran's Zartoshtis, there is the cultural history of Islamic Iran. Iran was the first land to which Islam spread where Arabic did not displace the local language as the vernacular. Through fourteen centuries, Iranians, while Muslim in religion, thought of themselves as Persian in culture. The glories of the Achaemenian and other ancient empires were dear to the hearts of many. Indeed, tradition preserved the legends of heroes in several dynasties prior to the Achaemenians. The greatest Persian poet, Abū al-Qāsem Manṣūr (c. 935–c. 1020), who took the pen name Ferdowsī, assembled these stories into a national epic, the *Shāh Nāmeh* (Book of Kings), completed in 1010. It was a *tour de force* partly because it proudly used the older vocabulary of Persian, avoiding the Arabic loan-words that were already flooding into Farsi. Iranians' attitude of cultural pride in their pre-Islamic past has resembled European pride in the Greek and Roman heritage; just as children in the West have been given names from Greek legend like Jason, children in Iran have been named for Iran's legendary heroes like Rostam.

Reza Shah (r. 1925–41) and Mohammad Reza Shah Pahlavi (r. 1941–79) ruled Iran through half the twentieth century with an ideology that was more culturally nationalist than Islamic. In 1971, the Shah celebrated the 2,500th anniversary of the founding of the Persian Empire by Cyrus, holding a huge gathering of international dignitaries with elaborate pageantry in a tent city set up at Persepolis. During the Shah's era, Iran's Zoroastrians witnessed an elevation of the

Permanent shelters at the shrine of Pīr-e Sabz, in mountains northwest of Yazd, Iran, accommodate Zoroastrians taking part in the annual pilgrimage to the site. (Willard G. Oxtoby)

cultural status of their ancient faith, and some even hoped for large numbers to reconvert to it. On a visit to Bombay, the Shah spoke to a gathering of Indian Zoroastrians and reportedly urged them to 'come home' and migrate to Iran. The fall of the Shah in an Islamic revolution in 1979 marked an end to this era. Some Zoroastrians, particularly any with clear ties to the Shah's establishment, emigrated to the West. In the Islamic republic, Zoroastrians did not initially suffer the same difficulties as Bahā'īs, for Zoroastrians' theological status in a Muslim view is as predecessors of Islam. This point was clear to the generation of Muslim leaders that came to political power in 1979, for they previously rose through the ranks of religio-legal scholarship. Under future generations, the situation could change.

The Parsi Experience in India

Some time after the Islamic conquest of Iran, Zoroastrians migrated to western India, settling in Gujarat, the coastal region north of Bombay today. There they became known as Parsis ('Persians') because of the land of their origin. As a minority in a caste-structured Hindu society, they maintained a separate identity over the centuries, generally marrying within their own group. As a closed ethnic group, they came to understand the Zoroastrian faith as something one was born and raised in, not one to which one converted.

Zoroastrian settlements in Gujarat are documented by inscriptions and travellers' accounts as early as the tenth and eleventh centuries. Historically, Iranians had contact with India over many centuries. King Darius, the Achaemenian, extended his empire to Sind, that is, to the plain of the Indus River or present-day Pakistan in the sixth century BCE. Inscriptions in Pahlavi have been found in South Indian Christian contexts and imply religious contact between Iran and India in the early Christian centuries. During the same era there were extensive trading contacts as well.

Some Zoroastrians were apparently located outside Gujarat. Muslim travellers in the tenth century mention various parts of India as inhabited by *gabar*s. Enough of these locations are in inland North India to suggest an overland migration pattern. Persians also went to China; the last Sasanian king, Yazdegerd III, appealed to the Chinese emperor for help after his losses to the Arabs in the sixth century, and *muhapas* (from Persian *mobed*, 'priest') are mentioned in southern China in the mid-ninth. However, all the migrations to areas other than Gujarat left no discernible Zoroastrian survival into modern times, and the Gujarat Parsi literary tradition ignores them.

In the literary narrative, there is only one migration, by sea rather than overland. It is told in the *Qisseh-e Sanjan* (Story of Sanjan), in 400 lines of Farsi verse composed in 1600 by a priest, Bahman son of Kaikobad. The *Qisseh* gives time spans in round numbers and acknowledges its indebtedness to oral tradition. It likely simplifies what was a more gradual and complex migration when it has Zoroastrians fleeing Muslim persecution in Iran spend '100 years in the mountain region' and then, on the advice of an astrologer, sail in one convoy together from the Persian Gulf to India.

Upon landing, the Parsis in the *Qisseh* proceed to the court of a local ruler, Jadi Rana, and ask him for shelter in his city and kingdom. The king, sensing them to be an alien group, specifies five conditions for his welcome: that they explain their religion, that they switch from Persian to the local vernacular, that they adopt local dress, that they go unarmed, and that they perform marriage ceremonies in the evening rather than by day. The local sovereign has accepted the Parsis as a distinct and tolerated minority.

Parsis accord the account in the *Qisseh* the status of a constitutional charter, the precedent setting the terms and conditions of their identity in India. Parsis cite a story very similar to what one finds in the biographies of Indo-Muslim saints in the Mughal era: that the king offered the new arrivals a pitcher of milk, brim full (signifying that his realm was already crowded), and that the Parsi priest responded by slipping something valuable into the milk—a pinch of sugar, his ring, or a coin, depending on the version (signifying that the Parsis would fit in and would enhance it). Many believe the *Qisseh* to contain the pitcher-of-milk account, though it does not. Nor does it mention a promise not to proselytize as one of the undertakings given to Jadi Rana. Parsis associate with the *Qisseh* features of their situation in India that are not literally in the text but are compatible with its spirit.

Parsis share many features of religion and custom with their Hindu neighbours. Some of these are shared because they go back more than three millennia to a common Indo-Iranian heritage; the role of priests, the notion of acoustic efficacy for the words of prayers, and the wearing of a cord on the body after one's ritual initiation are examples. If a shared feature goes back to Indo-Iranian antiquity, we should expect it to be present among Iranian Zoroastrians as well. Other Parsi-Hindu resemblances, which Iran's Zoroastrians do not share, have to be attributed to more recent centuries of Parsi life in India: women's wearing of *sāris*, for example, the household garlanding of pictures of Zoroaster with strings of marigolds, the stencilling of white powder designs at doorways after morning sweeping, and of course the definition of the community itself as a hereditary one.

Parsis became spectacularly successful in Bombay. The scrupulous honesty mandated by their religion was a factor in their success, as they were highly trusted by the ruling British for managerial and administrative responsibilities. Another factor was their involvement in industrial and manufacturing ventures where brahmin Hindus felt inhibited by traditional caste and purity regulations. By the beginning of the twentieth century, Parsis formed Bombay's dominant element in trade and industry. Half the Bombay city council were Parsis. Parsis were leaders in philanthropy and in education, pioneering in education for women, which liberated many to pursue successful careers in business, the professions, and the arts. The Parsis' position of influence before and after the First World War stands in retrospect as a kind of golden age for their community and its institutions.

Although Bombay is in Maharashtra, where Marathi is the vernacular, Parsis kept Gujarati as their household dialect. One expects to find in an older household a printed copy of the *Khorda Avesta*, the Zoroastrian prayer-book, not translated but transliterated into the Gujarati script. A treasured book among families with some education was the Gujarati translation of Ferdowsī's Farsi *Shāh Nāmeh*. Increasingly, however, Parsis were educated in English and used Gujarati only as a spoken language. Newer homes have copies of the *Khorda Avesta* transliterated into the Latin alphabet.

Through their links with the British, the Parsis were a westernizing and modernizing element in Indian society and politics. Dadabhai Naoroji (1825–1917) went to London, where he became a member of the British Parliament. Ties with Britain were close; more than sixty Parsis were knighted by the British, mostly in the early decades of the twentieth century, their numbers exceeding the recognition for any other group in India. Parsis were also active in Indian politics; Pherozeshah Mehta (1845–1915) was a cofounder of the Indian National Congress, and another important political figure was the financier Dinsha Wacha (1844–1936). These leaders saw their national identity as Indians more fundamental than their communal identity as Parsis. To the extent that the leadership of Mohandas K. Gandhi (1869–1948) after the 1920s appealed to specifically Hindu values, and with national independence (1947) bringing a policy of secularization that forced formerly Parsi firms to hire non-Parsis, the patriotic spirit of Parsis has been put to the test. On the whole, the end of British colonial rule in India affected the Parsis adversely.

While fire temples have their own endowments and boards of trustees, most other Parsi institutions are usually managed on a citywide basis by the *anjuman*, or community organization. In Bombay, Pune, and Surat, the *anjuman* council is known as the *punchayet*. A community's properties include the 'towers of silence'. These continue in use in Parsi settlements in western India that were founded before the late nineteenth century, though settlements elsewhere in India established burial grounds. *Anjuman* holdings also include subsidized housing blocks for Parsis and welfare endowments for the community's poor. Individual *agiaris* or fire temples often have their separate endowments and boards of trustees.

Among the concerns of India's Parsis in recent years has been the condition of the priesthood. The principal priest of a parish, called a *panthaki*, is in effect the proprietor and may hire other priests at a bare subsistence wage to assist him. Not surprisingly, other lines of work tend to attract the best minds in the community.

Throughout the twentieth century, Parsi population has been declining, for some decades at a rate of 1 per cent per annum. Reasons for this include late marriage and small family size. These choices are attributed partly to living in urban centres where housing is scarce and cramped, but crowding alone has not deterred population growth among other groups. It has to be considered in combination with the Parsis' relatively high socio-economic and educational levels and the expectations these produce. Emigration to other parts of the English-speaking world has also been a factor in the decline of Parsi numbers.

A most important factor also is intermarriage with other communities, formerly avoided as unmentionable, but more recently much discussed as inevitable. The marriage of a Parsi woman to a non-Parsi implies her departure from the community. In India, one is a Parsi by birth, the identity being derived through the male line. The community does not accept converts; a Parsi male who marries outside the community or who has children out of wedlock, however, may raise his children as Parsis.

The question of Parsi identity was hotly debated during the twentieth century. Priests who were willing to perform initiation ceremonies for adopted children and children of mixed marriages were subjected to censure by governing boards of the community's institutions in Navsari and Bombay. The pattern for twentieth-century India was decided by the civil courts in a 1909 case seeking the exclusion of a non-Parsi wife from fire temples and community institutions. In that decision, and again in 1925, the courts upheld the community's restriction of its properties to the children of Parsis and Irani Zoroastrians, plus duly initiated children of Parsi fathers by alien wives.

Migration Overseas

In their contacts with the British, Parsis followed commercial and cultural opportunities outside India, throughout and beyond the British Empire. During the nineteenth century, Parsi traders followed the sea routes of the Empire around the Indian Ocean and Southeast Asia. They settled to do business in such ports as Cape Town, Durban, Mombasa, Aden, Karachi, Colombo, Rangoon, Singapore, Hong Kong, Shanghai, and Kobe. They were involved especially in import-export trade, marine outfitting, banking, and the professions. In many cases they maintained close ties to India, regarding their residence elsewhere as temporary and returning to India to visit their families, to perform the initiation ceremonies of their children, and to find marriage partners for them. They also went to Britain, to trade, to study, and to settle.

In the middle of the twentieth century, Parsi migration took on different characteristics. On the one hand, migration and overseas communication became much easier, with the introduction of air travel and electronic communication. On the other hand, it also became less temporary. One no longer lived in an East African port and thought of home as Bombay; one settled now in an Australian or North American city that one considered one's new home. The late twentieth-century migration was much more a migration of entire households to take up a new citizenship and identity.

In the Zoroastrian diaspora, communities reached sufficient size by the 1960s and 1970s that they could form *anjumans* in such cities as Toronto, New York, Los Angeles, and Sydney. The Toronto community reckoned its numbers at 300 in the early 1970s and had grown to over 3,000 in the early 1990s despite fluctuations in employment opportunity. Similar growth can be charted for Los Angeles. These and other *anjumans* acquired property and built or renovated buildings that combined the facilities for fire rituals with the social and assembly space that are considered requisite for maintaining group identity in the North American pattern. But establishing continuous temple fires was not practical and not a high priority; diaspora worship has consisted largely of family prayers and *jashan* (thanksgiving) ceremonies employing a fire kindled *ad hoc*.

The years after 1979 brought a change of complexion to the overseas

Zoroastrian community. What had been a largely Parsi diaspora, proud of its Iranian history but largely ignorant of the Iranian Zoroastrians' ways, now began to receive a new wave of immigration: Zartoshti emigrants from Iran in the wake of the Shah's demise. In each overseas centre in the English-speaking world the question was the same: how to incorporate a growing number of Iranian Zartoshtis into what had been primarily a Parsi *anjuman*. The newcomers were more at home in Farsi than in English; at banquet times they had no particular attachment to Parsi foods such as *dhansak*, the characteristic lentil curry; and they might understand or perform the rituals differently. The answer to the question varied. In Los Angeles, different *anjumans* were organized representing different Zoroastrian origins. In Toronto, one *anjuman* remained, but with special concessions to accommodate Iranian Zartoshtis' ways and a Farsi section in its previously all-English newsletter.

New needs could be observed among the youth generation of the Parsi migrants to the West. In Indian society, one is not usually pressed to explain why one is a Parsi or what the meaning of Zoroastrian identity is; though the country is constitutionally secular, the society is structured with a religio-ethnic pigeonhole for everyone. In North America, religion is considered more of a personal option, and one may be called on to justify one's religiosity as the consequence of conscious choice. Zoroastrians, like others, are asked to articulate their religious faith and practice intellectually in order to explain it to others. Moreover, the terms in which modern Westerners understand their religious traditions often bring a considerable presumption of historical development and cultural relativism to what they describe, with the result that young people in the Zoroastrian diaspora are not always convinced or excited about their parents' and grandparents' explanations of the meaning and efficacy of traditional rituals.

In the Zoroastrian diaspora today, small numbers and decentralized patterns of residence mean that the majority of most young Zoroastrians' close acquaintances are likely to come from outside their own religious community. Such a setting demonstrably increases intermarriage and brings to the fore the definition of Zoroastrian identity. Neither in the Indian environment nor in the Iranian was Zoroastrianism accustomed to receiving converts. The reasons were different in the two cases—a caste structure in Indian society and a theologico-legal ban on defection from Islam in Iranian society—but the net effect was parallel. Neither of these inhibiting structures obtains in the English-speaking world, so the conversion question is discussed anew. Recent Indian and Iranian experience are precedents, to be sure, but it is also clear that in its Sasanian heyday, Zoroastrianism was a religion for everyone.

In the past, the maintenance of temples and rituals was thought to ensure the continuity of the religion, and many orthodox Zoroastrians still think this. However, maintaining the rituals is not easy with a shrinking and scattered community and a dwindling number of active priests. Moreover, there is serious questioning of ritual institutions in today's climate that repudiates male gender preferences in traditional religion. Since Zoroastrian priests have always been males only, a feminist outlook could imply, priesthood itself is an anachronism in today's or tomorrow's gender-balanced climate. Particularly offensive to modern feminist consciousness is the ritual isolation of women in a separate part of the house during menstruation. With dissatisfaction of this sort, the credit balance that earlier twentieth-century Parsis and Iranian Zartoshtis might enjoy for their practical advances in women's education and career achievement is reduced to zero, if not overdrawn.

Whatever one may say for ritual, Zoroastrians still discover much support among their own young and among interested non-Zoroastrians for the symbolic spiritual values and lofty ethical teachings of their religion. Although teaching was not the pre-modern role of a priest, educated priests can help at this task. Even in past generations, persons in other lines of work have articulated the tradition intelligently; in fact, one of the most intelligent and accessible presentations of Zoroastrianism is a 1938 book by a Bombay lawyer, Rustom Masani (1876–1966).

In our so-called information age, information may in fact form a new foundation for the continuation of the Zoroastrian tradition among future generations in the diaspora. As the number of active priests declines, the future promises a diminution in Zoroastrian ritual observances, in quantity if not in quality. But the future does not portend any diminution of interest in the ethical and spiritual message of Zarathushtra or in Iranian and Indian cultural history. The future of Zoroastrianism may depend on a renewal of dedicated learning, indeed with a new sophistication concerning what religion is all about. Iran's ancient heritage offers rich and challenging resources for such a quest.

KEY TERMS

(If two forms of a term are given, the first is Avestan, the second Pahlavi.)

agiari. A fire temple, where a consecrated fire is maintained by priests and stoked five times a day.

Ahuna Vairyo (Ahunavar). The principal Zoroastrian prayer, composed by Zarathushtra. It is short, and can be recited within fifteen seconds.

Ahura Mazda (Ohrmazd). The supreme divinity, whose name means 'Wise Lord'. His principal opponent is the evil spirit, Angra Mainyu (Ahriman).

Amesha Spentas (Amahraspands). Seven divine entities that personify beneficial qualities of Ahura Mazda: his Holy Spirit, Good Intention, Truth, Dominion, Devotion, Wholeness, and Immortality.

anjuman. Term for the community organization of Zoroastrians in most Indian, Iranian, and overseas locales. In the Indian cities of Bombay, Surat, and Pune, the comparable organization is a Panchayat ('council of five').

Ashem Vohu. 'Righteousness is the best thing', the opening words of one of the principal standard Zoroastrian prayers.

atesh Behram. 'The fire of Varahran (Behram)', designation of the highest grade of consecrated fires, established through elaborate ritual. In modern times there have been eight *atesh Behrams* in India and one in Iran.

Avesta. The corpus of literature preserving the oldest Zoroastrian ritual texts. Its language, named Avestan, is similar to the Sanskrit of the Hindu *Vedas*.

dakhma. A walled enclosure open to the sky, used for the disposal of the bodies of the dead by exposure to birds of prey.

dastur. Title for the highest grade of Zoroastrian priest.

farohar. The winged disk surmounted by a humanlike figure with royal robes and headgear. It accompanied Achaemenian royal inscriptions as early as the sixth century BCE and became adopted as a the principal Zoroastrian symbol.

fravashi. The spirit associated with an individual in an angelic or protective role.

gahambars. Seven seasonal festivals throughout the year, associated with the Amesha Spentas and with the domains of creation. These are occasions for community feasts.

haoma. An intoxicant plant extract ritually prepared and ritually consumed by priests. In name and function, it was like the *soma* of the *Ṛg Veda*, and its lost ancient identity is a matter for speculation. Zoroastian priests use a *haoma* substitute in ritual today.

jashan. A thanksgiving ceremony that may be performed at any time or place outside a fire temple, and that therefore is now widely used among Zoroastrians scattered overseas.

kusti. A long, woven tubular cord tied three times around the waist. Personal devotional prayers are said when tying it at stated times and when dressing or performing personal hygiene.

mobed. Term for an ordinary Zoroastrian priest, from the ancient word *magu*. In Christian tradition, priests from the East (Latin plural, *magi*) had a reputation as sages possessing an exotic wisdom.

navjote. 'New birth', the initiation ritual performed usually before adolescence, in which the young Zoroastrian is ceremonially provided with the *sudreh* and *kusti* and assumes responsibilities of the faith.

Nowrūz. Literally, 'new day'. The new year's festival, which in Iranian national tradition occurs at the spring equinox.

Pahlavi texts. Literature composed during the Sasanian era (226–642) as well as for some time after the empire fell to Arab conquerors. The name 'Pahlavi' means 'Parthian', as the middle Iranian language came into use under Parthian rule from the third century BCE onward.

revāyets. Correspondence in the Persian Islamic era among Zoroastrian communities in Iran and India on matters of ritual and theological precedent and interpretation.

sudreh. A plain, lightweight short-sleeved shirt worn under one's street attire and first worn in the *navjote* or initiation ceremony. It has a V-neck, at the apex of which a little pocket serves as a symbolic repository of one's good deeds.

Tan Dorosti. A prayer for health, long life, and virtuous living. The name literally means 'healthy body'. It serves as a concluding benediction in the *jashan* ceremony.

yasht. A liturgical hymn in praise of a divine being. The Avesta contains *yasht*s to various Iranian divinities and spirits, all now seen as agents, helpers, or manifestations of the power of Ahura Mazda.

yazata. A being worthy of worship. Possibly diverse in their historical origin, the divinities and spirits of ancient Iranian religion have all been incorporated into the worship of Ahura Mazda, to whom Zoroaster directed all his devotion.

FURTHER READING

Boyce, M. 1979. *Zoroastrians: Their Religious Beliefs and Practices*. London: Routledge and Kegan Paul.

______. 1984. *Textual Sources for the Study of Zorastrianism*. Manchester: Manchester University Press.

Duchesne-Guillemin, J. 1958. *The Western Response to Zoroaster*. Oxford: Clarendon Press.

______. 1973. *Religion of Ancient Iran*. Bombay: K.M. JamaspAsa.

Hinnells, J.R. 1973. *Persian Mythology*. London: Hamlyn.

Insler, S., trans. 1975. *The Gāthās of Zarathustra*. Leiden: Brill.

Katrak, S.K.H. 1958. *Who Are the Parsees?* Karachi: S.K.H. Katrak.

Masani, R. 1938. *The Religion of the Good Life: Zoroastrianism*. London: Allen & Unwin.

Modi, J.J. 1938. *The Religious Ceremonies and Customs of the Parsees*, 3rd ed. Bombay: Karani.

Zaehner, R.C. 1961. *The Dawn and Twilight of Zoroastrianism*. London: Weidenfeld and Nicolson.

REFERENCES

Boyce, M. 1984. *Textual Sources for the Study of Zoroastrianism*. Manchester: Manchester University Press.

Kent, R.G. 1953. *Old Persian: Grammar, Texts, Lexicon*. New Haven: American Oriental Society.

Malandra, W.W. 1983. *An Introduction to Ancient Iranian Religion*. Minneapolis: University of Minnesota Press.

Zaehner, R.C. 1956. *The Teachings of the Magi*. London: Allen & Unwin; New York: Macmillan.

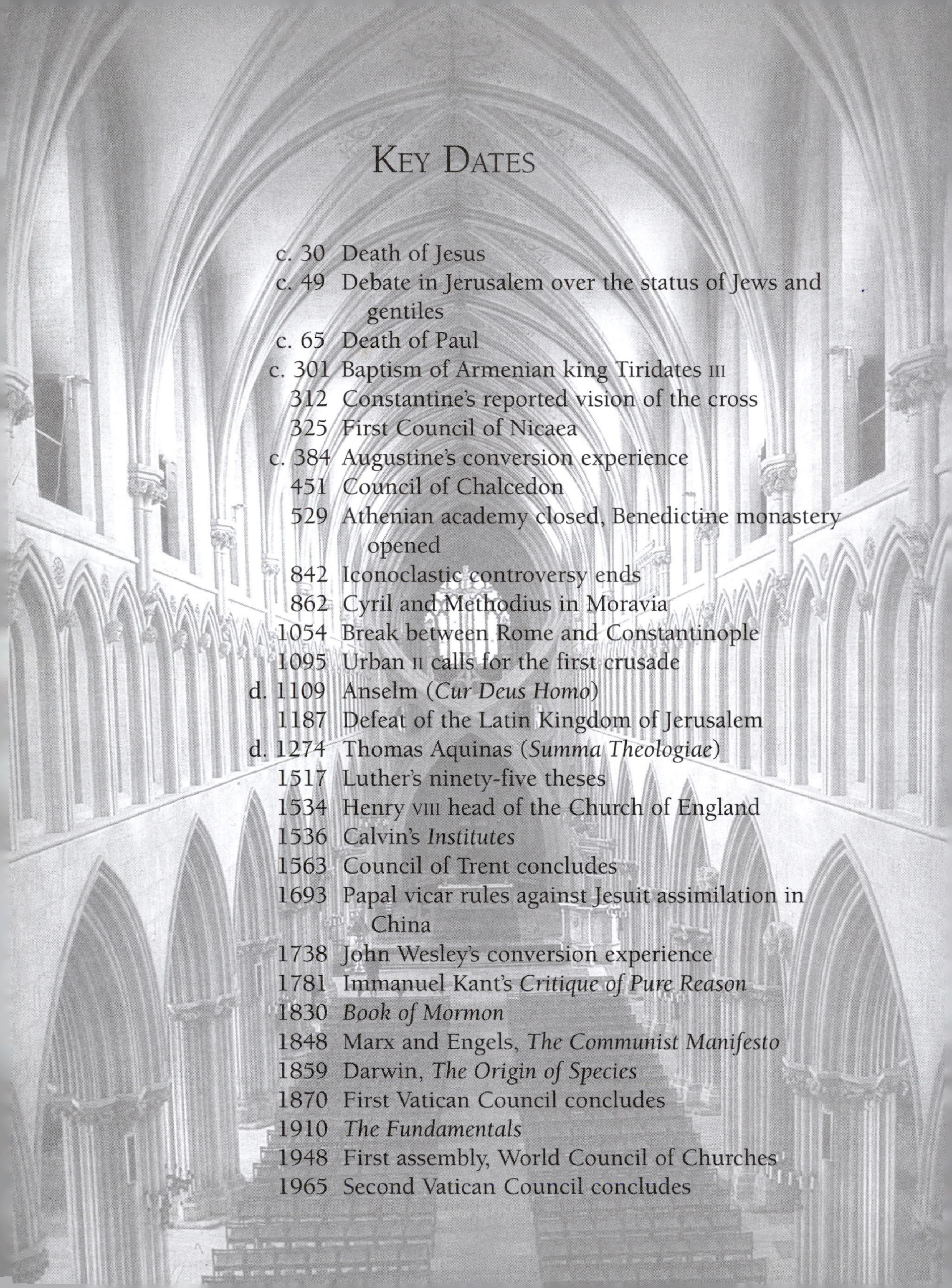

Key Dates

c. 30	Death of Jesus
c. 49	Debate in Jerusalem over the status of Jews and gentiles
c. 65	Death of Paul
c. 301	Baptism of Armenian king Tiridates III
312	Constantine's reported vision of the cross
325	First Council of Nicaea
c. 384	Augustine's conversion experience
451	Council of Chalcedon
529	Athenian academy closed, Benedictine monastery opened
842	Iconoclastic controversy ends
862	Cyril and Methodius in Moravia
1054	Break between Rome and Constantinople
1095	Urban II calls for the first crusade
d. 1109	Anselm (*Cur Deus Homo*)
1187	Defeat of the Latin Kingdom of Jerusalem
d. 1274	Thomas Aquinas (*Summa Theologiae*)
1517	Luther's ninety-five theses
1534	Henry VIII head of the Church of England
1536	Calvin's *Institutes*
1563	Council of Trent concludes
1693	Papal vicar rules against Jesuit assimilation in China
1738	John Wesley's conversion experience
1781	Immanuel Kant's *Critique of Pure Reason*
1830	*Book of Mormon*
1848	Marx and Engels, *The Communist Manifesto*
1859	Darwin, *The Origin of Species*
1870	First Vatican Council concludes
1910	*The Fundamentals*
1948	First assembly, World Council of Churches
1965	Second Vatican Council concludes

CHAPTER THREE

THE CHRISTIAN TRADITION

WILLARD G. OXTOBY

CELEBRATING A BIRTH

Throughout the Western world, the year reaches a climax towards the end of December. At that season, Christians celebrate the birth of Jesus, whom they regard as the manifestation of divine nature and purpose in a human life. The birth took place in Palestine about 2,000 years ago. Christians assert that in him God has reached out, taking on and conquering humanity's weaknesses.

To declare Jesus lord and saviour of the world is to identify oneself as a Christian. And the heavy emphasis that Christians place on such a declaration is key for understanding Christianity's function as a religious tradition. To be a Christian involves making a faith commitment—expressed in one's conduct but also as affirmation of doctrine. Christians 'confess' or 'believe' Jesus to be the incarnate son of God and saviour of the world.

For better or for worse, Christians have generally expected other religious traditions to express themselves as statements of doctrine too. All too often they have represented other faiths as stubborn refusals to go along with Christian affirmations about Jesus. Some Christians share the joy of their Christmas holiday and its message of peace and goodwill with neighbours and visitors. But the holiday is tinged with shame when other Christians ostracize groups as outsiders resisting their message.

The name Christmas etymologically means 'the mass of Christ'. The mass or Eucharist is Christianity's central rite, a symbolic meal recalling or re-enacting throughout the year the self-sacrificing death of Jesus. Its solemnity figures as a theme even amid the optimism of Christmas. The ritual looks towards the Easter season in the spring, the most central Christian festival. Christians take their early community's Easter experience of Jesus as risen from the dead to be a confirmation of his divine lordship.

Christmas brings a blend of the religious and the cultural. Carols and hymns proclaim joy that the Christ-child is born. Greetings and family visits enhance a feeling of community solidarity. Elements of Christmas observance in the English-speaking world come from midwinter revelry in the pre-Christian culture of northern Europe: evergreen trees (German), holly and mistletoe (British), the yule-log (Scandinavian). They continue even in markedly different climates and seasons, such as in the Caribbean, California, Hawaii, or Australia. The jolly, avuncular figure of Santa Claus goes back to the third-century St Nicholas of Myra in what is now Turkey; he was a patron saint of sailors before becoming a bearer of children's gifts. To understand Christianity's varying vocabularies, one has to refer to regional and historical circumstances in the lands where it has developed.

Christians themselves consider many of the holiday season's cultural trappings secular rather than religious. In theory, they distinguish between the sacred and the secular. The distinction has roots in Christian origins; Christianity spent three formative centuries as a minority movement before becoming the established religion of any state. In Christian history, the distinction has not always been easy to apply; sorting out the spheres of church and state was a problem in the European Middle Ages and remains one today. And modern Christians expecting a state to be secular have had difficulty adjusting to states recently built on religio-communal identity, such as Islamic Pakistan or Jewish Israel.

Christianity faces not only secularism in modern society but an increase in another development: pluralism. Within what classical Christianity has claimed as the sphere of religion, Christianity has been losing its monopoly. It is no longer the undisputed frame of reference for European and American society even in religious matters. It used to be: in medieval France, theology, meaning Christian theology, was central to the universities' curriculum. Still today, in England, one's personal, or first, name is termed one's 'Christian' name. But there has developed an increasing acceptance of religious diversity within formerly Christian societies, accelerating since the mid-twentieth century.

With growing appreciation of the Jewish heritage and with the migration of Middle Eastern and Asian populations to Western countries, Christianity has come to be not *the* religion of society but one of several. Plurality within contemporary society has become a fact, and pluralism is the society's valuation of that fact as desirable. What had been 'Christendom', the domain of Christianity, became by mid-century 'our Judaeo-Christian culture' and is on the threshold of becoming referred to as a multi-faith culture. This development poses a current challenge to Christians' thought about the meaning of their heritage for the world.

Christians live in every part of the world. Estimates place their number at a billion and a half. Persons identified as Christian, of whom some are observant and others not, constitute the world's largest religious community, perhaps a quarter of the religious identity of the human family. Christians are the majority in Europe, throughout the Western hemisphere, and in Australia and New Zealand.

In Africa, Ethiopia was a traditionally Christian country, and the modern spread of Christianity has produced Christian majorities in many lands south of the Sahara. In the eastern Mediterranean, where Christianity originated, historic Christian communities remain, but were reduced to a small minority following the spread of Islam. Their largest percentage (though also now a minority) is in a state that emerged as a half-Christian enclave, Lebanon. In the rest of Asia, missionary Christianity has produced a majority only in the Philippines, and a significant minority, approaching one-third, in Korea.

How the Christian message emerged, how its interpretation has developed over the centuries, and what have been the manifestations of Christianity in society and culture: these points will be the agenda of our survey of the religious heritage of Christians. In the historical sequence we follow, certain centuries mark key transitions. Christianity became an independent new religion in the first century, and an established imperial religion in the fourth. The Latin Church went its own way from the Greek by the eleventh century and developed medieval Europe's characteristic thought and institutions. Northern Europeans threw aside the authority of the Roman pope in the Protestant Reformation of the sixteenth century. And in the nineteenth and twentieth centuries Christianity has felt a massive impact of modernity and change. These are the major branches of Christianity:

Nestorians	(about 200,000)
'Assyrians' of Iraq, Iran, and Turkey	
Nestorian Malabar Christians in India	
Monophysites	(about 30 million)
Copts in Egypt	
Ethiopians	
Jacobites or Syrian Orthodox	
Jacobite Malabar Christians in India	
Armenians	
Orthodox	(at least 150 million)
Greek	
Bulgarian, Serbian, and Romanian	
Russian and Ukrainian	
Catholics	(about 900 million)
Roman Catholics	
Eastern 'Uniate' churches	
(some Anglicans)	

Protestants (about 400 million)
- Sixteenth-century divisions
  - Lutherans
  - Anglicans
  - Reformed (Presbyterian) churches
  - Anabaptists
  - Unitarians
- Seventeenth- and eighteenth-century divisions
  - Congregationalists
  - Baptists
  - Quakers
  - Methodists
- Nineteenth-century divisions
  - Disciples
  - Seventh-Day Adventists
  - Jehovah's Witnesses
  - Christian Scientists
  - Mormons

CHRISTIAN ORIGINS

The Gospels and Jesus

In Mark's biography of him, Jesus, executed like a criminal, gasps his last breath on the cross. The Roman soldier standing by says, 'Truly this was a son of God.'

Mark has Jesus called son of God by a Roman soldier rather than one of Jesus's close disciples. This is fitting, for the Christian movement soon grew beyond its initial base as a Jewish sect. Within a generation after Jesus, the Christians decided that theirs was a message for everyone—that you didn't have to be a Jew first to be a Christian. And in that decision lay the seeds of Christianity's eventual spread to become, along with its predecessor Buddhism and its successor Islam, one of the world's three great missionary religions.

In the accounts of him, called gospels, Jesus performs miracles and heals ailments. Though miracle stories may have impressed people 2,000 years ago, they form a barrier to modern belief. But the insights into human personality and relationships that permeate his teachings and the confidence with which he was ready to challenge traditional scriptural and legal interpretations place Jesus on any short list of the world's most insightful and astute teachers. Jesus calls for love of one's enemies as well as friends, and in word and example gives a strong emphasis to forgiveness, an emphasis probably exceeded in no other of humanity's religious traditions.

If Jesus were living in our modern society, there might be masses of information about him: birth and medical records, school transcripts, employment and financial files, even the dates and durations of long-distance telephone calls. From antiquity, no such data banks exist. We rely for our picture of him on writings produced a generation and more after his career, by people who had a very partisan claim to make: that their teacher had been the long-awaited kingly deliverer, and that his humiliating death was a victorious martyrdom. Moreover, they said, he had come back from the dead, had gone up to heaven, and was coming back in triumph. They also asserted that Jesus was the Son of God and that through his self-giving sacrifice, he was the saviour of humanity. That the Christian accounts were not given to understatement does not make them any easier to corroborate.

Others will probably agree with Christians today on some points about Jesus's life. He was a Jew who lived in Palestine. He was born about 4 BCE; when Christians in the sixth century devised a calendar dating from his birth, there was an error in calculation. He grew up in the northern Palestinian town of Nazareth, and learned stoneworking or carpentry, his father's trade. At about the age of thirty he began to proclaim religious teachings and attract a following. At about thirty-three he went to Jerusalem and came into confrontation with the authorities. He was apprehended and tried, and was executed by being nailed to a cross.

As historical evidence, what does the early Christian literature substantiate for us? Scholars for more than a century have agreed that at least it demonstrates the existence of a community of faith that preached the message of Jesus as the risen lord. Whether or not Jesus actually did or said each particular thing the texts say about him, by the middle of the first century the Christian message was crystallizing into the form we find in the Christian narratives. The Christian movement was coming into focus, reporting the life of Jesus as life on earth, but also preaching an interpretation of that life as cosmically significant.

More than three centuries later, when Christianity became the established religion of the empire, church leaders listed the writings acknowledged to be scripture. That standard list, or 'canon', of books and letters is what Christians know as the New Testament. It includes the four gospels that had achieved universal acceptance throughout Christendom. But in the late first and early second centuries, when these and a number of other gospels were first written and circulated, the situation was much more fluid. It is helpful to think of each gospel as coming from an individual author with a particular interpretation and an intended readership.

Mark

Mark's gospel is the simplest and most straightforward. It is also considered the earliest of the four gospels that eventually came to be in the canon. Mark's

SAYINGS OF JESUS

[From the body of teachings of Jesus in Matthew *conventionally known as the 'Sermon on the Mount'* (in Luke, *the corresponding material is delivered on a plain). The translation is that of the* New English Bible *(Oxford University Press and Cambridge University Press, New Testament 1961).]*

If, when you are bringing your gift to the altar, you suddenly remember that your brother has a grievance against you, leave your gift where it is before the altar. First go and make your peace with your brother, and only then come back and offer your gift (5:23–4).

You have learned that they were told, 'Do not commit adultery.' But what I tell you is this: If a man looks on a woman with a lustful eye, he has already committed adultery with her in his heart' (5:27–8).

You have learned that they were told, 'Eye for eye, tooth for tooth.' But what I tell you is this: Do not set yourself against the man who wrongs you. If someone slaps you on the right cheek, turn and offer him your left. If a man wants to sue you for your shirt, let him have your coat as well. If a man in authority makes you go one mile, go with him two. Give when you are asked to give; and do not turn your back on a man who wants to borrow (5:38–42).

Do not store up for yourselves treasure on earth, where it grows rusty and moth-eaten, and thieves break in to steal it. Store up treasure in heaven, where there is no moth and no rust to spoil it, no thieves to break in and steal. For where your treasure is, there will your heart be also (6:19–21).

account starts not with Jesus's birth but with his mature ministry. In the account, John the Baptist (the baptizer), leader of a desert-based movement, performs his ritual on Jesus and declares that Jesus will be even greater. After a forty-day retreat in which he wrestles with Satan, and after the arrest of John, Jesus launches his ministry in the region of Galilee, proclaiming that the kingdom of God is at hand. His local reputation spreads as he performs healing miracles. He picks grain and heals on the Sabbath, and, when challenged, takes the notion of Jewish legal authority into his own hand by declaring that the Sabbath is made for people rather than people for the Sabbath. This apparent arrogance sets up for Mark a conspiracy on the part of the Pharisees to do Jesus in.

Jesus selects from those who follow him a group of twelve (in the traditions of Israel, the size of a complete set of months, tribes, prophetical books, and other lists) as his inner circle of disciples. Accompanied by them, he continues to heal and teach, and to challenge the priorities of religious authority. Eventually he goes to Jerusalem, arriving with an entourage that shouts 'Hosanna' (a cry for divine

Pass no judgement, and you will not be judged. For as you judge others, so you will yourselves be judged, and whatever measure you deal out to others will be dealt back to you. Why do you look at the speck of sawdust in your brother's eye, with never a thought for the great plank in your own? Or how can you say to your brother, 'Let me take the speck out of your eye,' when all the time there is that plank in your own? First take the plank out of your own eye, and then you will see clearly to take the speck out of your brother's (7:1–5).

[An account that appears in all three synoptic gospels (Matthew 22, Mark 12, Luke 20). *Here citing* Luke.*]*

[The lawyers and chief priests] watched their opportunity and sent secret agents in the guise of honest men, to seize upon some word of his as a pretext for handing him over to the authority and jurisdiction of the Governor. They put a question to him: 'Master,' they said, 'we know that what you speak and teach is sound; you pay deference to no one, but teach in all honesty the way of life that God requires. Are we or are we not permitted to pay taxes to the Roman Emperor?' He saw through their trick and said, 'Show me a silver piece. Whose head does it bear, and whose inscription?' 'Caesar's,' they replied. 'Very well then,' he said, 'pay Caesar what is due to Caesar, and pay God what is due to God.' Thus their attempt to catch him out in public failed, and, astonished by his reply, they fell silent (20:20–6).

deliverance in Hebrew prayer) and proclaims the coming of a king in the line of the Hebrew dynastic founder, David. During the course of a week in Jerusalem, he disputes with the religious authorities, celebrates the Passover with his disciples, is betrayed by one of them named Judas, and is arrested. Brought to trial before Pilate, the Roman governor, Jesus does not deny that he is the king of the Jews, and offers no defence.

Jesus is executed on the cross, crying out, 'My God, my God, why have you forsaken me?' As he breathes his last, the Roman centurion terms him a son of God, and before the start of the Sabbath, he is placed in a tomb sealed by a large stone. The day after the Sabbath, three women from among Jesus's following go to the tomb to anoint the body and find the stone rolled away and the body missing; a figure appears to them and informs them that Jesus has risen and will meet the disciples. In some manuscripts of Mark's gospel, Jesus appears to the eleven remaining faithful disciples at a meal, commands them to preach the gospel (i.e., the good news), and promises that they, too, will be healers.

The Parables and the Source 'Q'

One form of discourse used by Jesus is the parable. Basically, a parable is a story with a moral, a kind of fable. Some of Jesus's parables compare the extension of the kingdom of God with the growth of seeds, and compare Jesus's audience's receptivity to the fertility of soil. With an eye to earlier prophets and teachers, Jesus suggests that you can teach and teach, but people will not grasp the point. 'Whoever has ears should hear' is a recurring refrain. Some parables emphasize such values in interpersonal relationships as forgiveness and acceptance.

Frequently it is the humble or poor person, or the outsider to society, who turns out to have a truly worthy character. In the parable of the Good Samaritan, for instance, a man is mugged while going down from Jerusalem to Jericho and lies abandoned at the roadside. Various people of high status in the Jewish community pass by, ignoring him. A man from Samaria, with whom the Jews have no dealings for theological and ritual reasons, comes along and rescues the victim, arranging for him to be nursed back to health. Jesus's message to his fellow Jews is clear: the truly righteous person is one who will help a fellow human being, even if that person is from a rival community that one's own group shuns.

Besides the parables, Jesus delivers numerous shorter sayings. Many of these could be presented apart from any narrative as universally applicable human proverbs or maxims. In chapters 5 through 7, Matthew presents Jesus as delivering a collection of these on a mountain in northern Palestine; the material is thus known as the Sermon on the Mount. Luke has the same material, though in his gospel it is delivered on a plain. Indeed, *Luke* and *Matthew* overlap to a considerable extent, sometimes utilizing the details in Mark's narrative, but often sharing sayings that are not in *Mark*.

In the nineteenth century, scholars postulated a separate hypothetical source for this material not in *Mark*. They assumed that another document, containing teachings of Jesus, has not come down to us but was used by both Luke and Matthew. Since it was German New Testament scholars who were making that assumption, they referred to that document as 'Q', the initial letter of *Quelle*, the German word for 'source'.

Luke

Luke's biography of Jesus has two chapters of material not found in *Mark* detailing events before the adult baptism and ministry of Jesus. These contain visions and portents anticipating the birth of John the Baptist and the birth of Jesus. Jesus's birth is reported in Bethlehem, as is the appearance of angels (divine messengers) to shepherds, who come and pay their respects to the newborn infant as the messiah. (Luke does not mention any visit of wise men from the East, however; the *magi*, Persian for 'priests', are in *Matthew*.) At a newborn-purification ceremony in the temple, the devout Simeon is also inspired to proclaim this infant as the messiah. Luke's opening chapters also incorporate a number of hymns appropriate to the situation.

Evidently, in the circles for which Luke was writing, there was already an incipient liturgical use of messianic hymns and psalms. Omens, portents, and declarations would serve to strengthen any case that Jesus was the long-awaited messiah. Luke lends support, moreover, to the idea that Jesus was born into his role and destined for it, whereas someone reading only Mark's account could easily view Jesus as embarking on a ministry through an adult decision marked by baptism. You would not necessarily have to be Jewish to be attracted by Luke's portrayal; signs and portents, wonders, and miraculous works formed part of the biographical traditions of other teaching and healing figures in Greco-Roman antiquity, too. Indeed, Luke appears to have had a Greek readership in mind, presenting his Jewish saviour as important to the gentile world.

Luke also provides more information than does *Mark* regarding the trial and crucifixion of Jesus. For Luke, the charge against Jesus is that by claiming kingship, he was inciting rebellion. In *Luke*, the Roman governor, Pilate, declares Jesus innocent of any crime, but then yields to mob pressure to have him executed anyway. Luke's Roman centurion witnessing the crucifixion is concerned to declare Jesus's innocence, not (as with Mark's) Jesus's divine sonship. And after the discovery of the empty tomb, Jesus appears among and speaks to his followers. As with his handling of the infancy narratives, Luke seems to regard signs, portents, and experienced manifestations as convincing evidence of Jesus's special role. As to whether these signs explicitly constitute the fulfilment of Jewish sectarian expectations, in Luke's gospel the references to scriptural fulfilment are not numerous and appear as statements made by Jesus himself.

Matthew

Scriptural references are quite another matter in the biography by Matthew. As a writer, Matthew is clearly addressing a Jewish audience with his claim of Jesus's messiahship. Matthew's narration of Jesus's family's hasty escape from the slaughter of infants by King Herod, for instance, suggests the *Exodus* account of the Israelites' escape from the wrath of the Egyptian pharaoh. And like Moses, Jesus goes into the desert for a personal spiritual encounter.

Matthew presumes that for his readers, the Hebrew scriptures have a literal, textual authority. He narrates the life of Jesus with constant references to Hebrew biblical passages. The claims that they are fulfilled are Matthew's own, not usually spoken by Jesus. Matthew lifts some Hebrew passages out of their earlier context and recontextualizes them, finding their meaning in their new application.

As an example, consider chapter 11 of the Hebrew prophet *Hosea*, concerned with the love of God for his people. Hosea says on God's behalf, presumably referring to the childhood of the nation at the time of Moses and the Exodus from Egypt, 'When Israel was a child, I loved him, and out of Egypt I called my son.' In narrating the birth of Jesus, Matthew has King Herod (r. c. 37–4 BCE) worried that the child is to be the king of the Jews, so Herod plots to kill newborn babies to protect his own reign. An angel then warns Jesus's parents to take the child and escape to Egypt, where they remain for the balance of Herod's life. 'This,' writes Matthew, 'was to fulfil what the Lord had spoken by the prophet, "Out of Egypt have I called my son."'

Matthew's desire to back up his biography of Jesus through scriptural citations no doubt had a steering effect on the biography itself. Many scholars view details of Matthew's narrative as generated by the already extant Hebrew texts. Many conservative Christians over the years, on the other hand, have seen the content of the earlier texts as providentially placed there by God so that, at the time of Jesus, the words could be found to have a meaning that had been divinely intended for them all along. Let us consider a few of the more challenging cases.

Matthew opens his gospel by giving a genealogy of Jesus as the descendant of King David, in a lineage that runs through Joseph, husband of Mary. However, Matthew then bypasses this genealogy by asserting that Mary was pregnant with Jesus before Joseph married her. The child is fathered by the Holy Spirit rather than by Joseph. Part of Matthew's agenda in claiming such an unusual birth is to cite scripture. He quotes from the seventh chapter of *Isaiah*, 'Behold, a virgin shall conceive and bear a son, and his name shall be called Emmanuel (which means, "God with us").'

Now that passage in *Isaiah* must have had some contemporary meaning 700 years before Jesus, in order to have been understood and preserved. The context in that earlier time was Isaiah's advice to King Ahaz (r. 735–720 BCE) not to get involved in a coalition against the Assyrians, who were the principal world power of the day. Such is the unmistakable significance of another symbolic naming and a short-term prediction, in *Isaiah* 8. Such, similarly, must have been the significance of *Isaiah* 7. But in citing this passage, Matthew now supplies a new context for the scriptural text. And although the Hebrew of *Isaiah* mentions only a 'young woman', the Greek is ambiguous and can be read as 'virgin'. The stage is thus set for one of Christianity's more problematic teachings, the virgin birth of Jesus, a doctrine that grows out of a reading of *Matthew* and *Luke*, not the work of other New Testament authors.

Matthew's use of scripture does contain mistakes, as two instances show. First, to provide a scriptural context for Jesus's use of parables, Matthew in chapter 13 cites the passage, 'I will open my mouth in parables, I will utter what has been hidden since the foundation of the world.' He gives this as fulfilment of what was spoken by 'the prophet' (in some manuscripts, 'the prophet Isaiah'), but actually the passage is not in any prophet but in *Psalm* 78.

Second, in chapter 21, Matthew ignores the parallelism of biblical Hebrew poetry, in which the first half of a line states a subject and the second half often restates the same subject in other words. When Jesus and his disciples enter Jerusalem, the theme is that of *Zechariah* 9:

> Tell the daughter of Zion,
> behold, your king is coming to you,
> Humble, and mounted on an ass;
> and on a colt, the foal of an ass (*Matthew* 21:5 quoting *Zechariah* 9:9).

For this fulfilment, Matthew has Jesus obtain and ride two animals, whereas Zechariah's poetry sees the ass and the colt as one and the same.

The historical moment of profoundest significance for Christians is the suffering and death of Jesus on the cross. Christians recount certain details of that suffering, termed the Passion, as follows. Bystanders mock Jesus for having trusted in God, saying that God should now rescue him. Jesus says he is thirsty. His hands and feet are pierced. People cast lots to divide up his clothing. And Jesus cries out, 'My God, my God, why have you forsaken me?' Startlingly, the much older *Psalm* 22, which begins with this cry, contains all the other details as well.

How much, then, would an eyewitness to the crucifixion have observed? Jesus may well have cried out that he was forsaken, and quite possibly he had in mind the rest of *Psalm* 22, which concludes with trust in divine deliverance. But did the rest of our details, such as the mocking of the psalmist's trust, 'happen' at the cross, or were they supplied by association as scripture-conscious narrators like Matthew retold the narrative? This sort of question will probably never be settled to everyone's satisfaction. Christians and others will differ in how far they will go along with Matthew in linking the figure of Jesus and the text of Hebrew scripture.

And if the gospel writers have added associations and details to their stories of Jesus, what did he actually intend? On this, Christian opinion varies widely, but some points stand out with clarity. Jesus wants his fellow Jews to live up to ideals already present in their tradition. Like the Hebrew prophets before him, he places ethics ahead of ritual. He is ready to challenge traditional interpretations, repeatedly declaring, 'You have heard it said …, but I say to you …' He shares a popular expectation that the 'kingdom of God', which will in some way restructure society, is at hand. And he is willing to die a martyr's death for the cause. This much is a minimum core of Jesus's evident intent as a teacher, but his followers soon developed a preaching message that went much further in what it claimed for him.

John

Despite their differences, the three gospels sketched so far (*Matthew*, *Mark*, and *Luke* in their sequence in the New Testament) exhibit a fair amount in common when they are contrasted with John's, the fourth gospel. Scholars therefore refer to the first three as the 'synoptic gospels'. The term 'synoptic' (from Greek, 'viewing together') can be confusing. It does not mean that they offer a brief summary or synopsis. It implies, rather, that they have a unified perspective or viewpoint. John's gospel is a biography of another sort.

We have termed the gospel accounts interpretations. Even in the case of Mark's, the most direct, the selection and arrangement of material amounts to an interpretation. And we have described the scriptural-fulfilment agenda with which Matthew went about his task. But compared with these, John's gospel is a major theological essay. John's concern is to present not just the narrative but its cosmic significance. Beyond the parables and actions of Jesus as teacher and healer, John offers a declaration of Jesus's identity as messiah and saviour. Regarding his purpose as a writer, John is candid at the end of his twentieth chapter: 'Now Jesus did many other signs in the presence of the disciples, which are not written in this book. But these are written that you may come to believe that Jesus is the Messiah, the Son of God, and that through believing you may have life in his name' (*John* 20:30–1).

John's theoretical reflection may well have developed over some decades after the composition of the synoptic gospels, but even if contemporary with them it pursues a direction distinct from them.

In his opening passage, called by scholars the prologue, John shows his concern at once. 'In the beginning', he writes (with an overtone of the opening words of *Genesis* in the Hebrew scriptures) 'was the *logos*, and the *logos* was with God, and the *logos* was God; all things were made through him.' *Logos* is a Greek term with an important range of meaning in the philosophy and religion of the Greek world at the time of Jesus. It meant 'word' not just as a vocabulary item, but the whole idea of divine intelligence and purpose. A God who can create the world through his word, who can command the world through his word, and who can redeem the world through his word, is what John wants his hearers to appreciate here. This *logos* is 'word' with a capital W.

A few verses later in the prologue, John declares Jesus to be the incarnation of that divine Word. 'The *logos* became flesh and dwelt among us, full of grace and truth; we have beheld his glory, glory as of the only Son from the Father.' For John, the eternal divine purpose has now become a personal presence in human form, in the community's recent experience. John continues with the contrast that the early Christian movement as a Jewish sect was making between its message and the traditional Jewish law, the contrast of law versus gospel. 'For the law was given through Moses; grace and truth came through Jesus Christ.'

John is in step here with the writings of an early convert, Paul, who probably contributed as much as any one individual to the shaping of the early Christian message. And notice that John, like Paul, is now using the title 'Christ' (the Greek translation of the Hebrew word for messiah, 'anointed') practically as a second personal name for Jesus. John's view of the significance of Jesus is encapsulated in an often-quoted passage: 'For God so loved the world that he gave his only Son, that whoever believes in him should not perish but have eternal life' (*John* 3:16).

As the gospel proceeds, Jesus's messiahship becomes not just something to take as John's declaration but something Jesus repeatedly states in his own words. Whereas Mark's Jesus will neither confirm nor deny that he is the long-awaited king, John's Jesus has no such reticence. In the first chapter, when a questioner declares Jesus to be the son of God, Jesus adds to the picture: 'Truly, truly I say to you, you will see heaven opened, and the angels of God ascending and descending upon the Son of man.'

Repeatedly throughout John's gospel, Jesus declares himself in passages that begin with 'I am', making claims to be the means of salvation. In chapter 6: 'I am the bread of life; he who comes to me shall not hunger, and he who believes in me shall never thirst.' In chapter 8: 'I am the light of the world; he who follows me will not walk in darkness, but will have the light of life.' In chapter 10: 'I am the good shepherd. The good shepherd lays down his life for the sheep.' In chapter 11: 'I am the resurrection and the life; he who believes in me, though he die, yet shall he live, and whoever lives and believes in me shall never die.' In chapter 14: 'I am the way, and the truth, and the life; no one comes to the Father, but by me.' In chapter 15: 'I am the vine, you are the branches. He who abides in me, and I in him, he it is that bears much fruit, for apart from me you can do nothing.' John's Jesus is more than a teacher with an insight into human nature; he is presented as the definitive link between God and humanity.

Salvation, then, is John's agenda. We humans need to be delivered from the flaws and constraints of our condition. John is especially concerned with our mortality, and offers the hope of life. Paul, as we shall see, is also concerned with our sinfulness, and offers the hope of justification. In the final analysis, it is not we humans but only God who can save us from sin and death, from the limitations of our existence.

A major theological agenda is set, to which subsequent thinkers devoted centuries of reflection. How is it that the transcendent God enters into the human condition to perform these saving acts? Jesus's status as a manifestation of God was eventually spelled out in the doctrine of the Trinity, after the middle of the third century. The link between the divine and the human in Jesus continued to be a doctrinal issue well into the fifth century. And the process by which human sin is conquered or atoned for remained a central doctrinal question throughout the centuries. We shall return to these topics later in our treatment.

From Sect to Church

The small circle of Jesus's disciples who were left at the time of his execution bears little resemblance to the Church that a Roman emperor patronized three centuries later. The disciples were basically peasants from rural Galilee, whose teacher had stirred hopes that low-status and marginalized people (the poor, sinners, Samaritans, women, and so on) had a place in God's plan. As a group, they amounted to a little Jewish sect that expected not to have to wait long for the end of the age and a glorious return of their teacher.

Various explanations are offered for how the early Church transformed its identity from a Jewish sect to an independent missionary religion. In the New Testament book *Acts of the Apostles*, a sequel to his gospel, Luke presents the mandate in miraculous terms, as one might expect him to. In *Acts* 2 the disciples are gathered on Shavuoth, the festival seven weeks after the Passover on which Jesus was executed. They experience the Holy Spirit as a rush of wind and fire, and begin to speak—and be understood—in diverse languages, thus enabled to preach to all people.

Acts also provides more everyday information about the apostles, as the original circle of Christians are called. We see a genuine debate among them in *Acts* 15 on whether one needs to be circumcised as a Jew first in order to join the movement, or whether participation is open to gentiles, i.e., non-Jews. This occurred around the year 49, when the Christians had been preaching for nearly two decades. In *Acts*, Peter and Jesus's brother or kinsman James are depicted as leaders among the apostles, steering a middle course between exclusive Jewish and gentile definitions of the movement. In *Galatians* 2 we see that the Christians could come to a consensus that circumcision was not a requirement.

In his writings, Luke makes hardly any explicit reference to what must have been the century's watershed political event for any Jew. That event was the Zealot-inspired rebellion against Roman rule in Palestine in 66–73. The Romans crushed the revolt, and the temple of Jerusalem was destroyed in 70 in their siege of the city. The Christians, one may speculate, would be at pains to distance themselves from Jewish nationalist ambitions, now thoroughly discredited, and to some extent from identification with Judaism altogether.

If we look for traces of such an effort, we do find a few. *Luke* has Jesus entering Jerusalem for his final week in the city:

> And when he drew near and saw the city he wept over it, saying, 'Would that even today you knew the things that make for peace! But now they are hid from your eyes. For the days shall come upon you, when your enemies will cast up a bank about you and surround you, and hem you in on every side, and dash you to the ground, you and your children within you, and they will not leave one stone upon another in you' (*Luke* 19:41–4).

Luke was evidently writing with a pacifist emphasis in the 70s, with the destruction of the city fresh in mind. But while Jesus and his followers are often depicted as mild-mannered in word and deed, there are hints that the matter was more complicated. In their accounts of Jesus's last night with his disciples, *Mark* 14 and *Matthew* 26 report the group as armed and resisting arrest.

Paul

The principal figure to shape the direction of the early Church, however, was not one of Jesus's unprepossessing band of twelve, but an educated and sophisticated convert who took the name Paul. He was a cosmopolitan person, and had the privileged status of a Roman citizen. Paul was a Pharisee from the diaspora Jewish community in Tarsus, a place on the southern coast of Turkey today, who had come to Jerusalem for religio-legal study.

Paul had not known Jesus during his ministry with his disciples. But by Luke's account, while on the road to Damascus to arrest and charge Christians, Paul experienced in a vision a personal encounter with the postresurrection Jesus that reoriented his life. For the next quarter-century he travelled tirelessly around the eastern Mediterranean. His initial contacts were in the diaspora Jewish communities, but Paul preached a message that gentiles alike were heirs in Christ to the promises of God.

Paul carried on correspondence with these scattered convert Christian communities in letters whose content ranges from personal greetings through liturgical blessings to essays on questions of theology. Paul's letters are the earliest Christian literature, coming from a time before the gospels were written, and had a formative effect on Christian theology that can hardly be overestimated.

In his letters, Paul refers to himself as the apostle to the gentiles. He sides against the view that in order to follow Jesus one must first become a Jew, being circumcised (if male) and following the dietary regulations and the other commandments of Pharisaism. One's 'works', one's observant conduct, do not lead to salvation. Rather, salvation is accessed through faith, specifically through faith in Jesus as the messiah or Christ. Divine grace comes through Christ, and it frees people from bondage to the law of Moses. And Paul expresses his sense of this freedom with the certainty of intense personal experience.

At the same time, Paul engages in an agenda with his gentile audience. To educated citizens of the Greco-Roman world, goodness amounted to virtue, that is, the cultivation of right moral conduct. But action that is morally correct by gentile standards does no more to justify people in the sight of God than does action that is ritually correct by Pharisaic standards. Basically, human beings are inherently self-willed and sinful, as the Church was later to spell out in its doctrine of 'original' sin. The liberation of people from this sinful nature, Paul says, is what God was all about in sending Jesus to die a self-sacrificing death. So it is not through morally correct action, but through trusting faith, that people are saved.

Paul is responsible for still another major theme that pervades subsequent Christian theology. He contrasts life 'in the spirit', that is, a life centred on lasting religious values such as faith, hope, and love, with life 'in the flesh', the pursuit of what passes away, including worldly ambition or pleasure. If we are to live in the spirit, it is thanks to the grace of God. But what is the life of the flesh that we leave behind? Is it wealth or status? That would be a sacrifice for the privileged classes, but unlike Paul, most of the earliest Christians were slaves, labourers, and artisans. Is it our physical appetites, such as for food and sex? Partly, but even our good works do not endure. Whatever Paul intended, he left a path open to understand our bodies negatively, as something to be controlled or repressed, a major issue in later Christian theology.

Thanks to Paul's voyages, Christian communities were established in many of the port cities of the Roman Empire by the time he died, about the year 65. At the start of his involvement with Christianity, Paul had assisted the people who stoned the apostle Stephen to death, by holding their coats. Now at the end, Paul was to become a martyr (etymologically, a 'witness') himself, executed in Rome as part of the emperor Nero's (r. 54–68) crack-down on Christians.

Marcion and the Canon

If we single out Paul as the architect with a blueprint for Christianity, then Marcion (d. c. 160) surfaces as the draughtsman of a sketch that was rejected. In response to Marcion, Christianity identified some things it would *not* be. Marcion lived a century after Paul. The son of a bishop, he was a wealthy shipowner from Sinope, on the south shore of the Black Sea. He made his way to Rome, the capital, where his teachings led to his excommunication (formal expulsion) from the Church in 144. This did not deter him from his views, which he continued earnestly to advocate.

In his theology, Marcion pushes Paul's ideas to astonishing lengths. Paul's contrast between law and gospel becomes for Marcion a contrast between the Old Testament and New, not just between one scripture and another but between one god and another.

Marcion sees the 'Demiurge', the creator God in the Hebrew scriptures, who gives the law to Moses, as stern and fearsome, capricious, despotic, and cruel. The coming of Jesus reveals an utterly different God, a God of love and mercy, whose purpose is to overcome the Demiurge. Jesus reveals a God who has no connection with, is superior to, and should replace the God of the Hebrew scriptures.

And that means, of course, replacing the Hebrew scriptures, too. Matthew in chapter 5 has Jesus say that he comes not to destroy 'the law and the prophets' (i.e., scripture) but to fulfil them. Such is not how Marcion sees Jesus. Not only does Marcion scrap the entire Hebrew canon; he rejects *Matthew* as well. For Marcion, scripture consists only of ten letters by Paul and an edited text of Luke's gospel and *Acts*. And Marcion produced his own key to scriptural interpretation in his writing entitled the *Antitheses*.

Marcion had a following in some circles, particularly in Syria; it is elusive, and appears to have died out by the fifth century. His principal influence, however, is the response to him that other Christian theologians felt compelled to make. Emphatically, they affirmed over against Marcion that the Christian message is indeed rooted in the faith of ancient Israel. The Church staked its claim to the heritage of Moses and the prophets. It saw revelation and covenant in the past and looked to judgement and redemption in the future. It considered itself a religion legitimate in the empire with a historical pedigree, not an illicit innovation.

Marcion notwithstanding, Christianity had a Hebraic ancestry. This meant that the Hebrew scriptures were ratified as a part of the Christian message. Marcion's posing the issue of authority contributed to the Church's eventual definition of its scriptural canon, the list of writings comprising the Old and New Testaments.

The Gnostics

Paul was not the only writer to distinguish between the spirit and the flesh, nor Marcion the only one to distinguish between negative and positive divine principles. The early Christians had to face a spiritual and doctrinal challenge in the movement known as Gnosticism.

The Greek word *gnōsis* means 'knowledge'. The Gnostics claimed privileged, secret knowledge. To their Christian adherents they offered an inner meaning to Christianity (and to Jewish Gnostics, of Judaism). At the start, they were not a separate, boundaried, independent community. Instead, they were a school of interpretation, gaining recruits to their teaching within the network of the Christian churches.

Gnostic teaching offers a philosophical outlook in narrative form. It is dualistic; the divine powers of good are opposed by demonic forces of evil, and spirit is in a cosmic struggle with matter. At the beginning, the material world is created through the entrapment or fall and fragmentation of spirit into matter. Depending on the particular account, spirit is the victim of temptation, or treachery, or attack. In any case, there will be battles before the cosmos is redeemed and spirit restored to its proper place.

The Christian Gnostics understood Jesus as an emissary from the realm of the spirit. Jesus's earthly life is an apparition in human form, but he does not take on material existence. Instead, he brings to humans the saving, secret knowledge of how to rise above this life to the realm of spirit. And a practical agenda for religious life is implied too: if matter is evil, then physical comforts and satisfactions, even the procreation of succeeding generations, are to be avoided or at least ignored, and regimes of abstinence, celibacy, and asceticism followed.

Later Christian centuries knew about Gnostic teachings largely through reading arguments against them in the writings of early Christian theologians. Critics of Gnostic teachings termed them docetic (from Greek *dokēsis*, 'appearance') and claimed that treating Jesus as a spiritual apparition robbed the religion of the benefits accruing from divine incarnation in human form.

However, in the mid-twentieth century there was a major discovery of Gnostic manuscripts on papyrus at Nag Hammadi, an up-river site on the Nile in Egypt. Consequently a more sympathetic view of Gnostic concerns has been available to historians in recent decades. Among the Nag Hammadi texts is the *Gospel of Thomas*, one of many writings, Gnostic and otherwise, that did not gain ratification as scripture by the church at large; some think this gospel was written during Jesus's lifetime because it presents his sayings as though he were still alive and does not describe his death.

In addition, one small Gnostic community survived outside the Roman Empire till today: the Mandeans (named from Aramaic and Syriac *mandā*, 'knowledge') in southern Iraq. Because of their baptizing rituals, this tiny community was perceived as Christian in recent centuries and referred to as 'Christians of St John'.

In third-century Iran, to the east of the Roman Empire, a separate religion of the Gnostic type arose. Mani (216–c. 274), who was raised in Gnostic circles, proclaimed himself a prophet, produced scriptural writings, and organized an independent community. Mani was a synthesizer, claiming to sum up the teachings not only of Jesus but of Zoroaster and the Buddha. Manichaeism, the tradition of 'the living Mani' (in Syriac, *Mānī ḥayyā*), spread in the Roman Empire and competed with Christianity for adherents in the fourth and fifth centuries. It won converts in Egypt and North Africa, including the theologian Augustine, who was a Manichaean during his twenties.

The development of Christian doctrine responded to the challenges of Gnostic and subsequently Manichaean teaching. Christians came to stress the unity and sovereignty of God, the humanity of Jesus, and the goodness of life in the material world. Nonetheless, some motifs that Gnosticism supported, such as the reality of the devil as an antagonist to God, or the desirability of ascetical practices, continued to find a place in Christianity.

Emerging Organization

Spontaneous at first, the Christian movement became formally organized during the early centuries. Some role specialization developed, with teachers providing leadership in groups already established, probably on the pattern of synagogue study, and evangelists spreading the message to form new ones. Before long, individuals were qualified by ordination to perform ritual and administrative functions. The most basic grade of ordination was as a deacon, and women as well as men were so designated in the early church. During the first two centuries, women apparently performed a variety of ecclesiastical roles, but in later ages even the role of deacon came to be monopolized by males.

The ranking priest in a political jurisdiction was known as a bishop (from Greek *episkopos*, 'supervisor'). His was the responsibility to ordain deacons and priests, symbolized by the 'laying on of hands' on the head of the person inducted. Similarly, it was the bishop, making rounds in his diocese or administrative district, who would confirm the baptism of new initiates into the community, for any Christian could induct someone into the faith by performing the symbolic bathing ritual.

By the third century, four episcopal jurisdictions or 'sees' in the Roman Empire had gained prominence because of the importance of their cities: Alexandria in Egypt, Jerusalem, Antioch in Syria, and Rome. The bishops of these cities came to be known as patriarchs. A fifth patriarch was added in Constantinople with the move of the imperial capital there in the fourth century.

To give legitimacy to claims of authority, Christians often invoked the apostles, the first-century companions of Jesus. Thus an early affirmation of faith was called the Apostles' Creed, and the ordination lineage of bishops was referred to as apostolic succession. Various nations claimed that their peoples had been converted by the missionary activity of one or another of the apostles—Egypt by Mark, India by Thomas, Armenia by Thaddeus and Bartholomew.

In the New Testament, loyal members of the church were referred to collectively as 'saints' by that energetic letter writer, Paul. In the course of time, the Church came to reserve the title for individuals considered channels of divine grace or distinguished by an unusual degree of virtuoso piety. Contemporaries of Jesus, including, of course, faithful disciples, gospel writers, and early missionaries, became saints as a matter of course. Individuals who made the ultimate sacrifice for the cause, martyrdom, were singled out. So were leading theologians and bishops in the early Christian centuries.

Asceticism

In the eastern Mediterranean, the margin of the desert was a region to which people retreated to practise contemplation or austerity. In the gospels, Jesus withdraws to the desert, wrestles with his own calling, and resists the devil's temptation. John the Baptist and his movement are associated with the desert. The Hellenistic Jewish sect known as the Essenes, part of whose library survives in scrolls and fragments, already had a community life, conducted in a settlement they built near the shores of the Dead Sea.

Centuries before Jesus, Hindus had established it as normal that a man whose household was established might go on to a semipermanent life as a forest-dwelling, contemplative ascetic, and the Buddhists elaborated the rules for their religious specialists to live permanently as monks. There are even suggestions that the spiritual practices and communities of India might have served as models for early Christian monasticism, since Buddhist inscriptions in India claim contact with the world of the Greeks, but such suggestions remain tantalizing and undocumented.

At least four aims internal to Christianity may have contributed to the emergence of its ascetical tradition. Asceticism, the practice of a strict discipline, was widely felt to provide a personal experience of spiritual depth. During the second- and third-century persecutions, life in the desert became an alternative to martyrdom. In more secure periods, giving up comfort or wealth was a public statement, a repudiation of the laxity and complacency of the wider community, particularly after imperial patronage in the fourth century began to make Christianity fashionable and even opulent. In addition to these factors, some of the early ascetics wanted to prepare for and to await the end of the world and the return of Christ, which they expected imminently.

The origin of Christian monasticism is traced to Antony, who lived a reported 105 years (c. 251–356) in Egypt, withdrawing to the solitude of the desert frontier. The account of his life attributed to the Alexandrian theologian Athanasius describes the spiritual temptations Antony sought to overcome.

> The enemy would suggest filthy thoughts, but Antony would dissipate them by his prayers. The wretched devil even dared to masquerade as a woman by night. It was as though demons were breaking through the four walls of the little chamber and bursting through them in the forms of beasts and reptiles. All at once the place was filled with the phantoms of lions, bears, leopards, bulls, of serpents and asps, of scorpions and wolves. Antony said: 'It is a sign of your helplessness that you ape the forms of brutes' (Meyer 1950:22–8).

Antony and others who pursued their discipline in solitude are termed hermits, from the Greek *erēmos*, 'solitary'. Noteworthy was Simeon (c. 390–459) in northern Syria. After having already been a hermit for ten years, Simeon at the age of about twenty-six built a pillar and remained atop it for the remainder of his life, hauling up in a basket the supplies provided by his admirers. At first low, the pillar was gradually raised to a height of 18.5 m (60 ft). Simeon's example of dedication attracted converts and pilgrims, and other 'stylites' or pole-sitters copied him.

Although the monastic life came to be permanent and corporate, its origins appear to have been temporary and sometimes individual. As the Greek word *monos* ('one', 'alone') suggests, monasticism entailed a life apart from the wider society; but as the institution took shape, it was very much a life in community.

The 'desert fathers', as early ascetics were called, made a transition to group life as they took up locations near one another for safety and mutual support. Such groupings were informal at first. In Egypt, Pachomius (c. 290–346) established nine monasteries for men, and his sister Miryam (Mary) two for women. Such communities are termed cenobite, from Greek *koinobios*, 'community life'. Basil (c. 330–79), bishop of Caesarea in Cappadocia (east-central Turkey), drew up regulations for monks that included poverty and chastity, specified hours of prayer, and assigned manual tasks. Some communities in or near urban areas became dedicated to social service. Monasticism was coming to be formalized as a corporate discipline.

Emerging Worship

With the Easter experience of the risen Christ as their model, the early Christians gathered regularly in homes on Sunday mornings. Spontaneous, even trancelike, activity was accepted as a manifestation of the presence of the Holy Spirit, but more formalized ritual became the norm. It contained prayer, affirmations of faith, song, scripture reading and preaching, and the Eucharistic service. Many services concluded with a benediction or blessing by the officiating minister or priest.

Prayer is reverent and contemplative conversation with the divine, aligning one's attitudes and motivations with it. Christians can pray individually as well as in groups; indeed, Jesus says to his disciples not to make a show of prayer, but to pray in privacy. He teaches them what is known as the Lord's Prayer, or by its opening words, as 'Our Father' (in Latin, *Pater noster*). This prayer was in fairly wide use around the end of the first century, when the gospels were produced. It is shared by all branches of Christians. The only substantial variation in the text is the inclusion or separation of the last line, 'For the kingdom, the power, and the glory are yours for ever.'

> Our Father, who art in heaven, hallowed be thy name. Thy kingdom come; thy will be done, on earth as it is in heaven. Give us this day our daily bread, and forgive us our trespasses, as we forgive those who trespass against us. And lead us not into temptation, but deliver us from evil, for thine is the kingdom, and the power, and the glory for ever.

As it is the prayer known by practically all Christians, the Lord's Prayer is often repeated in unison by congregations. Many of the rest of the prayers in a service are said on behalf of the congregation by the priest or minister leading the service.

Music was part of Christian worship from the beginning. The Church inherited from Judaism the biblical psalms, sung in the temple. Hymnlike passages incorporated into the text of the New Testament, such as in the opening chapters of Luke's gospel, indicate additional compositional activity.

The Eucharist

The central Christian ritual, common to all branches of Christianity but known under different names, is a re-enactment of Jesus's last meal with his disciples. In the synoptic gospels, Jesus shares the Passover supper with them on the Thursday night of his final week in Jerusalem. He breaks some bread and passes around a cup of wine, declaring these to be his body and his blood, given for them, and asking them to do the same in remembrance of him.

Because Jesus gives thanks before distributing the bread and wine, the ritual is called the Eucharist, from the Greek word for thanksgiving. This name, though well-nigh universal among Christians, strikes many as a technical term. Roman Catholics commonly refer to the Eucharistic service as the mass, so called from the final words of the Latin Eucharistic ritual, *Ite, missa est*, 'Go; it has been delivered.' Many Protestants refer to the ritual as Holy Communion or as the Lord's Supper. Eastern Orthodox Christians frequently refer to the service as the Liturgy, from a Greek word meaning 'service'.

In the typical Eucharistic service, the heart of the ritual is the 'Eucharistic prayer'. The officiating priest or minister repeats in it the account of Jesus's last supper and invites the congregation to 'communicate', to receive communion, by taking a portion of the 'elements' of bread and wine. A communicant who takes the bread only is said to receive communion 'in one kind', whereas dipping the bread into the wine or sipping from a cup extends the communion to 'both kinds'.

Baptism

Baptism is the Christian ritual in which an individual is admitted into participation in the community. At the time of Jesus, such a ritual implied that one's prior uncleanness was washed away, so that one could enter a new condition. Various movements practised ritual bathing, including the one with which Jesus's forerunner, John the Baptist, was associated.

As long as Christianity remained a minority religion that one joined at some potential personal sacrifice, its initiation ritual was not something to be undertaken lightly. One was baptized into the faith only after a course of instruction in it. The content of that instruction was termed catechism; and the persons receiving it, catechumens.

The Concept of Sacrament

The Latin word *sacramentum*, originally meaning an oath of allegiance, came to be applied to a wide range of Christian formal actions. Augustine in the fifth century used it of formulas such as the Lord's Prayer and the creeds. In Latin Christianity in the twelfth century, as many as thirty sacraments were enumerated, but in the thirteenth century a list of seven emerged that has remained standard for the Catholic tradition: baptism, confirmation, the Eucharist, penance, anointing the seriously sick, ordination, and marriage. Many Protestants pared the list down to baptism and the Eucharist, as the two ritual actions inaugurated by Jesus. The Anglican prayer-book's words, 'an outward and visible sign of an inward and spiritual grace', sum up the way in which many Christians understand such rituals.

The Christian Year

The liturgical year for Christians is calculated largely from the two main festivals of Christmas and Easter. It begins with Advent, the series of four Sundays prior to Christmas. Today, four special candles in the sanctuary, lit cumulatively over the four weeks, often mark the anticipation of Advent.

Christmas

We do not know at what time of the year Jesus was actually born. For some time there was a wide range of speculation; one third-century text sets the date as 28 March by reasoning that the world would have to be perfect, with trees in leaf and flowers in bloom, and the day would have to be a Wednesday because in *Genesis* the sun and moon are created on the fourth day. But by the fourth century at the latest, dates around the midwinter solstice came to prevail. That season coincided with Roman festivals, including 25 December as the day celebrating the unconquered sun. The Christian idea of a birth that would bring new blessing seemed to be readily associated with the annual renewal of the sun's radiance.

Many early Christians gave greater attention to the baptism of Jesus than to his birth. This was true especially among the Greek-speaking churches of the eastern Mediterranean in the first several centuries. In the Latin West, however, a difference in theological emphasis apparently lay behind the shift of ritual emphasis to the feast of Jesus's birth. Latin Christianity in the fourth and fifth centuries was experiencing competition from outside teachings that bodily existence is inherently corrupt, and from Christian teachings that downplayed the human side of Jesus's nature in relation to the divine. A feast that celebrated the incarnation amounted to a strong declaration in the opposite direction.

Epiphany comes twelve days after Christmas, on 6 January in the Gregorian calendar. It has a double association: the visit of the *magi*, and the baptism of Jesus. Both aspects can be seen as marking a manifestation to others of his mission or lordship. Indeed, 'manifestation' is the meaning of the name 'Epiphany' in Greek. In some Christian countries, Christmas gift-giving is delayed until Epiphany, or is spread, one gift per day, over the 'twelve days of Christmas'. The date of Epiphany in Latin Christianity corresponds roughly to that of Christmas in the Julian calendar, which the Greek Orthodox follow.

Easter

While Christmas has a fixed date in the calendar because it relates to the solar year, Easter is related to the phases of the moon and therefore has a variable date. The first Easter occurred just after Passover, a spring festival in the Jewish lunar calendar. In the course of time, Christians diverged from Jewish calendrical calculations. The Latin Church eventually fixed Easter as the first Sunday after the first full moon after the spring equinox. Thus it can fall anywhere across a range of five weeks from late March through late April. The Greek Church's reckoning of the date of Easter follows slightly different calculations, coinciding with the Latin Easter only about one year in every four.

Easter, the feast of Jesus's resurrection, comes as the conclusion of a period of six-and-a-half weeks known as Lent, of which the last and climactic week is called Holy Week. Lent is for most Christians the time of the year for the greatest solemnity, most serious reflection, and most stringent discipline. Eventually, in Latin Christianity, abstinence from meat eating or other pleasures, 'giving it up for Lent', came to be common, with the cultural result that the last evening before Lent has been a time of wild partying. Shrove Tuesday, as it is called in English, is Mardi Gras, 'fat Tuesday', in French, notably in New Orleans, and Carnival, etymologically 'goodbye, meat', in the Hispanic culture of the Caribbean.

Lent consists of forty days before Easter, not counting Sundays, which accounts for such Latin-derived names as the French Carême, from Latin Quaresima. The English name is a description of the season, when the days 'lengthen'. Lent begins on Ash Wednesday, so named because in some Christian churches the ashes of palm-leaf decorations from the preceding year are daubed in cross-marks on the foreheads of worshippers.

The last Sunday before Easter is Palm Sunday, which inaugurates Holy Week. Churches are often decorated with palm branches, recalling the greenery decorating Jesus's processional route into Jerusalem as he begins the last week of his life. The Hebrew ritual exclamation *hosanna*, 'O save now', with which Jesus is greeted, expresses the optimism of this day.

In four brief days, the mood of Jesus's followers in Jerusalem shifts from enthusiasm to foreboding. This is reflected in the course of Holy Week. Thursday, the day of Jesus's last Passover supper with his disciples, is called Maundy Thursday in English for the commandment (in Latin, *mandatum*) to love one another which in *John* 13 Jesus gives on that occasion. In various traditional churches, a bishop or ranking priest, acting the servant role of Jesus, recreates Jesus's washing the disciples' feet by washing the feet of a dozen priests or of a group of poor people.

Friday of Holy Week is known as Good Friday. Explanations of this name call Jesus's self-sacrificing death on the cross 'good' for humanity, but the more convincing historical etymology is 'God's Friday'. This most solemn day of the Christian year is marked by services recalling Jesus's Passion, his suffering on the cross. Services can run from noon till three in the afternoon, more or less matching the hours of the crucifixion in the gospels other than *Mark*. Some follow the narrative of the Passion as told in one or another of the gospels; others follow the seven 'last words' or utterances of Jesus from the cross.

Easter day itself commemorates the disciples' experience the morning after the Sabbath that Jesus, whose body disappeared from his tomb, had risen from the dead. The layers of meaning that the Christian worshipper on Easter finds in a service, whether at sunrise or later in the day, include both Jesus's own resurrection and a sense of cosmic triumph over sin and death.

Like Passover, Easter is a spring festival associated with the renewal of life. In popular Christian culture, some traditional symbols with probable pre-Christian origins connote fertility: the egg, for instance, and the rabbit. The English name 'Easter' itself comes from Eostre, a pagan goddess. In most other European languages, though, as in the French name Pâques, the name is a derivation from Pesach, the Hebrew name of Passover.

Pentecost is from the Greek for 'fifty', and is the fiftieth day counting from Easter. It was the Jewish festival Shavuoth, the Feast of Weeks, when as *Acts* 2 tells the story, the Holy Spirit enables the apostles to speak in diverse languages. For Christians this marks the Church's launching as a missionary movement with a message for all people. In England, Pentecost is often called Whitsunday, on account of the white garments formerly worn by persons baptized on that day. In Latin countries, the day is generally referred to as the feast of the Holy Spirit.

Early Christian Art

We have scanty evidence for the first three centuries of Christian art. The earliest Christians did not have separate ecclesiastical buildings. Some, whose roots were Jewish, must have gathered on synagogue premises to preach their new message. Some may have met in secret places away from their homes, such as in the catacombs outside Rome, but it is more likely that the catacombs were used for burial, not for meeting. Most often, small circles met in private homes.

Thus the surviving early church buildings, such as the Christian building in the eastern Syrian frontier town of Dura-Europos, were in the form of Roman houses, with rooms off an interior atrium or courtyard. In such house churches, given the secrecy in which Christians sometimes needed to meet, the room for worship might need to be placed away from the direct line of sight from the street door.

With imperial patronage, in the fourth century, the Christians built ambitious large-scale sanctuaries. Earlier Christian sites that did exist, with architectural details or mural paintings, often were lost in later expansion or reconstruction. From the Dura sanctuary mural frescoes survive, now preserved at the art gallery of Yale University in Connecticut.

Archaeology often finds funerary art better preserved than other art because it is buried intact. Hence material from tombs, such as the sarcophagi or stone coffins of wealthy or venerated Christians, dominates. These can display elaborate panels with groups of figures in scenes from the biblical narrative of the past or representing an eventual final judgement.

Central to many of these tableaux, and also frequently represented alone, is the figure of Jesus. In early representations he is portrayed as a simple shepherd, sometimes carrying a lamb across his shoulders. This clearly evokes Jesus's description of himself as the good shepherd in the tenth chapter of John's gospel, but the pictorial form seems to derive from earlier Roman representations of the god Hermes (Mercury) as a shepherd. In some of the other early depictions of Jesus, he is a young man, beardless, with the simple attire of a pilgrim or ascetic.

The fish is among the oldest of the Christian symbols. Stylized fish designs appear, among other places, in the catacombs, a third-century tomb complex on the outskirts of Rome. Many interpreters see the introduction of the fish as a coding of a Christian declaration of faith: the Greek word for fish, *ichthus*, is made up of the initial letters of the Greek phrase *Iēsous Christos, Theou huios, sōtēr*, 'Jesus Christ, son of God, saviour'. Other interpreters find the origin of the fish symbol in the gospel account of Jesus's multiplying bread and fish to feed a crowd, or in his calling his disciples 'fishers of humanity'. Historians who argue for these more directly representative origins regard the acronym as an interpretation devised subsequently.

Persecution

Roman society had its civic gods and rituals, which the population at large was supposed to support. However, the Christians stood aloof from the public religion, holding it to be the worship of idols. From a biblical point of view, they were bearing witness to their heritage of exclusive Hebraic monotheism. From a Roman point of view, they were guilty of insubordination, something for which Rome characteristically had little patience. In today's world of interfaith dialogue, one could argue that from the standpoint of Christian morality, they were un-Christian—judgemental rather than accepting. But remember that the early

Church was a minority movement that one joined at some potential personal cost, and thus with understandable zeal.

To the technically justifiable charges of insubordination made against Christians from time to time, there were added false accusations of incest, cannibalism, and black magic. Such actions, some thought, provoked the Roman gods to mete out punishment in the form of epidemics and natural disasters. Persecutions of Christians for these charges were largely local or mob-inspired during the first and second centuries.

In the third century, however, the empire was in crisis with deepening military, administrative, and economic instability. The emperor Decius (r. 249–51), seeking to revitalize his shaky regime, commanded public sacrifices to the Roman civic gods, with the penalty of death or imprisonment for anyone who would not comply. Throughout the empire, in the years 250–1, Christians were systematically persecuted as a matter of policy, and a few years after Decius, in 257–9, Valerian (r. 253–9) conducted another widespread official persecution.

Martyrdom, that is, facing death for one's faith, became a test for many Christians, who modelled their own conduct on the self-sacrificing death of their lord. Theirs was the confidence that the reward for their faithfulness would be a life in the next world in fellowship with him.

'The blood of the martyrs is the seed of the church,' said Tertullian (c. 160–c. 220), from Carthage in North Africa, the first theologian to write in Latin. And Tertullian had a point. By making martyrs of Christians, the Romans contributed to the record of bravery and fidelity that the Christians could be proud of. Persecution had a reverse effect from the intended imperial policy. According to a number of accounts, the steadfast faith of the martyrs offered an example that attracted many pagans to become Christian.

The careers of Diocletian (r. 284–305) and Constantine (r. 306–37) mark a turning-point in the history of the Roman Empire, and in many ways the end of the ancient world. Diocletian recognized that the economic and cultural strength of the empire lay in the Greek-speaking East at least as much as in the Latin West, and established an eastern capital at the city of Nicomedia. Constantine, in turn, located his capital not far away at Byzantium, which was renamed Constantinople after him. Diocletian undertook to stabilize things by organizing an orderly succession to the office of emperor, with junior and senior emperors in the western and eastern ends of the empire, but that system did not outlast him; Constantine subverted it, eliminating rivals and taking sole power.

Late in Diocletian's career, in 303, came the last and fiercest of the official persecutions of the Christians. For the next nine years, Christians were killed, church properties destroyed, and Christian sacred writings burned. The 'Great Persecution', as it was called, was no more successful than the earlier persecutions.

IMPERIAL CHRISTIANITY

Constantine

Under Constantine came a shift of policy that forever changed Christianity's place in the world. Gradually, Constantine switched from persecution of the Christians to issuing an edict in 313 giving them liberty to practise their religion, to later giving them state support and patronage. Why did Constantine do this?

Eusebius (c. 260–c. 340), bishop of Caesarea in Palestine, lived through the transition. In his *Ecclesiastical History,* he finds the providence and plan of God in the events of his day. Like the J source in the *Pentateuch* (see the chapter on Judaism), Eusebius has a success story: a recent triumph has to be explained. In his *Life of Constantine*, Eusebius links Constantine's conversion to Christianity with the emperor's reported vision of the cross in the heavens, with the words 'conquer in this sign', coming on the eve of a decisive battle in 312 that gave him control of the western half of the empire in his rise to power.

Modern historians have speculated about Constantine's motives as well as those of Eusebius. The allegedly sudden vision does not square with the gradual pace of policy change. Christian symbols appear over time on Constantine's coinage, for instance, alongside pagan symbols, and only after some years do the pagan symbols disappear. Sunday did not become a public holiday until 321, and even then it coincided with popular worship of the sun, a kind of nature monotheism. Constantine was not baptized a Christian until he was on his deathbed. Defenders of his sincerity rationalize that delay, however, by arguing that people saw baptism to be a once-only total cleansing from sin, guaranteeing salvation, and therefore postponed it in order to enter heaven with as clean a slate as possible.

Whatever his religious motives—his mother was a Christian—Constantine must have been a shrewd enough politician to recognize in the Church the potential for stability that his empire so desperately needed. The Church was dispersed throughout the entire empire. It had developed a system of regional government through districts called dioceses after their secular counterparts, supervised by bishops. It seemed to be arriving at a coherent sense of its teaching, in response to doctrinal challenges. And it had remarkable discipline, both institutional and personal. Many Christians conformed to imperial policy. Among those who demurred were the martyrs, whose courage in the Great Persecution was fresh in memory. One could say such positive things of hardly any other institution in Constantine's empire.

Still, Christianity did not replace paganism overnight. The etymology of the word 'pagan' hints at the process; like our word 'peasant', it comes from the Latin for 'rural'. Christianity spread in the towns and along the trade routes, while in more remote areas the old ways remained. (Similarly, what survived in a heath or remote area in northern Europe is called 'heathen'. In intellectual circles, too, there was competition from other movements. Politically, the emperor Julian (r. 361–3) attempted unsuccessfully to bring back pagan worship and teaching; he stopped short of reintroducing persecution of Christians. It was only with Theodosius I (r. 379–95) that the empire became an officially Christian state.

The consequences of official establishment were far-reaching. No longer did one put personal security at risk by associating with the Church; now, if anything, it was a way to get ahead. In time, baptizing infants and young children became the normal practice, with the parents as sponsors undertaking to raise them in the faith and sometimes with additional baptismal sponsors, known as godparents, recruited from outside the family. No longer were bishops chosen and doctrines determined by the Church acting on its own; now rulers oversaw the appointment of bishops and convoked councils. And the state's enforcement of law extended to areas of conduct that had previously been only the concern of religion; what had been sins became crimes.

Church Architecture

No longer did Christians worship in houses, in seclusion. With state patronage, things changed. Now there was an emperor ready to erect sanctuaries and shrines appropriate to the Church's new status. Constantine's mother, Helena, visited Palestine looking for the places of Jesus's birth in Bethlehem and his crucifixion in Jerusalem. Large sanctuaries, the Church of the Nativity and the Church of the Holy Sepulchre, were erected on the presumed sites of both, virtually obliterating them.

Christianity, repudiating the religion of the Roman Empire as pagan, repudiated the forms of its temples also. (To find a Pantheonlike or Parthenonlike church, one has to look

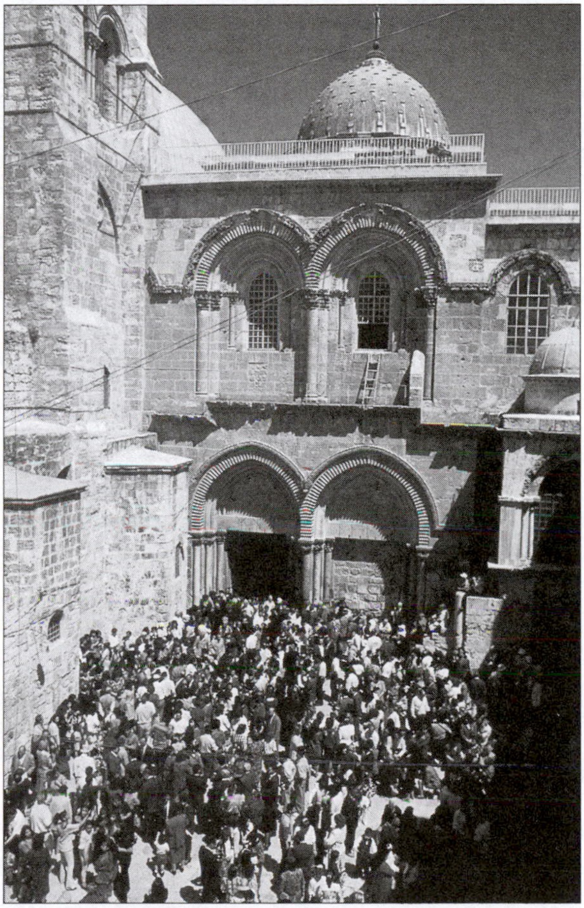

The Church of the Holy Sepulchre in Jerusalem, which is on the traditional site of Jesus's crucifixion and resurrection, was built during the time of the crusades. (Baruch Gian)

St Paul's cathedral in London, England, designed by Christopher Wren, features a style of round arches called Romanesque.
(British Tourist Authority)

to the fifteenth-century Renaissance and later.) The form that the Christians adopted, instead, was the building style of civil law courts and tribunals, known as the 'basilica', from the Greek word meaning 'royal'.

Basilicas had a dais raised a few steps at the end of the hall farthest from the entrance, and a nave or hall usually two stories high. The upper portion, with clerestory windows, rested on a row of columns along each side of the nave, beyond which were side aisles one story high. The dais end, called the apse, had a semicircular half-dome, or might occasionally be square. An option at the front entrance was an open, atriumlike forecourt with a low colonnade or portico around the sides.

In the hands of the Christians, the basilica form developed further. At the centre of the building, just before the steps up to the dais, the sides were extended by arms that came to be called transepts, thus giving the overall floor plan the shape of a cross and evoking Christian symbolism. From Byzantium to Rome to northern Europe, this plan became standard for the interior space of Christian sanctuaries, especially cathedrals, throughout the Middle Ages.

Not every church was built on the cruciform floor plan. A second pattern influential from the fourth and fifth centuries onward was the circle or octagon. Over the centre, where a shrine object could be situated, was a dome resting on a polygon or circle of columns and arches. As with the basilica, the central space was at least two stories high, with clerestory windows, and the surrounding space outside the columns was roofed at single-storey height. This radial plan, used in the eastern Roman Empire by the sixth century, served as the prototype for Islam's masterpiece, the Dome of the Rock in Jerusalem, constructed at the end of the seventh.

Symbols

Christianity's symbols imply a kind of coding of the tradition's message. Some interpreters think that during the years of persecution before Constantine, this helped the Christians escape notice. Others see in symbols a theological resistance to any picture making, a resistance we observe in rabbinic Jewish literature even though ancient synagogues actually had pictorial decoration. Whatever their origin, symbols had the capacity to survive times of challenge to pictorial images, such as eighth-century Byzantium or sixteenth-century Reformation Germany, both discussed later.

The cross, Christianity's chief symbol, is seldom found in Christian buildings and tombs before Constantine, but it came into widespread use during his reign, marking his patronage of Christianity. The crucifixion of criminals was abolished, now that the crucified saviour was seen as glorified. Now the symbol went wherever Christians did, with variety in its decoration and detail.

The Latin cross has an upright bar somewhat longer than the single transverse bar. The Greek cross has two transverse bars. In Ireland and Scotland, the cross of the Celts has a circle superimposed on it. Associated with Malta is the cross with twin flared points at the end of the four arms of equal length. The Copts of Egypt were known sometimes to represent the top arm of the cross as a loop, thus associating the cross with the ancient Egyptian *ankh*, a symbol of life.

Devout Catholics and Orthodox touch their face, chest, and shoulders to make the sign on their own bodies. Medieval warriors placed crosses on their shields, which survive in the heraldry of arms and in national flags. Each of the Scandinavian countries' flags features a cross, as do the Swiss and the Greek; and Britain's flag, the Union Jack, is formed by superimposing three crosses, one of them the diagonal Cross of St Andrew, representing the Scots.

The hot cross buns traditional in the English-speaking world around Easter are survivals of cross-marked cakes that pre-Christian Saxons ate at the spring festival of Eostre, their goddess of light. Rather than resisting the custom of distributing such cakes, the Christian clergy in England introduced their own cross-marked cakes, made from the same dough as the Eucharistic wafer, given to the congregation at the close of the Easter service.

Constantine's crosslike monogram, called the *labarum*, is used in both the Latin and the Greek Christian world. It superimposes X and P, *chi* and *rho*, the first two letters of the name Christ in Greek.

Another monogramlike usage is IHS, the first three letters of the name of Jesus in Greek. In the Latin-speaking world, this origin was forgotten and Latin explanations for the letters were offered: *in hoc signo*, 'in this sign [you shall conquer]', associated with reports of Constantine's vision of a cross in the heavens; and *Iesus hominum Salvator*, 'Jesus, humanity's saviour'.

Alpha and omega are the first and last letters of the Greek alphabet. They associate Jesus with the divine claim to be lord of all time, 'I am the first and the last,' in the *Apocalypse* or *Revelation* to John, the closing book of the New Testament.

A lamb representing Jesus recalls the first chapter of John's gospel, where John the Baptist declares Jesus to be the sacrificial lamb of God, who takes away the sins of the world. God's Holy Spirit is represented by a dove. The spirit could also be represented by a youthful or mature male figure, equipped as often as not with birds' wings, in the manner familiar in depictions of angels.

The orb, representing the world, is a little globe, without a map but with a cross at the top, usually about grapefruit- or cantaloupe-sized in relation to the accompanying figures. Present with depictions of God the Father in royal attire, it is supposed to signify his role as creator, sustainer, and judge of this world. People long before Columbus thought the world (i.e., the universe) was round.

Creeds and the Trinity

Very early in the history of Christianity, the Church arrived at formulations of the content of its faith. Especially before Constantine, such statements served as tests of the seriousness and commitment of individuals joining the movement. The use of creeds (the term is from the Latin for belief) has had a lasting influence on Christian understanding of themselves and of others. Christians have defined themselves as people who believe such-and-such about Jesus or about God and the world, and—often misleadingly—they have expected other traditions to be formulated in terms of belief as well.

Perhaps as early as 150 but certainly by the early third century, a formulation known as the Apostles' Creed was coming into use, especially in the Latin-speaking or western part of the Mediterranean. The apostles had been the first generation of the Christian Church. We have no historical evidence that this formulation was used at their time; indeed, if it had been used, it ought to be present in eastern Christianity to a degree that it is not. But the ascription of this creed to the first Christian generation clearly represents a claim of authority and legitimacy for it. It is frequently recited by congregations in services of worship:

> I believe in God, the Father almighty, maker of heaven and earth; and in Jesus Christ his only Son our Lord, who was conceived by the Holy Spirit, born of the Virgin Mary, suffered under Pontius Pilate, was crucified, dead and buried. He descended into hell; the third day he rose again from the dead; he ascended into heaven, and sits on the right hand of God the Father almighty; from thence he shall come to judge the living and the dead. I believe in the Holy Spirit; the holy catholic church; the communion of saints; the forgiveness of sins; the resurrection of the body; and the life everlasting.

The other best-known ancient formulation is called the Nicene Creed, named for the Council of Nicaea in 325 but ratified in its present form in 381. Somewhat longer than the Apostles' Creed, it covers many of the same topics in more detail. The Nicene Creed is recited in Eucharistic services in the Catholic tradition.

> We believe in one God, the Father almighty, maker of heaven and earth, and of all things visible and invisible; and in one Lord Jesus Christ, the only-begotten Son of God, begotten of the Father before all worlds, God of God, light of light, very God of very God, begotten not made, being of one substance with the Father, by whom all things were made, who for us men and for our salvation came down from heaven, and was incarnate by the Holy Spirit of the Virgin Mary, and was made man, and was crucified for us under Pontius Pilate. He suffered and was buried, and the third day he rose again

> according to the scriptures, and ascended into heaven, and sits on the right hand of the Father, and he shall come again with glory to judge both the living and the dead; whose kingdom shall have no end. And we believe in the Holy Spirit, the Lord and giver of life, who proceeds from the Father (and the Son), who with the Father and Son together is worshipped and glorified, who spoke by the prophets. And we believe in one holy catholic and apostolic church. We acknowledge one baptism for the remission of sins. And we look for the resurrection of the dead, and the life of the world to come.

Comparing these two texts, we see that the Nicene Creed is more specific about the Holy Spirit and more inclined to mention the Spirit along with God the father and Christ the son as part of a triadic list. This reflects the emergence of the explicit doctrine of the Trinity, a central Christian teaching and a problematical one. Following its roots in the insistently monotheistic Judaic tradition, Christianity has resisted asserting a plurality of distinct gods, but it has wanted to maintain a plurality of divine 'persons' or divine manifestations.

Christians today often think of the Trinity as a doctrine present in their tradition from its very beginning, almost as though foreordained by God from the foundation of the world. Actually, the Trinity as such is hardly mentioned in the New Testament. The text here and there speaks of God as father and of Jesus as son, and of God's spirit, but almost nowhere puts the three together in an explicit list. To settle on a doctrine that would hold the three in balance and preserve a monotheistic stance took the Church several centuries. (*Matthew* 28:19 is thought by some scholars to be a late addition to the text.)

In the interim, discussions were like preliminary findings in any research. At stake was the interrelationship of the three divine 'persons' or manifestations: God as heavenly father and creator, Jesus as son and redeemer, and the Holy Spirit as a continuing source of inspiration, guidance, and comfort. The thinker Origen (c. 185–c. 254), of Alexandria, wrote: 'With regard to the Holy Spirit it is not yet clearly known whether he is to be thought of as begotten or unbegotten, or as being himself a Son of God or not, but these are matters which we must investigate to the best of our power from holy scripture' (Stevenson 1957:213).

The emerging doctrine of the Trinity dominated discussion in the early fourth century. Today we may wonder how Christians could have become so consumed by fine points and theoretical distinctions. For an answer, we need to see the politicization of doctrine as a consequence of Christianity's emergence as the empire's establishment religion. Doctrinal issues were rallying points around which regional and personal rivalries for church leadership crystallized. It was not so much that the issues were unbridgeable as that people were frequently unwilling to bridge them.

Because of the political implications, the population was intensely interested in theological issues. In the new capital, Constantinople, the fourth-century climate was portrayed by one bishop as follows:

> If in this city you ask anyone for change, he will discuss with you whether God the Son is begotten or unbegotten. If you ask whether the bread is any good, you will receive the answer that 'God the Father is greater, God the Son is less.' If you say that you need a bath, you will be told that 'there was nothing before God the Son was created' (adapted from Frend 1965:186–7).

What is orthodoxy, that is, 'right teaching'? Heresy and orthodoxy are known in retrospect. As with judicial findings, one has to wait to see what view will prevail. One calls a view heresy when someone else, having failed to persuade the majority of its viewpoint, 'adheres' tenaciously to it following its rejection. Orthodoxy is the consensus one affirms with the wisdom of hindsight as having been intended all along.

What was permitted by consensus at one moment might not necessarily remain so later. Paul of Samosata (a town on the Euphrates River now in eastern Turkey) was chosen bishop of Antioch about 260 partly for his theological acumen. At the time of his baptism and ordination he had a binitarian theology of God as father and son. He described God as father, wisdom, and Word, and saw the Word as resting on, but not identical with, Jesus. During his career he maintained these views; one could consider him conservative. But Trinitarian theology was developing, and in 268 the very views that had led to his appointment were condemned as heretical and became grounds for deposing him. Unemployed as a bishop, he found work as an administrator for Queen Zenobia of Palmyra (r. 267–72).

Just at the time of Constantine, the Libyan-born Arius (c. 250–c. 336) was ordained and put in charge of a major church in the port city of Alexandria, Egypt. Arius proposed that the son of God was not eternal, but was created by God the father as an instrument for the creation of the world; in other words, 'there was an existence when the Son was not'. This meant that the son was not eternal by nature, but rather was subject to change.

Arius's view was opposed by another Alexandrian, Athanasius (c. 296–373), who asserted the coeternity and coequality of father and son. One of the benefits of so doing was to stress the power of the son to be a saviour. The conflict has been termed a battle over a Greek diphthong, the Athanasians calling the son *homoousion* (of the same substance) in contrast to the Arian *homoiousion* (of similar substance).

On the assumption that a unified Church would promote stability in his empire, Constantine called the bishops to meet in Nicaea, not far from Constantinople, in 325. The dispute between Arius and Athanasius was part of the agenda, and the decision went against Arius. But the matter was not laid to rest as the emperor had intended it to be. Arian views continued to enlist support, and for half a century they surfaced in various attempts at compromise formulas, even in 359 prevailing for a time, before being rejected under the emperor Theodosius I at the Council of Constantinople in 381.

Banned from the Roman Empire, Arianism took root among the Teutonic tribes beyond its northern frontier. It was carried to the Goths by the Gothic-born missionary Ulfilas (c. 311–83), who translated the Bible into his language. Among these people there lingered a hostility towards the Athanasian orthodoxy that dominated especially the Latin or western portion of the empire. This rendered Latin Christians vulnerable to persecution by fifth-century Teutonic invaders. Eventually, the influence of Arianism came to an end with the conversion of the Teutonic Franks to Catholicism in 495.

No sooner had the empire's dust settled on the debate over the Trinity in 381 than a corollary to Athanasius's position cried out for attention. If, as was now declared to be orthodoxy, the eternal son is coequal with the father, then how does the eternal divinity of Jesus relate to his historical humanity? Trinitarian doctrine had occupied the fourth century; now Christological doctrine, that is, doctrine regarding the incarnation of God in Christ, was the obsession of the fifth.

Around three principal options on this issue, regional divisions of Christendom emerged. The incarnate Christ could be:

- Two separate persons, one divine and one human. The Nestorians, stretching eastward across Asia, held this.
- One person, with only a divine nature. The Monophysites, from Ethiopia and Egypt to Syria and Armenia, held this.
- One person, but with both a divine nature and a human nature. The Greek- and Latin-speaking churches held this.

Each of these fifth-century options has continued to command Christian adherents to the present day.

The Nestorians

The split that produced the Nestorian churches was a blend of doctrinal dispute and political rivalry. Doctrinally, the issue was between theologians in Alexandria and others in Antioch, not far from the north Syrian coast.

The theologians of Alexandria, such as Cyril (d. 444), saw Jesus Christ in terms reminiscent of the prologue to *John*. The eternal *logos* or Word, they said, was what underwent the changes of being born, gaining wisdom, suffering, and dying. By contrast, the Antiochenes, such as Theodore of Mopsuestia (in Cilicia, today southern Turkey; c. 350–428), held the eternal son of God to be above such vicissitudes. They saw the *logos* as an entity distinct from the human personality of Jesus but having a controlling influence over him, more like the way in which a Hebrew prophet might be possessed by the spirit of God.

The differences came to a head when applied to the status of Mary, mother of Jesus. For the Alexandrians, Mary was *theotokos* (in Greek, 'bearer of God'). But for the Antiochenes, she was *christotokos* ('bearer of Christ'), that is, mother of the man Jesus but not of the eternal son of God. Not only doctrine but the allegiance of popular devotion was at stake if one would side with Antioch against the Alexandrian *theotokos* concept.

Politically, the rivalry was between Cyril, who became patriarch of Alexandria in 412, and Nestorius (d. 451), who became patriarch of Constantinople in 428. Nestorius, for whom Nestorianism is named, was not so much a principal author of the Antiochene position as he was a sponsor of it. Soon after his appointment, Nestorius opened a can of worms by supporting the Antiochene criticism of references to Mary as mother of God. Within three years, at the Council of Ephesus in 431, Cyril succeeded in having Nestorius deposed; by 435 the emperor Theodosius II (r. 408–50), who had appointed Nestorius, condemned his writings; and the following year Nestorius was banished to a monastery in southern Egypt.

Though repudiated within the Roman Empire, Antiochene Christology and the views of Nestorius survived farther east. Until the mid-fifth century their centre was the city of Edessa, in northeastern Syria (today in southeastern Turkey), where an Aramaic derivative, Syriac, was established as the Nestorian liturgical language. Edessa was a gateway to the eastern rival of Rome, namely, the empire of the Sasanian Persians, who ruled what is today Iraq as well as Iran. The Sasanian king Peroz (r. 457–84), though a Zoroastrian himself, gave patronage to the Nestorians, perhaps because of his own political rivalry with Constantinople. The headquarters of the Nestorian patriarch were established at Seleucia-Ctesiphon, the Sasanian capital, in Mesopotamia. Arab Muslim rule replaced Sasanian rule after 640, and Baghdad became the capital in 762; the patriarch moved there from Ctesiphon in 775.

From Persia, Nestorian Christianity spread overland through Central Asia, reaching the western cities of China. Though it did not establish an enduring community in China, it left its mark in a monumental stone tablet inscription of 781 at Xi'an that Roman Catholic missionaries found when they arrived there in 1625. The Nestorians also reached Malabar, the southwestern coastal region of India, where they survive to this day, as one of the branches of indigenous Christianity in India.

Nestorian missions were successful for some time among the Mongols in inner Asia. For instance, the wife of the Mongol ruler Hulagu (r. 1256–65), whose armies sacked Baghdad in 1258, prevailed on him to spare the Nestorians there. And the Mongolian monk Yahb-allaha, whose state emissary to Europe in 1288 was received by Pope Nicolaus IV in Rome, came close to Christianizing the Turkic and Tatar peoples of Central Asia. But the momentum of Nestorian Christianity was lost around 1393 when the armies of the brutal Mongol ruler Timur (Tamerlane, r. c. 1360–1405), a Muslim, wiped out much of the urban population of Persia and Iraq, Christian and Muslim alike. Central Asian

Nestorian influence disappeared, except for the survival of the Syriac alphabetic script (rotated 90° to read vertically) in Mongol and Manchu writing.

The mountainous terrain of Kurdistan became the refuge for the Nestorians who survived the Mongol devastation of Baghdad. Under modern political boundaries, Kurdistan is a frontier region. The Christians form a minority in northern Iraq, and an even smaller one in adjacent northwestern Iran and south-eastern Turkey. Because Europeans found them in the area that had been the heartland of the ancient Assyrian Empire, these Christians came to be called 'Assyrian', even though that empire had collapsed in the seventh century BCE.

The Monophysites

Following the Council of Ephesus in 431, theologians sympathetic to Cyril of Alexandria rather than to Nestorius swung the doctrinal pendulum in a direction opposite to the now discredited two-person Nestorianism. A key figure in this development was Eutyches (c. 378–454), who headed a large monastery near Constantinople and had influential connections at the court of Theodosius II. Eutyches taught that the union of the divine and the human in Jesus Christ produced only one nature, a divine one. The human was fully absorbed into or replaced by the divine. Christ thus had only one *phusis* (Greek, 'nature'); hence the name 'monophysite' for this position.

At the midpoint of the fifth century, the challenges to Eutyches's teaching made for political reversals on an annual basis. He was summoned by the pro-Antiochene patriarch to a synod or gathering of bishops in Constantinople in 448, which condemned and deposed him for not acknowledging two natures in Christ. In 449 the next patriarch, pro-Alexandrian, convoked what has been called the 'Robber Synod' to reverse these actions and condemn Eutyches's opponents. In 450 Theodosius II died, and with the loss of imperial favour, Eutyches was expelled from his monastery. The new regime convoked a council that met at nearby Chalcedon in 451, which repudiated Eutyches's views and the actions of the Robber Synod, while also reconfirming the rejection of Nestorianism in the opposite direction.

The formula produced at Chalcedon, which we shall discuss later, was one that both the Greek Church in Constantinople and the Latin Church in Rome found congenial. But it did not sit well with the Egyptian Christians, who continued to hold out for the one-person Christology of the Alexandrian school. Over the next century and more, there were attempts at compromise formulations, such as a circular letter by the emperor Zeno (r. 474–91) in 482, a conference called by the emperor Justinian in 532, and another circular letter by the emperor Justin II (r. 565–78) in 573. But what satisfied Rome tended to fail in Alexandria, and vice versa. When push came to shove, Constantinople found it had more in common with Rome and with the formula of Chalcedon than with Egypt, thus isolating the Monophysites.

In the reign of Justinian (r. 527–65), national churches in three distinct eastern regions went their separate ways from Constantinople as Monophysite churches. These were the Coptic Christians of Egypt and Ethiopia, the Jacobites of Syria, and the Armenians. All these branches survive to the present day.

Copts

The indigenous Christians of Egypt are called Copts from Arabic *Qubṭ*, with that name's core consonants coming from the Greek *Aiguptioi* ('Egyptians'). They say that the gospel writer Mark brought their faith to Egypt. They were early pioneers in the development of monasticism with Antony (c. 251–356). Coptic, the language of their liturgy, is like ancient Egyptian but containing theological vocabulary from Greek and written in an alphabet derived from Greek. After the Islamic conquest in the seventh century, Egyptians who remained Christian were a minority, but a significant one. The Copts have maintained a sense of cultural pride as 'original' Egyptians to the present day.

Christian influence extended to Ethiopia by the fourth century. There, the ancient South Arabic script was adapted to write Ethiopic, like Arabic a Semitic language. But Ethiopia, which gave asylum to Muslim emigrants, was not subjugated by Islam. It remained Christian, solidly Monophysite, recognizing the authority of the Coptic patriarch in Cairo and maintaining a window on the world through its own priests and monks in Jerusalem. The Ethiopians were later exposed to non-Monophysite Christianity, which sparked some Christological debates. The doctrines came from Portuguese priests accompanying their country's sixteenth-century Indian Ocean expeditions to aid Ethiopia against the Turks. The Ethiopian church remained essentially Coptic, though it has been formally independent of Cairo since the mid-twentieth century.

Jacobites or Syrian Orthodox

In Syria, where Antiochene theology and Nestorianism had been strong, Monophysite teachings were promoted in the sixth century through the vigorous missionary activity of Jacob (c. 500–78), nicknamed Baradae ('ragged') because he disguised himself as a beggar to avoid arrest. From Constantinople to Egypt to the frontier of the Persian Empire, Jacob established congregations and organized a hierarchy. The surviving Syrian Orthodox Church, which is Monophysite, calls itself Jacobite, acknowledging his influence. Its liturgy, like the Nestorians', is in Syriac.

And, like the Nestorians, Syrian Monophysites spread their teaching to the Malabar Coast of southwestern India, where it has been maintained. A Jacobite reform offshoot of 1836, influenced by British missionaries, took the name Mar

Thoma (St Thomas) Church because legend credits Thomas, one of Jesus's twelve apostles, with having taken Christianity to India.

Armenian Orthodox

Legendary accounts also trace Armenian Christianity back to missionary activity of the apostles, in this case Thaddeus and Bartholomew. Armenians take pride in their tradition, claiming that the baptism of their king Tiridates III by Gregory the Illuminator in about 301 constitutes the first establishment of Christianity as a state religion anywhere.

Politics overshadowed theology in the history of Armenian Christianity. Armenia was in what is now eastern Turkey, to the south of the Caucasus mountains and of today's Armenian republic. The region was on the northern flank of the Roman and Persian empires. When Rome and Persia divided control of the region in 387, ties with the Roman Empire were loosened; Sahak, bishop from 387 to 439, acted independently and sponsored the translation of the Bible and the liturgy into the Armenian language by Mesrop Mashtots (c. 345–440).

Because of political and military conflict between Constantinople and Persia, the Armenians did not take part in the Council of Chalcedon in 451, and fifty years later they repudiated its position. That repudiation has caused them to be grouped together with the Monophysites of Syria, Egypt, and Ethiopia. The Armenians have not been particularly enthusiastic about Monophysite teachings, but at a number of points they have been anti-Byzantine. They preferred Latin to Greek influence during the Crusades, and succeeded in having themselves defined as a *millet* (religious community) separate from the Greek Christians under Turkish rule following the Turkish capture of Constantinople in the fifteenth century.

Armenian nationalist sentiment in the twentieth century met with brutal Turkish reaction and eventually massacres from 1909 to 1922. Some Armenians fled northeast to the Caucasus, where their chief ecclesiastical centre today is Echmiadzin, in formerly Soviet Armenia. Others fled south to the Arab lands of the Mediterranean, where they were to become a factor in the intercommunal politics of Lebanon. The modern Armenian diaspora also includes such countries as France, Britain, Canada, and the United States.

Orthodoxy in the Greek World

The Council of Chalcedon in 451 was composed almost exclusively of eastern bishops, but it arrived at a Christological formulation in response to the Monophysite challenge suitable to Rome as well as to Constantinople. Its declaration reads, in part:

> … our Lord Jesus Christ, the same perfect in godhead and perfect in manhood; truly God and at the same time truly man of a reasonable soul and a body; consubstantial with the Father according to his godhead, and consubstantial with us according to his manhood, in all things like unto us apart from sin; begotten before all worlds (ages), of the Father according to his godhead, and also in these latter days, on account of us and our salvation, of the virgin Mary, the Mother of God, according to his manhood.

Chalcedon steered a middle course between the Nestorians, who compromised the eternal deity of Jesus, and the Monophysites, who compromised his humanity. The middle position, that the incarnate Christ was one person but with both a divine and a human nature, still left plenty of ambiguity. Chalcedon did not attempt to resolve everything, but only to state the acceptable limits of debate.

Indeed the debate was not over. In the early seventh century, there was what amounted to a rerun of the Monophysite controversy. In an attempt to win back the Monophysite Christians to the east, it was proposed that Christ had two natures, divine and human, but only one mode of activity, *energia*, or, as it came to be stated, one will (in Greek, *thelēma*), hence the name Monothelite for this view. But by late in the century, this effort was repudiated, and much of the Monophysite world was being lost to Islam anyway.

The main portion of the empire in the eastern Mediterranean remained orthodox within the terms of Chalcedon's doctrinal formulation. The Byzantine, or eastern Roman, Empire, was a comparatively stable and prosperous region. In the seventh and eighth centuries, circumstances were far more conducive to intellectual life in the Greek-speaking east than in the Latin-speaking western Mediterranean. The Latin world was struggling after the barbarian invasions, but the Greek world, including the regions where Islam triumphed from the seventh century onward, achieved a high level of culture and sophistication.

Byzantium lasted for more than a thousand years after Constantine. Even the slow but steady spread of the Turks, resulting in the fall of Constantinople in 1453, did not mean the end of the Greek Church. Formally tolerated under Islam though now forbidden to proselytize, the Byzantine Church became a self-governing religious community under the Ottoman Turks, with the patriarch as its civil ruler. Greece gained independence from Turkey in a rebellion that began in 1821, but Constantinople (named in Turkish Istanbul, with the same core of consonants) has remained Turkish.

Characteristic of Byzantium and also of the other Orthodox traditions is a close association of religion with the ruling regime and the national language. Historians refer to the involvement of the emperors in the affairs of the Church as 'caesaropapism'; and Orthodox Christianity displayed a number of other features one could term imperial.

Byzantine Art and Theology

One can see the Byzantine imperial tradition reflected in pictorial representations of Jesus. After the patronage introduced by Constantine, the Jesus figure changes. Instead of the young shepherd of the early centuries, he is now older, bearded, and portrayed as a king or a judge, attired in robes reflecting the dignity of his office. And he is seen more and more with that symbol of glory, the halo or nimbus. Even though the word 'nimbus' means a cloud, albeit possibly a luminous one, the obvious origin of the halo is the association of the revered figure with the radiance of the unobscured sun. The halo likely goes back to Persian usage, as the third- to seventh-century Sasanian kings were portrayed with halos. And not only did Christians carry it westward, but Buddhist art picked it up and carried it throughout Asia for representations of the Buddha as well.

The figure of Jesus is promoted yet further in Byzantine art, as we see in mosaics from the sixth-century emperor Justinian onward. Now Christ is represented as enthroned in the heavens, the ruler of creation. The Greek term is *pantokrator*, 'ruler of all'. Given a place of honour such as directly above an altar, these formal, frontal Byzantine representations feature him in the centre, flanked by attendant figures in a kind of heraldic symmetry. The cosmic ruler-Christ generally has a far older and more distinguished appearance than the carpenter from Nazareth who was crucified when only in his thirties.

Icons

The Orthodox churches, such as the Greek and the Russian, developed a distinctive technique of rendering portraits of Jesus, Mary, and other religious figures. These portraits are known as icons, from the Greek word for image. An icon might be an entirely two-dimensional painting, often on a piece of wood, but it might be overlaid in low relief, in wood or precious metal, and often ornamented with jewels. While the robes of the figure were executed in relief, the hands and face characteristically remained two-dimensional, so that the flesh portions of the portrait peek through what amount to openings in the relief.

An Orthodox sanctuary has a screen across the church in front of the altar, often three times a person's height, shielding the altar from the main portion of the sanctuary. The screen is called the iconostasis, or place for icons, and can accommodate a row of them each the size of a newspaper page. Smaller icons can be hung in private homes; some, as small as a pocket diary, are equipped with folding covers and may be carried on the person, especially by travellers.

Christianity's classic dispute over the place of images was carried on in the Greek Church in the seventh and eighth centuries. Known as the iconoclastic controversy, it pitted one faction in Constantinople, the iconoclasts ('icon breakers') against another, the iconodules ('icon worshippers'). Like other controversies in Christian history, the two sides of the issue were rallying points for groups

On the floor of a Byzantine church in Madaba, Jordan, is a mosaic map depicting Jerusalem before the arrival of Islam.
(Willard G. Oxtoby)

whose antagonisms were partly political or regional. But points of principle were nonetheless at stake, and serious theological discussions concerning the justification and role of images in worship were carried on among Byzantine intellectuals. It was important, for instance, to distinguish between worshipping an image and venerating it.

Historians continue to wonder whether these issues were entirely intra-Christian, flowing from the political and theological situation in Constantinople, or whether they were also a response to the success of an iconoclastic competitor—Islam—in the regions bordering Syria where the iconoclastic movement seemed to have a particular impetus. In any event, the iconodules prevailed in the end, and eastern Christendom retained its tradition of icons.

Theology

Representative of the eastern Mediterranean's cultural sophistication in that age was the Greek theologian John of Damascus (c. 675–c. 749), who for a time followed in his father's footsteps as representative of the Christians to the Muslim caliph. He was a defender of images in the iconoclastic controversy. His major work, *Pēgē gnōseōs* (Fountain of Wisdom), is a comprehensive treatise on theological topics.

Medieval Byzantine theology enjoyed a rich development of devotion and mysticism. Simeon (949–1022) headed a monastery in Constantinople and wrote of the profundities of the spiritual life. He was sufficiently respected that he was called the 'New Theologian', ranking him in Greek estimation next to a fourth-century figure, 'the Theologian' Gregory of Nazianzus in Cappadocia (east-central Turkey), who defended the Nicene Trinitarian formula against Arianism. What pervades Simeon's work is God's closeness to the faithful:

> I know that the Immovable comes down;
> I know that the Invisible appears to me;
> I know that he who is far outside the whole creation
> Takes me into himself and hides me in his arms.
> … I know that I shall not die, for I am within the Life,
> I have the whole of Life springing up as a fountain within me.
> He is my heart, he is in heaven.
> (McManners 1990:147–8)

By the fourteenth century there developed a movement termed hesychasm, from *hesuchia* ('inner stillness'). The Hesychasts repeated with each breath a mantralike formula known as the Jesus Prayer: 'Lord Jesus Christ, son of God, have mercy on me, a sinner.' Their practical spiritual discipline was challenged by Barlaam the Calabrian (c. 1290–c. 1350), a philosopher in Constantinople, who held that one could only see and know God directly in the next life.

To the defence of the Hesychasts, there came another great Byzantine theologian, Gregory Palamas (c. 1296–1359). Gregory distinguished between God's essence and his energies, agreeing with Barlaam that God transcends this realm, but arguing that God's energies come through to humans like the radiance of the transfigured Christ in *Mark* 9 and *Matthew* 17. Palamas held in balance divine transcendence and divine contact with humans: 'He is being and not being; he is everywhere and nowhere; he has many names and cannot be named; he is both in perpetual movement and immovable; he is absolutely everything and nothing of that which is' (Meyendorff 1964:209). Dialectical argument and paradoxical language of this sort have often been found appealing in religious thought, since while they rely on logic for their effect, they suggest that religious insight is beyond what can be grasped with strict logic.

Worship in the Greek Church

Religious services in the first centuries of Christianity must have involved chanting, though our documentation of it is only fragmentary. We can infer a common background, however, from similarities in the musical idioms of later communities. Medieval Roman Catholic, Greek Orthodox, Muslim, and Jewish melodies and harmonies have features in common. The emergence of systems of musical notation in the Byzantine era shows contact across the religious communities: specific signs employed in Byzantine chant are virtually identical to those recording Jewish cantorial tradition in medieval Hebrew biblical manuscripts. Premodern Mediterranean music had a number of different musical modes, that is, sequences of intervals giving a particular character to a scale in that mode; if they sound exotic to modern Western ears, it is because of the subsequent development of harmonic and rhythmic conventions in the western European baroque and classic periods.

Many Christians celebrate the eve of Easter with a vigil service where a flame, symbolizing Jesus's resurrection, is passed from candle to candle among the worshipping congregation. The ceremony is particularly spectacular in the Greek Orthodox service in the Church of the Holy Sepulchre in Jerusalem. Hundreds of worshippers, each carrying a candle or a whole bundle of tapers, pack the church's rotunda. A priest is ritually searched to see that he is carrying no matches. He then enters the chamber at the centre of the rotunda, which marks the traditional site of Jesus's tomb. After a time he extends his arm from the chamber with a burning taper, kindled presumably miraculously since no source of fire had been seen taken in. The people nearest light their candles from his, and share the fire with others, so that within moments the whole vast rotunda is a sea of flame. Outside the church, the fire is carried by runners to Orthodox congregations elsewhere. This ritual impressively symbolizes the spreading of the Easter light and the going forth of the gospel message.

Another ceremony in Jerusalem on the eve of Easter is the Ethiopians' searching-for-the-body service. Because their branch of Christianity lacks historic rights at the shrines and altars inside the Church of the Holy Sepulchre, they pitch their tents on the flat portion of the roof of the building. At a certain point in their colourful ritual, they go out in procession around the dome looking for the body of Jesus. When it is not to be found, they joyfully exclaim that he is not there but is risen.

A treasure of Byzantine architecture is the church known as Hagia Sophia, the Church of the Divine Wisdom, built in Constantinople during Justinian's reign. It combines features of the basilica and the octagon shrine discussed earlier. The nave, surmounted by a central dome, is so broad and so high in relation to its length that the interior effect is that of a central-domed radial shrine. The technical accomplishment of the Byzantine architects was to rest the dome on a rectangular base of four arches, but to employ quarter-sphere corners (called pendentives) to provide a horizontal circular base just above the tops of the arches on which the dome might rest. The resulting achievement is the enclosing of an interior space that is both broad and high. Interiors of this and other Byzantine churches were often sumptuously decorated with gilded mosaics, while the exteriors of such churches might be relatively unprepossessing.

An institutional centre of Byzantine spirituality is Mount Athos, a peninsula in the Aegean Sea that projects from the Macedonian coast of northern Greece. It is dotted by twenty monasteries that have been founded over the last thousand years. Numerous valuable icons and other artworks decorate their chapels and treasuries, and manuscripts fill their libraries. The entire peninsula is a preserve of male monks, and no women are permitted to set foot there.

Christianizing the Slavs

Eastern Orthodoxy is the name we use for the form of Christianity that was spread from Byzantium to various peoples in eastern Europe. In the ninth century, Orthodox missions to the Slavic peoples made significant headway. Language was important in their effort. The Byzantines, though they used Greek throughout their empire, used local vernaculars in their missionary activity beyond the imperial frontier. This encouraged the development of independent local churches with a strong sense of national identity based on language.

The activity was sparked by two brothers, Cyril (826–69) and Methodius (c. 815–85). In 862, they went to Moravia (the region of today's Czech Republic). They preached in the local vernacular, and produced translations of the Bible and the liturgy into Slavonic. Following Cyril's time, a new alphabet, a modification of the Greek, was devised. Known after him as the Cyrillic alphabet, it was adopted for Slavic languages whose speakers are mainly Orthodox, such as Bulgarian, Serbian, Ukrainian, and Russian. Romania, originally colonized by Rome as the province of Dacia, was Christian from the fourth century and uses a Latin alphabet, but its Church later came into the eastern Orthodox orbit during Bulgarian rule.

Meanwhile, Roman Catholic missionaries reached other Slavic peoples, maintaining a Latin liturgy and more centralized church control, and spreading the Latin alphabet. Thus Latin characters are used to write languages of the dominantly Catholic Slavic peoples, such as the Croats, Slovenes, Czechs, Slovaks, Poles, and Lithuanians. The Hungarians, also mainly Catholic, use the Latin alphabet, too, but for a language that is not of the Slavic group.

As with Tiridates in the Armenian and Constantine in the Roman Empire, the conversion of the ruler to Christianity could mean the conversion of his population. Missionaries tried to reach the ruler through an adviser or a consort.

The early centre of Russian Orthodoxy was Kiev, in the Ukraine. There, the fearsome pagan ruler Vladimir married the sister of the Byzantine emperor, who was a Christian, in about 987. Through her influence he became a vigorous promoter of Christianity. Some stories indicate that his new faith caused him to rule

Church buildings in the New World reflect old-country architectural styles. This is Cook's Creek Ukrainian Catholic church near Winnipeg, Manitoba. (Chris Lund/National Film Board of Canada)

more gently, without capital punishment; but other accounts suggest that his promotion of Christianity among his subjects was coercive. Kiev suffered a Mongol invasion in 1237, after which Moscow replaced it as the centre of Russian religion and politics.

Russian ecclesiastical and diplomatic interests coincided during the nineteenth century as Moscow sought to establish a presence in the Holy Land and also sent missionaries to the native peoples of Siberia.

Communism after 1917 ushered in a different era, as for seventy years the state was hostile to religion, regarding its practice as superstition and its institutions as museums. But Christianity survived, transmitted in the family often from baby-sitting grandmother to grandchild.

The nation- and language-based aspects of Slavic Christianity re-emerged after the collapse of the communist order in 1989. In the Balkans, these passionately held markers of identity proved particularly divisive, as secular Yugoslavia disintegrated in the early 1990s into religio-ethnic strife among Catholic Croats, Muslim Bosnians, and Orthodox Serbs.

Rome and Constantinople

With the passage of time after the Council of Chalcedon in 451, Greek and Latin Christianity grew further and further apart. Differences in language and culture were underlying factors, but again a theological formulation provided the rallying point for primarily political differences. At issue was a single word, *filioque* (Latin, 'and from the son'). Did the Holy Spirit 'proceed' from God the father, as the Greek Church had it in the Nicene Creed, or from the father and the son, as the Latin Church came to hold? Photius (c. 810–93), patriarch of Constantinople, in 867 denounced the intrusion of Latin missionaries into Bulgaria, which he took to be Greek territory, and also objected to the insertion of *filioque* into the creed. For the next two decades, one party in Constantinople repudiated the term and condemned the pope, while opponents rehabilitated the term and condemned Photius.

Behind the theological niceties lay the basic issue of authority. Rome had added *filioque* to the creed without the action of a universal church council. This pitted the Roman claim to be the centre of authority against a Greek notion of Rome as one among five equally important patriarchates. It set the Roman notion of papal authority against a Greek understanding of authority vested in councils of bishops. The mutual recriminations of Rome and Constantinople led to a break conventionally dated to 1054, though it was in the making before then and there were attempts for a while after that date to heal it.

Uniate Churches

Rome's efforts to recruit the allegiance of Christians in the Eastern Orthodox world subsequently produced the bodies known as Uniate churches. The name, first used by those who disapproved of the connection, derives from the Union of Brest-Litovsk, east of Warsaw, in 1595, when a church of the Ukraine affiliated with Rome. Other unions with churches of the Byzantine rite included the Ruthenians of Hungary in 1595, Serbs in 1611, Rumanians in about 1700, Melkites in the Levant in 1724, and Bulgars and Greeks in 1860.

Compromise with eastern usage was the order of the day as Rome sought satellites in the eastern Christian world. The Uniate churches retained their own liturgies in eastern languages rather than Latin. They often continued to administer the Eucharist in both kinds and to baptize by immersion rather than sprinkling. Significantly, they retained married clergy.

A number of the Uniate churches came from rites other than the Byzantine, that is, from eastern Christian minorities surviving in the Muslim Middle East and beyond. The Maronites of Lebanon were united with Rome during the Crusades, in 1182. Other affiliating groups were recruited from the Armenians of Cilicia in 1198, the Chaldeans of Iraq in 1551, the Copts of Egypt in 1741, and the Ethiopians in 1839. There was also a complicated interaction of Chaldean and

Portuguese influences among the Malabar Christians of southwestern India from the late sixteenth century onward.

THE MEDIEVAL LATIN WORLD

The Papacy

The Church centred in Rome thought of itself as 'catholic', that is, universal. Its interaction with political regimes in the Latin world (the western Mediterranean and northern Europe) produced the synthesis of religion, culture, and governmental and social structure often referred to as Christendom (the 'domain' of Christianity).

The bishop of Rome had unchallenged ecclesiastical authority in the Latin-speaking West of the empire, ranking with the bishops of such Greek-speaking centres as Alexandria and Antioch. His office was important because Rome was the capital, but some also thought it special because of Jesus's play on the etymology of the name Peter in *Matthew* 16:18: 'You are Peter, and upon this rock I will build my church.' There, Jesus clearly sees Peter's kind of faith as a foundation, but Christians have disagreed over whether the words also intend an institutional lineage from Peter that bishops could inherit.

Bishops of Rome, called popes (from *papa*, 'father'), were claiming theological primacy as successors of Peter by the third century. Their practical influence in matters of government, however, increased dramatically after the fifth century, when government in the western part of the empire collapsed under Germanic invasions. In those chaotic times, the Church was the principal source of organization and continuity. Culturally and religiously, Latin Christianity conquered the populations that were the military victors over Rome.

A remarkable leader, Pope Gregory I 'the Great' (r. 590–604) performed ecclesiastical and imperial administrative duties simultaneously. His reputation was such that the seventh- and eighth-century activity of collecting and editing a repertory of ancient musical melodies, carried on after his time, was attributed to him. It included over 600 compositions for various parts of the mass, as well as 3,000 antiphons and responses for other services. Gregorian chant was not the only such collection, but it was the most influential religious source for the later development of European music. The term 'Gregorian' applied to the calendar, however, denotes another Gregory a thousand years later. In 1582, an adjustment under Pope Gregory XIII set the calendar of western Europe ten days ahead of the Julian calendar, which continued to be used by the Orthodox churches.

Theology in the Latin Church

In Constantine's century, Latin-speaking Christians in the western Mediterranean

The present structure of St Peter's, which dates from the sixteenth century, replaced an older structure built by Constantine on what was believed to be the site of St Peter's crucifixion in Rome. (M. Dale Davis)

generally shared the doctrines agreed on by the councils held around Constantinople in the Greek-speaking East. However, in the course of time, Latin theologians went their own way. In the East the dominant issue was the nature of divinity in God and Christ, but for the West the central topic was human sinfulness and divine redemption.

A landmark figure was Aurelius Augustine (354–430), born in what is now Algeria. In his dramatic and passionate life, several currents flow together. He had a pagan father, and studied classical philosophy and rhetoric as well as Neoplatonism, the mystical and emanationist spin put on Plato's philosophy by Plotinus (205–70). He sowed his wild oats in his student years, including having a child by his common-law companion. He was a Manichaean between age twenty and age thirty, but after a vivid conversion experience returned to the Christian faith in a far more sophisticated form than that in which he had been raised by his devout mother, Monica. He became a priest and a prolific theological writer, and an active campaigner against heresy also as bishop of Hippo, in North Africa.

The concerns Augustine had while a Manichaean—of the struggle between good and evil, spirit and matter—remained in his Christian writing. He exhibits the tension between the spiritual and the carnal that we find abundant in Mani but also implied by Paul. Augustine's ideas shaped medieval Christianity's view of the human self and personality, as dependent on God. They also underscored a sense of guilt about the human body's appetites. Indeed, medieval Latin theology followed Augustine in its central concern with liberation from guilt.

An often-cited writing of Augustine's is his *Confessions*, in the form of a lengthy rhetorical prayer. Augustine relates his own spiritual struggles, the tension between his conscience and his will. He tells how he came to a Christian faith, and follows this with a briefer systematic statement of how it is in principle possible for anyone to follow the same trajectory. He describes the moment of his conversion:

> I was greatly disturbed in spirit, angry at myself with a turbulent indignation because I had not entered thy will and covenant, O my God, while all my bones cried out to me to enter ... It was I who willed and I who was also unwilling. In either case, it was I ... Suddenly I heard the voice of a boy or a girl—I know not which—coming from the neighboring house, chanting over and over again, 'Pick it up, read it' ... In silence I read the paragraph on which my eyes first fell: 'Not in revelling and drunkenness, not in lust and wantonness, not in quarrels and rivalries. Rather, arm yourselves with the Lord, Jesus Christ; spend no more thought on nature and nature's appetites' (Outler 1955:170–6).

The citation of scripture—in this case, the thirteenth chapter of Paul's letter to the Romans—is not unique to this passage. Augustine regularly cites scripture; he will come to a reasoned conclusion and then show that it accords with a text from the Bible. In this sense Augustine sets a pattern for much medieval Christian thought. The pattern is symptomatic of medieval philosophy's role as 'the handmaid of theology'. That is, it attempted to show revelation, authority, and faith to be reasonable and to spell out their consequences.

Christian theories of divine predestination and grace draw heavily on Augustine. There was a strong challenge raised by the lay monk Pelagius (c. 360–418), from Britain, who encountered Augustine's views in Rome and disputed them there and in Augustine's North Africa. Quoting Jesus's words, 'Be therefore perfect as your heavenly father is perfect', Pelagius emphasized the possibility of humans achieving such perfection through their own moral efforts. Pelagius did not actually deny the grace of God, but his critics, including Augustine, combatted his view as not giving adequate scope to a doctrine of divine grace as important in overcoming human frailty.

One of Augustine's most influential works was a response to political events of his day. Although we have suggested that the New Testament seems largely unwilling to talk about the fall of Jerusalem in 70, we find Augustine tackling head-on the trauma of the Goths' sack of Rome in 410. Augustine's occasion for writing was to refute the pagan charge that the Christians had brought on the collapse of the empire.

But his book *The City of God* is far more. It is a monumental theology of history, from biblical to Roman civilization. His judgement is that culture and institutions, even the Roman Empire itself, are of no enduring value in the sight of God. The earthly city, while sinful, is part of the divine plan. Kings are divine representatives and rule by divine mandate, in a fashion we can see paralleled in ancient Babylonia and classical China in texts that were not accessible to Augustine. But people must in the end flee the earthly for the heavenly city, to the community to whom God has promised salvation. The Church both symbolizes this city of God and is the means of reaching it. The idea that

> Crowns and thrones may perish,
> Kingdoms rise and wane,
> But the cross of Jesus
> Constant will remain,

to quote a hymn written in 1865, echoed through the centuries in the thinking of Christians. Christian political theory built on Augustine, seeing the church as transcending, and far more enduring than, the state.

The Monastic Life

In medieval Christianity, monastic communities developed a highly structured form of religious discipline. There were all-male communities of monks and all-female communities of nuns. To join a community, one made solemn vows of poverty, chastity, and obedience. One stayed within the physical precincts of the community, a status termed 'stability', and one followed the community's rule.

In both the Greek and Latin churches, monks played an important role. Technically, since monasticism started as an alternative to established religion, monks were laity rather then priests, but they made a demanding schedule of prayer and worship part of their practice. A distinction was drawn between 'religious' or 'regular' clergy, that is, those who followed a monastic rule, and on the other hand 'secular' clergy, those who worked in the world. The Greek Church permitted its secular clergy to marry, but came to choose its ecclesiastical hierarchy from among the celibate (unmarried) monks. Greek Orthodox monks follow the Rule of St Basil in a revision made by Theodore (759–826) of Studios, a monastery in Constantinople.

For Christianity in the Latin West, the Rule of St Benedict is fundamental

FROM THE RULE OF ST BENEDICT (FIRST HALF OF THE SIXTH CENTURY)

XXIII. *Of Excommunication for Faults*. If a brother be found contumacious or disobedient, proud or a grumbler, or in any way acting contrary to the holy Rule and despising the orders of his seniors, let him, according to the Lord's commandment, be privately admonished once and twice by his seniors. If he do not then amend, let him be publicly rebuked before all. But if even then he do not correct himself, let him be subjected to excommunication, if he understands the gravity of this penalty. If, however, he is incorrigible, let him undergo corporal chastisement.

XXXIV. *Of the Extent of Excommunication*. The extent of the excommunication or discipline is to be regulated according to the gravity of the fault; and this is to be decided by the abbot's discretion. If a brother be found guilty of a lighter fault, he shall be excluded from the common table; he shall also intone neither psalm nor antiphon in the oratory, or read a lesson, until he has atoned. He shall take his meals alone, after those of the brethren; if, for example, the brothers have their meal at the sixth hour, he shall have his at the ninth ...

XXXIII. *Whether the Monks should have anything of their own*. More than any thing else is this vice of property to be cut off root and branch from the monastery. Let no one presume to give or receive anything without the leave of the abbot, or to retain anything as his own. He should have nothing at all: neither a book, nor tablets, nor a pen—nothing at all. For indeed it is not allowed to the monks to have bodies or wills in their own power. But for all things necessary they must look to the Father of the monastery; nor is it allowable to have anything which the abbot has not given or permitted. All things shall be common to all, as it is written: 'Let not any man persume or call anything his own' [*Acts* 4:32] (Bettenson 1977:118, 120).

to the definition of monastic life. Benedict (c. 480–550) came from Nursia, east of Assisi in Italy. In about 529, he moved with a small band of monks to Monte Cassino, a summit overlooking the route between Rome and Naples. The instructions for community religious life that he elaborated include spiritual discipline as well as such practical matters as economic self-sufficiency. Benedict's sister, Scholastica (c. 480–c. 543), established a convent for women at nearby Plombariola. Many Benedictine monasteries were founded in western Europe. For several centuries they were individually self-governing, each following Benedict's Rule.

A monk or nun in the Catholic tradition is referred to as 'a religious'. Such a person has taken a vow to live by the spiritual discipline, and under the community rule of, a religious community. Daily living involved many menial tasks.

The monasteries and convents of the Middle Ages had to support themselves, often through the sale of the products of their own fields and vineyards.

The discipline of the community also included a life of prayer services at specified hours, and the serious reading and study of the scriptures. For their cultivation of study, the medieval monasteries have received credit from history as the custodians of culture. Their scholarship and libraries preserved much ancient learning that might have otherwise been lost.

The devotion of the monasteries could serve the wider society. The religious within the cloister walls could, for instance, perform penance on behalf of those outside, earning spiritual credit or meeting spiritual obligations. Frankish knights were barred from fighting during periods of penance the bishops imposed after the battle of Soissons, northeast of Paris, in 923, periods amounting to a third of the year. By engaging the monks to do their penance for them, the knights could fight on without interruption.

The monastic institutions have received criticism for their worldliness. Large donations and bequests made some of them wealthy indeed, to an extent that would have dismayed the early ascetics. The monasteries were useful to the aristocracy where division of land among heirs was not practised. The first son inherited the estate, but younger sons might find a respectable niche in the clergy. Monasteries tended to become the preserve of the wealthy, and the manual tasks that had once been an integral part of ascetic discipline could now be performed by servants and serfs.

Medieval Monastic Orders

From the tenth century onward, a number of major religious orders were founded, organized by individuals with a spiritual sense of mission. From an order's principal centre a network of houses and communities spread out. And the Benedictine tradition, where for several centuries local communities had had considerable autonomy, began to think of itself as a centralized order like the others now being organized.

Cluniac Fathers

Cluny, north of Lyon in France, was the site of one of the most influential monasteries, founded in 910 by William the Pious, Duke of Aquitaine (r. 893–918). During the next two-and-a-half centuries, the order of Cluny founded more than 300 satellite religious houses across Europe. Its organization and authority were a stabilizing factor at a time of political fragmentation and turbulence, in a way like what the Church itself had been at the time of Constantine. Cluny's abbey church, begun in 1080 and consecrated after completion in 1231, was 171 m (555 ft) in length, making it the largest church in Europe at the time.

Cistercians

The opulence of Cluny prompted a reaction from Robert of Molesmes (c. 1027–1110) in 1098. He founded the Cistercian order, called after the Latin for Cîteaux, its centre north of Cluny near Dijon. The Cistercians pressed for a return to austerity, with simple undyed wool habits, vegetarian meals, and sparely decorated churches. Within a century there were 500 Cistercian abbeys. Though the Cistercians had refused lavish endowments, rising land values in the more marginal areas where they established themselves eventually made the Cistercian order wealthy too.

Cistercians kept an austere silence within the community. The Trappists, known for this practice, are Cistercians of the Strict Observance. Trappist ideals have been made known in modern times partly through the writings of the mystic Thomas Merton (1915–68), who was active in social protest in the 1960s and also became interested in Asian spirituality.

Carthusians

Also influenced by Robert was a German named Bruno (c. 1032–1101). He turned to the religious life in his mid-forties and followed Robert's spiritual direction until founding his own order in 1084. Known as the Carthusian order, it, too, has a vow of silence and considerable austerity. The headquarters are at La Grande Chartreuse, near Grenoble in France. Like the Benedictine abbey of Fécamp, the Chartreuse abbey supported itself in part by perfecting and selling a famous liqueur, in this instance one that gave the Carthusian name to its greenish colour.

The idea of knightly chivalry led to the idea of fighting on all fronts against the perceived enemies of the faith. So leading Cistercians helped to found spiritual orders of knights, like the Knights Templar, the Knights of St John, and the twelfth-century Teutonic order. Their members served pilgrimages to the Holy Land, and their biblical model was the Maccabees, Jewish patriots of the second century BCE.

Mendicant Orders

The monastic response to the secular world had been to withdraw from it, even if as monasticism developed, withdrawal turned out to be more in theory than in practice. The growth of towns and cities in Europe posed new situations: urban intellectual sophistication and urban poverty. To respond to these needs there emerged a new type of religious order, one that served in the towns rather than apart from them.

Already in the eleventh century there had developed the religious lifestyle of the cathedral canons, people attached to the standard or 'canon' of a cathedral. Many of these followed the Rule of St Augustine, which called for renunciation of personal property, obedience to a superior, and 'stability' in a place. They became a model for groups devoting themselves to pastoral work.

The thirteenth century saw the rise of 'mendicant' orders, as they are termed. They represent a protest against the Church's wealth. Their members worked or begged for their living and were not bound to one convent by a rule of stability. The mendicant orders were for men, women, and laypeople (a 'third order'). Their members were called friars, from the Latin *frater* ('brother'). In England, the chief mendicant orders were identified by the colour of the mantle worn over their habit or religious uniform.

Franciscans

Francis (1182–1226), of Assisi in Italy, grew up as the son of a wealthy cloth merchant, but rethought priorities during an illness in his twenties. On a pilgrimage to Rome, he was moved by the presence of beggars outside St Peter's cathedral and exchanged places and clothing with them for a day, which he spent begging. Back in Assisi, he ministered to lepers and repaired a run-down church. Francis's rule of life, emphasizing poverty, received papal approval in 1209. Clara of Assisi was attracted to Francis's movement and formed a Franciscan women's order, the Poor Clares, about 1212.

Among other things, the Franciscans were assigned the custody of Latin sites in the Holy Land. Francis and his associates wore simple sandals and a rope belt, both of which became distinctive features of the Franciscan habit. Often the habit is brown, but in England Franciscans are called 'Grey Friars'. The Capuchins, an offshoot of the Franciscans, drew up their own separate rule in 1529.

Dominicans

Dominic (1170–1221) was from northern Spain. In nearby southwestern France, there was a movement, particularly strong among the inhabitants of the city of Albi and therefore called Albigensian, which taught about a struggle between light and darkness. Their doctrine, termed dualistic because of its references to these two opposing forces, was thought to be a recurrence of Manichaeism. Dominic received a papal mandate in 1216–17 for a preaching order to combat the Albigensians. As itinerant preachers of doctrine, Dominicans like Thomas Aquinas (1225–74) rapidly established their influence in such university centres as Paris. In England, they are called 'Black Friars' for the black mantle worn over their white habits.

Carmelites

Other mendicant orders included the Carmelites, the hermits of Mount Carmel organized by Berthold (d. 1195) in Palestine in 1154 during the crusades. They were given a rule by the patriarch of Jerusalem. With the decline of the Crusader presence in the Holy Land, they established themselves in Europe, and in England were termed 'White Friars'. Another mendicant order, the Hermits of St Augustine ('Austin Friars'), is the one to which Martin Luther belonged.

The insistence that priests be celibate became stronger in the Middle Ages than earlier, and much stronger in Latin Catholicism than in Greek Orthodoxy. Celibacy is an option only to religious traditions that have a vocational rather than a hereditary priesthood. Indeed, it counteracts the tendency for institutional influence to be concentrated in particular families. Rationales for priestly celibacy include the spiritual benefit of surmounting worldly and physical desires, and the practical benefit of being free to risk one's life or security in dangerous situations where a husband or parent might choose a safer but more timid course of action.

Popes and Princes

From the ninth century onward, popes and princes vied for legitimacy and supremacy. Charlemagne, king of the Franks (Charles the Great, r. 771–814) was crowned emperor by Pope Leo III in 800. For the Franks this was an endorsement of their German-based kingdom with its court at Aachen: it was heir to the political mantle of Rome. (Historians have quipped that this 'Holy Roman Empire' was neither holy, nor Roman, nor an empire.) Later in the ninth century, as Charles's dynasty faltered and the popes were strong, the papal argument was that the coronation illustrated the Church's role as king maker.

In the tenth century, the bishopric of Rome, like other bishops' jurisdictions, came increasingly under the influence of princes. The German (Holy Roman) emperor Henry III (r. 1039–56) in 1046 marched into Italy, deposed three rival claimants to the papacy, and imposed his own. And the operation of the Church was in need of reform. Ecclesiastical appointments could be bought and sold. The prince could confer the office of bishop or abbot on his own nominee, that is, 'invest' his appointee.

The investiture controversy erupted in 1059. Pope Nicholas II took advantage of a fluid political situation to decree that the selection of popes should be by an assembly of senior clergy of important churches in Rome, called cardinals. In 1075, two years after being elected pope, Gregory VII issued a decree that threatened expulsion from the Church—excommunication—for any prince who would invest anyone with an ecclesiastical office. And the pope, he claimed, could depose emperors.

The confrontation that continued over the next two centuries was basically a stand-off, neither side fully able to dislodge the other, but the rationale for defining the relative spheres of popes and princes developed during the period. The theory of two swords, stated in the eleventh century (as an application of the distinction between temporal and spiritual power drawn much earlier by Pope Gelasius in 494), held that the pope is given both the sword of spiritual power and the sword of temporal power, but delegates the temporal to a secular ruler, who is therefore accountable to him. In the 1050s, the two sides were making relatively simple claims of possession and scriptural precedent. By 1300 they were disputing political philosophy.

The Church grew to be like the secular states with which it competed. It was dependent on tax revenues, which it was often unable to collect. It was subject to coups from within and without. French mercenaries arrested Pope Boniface VIII in his family villa in 1303, and the popes deserted Rome to spend the years 1309–77 at Avignon in southern France, a period sometimes called the 'Babylonian captivity' of the papacy.

The so-called Great Schism of 1378–1414 occurred just after the return to Rome. A disputed papal election produced at first two and then three rival claimants at a time to the papal office for the course of a generation. This turbulence was settled in theory when the Council of Constance in southern Germany in 1414–18, mandated the papacy to be accountable to councils, but this was observed in the breach until more than a century later. Real power during the fifteenth century was largely in the hands of national rulers in different parts of Europe, and the popes behaved increasingly like Renaissance princes.

The Crusades

In a series of military campaigns spanning two centuries, Latin Christians from western Europe struggled to recover Jerusalem from Muslim control. The history of these campaigns is complicated. A major impulse came from the fusion of pilgrimage and religious war. There was an old tradition of pilgrimage to the Holy Land, often undertaken as a penance or in fulfilment of a vow, on the part of western European Christians who were also looking to acquire relics.

In today's climate of mutual appreciation among religious communities, the confrontations of a thousand years ago evoke ambivalent responses. To be sure, brave knights did valiant deeds in the name and symbolism of the cross, red on their white cloaks. But the crusades brought out both the best and the worst in people: valour and devotion, but also violence and greed.

In the spread of Islam in the Middle East, the Arab Muslims captured Jerusalem in 637. Thereafter, local populations that remained Christian were a formally tolerated minority under Muslim rule. Christian pilgrims could also continue to come to Jerusalem from lands outside the world of Islam. These Christians included what the Arabs called 'Romans', that is, from the Byzantine Empire with its capital at Constantinople. They included also what the Arabs called 'Franks', from the kingdoms in western Europe such as that of Charlemagne, with his court in Germany.

Changes in the eleventh century disrupted Latin pilgrimage to Jerusalem. These included the burning of the Church of the Holy Sepulchre by the mad caliph al-Ḥākim in 1010, the split between Rome and Constantinople in 1054, and the capture of Jerusalem in 1071 by the Seljuq Turks, who as recent converts to Islam were less accommodating than the Arabs. The Byzantine emperors felt threatened and appealed for Western help.

In 1095, Pope Urban II, declaring 'God wills it' in an eloquent address in Clermont, France, called for an expedition to the east and met with an enthusiastic reception. Thousands of French, Norman, and Flemish knights responded by 'taking the cross' in a public act signifying their commitment to the cause. The crusaders won some bloody victories, capturing Antioch and Jerusalem (1099) and even Edessa in northeastern Syria.

The crusaders formed military orders, the Knights Templar and the Knights Hospitaller. To hold on to the conquests, small crusader states such as the Latin kingdom of Jerusalem were organized along the Syro-Palestinian coast. As a small force controlling a large area, they maintained their control through a series of castles up and down the coast. For about a century, the crusaders held Jerusalem, but they were driven out by Salāḥ al-Dīn (Saladin, r. 1164–93) in 1187.

Crusader losses, beginning with the fall of Edessa in 1144, led to the organization of further expeditions in Europe to bolster the crusader enterprise. These follow-up crusades were often disastrous, their energies as often as not distracted by objectives short of Jerusalem. The second crusade, for instance, was diverted in 1148 to the unsuccessful siege of Damascus, a city that had been at peace with the kingdom of Jerusalem. In the third crusade, Richard I ('Lion-hearted') of England (r. 1189–99) took Cyprus from the Byzantines in 1192. Troops of the fourth crusade in 1204, bound for Egypt, switched to Constantinople, which they looted disgracefully. They placed on the throne a ruler from Flanders. In 1261, the Byzantines recaptured the city, but the relations between Western and Eastern Christians did not recover.

Among the other campaigns, in the so-called sixth crusade in 1228, the Holy Roman emperor Frederick II of Hohenstaufen (r. 1211–50) negotiated the return to crusaders of territories that included Jerusalem. There, he had himself crowned king, in spite of an excommunication order he was still under. Jerusalem was once more lost to Muslims in 1244. There was also a tragic children's crusade in 1212, when young boys sought to go to the Holy Land, only to lose their way while still in Europe after crossing the Alps.

Crusades often turned a religious project into a worldly one. Large numbers found scope for their ambitions as warriors. The people of Venice were particularly interested in opening up trading contacts, and profited from the spoils of Constantinople in the fourth crusade in 1204. Papal condemnation was harsh:

> It was not heavenly riches upon which your minds were set, but earthly ones. Nothing has been sacred to you. You have violated married women, widows, even nuns. You have despoiled the very sanctuaries of God's church, stolen

Westminster Abbey, where English monarchs have been crowned, was built in stages from 1050–1745. This chapel was begun in 1605. (British Tourist Authority)

> the sacred objects of altars, pillaged innumerable images and relics of saints. It is hardly surprising that the Greek church sees in you the works of the Devil (Bradford 1967:184).

Venice became a prosperous city, while Constantinople declined.

While they flourished, the crusades strengthened papal as well as national authority in Europe. They fired the enthusiasm of many people, inspiring chronicles, poetry, and heroic stories in Latin as well as the vernacular. They broadened European geographical and intellectual horizons, perhaps preparing the way for later discoveries, such as the New World. But the Latin states in the Holy Land failed militarily, and the misled efforts against the Byzantines led to much ill will.

The crusaders engaged as Christians in what critics have termed 'holy war'. Possibly, their enterprise encouraged a response of *jihād* (struggle in defence of the faith, also critically termed 'holy war') with Turkish campaigns in the Balkans that eventually threatened central Europe. To some extent, Westerners learned to distinguish between Turks and Arabs. On their side, Muslims learned to distinguish the Byzantines from the western Europeans, with whom they continued to trade after the crusades. More recently, however, Muslims have begun to look back to the crusaders as precursors of Western infiltration and intrusion into the territory of the Middle East.

Medieval Church Architecture

In the western Mediterranean, as in Byzantium, the round arch that the Romans had developed was the characteristic shape used in the churches, many of them cruciform. In northern Europe after about the eleventh century, a new style of arch came into fashion. Called the Gothic arch, it has two curved sides rising to a point at the top. Churches built with it could achieve a greater sense of height, and indeed the Middle Ages in Europe witnessed an attempt on the part of architects to build churches whose interior space rose ever higher. The height of a Gothic cathedral's nave might be as much as five times its width. Many writers on Gothic architecture have claimed that these high structures directed the thoughts of the worshippers heavenward.

In any case, the architects were pushing the capacity of their material, stone, to the limits. The arched crossing (the meeting of the nave and transepts) of Wells cathedral in England had to be reinforced from within with X-shaped stone bracings, producing an hourglasslike double arch. And many Gothic churches had to be buttressed from without to keep the weight of the roof from forcing the upper parts of the walls outward. Some supports, when they stood free of the wall and bridged to it with half-arches, were called 'flying buttresses'; these can be seen, for instance, in the elaborate exterior stonework of the cathedral in Milan, Italy.

Gothic exteriors were much more elaborate, on the whole, than Byzantine or Romanesque, but the interiors of Gothic churches could also contain much ornamental detail. Carvings in stone and in wood, usually brightly painted, depicted the many events in the life of Christ and of the saints. Above the altars in the side aisles of a church there might be paintings, often an arrangement of a central and two flanking paintings, called a triptych.

Stained-glass windows are a feature that developed in the Middle Ages. They are pictorial windows made up of thousands of pieces of coloured glass, joined by strips of lead. The earlier medieval churches with them were dark and had a small area of windows compared to their overall wall space. Hence deep, clear blues and reds could be seen as brilliant from within the sanctuary. As the area of windows increased relative to the wall space—in seventeenth-century

The Gothic architecture of York Minster in York, England includes the Great East Window, one of the largest expanses of medieval stained glass.
(British Tourist Authority)

Tudor architecture in England, for example—the interior space became lighter, and therefore lighter tones were chosen for the glass of the windows. By the nineteenth century, Victorian glass was often quite light, and painted as much as stained.

Scenes from the biblical narratives, or of an eventual final judgement, were repeated on church walls in sculpture, painting, tapestry, or stained glass. Often arranged in sequence like the panels of a comic strip, they were one of the chief means before printing and widespread literacy by which the average person could learn and review the Christian story of the Bible, the Church, and the world to come.

This view of the nave of Wells cathedral shows the reinforced double arch. (British Tourist Authority)

As late as the fifteenth century, the participation of the actual worshipping Christian in a service was dominantly oral. The clergy had texts in writing, but the laity on the whole knew more *that* the texts were written than they knew *what* was written. They attended the services, listened, and responded. The stories of the faith were conveyed orally and in the visual art that decorated the churches.

A feature of church arrangement unique to Roman Catholic churches is a sequence of fourteen locations, usually along the side of the nave of the church, called the 'stations of the cross'. They may be paintings, or plaques, or sculptures, or even, in austerely decorated churches, simply Roman numerals or crosses. This sequence recalls events from Jesus's trial to the placing of his body in the tomb. During Lent, the individual worshipper proceeds from one station to the next, meditating on Jesus's final suffering. The practice developed in medieval Jerusalem as a Good Friday itinerary through the streets of the city to the Church of the Holy Sepulchre, and it is still followed there by Catholic pilgrims. The itinerary was promoted by the Franciscans, the Latin order given principal custody of sites in the Holy Land. The present enumeration of the fourteen stations was finalized only within the past two centuries.

York Minster, which dominates the city of York, was begun in 1220 and finally completed in 1472. (British Tourist Authority)

Saints

The Church eventually developed criteria for sainthood (including the performance of attested miracles), a canonical list of saints, and a rigorous procedure for screening new nominees for the title.

The saints, collectively, came to be thought of as a kind of heavenly senate or honour society. Any of their number could be said to possess merit or virtue, a kind of personal credit in the economy of blessedness that could be drawn on by the believer who wanted the saint to intercede with God on his or her behalf. Prayers addressed to the saints, or ritual acts such as pilgrimages performed at their shrines, might win one release from punishment in the next existence and from guilt in this one. The saints could, in short, be powerful allies in one's quest for spiritual benefit.

In the Christian year, particular saints are honoured on particular days. Their profile was high in Latin Christianity, such that for instance Spanish and Portuguese explorers in the sixteenth century named features of the coastline in the New World for the saints on whose days they arrived at these places.

Well developed in the European Middle Ages was a large vocabulary of specific pictorial associations with particular saints. Visitors to Venice, for instance, learn that the lion symbolizes the gospel author St Mark. Similarly, a bishop portrayed carrying a beehive is likely St Ambrose, the fifth-century bishop of Milan, whose name connotes nectar; reportedly, Ambrose's mother dreamed that as a boy he swallowed a bee, which made him sweet of speech. But the beehive is shared with the twelfth-century St Bernard of Clairvaux, who was called the 'honey-mouthed teacher'. Keys? The apostle Peter, of course, to whom in a famous passage in *Matthew* 16 Jesus promises the keys to earth and heaven, but there are at least nine other saints who have also been represented with keys. And the orb appears not only with God but also with Dominic, the twelfth-century founder of the Dominican order with a mission to bring light to the world.

Pre-Christian local traditions and symbolism survive in the veneration of the saints. The eighth-century English church historian Bede (672–735) reports correspondence from Gregory the Great a hundred years before him: 'On the day of the dedication or the festivals of the holy martyrs, whose relics are deposited there, let them make themselves huts from the branches of trees around the churches which have been converted out of shrines, and let them celebrate the solemnity with religious feasts. Do not let them sacrifice animals to the devil, but let them slaughter animals for their own food to the praise of God' (*Ecclesiastical History*, ch. 30; Colgrave 1969:109). And the legendary St Ursula, with her ship and her company of maidens, sails the Rhine at Cologne, in the fashion of the earlier Teutonic moon goddess Urschel, and for that matter resembling such other pre-Christian deities as Diana and Isis. And St Christopher, who finds the child Jesus on his shoulder as heavy as the universe, does bear a striking resemblance to Hercules or Atlas, bearers of the weight of the world in classical mythology.

Some in southern France proposed one Decimil for canonization as a martyred saint; they had found what they took to be his tombstone, inscribed in Latin letters. Only later did people realize that the inscription was a partly obliterated milestone marking an old Roman road in Gaul.

The Figure of Mary

Early in both Greek and Latin Christianity, piety accorded a high place to Mary, mother of Jesus, as pre-eminent among Christianity's saints. The development of that place has roots in the biblical record, but began to flower after Constantine.

Mary's role in the gospels is particularly as virgin mother in *Matthew* and *Luke*. She is largely in the background in the accounts of Jesus's public ministry, but is prominent in *John* 19 as present at the crucifixion.

From scanty biblical details, Christian regard for Mary developed along two parallel lines. She became the recipient of popular devotion, both as the principal feminine point of access to the Trinity and as a model of sorrow-enduring love in her own right. Marian holidays, recalling events in her biography, developed in the Greek east and spread elsewhere. These included the Annunciation of her pregnancy (25 March), and the Purification (2 February). The fifteenth of August became the date for her Dormition (i.e., falling asleep).

At the same time she was a subject of theological speculation as the expression *theotokos* ('bearer of God') became a contested matter in the fifth-century Nestorian controversy. Later accounts speak of her bodily assumption into heaven, and regard her as now reigning with her son, and as mediatrix with him. There was a long debate in the West over her sinlessness, with the Dominicans opposing the feast of the Immaculate Conception (8 December) and the Franciscans promoting it. Mary even became regarded as the mother of the Church, for bringing forth Christ, head of the Church.

Widespread among Roman Catholics is the use of the rosary. It is a string containing fifty-eight beads and a small crucifix, that is, a cross bearing the image of the suffering Christ. The structure of the rosary serves as a reminder of which prayer to say. The rosary has five sequences of ten beads, separated by single beads of a different colour or size. (The English word 'bead' comes from the same origin as the German *beten*, 'to pray'.) Depending on the time in the life of Mary and therefore on her awareness of her son Jesus, three different cycles or 'mysteries' are defined: joyful, sorrowful, and glorious. The person using the rosary will say one Our Father (the Lord's Prayer, discussed earlier) and ten Hail Marys following the sequence of the beads. The Hail Mary is a brief prayer whose first phrase is found in the first chapter of Luke's gospel: 'Hail, Mary, full of grace, the Lord is with you; blessed are you among women, and blessed is the fruit of your womb, Jesus. Holy Mary, mother of God, pray for us sinners now and at the hour of our death.'

In Latin Europe the artistic depictions of Mary developed a set of conventions all their own. Historians see a debt to the worship of the pre-Christian goddess Isis in rural Italy, but the medieval images of Mary as virgin mother develop far beyond the infancy of Jesus and the figure of Isis. She becomes the mature woman who grieves at the martyrdom of her adult son. She is seen as the model of purity and incorruptibility, of devotion and fidelity, of sorrow and compassion. Many statues and paintings of the virgin Mary present her alone, as a model of selflessness to which not only females but males might aspire.

Among Protestant reformers (whom we shall discuss later) some, like Martin Luther, seem at times to have affirmed the Immaculate Conception and the Assumption, finding these to imply a high status for Christ. John Calvin praised her as 'holy virgin', but had reservations about her title as 'mother of God'. As the Catholics placed more emphasis on the Marian cult after the Reformation, Protestants tended to shy away more from her. Eastern Orthodox Christianity has maintained a high regard for Mary, but without the dogmatic formulations of Roman Catholicism.

In 1854, Pope Pius IX defined as dogma the Immaculate Conception: that

Mary herself was conceived without sin. In 1950, Pope Pius XII defined the Assumption as a dogma: that upon death she was taken up bodily to heaven. The Second Vatican Council (1962–5) did not add to her titles, as some had wished. Paul VI proclaimed her Mother of the Church; John Paul II has also spoken in traditional terms of Marian piety, but in general, there is more discretion and restraint in Catholic Mariology today.

Because of differences between Catholics and Protestants, Marian theology is sometimes considered a stumbling-block in ecumenical relations. The figure of Mary has also become something of a problem in today's world, with the development of feminism. Is Mary a stereotype representing feminine submissiveness in a patriarchal society, or has she something to say for the feminist as well? This question is still open.

Pilgrimages and Relics

In the early Church, people had drawn close to the saints and martyrs. Before long, the bodies of saints began to be placed in churches. By the fourth century, it became customary to celebrate the Eucharist with altar cloths that had fragments of saints' bones sewn into their hems. And at the Second Council of Nicaea in 787, it was declared mandatory to have a relic—that is, part of the body or personal paraphernalia of a venerated individual—in order to consecrate a church sanctuary.

The function of relics in medieval popular piety can hardly be overestimated. They were tangible, not abstract, and required little schooling to appreciate. They were widely thought to contain an almost magical power. They provided a link with specific individuals and events in the past history of the tradition. And while their physical location could be a focus of devotion and pilgrimage, their portability could also contribute to the

The city of Canterbury, which was a destination for devout pilgrims in the Middle Ages, is the seat of the Anglican Primate, the archbishop of Canterbury. (British Tourist Authority)

geographical spread of Christianity in the Mediterranean and northern European world.

For people whose lives' horizons were principally the fields and the towns where they lived and worked, pilgrimage was an experience to look forward to. It was almost the sole form of tourism in the Middle Ages. Organized groups took in the highlights of various centres and shrines, much in the manner of today's package tours to cultural or recreational destinations. In the *Canterbury Tales* by Geoffrey Chaucer (c. 1342–1400) we see pilgrim personalities in fourteenth-century England, including a character ready to make a quick profit producing fraudulent relics in response to demand for them.

There was indeed a lively demand for relics. In the economy of piety, they might bring rewards in the next world, but in the interim tangible economic benefits from the pilgrimage trade accrued to the centres that possessed them, comparable to income from tourism today. Princes and priests made deals to acquire relics, bought them, fought to capture them, stole them, or fabricated them. A bishop of Lincoln, England, himself on a pilgrimage and kneeling to venerate a bone of Mary Magdalene, reportedly bit off the end of the bone and brought it back to Lincoln, receiving local praise for having done so.

Rarely did a saint's bones remain together in one place. A major pilgrimage destination was Santiago (i.e., St James) de Compostela in northwestern Spain, but the same saint's body could be visited in half a dozen other places, not to mention detached parts like arms dispersed elsewhere. Nobody had talked of cloning in those days, but the effect was the same, as half a dozen hands of the same saint might overcome distance and inspire the faithful in several places at once.

The most treasured relics were those associated with Jesus himself, especially with his suffering and death. Highly prized were chips and slivers of wood, and assorted nails, purporting to be from the True Cross. Also revered were spines from, or examples of, the Crown of Thorns placed on Jesus. Various pieces of cloth were preserved for impressions Jesus may have left on them: his face enroute to the crucifixion, on Veronica's veil, and his entombed body on a shroud that turned up in France in the fourteenth century and later came to be kept in Turin, Italy.

A relic of Jesus's mother, Mary, venerated at Chartres in France, was *la Sainte Chemise* or holy undergarment, reportedly worn when she was giving birth to Jesus. This was by no means the most intimate Christian relic. Since doctrine held that Jesus and also Mary had been taken bodily into heaven, their bodies were ineligible as sources of relics except for pieces or substances separated during their lifetimes. Hence a prize at Chartres was *le Saint Prépuce*, a trimming from the circumcision of the infant Jesus, and it was only one of between six and a dozen of his foreskins venerated here and there in Europe. As for Mary, the mother's milk she allegedly spilled while nursing Jesus was preserved in surprisingly large amounts, and pilgrims to Bethlehem over the centuries have been able to visit a Latin chapel and bring away packets of the soil from the reported site of the event.

Relics carried on one's body were contained in amuletlike pieces of metal jewellery, with the piece of bone or sliver of the cross visible through glass like the bubble in a carpenter's level. Relics kept in a church for the veneration of the faithful were displayed in reliquaries, ornate containers at least the size of a candlestick, often with a crystal window for viewing the item itself. Reliquaries made of gold or silver could be quite costly, and took a variety of forms from treasure chests to models of church buildings. The most ambitious reliquary, in a sense, is the entire sanctuary in Paris known as *la Sainte Chapelle* ('the holy chapel'), built by Louis IX (r. 1226–70) to house the Crown of Thorns acquired in Constantinople. With its stained-glass windows, this chapel itself is one of the truly great treasures of medieval Christian art.

Struggling with Evil

Does the devil exist? Today many Christians who are quite ready to talk of God in personal terms are very reluctant to suppose that a comparable being exists as his adversary. Things were different in the Middle Ages. Not only did God have an angelic host, but the devil—Satan, or the Antichrist—commanded a corresponding host of demons.

Belief in evil spirits or demons is near-universal in traditional religions. Some theorists associate such belief with the fear of threatening forces in the natural world, including ferocious animals. Others locate a strong impetus towards fearing the spirits in the expectation that angry ghosts of the dead may return to settle old scores or to berate the living for ignoring them.

Likewise widespread among societies is belief in good or protective spirits. As far as the biblical tradition is concerned, the term 'angel' meant 'messenger', often a male herald. From this rather military aspect, representation of angels in Christianity developed over time into the winged and haloed feminine creatures portrayed with musical instruments, not weapons. But the belief remained till modern times that each individual is supervised by a guardian angel.

Medieval theologians devote considerable speculation to angels. Several authors, doubtless influenced by Neoplatonism's view of the cosmos as nine emanating spheres, rank angels in a nine-level hierarchy. Angels are thought to be created, not eternal. Not having physical bodies, they for instance do not eat, but they are considered to be localized in only one place at a time. (From the discussion of how much space they occupy follows the question of how many can dance on the head of a pin.) Angels have will, but not emotion. They know God more fully than humans do, but still not completely. How can one be so sure of such description? In a sermon on the feast of St Michael and All Angels, the German Dominican Johann Tauler (c. 1300–61) cautioned: 'They have neither hands nor feet, neither shape nor form nor matter; and what shall we say of a being which has none of these things, and which cannot be known by our senses? What they are is unknown to us ... Therefore we speak of the works which they perform towards us, but not of their nature' (Pass 1911:583).

Possibly as old as monotheism is the notion of the devil, a single adversary leading the host of demonic powers. The Greek *diabolos* ('slanderer') matches the name Satan ('accuser' or 'adversary') in Hebrew. He is also called Ba'al-zabul ('mighty lord'), corrupted to Ba'al-zabub ('lord of the flies').

A view common among early Christian writers is that the devil started as an angel. Through pride he tries to take over God's role, and so falls from grace. This is the implication of the name Lucifer ('bearer of light'): a star that has fallen from heaven, on the pattern of *Isaiah* 14. Biblical tradition speaks of humankind (personified as Adam) as fallen from the paradise of Eden through an act of selfishness, and Christian theology made selfishness central to its notion of innate or 'original' sin. The notion of the devil as fallen from heaven in a parallel fashion afforded little comfort but plenty of opportunity for moral admonition.

Lucifer falls to, and presides over, the realm of hell. It is the destiny of the wicked after their present life. The medieval imagination mapped and depicted this realm in gory detail, with a grotesque fascination reminiscent of disaster and deformity stories in tabloid newspapers today. The torments of the wicked could be extreme cold, far from the divine light; but much more graphic were the images of them prodded, speared, and boiled in cauldrons. Whatever morbid enjoyment people may have derived from imagining their own tormentors similarly barbecued was probably offset by the fear that one might oneself incur such punishment for wicked thoughts, if not wicked deeds.

With a basis partly in peasant superstition, medieval Christian society tended to identify individuals as witches, practitioners of malevolent magic. Witches were thought to be the devil's agents on earth and to have intimate sexual relations with him. A handbook for Christian witch-hunting was the *Malleus Maleficorum* (Witches' Hammer), published in 1486 by the German Dominicans Heinrich Kraemer and Johann Sprenger, who two years previously had been authorized by Pope Innocent IV to eradicate witchcraft from Germany.

Society's efforts to hunt down, prosecute, and execute such individuals by burning demonstrate how devastating the fear of non-conforming behaviour can be. Very often, personal grudges led to witchcraft accusations. In records of sixteenth- and seventeenth-century witchcraft trials in England, the most frequent charge attributed the accuser's misfortune to the alleged scheming of a neighbour, often an old woman, previously rebuffed by the accuser. Some behaviour explained as demonic possession may have had physiological causes unrecognized at the time; records of the witchcraft trials of 1692 in Salem, Massachusetts, have suggested to modern researchers the symptoms of poisoning by ergot, a grain fungus.

The medieval Christian world seems obsessed with the realization that death comes to us all. Death was unpredictably close at hand, given the conditions of warfare and disease, particularly when more than a third of the population of western Europe was wiped out by plague, the Black Death, in the late 1340s. But death was also often considered the consequence of sinfulness and marked the occasion to proceed to punishment in the hereafter. Rituals reminding people of our limited human condition included a dance of death in which people dressed as skeletons. And the walls and ceiling vaults of a basement chapel belonging to the Capuchin order in Rome have a gruesome decoration made entirely from the bones of deceased friars.

To the modern mind, the Latin Christianity of the Middle Ages also seems obsessed with sin. Humans are considered subjectively or 'originally' sinful with their pride and self-will, but specific actions are also objectified as sins. Medieval theologians saw such sins as contributing to the individual's mortality. Referring to the first New Testament letter of John (*1 John* 5:16), they drew a distinction between 'mortal' and 'venial' sins. A mortal sin, one that deprives the soul of God's grace, had to be committed both knowingly and wilfully and to concern a 'grave matter'. The Church required that such an act be reported in private confession to a priest, who could prescribe penance and absolve the offender. Lesser sins, termed venial, did not require confession before one attended the Eucharist.

For moral edification, the Church also warned the faithful against the Seven Deadly Sins: pride, covetousness or avarice, lust or lechery, envy, gluttony, anger or wrath, and sloth. A list of seven was established as early as the beginning of the seventh century by Pope Gregory I, although his seventh sin is despair rather than sloth.

Earlier Scholastic Philosophy

Scholasticism, the dominant expression of thought in western Europe in the Middle Ages, means different things to different people. Institutional definitions of it describe it as the work of the clergy in the 'schools', that is, the medieval universities. In emerging centres like Paris, Bologna, and Oxford, theology was a central subject in the curriculum. The clerical base of scholarship a thousand years ago is reflected in the traditional gowns, similar to monks' robes, used today in academic costume.

Intellectual definitions of the movement, on the other hand, characterize scholasticism in terms of its assumptions and goals. Faith and reason, for scholastics, are mutually confirming; philosophy is termed the 'handmaid' of theology. We find the view that it is 'faith seeking understanding' in the early fifth century in Augustine, and in the early sixth century in Italy in the government administrator Boethius (c. 480–c. 524).

Boethius wrote *The Consolation of Philosophy* while awaiting execution under the Gothic ruler Theodoric (r. 489–526). And at the end of a shorter work on the Trinity, he wrote, 'As far as you are able, join faith to reason.' He was perhaps the last important layman for a thousand years in Christian philosophy, for in 529 the emperor Justinian closed down the Platonic academy in Athens and in that very same year Benedict founded his abbey at Monte Cassino. The centre of gravity shifted to the clergy as custodians of faith and learning.

John Scotus Erigena (c. 810–c. 877), who was born in Ireland and taught in Paris, expanded on Augustine's distinction between authority and reason. Scripture, for Erigena, is the source of authority, but it is the duty of reason to examine and expound it.

Early scholastic teaching was based on following the *lectio*, the reading of scripture. This it shared with the scriptural schedule of monastic life, which had devotional services at specified hours. Early on, the scholastics were seeking to distil and summarize scripture and arrive at a rational grasp of its meaning.

Anselm

As time went on, however, scholastic teaching evolved to a dialectical, thesis-and-objections structure. A proposition of doctrine was stated, objections raised, and the objections dealt with. Anselm (c. 1033–1109), a native of the Italian Alps who became archbishop of Canterbury in England, moved away from the principle of scriptural authority, asserting that faith itself has a kind of rationality. One of the formulations for which he is famous is the statement, 'I believe so that I may understand.'

The most tantalizing of the medieval proofs for God's existence is Anselm's 'ontological argument'. Unlike later proofs that infer God's existence from inspection of the universe, Anselm's reasoning finds it implied in the idea of God itself. Characterizing God as 'a being greater than which nothing can be conceived', Anselm argues in the second chapter of his treatise called the *Proslogion* in a warm-up passage that such a being must exist, not only in the mind but in reality, since if it did not exist, some other being that did exist would be greater. In the next two chapters of the same treatise, Anselm pursues the argument in a second and more substantial form: a being that cannot be conceived not to exist is greater than one that can. As philosophers understand this, all other being is contingent, whereas God's being is necessary.

If the reader is tempted to see this line of argumentation as implying existence by definition, he or she is not far off the mark. Even in Anselm's own time, there were people such as the French monk Gaunilon, who held that the idea of perfection did not necessarily imply existence. But it was in a later period, the Enlightenment, that the German philosopher Immanuel Kant (1724–1804) made clear the objection that existence is not a description or 'predicate'. As Kant put it, the idea of a perfect being does not of itself cause a perfect being to exist any more than the thought of a hundred dollars actually puts them into one's pocket.

Nonetheless Anselm's thinking has resonated for centuries in Christian theology because it expresses the uniqueness and majesty of God's being. It is not existence like that of objects in the universe, but the ground and basis of the universe's existence. Indeed, some thinkers refused to speak of God as existing, since to do so would be to diminish God. The strategy of denying descriptions of the divine in order to move beyond their limitations is known as the *via negativa* or 'negative way' in theology. We have already seen it in Gregory Palamas; it was also used by late medieval Latin mystics.

However much philosophers have been intrigued by the ontological argument, Anselm's main impact on theology resides in his contribution to Christian atonement theory. For the Church fathers in the centuries prior to Anselm, God enters into the world to overcome the sin and death that hold humankind in bondage. In their classical atonement theory, by becoming incarnate and suffering, God rescues humanity from the power of the demonic.

What propels Anselm's thought is more a juridical notion of punishment than an incarnational theology. For Anselm, the compensation for sin to satisfy divine justice must be made by the guilty party, which is humankind. And since ordinary people cannot measure up to this obligation, Jesus appears as the man who can make the payment. Indeed, Jesus's self-sacrifice is the highest human gift to God. For Anselm and his medieval Latin successors, God does set the terms and conditions, and he does send his son to help meet them, but Christ's human nature is sufficient to accomplish the payment. Anselm's view of the atonement contributed, among other things, to medieval Latin interpretation of the Eucharist as the re-enactment of a sacrifice.

As scholastic thinking developed, so did the philosophical resources at its disposal. The tradition on which early scholastics relied came through Augustine and Boethius. Based on the thought of the fourth-century-BCE Greek philosopher Plato, it was dominated by consideration of abstract ideas. The twelfth century saw Latin Christianity discover the thought of Plato's contemporary Aristotle, which gave more scope for practical considerations and an examination of the material world. What people thought of as 'reason' came to consist of more than logic; it became more empirical, taking in the observation of phenomena. Aristotle's thought reached western Europe first via Arabic translations used by Muslims and Jews in medieval Spain, and then also in Greek by way of the Byzantines. The first major Latin theologian to take up Aristotle was Albertus Magnus (c. 1200–80), from northern Italy, who taught in Germany.

Thomas Aquinas and the Five Ways

The greatest of the Aristotelian scholastics was Thomas 'Aquinas' (i.e., of Aquino; c. 1225–74), a Dominican from near Naples who taught in Paris. Foremost among his works is his *Summa Theologiae* (Summation of Theology). In it and other writings Thomas sharpened the distinction between reason and faith. For him a large area of Christian faith assertions, such as the doctrines of the Trinity and the incarnation of God in Christ, lie beyond reason, but that does not mean that they are contrary to reason. But other Christian affirmations, such as the existence of God, he held provable by reason.

Thomas wrote of five 'ways' of proving God's existence. Most of these describe some feature of the extant world and argue that without a God such a world could not exist.

The first three of Thomas's ways overlap as variations on what philosophers term the 'cosmological argument' for God's existence. In the first way, change or motion in the universe is evidence that there must be a Prime Mover to sustain the process. In the second, the pattern of cause and effect points to God as a First Cause. In the third, things have the possibility of existing or not existing, being generated or corrupted, but in order for there not to have once been nothing at all, there must have been some being that existed out of necessity, and that is God.

The fourth of Aquinas's five 'ways' argues that there are gradations of goodness, truth, and nobility in what we experience, and that therefore there must be a being that is supremely good, supremely true, and supremely noble. If one argues that there is goodness in the universe and that such extant goodness is inexplicable without a good God causing it, then we have a type of cosmological argument. It is less clearly Thomas's intent, but if one argues that there is an idea of goodness that because of its own implied perfection has no possibility of not existing, there is an overtone of the ontological argument.

Aquinas's fifth 'way' illustrates the type of argument termed 'teleological' (from Greek *telos*, 'end' or 'purpose'). Arguments based on design or purpose in the universe can be found as far back as ancient Greek philosophy, in Plato's *Timaeus*. The plan observable in the universe, in this view, is evidence of a divine planner.

Thomas was convinced that in a doctrine of God as creator, he could maintain a foothold in a doctrine of biblical authority at the same time as he explored the characteristics of the secular world. The tension between these two concerns proved controversial among scholars who paid attention to his thought. Three years after Thomas died, the archbishop of Paris formally condemned a list of propositions close to what Thomas had taught. But the comprehensiveness of Thomas's system commended itself to later generations. In 1567, in the time of the Catholic Reformation, Pope Pius V declared him 'Doctor of the Church'. In

FROM THOMAS AQUINAS

[In his Summa *Theologiae of 1265–73, Book ii, Question xi, Article iii, he considers whether heretics should be tolerated.]*

With regard to heretics, two considerations are to be kept in their mind, 1) on their side, 2) on the side of the church.

1) There is the sin, whereby they deserve not only to be separated from the Church by excommunication, but also to be shut off from the world by death. For it is a much more serious matter to corrupt faith, through which comes the soul's life, than to forge money, through which temporal life is supported. Hence if forgers of money or other malefactors are straightway put to death by secular princes, with much more justice can heretics, immediately upon conviction, be not only excommunicated but also put to death.

2) But on the side of the Church there is mercy, with a view to the conversion of them that are in error; and therefore the Church does not straightway condemn, but after a first and a second admonition, as the Apostle teaches [*Titus* 3:10]. After that, if he be found still stubborn, the Church gives up hope of his conversion and takes thought for the safety of others, by separating him from the Church by sentence of excommunication; and, further, leaves him to the secular court, to be exterminated from the world by death (Bettenson 1977:133–4).

1879 Pope Leo XIII opened a modern era for Thomism as the official theology of the Roman Catholic Church, to counteract modern thinking, making him required reading for theology students.

Medieval Mystics

The fourteenth-century reaction to Thomas's views included further discussion of the limits of reason in certifying the content of faith. But there was another development afoot that rendered those limits to some extent irrelevant. The late Middle Ages saw a remarkable flowering of mysticism.

'Mysticism' does not mean simply anything unclear, uncertain, or mysterious. Rather, mysticism is a specific tradition that emphasizes the certainty of profound personal experience. The certainty of God that a mystic has is based not on logical proof but on a moment of vivid, intense awareness. At such a moment one may experience ecstasy (from Greek, 'standing outside oneself'), or being displaced from one's ordinary mode of awareness. And characteristic of that experience is a sense of union with, or vision of, the divine—a temporary dissolving or bridging of the gulf that separates the human person from God.

As indicated, such moments are temporary. The mystic comes down from the experiential heights, returning to more mundane awareness. If a mystic writes about the experience, it is afterward, on the basis of memory. A number of medieval Christian mystics did indeed write in vivid detail of what they had experienced, and some have engaged in a certain amount of theoretical writing on how such experience is in principle possible and what its implications are.

Medieval mysticism picked up on a long tradition of Christian cultivation of the interior life. In Christianity, that life is usually termed spirituality. It is parallel to, and complements, the ethical life where virtue is practised in one's relationship with others. In spirituality, the heart or conscience savours its own presence, opening itself to the divine through prayer and contemplation. For many Christians, spirituality is viewed as the essence of religious experience, and credit for it is given to the action of the Holy Spirit on the individual self or soul.

Christian spirituality did not emerge out of a vacuum. It had roots in Jewish contemplation of the mystery of God's presence with his people. It included the 'desert fathers'—and mothers—whose asceticism was the forerunner to the life of the medieval religious communities. Christian spirituality developed very much in the bosom of the monastic life.

In the Greek world, mysticism was especially influenced by the younger brother of St Basil, Gregory of Nyssa (c. 330–c. 395) in Cappadocia, who likens the knowledge of God to the soul's groping towards the light, with the desire of love, in a dark night of unattainability and unknowing. In sixth-century Syria, another writer in Greek put forward his or her ideas under the name of Dionysius, a convert who had heard the apostle Paul preach in Athens. Pseudo-Dionysius, as we designate this author, speaks of a divine reality beyond all names, including such formulations as the Trinity. Pseudo-Dionysius, whose ideas show the influence of Plotinus's Neoplatonism, negates all forms, proposing a spiritual ascent to the nameless One.

In medieval Europe, the most formidable systematizer of mystical thought was the German Dominican Johannes ('Meister') Eckhart (c. 1260–1327). He combined Gregory's and Pseudo-Dionysius's ideas with Augustine's psychology of the self. For Eckhart, human life is as an image of God, but it is finite and creaturely and therefore obscures the divine. The mind of the spiritual person permits an actualization of the divine nature that the human soul contains. The individual mystic becomes aware of the divinity of his or her being. Eckhart's mysticism is unitive, tending to dissolve distinctions between self and God.

The Flemish mystic Jan van Ruysbroeck (1293–1381) took up the problem of differentiation and related it to the persons of the Trinity. God as Father, he said, is the One. But the other parts of the Trinity are related to the movement of creation in the cosmos and a movement of awareness in the self.

While Eckhart and Ruysbroeck seek to identify the self with the image of God, the alternative is to see God in all the nearness of humanity. Likening the awareness of God to the awareness of one's beloved is a move made not only by Muslim Ṣūfīs but by the French Cistercian Bernard (1090–1153), abbot of Clairvaux. Unity of the spirit with God, he says, is a concurrence of wills, not a union of essences. Like the ecstasy of love, this union is fleeting, but no less intensely experienced: 'To lose yourself so that you are as though you were not, to be unaware of yourself and emptied of yourself, to be, as it were, brought to nothing—this pertains to heavenly exchanges, not to human affection' (O'Brien 1964:122).

In Bonaventure (1221–74), an Italian Franciscan who taught at Paris and wrote a text, *Journey of the Mind to God*, the orientation moves to a meditation on the humanity of Christ as the point of experiential contact with the divine. Later, in the writings of St John of the Cross (1542–91), a Spanish Carmelite, the soul seeks to purify itself. John speaks of the 'dark night of the soul' when it is purged of its attachments, and rises to God in a union described in the language of a pure flame.

A striking feature of late medieval mysticism is the scope it afforded for achievement by women. However much women might be held back from full participation in clerical activities and given supporting roles in the women's reli-

SOME WOMEN MYSTICS

Hildegard of Bingen

[From Scivias *(Know the ways [of God], written by Hildegard of Bingen between 1141 and 1151, Book II, section 2.6].*

On the Trinity: Just as the flame contains three essences in the one fire, so too, there is one God in three persons. How is this so? The flame consists of shining brightness, purple vigour and fiery glow. It has shining brightness so that it may give light; purple vigour so that it may flourish; and a fiery glow so that it may burn.

In the shining brightness, observe the Father who, in his fatherly devotion, reveals his brightness to the faithful. In the purple vigour contained within it (whereby this same flame manifests its power), understand the Son who, from the Virgin, assumed a body in which Godhead demonstrated its miracles. And in the fiery glow, perceive the Holy Spirit which pours glowingly into the minds of believers.

But where there is neither shining brightness, nor purple vigour, nor fiery glow, there no flame is seen. So too, where neither the Father nor the Son nor the Holy Spirit is honoured, there God is not worthily revered.

And so, just as these three essences are discerned in the one flame, so too, three Persons are to be understood in the unity of Godhead (Bowie and Davies 1990:53, 75).

Teresa of Ávila

[From the Life *of the sixteenth-century Spanish Carmelite Teresa of Ávila, chapter 18.]*

Previously, as I have said, the senses were permitted to give some indication of the great joy they feel. But now the soul enjoys incomparably more, and yet has still less power to show it. For there is no power left in the body—and the soul possesses none—by which this joy can be communicated. At such a time anything of the sort would be a great embarrassment, a torment and a disturbance of its repose. If there is really a union of all the faculties, I say, then the soul cannot make it known, even if it wants to—while actually in union I mean. If it can, it is not in union.

How what is called union takes place and what it is, I cannot tell. It is explained in mystical theology, but I cannot use the proper terms; I cannot understand what mind is, or how it differs from soul or spirit. They all seem one to me, though the soul sometimes leaps out of itself like a burning fire that has become one whole flame and increases with great force. The flame leaps very high above the fire. Nevertheless it is not a different thing, but the same flame which is in the fire (Happold 1963:321).

Marie de l'Incarnation

[Marie de l'Incarnation writes to her son, the French Benedictine Dom Claude Martin in her Relation *of 1654, describing her experience after becoming an Ursuline nun and serving in Québec. She identifies thirteen stages of progress in prayer.]*

The state which I now experience, compared with what I have previously described, is a completely extraordinary clearness about the ways of the adorable Spirit of the Word Incarnate. I know, experientially in great pureness and certainty, that here is Love Himself intimately joined to me and joining my spirit to His and 'all that He has said has spirit and life [*John* 6:63]' in me. Particularly does my soul experience being in this intimate union with Him …

I find myself frequently saying to Him: 'Divine Spirit, guide me in the ways of my Divine Spouse.' I am continuously engaged in this divine exchange in a fashion and a manner so delicate, so simple, and so intense that there is no way of expressing it. It is not an act. It is not a sigh. It is an air so gentle in the center of the soul where God has His dwelling that, as I have already said, I cannot find words to express it. My converse with the adorable Majesty contains only what the Spirit makes me say. It is by Him that I speak because in this language of the spirit in such exchanges as these wherein His Divine Majesty wills to dignify my lowliness I am entirely incapable of doing anything except through his very delicate urging (O'Brien 1964:297–8).

gious orders, there was no limit to the experiential depth and profundity they could attain in their devotion.

Hildegard of Bingen, on the Rhine near Mainz (1098–1179), a Benedictine abbess, had a creative life in writing and music, but was also involved in politics and diplomacy. Clergy and feudal nobility sought the counsel of 'the Sybil of the Rhine', as she was called. When she became abbess in 1141, she had a vision of tongues of flame from the heavens settling on her, and over the next ten years she wrote a book of visions, *Scivias* (Know the ways [of God]).

Catherine of Siena (1347–80 or 1333–80) in Italy was a member of the Dominican third, or lay, order. She was actively involved in the religious politics of the day, but her *Dialogue* records her mystical visions.

Julian of Norwich (c. 1342–c. 1413) in England, attached to a church there, experienced visions during a five-hour state of ecstasy, and one the next day, when she was thirty, and at fifty after two decades of reflection on their content she wrote a description and analysis of them in her *Sixteen Revelations of Divine Love*. To her, evil is a distortion introduced by the human will, serving to reveal by contrast all the more clearly the divine love of God.

Later, Teresa of Ávila (1515–82) was a Spanish Carmelite in the same spiritual milieu as John of the Cross. At the age of forty she decided to seek spiritual perfection while praying before a statue of the scourging of Christ, and within about two years she experienced her first mystical ecstasy. Over the next fifteen years, while actively working to establish religious houses, she deepened her spiritual life until in 1572 it reached the state of 'spiritual marriage'. Her writings produced during this period are noteworthy because they treat the life of prayer comprehensively, describing its steps and intermediate stages between 'discursive' prayer (i.e., prayer mentioning specific needs) and ecstasy.

THE PROTESTANT REFORMATION

The World after 1450

In the fifteenth century, Christianity was essentially a European phenomenon. Apart from the ancient Eastern churches of Ethiopia and southern India, and some remnant minorities in the eastern Mediterranean, Christendom had long earlier lost Asia and northern Africa to Islam. When Constantinople fell in 1453 to the Ottoman Turks, the event sealed the victory of Muslims over Byzantine Christians after seven centuries of rivalry since the Arab attempt to take the city. The Turks then campaigned in the Balkans, their armies reaching Vienna in 1529 and again in 1683. Muslim populations remaining in Bosnia and Albania to the present are a legacy of the Turkish advance in the region.

But the balance of civilizations in the world changed after 1450. Christendom's horizons were vastly broadened, not reduced, a generation after

ERASMUS

[From Desiderius Erasmus. The Dutch classical scholar and humanist wrote Encomium moriae *(The Praise of Folly) in 1509 after a visit to Rome, while staying in England with his friend Sir Thomas More, whose social critique* Utopia *(Nowhere) was published seven years later.]*

[Some questions have] been discussed threadbare. There are others more worthy of great and enlightened theologians (as they call themselves) which can really rouse them to action if they come their way. What was the exact moment of divine generation? Are there several filiations in Christ? Is it a possible proposition that God the Father could hate his Son? Could God have taken on the form of a woman, a devil, a donkey, a gourd, or a flintstone? If so, how could a gourd have preached sermons, performed miracles, and been nailed to the cross? And what would Peter have consecrated if he had consecrated when the body of Christ still hung on the cross? Furthermore at that same time could Christ have been called a man? Shall we be permitted to eat and drink after the resurrection? We're taking due precaution against hunger and thirst while there's time. There are any amount of quibbles even more refined than these, about concepts, relations, instants, formalities, quiddities, and ecceities, which no one could possibly perceive unless like Lynceus he could see through blackest darkness things which don't exist (Radice 1986:126–7).

the fall of Constantinople when the Portuguese navigator Bartolomeu Diaz (d. 1500) sailed around southern Africa in 1488, outflanking the Turks. Another Portuguese, Vasco da Gama (1460–1524), arrived on the shores of India in 1498. From the sixteenth century onward, European colonial powers established a presence in the ports of India, Southeast Asia, and China.

In these same years Spanish navigators reached the New World, taking Christianity with them. The indigenous religious traditions of the New World yielded to Christian missionary activity. So in both Eastern and Western hemispheres, Christianity, a mainly European religion, encircled the planet. Christianity now became global, as part of European civilization's emerging dominance. The missions will be discussed later in more detail.

Ironically, just as European Christianity was poised for this global expansion, it was fragmented within Europe by a crisis of institutional and spiritual authority: the challenge of Protestantism.

Luther

The main narrative of Protestantism begins with Martin Luther in Germany in 1517, but even before him, pressures for change were building up. Political challenges included the rivalries of princes north of the Alps with the power of the papacy in Rome. An intellectual challenge was humanism, exemplified in the Dutch classical scholar Desiderius Erasmus (1466–1536), who wanted to replace complicated scholastic theology with the simple morality of Jesus, reached through critical textual study of scripture. Literacy was becoming more widespread, and local vernacular dialects were developing into recognizable regional languages.

In the life of the church, there were challenges too. John Wyclif (1329–84) in England and John Hus (c. 1369–1415) among the Czechs both wanted to replace Latin with the vernacular in worship and to translate the Bible into the languages of the people. Ulrich von Hutten (1488–1523) and Crotus Rubianus (Johann Jäger, c. 1480–c. 1539) wrote *Letters of Obscure Men*, mocking the intricacy and futility of church regulations. There was also criticism of lavish and corrupt practices by the clergy.

These danger signals had been in evidence for decades, but the stubborn and uninhibited personality of Martin Luther (1483–1546) ultimately enabled the Protestant Reformation in Germany to erupt as it did. The specific issue triggering his objections was the sale of indulgences—that is, releases from time in purgatory, a holding area for the soul in its passage from death to the next existence—and their association with sacred relics.

Prince Frederick (r. 1486–1525) in Wittenberg, Luther's town north of Leipzig, had a collection of several thousand relics. Someone visiting them on the appropriate days, and making the appropriate contributions of money, could be granted exemption from many thousands of years in purgatory. But a competing collection of relics arrived in the nearby town of Jüterbog in the possession of Johann Tetzel (1465–1519), as part of a campaign by the new archbishop of Mainz. Half the proceeds were to go to build St Peter's basilica in Rome, and the other half to reimburse the archbishop's installation fee.

Frederick was not amused, as Tetzel's relics might cut into his own revenues on All Saints' Day, 1 November, a big day for his collection. He therefore supported the objections to Tetzel's huckstering raised by Martin Luther, an Augustinian monk and theological scholar at the university in Wittenberg, but Luther's reasoning was more far-reaching. It was better, Luther held, for St Peter's to remain unbuilt than to impoverish the German people; if the pope had any jurisdiction over purgatory, he should free its denizens; and, most importantly, the treasury of scripture outweighs the merits of the saints.

In the standard manner of posting a topic for debate, Luther tacked up on the church door a list of ninety-five propositions or 'theses', a critique not just of selling indulgences but of other aspects of Church practice. News of the challenge spread like wildfire, doubtless exceeding Frederick's or Luther's expectations. People with various spiritual and political aims were ready to support him.

Luther had to defend himself against charges of political subversion at an imperial council called a diet, held in 1521 at the German city of Worms, south

LETTERS OF OBSCURE MEN

[From the Letters of Obscure Men *by Ulrich von Hutten and Crotus Rubianus, a satirical publication of 1513–5.]*

Heinrich Schafmaul [sheep's mouth] to Magister Ortuinus Gratius, many greetings. Inasmuch as before I journeyed to Court you charged me to write to you oft, and propose from time to time knotty points in Theology, which you would straightway resolve better than the Courticians [court ministers] at Rome: therefore, I now write to ask your reverence what opinion you hold concerning one who on a Friday, that is on the sixth day of the week—or on any other fast-day—should eat an egg with a chicken in it?

For you must know that we were lately sitting in an inn in the Campo dei Fiori, having our supper, and were eating eggs, when on opening one I saw that there was a young chicken within.

This I showed to a comrade; whereupon quoth he to me, 'Eat it up speedily, before the taverner sees it, for if he mark it, you will have to pay a Carline or a Julius for a fowl. For it is the rule of the house

of Mainz. When he refused to retract his views, he first received an imperial censure, while the religious excommunication followed only later. German support for Luther's ideas enlisted local and regional sentiments, taking on a concrete political form. It was two decades before the Roman Catholic Church responded with religious reforms, in the Council of Trent, 1545–63, discussed later.

Like others, Luther complains in his writings about the Church's lavishness and corruption, but the core of his challenge is theological. Luther wants to recast Christian understanding of the very nature of sin and redemption. He rules out a transactional notion, in which the individual confesses particular sins and expiates them through particular acts of penance. Instead, Luther emphasizes that in Jesus divine grace reaches out to each human being, saving and redeeming individuals regardless of their merit or performance.

Taking up a key theme in Paul's New Testament letter to the Romans, Luther insists that humans are justified by faith alone. Both Paul and Luther take their stand on a confident experiential certainty. Luther refers to this as the inner guidance or testimony of the Holy Spirit. For Luther as for Paul, the dialectic is between faith and works. While the works Paul was downplaying were observance of Jewish commandments, the works that Luther downplays are the procedures of confession and penance in Latin Christianity. Paul's reaction was against the literal Torah, pitting against it the gospel or 'good news' about Jesus, which was a preaching message in Paul's day but not yet a scriptural text. Now Luther, in contrast, makes scripture a key authority, indeed the fulcrum from which to exert leverage against the institutional Church.

that once the landlord has put anything on the table you must pay for it—he won't take it back. And if he sees that there is a young fowl in that egg, he will say "Pay me for that fowl!" Little or big, 'tis all one.'

In a trice I gulped down the egg, chicken and all.

And then I remembered that it was Friday!

Whereupon I said to my crony, 'You have made me commit a mortal sin, in eating flesh on the sixth day of the week!'

But he averred that it was not a mortal sin—nor even a venial one, seeing that such a chickling is accounted merely an egg, until it is born.

He told me, too, that it is just the same in the case of cheese, in which there are sometimes grubs, as there are in cherries, peas, and new beans: yet all these may be eaten on Fridays, and even on Apostolic Vigils. But taverners are such rascals that they call them flesh, to get more money.

Then I departed, and thought the matter over.

And by the Lord, Master Ortwin, I am in a mighty quandary, and know not what to do.

I would willingly seek counsel of one of the Courticians, but they are not devout men (Stokes 1909:445–6).

From his 1517 challenge until the diet at Worms in 1521, Luther was given the opportunity to retract his challenges. Had any settlement been negotiated, Luther's reform might have been defused, but Luther stood his ground. Historians dispute that at the diet he declared the words attributed to him, 'Here I stand; I can do no other.' But the sentiment is in keeping with what he likely did say: 'Unless I am convicted by Scripture and plain reason—I do not accept the authority of popes and councils, for they have contradicted each other—my conscience is captive to the Word of God, I cannot and I will not recant anything' (Bainton 1974, 15:551).

The emperor, Charles V (r. 1519–56), termed Luther a threat to order and banished him. During the few days he was given to leave under safe conduct, Luther was intercepted by some armed men along the highway and disappeared for more than a year. Many thought him dead, but he was actually hidden in the Wartburg castle under an assumed identity by his protector, Prince Frederick. Luther made use of this seclusion to produce a string of theological writings and to translate the New Testament from the original Greek into a direct, lively German that eventually gave the Luther Bible a profoundly influential place in German literature.

In the form it took, the Protestant Reformation could not have happened much before it actually did. The technology of printing from movable type had only been introduced in Europe a half century earlier, with a Latin Bible coming off Johann Gutenberg's (d. 1468) press in Strasbourg in 1456. Though prohibitively costly at first, printed materials soon became economical to produce. The topics of Luther's challenge were disseminated rapidly as pamphlets, reaching a wide popular audience. As many as a million pamphlets were reportedly produced between 1521 and 1524. Of Luther's own short tracts or pamphlets, there were at least 1,300 different printings by 1523. Luther's accessible translation of the Bible had an impact, too, its New Testament appearing in 1522 and its Old Testament in 1534.

By the mid-1520s the forces Luther had unleashed were pulling in diverse directions. Different people expected different things of reform. On one agenda, the life of a priestly or monastic vocation, he set a personal example. His teachings spurred a dozen nuns to leave the convent in Wittenberg, three of whom went back to their families but the other nine of whom were now homeless. Luther as a matchmaker found husbands for eight, and then took the last, Katherina von Bora, as his own wife. We do not have the details, but surmise that moral concern, even ideological conviction, played a greater initial role than romance. In the course of time they had six children and also adopted four orphans. In his writing *Concerning Married Life*, Luther suggests that even washing diapers is an act that can be ennobled by faith. And he set a pattern for married clergy in Protestantism that, whatever else may be said for it, has at least pressed clergy to counsel the married people among their flocks on the basis of practical experience as well as theory.

There were broader theoretical aspects to Luther's view of clergy and the priesthood. In essence, Luther was taking priesthood off the pedestal of status and authority that it and the institutional Church had enjoyed since the time of Constantine. Luther took as authoritative not institutional tradition but the Bible and the inner guidance of the Holy Spirit. There is consequently no need for an intermediary between the Christian and God, to transmit human petitions or dispense divine grace. Protestants use the phrase 'the priesthood of all believers' to refer to this egalitarianism of spiritual access.

In politics, an uprising of German peasants demanded privileges and the redress of grievances. Luther's decision not to endorse all their demands placed him in a conservative position and left the radicals to follow a more strident leader, Thomas Müntzer (c. 1490–1525). Eventually they went in an antiestablishment direction in the Anabaptist movement.

On a theological agenda, Luther engaged in controversy with the Swiss reformer Huldrych (Ulrich) Zwingli (1484–1531) over the interpretation of the Christian Eucharistic ceremony. The reformers generally dismissed the notion of the Latin mass as a sacrifice, but they were unable to agree on the terms in which to state that divinity was present in it.

The debate illustrates a recurring issue for Protestants: if you use the Bible as your fulcrum of authority over against alternatives such as institutional tradition, then by what authority can you pick and choose when and when not to take the Bible literally? Luther's biblicism was simple: if the text says 'this is my body', then that must be so and a doctrine must be developed that says Christ's body is there in the bread and wine of the Eucharist. Others, like Zwingli, held that 'this is' means 'this represents', but in so doing implicitly had commit themselves to a more subtle notion of scriptural authority.

Division and diversity characterize the Reformation. Protestantism rejected central institutional control, but that rejection was a mixed blessing. Early reformers often advocated their breakaway doctrines with an ideological stridency that matched the authoritarianism of the Church in Rome they had only just left. At a practical level, redundancy and confusion developed when independent bodies went their own way and competed for adherents. A denominationally fragmented Church has been the legacy of the Protestant Reformation down to the present day.

Sixteenth-Century Branches

One identifies three main 'establishments' emerging from the sixteenth-century Reformation: the Lutherans, the Anglicans, and the Calvinists. After discussing these, we shall consider the Anabaptists and Unitarians as non-establishment branches.

Lutherans

The followers of Martin Luther's theological and political leadership flourished in Germany and Scandinavia. Like him, they stressed the authority of scripture and the guidance of the Holy Spirit. There was ample scope for rational and intellectual argument in the exposition of scripture, but Lutheranism also knew a deep sense of personal piety. Indeed, the notion of God as friend and companion comes through as strongly in the texts of Lutheran hymns as does the notion of God as warrior or judge.

In worship and in ecclesiastical organization, Lutherans departed in only some respects from the precedents of the Roman Church. Lutherans continued a Eucharist like the mass, but now celebrated it in the vernacular rather than Latin, and held that Christ's body becomes present along with the bread and wine of the sacrament, but is not produced out of them. Lutheran church organization retained a priesthood governed by bishops, but permitted clergy to marry. Ordination of women as priests is a recent phenomenon among Lutherans.

In most parts of Germany and Scandinavia, Lutheran Christianity became the state Church. The 'Evangelical' Church, as it is called in Germany, claims the preponderance of the population in northwestern and northeastern Germany, while Catholics are stronger in the south. To this day, Germany provides basic funding for churches out of tax revenues, the individual taxpayer paying a flat rate whether enthusiastic about religion or not, with the money directed to

Figure 3.1
CHRISTIANITY: Major Spheres of Influence

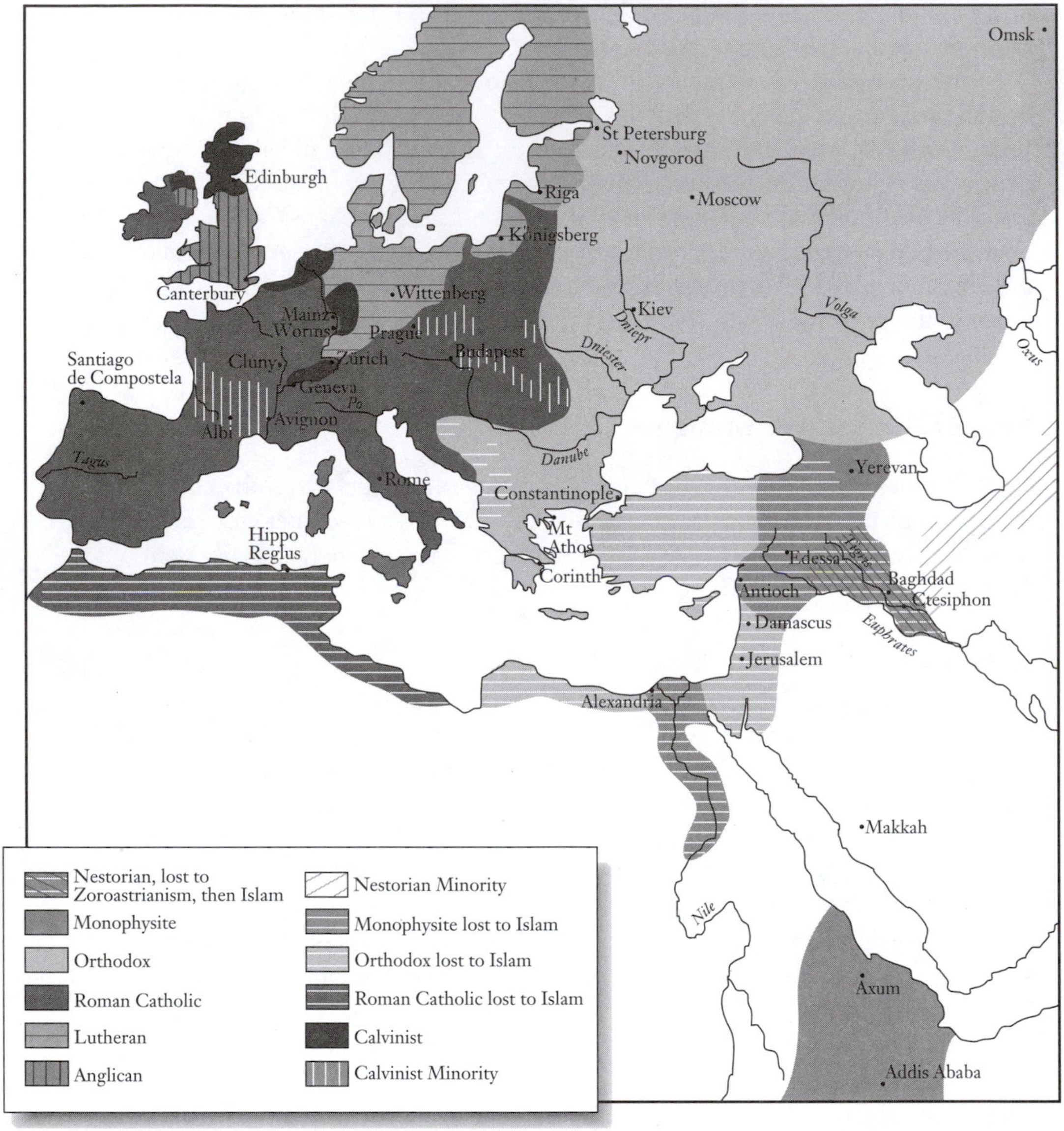

Evangelical or Catholic treasuries depending on the taxpayer's communal affiliation. In Scandinavia, tax monies similarly fund the Lutheran churches.

Outside Germany and Scandinavia, Lutheranism has spread through migration and missionary activity. Lutherans became influential in the United States and Canada during the nineteenth century, with German migration to such destinations as Pennsylvania, Ohio, Missouri, Ontario, and the shores of Lake Michigan. Scandinavian immigration was particularly strong in Minnesota and Wisconsin. The ethnic flavour of these North American Lutheran churches has become diluted over time, except where replenished by continuing immigration.

Anglicans

While the Reformation had been a popular movement in Germany, it was royal policy in Britain. Henry VIII (r. 1509–47) wanted a male heir, but Catherine of Aragon had not borne him one. In 1527, Henry requested an annulment of the marriage on the ground that Catherine had been his deceased brother's wife. Pope Clement VII, closer to the circle of Catherine's nephew (the Holy Roman emperor), refused to rule in Henry's favour, but European universities that were asked for rulings were divided. Henry, finding some advice supporting him, married Anne Boleyn in 1533 in the second of eventually six marriages.

At Henry's instigation, the English parliament in 1534 passed an Act of Supremacy. Implying that the king had always been such, the act 'for corroboration and confirmation' proclaimed the king and his successors by authority of Parliament 'the only Supreme Head in earth of the Church of England'. In fact, the act for the first time replaced the pope as head of the English Church with the king.

Divorce and a male successor were not the only things on Henry's mind. While one could interpret his break with Rome as consistent with a high-minded or principled notion of secularity, more convincing as a motive is the desire of rulers to expropriate vast ecclesiastical landholdings. Throughout England, ruins of the abbeys that Henry confiscated stand as a stark reminder, as do similar ruins elsewhere in northern Europe.

Like the movement of a pendulum, the direction of change in England underwent a pair of reversals in the years following Henry's reign, under his three children, by different wives, who succeeded him. Protestant ideas prevailed under Edward VI (r. 1547–53), Catholicism was brought back under Mary Tudor (r. 1553–8), and a synthesis emerged under leadership of the Protestant Elizabeth I (r. 1558–1603).

The key Protestant reformer under the young king Edward was his adviser Thomas Cranmer (1489–1556), archbishop of Canterbury, southeast of London. With German connections and convinced that the austere Reformation in Geneva was correct, Cranmer purged the English Church of its images, candles, and priestly vestments. He interpreted the Eucharist as a memorial meal around a table rather than a sacrifice at an altar. The features of Roman Catholic practice that Cranmer eliminated under Edward were all reintroduced under Mary, but Cranmer made an enduring contribution in the 1549 *Book of Common Prayer*, still a model for Anglican worship.

Cranmer was trapped between the Reformation in which he believed and the monarchy he served. He was charged with treason, but then spared, for having backed Lady Jane Grey, a losing aspirant, as Edward's successor. But Mary's regime then charged him with heresy. Sentenced, he tried at first to avoid execution by recanting his Protestant views and affirming papal supremacy and Latin Eucharistic theology. Finally, when he was burned at the stake anyway, he held to the flames the hand with which he had written the recantations, declaring, 'This hand has offended.'

Under Elizabeth I, the Church of England, weary of strife, settled into a balanced position reflected in Parliament by Protestant popular sentiment in the House of Commons and a Catholic nobility in the House of Lords. Elizabeth's course is characterized as a *via media* or 'middle way'. For example, the 1559 revision of the *Book of Common Prayer* preserves both Eucharistic theologies: the more Catholic sacrificial concept of 'this is my body, given for you', and the more Protestant memorial reading of 'take, eat in remembrance of me'.

In the end, the English Reformation, often directed from the top down, produced results comparable to the grass-roots Lutheran Reformation: an established state Church, but without links to Rome; a traditional mass as the liturgy, but conducted in the vernacular; a hierarchy with bishops, but with clergy who could now marry. The Church of England has remained a state Church, with the monarch as its titular head. (When the monarch is in Scotland, however, she or he is head of the Church of Scotland, which is Presbyterian.) The ranking bishop of the Church continues to be the archbishop of Canterbury.

Known in the United States as Episcopalian after its form of government by bishops, the tradition of the Church of England is elsewhere called Anglican. Wherever British influence has been dominant in the world, Anglicanism has taken root. That includes not only Australia, New Zealand, South Africa, and English-speaking Canada, but also the missionary churches of former British colonies and protectorates. In East Africa, West Africa, the Caribbean, India, the Polynesian islands, and Hong Kong, Anglican Christianity is in evidence today. Indeed, at worldwide meetings of the Anglican communion, the racial diversity of the human community is reflected among the participating bishops.

Over the centuries there has been a tension between what came to be the more liturgical and Catholic or 'high church' side of Anglicanism, and a more spontaneous and evangelical or 'low church' side. Some Anglicans, attempting to bridge the two, refer to a 'broad church'.

High-church Anglicanism has not lacked individual enthusiasm; around 1833 John Keble (1792–1866), John Henry Newman (1801–90), and others at Oxford sparked the Oxford movement, promoting a view of the Church as independent of the state. It developed a revival of Anglican interest in the aesthetics of the liturgy and the dignity of priesthood. The movement effectively countered evangelical fears of a resurgence of Catholicism, deriving partly from famine-induced Irish immigration. Did it succeed in making Catholicism more attractive?

Newman himself left to become a Roman Catholic in 1845, and in 1879 was made a cardinal.

Reformed Churches

In the 1520s to 1560s, the first decades after Luther's challenge to the theology and practice of the Church of Rome, the Reformation movement in and around Switzerland departed from Luther's position on several points. As mentioned earlier, Huldrych Zwingli in Zürich disputed Luther's Eucharistic theology, holding that 'this *is* my body' means 'this represents', but not that Christ's body is in any real physical sense present. Martin Bucer (1491–1551) in Strasbourg increased the role of the laity at the expense of the clergy in matters of ecclesiastical organization and discipline.

And in Geneva, John Calvin (1509–64), trained as a lawyer and classical scholar (even a Renaissance humanist) and the Reformation's dominant intellectual leader, ruled the city in conformity to strict, austere norms of doctrine and conduct. Calvin's Geneva has been termed theocratic and has been compared with the rule of religio-legal scholars in late-twentieth-century Iran; however, to the followers of Calvin a trust in God's power and caring providence brought joy at least as much as it brought fear.

Calvin's key theological treatise, published in 1536 just prior to his active involvement in Geneva's civic life and extensively expanded over two decades in later editions, bears a title commonly translated as *Institutes of the Christian Religion*. In form, it is a manual of spiritual discipline, such that the title could more aptly appear as 'instruction in Christian piety'. Calvin echoes the words in Augustine's *Confessions* that humans are created for communion with God and lack rest until they arrive at it. The human approach to God is both intellectual and spiritual; Calvin uses the term 'knowledge' practically synonymously with 'faith'. Calvin's *Institutes* have a systematic overall structure, contrasting with the writings of Luther that were more often responses to specific situations.

God, for Calvin, is absolutely sovereign, initiating all actions, both creating and redeeming. Two consequences of this teaching were given a central place by Calvin's interpreters, making it a struggle for the Reformed tradition in the centuries since Calvin to defend them: the notion that humans, dependent on divine grace, are utterly sinful and powerless to achieve salvation; and the notion that the sovereign God, both omniscient and omnipotent, predestines humans to salvation or damnation. There is a juridical flavour to Calvin's system that resonates with Anselm's views discussed earlier, and atonement theory has had a key place alongside the work of the Holy Spirit and the authority of scripture in Calvin's thought. So strong was Calvin's influence that the Reformed churches are often referred to as Calvinist.

From sixteenth-century Geneva, the ideas of the Swiss Reformation spread to other lands, notably to France (the Huguenots), the Netherlands, Hungary,

England, and Scotland. In the Netherlands and Hungary, the Calvinist churches have been known as 'Reformed' churches, after their theological tradition. In England, the tradition was called Presbyterian, after its form of government by representatives called elders or 'presbyters'. The established state Church of Scotland is also termed Presbyterian. Reformed churches like the Presbyterians do not have bishops; the regional representative assembly, the presbytery, corporately performs the traditional tasks of a bishop, including the supervision, examination, and ordination of candidates for ministry. And Presbyterians term a multipresbytery gathering a synod, taking the old term for a meeting of bishops.

Through migration Presbyterianism has taken root on other continents. Presbyterians from England and Scotland settled in the middle Atlantic American states and eastern Canada, as well as in New Zealand and Australia. Dutch Reformed settlers carried their tradition to South Africa and to New Amsterdam (i.e., New York) and Michigan. In the nineteenth and twentieth centuries, Presbyterian missions from Britain and North America reached many parts of Asia and Africa. In most lands the 'younger churches' founded by missionaries remained small. Indeed, in the Islamic world the recruits were generally not from Muslim populations but, as in the case of Rome's Uniate churches, from indigenous eastern Christian populations. But the Presbyterians did become a sizable minority in one Asian land: Korea.

Anabaptists

Each of the three branches of the Reformation named so far was willing, even eager, to take over the governance of its local European society. Each was content to replace established institutions by becoming an establishment itself. It was different with another strand of the Reformation, a somewhat more diverse and less cohesive group whom sixteenth-century writers called 'Anabaptists'. The name, meaning 'rebaptizers', connotes the movement's emphasis on baptism of adults rather than infants.

That emphasis was part of a voluntaristic conception of the nature of the Church. Individuals should, on the basis of mature personal commitment, seek to be baptized. The Church should seek to restore the close-knit sense of community of the apostolic era. And it should remain apart from political institutions and structures. Through the years, Anabaptist groups have tended to be pacifists when it came to the military aims of the state, even if they might be stubborn or quarrelsome in their own internal sectarian differences.

Anabaptist origins are diffuse; there were varied local scenarios of dissatisfaction with the pace of change as the first decade of the Reformation unfolded. One of the opening breaks with the 'establishment' Reformation was a dispute with Zwingli in Zürich in 1525, in which the dissidents administered adult believers' baptism. Essentially, the Anabaptist movement emerged as an antiestablishment, underground movement within central European Protestantism, relying on lay preachers rather than trained clergy.

In the Westphalian (northwestern German) town of Münster in 1533–5, Anabaptist enthusiasm that the New Jerusalem was about to be ushered in, and attempts to establish the kingdom of God by force, produced a crack-down by Catholic and Protestant authorities. Thereafter a former Dutch priest, Menno Simons (1496–1561), led the movement into a largely otherworldly and non-violent path, urging withdrawal from society since the chance of removing the authorities was near zero. Simons's followers were known as Mennonites. In the Netherlands, they enjoyed toleration and by the middle of the nineteenth century had largely assimilated to the modern and secular climate of the Enlightenment. But elsewhere, Mennonite withdrawal often entailed migration, as the movement spread eastward through Germany and Austria to the Ukraine.

Some Mennonites escaped hardship or persecution in Europe by migrating to the Americas, particularly to Pennsylvania and subsequently to Ontario and the Canadian prairies. In Pennsylvania, where some arrived as early as 1663, they came to be known as Pennsylvania Dutch (the word is from Deutsch, meaning 'German'). While most Mennonites use modern technology, some branches, such as the Old Order Amish farmers in Pennsylvania and Ontario, practise a traditionalism in dress and conduct comparable to that of Hasidic Jews. They continue to farm with the draft animals and simple tools of a century ago, resisting machinery and gadgetry as part of the moral temptation and corruption of today's life.

Unitarians

If Christianity is strictly defined as faith in Jesus as son of God, one may legitimately wonder whether Unitarianism belongs in a survey of Christianity. However, it has emerged within Christendom as individuals have struggled intellectually with the admittedly difficult doctrine of the Trinity and then concluded that they could not affirm the divinity of Jesus. Unitarianism can only make sense historically in the context of traditional Christianity. And we may well think of it as a recurring idea, without trying to connect every instance of it into one movement.

As early as 1527 in Strasbourg, Martin Cellarius (1499–1564), a pupil of the German humanist Johann Reuchlin (1455–1522), rejected views of the Trinity and preferred to speak of God as a single person. Others expressed similar views. Subsequently, Unitarian communities emerged in several lands. In Poland, an Italian named Giorgio Biandrata (1515–88) launched Unitarian ideas in 1558 and was followed by Fausto Sozzini (1539–1604) in 1579; Socinianism, as the teaching was called, was banished from Poland in 1658. The same Biandrata planted Unitarian ideas in Hungary in 1553, winning the support of the king, John II Sigismund Zápolya (r. 1540–71), but from the end of his reign that movement was persecuted.

In England, the figure considered the father of Unitarianism was John Biddle (1615–62), who began to publish tracts in 1652, but it was more than a century later, 1773, before a Unitarian denomination was organized in England by Theophilus Lindsey (1723–1808), who broke with the Church of England.

In New England, Unitarianism represented a left-wing theological break with Congregationalism (which will be discussed later) in the career of William Ellery Channing (1780–1842). Channing preached a sermon in Baltimore in 1819 that American Unitarians have taken as a kind of denominational manifesto, yet Channing declined to think of the Unitarians as a separate group and claimed to belong 'not to a sect, but to the community of free minds'.

North American Unitarianism continued in the nineteenth and twentieth centuries to appeal to a humanist and rationalist clientele, often in university circles. In 1961, the Unitarians merged with a kindred group, the Universalists. Unitarianism in the twentieth century has had a sociological as well as an intellectual appeal: in more than a few instances, because of its minimal creedal demands, it has been the denomination of choice for couples in mixed Jewish-Christian marriages.

Puritanism

A movement in English and colonial American Protestant churches rather than a boundaried denomination in itself, Puritanism flourished from the middle of the sixteenth to the middle of the seventeenth centuries. Some of its early advocates, exiles from the Catholic reign of Queen Mary in 1553–8, had absorbed Calvinist ideas in Geneva and after the accession of Elizabeth I in 1558 sought to 'purify' the Church of England of the remnants of Catholic usage that it retained in church vestments, furnishings, and ecclesiastical organization. Around the end of the seventeenth century, responding to these trends, Anglican theologians such as Richard Hooker (c. 1554–1600) and William Laud (1573–1645) made use of the ideas of the Dutch theologian Jacobus Arminius (1559–1609), who had opposed the strict Calvinistic doctrine of predestination.

Reacting now to this emerging Anglican position, Puritan thinkers committed their movement to a rigorous Calvinistic notion of human sinfulness and divine predestination. The consequence of this for the individual was a strict, sometimes smug, sense of moral vocation, of living up to one's being chosen by God. The Puritan ideal of society was morally activist, and stressed moderation in behaviour. The poetry of John Milton (1608–74) and the *Pilgrim's Progress* of John Bunyan (1628–88) provide well-known literary examples of the Puritan ideal.

A seminal modern interpretation of that ideal has been the 1904–5 essay by the German sociologist Max Weber (1864–1920), *The Protestant Ethic and the*

Spirit of Capitalism. Weber explores the Calvinist incentives for zealous and self-denying action to transform the world of the here and now, however uncertain one's fate in the hereafter might remain. Although Reformation leaders preached otherworldly values and scorned the direct pursuit of riches, doing well enters by the back door as a by-product of doing good. As Weber puts it, Calvinists (including Puritans) who are motivated both to work hard and to live simple lives tend to accumulate savings and thus to play a capitalist role. Nearly a century after publication, Weber continues to be invoked and discussed. Few dispute his view of the Puritans as frugal, but some wonder what explanatory power his thesis has with respect to the work ethic of others such as modern Confucians.

Puritans and English Presbyterians found themselves in substantial agreement in the Westminster Confession of Faith in 1647. Oliver Cromwell (1599–1658), who came to power in 1649, sought to unite Congregationalists, Presbyterians, and Baptists in a Puritan state Church. The Church of England largely rid itself of Puritanism in the 1660 Restoration of Charles II (r. 1660–85). In England Puritanism ceased to have a coherent existence as a movement, though its ideas had a ripple effect in the so-called non-conformist (i.e., non-Anglican Protestant) churches.

But the demise of Puritanism in England came only after the movement's influence had already spread elsewhere. Puritans had migrated to New England in the 1630s, where they established Congregational churches in Massachusetts and Connecticut.

Seventeenth-Century Denominations

Congregationalists

As a denomination, the Congregational churches trace their roots to 'separatist' clergy in the time of Elizabeth I (r. 1558–1603), but they became a significant force in England as the 'Independent' clergy in the era of Cromwell after 1649. As far as doctrine is concerned, there is little to distinguish Congregationalism from Presbyterian Calvinism. As the name implies, though, the denomination is described in terms of its church government. Pursuing the notion of the priesthood of all believers towards a logical conclusion, the tradition accords each individual congregation the ultimate authority to determine its theological and institutional affairs, regarding only God as a higher power.

In England, Congregational churches formed a Congregational Union in 1832 and were active in political and missionary causes throughout the nineteenth century. Meanwhile, the greatest strength of Congregationalism emerged in Massachusetts, including both the Puritans of Massachusetts Bay and the Separatists of Plymouth. Harvard was founded by Congregationalists in 1637 in order not 'to leave an illiterate ministry to the churches, when our present ministers shall lie in the dust'. Yale, founded in 1701, and other educational institutions in the American northeast were also of Congregational foundation.

Baptists

Like the Anabaptists on the European continent, the English Baptists stressed the baptism of mature believers rather than of infants. The denomination's affinities, however, are much more intimately connected with the Puritan movement in England than with the Anabaptists of the Continent. What was important to these Puritan separatists at the start of the seventeenth century was that people should choose their religion rather than be born into it, and that such a choice ought to be private and beyond any interference of the state in religion. England's non-Calvinist Baptists, called 'General' Baptists because they proclaimed a general redemption for humanity, were augmented in the 1630s by Calvinist or 'Particular' Baptists, so called because they limited redemption to a particular sector of humankind. Already the Particular Baptists were practising the ritual of baptism by total immersion rather than by sprinkling the initiate.

The early Baptist presence in America was small. Roger Williams (c. 1604–83), exiled from Massachusetts in 1636, founded Rhode Island on the principle of religious tolerance, but other groups also settled there, and the Baptists were divided. The real growth of the Baptists in the United States began only a century later. It followed the revival of 1740–3 known as the Great Awakening; Baptists, though not among its principal protagonists, made massive numerical gains in its wake. They positioned themselves to become the largest American Protestant denomination partly through their successful appeal to the Black population; by the middle of the twentieth century, two out of every three American Black Christians were Baptists.

Quakers

George Fox (1624–91), an Englishman who spent three years in search of spiritual enlightenment, claimed in 1646 that he had found what he sought. He began to preach that moral and spiritual peace was not to be had in the institutional churches but in reliance on experience of the 'inner light' of the living Christ. Fox's moral and spiritual earnestness won him a following whom he called Friends of the Truth. In 1650, his initially impulsive group was pejoratively called 'Quaker' by Justice Bennet, whom he had admonished to tremble at the word of the Lord. The name now used, Religious Society of Friends, dates from the nineteenth century. In 1682, the colony of Pennsylvania was founded by William Penn (1644–1718) as a place where Quakers might find religious toleration and free expression. There they became staid, solid citizens.

Quakers at worship combine intellectual and spiritual reflection. Seemingly with no fixed ritual, they sit silently until moved by the Holy Spirit to speak. Actually, there is more formality than first meets the eye: one seldom speaks before a third of the hour has elapsed, one's declaration is expected to be logical and thoughtful, and one often waits till senior members of the meeting (which is what Quaker congregations are called) have spoken.

Quakers are not numerous, claiming only about 100,000 worldwide, but their humanitarian involvement in peace and refugee-relief causes has far outweighed their numbers and has earned the movement the respect of many. The Quakers are strongest in Pennsylvania and Indiana, and around university centres.

Diverse though they are in their detail, the three Anglo-American denominations we have just sketched are variations on a central theme of the Reformation: the rejection of external human authority. The Congregationalists' authority was corporate, but local; the Baptists were wary of the state; the Quakers looked inward for insight.

Protestant Worship

The Protestant break with the Church of Rome was reflected in both the theory and the practice of Protestant worship. Like the spectrum of denominations themselves, Protestant rationales and forms of worship came to express varying degrees of departure from the earlier Roman model. For instance, making the sign of the cross on one's own body (touching face, chest, and shoulders) is a characteristic act of Orthodox and Catholic Christians, but avoiding doing so is equally salient among Protestants.

One central issue was the status of the officiating clergy. For medieval Latin Christianity, the priest was a representative of the divine, practically a dispenser of miracles. Now Protestants stressed the human side, making the officiant more a representative and spokesperson for the congregation. Protestants claimed that the Christian needs no human intermediary—no living priest, no dead saint—for access to God.

No human intermediary needed.

At the Catholic end of the spectrum, such as the 'high church' wing of Anglicanism, the clergy were still termed priests and addressed as 'father', though Protestants eliminated celibacy from the job description. Low-church Anglicans and most other Protestants declined to call their clergy priests, preferring the terminology 'minister' with reference to their role as leader of worship or 'pastor' as spiritual counsellor of a congregation. Protestants gave an increased role to the laity as preachers and leaders of worship. A few denominations, such as the Quakers, were dominantly lay-led.

Protestants also departed from Rome in interpreting the sacramental rituals, particularly the Eucharist. Some Anglicans and Lutherans sought to retain a sacrificial understanding of the Eucharist, holding that the body and blood of

Christ are present in or together with the bread and wine of the ceremonial meal. In Switzerland the sacramental theology of reformers such as Zwingli and Calvin set the tone for most subsequent Protestant understanding of the Eucharist as a memorial more than as a sacrifice, in which the bread and wine represent Christ's body and blood symbolically.

Practice for receiving communion varies. In the Catholic tradition, people line up near the altar, while many Protestant congregations remain seated as elders or ushers serve the bread on trays and the wine in little individual glasses. The materials used as bread and wine have also varied: often, the Catholic tradition has used unleavened wafers for bread, and many Protestant churches use unfermented grape juice instead of wine. In some parts of the world to which Christianity has spread, both bread and wine are exotic diet items; thus in the Philippines, for example, some Protestants share rice cakes and fruit juice or cola.

In the later Middle Ages, the Eucharist might be open to participation as infrequently as twice a year. The Reformation sought greater participation by the people. Ironically, most Protestant denominations have since come to celebrate the sacrament less often—in some congregations, only once every three or four months. Protestants emphasize the reading of scripture and the interpretation of it in a sermon frequently taking up a third of the worship hour.

The first decades of the Reformation in Germany and England saw the elaboration of lectionaries not unlike the medieval monastic 'offices' or schedules for the reading of scripture. The lectionaries were systematic plans to read consecutive portions of the entire Bible in the daily services of morning and evening worship. Each testament was covered twice during the year. The *Genesis* account of creation would thus be read on New Year's Day, and Jesus's crucifixion might come up closer to Christmas than to Good Friday. In the course of time, as it became clear that many would not be going to church twice a day, more selective lectionaries were designed. These scheduled the texts judged more important on consecutive Sundays and sought to cover the highlights of scripture in a three-year cycle. Practice varies quite widely today, but in churches that maintain more formal worship, the norm is to preach from a passage assigned for the day.

Spontaneous and extemporaneous prayers are especially frequent in Protestant denominations. Rejecting priestly mediation, Protestants looked for signs of the direct activity of the Holy Spirit. Ordained clergy in some Protestant denominations came to cultivate an ad-lib and *ad hoc* style of prayer, regarding it not as impromptu rambling and folksiness but as evidence of the Spirit's immediate presence. In other Protestant circles, what is intended as unstructured worship can ironically be highly formalized; the reasoned manner of speaking at Quaker meetings, mentioned above, is an example.

In the sixteenth and seventeenth centuries, it was typical for an emerging

Protestant movement to draft its own affirmation of faith, or 'confession'. In services of worship, however, many Protestant denominations continued to use the Apostles' Creed or the Nicene Creed; the Reformation confessions on the whole were too lengthy.

Protestant architecture in northern Europe was not markedly distinct from earlier Catholic forms, since in many cases Protestants took over extant churches. Within a sanctuary, however, Reformed churches rearranged the furniture in keeping with their sacramental theology. Instead of an altar at the end wall that the priest faced with his back to the worshippers, Protestants shifted to a communion table behind which the minister stands and faces the congregation.

The sixteenth-century reformers had little patience for images, especially those of Mary and the saints, and they preferred an empty cross to the crucifix with the suffering Jesus on it. Statues and paintings were trashed with fanatical zeal. Some Protestants are proud of this accomplishment as a blow against what they consider image-worship, and have kept church interiors bare and austere, though stained-glass windows have proven more acceptable than statues. Others regret that much fine art was lost, and have at least an aesthetic affection for Renaissance madonnas, paintings of Mary with the infant Jesus. Having survived the image-bashing of the Reformation, Mary appears in Protestantism at the Christmas season, but manifestly subordinated to the figure of Jesus himself and associated largely with his infancy.

Protestant austerity in the visual arts did not on the whole carry over to music, where there was a major cultural contribution. Alongside Gregorian chant, the premodern European world knew folk songs and dances. Frequently the Reformation took over the tunes of folk songs and used them in worship. Especially among the Lutherans in Germany, there was a rich development of the chorale form, many of whose finest examples are still in regular use. One of them, by Martin Luther, is probably the most widely cherished hymn among Protestants, and since the rapprochement of Protestants and Roman Catholics in the 1960s has been widely used by Catholics as well. We quote the first two stanzas in English translation:

A mighty fortress is our God, a bulwark never failing;
Our helper he amid the flood of mortal ills prevailing.
For still our ancient foe doth seek to work us woe;
His craft and power are great; and armed with cruel hate, on
earth is not his equal.

Did we in our own strength confide, our striving would be losing,
Were not the right man on our side, the man of God's own
choosing.

Dost ask who that may be? Christ Jesus, it is he,
Lord Sabaoth [i.e., Lord of hosts] his name, from age to age the
same, and he must win the battle.

Protestants have composed countless hymns for worship. Hymns are often tuneful and musically simple, usually consisting of four lines in which the fourth returns to the melodic material of the first two. They reflect in their texts a wide range of religious concerns—from praise to God as creator, to calls for social justice and world peace, to hopes for individual strength and divine guidance. Indeed, Protestants were quite willing to depict in words the suffering of the crucified Christ, even while rejecting the bleeding statuary of the crucifix as excessively gory. The third stanza of Isaac Watts's hymn, 'When I Survey the Wondrous Cross', written in 1707, reads:

See, from His head, His Hands, His feet,
Sorrow and love flow mingled down:
Did e'er such love and sorrow meet,
Or thorns compose so rich a crown?

Among the Calvinists in Switzerland and Scotland, the musical development that first replaced the Latin mass was the setting of translations of the biblical psalms to music. During the sixteenth century the 'psalter', as the collection of psalm settings was called, was the principal musical repertory of the Reformed churches. The tunes of the sixteenth-century Genevan Psalter include a familiar setting of *Psalm* 100, to which Protestants often sing the doxology (song of praise):

Praise God from whom all blessings flow;
Praise him all creatures here below;
Praise him above, ye heavenly host:
Praise Father, Son, and Holy Ghost.

To that tune the words of *Psalm* 100 were rendered in seventeenth-century English verse. We cite two of the stanzas:

All people that on earth do dwell
sing to the Lord with cheerful voice;
Him serve with mirth, his praise forth tell,
come ye before him and rejoice.

O enter then his gates with praise,
approach with joy his courts unto;

Praise, laud, and bless his name always,
for it is seemly so to do.

The psalms were likewise the principal focus of congregational song in the Church of England following the Reformation. The pattern, still in use to the present day, has a cadence or progression of chords at the middle and the end of each line, with the earlier part of the line, regardless of length, holding a single note, as follows:

[*reciting tone*] Glory be to the Father, and
[*half-close*] to the Son
[*reciting tone*] And [*closing*] to the Holy Ghost;
[*reciting tone*] As it was in the beginning, is
now and [*half-close*] ever shall be,
[*reciting tone*] World without [*closing*] end,
Amen.

ROMAN CATHOLICISM AFTER 1500

The Catholic Reformation

The abuses of ecclesiastical power that Luther condemned were abuses that the Catholic Church realized it had to rectify. These included the sale of indulgences, and a lavish and permissive clerical lifestyle. The Latin Church returned to a sense of discipline and accountability, a sense that spiritual and moral matters were its primary objective, and a sense of faithfulness to ecclesiastical and historical tradition. It came to think of itself as having had its own reformation.

The Council of Trent

This Catholic reformation, frequently referred to as the 'Counter-Reformation', included the consultative sharing of papal power with the bishops. Unwilling at first to heed the secular princes' calls for such action, the papacy overcame its resistance and convoked a council that eventually met on and off from 1545 at the Italian city of Trent, in the lower reaches of the Alps northwest of Venice, finishing with a burst of decisive energy in 1563.

Trent's formulations—the adjective for them is 'Tridentine'—stood as the Roman Catholic Church's self-definition for four centuries. The decrees cover the whole range of practical and theoretical issues that had come to a boil in the Reformation. It may surprise some today to learn that Protestants were in attendance at some of the sessions, and that there had been the hope for reconciliation and reunion, but compromise could not be achieved.

Historians differ in assessing the Roman Catholic response to the Reformation. Protestants see the post-Tridentine era as one of repression, pointing to the *Index of Prohibited Books* and to the Church's investigative tribunals known as the Inquisition as examples. Catholic interpreters do not deny that there was an *Index* or an Inquisition, but point to the need for discipline and to a genuine fidelity to truth understood conservatively as well as to a genuine desire for renewal.

The council acted to enforce discipline and reform practice, ending the abuses and excesses that had so weakened the Church's credibility as an institution. However, the council stood its ground against some of the Protestants' theoretical positions. It reaffirmed the authority of institutional tradition alongside scripture. It upheld the idea of a distinct status and function as intermediaries for the priesthood, which would have to remain celibate. It instituted seminaries for their training.

Trent reiterated an understanding of the mass as a sacrifice. Theology held that in the re-enactment of Jesus's supper with his disciples, the words 'this is my body' and 'this is my blood' are literally and mysteriously effective. That is, at a certain moment during the service of the mass, the wafer and the wine are transformed into the body and the blood of Christ. This doctrine is known as transubstantiation.

The Tridentine text of the mass, in Latin, was standard throughout the Catholic world for four centuries after Trent. As Latin was a language no longer spoken by the congregation, the moment of transubstantiation was indicated by ringing a small bell. For the faithful the moment has been one of mystery and miracle, while others have dismissed it as a show; the English expression 'hocus-pocus' is a garbling of the words 'this is my body' said in Latin by the priest, *hoc est corpus meum*.

In medieval Europe, the entire Latin mass had been chanted with varieties of musical settings in a melodic musical form known as plainsong. With the Renaissance, Europeans made increasing use of polyphony, where different musical lines were sounded at the same time by different instruments or voices. The harmonies familiar in classical Western music developed especially from the eighteenth century. Clearly, since polyphonic music was more suited to groups than to individuals, it was more suitable for the choral or congregational responses than for the solo parts of the mass said by the officiating clergy.

Choral settings of the Latin mass generally do not contain the entire text of the service with the Eucharistic prayer, but rather the congregational or choral responses. These sections include:

- the Kyrie: '*Kyrie eleison, Christe eleison*' [Greek for 'Lord, have mercy; Christ, have mercy']

- the Gloria: a long section that begins '*Gloria in excelsis Deo* ...' [Latin for 'Glory to God in the highest']
- the Credo: the entire Nicene Creed, beginning, '*Credo in unum Deum* ...' ['I believe in one God']
- the Sanctus: '*Sanctus, sanctus, sanctus, Dominus Deus sabaoth* ...' ['Holy, holy, holy, Lord God of hosts']
- the Benedictus: '*Benedictus qui venit in nomine Domini; hosanna in excelsis*' ['Blessed in the name of the Lord is he who comes; hosanna in the highest']
- the Agnus Dei: '*Agnus Dei, qui tollis peccata mundi, miserere nobis; dona nobis pacem*' ['Lamb of God, who takest away the sins of the world, have mercy on us; give us peace']

European composers also produced many substantial choral settings for parts of the requiem mass (the mass for the dead), which has a different Latin text. And another Latin text frequently set to music was the hymn of praise that begins, *Te Deum laudamus, Te Dominum confitemur* ('We praise you, O God; we acknowledge you to be the Lord'). Also popular among Catholic composers was a long medieval Latin devotional poem, *Stabat Mater*, meditating on and identifying with Mary's grief at the crucifixion of Jesus. Here is its first stanza:

Stabat mater dolorosa
Juxta crucem lachrymosa
Dum pendebat filius.

The mother stood sadly
By the cross, in tears
As her son hung there.

The Jesuits

The Jesuit order, influential in the Catholic Church following the Reformation, exemplifies three principal areas of renewal: spiritual discipline, education, and missionary expansion. Called the Society of Jesus, it was inaugurated by Iñigo (c. 1495–1556), of the family of López of the northern Spanish town of Loyola. History knows him by the name Ignatius, which he used after the age of forty. In his twenties, Iñigo was practically a soldier of fortune, serving with bravado in the retinue of nobles until wounded in the leg by a cannonball. He chose painful corrective surgery, in an age without anaesthesia. Available reading during his convalescence included the lives of saints, which may have influenced his decision at about thirty to take religious vows of poverty, chastity, and obedience.

While following a regimen of prayer and bodily self-denial, he wrote his *Spiritual Exercises* in 1522–3. This concise text is a how-to manual for Christian meditation, a theological reflection on Christ's incarnation as a divine intervention in human history, and a call to arms to join a spiritual crusade. It is a classic of Catholic piety; an encyclical of Pope Paul III in 1548 gave it the best papal endorsement for any book ever with the possible exception of the Bible, and in 1922 Pope Pius XI named Ignatius, canonized exactly 300 years earlier, as the patron saint of spiritual exercises.

Turned down for permanent residence in Turkish-controlled Jerusalem, Ignatius returned to Spain in 1524, where he gained followers for his spiritual exercises and studied philosophy. The heresy-hunting climate in Spain meant restrictions on his activity, so he moved to Paris in 1528 and with six friends in 1534 formed a society vowing strict poverty and service to others. In the next few years they moved to Italy, where several, including Ignatius, were ordained as priests. In 1540, Pope Paul III approved the society as a religious order, which Ignatius led as 'general' for fifteen years until his death.

As time passed, Jesuits became important as a teaching order, well known for their methods as well as their schools. Some institutions are named to honour some of the great figures in the order's first century: Loyola, for instance, and Robert Bellarmine (1542–1621), Peter Canisius (1521–97), Aloysius Gonzaga (1568–91), and Francis Xavier (1506–52).

The most prominent Catholic teaching order of women dates from exactly the same period. The Ursulines were founded in 1535 in Italy by Angela Merici (1474–1540) and received papal approval in 1544. They became influential particularly in France and Canada. One of the most famous Ursulines was the mystic Marie Guyard (1599–1672), known as Marie de l'Incarnation. First a mother and then a widow in France, she became a nun at the age of thirty-one and was invited by the Jesuits to found a convent in Québec in 1639, when she was forty. Her writings describe stages of progress in the personal development of the mystical life, and some say she advanced beyond Teresa of Ávila.

The Jesuits' educational efforts could yield political advantage. For example, in the Thirty Years' War between Protestant and Catholic states in Europe in 1618–48, the Jesuit education of Hapsburg emperor Ferdinand II (r. 1619–37) may have invigorated his efforts to enforce a Catholic restoration in central European regions like Bohemia. The Jesuits came to be both envied and criticized for their role in a number of courts as the confessor priests of royalty, and their casuistry, that is, the use of technicalities and rationalizations, earned them the connotations of the adjective 'Jesuitical'. After the middle of the eighteenth century, this influence backfired, being seen as a foreign influence: they were expelled from Portugal, France, and Spain. Rome suspended the order in Latin countries in 1773. The suspension never took place in Russia, and individual Jesuits continued to teach in Germany and Austria. Rome reinstated the order in 1814.

Catholic Missions in Asia

India

The Portuguese opened up the trade route to India in the sixteenth century. King John III of Portugal (r. 1521–57) sent the Spanish Jesuit Francis Xavier, one of Ignatius's original circle, to evangelize the East Indies. Francis reached India in 1542, made Goa his base, and began to establish communities of converts elsewhere on the Indian and Sri Lankan coast and the Malay peninsula. Despite chronic seasickness, Francis went on to Japan in 1549, introducing Christianity there, too. He then set out for China in 1552, but fell ill and died en route from Goa at the age of forty-six. The Jesuits have attributed 700,000 conversions to Francis.

For a time, Roman Catholic Christianity in India claimed the indigenous Syriac Church ('the Christians of St Thomas') of the Malabar Coast, as in 1599 the archbishop of Goa persuaded them to repudiate the patriarch of Baghdad and give allegiance to Rome. But fifty years later many of this community, disappointed with the way the Jesuits ran things, transferred their allegiance to the Syrian Orthodox Church.

Much of Christian growth in Portuguese territories, it has been argued, came through conversions from Hinduism, where there were often inducements. Christians enjoyed special privileges, while there were economic and social disabilities for Hindus. During the first half of the seventeenth century, the Italian Jesuit Robert De Nobili (1577–1656) gave a new flavour to Catholic missions in India: he wanted to indigenize Christianity in the terms of Indian culture. An Italian aristocrat himself, he aimed to reach the brahmin class of Hindus by adopting the discipline of Indian holy men and by not challenging the caste structure of Indian society. He gained some acceptance, avoiding contact with outcastes and advocating the appointment of different missionaries to preach to different Hindu castes. He studied Sanskrit, Tamil, and Telugu, and wrote books, hymns, and poems in these languages. He is said to have made 100,000 converts, but his assimilationist methods evoked criticism from other missionaries, and he was summoned to appear before the archbishop of Goa to respond to complaints. He was allowed by Rome to continue, but the theme of assimilation versus rejection of the target culture remained a perennial issue in Christian missions.

Japan

In Japan, assimilation at first produced remarkable success. Francis Xavier spent three years there, 1549–52, during which time Portuguese priests admired the

Japanese, finding the feudal class's military discipline something they could relate to. For their part, the Japanese seem to have found the Jesuits both disciplined and learned, something they were accustomed to among their own Zen monks. Christianity at first seemed to be another Buddhist sect. It was policy to follow Japanese etiquette, as indicated by Alessandro Valignano (1539–1606) on his inspection visit to Jesuit missions there in 1579. He stipulated that all local customs not explicitly in contradiction to Christianity should be observed. Especially on the southwestern island of Kyushu, various local Japanese lords, eager to build up trade, encouraged the missionaries, espoused Christianity, and imposed it on their realms. An estimated 150,000 Japanese became Christians by 1582, a figure that doubled in the next two decades and rose to perhaps 500,000 by 1615.

But Japanese rulers were arising who saw the Christian and foreign influence as a threat. The *shōgun* Hideyoshi Toyotomi (r. 1582–98) ordered missionaries banished in 1587, though he did not enforce the ban until 1597, when he executed nine missionaries and seventeen Japanese Christians. The Tokugawa *shōgun* Hidetada (r. 1605–23) consolidated power in central Japan and after a few years of anti-Christian edicts undertook in 1614 to round up the 150 Christian missionaries who were in Japan at the time and deported them, but about a third of them managed to find their way back.

Under Hidetada, persecution of Christians intensified, reaching a peak in the early 1620s. Tortures awaited those who would not comply when asked to step on an image of Christ or Mary. The Roman Catholic Church counts 3,125 as martyrs in this period in Japan. Around Nagasaki, where Christians had been strongest, resentment of the central Tokugawa government prompted an uprising in 1637–8, but the resistance was crushed under siege and marks the end of Japan's 'Christian century'. Catholic Christianity ceased to be a presence in Japan, but when the country was opened up to renewed foreign contact two centuries later, in 1858, missionaries discovered a small remnant community that had kept the faith alive, if in a garbled form.

China

When the Italian Jesuit missionary Matteo Ricci (1522–1610) landed at the southern Chinese port of Macau in 1582, he was far from the first to have taken Christianity to China. We know of two previous waves: one was the Nestorian branch of Christianity, which had arrived overland in Xi'an in 635, and the other a Catholic mission under the Franciscan John of Monte Corvino (d. c. 1330), arriving overland in Beijing in 1294. These two earlier waves had left no Christian community that survived, but there was a monument: the Nestorian inscription on a large standing stone that the Jesuits found in Xi'an almost a thousand years after it had been carved.

Ricci attempted not to seem alien to the vast and ancient land of China. When he and his Jesuit companions first made their way into southern China after 1582, they assumed clothing similar to that of Buddhist monks, and conducted themselves unobtrusively. Ordered in 1589 to leave one southern locale, they seem to have acted on the advice of a local convert and changed to presenting themselves as Confucian-style scholars rather than Buddhist-style monks.

Ricci and the Jesuits won favour at the imperial court in Beijing. After all, the foreigners in scholars' robes bore exotic gifts that fascinated the Chinese. They had mechanical clocks that struck the hours. They had European maps. They had lenses and prisms. Such gifts pleased the emperor, and the Jesuits were invited to stay, even receiving a monthly stipend. Ricci remained in Beijing nine years until his death at the age of fifty-seven from illness. These years were a time of active cultural exchange, in which translations of Chinese philosophical and religious texts were made, and European scientific and mathematical texts were translated into Chinese.

One of Ricci's successors, the German Jesuit Adam Schall von Bell (1591–1666), with training in Galileo's astronomy in Rome, arrived in China in 1619, was given a post in the imperial bureau of astronomy in 1629 with responsibilities for reforming the calendar, and was made chief of the bureau in 1645 when he had also helped cure the empress dowager of an illness. In 1650, Schall, then sixty, was able to build a church in Beijing that the emperor even attended. Only in his mid-seventies would Schall be sentenced for plotting against the state, probably because of complaints from individual jealous Chinese astronomers.

There were complaints by Europeans, too, concerning the Jesuits and their cultural-assimilationist strategy. Schall's successor was the Flemish Jesuit Ferdinand Verbiest (1623–88), during whose time in China from 1657 until 1688 the so-called 'Chinese Rites controversy' erupted. As with so many Christian theological controversies, there was an interplay of intellectual issues and political interests.

Intellectually, three issues revolved around the extent to which the Chinese cultural tradition could be considered valid by Christians. First, there was the matter of participating in rituals honouring Confucius, presumably thereby endorsing his moral system as compatible with Christianity. Second was the question of the Chinese rituals called 'ancestor worship', honouring deceased family members with prostrations, incense, and food offerings. And third was the question of 'terms', that is, whether Chinese terms such as T'ien, 'heaven', or Shang-ti, 'the Lord above', meant the same thing as the Christian idea of God.

Politically, the Jesuits were walking a tightrope. On the one hand, they wanted to win over the Chinese mandarins, and so needed to offer a subtle and judicious endorsement of Chinese culture. On the other hand, they were being challenged by rival orders, notably the Franciscans and Dominicans, whose medieval experience in Europe and recent experience among tribal populations in places like the Philippines had conditioned a knee-jerk response of condemnation towards anything that smacked of paganism.

The confrontational evangelism of these orders in China embarrassed the Jesuits before the Chinese authorities. Meanwhile, in 1639, a Dominican complained about the Jesuits in an appeal to Rome, correctly describing the Jesuits on some points (such as that they did not declare Confucius to be in hell) and misrepresenting them on others. In the face of Rome's essential agreement with the charges, it took the Jesuits fifteen years to get them cleared.

The closing years of the seventeenth century saw a renewed suspicion of Jesuit accommodation, this time voiced by French missionary priests. The upshot, in 1693, was a ruling by a papal vicar in coastal China, Charles Maigrot (1652–1730), that condemned Ricci's teachings, participation in the Chinese rites, and the use of Chinese terms for God. The emperor, who had just issued an edict of toleration, remained sympathetic to the Jesuits. When a papal legate, Charles Thomas Maillard de Tournon (1668–1710), turned up in China in 1705, he and Maigrot showed themselves utterly uninformed about Chinese culture, and the emperor banished them.

The emperor subsequently gave residence permits only to pro-Ricci missionaries. But with his death in 1722, any Christian hope for the evangelization of China from the top down was at an end. Within a few years, there were hardly any Christians left among the Chinese literati. And Maigrot's restrictions of 1693, renewed by papal constitutions in 1715 and again in 1742, severely curtailed the ability of Catholic missionaries in China to state the tradition in indigenous terms.

Three centuries after Vasco da Gama and Columbus, Catholic missions in Asia were left with practically nothing apart from the Philippines to show for their efforts. European Christianity had come up against the religious traditions of high civilizations, with their social institutions and sophisticated intellectual heritages, and had failed to displace them. In those same three centuries in the Western hemisphere, the story was just the opposite. Latin America was to become a new heartland of Catholicism.

Missions in the Americas

Christopher Columbus (1451–1506) landed in Santo Domingo in 1492. His second expedition, the following year, included laity and clergy eager to win territory and populations in the name of Christ as well as of Spain. The native peoples in the Caribbean, and their nature-related religion, offered Spanish Christianity less resistance than the Judaism and Islam that were at that time being expelled from Spain.

But when Hernán Cortés (1485–1547) reached Mexico in 1519 and Francisco Pizarro (c. 1475–1541) conquered Peru in 1532–3, they encountered social institutions and religious conceptions of a rather more sophisticated order. Still, the great pre-Conquest civilizations of the Americas—the Aztecs and Mayas in Mexico and the Incas in Peru—seemingly fell before small numbers of Spanish conquerors like a row of dominoes.

One looks for explanations of so dramatic a collapse. Some historians point to Spain's advantage in weapons. The Spanish had horses, which the indigenous peoples of the Americas did not. The Spanish carried diseases to which they themselves had immunities but which devastatingly depleted the unprepared populations in the New World.

The Aztec ruler in Mexico, Moctezuma II (Montezuma, r. 1502–21), welcomed the Spaniard Cortés with gifts rather than wiping out the tiny Spanish force he led. One reason adduced for this is that Cortés's arrival matched the timing of an Aztec messianic expectation. People were waiting for the god Quetzalcoatl to appear in the form of a fair-skinned Toltec king. He would come from the east at a particular moment in the fifty-two-year Mexican calendrical cycle. So Cortés and his men may have appeared to Mexico as the fulfilment of Mexican expectations.

On the whole, the priests and friars who accompanied the conquerors had no use for Mexican religion. It was to be destroyed, not fulfilled. It was to be displaced, not built upon. Cortés was of this view; if he recruited a Mexican tribe in an alliance against Moctezuma, they would have to destroy their sacred images. The native populations flocked to Christianity in large numbers, so quickly as to raise questions about the profundity of any conversion. One Franciscan friar figured that within ten years after Cortés's arrival, he had baptized 200,000 locals, as many as 14,000 in a single day. Some of the clergy spoke no Indian language, putting their message forward with pictures, symbols, and gestures. And even those who did learn the local languages found that often the Spanish rituals and festivals they introduced were the feature of Christianity to which the Indians of Mexico could relate.

Among the Spanish missionaries there were those who did make a serious effort to study the native languages, to appreciate the native myth and symbol and ritual, and to document their culture. One such was the Spaniard Bernardino de Sahagún (c. 1490–1590), whose *Historia de las cosas de Nueva España* (History of Matters in New Spain) is a valuable ethnographic record of Mexico at the time of the conquest.

There were missionaries who committed themselves to the well-being of the local population. They became the voice of prophetic protest against exploitation of the natives: each Spaniard in the conquest had been allocated a grant of land and a number of Indians to work it, and their treatment often amounted to slavery. Strictly speaking, slavery was illegal; but then, laws promising safeguards are one thing and their implementation can be something else.

The greatest defender of the rights of the Indians was Bartolomé de Las Casas (1474–1566), a Spanish priest. As a participant in the conquest of Cuba in 1513, he had received an allotment of serfs with his land grant, but the following year he declared he would not keep them. Over several seasons he sailed back and forth between Spain and Mexico, winning in Madrid a hearing for the rights of the Indians and favour with King Charles I (r. 1516–56) while failing to make an impact on the practice of the colonists in Mexico. He joined the Dominican order, and wrote a monumental *Historia de las Indias* (History of the Indies), detailing abuses in Mexico, which was published only after his death. Named bishop of Chiapas in Guatemala at the age of seventy, Las Casas denied absolution in his diocese to any slave-holders in his constituency.

He returned to a much warmer welcome at the Spanish court. In 1550, when he was seventy-six, he faced the scholarly Juan Ginés de Sepúlveda (1490?–1573) in a great debate at Valladolid, Spain, on the inferiority versus the equality of the peoples of the New World and European Christians. The manner of the debate was academic, both sides basing their arguments on the ancient Greek philosopher Aristotle. The issues at stake, though, were anything but, for King Charles was putting a moratorium on any further conquests until it could be shown that they were morally justifiable. The debate was somewhat inconclusive, but questions concerning cultural imperialism and the use of force remain lively to the present day.

Church and Society in Latin America

An intimate relationship between Church and state prevailed from the very start of Spanish and Portuguese influence in the New World. Discovery and conquest themselves were conducted under what amounted to a licence granted in 1493 by Pope Alexander VI. In this, Spain was awarded all territory beyond a certain point west of the Azores, and Portugal everything east of that. Thus not only were Africa and Asia Portugal's concession, but so was Brazil, while the rest of Latin America was Spanish.

The papal licence linked conquest and mission: along with the allocation of the territory went the responsibility to evangelize its population. And it meant that the kings' representatives ruled the affairs of the Church in the Spanish New World, centring first on New Spain (Mexico) and Peru, with later centres in Granada (Colombia) and the Plata (Argentina).

The missionaries were chiefly members of religious orders such as Franciscans, Dominicans, and Jesuits. In their expansion, to Paraguay and Argentina in the south and to California in the north, they were accompanied by soldiers who established *presidios* (garrisons) and by civilians. The Spanish missionaries established autonomous villages known as *reducciones*, 'reductions'. Among the politically most significant were the Jesuit reductions in Paraguay, which, since they lay along the frontier between Spanish and Portuguese territory, heightened the Jesuits' involvement in political intrigue in eighteenth-century Europe.

Indians who lived in *reducciones* were protected from colonial enslavement, but became dependent on another kind of paternalism in exchange: they had their life and work strictly laid out for them, with little encouragement of initiative. By the end of the colonial era, according to some estimates, the Church controlled half of the productive land under Spanish rule.

Outwardly, Catholic Christianity seems to have scored its most spectacular successes in Latin America. Half the world's Roman Catholics live there today, and from Mexico to the South Pole, the Catholic faith is the majority religion. Is Latin America the region of the world's most salient triumph of Christianity? It would at first seem that there are no rivals.

On closer inspection, the alternative that Catholic Christianity lacks from without (though there are some rapidly growing Latin American Protestant groups, particularly Pentecostal churches) seems to confront it from within. The Spanish and Portuguese conquest did not in fact result in the total displacement of native traditions. Behind Christian altars in Mexico there were pagan images. Inside early Mexican crucifixes are Aztec cult objects. In coastal Brazil, the tribal deities of West African Blacks who were brought to the New World turn up as Catholic saints in the cults called *candombles*.

Across the hemisphere, the phenomenon of combination of religious elements, often termed syncretism, is accessible to all who look for it. Whereas interfaith dialogue and encounter may be today's agenda for Christians in other religiously diverse regions such as India or North America, in Latin America the dialogue is with the Native past and is internal to the Christian community.

Latin American syncretism solves the problem of indigenization, for it furnishes religious figures with whom the people can identify as one of their own. At the folk level in Mexico, no challenger displaces the Virgin of Guadalupe. Her cult goes back to 1531, and to a hill near Mexico City that was sacred to the Aztec goddess Tonantzin, herself a virgin mother of gods. A Christian convert named Juan Diego reported an apparition of a beautiful lady, who said she was 'one of his own people' and instructed him to gather flowers from the hilltop and present them before the bishop. He wrapped them in a piece of cloth, and when he unrolled them before the bishop, an image of the Virgin appeared to be visible on the cloth. The cloth is still venerated at a basilica at the foot of the hill, and the popular piety that attends it is reminiscent of medieval Christianity in Europe.

Catholicism in North America

North America is a region where various regional Roman Catholic influences have met and interacted. These involve both mission and migration.

The Spanish missionary activity in Latin America contributed diverse legacies to North America. Florida was an area of early settlement direct from Spain. Texas and New Mexico were part of, and influenced by, Mexico until the mid-nineteenth century. In California, the Franciscans extended a chain of missions along the coast, the last and northernmost being established at Sonoma, about 65 km (40 mi.) north of San Francisco, in 1823.

As Russian settlers had established Fort Ross, with an Orthodox chapel, only that same distance farther north along the coast, there was an element of competition between the Spaniards, who had come by the Atlantic, and the Russians, who had arrived via Siberia. Arguably, the encounter between the Spanish and the Russians in California marks the moment when Christianity's overland spread encircled the globe.

The Spanish and Portuguese were not the only missionaries to the New World. Farther to the north, there were the French. The explorer Jacques Cartier (1491–1557) sailed up the St Lawrence River in 1535–6, past the site where Québec would stand, and got as far as the vicinity of Montréal, where the first rapids are. He called the spot Lachine, since he was looking for a route to China. But a permanent French settlement on the St Lawrence had to await the arrival of Samuel de Champlain (1567–1635) in 1603. Champlain explored upstream to Ottawa and the Great Lakes.

Missionaries followed: four Recollet friars in 1615 and five Jesuits in 1625. The Jesuit Jacques Marquette (1637–75) arrived in Québec in 1666 at the age of twenty-nine and two years later founded a mission at Sault Ste Marie (i.e., St Mary's rapids) at the northern end of Lake Michigan. With the Québec-born layman Louis Jolliet (1645–1700), he explored southward along the Mississippi River. French missionary activity among the Iroquois and other Native American peoples was handled largely by the Jesuits. Their sensitivity to Native ways resulted in the adoption of Christianity by the Native peoples, but not in the complete eradication of Native traditions. In recent years, there have been initiatives to recover an appreciation of Native traditions of respect for the creator and for all species of creatures, in a manner not out of keeping with Jesuit sensitivity to local ways in the seventeenth and eighteenth centuries.

The other principal influences of European Catholicism in North America are due to migration. French settled along the St Lawrence in Lower Canada (i.e., Québec), as well as at the mouth of the Mississippi River (New Orleans). The colony of Maryland reflects Catholicism from England; in 1632, Lord George Calvert Baltimore (1580–1632) was granted a charter for this colony, where English Catholics might find refuge from persecution in Britain. Other regions, such as Upper Canada (that is, Ontario) also attracted Catholic settlers from England.

From the mid-nineteenth century, the growth of industrial cities along the East Coast of North America attracted migrants in large numbers from Ireland and then from Italy. The ecclesiastical hierarchy of the Catholic Church in North America mirrors to some extent the recent history of immigration. One finds bishops in Canada whose ancestors were French or English, whereas a great many of the United States bishops are of Irish descent, with their dominance now giving way to clergy of Italian and Hispanic background. There are newer immigrant communities of Portuguese, Filipinos, and others. Modern migration reflects the fact that Christianity has spread worldwide; in fact, because of their links with the Western Christian world, Christian minorities in different parts of Asia are somewhat overrepresented in the flow of migrants to the West from their lands.

THE MODERN WORLD

The Enlightenment

Modernity has had institutional and intellectual aspects, both of which have challenged traditional Christianity and transformed its role in Western civilization.

By 'the Enlightenment' is meant an era in European history, cresting in the seventeenth and eighteenth centuries, when human reason was claimed to have a central role. Thinking of human beings as rational was hardly new; the ancient Greeks had done this, as had the medieval Muslims. However, the European Enlightenment gave particular privilege to reason in proposals for the regulation of public life. Theories of human nature were implicit, if not explicit, in political rhetoric and journalistic comment. People discussed the nature and purpose of government and the proper training of rulers and administrators. Towards the close of the eighteenth century, some of these ideas were implemented in practice in the American and French revolutions.

Secularism

Institutionally, the American and French revolutions signalled a change from Christianity's status as the established religion. The new secularity was more a bending of the past than a break with it, however. From national flags to the health-care professions, the cross has remained despite the secularization of politics and medicine. Christian symbols and values continue to permeate Western culture. And as republics replaced monarchies in nineteenth-century Europe, the old linkages between Church and politics survived in the names of European political parties such as Christian Democrats and Christian Socialists. In North America, too, politicians continued to invoke religious sentiments and values.

In Latin America, a number of emerging states promulgated constitutions that were secular in principle and implied religious liberty, but in many cases the Roman Catholic Church remained officially subsidized, and its missions to tribal populations were a means of state cultural control. The principal break in Latin America was the Mexican revolution of 1917, when the state confiscated all Church landholdings and took over control of education. Lay Catholics formed Christian Democratic parties in several Latin American countries, seeking to maintain through the electoral process the influence that had been jeopardized by the secularization of the state.

Intellectually, the eighteenth-century Enlightenment displayed a spirit of confidence in human reason. Like the Renaissance that preceded it, the Enlightenment also took pride in the cultural heritage of ancient Greece and Rome. In these respects the culture looked to sources outside traditional Christianity for its symbols and values.

Galileo

A growing understanding of science eventually resulted in a recasting of our understanding of the nature and place of religion. This happened despite vigorous opposition from traditionalists.

The 'Copernican revolution' in astronomy was a reorientaton from a geocentric to a heliocentric view. Consensus had held, with the ancient Greek astronomer Ptolemy, that the sun and the planets moved around the earth, the apparent reversals of their movements in the sky being due to complex subsidiary circles termed epicycles. Supposing the sun to be at the centre, the Polish astronomer Nicolaus Copernicus (1473–1543) was able to offer an explanation elegantly simple by comparison. It was published in 1543. By 1609, the Italian mathematician Galileo Galilei (1564–1642) had developed improvements to a recent invention, the telescope, and he began to make observations of sunspots that confirmed the Copernican theory.

Galileo's observations, published in 1613, gained a popularity that worried conservative scholars. Some of them appealed to the authorities of the Roman Catholic Church, contending that the heliocentric theory was in conflict with the Bible. His views were also a challenge to the current theology's investment in the worldview of the ancient Greeks, particularly Aristotle. Galileo stated his side of the case to the authorities, recalling in his letters that in past cases of conflict with science, the Church had interpreted scripture allegorically. It would, he warned, be 'a terrible detriment for the souls if people found themselves convinced by proof of something that it was made then a sin to believe'.

Cardinal Robert Bellarmine chose, however, to try to contain the Copernican theory by having it declared 'false and erroneous' in 1616 and placing Copernicus's book on the *Index* of prohibited writings. Avoiding public exposure, Galileo worked for a number of years on a book comparing the Ptolemaic and Copernican systems, publishing it in 1632. Ostensibly a comparison between the two, it came out with the Roman Catholic censors' licence to publish, called an *imprimatur*. Once published, the work was seen to be a defence of the Copernican theory and a threat to doctrine, but since it had been licensed it could not be suppressed directly. Instead, research 'discovered' an injunction Bellarmine had allegedly given Galileo back in 1616 not to discuss Copernican theory further.

Summoned to trial before the Inquisition in Rome in 1633, Galileo, then aged sixty-nine, denied having received any such injunction; historians have tended to side with Galileo. But he was made to 'abjure, curse, and detest' his errors and lived the remaining eight years of his life under house arrest. Three-and-a-half centuries later, in 1992, evidently able to resist the accumulating data of space research no longer, Rome rehabilitated Galileo, issuing a retraction of its condemnation of him.

The Deists

Deism was a philosophical position that gained a considerable following in England in the seventeenth and eighteenth centuries. The universe manifests regular patterns that can be described as laws of nature, the Deists said; and they were unwilling to admit the suspension of these patterns by divine intervention. On the other hand, though, they were willing to think of the universe as the result of a creative divine intelligence. The creator God of the Deists, like a divine clock maker, assembles or shapes the universe and then leaves it to run on its own.

In his *Natural Theology*, published in 1802, the English philosopher William Paley (1743–1805) argues for this view. If we found a watch on a desert island, Paley says, we would never need to have seen any other watch to posit a maker, the watch would not have to work perfectly, nor would we have to understand the function of every part. This is similar with humans and the universe as evidence for God: even if the universe is imperfect or not fully comprehensible, we can still think of a perfect creator deity.

Newton

A towering figure in late seventeenth-century and early eighteenth-century science was England's Isaac Newton (1643–1727). His insight was that the earth's gravitational force might extend to the moon. Therefore the fall of an apple to the ground and the maintenance of the moon's trajectory in its orbit are instances of the same force of attraction between physical objects. The universe is thus a manifestation of a single harmonious order, though for Newton it was of forces and masses whereas for the medieval theologians it had been a gradation of orderly purposes. Newton, not wanting to limit God to a Deist-type role only as first cause, did hold that God might make occasional interventions to adjust the universe, as in the case of variations observed in planetary orbits. Later scientists found no need of such adjustments and contended that Newton postulated them because of deficiencies in his own data.

For scientists in Newton's and the Deists' day, the teleological or design argument for God was persuasive. They had imbibed the Puritan notion of a benevolent and provident creator, and from the Middle Ages long before Puritanism a view of the world as intelligible. Seeing the universe as a mechanism that obeyed regular laws was not in itself antithetical to religious faith. Indeed, the religious climate of the eighteenth century was remarkably favourable to the investigation of the mechanisms of the universe, as each new discovery was taken to be the unfolding of a new detail of the marvels of a divine creation. To the extent that we today think of science and religion as antithetical, it is not Newton's era but an earlier one (Galileo's) or a later one (Darwin's) on which that impression is built.

Philosophy

The eighteenth century saw philosophical scepticism about claims for the transcendent. Thinkers contended that one cannot substantiate the objects of religion through the operation of reason on sense data. Particularly decisive were the critiques of such philosophers as the Scotsman David Hume (1711–76) and the German Immanuel Kant (1724–1804). God as the First Cause cannot be proved; as Kant argued, causality is not part of the data of the physical world but part of the framework of thought by which human minds interpret it.

But what Kant showed to be in principle unprovable is by the very same token undisprovable. In place of cognitive assertions about the divine or transcendent, much modern philosophy of religion since Kant has preferred to speak of experience and feeling—that is, of the dynamics of the human response to the transcendent. The German philosopher Friedrich Schleiermacher (1768–1834), for instance, characterized religion as an 'intuitive sense of absolute dependence'. If one could not prove the existence of that on which one feels dependent, one could at least describe the intuition. In the same post-Kantian vein, the twentieth-century German philosopher of religion Rudolf Otto (1869–1937) coined the word 'numinous' for what people sense as an overpowering yet fascinating mystery.

Schleiermacher also contributed to a 'subjective' understanding of Christ's atonement, in which Jesus functions as a moral example, an embodiment of human awareness of God. In this view, Jesus as the second Adam is a better example than the first. For Schleiermacher, salvation comes first as a change in spiritual awareness, and atonement follows as a divine-human reconciliation.

Meanwhile, the nineteenth-century Danish philosopher Søren Kierkegaard (1813–55) pioneered the line of inquiry called existentialism. In existentialism, the focus is shifted from knowledge, already limited by Kant's strictures, to commitment, for which Kant himself sensed he was making room. It is no accident that much modern intellectual defence of religion sees it in analogy with love, which likewise rests on commitment rather than proof.

Commitment-based theologies have been influential, but they do not rule out one powerful classic argument against religious faith. We find it already in ancient literature such as the biblical book of *Job*; it is at least as old as monotheism. It is the problem of evil and suffering: how can one treat as both powerful and good, and hence worthy of worship, a deity that would allow either the evil that results from some human actions or the suffering that results from accident or chaos in nature? Even in a mechanistic theory, where after creation the deity does not intervene, the deity as creator does not escape responsibility. The modern world has in no way eliminated evil and suffering as an objection to theistic faith, nor has it come up with any striking new avenues to answer it. If anything, the modern world has only added new instances of human brutality to the inventory of grievances that theodicy (the term philosophers use for the enterprise of justifying God as good) must answer.

Pietism, Methodism, and Revival

The name 'Pietism' designates not a boundaried denomination but a movement that rippled through various Protestant denominations. It emphasized individual piety, seeking as a model the spirituality of the earliest Christians. After 1675, the followers of Philipp Jakob Spener (1635–1705), in Lutheran circles in Germany, were termed Pietists, but comparable tendencies emerged in Reformed (Calvinist) circles in the Netherlands.

Pietists were dissatisfied with doctrinal and institutional rigidity in the Protestant churches emerging from the Reformation. They sought a spontaneity of devotion, in which a complete renewal of faith would occur in the individual believer and be accompanied by a certainty of divine forgiveness and acceptance. For many, the feeling of certainty was all the evidence one needed—a position that certainly pitted Pietism in Germany against the emerging rationalism of the eighteenth-century Enlightenment, but which found intellectual articulation in the emphasis laid on feeling by Schleiermacher.

Pietism spread in Lutheran circles both in Europe and the Americas, and in the form articulated by the eighteenth-century Moravian count Nikolaus Ludwig von Zinzendorf und Pottendorf (1700–60), it influenced the Wesleyan movement in England and contributed to Methodism.

Methodists

In the late 1720s, John Wesley (1703–91), then an Anglican undergraduate at Oxford, collected fellow students in a circle others nicknamed the 'Methodists' for their methodical approach to Bible study and church attendance. The group included John's brother, Charles (1707–88), as well as George Whitefield (1714–70). All subsequently engaged in itinerant preaching careers. John and Charles embarked on a mission to evangelize Native Americans in Georgia in 1735–7, but their condemnation of slavery won them little welcome in the American South. The spiritual side of the Reformation on the Continent had a delayed impact on Anglicanism. After a visit to a Moravian Pietist community, and three days after his brother Charles's conversion experience, John Wesley in 1738 felt his heart 'strangely warmed'.

Wesley began to preach to public gatherings, often of miners and workers, outside the established churches. In the fifty-three years until his death, he preached over 40,000 sermons, averaging fifteen a week, and travelled 320,000 km (200,000 mi.), mainly on horseback. Though he had at first hoped his movement would tap Reformation spirituality and revitalize the Church of England from within, Wesley eventually oversaw its organization as an independent denomination and personally ordained leaders for it.

Revival

In the group phenomenon of revival, many at one time developed an intense feeling of blessing or spiritual perfection. The Great Awakening, a revival in New England in 1740–3, was sparked by the Calvinist preaching of the gifted and versatile theologian Jonathan Edwards (1703–58) in Massachusetts after a visit from the English Methodist preacher George Whitefield.

The Great Awakening's influence extended well beyond New England, altering the shape of American Protestantism as the nation expanded westward. Itinerant preaching, often in camp meetings, was well suited to the western frontier in the late eighteenth and early nineteenth centuries, and was engaged in by the various denominations. While Congregational and Presbyterian circles had been the locus of Edwards's activity, the Methodists and Baptists were more successful in making new recruits. The Methodists became the largest Protestant denomination in the American midwest and, after the Baptists, in the American South as well.

Many hymns expressing a confidence of having received divine favour were produced from the middle of the eighteenth to the end of the nineteenth centuries. They have a high frequency of the first-person pronoun in their texts and three or six beats to the measure in their music. An example, with words from 1779 often sung to a familiar early American tune:

> Amazing grace—how sweet the sound—
> that saved a wretch like me!
> I once was lost, but now am found,
> was blind, but now I see.

Holiness Churches

In time the main Methodist bodies in America became more organized and conventional, more sedate and mainline. But new independent churches and movements continued to spring from the revivalist roots of Methodism. For their emphasis on feeling intensely the achievement or the gift of holiness, these congregations are often referred to as 'Holiness' churches. Among them are the Church of the Nazarene, and the Church of God that started in Anderson, Indiana.

Holiness can bring striking changes in observable behaviour. Whether one rolls in the aisles of the meeting (hence the nickname 'holy rollers') or speaks out ecstatically in an exotic prayer language one has not previously known ('speaking in tongues', technically termed 'glossolalia'), the group interprets such conduct as prompted by the Holy Spirit. The term 'charismatic', from the Greek word for gifts, describes such groups. Charismatic tongue speaking was promoted in London in the 1830s by a Scottish Presbyterian, Edward Irving (1792–1834). In 1901, Charles Fox Parham (1873–1937), teaching at a Bible college in Topeka, Kansas, encouraged it as well. Though initially a Protestant phenomenon, charismatic activity has become visible also among Catholic Christians since the 1970s.

Pentecostalism

Protestant congregations that cultivate speaking in tongues are also termed Pentecostal, recalling the early Church's Pentecost experience. But unlike today's Pentecostal movement, *Acts* reports speech in exotic tongues that is intelligible rather than mystifying.

Evident to any observer is the group-supported nature of revivalism in general and of charismatic religion in particular: the gestures, the speech, the build-up of emotional intensity in worship, all follow conventionalized patterns. The community's anticipation of spiritual experience helps it to happen.

Many locate the birth of the modern Pentecostal movement in a revival held at a church on Azusa Street in Los Angeles in 1906. Its leader was a Black, William J. Seymour (1870–1922), whose parents had been slaves. Seymour had been influenced by Parham's work in Topeka. Newspaper coverage described the sounds of Seymour's meetings as a 'weird babble'. At the outset Blacks and Whites participated together, but as Pentecostalism diversified, it developed segregated congregations.

Pentecostalism, with its emphasis on immediate personal experience rather than on a textual or doctrinal tradition, can take a variety of forms and can appeal effectively to persons with little formal education. Its religiosity has a cross-cultural appeal; Pentecostal missionaries enjoy remarkable success in Latin America and Africa. Some consider Pentecostalism the fastest-growing segment of Christianity at the present time.

New American Denominations

With the autonomy that Protestantism gives the individual's faith there has inevitably come a bewildering diversity of expression. New denominations that emerged on the American scene in the nineteenth century illustrate this. People were experiencing economic and social changes that left many disoriented. Historians referring to upstate New York as 'the burned-over district' see it as a cradle of new movements in the nineteenth century much as California became in the twentieth.

Disciples of Christ

Following Presbyterian opposition to a revival in Kentucky in 1804, Barton Stone (1772–1844) left the Presbyterians to be a 'Christian only', and gained followers. Meanwhile, Thomas Campbell (1763–1854), a Presbyterian from Northern Ireland, became disaffected with the sectarian character of the Presbyterianism he encountered; he and his son Alexander joined Baptist associations, calling themselves Reformers. In 1832, the Stone and Campbell movements merged.

Stone's followers called themselves the Christian Church, while the Campbell element preferred the name Disciples of Christ. The merged movement, which used both names as well as 'Churches of Christ', spread with the westward expansion of the United States. The names bespeak an initial protest against sectarianism, though before long the movement became another denomination. An influential periodical, the *Christian Century*, was of Disciples origin and reflects pan-Protestant goals, as do some educational institutions such as Texas Christian University.

Seventh-Day Adventists

In 1831, in upstate New York, William Miller (1782–1849), a Baptist lay minister, began to preach that the second coming of Christ was imminent. Interpreting the mention of 2,300 days in *Daniel* 8:14 as 2,300 years, he expected it would happen about 1843. Following the 'great disappointment' of its non-occurrence, Miller's followers revised their calculations several times over two decades, but eventually became non-specific about them. Besides its eschatological expectations, Adventism characteristically stressed Saturday rather than Sunday worship.

From the 1840s until her death, the 'gift of prophecy' of Ellen Gould Harmon (1826–1915), who experienced trances and visions and married the Adventist preacher James White, was the confirming spiritual authority of the movement. As early as 1866, the Adventists began to promote health cures, opening a sanatorium in Battle Creek, Michigan. In the 1880s, they expanded their missionary activity, including sending medical missionaries around the world. The twentieth century saw Adventist ranks swell dramatically among Third World peoples. At the same time, Adventist intellectuals and scholars in the United States were growing more willing to ask critical questions about biblical interpretation and about the claims of Ellen White. This development marked the movement's transition from millenarian sect to established denomination.

Jehovah's Witnesses

Raised near Pittsburgh, Charles Taze Russell (1852–1916) was exposed to forecasts of the end of the world and the return of Christ, such as Miller's adventism. Russell was intensely interested in Bible study, but was largely self-taught. His understanding of scripture was as a quarry for proof texts rather than as the ancient cultural legacy of Israel and the early Church. The group he formed began publishing *Zion's Watch Tower and Herald of Christ's Presence* in 1879. Its predictions of the end did not eventuate, but the projected date of 1914 produced the First World War. The Witnesses have since held that Jehovah's Kingdom was inaugurated in that year in anticipation of the end.

The Witnesses meet in what they call Kingdom Halls, principally in preparation for the missionary activity that they conduct systematically on a door-to-door basis. Their evangelistic activity includes a vast output of their publications *Awake!* and *The Watchtower*. Witnesses regard Jesus Christ as a created being (as Arius did), rejecting the doctrine of the Trinity, but hold that by dying he brought humanity a second chance to choose righteousness and escape the punishment expected at the end.

Witnesses reject the authority of secular states, refusing to salute their flags or serve in their armies. This refusal is not on the grounds of pacifism but because they see themselves as citizens of another kingdom. Some countries have treated them harshly, but in the United States their demands for exemption from state allegiance and service have often been upheld in the courts. They also refuse blood transfusions and some medical treatments for their children, but on this issue secular courts have tended to rule in favour of the child's right to health ahead of the parents' right to religious expression.

Christian Science

Spiritual healing is the central concern of the Church of Christ, Scientist, founded in Boston in 1879 by a New England woman then known, in her third marriage, as Mary Baker Eddy (1821–1910). Seventeen years earlier, in 1862, at the age of 41, she had received help for her spinal condition from a healer from Maine, Phinehas Quimby (1802–66), who worked without medication. She began to write articles seeing in this the method of Jesus's healing. After Quimby died in 1866, her illness returned, and she suffered a bad fall. But, reading the New Testament, she recovered and began to write about spiritual healing, publishing in 1875 *Science and Health*, which came to be regarded as an inspired text second in authority only to the Bible by the following who attended her meetings.

In her youth, Mrs Eddy had come from New England Congregationalist roots, with Puritan affinities and with a longing for, or sense of, spiritual presence in tune with the thought of Jonathan Edwards and the eighteenth-century Great Awakening. But in her own thought, she departed from the standard Protestant view of God as creator of the material world, and saw in the resurrection and ascension of Jesus a motif of rising above the material world. Rather than constituting the hereafter, spiritual existence should be the characteristic of the here and now. And in such a perspective, evil, illness, suffering, even death, do not merit being thought of as real. The quest to realize and implement this on an individual level is optimistic to the point of wishful thinking. It has occupied most of Christian Scientists' energy, and apart from its publishing activity, the Church has not been conspicuously involved in social projects.

Mrs Eddy founded the Massachusetts Metaphysical College in Boston in 1881, teaching there until it closed in 1889. From 1883 the Church published the *Christian Science Journal* and from 1898 the *Christian Science Sentinel*, but it is the newspaper founded in 1908, the *Christian Science Monitor*, known for the integrity of its journalism, that has gained the Church the widest public respect. Apart from a religious page, the *Monitor* devotes little direct attention to the Church's teachings; but, perhaps in deference to its heritage, its coverage of world events sometimes contains more of an element of hope than do comparable stories in the commercial press. And for years, the *Monitor* declined to report that people 'died'; instead, they 'passed'.

Mormons

Joseph Smith, Jr (1805–44), living in upstate New York, claimed that in 1820 he was instructed in a vision of God and Jesus not to join any of the existing denominations. In subsequent visions he became persuaded that he had been divinely chosen to restore the true Church of Christ. The authority of that Church, Smith claimed, was revelatory, given by apostolic figures to him and his associate Oliver Cowdery (1806–50) in 1829.

As a textual basis for the enterprise, Smith published the *Book of Mormon*, which he said was translated from gold plates inscribed in 'reformed Egyptian' that had been divinely vouchsafed to him. While subsequent editions call him 'translator', the title page of the 1830 first edition declares Joseph Smith 'author and proprietor'.

This book, reflecting the usage of the 1611 *King James* translation of the Bible and religious ideas of Smith's own day, gives an otherwise undocumented history of migrations to the New World prior to Columbus and states that Christ after his crucifixion visited the Western hemisphere to teach the gospel and inaugurate a new church. Mormons regard the book as a scripture of God's dealings with the Western hemisphere, parallel with the Bible and its account of events in the Eastern hemisphere.

Also scriptural for Mormons are Smith's *The Pearl of Great Price*, presented as revelations and translations, and *Doctrine and Covenants*, a collection of Smith's *ad hoc* revelatory declarations. Passages in this latter work address specific individual moments in the Church's early years. General reflection is interspersed with guidance for particular circumstances in a manner reminiscent of the letters of Paul—or certain *sūrahs* of the *Qur'ān*.

Smith's followers soon established settlements in Ohio and Missouri. Driven out of Missouri in 1839, Mormon refugees settled in Nauvoo, Illinois, on the Mississippi River. By now, the Mormons referred to themselves as the Church of Jesus Christ of Latter-Day Saints. In Nauvoo, Smith continued to develop unusual practices such as baptism for the dead, introduced secret polygamy, and declared himself a candidate for the American presidency. Some of these innovations caused strife between different factions of the Latter-Day Saints, and an anti-Mormon mob killed Smith and his brother in 1844. Some of the traditionalist, antipolygamy Mormons decided to maintain themselves in the midwest as the Reorganized Church of Latter-Day Saints, with headquarters in Independence, Missouri.

The migration of a major portion of the Mormons to Utah took place in 1847 under the leadership of Brigham Young (1801–77), who had been president of an inner council of twelve that Smith had organized on the pattern of the apostolic Church. For the next thirty years, Young led the Mormons as they dominated Utah. They were unsuccessful in their bid to make Utah a Mormon state, but Young was chosen by Washington as governor of the Utah Territory. However, polygamy, publicly announced by the Mormons in 1852, was dropped in 1890 as the federal government threatened its abolition following an 1870 Supreme Court ruling. Thereafter, the Mormons set their community apart with a code of behaviour that included not only a rigid sexual morality but strict abstinence from stimulants: tea and coffee as well as alcohol and tobacco.

The Church expects of its young adults two years' volunteer service as missionaries. Distinctive Mormon doctrines include the notion that God is increasing in perfection, as human beings improve to where God once was. Distinctive practices include the augmentation of the spiritual community through baptism by proxy of persons, with the result that some of the world's most energetic genealogical research goes on in Utah. Mormons have also been interested in Western-hemisphere archaeology for any light it might throw on the content of the *Book of Mormon*. Cultural parallels between the Eastern and Western hemispheres are thought by Mormons to lend plausibility to their claims of historical transmission.

Protestant Missions

The colonial policies of the northern European nations and the missionary efforts of Protestants peaked in the second half of the nineteenth century. In Africa, one of their main objectives, the aims of Church and state went hand in hand. The British established themselves on large stretches of the African coasts, moving into the interior of the continent by river and road, and later by rail. Although formerly active in slave trading from West Africa to the New World, Britain now opposed slavery in its competition with the Arab sultanates of the Gulf, who were the slave merchants of East Africa. In 1857, David Livingstone (1813–73), a Presbyterian missionary on a return visit to Britain from East Africa, put the challenge of evangelism and empire to a Cambridge audience: '[Africa] is now open; do not let it be shut again! I go back to Africa to try to make an open path for commerce and Christianity. Do you carry on the work I have begun. I leave it with you' (Livingstone 1858:24).

Elsewhere in the world there were comparable opportunities. A missionary to the southwestern Pacific reported in 1837: 'at the lowest computation 150,000 persons, who a few years ago were unclothed savages, are now wearing articles of British manufacture.' And though an atheist himself, Sir Harry Johnston (1858–1927), a British colonial administrator, saw the missionary enterprise as essential to colonialism:

> As their immediate object is not profit, they can afford to reside at places till they become profitable. They strengthen our hold over the country, they spread the use of the English language, they induct the natives into the best kind of civilization, and in fact each mission station is an essay in colonization (Oliver 1957:297).

Missionaries sometimes opposed colonial policy. The colonial British East India Company was not interested in having destabilizing influences within in its sphere of operations, and found the missionaries destabilizing. The company preferred to ground its authority in the 'ancient laws' of Indian tradition. It excluded missionaries from India until 1813, when Church pressure in Britain for evangelism forced it to allow their entry.

Opinion remained mixed on the subject of missionaries: even Rudyard Kipling (1865–1936), whom we stereotype as seeking British cultural domination in India, criticized the missionary enterprise in a letter to a clergyman: 'it seems to me cruel that white men … should amaze and confound their fellow creatures with a doctrine of salvation imperfectly understood by themselves and a code of ethics foreign to the climate and instincts of those races whose most cherished customs they outrage and whose gods they insult' (Faber 1966:106–7).

Protestant missionaries from Canada and the United States were likewise often unconsciously bearers of political and cultural tidings along with their gospel. Where they encountered the other great religions, Christians recruited fewer converts. Even among the great Asian cultures, though, Protestant medical and educational institutions provided a significant transfer of technology and culture. From the 1870s and 1880s to at least the middle of the twentieth century, colleges and universities founded under missionary auspices in China, India, and the Middle East had a visible influence. For instance, the alumni of the American

University of Beirut provided a pool of talent for many Middle Eastern lands; it has been claimed that the founding conference of the United Nations in 1945 had more delegates who were AUB alumni than of any other university in the world.

The Student Volunteer Movement was an example of the vast North American outpouring of missionary energy. It was propelled by some Protestants' expectation that the second coming of Christ was almost at hand and that they should prepare the world for it. Calling for 'the evangelization of the world in this generation', at huge quadrennial missionary conferences from 1891 to 1919, the SVM recruited more than 8,000 missionaries. Missionaries often stressed a rejection of old ways as a precondition for entering into the promise of the new, a message that was not always clear in the minds of their Asian and African audiences.

By the 1930s, Protestant missionary thinking was undergoing re-evaluation and retrenchment. As the Anglican mission secretary Max Warren (1904–77) put it, 'We have marched around alien Jerichos the requisite number of times. We have sounded the trumpets. And the walls have not collapsed' (Smith 1963:110). Should one continue to spend so much money and effort on evangelistic preaching? In recent decades, liberal Protestants have moved towards a view of mission as a low-key sharing of human experience with the target community, while more conservative Protestants have continued to see the preaching of the gospel as a confrontational effort aimed at rescuing the other from ignorance and damnation.

Creation and Evolution

As the nineteenth century opened, most biology in England was 'creationist', that is, scientists held that each individual species of plants and animals, as well as the human race, had been created by God with specific characteristics. The work of Charles Darwin (1809–82) definitively overturned this view.

At the age of twenty-two, Darwin embarked on a five-year voyage as a naturalist. By the time of his return to England, he had become persuaded of gradual change in biological species. Two years later, reading the population-competition theories of Thomas Malthus (1766–1834), he hit on the idea of a mechanism for such change: competition, and the survival of those organisms whose variation made them adaptively the fittest.

Darwin's epoch-making study, *The Origin of Species*, appeared more than twenty years later in 1859; the refinement of its material and argument clearly took time, but Darwin also seems to have proceeded cautiously because, having had theological training, he knew the resistance he would encounter. He was not merely seeking to demonstrate as credible his new theory of evolution, that is, the emergence of new types of organisms from previous types. He was at the same time trying to refute the previously held consensus regarding biological creationism. And he was aware that 'natural' selection was antithetical to the theological argument from design. He saw the natural world as completely self-regulating, which would render superfluous the notion of a supervising deity. Admittedly, in *The Origin of Species* he referred to the laws of nature as 'secondary causes' established in the beginning by the Creator. But he left the way open for those who might say that one does not need to postulate such a creator for the laws to work.

Darwin had said little in *The Origin* about the human race; his *The Descent of Man* came out twelve years later. That was after evolution had gained considerable acceptance and eight years after books by Thomas Huxley (1825–95) and Charles Lyell (1797–1875) had explored what it meant for a view of humankind. In *The Descent*, Darwin stressed the continuities between animal and human development, with attention to the detailed similarity of their bodily organs. The human brain is not exempt from such continuity; for Darwin, all its intellectual activity, including language and social morality, is the adaptively advantageous product of natural selection.

Thanks to Darwin's theories, we are more cognizant of our kinship with the animals, not only in medical and biological research but in our concern for a viable ecological future. In this century, modern Christian theologians assessing the place of human life in the universe have tended to shift the locus of human distinctiveness from special physical creation to a unique intellectual and spiritual capacity for transcendence. It is not so much human descent in the past but human ascent in the future that has become the agenda for religious thinkers persuaded by Darwin's discoveries.

Contextualizing the Bible

Europe in the Renaissance and the modern era knew the exploits of the Greek gods of Olympus and the epic tradition that located the events of an emerging Greek identity in a war with the people of Troy. But these narratives, standing outside the Christian tradition, were readily dismissed: stories of superhuman beings were 'only' myths, and stories of human heroes were 'mere' legends.

The Bible's narratives of Israelite origins, on the other hand, were something different. They were scripture. The Bible, most people believed, contained a factual account of the creation of the world, the origins of the human race, and the emergence of the Israelite nation. For Christians the Bible was a unique book, constituting or containing the word of God. A set of converging circumstances in the nineteenth century took the Bible off its special pedestal to treat it as a book like other books, as the word of human beings.

A historical context for ancient Israel was pieced together. Apart from the Greek epics, Europe prior to the nineteenth century possessed no narratives of its cultural antiquity other than those of the Bible. The Egyptians, the Babylonians, the Assyrians, the Hittites, the Canaanites or Phoenicians: all were the naughty neighbours of Israel, a mere supporting cast in the biblical drama.

But when Napoleon (r. 1799–1815) took a campaign to Egypt in 1798 (to try to counter British influence in India), he took scientists along, beginning direct European investigation of the ancient Egyptians' own monuments and documents. During succeeding decades European archaeologists dug the stratified city-mounds of Mesopotamia, today's Iraq, on the trail of the Babylonians and Assyrians. By the end of the nineteenth century, historians could situate the Bible in an ancient cultural context in a way that no previous Christian century had been able to do.

The context did not necessarily present things the way the Bible did. Mesopotamian and Egyptian civilizations were already old long before the Hebrews appeared on the scene, and had larger populations than Israel. The Hebrews, as it now appeared, were provincial locals, on the receiving end of ideas and technology from these major centres of empire. Mesopotamia and Egypt had had writing systems for more than a thousand years before Abraham, and nearly 2,000 years before Moses. What is more, their literature included prototypes of references and narratives found in the Bible.

Striking among these is the Mesopotamian epic whose hero is named Gilgamesh. In one of its episodes, he visits an ancient sage named Utnapishtim, who has survived a primeval flood. Utnapishtim tells Gilgamesh how he built a boat and took pairs of animals aboard in order to survive the all-submerging deluge. When the flood waters receded, says Utnapishtim, he sent out birds to see whether there was dry land; at first they returned, but then they did not. To scholars, the Mesopotamian narrative is manifestly the source of the biblical account of Noah and his ark, and is a challenge both to the originality and to the historicity of Noah. And one glance at the topography of Iraq as compared with that of the West Bank will make it clear that a flood covering everything in sight was a plausible enough occurrence in the flat plain of the ancient Mesopotamians but hardly likely in the hill country of the Hebrews.

Admittedly, much archaeological work can neither confirm nor contradict the biblical accounts; if one excavates a destruction level in the mound of ancient Jericho, and finds the debris of an appropriately datable wall, there is no way of knowing whether the sound of the trumpet in the sixth chapter of *Joshua* is what caused it to fall. But pervading the nineteenth century's historical and archaeological investigations was a presumption of biblical events occurring on a human scale, comparable and compatible with what one was now coming to know of neighbouring peoples.

In general, historians were no longer looking for unique instances of divine intervention, whether cataclysmic or subtle. To argue for the suspension of the everyday order of things would not constitute a historical explanation, whereas to demonstrate a parallel to another feature close in space and time would be to make a plausible historical case. In this sense, nineteenth-century historians were looking for uniformity in cultural processes in a way comparable to what their geologist and biologist contemporaries sought in the realm of nature.

Literary criticism of the Bible, which was centred in Protestant circles but influential eventually in Catholic and Jewish ones as well, removed it from scrutiny as a unique text and treated it instead as the product of human circumstances, genres, and motives. One no longer asked, as centuries of pious Christian and Jewish commentators had asked, why God had placed or inspired a particular passage to be read in a particular way. Instead, one asked what person or group, with what information and what theological agenda, would have been motivated to introduce or to preserve the passage under consideration.

Applied to the first five books of the Hebrew scriptures or Christian Old Testament, this approach distinguished northern and southern Israelite tribal traditions and the theological agendas of the Deuteronomic and priestly schools. Applied to the psalms, it posited plausible individual and corporate settings for their composition and continued use. Applied to the four gospels of the New Testament, it produced the presumption of different audiences and editorial strategies that we have assumed in the presentation of that material earlier in this chapter. Indeed, though scholars continue to debate detail, many key assumptions and the main outlines of nineteenth-century biblical criticism have stood the test of time and have been incorporated into contemporary Christians' understanding of their own tradition.

Historical development is a key modern category for understanding the postbiblical development of the Christian tradition as well. Doctrines presented as perennial and unchanging can often be profitably situated in the contexts in which they were articulated. To take only one example, one might appreciate the Calvinists' insistence on predestination as a logical working out of their sense of God's sovereignty, and Arminius's followers' reaction to it as flowing from a desire to stress human responsibility. To contextualize each of the two concerns is a different enterprise than to brand one everlastingly true and the other therefore false. And it is clear that many modern Christians have developed a historian's perspective on the claims of their tradition without diminishing their fascination with it, affection for it, or loyalty to its community.

Evangelicals and Fundamentalists

Seen in its broadest compass, twentieth-century Protestant evangelicalism is a multifaceted emphasis or movement cutting across the major denominations. It is not a denomination as such, although some denominations are solidly evangelical. It draws on earlier themes, notably the individual's confident assurance of God's grace and acceptance that characterized Reformation pietism on the European continent and the revivalist movements of England and North America. Evangelicals refer to this assurance of grace as a spiritual rebirth, an experience of being 'born again'. As their name, drawn from the Greek for the gospel or 'good news', indicates, evangelicals are frequently active in preaching their message of standards for belief and personal conduct, and they often do so with the conviction that it, and no other, is valid.

Because Protestantism had put so many of its eggs in the basket of scriptural authority over against the institutional Church, biblical criticism was bound to provoke a particularly sharp reaction among Protestants. Committed, like earlier Protestantism, to the literal authority of the scriptures, evangelicals fought a rearguard battle against the findings of modern historical and literary study of the Bible in the late nineteenth and early twentieth centuries.

In the United States in 1910, a series of booklets titled *The Fundamentals* contained articles affirming the inerrancy of the Bible and of traditional doctrines. Three million copies were distributed free to Protestant clergy, missionaries, and students through the anonymous sponsorship of 'two Christian laymen', who were in fact William Lyman Stewart (1867–1930) and his brother Milton, major figures in the Union Oil Company of California. Advocates of inerrancy came by 1920 to be called 'fundamentalists'.

The test case for fundamentalism was the 1925 trial of a high school teacher, John T. Scopes (1900–70), for violating a Tennessee law enacted earlier that same year barring the teaching of evolution in contradiction to the Bible. The court found for the prosecution's traditionalist oratory of William Jennings Bryan (1860–1925) against the defence of Clarence Darrow (1857–1938) and fined Scopes $100. So extensive was news coverage, however, that fundamentalism itself was on trial nationwide in the court of public opinion, where Darwin, Scopes, and Darrow emerged the clear victors among the population at large. Scopes's conviction was overturned in 1927 on appeal, on the technicality that the fine was too high, and the Tennessee law was eventually repealed in 1967.

People mean a variety of things by the word 'fundamentalism'. Most speakers use it pejoratively; conservative Protestants often distinguish between their own position as evangelical and more extreme views that they dismiss as fundamentalist. 'Fundamentalism' denotes an orthodoxy centring on a defence of literal inerrancy. It also suggests orthopraxy, conformity to a strait-laced code of social and personal conduct. In either case, it connotes as well a militant spirit in defence of a particular understanding of tradition; fundamentalists have been known to attack as diabolical those whom they see as subverting it through doubt or permissiveness.

Fundamentalism is a modern development, for it is a reaction to modernity. From the 1970s onward, the term came into wide use to describe phenomena in traditions other than Christianity, such as religiously based ultraconservative movements in the politics of the Middle East and South Asia. Such movements can be reactionary in doctrine or social morality or both, but it is usually their militancy that prompts the use of the word.

Fundamentalists and some evangelicals sense a struggle between good and evil forces in the world, and have a greater-than-average readiness to see evil personified in Satan or tangibly manifested in social groups and forces with which they take issue, such as those who are pro-choice on abortion or advocates of gay rights. They also display a noticeable apocalypticism, that is, a sense that a final showdown between the forces of good and evil in this world is imminent. Though criticized as having simplistic views on complex social and ethical issues, evangelicals are generous givers to charitable causes like famine relief, particularly where the needy recipients can be viewed as individuals.

Heirs to the revivalist tradition, some twentieth-century Protestant evangelical preachers have engaged in itinerant visits and short-term campaigns or 'crusades', filling large auditoriums and calling for 'decisions for Christ'. The decision is termed a conversion—in this case not from some other religion to Christianity, which would be desired and welcomed, but from a lapsed or inactive form of the faith to a revitalized one. The conversion experience is accompanied by a confession of one's sinfulness and dependence on God, and confession comes as the climax following the sermon, rather than coming early in the service as in classical Protestantism.

Radio was the first medium to render possible preaching to a widely dispersed, unseen audience. In the United States, Charles E. Fuller (1887–1968) conducted 'The Old-Fashioned Revival Hour' on radio in the 1940s; the scattered 'congregation' of his listeners could make their offerings by mail. Among the most successful evangelical preachers from 1949 onward was the Southern Baptist Billy Graham (b. 1918), a welcome guest under several presidents at the White House. His evangelistic missions to live assemblies were broadcast on radio, and on television as that medium developed.

Graham's successful use of television to reproduce the message of his assemblies in people's homes gave rise by the 1980s to a succession of preachers nicknamed 'televangelists', who like Fuller made the electronic audience their primary 'congregation' and solicited responses by mail and telephone. Several of these highly entrepreneurial televangelists, operating independently of established denominations, built what amounted to personal empires. Success could lead into temptation, and did not necessarily deliver from evil. Financial and marital scandals involving a small number of the most visible televangelists brought the medium into some disrepute at the end of the 1980s.

Vatican I and Vatican II

Modernity for modern Roman Catholics has posed challenges on varied issues of faith and practice. These include, to name only a few, philosophical justifications for doctrine, the status of Mary and the saints, the theology of the sacraments, clerical celibacy, and the standards for lay Catholic practice in sexuality and reproduction.

A focus in all of these—arguably the heart of the matter for many committed Catholics—is the authority of the institutional church itself, especially that of its head, the pope. The more progressive have tended towards demythologizing the institution, the more conservative towards idolizing it. A move made by some reform-minded scholars is to take the claims for authority as themselves the product of historical circumstance and development, while the conservative position more commonly works out a derivation of authority as the implication of divine promises.

Since the mid-nineteenth century, we have suggested, historical criticism of the Bible spurred the fundamentalist or evangelical reaction in Protestantism. Protestants had made the Bible their mainstay when differing with Rome during the Reformation, and now its literal authority was under threat not from Rome but from modern historical assumptions. Comparably, Catholics had committed themselves to the teaching tradition of the Church, the *magisterium* as it is termed, and its authority was now under threat not from the Protestants but from modern assumptions.

The Catholic Church has often framed its claims to authority in juridical terms. Jesus delegates it to his disciple Peter, who becomes the first bishop of Rome. In New Testament accounts, Peter himself is fallible, indeed lapses into denial of Jesus. Jesus even calls him Satan. But as the centuries passed, the institution increasingly referred to the legacy of Peter as authoritative. By the Middle Ages, the Church developed its own internal legal system, known as canon law, and acted in its courts to enforce correct belief as well as correct conduct. Medieval canon lawyers and theologians spoke of the Church's guidance. Increasingly after the sixteenth-century Council of Trent, that guidance was described as infallible.

A key tenet of Christian faith is that God guides the Church through the continuing presence of the Holy Spirit. Catholics have held that such guidance includes the formulation and maintenance of its doctrines, and it may follow from such a view that the truth of such doctrines is divinely supported—that is, that in doctrine the Church cannot err. But surprisingly enough, no precise definition of the infallibility claimed for the Church was ever formally enacted.

Vatican I

The council that met at the Vatican in 1869–70, during the papacy of Pius IX, was to address the matter. In a draft it considered on the nature of the Church, a clause asserted that the Church is enabled 'to conserve in its entirety and without alteration the already revealed Word of God contained in Scripture and Tradition'. Elsewhere the document clarified that keeping Christ's revelation intact was the collegial or corporate task of the apostles and their successors, not the sole responsibility of the pope as their leader. But that document never made it to ratification before the council closed with the outbreak of the Franco-Prussian war.

Instead, the First Vatican Council devoted its political energies to spelling out a monarchical view of the role of the pope. Papal infallibility, as extrapolated from ecclesiastical infallibility, was part of that agenda. Nobody had proposed papal infallibility before the thirteenth century when a Franciscan, Peter John Olivi (c. 1248–98), did so, and his views were condemned by Pope John XXII in 1324 as the work of the devil. Nor did the Council of Trent spell out papal infallibility. The classic view was that even though its head might err, the Church as a whole would not go astray. But Vatican I broke new ground by defining papal infallibility as follows:

> The Roman Pontiff when he speaks *ex cathedra*, that is, when exercising the office of pastor and teacher of all Christians he defines with his supreme apostolic authority a doctrine concerning faith or morals to be held by the universal Church through the divine assistance promised to him in St Peter, is possessed of that infallibility with which the divine Redeemer willed his Church to be endowed in defining doctrine concerning faith and morals: and therefore such definitions of the Roman Pontiff are irreformable of themselves and not from the consent of the Church.

Thus papal infallibility, a disturbing innovation when Olivi proposed it six centuries earlier, became conservative tradition in 1870. And the theological system of Thomas Aquinas, also a disturbing innovation six centuries earlier, was given official status by Pope Leo XIII in 1879. A small group of German, Austrian, and Swiss Catholics who refused to accept infallibility and papal authority broke away from Rome, becoming known as Old Catholics; but for the Catholic Church at large, there was a wait of nearly a century for the winds of renewal to blow.

Vatican II

When Italy's Angelo Giuseppe Roncalli (1881–1963) was elected pope (John XXIII) in 1958, few had any inkling of the changes that lay in store for the Roman Catholic Church. Though already in his late seventies, this man of great human warmth proved to have a vision for his Church, and a fearless openness to change. John XXIII convoked the Second Vatican Council, which met from 1962 to 1965. He called for *aggiornamento*, Italian for 'updating'.

The changes set in motion at the council ushered in a new era for Catholicism. In worship, the language of the mass was shifted from Latin to the local vernacular, and the officiating priest now turned to face the congregation (though the doctrine of transubstantiation was retained). The dress of priests and nuns was modernized and in many cases secularized. Emphasis was laid on the pope's role in council with the bishops, as contrasted with Vatican I's monarchical role. The conditions of biblical and theological scholarship were improved. Efforts were made to restore relations with Protestants, the Eastern Orthodox, Jews, and adherents of other religions. A Church that had hardly assimilated either the Reformation or the Enlightenment now had to try to down both in one gulp.

The agenda of the council is unfinished, as pressing problems remain. Priesthood today is an institution under threat, with declining numbers of vocations. Clearly, the demand of celibacy, on which the Church did not budge, has reduced its appeal to modern Roman Catholics. There is the further danger that among Catholics and others the traditional ritual activities of priests and ministers are no longer perceived to offer an intellectual challenge to compete with such professions as law, medicine, or engineering. With priests aging and a shortage of replacements, the future of the role is far from clear.

A major breach developed shortly after the council in 1968, when Pope Paul VI, John's successor, in his encyclical *Humanae Vitae* (On Human Life) prohibited the use of artificial birth control by Catholics. It was in part a breach between the hierarchy and the modern laity, as the gap has widened between the Church's official stand on sexuality and the actual practice of many of its faithful. Many Catholics have ceased to take seriously the Church's teachings in whole areas of their practical decision making.

Humanae Vitae also exacerbated the theological tension between reform and traditionalist wings in the Church's hierarchy. Progressive Catholics saw the encyclical, which while not *ex cathedra*, nonetheless was coming from the pope without the consensus of bishops in council, as an erosion of Vatican II's accomplishments and an attempt to turn the clock of authority back to Vatican I. The Swiss theologian Hans Küng (b. 1928), outspokenly critical in his 1970 book *Infallible? An Inquiry*, was removed from approved status as a Catholic theological teacher in a German faculty (though not from status as a priest) in 1979, the year he published a preface to *How the Pope Became Infallible*, by his student August Hasler (1937–80). Evident in the Church's move was a 'fundamentalism' of ecclesiastical authority, parallel to Protestant fundamentalism of scriptural authority. Rome's attempts to silence progressive theologians may in the long run enjoy no greater success than the Scopes trial's attempt to suppress evolution.

Ecumenism

Exported to Africa and Asia, the historical divisions of Euro-American Christianity seemed to have very little sense or relevance. What did it matter in India whether one was Anglican or Presbyterian? What difference would the distinction between Baptists and Congregationalists make in China? From 1910 onward, the mainline Protestant denominations began to overcome four centuries of separation.

Part of the movement towards union was rooted in collaboration on the mission field. Denominational mission boards divided overseas territories to reduce redundant competition, and the International Missionary Council grew in effectiveness. Also significant was collaboration in youth work, with such interdenominational efforts as the Student Christian Movement. And in the United States, the Federal Council of Churches was particularly devoted to interdenominational collaboration on economic and social issues.

By mid-century, a generation of Church leaders who had grown up with these enterprises had come into positions of responsibility in their denominations. The time was ripe for worldwide collaboration. The World Council of Churches was formed in 1948 with representation from most major Protestant and Orthodox bodies.

Ecumenism (from the Greek *oikoumene*, 'inhabited world') offered a climate of mutual acceptance and common purpose, an emphasis on unity within diversity. Protestants agreed to go on disagreeing on many issues that had historically separated them. They found that they could readily make common cause on such matters as refugee relief, but had lingering disputes on such 'faith and order' questions as Church discipline and Eucharistic theology. They could more readily affirm one another's agendas regarding social justice (or, later, ecological concern) than recognize one another's ordination or take communion together.

Nonetheless a number of denominational mergers took place in the twentieth century. Methodists, Congregationalists, and a majority of Canada's Presbyterians formed the United Church of Canada in 1925. A similar mix is the Uniting Church formed in Australia in 1977. In England in 1972, the Presbyterians and Congregationalists merged to form the United Reformed Church. In the United States, the Congregational-Christian merger with the Evangelical and United Brethren in 1961 produced the United Church of Christ.

Other broader and more ambitious twentieth-century attempts at Church union remain unconsummated. Consultations in the United States and New Zealand involving Anglicans, for instance, could not resolve differences over ordination and the Eucharist. However, the Church of South India, formed in 1947, includes Anglicans, and was followed by similar regionally defined unions in North India, Pakistan, and Bangladesh. Anglican hesitation to rush into union with Reformed churches, it should be added, stems partly from the desire to conduct conversations also with Lutherans and with the Roman Catholic Church.

For years, the goal of ecumenism for Catholics had been what they termed the return of 'separated brethren' to the Roman Church. This frequently amounted to a unilateral stipulation of terms, but there were straws in the wind that concessions might be made. The Belgian cardinal Désiré-Joseph Mercier (1851–1926) sponsored ground-breaking conversations with Anglicans in his city, Malines, from 1921 to 1926. Elsewhere, too, intellectual, spiritual, and personal contacts were replacing political confrontation.

Rome's twentieth-century move into ecumenism is associated primarily with the 1958–63 papacy of John XXIII. A permanent Secretariat for the Promotion of Christian Unity was established in 1960. Important on the agenda of the Second Vatican Council was the drafting of documents and declarations that might bring about a rapprochement with other Christians.

The spirit of reunion was in the air. By the end of the 1960s, Protestant and Catholic institutions for the study of theology and the training of clergy were entering into collaborative arrangements of all sorts, now attending the same lectures and reading the same books. No matter how much conservative Protestants or Catholics might subsequently try to reverse such a development, it would be impossible to unscramble the ecumenical omelet. A gulf that had separated Western Christendom for four centuries was being bridged.

Reforming Society

The denominations that Puritanism influenced looked for personal morality, and expected it to bear fruit in society. To Quakers or to English Congregationalists, for instance, and to some Methodist-derived movements such as the Salvation Army (organized by William Booth, 1829–1912, in London after 1865), one test of any renewal was whether it improved food, clothing, shelter, or education for the population at large.

In the middle of the nineteenth century, the question of slavery tore the United States apart. It erupted politically in the Civil War of 1861–5, but its effects were also felt in the Christian denominations. Some, such as the Presbyterians, separated into northern and southern churches that took a century to reunite. By and large, the Christian conscience was antislavery, but there was more at risk, more interests to be offended, in the southern White constituencies than the northern.

In the mid-twentieth century, the political issue of race continued to enlist religious energies. When the bid to bring the Black population of the United States into a share of public life developed during the early 1960s, the Black community had few institutional structures other than churches, so the ministry was at first practically the only source for Blacks as leaders. Pivotal in the civil-rights movement were Martin Luther King, Jr (1929–68), and his Southern Christian Leadership Conference. But also important was the support of White religious leaders in America, who were ready to join marches and demonstrations in the cause of racial equality.

Religion has been invoked on both sides of the race issue. Some conservative Protestants have maintained the view that a God who created the races different meant for them to remain separate; the Mormons in America long resisted Black leadership, even membership. The Afrikaner settler population of South Africa, who constitute a three-fifths majority of South Africa's Whites and whose National Party came to power in 1948, have a Dutch Calvinist background. Theirs was the term 'apartheid' ('apartness') for the racial separation that was South Africa's pattern after its union was formed in 1910, and they gave theolo-

Martin Luther King

[From Martin Luther King, Jr, 'Letter from Birmingham Jail', 16 April 1963. King, a Baptist minister and civil-rights leader, is responding to a published statement by eight clergymen criticizing his protest activity against racial segregation in Birmingham, Alabama.]

So I, along with several members of my staff, am here because I was invited here. I am here because I have organizational ties here.

But more basically, I am in Birmingham because injustice is here … I am cognizant of the interrelatedness of all communities and states. I cannot sit idly by in Atlanta and not be concerned about what happens in Birmingham. Injustice anywhere is a threat to justice everywhere. We are caught in an inescapable network of mutuality, tied in a single garment of destiny. Whatever affects one directly, affects all indirectly. Never again can we afford to live with the narrow, provincial "outside agitator" idea. Anyone who lives inside the United States can never be considered an outsider anywhere within its bounds …

You express a great deal of anxiety over our willingness to break laws … One may well ask: "How can you advocate breaking some laws and obeying others?" The answer lies in the fact that there are two types of laws: just and unjust. I would be the first to advocate obeying just laws. One has not only a legal but a moral responsibility to obey just laws. Conversely, one has a moral responsibility to disobey unjust laws. I would agree with St. Augustine that "an unjust law is no law at all" …

I have traveled the length and breadth of Alabama, Mississippi and all the other southern states. On sweltering summer days and crisp autumn mornings I have looked at the South's beautiful churches with their lofty spires pointing heavenward. I have beheld the impressive outlines of her massive religious-education buildings. Over and over I have found myself asking: "What kind of people worship here? Who is their God? … Where

gical as well as practical reasons for segregation. Vehement condemnation of the policy from outside, by member states in the United Nations and the British Commonwealth, brought about South Africa's withdrawal from the Commonwealth in 1961 and its expulsion from the UN. But within South Africa there was equally vocal opposition to the policy from both Black and White Christians, many of them Anglicans. By 1994, when Blacks first voted in South African elections, the Reformed Church had also pulled back from justifying *apartheid*.

Similarly, Christians have not been of one mind on economic policy. A

were they when Governor Wallace gave a clarion call for defiance and hatred? Where were their voices of support when bruised and weary Negro men and women decided to rise from the dark dungeons of complacency to the bright hills of creative protest?" …

There was a time when the church was very powerful—in the time when the early Christians rejoiced at being deemed worthy to suffer for what they believed. In those days the church was not merely a thermometer that recorded the ideas and principles of popular opinion; it was a thermostat that transformed the mores of society. Whenever the early Christians entered a town, the people in power became disturbed and immediately sought to convict the Christians for being "disturbers of the peace" and "outside agitators." But the Christians pressed on, in the conviction that they were "a colony of heaven," called to obey God rather than man …

But the judgment of God is upon the church as never before. If today's church does not recapture the sacrificial spirit of the early church, it will lose its authenticity, forfeit the loyalty of millions, and be dismissed as an irrelevant social club with no meaning for the twentieth century. Every day I meet young people whose disappointment with the church has turned into outright disgust …

Yes, they [some clergy] have gone to jail with us. Some have been dismissed from their churches, have lost the support of their bishops and fellow ministers. But they have acted in the faith that right defeated is stronger than evil triumphant. Their witness has been the spiritual salt that has preserved the true meaning of the gospel in these troubled times. They have carved a tunnel of hope through the dark mountain of disappointment.

I hope the church as a whole will meet the challenge of this decisive hour …

Let us all hope that the dark clouds of racial prejudice will soon pass away and the deep fog of misunderstanding will be lifted from our fear-drenched communities, and in some not too distant tomorrow the radiant stars of love and brotherhood will shine over our great nation with all their scintillating beauty (King 1964: 76–95).

dominantly agricultural and town society gave way in the nineteenth century in Europe and in the English-speaking world to an urban and industrial one. In several Protestant constituencies, the ownership and managerial class came into prominence, while the industrial workers were often from populations of Roman Catholic origin.

The wealthy often had a religious commitment and conscience; religious institutions were indebted to the philanthropy of such families as the petroleum Rockefellers and railroad Vanderbilts in the United States or the department-store Eatons and jewellery Birkses in Canada. It was sometimes hard for the Church to bite the hand that fed it; affinities between the political right and the religious right continued to be evident, for instance in the United States during the 1981–9 presidency of Ronald Reagan.

From the 1860s onward, socialism in Europe addressed the growing gulf between owners and workers. On the Continent, it was largely antichurch, but in Britain there was a significant Christian socialist movement, sparked by the Anglican theologian Frederick Denison Maurice (1805–72) and the Anglican clergyman-novelist Charles Kingsley (1819–75).

Their influence had a ripple effect across the Atlantic. A principal moral concern of late nineteenth-century Protestants had been alcohol abuse, as temperance movements enlisted many of their energies. But as the twentieth century opened, broader issues of social and economic justice received emphasis. For example, the Canadian Methodist board of Temperance, Prohibition and Moral Reform was renamed Evangelism and Social Service.

In the United States, Christian critics of the civic and corporate order in the decade before the First World War called for the Christianization of the economy. The leading theologian of the 'social gospel' movement was Walter Rauschenbusch (1861–1918). While a Baptist pastor in New York City, he supported a radical candidate for mayor. Subsequently as a theology professor in Rochester, New York, he campaigned to make the gas company, the transit system, and the public schools more responsive to people's needs. Another leader was Washington Gladden (1836–1918), a Congregational minister, who served on the city council in Columbus, Ohio, coordinated social service agencies, mediated in labour disputes, and lobbied the United States Congress to create a commission on industrial relations.

In Canada, the Nova Scotia Presbyterian George M. Grant (1835–1902), who became head of Queen's University in Kingston, Ontario, was a spokesman for interdenominational and national unity and also for a social conscience in public affairs. More dramatic was the voice of the Manitoba Methodist James S. Woodsworth (1874–1942), son of a mission superintendent. For criticizing the use of churches as recruiting centres during the First World War, he was ousted from the secretaryship of his denomination's Bureau of Social Research. He later left the clergy and became a Vancouver longshoreman, and eventually one of the founders of a socialist political party, the Co-operative Commonwealth Federation. Thus the roots of what became the New Democratic Party, occupying the left band of Canada's political spectrum, can be located not only in secular socialism but in Christian calls for economic justice, especially in the Depression era between the two world wars.

Issues of war, peace, and international justice have gripped Christians, and on these they have often been divided. Pacifist objection on grounds of conscience or ideology to participation in armies and wars has generally been a minority position. It has been more common among the individualist denominations such as Quakers and Anabaptists than among the 'establishment' branches such as Catholics, Lutherans, and Anglicans. When the rationalizations for fighting seemed relatively simple, such as in the two world wars, most served in the military when called. The military chaplaincy often saw little to choose between God and Caesar. An American popular song about an artillery chaplain in the Second World War had the refrain, 'Praise the Lord and pass the ammunition.'

Following the Second World War, the forty-year cold war between the West and the Soviet bloc often evoked simplistic responses. The communist world was portrayed as formally atheist, even if only debatably diabolical. Religious support of the United States' national policy was fragmented during the 1960s, however, as America found itself mired in an ambiguous and confusing war in Vietnam. On an unprecedented scale, American Christians opposed this war at least, if not all war, in the name of religion. But more than a few leaders who were 'doves' on Vietnam were 'hawks' when it came to Israel's conquests in 1967.

Christians spoke out in increasing numbers against American encouragement of regimes around the world that they judged repressive. Such criticism could often be selective, one person's terrorist being another's freedom fighter. And it depended on the affinities and information one had, often conditioned by what coverage the communications media gave to Latin America, Africa, the Middle East, or Southeast Asia. But the Christian ideal for society remains one of peace, justice, and reconciliation.

Marxism in Theory and Practice

The thought of Karl Marx (1818–83), with his critique of traditional religion, remains a major intellectual development of the modern world. We may still be too close to the collapse of Soviet and eastern European communism in 1989 to judge whether Marx's ideas remain contemporary or now belong to the recent past. After all, one-fourth of the human race, namely China, remained officially communist after 1989, though popular sentiment was for democracy.

Marx was raised in Germany in a Jewish family but a secularist one. The prevailing climate was one of social emancipation and assimilation, so much so that in 1824, then aged six, Karl was formally baptized a Christian. In the mid-1840s, after having written a doctoral dissertation on the philosophy of G.W.F. Hegel (1770–1831), Marx came to know Friedrich Engels (1820–95), the Calvinist son of a wealthy German industrialist who owned cotton mills in England. Following Engels's publication of *The Condition of the Working Class in England*, Marx collaborated in Brussels with Engels, and in 1848 they published *The Communist Manifesto*. Unwelcome in Belgium or in his Prussian homeland, Marx spent the next three decades as an exile in London, where with Engels he pursued his writing and was involved in the movement to organize industrial labourers.

Marx's atheism is evident in his reliance on Feuerbach's notion of projection. Ludwig Feuerbach (1804–72) published *The Essence of Christianity* in 1841. Feuerbach took Hegel's notion of the divine spirit as motivating and moving humankind and reversed it: instead, the divine is a projection of human powers and attributes. This view gained Feuerbach no acceptance in the German philosophical establishment. Nor did Marx have any illusions about its acceptability in religious circles in Britain. Marx was convinced, with Feuerbach, that putting humankind first, as over against the divine, was the move one had to make if humanity was to be fulfilled.

Although Marx wrote as an atheist, his is not a philosophical critique of the possibility of believing in God. Rather, it is a social critique of the function of institutional religion. Marx picked up and popularized a phrase describing religion as the 'opium of the people'. That is, in the hands of its practitioners religion numbs people to the injustices they suffer, promising them pie in the sky when they die by and by, instead of working for their material betterment in the here and now.

Putting humankind first was largely an intellectual priority for Feuerbach, but it became a social one for Marx. The Marxist criterion of success was thus whether any institution actually improved the conditions of human existence. Marx found religion wanting, by this criterion. Before the twentieth century ended, many in eastern Europe and the Soviet Union found the socialist system wanting, by the same criterion. Marx judged religion by its achievements, not its ideals. And the world would judge Marxism similarly.

There are striking affinities between Marx's thought and the Judaeo-Christian religious heritage. Both display a profound protest against social injustice. Both look to the end of the present world order and to a radical reshaping of things that will compensate those who currently suffer. This ideal has resonated in Latin America. The Latin American Council of [Catholic] Bishops, meeting in 1968 at Medellín, Colombia, called for the Church to identify with the situation of the poor rather than with the ruling élite.

Liberation theology, advanced by such figures as the Peruvian priest Gustavo Gutiérrez (b. 1928) and the Uruguayan Jesuit Juan Luis Segundo (b. 1925), makes use of Christian biblical and theological resources that parallel Marxist thought. Like Marxism, it asks on behalf of the rural peasantry and the urban working class for a share in the material benefits of economy and society. Liberation theology has attracted the attention of concerned Catholics and other Christians outside Latin America. Since gross inequalities of wealth and poverty in Latin America persist, liberation theology might considerably outlast the 1989 collapse of Marxism as a political ideology in Europe. It offers a rationale for social action that addresses an enduring problem.

Twentieth-Century Theology

'I believe because it's absurd,' said the early third-century Latin theologian Tertullian. 'What does Athens have to do with Jerusalem, the Academy with the Church?' he also asked. His provocative remarks challenge the rational consensus of Greek and Roman philosophy, but at the same time they show that the philosophy of the age frames issues for debate.

Through the centuries Christian theologians have used the resources of current thought to express their preaching. In the ancient world, the narrative message of a Jewish-based movement was stated in terms where stability and permanence were often valued ahead of development or change. How faith relates to reason was a central question in the Latin Middle Ages for theologians, who regarded the two as mutually confirming.

For Roman Catholics, Thomas Aquinas's Aristotelian principles and methods were explored for modern purposes by a number of twentieth-century theologians and philosophers. Innovative and wide-ranging was the German Jesuit Karl Rahner (1904–84), who taught in Innsbruck and Munich. Concerned with the theory of knowledge was the Canadian Jesuit Bernard Lonergan (also 1904–84), who taught in Rome for half his career. A neo-Thomist with conservative views on numerous issues was the French philosopher Jacques Maritain (1882–1973), a convert to Catholicism while a student, who taught in Paris, Toronto, and Princeton. Widowed at seventy-eight, he joined the Dominicans in a French monastery for his last years.

Tradition-based theologies also continue to command adherents among Protestants. A commentary on Paul's New Testament letter to the Romans propelled the Swiss theologian Karl Barth (1886–1968), of Basel, into prominence at the end of the First World War, a time of disillusionment with the idea of inevitable human progress. Barth's theology draws a sharp dialectic between what humans can do or know by themselves on the one hand and the gift of saving grace by God on the other; the Barthian position has been popular in conservative Protestant circles.

Reason and empirical investigation had already proved to be a challenge to faith in the European Enlightenment. The dominant mood in Anglo-American philosophy in the twentieth century was empirical and logical, declining to confirm the content of most theological assertions. By contrast, existentialism has had more scope on the European continent. Existentialist thought faces up to religion's unprovability by asserting that valuing and commitment are something different than proof. Theologians trained on the continent put existentialism to use. Noteworthy among these is the German Paul Tillich (1886–1965), who settled in the United States in the 1930s. Tillich characterizes the agenda of religion not from God downward, as Barth does, but from the human experience upward:

religion is, in Tillich's words, 'ultimate concern'. Tillich's formulations were widely influential during the second half of the century.

Another twentieth-century movement is process thought. Alfred North Whitehead (1861–1947), who also settled in the United States, was one of the century's relatively few English-speaking philosophers to make a substantial contribution to metaphysics, the branch of philosophy that speculates on the nature of ultimate reality. Whitehead sees reality as dynamic rather than as static:

> It is as true to say that God is permanent and the world fluent, as that the World is permanent and God is fluent. …
>
> It is as true to say that the World is immanent in God, as that God is immanent in the World (Whitehead 1929:410–11).

Drawing on Whitehead, process theology has emerged as a distinctly American movement, with an appeal to persons who associate change with modernity. For its principal thinkers, such as the American Charles Hartshorne (b. 1897), creation is unfinished, and God is developing too. The idea of God is the idea of a dynamic power open to virtually unlimited possibility.

In recent decades few systematic thinkers have made as significant an impact as Barth and Tillich among Protestants at mid-century, or as Rahner among Catholics at the time of Vatican II. With few exceptions, progressive theological thinkers have not enjoyed success in presenting to their public the meaning of scripture, tradition, and religious experience. Fashion has favoured responses to the world or to culture that are not so much statements of Christianity's classic message but applications of it: theologies of social liberation, feminist empowerment, global ecology, and the like. We have characterized fundamentalism in both its Protestant and Catholic forms (biblical and magisterial infallibility) as a defensive reaction against modernity. Recent liberal theology, while more accepting of modernity, has unfortunately also come across as reactive rather than assertive. Hence conservative movements find widespread sympathy when they urge going back to basics.

Psychology and Religion

Freud

If the nineteenth century revised the way people thought about human bodily existence, the twentieth century has revised our view of the functioning of the self. Of the many who have contributed, the Austrian psychoanalyst Sigmund Freud (1856–1939) belongs on any short list. Freud assembled evidence of a domain of personality operating below the level of conscious thought and volition. His theories have had so wide an influence that many who have never actually read Freud make use, when interpreting their own behaviour, of terms introduced by Freud and the Freudians: 'repression', 'Freudian slip', 'identity crisis'.

What Freud did was to convince many that the human self is not a static entity, but rather an arena in which conscious intellect and choice are in battle with unconscious impulses, drives, fantasies, and emotions. If one follows Freud, a seemingly ordered and rational personality is only superficially stable, like the thin crust of the earth resting on a deep interior of churning molten rock. The consequences of this view for any religious expectation of fundamental serenity may be devastating; on the other hand, the need for therapy, from whatever source, is accentuated.

In Freud's own life, the concrete instances of religion that he experienced ran counter to his instincts as a scientist. For fostering obscurantist mythology, moral injustice, or intergroup hostility, religion earned little respect. The shaping of Freud's attitudes began in a secular Jewish family environment where about the only observance was the annual Passover celebration. He encountered strident anti-Semitism in the society of late nineteenth-century Vienna.

But it was as much as anything the expectations and inhibitions Freud observed in patients in his clinical practice that served as a springboard for his views of religion as infantile dependency and wishful thinking. Religion, for Freud, is the individual's mechanism for tolerating infantile helplessness. Modern religious thinkers have had to admit the force of Freud's arguments, and agree that religion indeed does function to meet psychic needs, not just infantile ones but profound ones.

Jung

Some sympathetic to religion have found more congenial the theories of the Swiss psychoanalyst Carl Gustav Jung (1875–1961). The son of a Protestant pastor, Jung broke with Freud in part over religion. He finds rich levels of meaning in religious symbolism, including magic and alchemy. But Jung, who refers to religion as the collective unconscious, is like Freud to the extent that he sees religion as a product of psychological processes. The challenge for modern religious thought is to assert convincingly, even if one cannot directly demonstrate, that what serves to meet psychic needs is not necessarily nor merely the product of those needs.

Modern Roles for Women

The twentieth century, particularly the second half of the century, has brought dramatic changes in the cultural expectations of the role of women in society. The notion of females as subordinate to, or inferior to, or the property of, males is a notion now in rapid retreat, a notion that from today's perspective is quite justly discredited.

In North America, liberal Protestant denominations have ordained women as clergy, and the Anglican communion has followed suit more recently. Several American and Canadian denominations have had women as presiding officers. A Black woman, Barbara Harris (b. 1930), became an Episcopalian bishop in Massachusetts in 1989. Lois Wilson (b.1927), a minister of the United Church of Canada, served as one of the presidents of the World Council of Churches from 1983 to 1991.

The Roman Catholic and Eastern Orthodox churches do not yet ordain women as priests, let alone admit women to the senior hierarchy. In both Greek and Latin Christendom, where one looks to institutional and historical precedent, the subordination of women has been precisely that precedent, and has proven difficult to overturn. Formerly women were not allowed by Rome to take degrees in theology, but in recent decades Catholic lay-women and members of religious orders have made substantial contributions as scholars in the subject. Still conspicuous as a minority, they often encounter the inertia of males' assumptions in both the substance and the environment of their scholarship.

Women, and sympathetic males as well, have sought in recent decades to redress the patriarchal bias of two millennia of Christian tradition. The attempts at correcting the picture have run along several lines in addition to seeking ordination for women.

First, there has been attention given to the role of the feminine principle, of female figures and symbols, in the history and psychology of religion. A kind of comparative psychology of religion is implied in studies of mother goddesses in various religions that sometimes link their findings with an appreciation of the function of Mary as archetypal mother in Roman Catholic piety.

It may not be enough to point to female symbols of divinity if one persists in conceiving of the Christian God as masculine only, as God Himself. Consequently some Christians now pray to God as equally masculine and feminine, addressing God as 'Our Father and Mother'. But, others argue, a gender-balanced God who is equally masculine and feminine is still an anthropomorphic god, a deity in human form. For such persons, the God who transcends the world must necessarily transcend gender.

Second, there has been an effort to emphasize the contribution made by gifted women in the history of Christianity, particularly in devotional spirituality. The fourteenth-century English mystic Julian of Norwich, the sixteenth-century Spanish mystic Teresa of Ávila, and the seventeenth-century French-Canadian mystic Marie de l'Incarnation are only three examples of individuals on whom the number of research papers has expanded in recent years in comparison with those on their male counterparts.

Third, critics have heaped assorted praise and blame on Christianity for the virtues and faults of Western culture's treatment of human sexuality. On the tangled issues involved, contributors to the discussion look to history for heroes and scapegoats. Some praise the Church for its ideals, such as the ideal of fidelity and equal partnership in marriage. They have contended that the Christians offered an alternative, for instance, to practices in the Roman Empire where the male head of a household slept freely with the slave-girls. Clearly, Christians, too, have on occasion fallen short of such an ideal.

Others blame Christianity for psychologically repressive and socially restrictive standards. 'The pathologization of sex' is one phrase that has been applied to Christian rejection of bodily appetites as sinful. If the purpose of sexuality is taught to be reproduction exclusively, critics argue, then vast amounts of guilt are laid on women and men for enjoying doing what comes naturally. And the Roman Catholic Church's continuing rejection of birth control, it has been observed, is both unrealistic in the light of survey information on the laity's actual behaviour and grossly irresponsible in the face of global population forecasts.

Fourth, there has been a shift in the use of English, referred to as 'inclusive language', that since the early 1980s has transformed the meanings people find in the third-person pronoun 'he' and the noun 'man'. Formerly accustomed to thinking of 'the salvation of man' as meaning humankind, many English-speaking Christians have come to see such a wording as connoting males only.

People therefore seek to substitute expressions such as 'humanity'. The English texts of hymns have been revised, with non-rhyming but politically correct gender sometimes prevailing over the original rhymes. Unquestionably, inclusive language is desirable in texts used in a worship setting, where an absolutely top priority is that women in the congregation feel an equal share in the words that are spoken or sung.

The influential mid-twentieth-century *Revised Standard Version* of the Bible (New Testament 1946, Old Testament 1952) has been redone in inclusive language in the *New Revised Standard Version* of 1989. Generally the choices of wording are felicitous, including rendering 'Son of man', a recurring divine call or address to the prophet in *Ezekiel*, as 'O mortal'; the NRSV here offers a paraphrase of one presumed implication of the Hebrew text. The pre-1980s RSV, with 'Son of man', continues to furnish a more direct translation of such passages and so remains useful for historical study even while replaced in worship.

The Faith of Others

Increasingly since the middle of the twentieth century, international communication and travel have intensified. The age of discovery that began at the end of the fifteenth century has given way to an age of world integration by the end of the twentieth.

Besides the experience of travel, modern society has seen large-scale migration. People of previously isolated cultural backgrounds now live side by side as neighbours, whether in Hong Kong or Montréal, Trinidad or London. In varying fashions, lands built on immigration like Canada, the United States, and Australia have come to accept this diversity as part of their national fabric and to value it. In the workplace, adherents of diverse traditions are seeing the erosion of barriers to the observance of their religious holidays and dress codes. Sikh members of the Royal Canadian Mounted Police, for instance, may now wear the turban when in uniform instead of the conventional RCMP headgear. The front lawn of the Ontario parliament buildings has sported a Ḥanukkah candlestick each Christmas season, recognizing the concurrent Jewish holiday. The plural nature of ethnic and religious heritages is a simple fact; the acceptance of that fact as desirable is what we now refer to as plural*ism*.

The issues surrounding pluralism in the late twentieth century are complicated because of societies' different degrees of commitment to it. Within North America, urban centres such as Toronto, Vancouver, and Los Angeles experience a far greater diversity through immigration than do many rural areas, such as in Newfoundland, Tennessee, or South Dakota.

Worldwide, too, older societies not built on immigration are less likely than Canada and the United States to adopt pluralistic views regarding religion. Swedes, for instance, can afford travel but do not so often know people from the Hindu or Buddhist worlds as neighbours in their own society. France, with a history as a colonial power, is cosmopolitan; but in the two centuries since the Enlightenment and the French Revolution, it has had a secular ethos that the Algerian Muslims living in France today find problematical. England is aware of the diversity in its society contributed by Muslims, Hindus, and Sikhs from the Indian subcontinent, but it is still one thing to live *in* England and quite another thing to be *of* it. And Germany maintains formal ties with Christianity in its culture, ties that allow little scope for the identity of Turkish Muslims living in the country today.

The faith of other communities is a theological problem not for those communities but for Christianity's claim to be a message both universal and unique. In ancient times, Christians already pondered the issue of salvation for pre-Christian pagans whose morality was above reproach, and one theory treated positive features of pagan religion resembling Christianity as demonic imitations set as traps to test the unwary Christian faithful.

Medieval Latin Christianity reasoned that God must necessarily will the salvation of all in Christ, whereas the logic of Calvinism held that God predestines some to eternal damnation. Twentieth-century theologians have continued to work from these premises. The Catholic Karl Rahner takes up the idea of universal salvation, considering Hindus, Buddhists, and others to be 'anonymous' Christians—that is, implicitly Christian without their acknowledging it. The Protestant Karl Barth applies the dialectic between God's chosen and others to view all other religions as mere human striving, in contrast to the gift of divine grace and revelation he holds to be unique to the cross. Each of these views operates within a syllogistic doctrinal circle.

By what Christian standards can the late twentieth-century Church convince itself that it should listen to, and appreciate *on their own terms*, the views of others? I have argued in a 1983 book that the figure of Jesus provides a model and warrant for openness to the identity of one's fellow human being. The personal and moral example of Jesus is surely as central to the Christian tradition as its doctrinal formulations are. Many Christians remain convinced that their gospel tolerates no concessions to rivals. But while logically one is to assert doctrine as true, morally one is to love one's neighbour. Pluralism presumes a human community whose common values may yet override the particularism of traditional Christian theology.

Christianity and Change

In the twentieth century, the impact of modern thought and preferences for more modern language have spurred denominations to formulate short statements of affirmation that can be used in a worship setting. An example particularly successful for its freshness and directness and, indeed, for its openness to modern critical thought when compared with the Apostles' Creed, is the statement introduced by the United Church of Canada in 1968:

> Man is not alone, he lives in God's world. We believe in God: who has created and is creating, who has come in the true man, Jesus, to reconcile and make new, who works in us and others by his spirit. We trust him. He calls us to be his church: to celebrate his presence, to love and serve others, to seek justice and resist evil, to proclaim Jesus, crucified and risen, our judge and our hope. In life, in death, in life beyond death, God is with us. We are not alone. Thanks be to God.

Time does not stand still. In only twenty years this contemporary statement was obsolete because of change in language usage. By the 1980s, the word 'man' connoted exclusively males, rather than the entire human race intended when the statement was drafted. As revised, the statement begins, 'We are not alone'.

What, then, has modernity meant for the Christian tradition? Modernity has brought new outlooks on the nature and possibilities of thought and knowledge. It has offered new insights into the nature of the physical universe, living creatures, and the structure of personality. And it has meant new outlooks on the character of human culture, history, and society. It has meant change. As the Canadian religion scholar Wilfred Cantwell Smith (b. 1916) has said, to be modern is to be self-conscious about the fact of change and to take an active hand in shaping change itself.

We have sampled the elaboration and differentiation of the Christian tradition over 2,000 years. Christianity is many things to many people because of the contexts and circumstances in which it has been shaped by individuals—individuals who have borne witness to the faith of their ancestors but who have responded to the new needs that unfolded in their own times.

We may long for the comfortable, self-contained world of an earlier Christendom; many Christians have a particular fondness for the art and thought of the European Middle Ages. That is an age from which modernity has sometimes mercifully, sometimes rudely, banished us. One thing, at least, is clear: change has been a feature of Christian history in every age. One would be ill advised to rule out the possibility of dramatic and creative change in the future.

KEY TERMS

Advent. Start of the Christian liturgical year, a period including four Sundays immediately preceding Christmas.

Apostles' Creed. A brief statement of Christian doctrinal belief, dating from about the third century but ascribed to the apostles or first-generation followers of Jesus, and often recited in unison by congregations.

atonement. Christ's restoration of humanity to a right relationship with God, variously interpreted as divine victory over demonic power, satisfaction of divine justice, or demonstration of a moral example.

baptism. Sprinkling or immersion in water, the ritual by which a person is initiated into membership in the Christian community. Baptism is considered a cleansing from sin.

basilica. Architectural form of a church building, with a nave or main hall separated from side aisles by columns and with transepts producing a cross-shaped floor plan, and a rounded apse containing the principal altar at the end opposite the main entrance.

bishop. The supervising priest of a district called a diocese. In some branches of Christianity the bishop has charge of ordaining priests as well as confirming baptisms.

canon. A standard. A scriptural canon is the list of books acknowledged as scripture. Canon law is the accumulated body of Church regulations and discipline. Clergy subject to the rule of a particular cathedral or congregation are also sometimes termed canons.

charismatic. Characterized by spiritual gifts, especially the gift of strange and impulsive speech or other possession-type behaviour.

Christology. One's doctrine of how the divinity of Jesus Christ relates to his humanity.

crucifix. A cross with an image of the suffering Jesus mounted on it.

ecumenism. Movement for reunion

or collaboration between previously separated branches of Christianity.

Epiphany. The festival twelve days after Christmas commemorating the manifestation of Jesus's divinity, associated with the visit of wise men from the East to the infant Jesus.

Eucharist. The ritual re-enactment of Jesus's self-giving sacrifice, patterned after his sharing bread and wine as his body and blood at his final Passover meal with his disciples. The Orthodox term it the liturgy, Catholics the mass, and Protestants the Lord's Supper or Holy Communion.

Evangelical. In Germany, a name for the Lutheran Church. In the English-speaking world, a description of conservative Protestants with a confident sense of the assurance of divine grace and the obligation to preach it.

excommunication. Formal expulsion from the Church, particularly the Roman Catholic Church, for doctrinal error or moral misconduct.

friar. A member of a Latin mendicant order such as the Dominicans, Franciscans, or Carmelites.

fundamentalism. A twentieth-century reaction to modernity by Protestants who advocated strict literal inerrancy of scripture and doctrine. 'Fundamentalism' has come to connote calls for strict conformity in conduct as well as militancy in defending tradition and attacking modernity.

glossolalia. Speaking in strange tongues, which is a principal feature of charismatic behaviour.

Gnosticism. An ancient movement that understood the material world to be the result of a fall from pure spiritual existence. Christian Gnostics viewed Jesus as the bearer of a secret, saving knowledge enabling the faithful to be redeemed from this material realm.

Good Friday. The solemn holy day recalling the Passion or suffering and death of Jesus on the cross, two days before Easter.

Hesychasm. This is the fourteenth-century devotional movement in the Greek Orthodox Church that made extensive use of the Jesus Prayer, repeated like a mantra with each breath.

Holiness Churches. Protestant Churches emphasizing spiritual perfection as a gift one can be intensely aware of already having received from God. Developing out of Methodism as it became more sedate, they remain more sedate than Pentecostalism in not promoting exotic speech as a mark of such a gift.

Iconoclasts. The party in seventh- and eighth-century Constantinople that fought, ultimately unsuccessfully, to eliminate the use of icons or pictorial images of Jesus, Mary, and the saints.

Immaculate conception. The doctrine that the virgin Mary was herself conceived without sin, defined as Roman Catholic dogma in 1854.

imprimatur. Permission given by a Roman Catholic ecclesiastical official before a book on a theological or moral subject may be printed.

indulgences. Releases from specified amounts of time in purgatory, a realm to which in Catholic doctrine the soul proceeds after death for an unspecified period of preparation to enter heaven.

investiture. Conferring the insignia of office on a new appointee such a bishop or abbot. The competing rights of princes and popes to make such appointments were disputed for years after the papacy asserted its claim in 1059.

lectionary. A schedule assigning particular scriptural passages to be read in worship on particular days.

Lent. The period preceding Easter, consisting of forty days not counting Sundays. It is the season for most serious Christian spiritual reflection.

logos. 'Word' in the sense of eternal divine intelligence and purpose, an idea prominent in Greek thought at the time of Jesus.

mass. The eucharistic ceremony of Roman Catholics, with bread and wine eaten as the body and blood of Christ. It was celebrated in Latin until 1965, in local languages since then.

mendicant orders. Medieval Latin religious orders operating in the cities and towns rather than in monasteries apart from them. Members worked or begged for a living, originally as a protest against the monasteries' wealth.

Monophysites. Fifth-century advocates of the view that Christ had a divine nature fully absorbing or replacing his humanity. Churches from Ethiopia through Egypt and Syria to Armenia remain Monophysite till today.

mysticism. A tradition cultivating and reflecting on the content of moments of intensely felt spiritual union with the divine.

Nestorians. Fifth-century advocates of the view that the incarnate Christ was two separate persons, one divine and one human. Nestorian Christianity spread from Syria across Central Asia to China, with a remnant still surviving in Iraq.

Nicene Creed. An ancient doctrinal formulation longer and more explicit than the Apostles' Creed and still in use through regular recitation in the Catholic mass.

ontological argument. An argument based on logic holding that God must necessarily exist, formulated by the eleventh-century theologian Anselm.

Passion. The suffering and death of Jesus on the cross.

Pentecost. The fiftieth day after Easter, commemorated as the occasion when Jesus's followers experienced dramatically the presence of the Holy Spirit and the ability to preach and be understood in different languages.

Pentecostal Churches. These are modern

Protestant groups emphasizing outbursts of exotic, generally unintelligible, speech as a mark of the Holy Spirit's presence and of the individual's holiness or spiritual perfection.

Pietism. A movement originating in late seventeenth-century Lutheran Germany, expressing a spontaneity of devotion and a confident certainty of forgiveness, over against institutional rigidity. It contributed to Methodism in eighteenth-century England.

predestination. The notion, developing from faith in God as all-powerful and all-knowing, that God anticipates or controls human actions, foreordaining people to salvation or damnation.

Puritanism. A movement in England from 1558 to 1660 seeking to 'purify' the Church of England of Catholic influences in favour of Calvinist ones. Before running its course in England, it became a major influence in Congregational Churches in New England.

Reformed Churches. Churches that are Calvinist in doctrine and often Presbyterian in Church government, strong in the Netherlands and Scotland and also found in France, Switzerland, Hungary, and places on other continents populated by settlers from these lands.

rosary. A string with fifty-eight beads and a small crucifix, used in Catholic devotion to keep count when repeating Our Father and Hail Mary prayers.

sacrament. A ritual action seen as signifying divine grace. Most widely accepted as sacraments are baptism and the Eucharist; the Catholic Church has regarded these plus five others as sacraments since the thirteenth century.

Stations of the Cross. Fourteen locations marked in the nave of a Catholic church, recalling events along the pilgrim route in Jerusalem from Jesus's trial to his crucifixion.

transubstantiation. The Catholic doctrine that the bread and wine of the Eucharist are at the moment of consecration in the service miraculously transformed into the body and blood of Christ.

Trinity. The conception of God as having three 'persons' or manifestations: as father, as son, and as Holy Spirit. The doctrine emerged during the late third century and was adopted after vigorous debate in the fourth.

Uniate Churches. Churches in the Eastern Orthodox world and farther east with which the Roman Catholic Church established relations, recognizing their distinctive rites in Eastern languages and their married clergy.

FURTHER READING

Allen, E.L. 1960–1. *Christianity among the Religions*. London: Allen and Unwin; Boston: Beacon.

Aulén, G. 1930. *Christus Victor*. London: SPCK; New York: Macmillan.

Barraclough, G., ed. 1981. *The Christian World: A Social and Cultural History*. London: Thames and Hudson; New York: Abrams.

Charlesworth, M.J. 1972. *Philosophy of Religion: The Historic Approaches*. London: Macmillan.

Gascoigne, B. 1977. *The Christians*. London: Jonathan Cape.

Gilson, E. 1955. *History of Christian Philosophy in the Middle Ages*. New York: Random House.

Grant, J.W. 1984. *Moon of Wintertime: Missionaries and the Indians of Canada in Encounter Since 1534*. Toronto: University of Toronto Press.

Isichei, E. 1995. *A History of Christianity in Africa: From Antiquity to the Present*. London: SPCK.

Küng, H. 1976. *On Being a Christian*. London: Collins; New York: Doubleday.

Lewis, C.S. 1952. *Mere Christianity*. London: Blès.

McManners, J., ed. 1990. *The Oxford Illustrated History of Christianity*. Oxford: Oxford University Press.

Pelikan, J. 1985. *Jesus through the Centuries: His Place in the History of Culture*. New Haven: Yale University Press.

Roeder, H. 1951. *Saints and Their Attributes*. London: Longmans, Green.

Ruether, R., and E. McLaughlin, eds. 1979. *Women of Spirit: Female Leadership in the Jewish and Christian Traditions*. New York: Simon and Schuster.

Zernov, N. 1961. *Eastern Christendom: A Study of the Origin and Development of the Eastern Orthodox Church*. London: Weidenfeld and Nicolson; New York: Putnam.

References

Bainton, R.H. 1974. 'Reformation'. In *Encyclopaedia Britannica*, vol. 15, 547–57. Chicago: Encyclopaedia Britannica Inc.

Barbour, I. 1966. *Issues in Science and Religion*. Englewood Cliffs: Prentice-Hall.

Barrett, C.K. 1989. *The New Testament Background: Selected Documents*, rev. ed. San Francisco: Harper & Row.

Barrett, D.B., ed. 1982. *World Christian Encyclopedia*. Nairobi: Oxford University Press.

Bettenson, H.S. 1977. *Documents of the Christian Church*, 2nd ed. London: Oxford University Press.

Bowie F., and O. Davies, eds. 1990. *Hildegard of Bingen: Mystical Writings*. New York: Crossroad.

Bradford, E. 1967. *The Great Betrayal: Constantinople 1204*. London: Hodder & Stoughton.

Buttrick, G.A., ed. 1962. *The Interpreter's Dictionary of the Bible*, 4 vols. New York: Abingdon.

Colgrave, B., ed. 1969. *Bede's Ecclesiastical History of the English People*. Oxford: Clarendon Press.

Cross, F.L., ed. 1974. *The Oxford Dictionary of the Christian Church*, 2nd ed. London: Oxford University Press.

Faber, R. 1966. *The Vision and the Need: Late Victorian Imperialist Aims*. London: Faber.

Frend, W.H.C. 1965. *The Early Church*. Oxford: Blackwell.

Halverson, M., and A.A. Cohen, eds. 1958. *A Handbook of Christian Theology*. Cleveland: World.

Happold, F.C. 1963. *Mysticism*. Harmondsworth: Penguin.

King, M.L. 1964. *Why We Can't Wait*. New York: New American Library.

Kittel, G., ed. 1964–76. *Theological Dictionary of the New Testament*, 10 vols. Grand Rapids: Eerdmans.

Livingstone, D. 1858. *Cambridge Lectures*. Cambridge: Deighton.

McManners, J., ed. 1990. *The Oxford Illustrated History of Christianity*. Oxford: Oxford University Press.

Meyendorff, J. 1964. *A Study of Gregory Palamas*. London: Faith Press.

Meyer, R.T., trans. 1950. *Athanasius, Life of St. Anthony.* Westminster, MD: Newman Press.

National Council of Churches of Christ in the United States of America. 1946/52. Revised Standard Version Bible. New York: Thomas Nelson & Sons.

______. 1989. *New Revised Standard Version Bible*. New York: Thomas Nelson & Sons.

New Catholic Encyclopedia, The, 15 vols. 1967. New York: McGraw-Hill.

O'Brien, E. 1964. *Varieties of Mystic Experience*. New York: Holt, Rinehart and Winston.

Oliver, R. 1957. *Sir Harry Johnston and the Scramble for Africa*. London: Chatto & Windus.

Outler, A., trans. 1955. *Augustine: Confessions and Enchiridion*. Philadelphia and London: Westminster/SCM.

Oxford University Press and Cambridge University Press. *New English Bible*. New York: Oxford University Press and Cambridge University Press.

Pass, H.L. 1911. 'Demons and Spirits'. In *Encyclopaedia of Religion and Ethics,* edited by J. Hastings, 578–83. New York: Scribner.

Radice, B., trans. 1986. 'Moriae encomium' by Erasmus. In *Collected Works of Erasmus*, vol. 27. Toronto: University of Toronto Press.

Rahner, K., ed. 1968–70. *Sacramentum Mundi*, 6 vols. London: Burns & Oates; New York: Herder and Herder.

Schlesinger, A. 1974. 'The Missionary Enterprise and Theories of Imperialism'. In *The Missionary Enterprise in China and America*, edited by J.K. Fairbank, 336–73. Cambridge, Mass.: Harvard University Press.

Smith, W.C. 1963. *The Faith of Other Men*. New York: New American Library.

Stevenson, J., ed. 1957. *A New Eusebius*. London: SPCK.

Stokes, F.G., trans. 1909. *Epistolae obscurorum virorum*. London: Chatto & Windus.

Whitehead, A.N. 1929. *Process and Reality*. Cambridge: Macmillan.

Key Dates

622	Muḥammad's *hijrah* from Makkah to Madīnah
632	Muḥammad's death; community leadership passes to the caliph
661	Mu'āwiyah, Umayyad caliph, moves capital to Damascus
680	Death of Ḥusayn at Karbalā', commemorated as martyrdom by Shī'īs
711	Arab armies under Ṭāriq reach Spain
d. 728	Ḥasan al-Basrī, early Ṣūfī ascetic
732	Battle of Poitiers puts a stop to Muslim expansion in France
762	Manṣūr establishes Baghdad as 'Abbāsid capital
833	'Abbāsid caliph al-Ma'mūn's decree enforcing a Mu'tazilī teaching
922	Execution of al-Ḥallāj for claiming to be one with the Truth
d. 935	al-Ash'arī, theologian of Sunni *kalām*
1071	Seljuq Turkish victory over Byzantines
d. 1111	al-Ghazālī, theological synthesizer of faith and reason
d. 1240	Ibn al-'Arabī, philosopher of the mystical unity of being
1258	Ruin of Baghdad in Mongol invasion
d. 1273	Rūmī, Persian mystical poet
1492	Christian domination of Spain (official expulsion of Muslims in 1602)
1529	Ottoman Turks reach Vienna (again in 1683)
1582	Emperor Akbar in Mughal India promulgates the 'Divine Religion'
d. 1792	Ibn 'Abd al-Wahhāb, leader of traditionalist revival in Arabia
d. 1897	al-Afghānī, promoter of modern Islamic cultural revival
1924	Atatürk, modernizer and secularizer, abolishes the caliphate in Turkey
1930	Iqbāl proposes a Muslim state in India
1947	Pakistan formed as an Islamic state from parts of British India
1979	Khomeini heads a revolutionary Islamic regime in Iran

Chapter Four

The Islamic Tradition

Mahmoud M. Ayoub

The Name and the Concept of Islam

Islam is the last of the three historic monotheistic faiths that arose in the Middle East, coming after Judaism and Christianity. Its name signifies the commitment of its adherents to live in total submission to God. *Islām* is an Arabic word meaning submission, or surrender. The three-consonant root *s–l–m* contained in it connotes peace (*salām*), soundness, and safety. In its etymological associations, therefore, Islam is a person's total submission to the will of God, which gives one inner peace and soundness of nature in this life and safety from divine retribution in the life to come.

A person who professes Islam is called a Muslim, again a term displaying the sequence of these three consonants. The vowels in the earlier English rendering of this word, 'Moslem', reflect other languages more than Arabic, and this spelling is now less often used. In Iran, the Persian form *musulmān* was derived from the Arabic *muslim,* and this usage spread to the Indo-Pakistan subcontinent and found its way into French, where it is accepted.

An older term sometimes still encountered is 'Mohammedan'. Used by Westerners analogously to the terms 'Buddhist' and 'Christian', it misleadingly suggested Muslim worship of the prophet Muḥammad. The term was considered offensive by Muslims, and neither they nor serious non-Muslim scholars lament its disappearance from active use.

Who is a Muslim, or included in Islam? The *Qur'ān*, the Islamic scripture, offers a very inclusive view. It presents Islam as the universal and primordial faith of all the prophets from Adam to Muḥammad, and of all those who believe in God, the one sovereign Lord, creator, and sustainer of all things. Islam, moreover, is God's eternal way for the universe.

Islamic thought on this matter distinguishes between nature and choice.

Inanimate things, animals, plants, as well as the angels, are *muslims* to God by nature or instinct. Only human *islām* is an *islām* of choice. Muslims hold it to be the universal faith of all those who affirm the oneness of God, in total submission to his will. Human beings may voluntarily accept or wilfully reject faith, but on the Day of Judgement, they are to face the consequences of their choice. They can expect to be rewarded for their faith, or punished for their rejection of faith.

In practical implementation, a Muslim is often someone born to a Muslim family and thus a member of the Muslim community. Or one can become a Muslim by repeating before two Muslim witnesses the *shahādah*, or profession of faith: 'I bear witness that there is no god except God, and I bear witness that Muḥammad is the messenger of God.' By so doing, such a man or woman becomes legally a Muslim with all the rights and responsibilities this new identity entails. Whether what this person publicly professes with the tongue is what he or she truly holds in the heart, Muslims assert, is only for God to judge. There is no other ceremony required for one to become a Muslim.

Muslims see the choice to affirm Islam as the choice of something for which all human beings are naturally prepared or endowed by God as their creator. Thus besides the historical and social community, there is an inner source of Islam: the natural inclination of every person towards faith, or the inner human capacity to know God. This is seen as an original state of purity or innocence in the *Qur'ān*'s references to *fiṭrah*, the original creation 'upon which God originated humankind; there is no altering of God's creation' (*Q.* 30:30). This innate *islām* is the 'pure religion of Abraham' to which the prophet Muḥammad came to call his people: 'It is the religion of your father Abraham; he called you *muslims* aforetime' (*Q.* 22:78).

HISTORICAL BACKGROUND

The Faith of Abraham

In the *Qur'ān*, the Hebrew patriarchal figure Abraham, through his own innate reasoning capacity, is guided from the idol worship of his people to the knowledge of God. As a youth he discerns that idols made of wood or stone cannot hear the supplications of their worshippers, and therefore can do them neither good nor harm. He gazes one night at the full moon and thinks it to be God on account of its splendour. But when the moon sets, Abraham says, 'I love not those that set.' He then gazes at the bright sun and says, 'This is my lord, this is bigger!' But when the sun, too, sets, Abraham exclaims, 'I turn my face [that is, entire person] to him who originated the heavens and the earth, a man of pure faith, and I am not one of the Associators [that is, of other things or beings with God]' (*Q.* 6:77–9).

Accounts of Abraham link him to the Arabs and to Islam. Physically the Arabs, including Muḥammad, the Prophet of Islam, are said to be the descendants of Abraham through his son Ishmael (Ismā'īl in Arabic). Religiously, Abraham's faith in the One God, long before the Jewish Torah and the Christian Gospel are revealed, is the true *islām* that, according to the *Qur'ān* and Islamic 'tradition' (that is, the body of oral tradition traced to Muḥammad), provides the basis for the Islamic faith. The *Qur'ān* and Islam affirm a close theological and spiritual kinship with the biblical heritage of the Judaic and Christian religious traditions.

Arabian Society before Islam

The long period of pre-Islamic Arab history is called by the *Qur'ān* and Muslim tradition the age of *jāhilīyah* ('foolishness' or 'ignorance'). As scholars have observed, the term *jāhilīyah* designates not so much a state of cognitive ignorance or lack of knowledge (*'ilm*) as it does a lack of moral consciousness, magnanimity, or prudence (*ḥilm*).

Allāh is Arabic for 'the God'. The Arabs before Islam recognized Allāh as the supreme creator god, but he was not the central recipient of worship. Among the many gods the Arabs worshipped in and around the shrine called the Ka'bah were the three goddesses Al-Lāt, al-'Uzzah, and Manāt, and the god Hubal. Manāt may have been a vague representation of the goddess of love, known to many ancients as Venus. Hubal may have originally been a rain god, as the name means 'vapour'. The three goddesses were believed to be the daughters of Allāh. They were worshipped in order to bring the devotee closer to him (see Q. 39:3). The *Qur'ān* repudiates these goddesses, calling them mere 'names which you [the Arabs] and your fathers named; God sent down no authority concerning them' (53:20–3).

Arabs shared the general Semitic idea of a sacred place (*ḥaram*) where no living thing—plant, animal, or human—could be harmed. For Makkah (Mecca) and most of Arabia, the chief *ḥaram* was the shrine of the Ka'bah and its environs. It was believed to have been built by Abraham and his son Ishmael, brought by Abraham with his mother, Hagar, to settle in the valley of Makkah (see Q. 14:37). The Ka'bah is an ancient square building that contained a large number of idols or images of gods and goddesses, perhaps including crudely painted images of Jesus and his virgin mother Mary. It still contains at one corner an unusual black stone, thought by some to be a meteorite.

Before Islam, the Ka'bah was a pilgrimage site to which people came from far and near. The pilgrimage season was also a trade fair, which gave Makkah a special prestige and economic status in Arabia. The pilgrimage was later purged of its idolatrous elements and adopted by Islam as one of its rites of worship, and the sanctity of the Ka'bah was greatly enhanced by making it the direction of prayer for Muslims everywhere.

The Arabs before Islam believed time to be synonymous with death or fate, which in the end will spare no one. Therefore, while a person can, he or she should make the most of this life. Arab society was thus largely given to hedonistic pleasures, finding no other meaning in existence. The *Qur'ān* describes this attitude as gloomy: 'They [the Arabs] say there is only this life of ours; we live and we die, and time alone will destroy us all' (Q. 45:24). These sentiments were expressed in eloquent odes recounting deeds of chivalry and generosity, deploring fate, and praising the wise man who drowns his sorrows in the pleasures of wine, women, and sentimental verse, but is sure to leave behind a good name for his tribe to boast of after him.

Like the ancient Hebrews, the Arabs before Islam did not believe in an afterlife. To them the only form of life after death was the ghost of a slain man, which would linger around crying for revenge until such was exacted from the killer himself or any man of similar status in his own tribe. This belief, coupled with the virtue of manly prowess and tribal solidarity, often led to long and deadly feuds that decimated many tribes and forced others to migrate.

Many ideals and customs of Arab society were taken over or transformed by Islam and included in its comprehensive religious system. Manliness, hospitality, family honour, neighbourly protection of a defenceless person, and keeping one's covenant were among the values to which Muslims gave a religious and moral purpose. Manliness was transformed into religious zeal, and hospitality into almsgiving and care for the poor, orphan, and wayfarer. Family honour was transformed into moral chastity and respect and love between parents and children, and keeping one's covenant into a system of socio-political, religious, and economic relations between the Muslim community and other communities, notably Christians and Jews.

Jewish and Christian communities existed in Arabia long before the emergence of Islam in the seventh century. The city of Makkah, in which Muḥammad was born, was a caravan station on the trade routes between Syria and the Mediterranean to the north and west and the Red Sea, Africa, and India to the south and east.

Like the rest of the Arabian peninsula, it was open to diverse cultural and religious influences, and thus permeated with Jewish and Christian moral and devotional ideas. The desert monks, who preached and practised holiness and healing, exercised a deep influence on many Arab seekers after a moral and spiritual life.

A group of Makkan Arabs known as *ḥanīfs* ('pious ones') accepted the ethical monotheism of Judaism and Christianity, but did not join either of these two religious communities. The Makkans may have resisted Christian proselytizing, hoping for a scripture of their own (see Q. 35:42 and 6:157, where such expectations are alluded to). They may also have been put off by the discord and hostility between the two communities; the *Qur'ān* reports: 'The Jews say the Christians have nothing on which to stand, and the Christians say the Jews have nothing on which to stand, yet they both recite the scriptures' (Q. 2:113).

One custom Islam repudiated, but could not fully eradicate, was tribe or kinship solidarity, which often took priority over the bond of religion. Although Islam substituted for this custom the ideal of the brotherhood of faith, tribal interests and intertribal conflicts dominated the social and political life of early Muslim society, as will be demonstrated later.

Makkan society consisted largely of one tribe, the Quraysh, which was divided into various clans. As Makkah was in an arid land, its people lived less on agriculture than on trade and the revenues of the Ka'bah. The significance of these two sources of livelihood is vividly described in the following brief *sūrah* (chapter) of the *Qur'ān*:

> This [the sparing of the Ka'bah; see below] is for the sake of the pact of safety of the Quraysh, for the sake of their safety during the winter and summer journeys. Let them then worship the Lord of this House who provided them with food against hunger, and make them secure from fear (Q. 106).

The Life of Muḥammad

Muḥammad, of the tribe of Quraysh, was born in about 570. His father died before his birth, while on a caravan journey, and his mother died a few years later. Muḥammad thus grew up an orphan, and was cared for first by his paternal grandfather, 'Abd al-Muṭṭalib, and when he died while Muḥammad was still a youth, by his uncle Abū Ṭālib.

Little is known about Muḥammad's youth. He may have accompanied his grandfather on one or more caravan journeys to Syria. He then worked as a merchant for a rich widow, Khadījah, who may have been considerably older than he was, but whom he married at around the age of twenty-five. His marriage to Khadījah freed him from financial cares and allowed him to turn his thoughts to spiritual things. Muḥammad is described in the early biographical sources as a contemplative, honest, and mild-mannered young man. He was called al-Amīn ('the faithful' or 'trustworthy') because of the confidence he inspired in people.

Tradition reports that Muḥammad loathed the idol worship of his people, considering their ways immoral and foolish. Quite possibly he belonged to the small circle of the *ḥanīfs*, already mentioned. Once a year, during the hot summer month of Ramaḍān, Muḥammad spent days in seclusion in a cave on Mount

Ḥirā', a short distance from Makkah. During one of these retreats he receives the call to prophethood and the first revelation of the *Qur'ān*.

As Muḥammad sits one night in the solitude of his retreat, an angel, later identified as Gabriel (Jibrīl in Arabic), appears to him. Taking hold of him and pressing him hard, the angel commands, 'Recite [or read]!' Muḥammad answers, 'I cannot read.' After repeating the command for the third time, the angel continues, 'Recite in the name of your Lord who created, created man from a blood clot. Recite, for your Lord is most magnanimous—who taught by the pen, taught man that which he did not know'(Q. 96:1–5). Muḥammad runs home frightened and asks the people of his household to cover him, as he is shivering with fear and apprehension. This experience fills him with misgivings, so that he wanders aimlessly among the Makkan hills trying to understand the meaning of the encounter. Often, tradition reports, the angel would appear to him seated on a throne filling the horizon and would say, 'O Muḥammad, I am Gabriel, and you are the Messenger of God.' Khadījah always consoled and encouraged him, asserting that what he saw was not an evil spirit. She reportedly took him to her cousin, a Christian savant, called Waraqah b. Nawfal. Waraqah confirmed Muḥammad in his mission, declaring him to be the Prophet sent by God with a sacred law like that of Moses.

The Arabs of Muḥammad's time believed that a poet was possessed by a spirit of the demons or *jinn*, which inspired him while he recited his verses. Their nearest parallel to the priest or prophet of the ancient religious civilizations of the Middle East was the *kāhin* or soothsayer, who was often a poet. Such a man or woman spoke in rhymed and mysterious phrases that were meant to announce an important event, answer a perplexing question, or evoke fear and wonderment in the *kāhin*'s listeners.

But the idea of a prophet, called in both Arabic and Hebrew *nabī*, was not unfamiliar to Muḥammad's people. In fact, tradition frequently asserts that the Arabs did expect a prophet of their own. Nor was Muḥammad the only person to claim to be such a prophet.

For twelve years Muḥammad the Prophet of Allāh preached the new faith in the One God to his people, meeting with little success. His message was not only religious but also moral and social. The Makkans objected to the consequences they feared it would have for their social customs and for the religious and economic status of the Ka'bah. They did not wish to abandon the ways of their forebears; the *Qur'ān* reports their saying, 'We found our fathers following a custom, and we shall follow in their footsteps' (Q. 40:22).

Muḥammad admonished the Makkans to give alms, to care for the orphaned, to feed the hungry, to assist the oppressed and destitute, and to offer hospitality to the wayfarer. He warned them of an impending doom, on a day 'when men shall be like scattered moths, and the mountains shall be like fluffed tufts of wool' (Q. 101). On that day of the last judgement, the deeds of every human being will be weighed in the balance: 'As for him whose scales shall weigh heavy [that is, with good deeds], he shall be in a pleasing life. But as for him whose scales shall weigh light, his mother [i.e., abode] shall be the pit' (Q. 101). It is 'a fire hotly blazing'.

The first to accept the new faith were the Prophet's wife Khadījah, his cousin and son-in-law 'Alī b. Abī Ṭālib, his slave Zayd b. Ḥārithah—whom he later freed and adopted—and his faithful companion Abū Bakr. Slowly a small band of believers, consisting of slaves and the poor of society, began to form. Soon the piety, moral uprightness, and egalitarianism that characterized the small community of Muslims attracted men of substance and prestige, such as 'Umar b. al-Khaṭṭāb and 'Uthmān b. 'Affān, who would be the second and third caliphs.

Muḥammad and his followers were often vilified, and those who had no tribal protection were severely persecuted. The Prophet thus advised a group of such people to migrate across the Red Sea to Abyssinia (Ethiopia), a Christian country, where they were well received. With the death of Muḥammad's uncle Abū Ṭālib and his wife Khadījah within the space of no more than two months, he, too, lost all support and protection. Among his most bitter enemies was his uncle Abū Lahab, who is singled out in the *Qur'ān* for damnation (see Q. 111). Accordingly, the Prophet went around the neighbouring tribes and towns, asking in vain for protection to preach his new faith.

The First Muslim Community

In 622, after negotiations, the Prophet was invited to arbitrate between two feuding tribes in a city called Yathrib, about 400 km (250 mi.) north of Makkah. He was also to unite the tribes of Yathrib into a new Muslim community. His migration (*hijrah*) to Yathrib, a place that henceforth came to be known as 'The city of the Prophet' or Madīnah ('the city'), marked the beginning of community life under Islam, and thus of Islamic history.

HIJRAH

Muslims very early adopted the *hijrah* as the beginning and focus of their calendar, and thus events are dated before or after the *hijrah*. The abbreviation AH used with such dates is from Latin for 'year of the *hijrah*'. Since the lunar year is eleven days shorter than the solar year, *hijrī* dates gain one year approximately every thirty-three solar years, and reached 1400 AH in 1979 CE. In Iran, however, where a solar year based on the national tradition was implemented in the twentieth century, the date had reached only 1357.

In Madīnah, the Prophet established the first Islamic commonwealth. Headed by a prophet who was believed to be ruling in accordance with the dictates of a divine scripture, it was a truly theocratic state. As such, it has provided an ideal that subsequent Islamic states have never fully realized. The Prophet's legacy was the broad sources for a sacred law, in the *Qur'ān* and his own life-example, the *sunnah*.

The society of Madīnah, an oasis city with an agricultural economy, had a far more heterogeneous social structure than that of Makkah. Besides having a substantial Jewish community, the city consisted largely of two hostile tribes, the Aws and the Khazraj, whose old rivalries kept it in a continuous state of civil strife.

Muḥammad sought to weld these disparate elements into one social unit. While he lived, he achieved this with remarkable success. He issued a brief constitutional document known as the covenant of Madīnah. This covenant stipulated that all the people of Madīnah should henceforth be one Muslim commonwealth. The covenant granted the Jews full religious freedom and equality with the Muslims, provided that they support the state and not enter into any alliances against it with the Quraysh or any other tribe.

The *Qur'ān*'s narratives and worldview are closely akin to the prophetic view of history in the Hebrew Bible. The Prophet expected the Jews of Madīnah to recognize this kinship and thus be his natural allies. He adopted a number of Jewish practices, including the fast of the Day of Atonement, Yom Kippur. It seems, moreover, that, as in Jewish usage, the Muslims had from the beginning been facing Jerusalem in their prayers.

The Madīnan Jews, however, rejected Muḥammad's claim to be a prophet and that of the *Qur'ān* to be a sacred book. This led to great tension in the relations between the two communities, which is clearly reflected in the *Qur'ān*'s treatment of the Jews. Increasingly, therefore, Islam began to distinguish itself from Judaism, so that within two years of the Prophet's migration to Madīnah, the *qiblah*, or direction of prayer, was changed from Jerusalem to the Ka'bah in Makkah, and the fast of Yom Kippur was dropped in favour of the fast of the month of Ramaḍān.

In the *Qur'ān* the people of Madīnah are called Anṣār, meaning 'helpers' or 'supporters', that is to say, the first supporters and protectors of Islam and the Prophet. As the flow of Muslim immigrants from Makkah increased, a new social group was added to an already diverse society. The new immigrants, along with those who came with or shortly after the Prophet, were appropriately called Muhājirūn, meaning 'immigrants'. The Immigrants were predominantly members of the tribe of Quraysh. Thus they soon came to form a closely knit and powerful group in the Muslim community during that formative period of its history.

The *Qur'ān* presents an increasingly widening scope of Muhammad's mission. At first he is enjoined to limit his call to his nearest kinsfolk. Then he is commanded to proclaim his message publicly, then 'to warn [Makkah] the mother of towns and its environs' (Q. 6:92). Finally he is ordered to declare: 'O people, I am God's Messenger to you all' (Q. 7:158). This no doubt reflects the

Prophet's own growing consciousness of the potentially universal scope and significance of his new religion.

The Incorporation of Makkah

If Islam was to grow beyond the confines of its new home in Madīnah, Makkah would have to be restored to a place of prominence. Without Makkah Islam would be incomplete, and without the rest of Arabia it would remain powerless.

To this end, the Prophet adopted the familiar strategy of economic and military pressure against the intransigent Makkans. The Muslims intercepted and raided the Makkan caravans on their way from Syria. The Makkans were forced to send an army of about a thousand men, which met a 300-man detachment at the well of Badr in 624.

Poorly equipped and far outnumbered but highly motivated, the Muslims inflicted a crushing defeat on the Makkans. Thus the Battle of Badr remains one of the most memorable events of Muslim history. It is celebrated in the *Qur'ān* as a miraculous proof of the truth of Islam. The *Qur'ān* declares: 'You [Muḥammad] did not shoot the first arrow when you did shoot it; rather God shot it' (Q. 8:17), and 'God supported you [Muslims] at Badr when you were in an abased state' (Q. 3:123).

The victory at Badr gave the Muslim state much prestige among the neighbouring tribes and forced the Makkans to deal with it on a basis of equality. The Makkans decided, however, to avenge the defeat of Badr and met the Muslims the following year by Mount Uḥud, not far from Madīnah. At Uḥud the Muslims were not only defeated; they were also demoralized because their defeat was largely due to their negligence and lack of motivation. The Prophet was badly injured, and rumours quickly circulated that he had been killed.

The defeat at Uḥud was not decisive because the men of the Quraysh did not pursue their victory further, and the Muslims quickly recovered. The Prophet then decided to expel the Jews from Madīnah and its neighbouring settlements. The reason given was the Jews' revocation of their covenant of protection with the Muslims. The motive behind this measure may have actually been to free the Muslim state of outside influences at this critical formative stage of its history.

As the Muslims grew in strength and the occasional skirmishes with the caravans of the Quraysh continued, the Makkans decided to attack Madīnah. On the advice of Salmān the Persian, a former slave, the Prophet had a trench dug around the exposed parts of the city, to prevent Makkan cavalry from advancing towards it. In 627, the men of the Quraysh, along with a large coalition of other tribes, besieged Madīnah in what came to be known as the 'Battle of the Trench' or the 'Battle of the Confederates'. As the siege failed to achieve its aim, the attacking armies became discouraged and left.

This event was a turning-point in the Prophet's goal of Islamizing all of Arabia. Islam was quickly spreading throughout Arabia and beyond, including Makkah. Finally the Makkans were impelled to seek a truce with the Muslims. The truce of Ḥudaybīyah was concluded in 628 and allowed the Prophet to consolidate the nascent state's diplomatic as well as military gains.

Two years later, in 630, the Prophet led a large army to conquer Makkah, the Quraysh having breached the truce. There was no fighting, however, as the Makkans capitulated and accepted Islam en masse.

The Prophet granted amnesty to all in the city. Whenever an individual or tribe accepted Islam, all hostility was to cease and the enemy were to become brothers in faith. Clearly powerless after the Prophet's victory over them, the Makkans asked him what he intended to do with them. He answered, 'I will do with you what Joseph did with his brothers. Go; you are free.' Then quoting Joseph's words to his brothers, he continued, 'There is no blame in you today; God forgive you' (Q. 12:92).

Muḥammad regarded his victory over Makkah not as his own but as God's victory. The victory and its purpose are represented in the *Qur'ān* in the words not of a conqueror but of a thankful servant: 'When support from God comes, and victory, and you see men enter into the religion of God in throngs, proclaim the praise of your Lord and seek His forgiveness, for He is truly relenting' (Q. 110).

The Prophet did not remain in Makkah as might be expected, but returned to Madīnah to spend the last two years of his life. Before his death, Muḥammad led the Muslims on his farewell pilgrimage to Makkah and its sacred shrine, the Ka'bah. With this ritual officially instituted, Islam is seen as complete, as we shall illustrate in our discussion of pilgrimage below.

Muḥammad was always known as *rasūl Allāh* ('the Messenger of God'), not as a ruler or military leader, although he was all of these. He waged war and made peace, and laid the foundations of an Islamic order. He established laws and social and religious institutions that are all accepted as Islamic laws and institutions. In the society of Arabia, Islam thus came to be the standard encompassing all of life. The community (*ummah*) he established was ideally to be a religious community (in Arabic, an *ummah muslimah*).

Before Muḥammad died after a short illness in 632, he had firmly established Islam in Arabia and sent expeditions to Syria. After the conquest of Makkah, Arab tribal energies were turned outwards towards the Persian and Byzantine empires. Within eighty years after the Prophet's death, the Muslims administered an empire stretching from the southern borders of France through North Africa and the Middle East into Central Asia and to India.

Muhammad die from illness

PROPHETHOOD AND REVELATION

Prophets and Messengers

According to the *Qur'ān* and Islamic tradition, God's role in human history is not played by him directly through self-disclosure or incarnation in a divine human being, as Christians affirm of Jesus. Rather, God operates through his prophets and messengers, who convey his will in revealed scriptures and seek to establish his sacred law in the lives of their communities. From the Islamic point of view, therefore, human history is prophetic history.

Adam, a figure known from the Hebrew Bible, is the father of humankind. He is the first sinner; his sin is his violation of the principle of submission (*islām*) to God, through disobedience. The story of Adam in the *Qur'ān* shows humankind's proclivity to evil. Yet God fashions this sinful earthly creature with his own two hands and breathes into him his spirit. (For the story of Adam in the *Qur'ān*, see *sūrahs* 7:12–26 and 20:114–27. But for a major difference from the *Genesis* account of Adam's creation and fall, see 2:30–9.)

But Adam is also the first prophet. Before he and his spouse disobey God and eat of the forbidden tree, 'God taught Adam all the names' (*Q.* 2:31). With this revelation to his earthly creature, God challenges the angels. This is because they have protested against God's choosing such an insignificant creature and his potentially wicked progeny to be his stewards on earth. God orders the protesting angels to bow down reverently before him. They all do, except Satan, who is also called in Arabic Iblīs (many consider the name's resemblance to Greek *diabolos* coincidental). Satan arrogantly refuses to bow down before a creature of clay, while he himself has been created of fire and thus thinks himself to be better than Adam. Because of this sin of arrogant rebellion, Satan is expelled by God from the company of the angels. He is allowed, however, to tempt Adam and the weak among his descendants into disobeying God till the Day of Resurrection.

After Adam and Eve, and by implication the rest of humankind, are expelled from the garden, God promises them salvation through revelation: 'There shall come from me to you [humankind] guidance, and whoever follows my guidance, no fear shall come upon them, nor will they grieve' (*Q.* 2:38).

Beginning with Adam, Islamic tradition asserts, God sends 124,000 prophets at various times and to every community to remind people of their obligation to the one and only sovereign Lord and warn them against heedlessness and disobedience. The *Qur'ān* declares, 'There is not a nation but that a warner was sent to it' (*Q.* 26:207).

The *Qur'ān* mentions by name, however, twenty-six prophets and messengers, most of whom are well-known biblical personages. These include Abraham, Moses, David, Solomon, Elijah, Jonah, John the Baptist, Jesus, and others. The

Qur'ān also mentions three Arabian prophets: Shu'ayb (possibly Jethro, Moses's father-in-law), Hūd, and Ṣāliḥ. These are sent to Midian and the Arabian tribes of 'Ād and Thamūd respectively. Their people stubbornly reject them and their message and are utterly destroyed by God in punishment for their denial of his prophets.

When a community wilfully denies the prophet sent to it, it is destroyed, and thus becomes an example for future generations. The *Qur'ān* warns the Arabs of Muḥammad's time: 'We have destroyed [many] generations before you, when they committed wrongdoing. Their messengers came to them with elucidations, but they would not accept faith. Thus do We recompense sinful people (Q. 10:13). Revelation for Muslims is not only a source of salvation through faith in and obedience to God but also a criterion of judgement and damnation for those who knowingly disobey God and reject faith in him and his messengers.

Islamic tradition distinguishes between prophets and messengers. A prophet (Arabic *nabī*) is one who conveys God's message to his people, warning them of God's wrath if they are wicked and promising them blessing and prosperity if they are righteous. The message conveyed is limited to a specific people and for a particular time. It does not therefore constitute a sacred law or new religious dispensation. An example of such a limited prophetic mission is that of the prophet Jonah, who is sent by God to one city to call its people to repent of their evil ways. (See the story of Jonah in the Hebrew Bible, the book bearing his name, and in the *Qur'ān*, 10:98 and 37:139–48.)

A messenger (Arabic *rasūl*) is also a prophet sent by God to a specific community, but with a universally binding sacred law (*sharī'ah*). Moses and Muḥammad are the two best examples of persons with such a mission. This is because they not only come with a new and universal religious dispensation, but each founds an actual community wherein God's law is to be implemented.

Although Moses is given the Torah on Mount Sinai for the ancient Hebrews, the Torah remains binding on all those who know it, Hebrews and others, till the coming of the subsequent revelation, which is the Gospel (*injīl*; cf. Greek *euangelion*) of Jesus. Thenceforth, the Torah is still binding, but only as modified by the scripture revealed by God to Jesus. Jesus declares in the *Qur'ān*, addressing his fellow Jews, 'I shall confirm the Torah that was before me, and will make lawful for you some of the things which were before unlawful for you' (Q. 3:50).

The Five Major Prophets

According to the above schema, not every prophet is a messenger, but every messenger is a prophet. Among the prophets, five are called *ulū al-'azm* ('prophets of power or firm resolve', Q. 46:35). These are: Noah, Abraham, Moses, Jesus, and

Muḥammad. Their special significance lies in their receiving revelations from God. These, whether still extant or not, contain laws or precepts that are important landmarks in the long and progressive process of divine revelation, and hence of human religious development.

Noah

Noah, the father of humanity's second start, is sent to an obstinate people. In vain for 950 years he calls them to turn to God before God destroys them by the flood (see Q. 29:14 and 11:25–49). Noah receives dietary and marriage laws that constitute the first *sharī'ah*, or sacred law. The Noachic laws reported in Muslim tradition closely correspond to the Noachic covenant in Jewish tradition.

[margin note: humanity's 2nd start]

Abraham

The primary mission of all prophets is to warn people of their moral and religious obligations to serve and worship God alone without associating any partners with him. Thus Abraham is to convert his people from idol worship to the worship of God alone. Were his people to accept his message, there would be no reason for Abraham to migrate to a new land. The covenant that God makes with Abraham is similar to the covenant he makes with all prophets before and after him. The *Qur'ān* states: 'Remember when God made a covenant with the prophets saying, "Whereas I have given you the Book and wisdom, then an apostle shall come to you confirming that which is with you, you will have faith in him and assist him."' The prophets who follow Abraham are largely his descendants through his two sons, the Arabian through Ishmael and the Hebraic through Isaac.

[margin note: —convert people from idol worship to the worship of God alone]

Moses

Because Muslim tradition presents Muḥammad in many ways as 'a prophet like Moses', Moses occupies more space in the *Qur'ān* than any other prophet, including Muḥammad; he is mentioned over 200 times. Like Muḥammad, Moses grows up like an orphan, away from his parents' home. His mission begins, like that of Muḥammad, in solitude with God in the wilderness. The scripture revealed to him, the Torah, is for Muslims second in importance to the *Qur'ān* and most like it in content and purpose.

[margin note: Torah is revealed.]

Moses is sent as a messenger of God not only to his own people, but to Pharaoh and his people. The *Qur'ān* summarizes Moses's mission thus: 'His Lord called out to him ... "Go to Pharaoh, for he has waxed arrogant!" ... He [Pharaoh] cried out and proclaimed, "I am your lord most high!" But God seized him with the torment of both the next world and this' (Q. 79:15–25). Pharaoh persists in the sin of claiming parity with God for himself, discussed later as *shirk*. But the magicians he brings to counter God's miracles, wrought at Moses's hands, are themselves converted and die as martyrs for their faith. In Muslim tradition,

Pharaoh's wife, too, accepts faith in God and dies a martyr. As for Pharaoh, his declaration of faith in 'the God of the children of Israel', coming at the point of death by drowning, is too late to save him (see Q. 10:90).

Muslims believe that every major prophet is supported by evidentiary miracles in his claim to be a prophet sent by God. These miracles must suit the prophet's mission as well as the condition of his people. The miracles of Moses, for instance, are meant to affirm God's power and wisdom against the magic and might of the Egyptians.

Jesus

Jesus is presented in the *Qur'ān* as a miracle in himself. His virgin birth, healing the sick, feeding the hungry, and even raising the dead are seen as life-giving miracles. They are meant to affirm God's creative and life-giving power against the denial by many Jews and non-Jews of his time of the resurrection and life to come. Furthermore, they are performed at a time when Greek medicine, science, and philosophy question the sovereignty, power, and wisdom of God as the sole creator and Lord of the universe. The miracles of Jesus therefore serve to assert the power of God over human science and wisdom.

The *Qur'ān* presents Jesus as a messenger of God to the children of Israel with the message: 'God is surely my Lord and your Lord. Worship him, therefore; this is the straight way' (Q. 3:51). For Muslims, particularly the mystics, Jesus is an example of a world-renouncing ascetic, a wandering prophet with stern piety but deep compassion for the poor, suffering, and oppressed, whoever they may be. He has no home or possessions; 'his mount was his two feet and his servant his two hands.'

Jesus is a great prophet for Muslims, but the *Qur'ān* categorically denies his divinity and divine sonship (see Q. 5:116, 19:34–5, and 5:17 and 72). His role extends far beyond his earthly existence as a prophet into sacred history. Jesus, the *Qur'ān* insists, did not die, but was lifted up by God to heaven (Q. 4:157–8). He is to return at the end of time as 'a sign of the knowledge of the Hour [that is, the Day of Resurrection]' (Q. 43:61). He shall kill the anti-Christ (al-Dajjāl, the deceiver), and establish true Islam on earth.

Each prophet must, in accordance with God's covenant with all prophets, prepare for and support the prophet to come after him. Thus Jesus in the *Qur'ān* announces the coming of Muḥammad, saying, 'O children of Israel, I am the messenger of God to you, confirming the Torah that was before me, and announcing a messenger who shall come after me whose name is Aḥmad' (Q. 61:6).

Muḥammad

Muḥammad is presented in Muslim tradition as 'the Prophet of the end of time'. He is 'the seal of the prophets', and the sacred book he receives directly from God, the *Qur'ān*, is the final revelation. His way or life-example (*sunnah*) provides for

Muslims the prophetic model that guides history till its final consummation in the Day of Judgement. Likewise, the *Qur'ān* is considered to be God's final revelation for humanity, confirming and supplanting all previous revelations (see Q. 5:48).

Muslims accord Muḥammad the highest spiritual prominence. In Makkah, he experiences a night-time journey to Jerusalem. This interpretation is based on a Qur'anic passage: 'Glory be to him who carried his servant by night from the Holy Mosque to the Further Mosque, the precincts of which we have blessed, that we might show him some of our signs' (Q. 17:1). The Prophet also experiences a brief journey to heaven. Termed *mi'rāj* ('ladder'), it parallels the heavenly ascents of prophetic figures described in visionary terms in Hellenistic and rabbinic Jewish religious literature.

In the context of Muslim piety, respect for Muḥammad is shown through the expression 'peace [and blessings of God] be [up]on him', spoken immediately after mention of his name or title. In writing, the formula is often abbreviated as p.b.o.h. or p.b.u.h. When the prophets as a group culminating in Muḥammad are mentioned, the corresponding expression is p.b.o.t.a., 'peace be on them all'. The gesture some Christians make, crossing themselves on mentioning the name of Jesus, is a usage in some ways parallel to the verbal formula used by devout Muslims.

The *Qur'ān*

The *Qur'ān* comes to the prophet Muḥammad as revelation over a period of twenty-two years. The moments of revelation are for him both a spiritual and a physical experience. During such moments, he falls into a trancelike state, the effects of which are visibly manifest in his behaviour. According to both the *Qur'ān* and Muslim tradition, the angel Gabriel appears to him, often in human guise, transmitting words that come to constitute the verses and *sūrahs* (chapters) of the *Qur'ān*. At times, it is said, the Prophet senses in his ears sounds like the ringing of a bell. These sounds he then apprehends as direct revelations from God and conveys to the people.

The Prophet's role as transmitter of revelation is reflected in the *Qur'ān*'s characteristic use of pronouns. Often, 'We' (that is, God) address 'you' (that is, the Prophet) to 'say' such-and-such (that is, to declare the message to the people).

The first revelation to Muḥammad, as we have mentioned in recounting his life, is a command to 'recite' or 'read' (*iqra'*). The term *qur'ān* is derived from the same triliteral root *q–r–'*, meaning 'to read' or 'recite'. The *Qur'ān* is, accordingly, meant to be recited or chanted aloud, rather than to be perused or read to oneself silently.

In size, the *Qur'ān* is nearly as long as the New Testament. Muslims understand it as revealed (literally, 'sent down') to Muḥammad in separate portions.

A DESCRIPTION OF THE DAY OF JUDGEMENT

[Qur'ān, sūrah 99, al-Zalzalah *(The Earthquake) in its entirety*.]

When the earth shall be shaken with a great quake, and the earth yields up its burdens, and man exclaims, 'What has happened to it!' On that day it shall recount its tidings—as your Lord had inspired it.

Whoever does an atom's weight of good shall then see it, and whoever does an atom's weight of evil shall then see it.

These can vary in length and content from one or a few verses, dealing with one or several unrelated themes or ideas, to a coherent and fairly lengthy *sūrah*.

Muḥammad began his prophetic mission within the framework of the *Qur'ān*. For twelve years in Makkah he recited the *Qur'ān*, and through it, he preached faith in the One God, Allāh, and warned his recalcitrant people of an impending divine chastisement if they would not mend their immoral and callous ways.

The early Makkan *sūrahs* are generally brief admonitions couched in terse and powerful verses. The later ones, in contrast, are didactic narratives or illustrative tales of earlier prophets and their communities. Through stories, parables, and exhortations, the *Qur'ān* aims at creating a society united by faith, an *ummah* enjoining good conduct and dissuading people from evil and indecent behaviour.

This aim continues in Madīnah, where following the *hijrah* the Prophet was not the powerless preacher of Makkah, but a lawgiver and head of a new Islamic commonwealth. The *sūrahs* revealed in Madīnah are fewer in number but longer, presenting didactic arguments, discourses, and legal pronouncements. This change of idiom, however, is not seen as affecting the essential message of the *Qur'ān*.

In Madīnah, moreover, the *Qur'ān* became intimately tied to the life of the community. Thus often verses are revealed in answer to a question or special situation touching the life of the people. Theological and social issues involving the 'People of the Book', that is, the Jews and Christians as scripture-using communities, are hotly argued, and relations between the Muslim community and members of these two communities are regulated.

The Status of the *Qur'ān*

As revelations came to the Prophet, he reportedly dictated them immediately to one of a group of men known as 'the scribes of revelation'. This he did because, according to the *Qur'ān* and Muslim tradition, he is an unlettered prophet, that is, he can neither read nor write. For Muslims this circumstance is an incontro-

ABRAHAM'S ICONOCLASM IN FIDELITY TO THE ONE GOD

[Qur'ān, sūrah 21, al-Anbiyā' *(The Prophets), verses 51–73.*]

When he said to his father and his people, 'What are these idols that you so fervently worship?' they said, 'We found our fathers worshipping them.'

He said, 'Both you and your fathers are in manifest error.' They said, 'Have you come to us with the truth, or are you one of those who jest?'

He said, 'Your Lord is indeed the Lord of the heavens and the earth, for he originated them; and to this I am one of those who bear witness. By God, I shall confound your idols as soon as you turn your backs.'

He thus destroyed them utterly except for the chief one, so that the people might turn to it [for petition].

They said, 'Who did this to our gods? He is surely a wrongdoer.'

Some said, 'We heard a youth called Abraham speaking of them.'

Others said, 'Bring him here in the sight of the people, so that they may all witness.'

They said, 'Did you do this to our gods, O Abraham?'

He said, 'No, it was their chief who did it. Question them—if they could speak.'

The people then turned on one another, saying, 'Indeed you are the wrongdoers!' Then they bowed their heads in humiliation, saying, 'You know well, [O Abraham], that these do not speak.'

He [Abraham] said, 'Would you then worship instead of God a thing that can do you neither good nor harm? Fie on you and on what you worship instead of God; do you not reason?'

They said, 'Burn him and stand up for your gods, if you would do anything.'

We [God] said, 'O fire, be coolness and peace for Abraham!'

They wished evil for him, but We turned them into utter losers. And We delivered him and Lot to a land that We blessed for all beings. We also granted him Isaac and Jacob as added favour, and We made them both righteous. We made them all leaders guiding others by our command. We inspired them to do good deeds, perform regular worship, and give the obligatory alms; and they were true worshippers of Us alone.

vertible proof that the words of the *Qur'ān* conveyed by Muḥammad to his people are not his own but revealed to him by God. It also means that his mind is not contaminated with human wisdom. Rather, it is seen as a pure receptacle for the divine Word, in the same way that Mary's virginity means for Christians that her body is a pure vessel fit to receive Christ as the Word of God.

Muslims believe that the *Qur'ān* is an immutable heavenly book, preserved by God in the 'mother of the Book' or source of all revelation. In fact, there is an

ON THE STATUS OF THE QUR'ĀN AS REVELATION

[Qur'ān, sūrah 46, al-Aḥqāf (*The Sand Dunes*), verses 7–12.]

When Our revelations are recited to them, clear as they are, the unbelievers say: 'This is plain sorcery.' Such is their description of the truth when it is declared to them.

Do they say: 'He has invented it [the *Qur'ān*] himself'?

Say: 'If I have indeed invented it, then there is nothing you can do to protect me from the wrath of God. He well knows what you say about it. Sufficient is he as a witness between me and you. He is the Benignant One, the Merciful.'

Say: 'I am no prodigy among the apostles; nor do I know what will be done with me or you. I follow only what is revealed to me, and my only duty is to give plain warning.'

... Since they reject its guidance, they say: 'This is an ancient falsehood.'

Yet before it the Book of Moses was revealed, a guide and a blessing to all men. This Book confirms it. It is revealed in the Arabic tongue, to forewarn the wrongdoers and to give good tidings to the righteous (Dawood 1990:502).

parallel to Christ + the Qur'āni

interesting theological parallel between Christ and the *Qur'ān*. Christ is for Christians the eternal Word of God, made incarnate at a certain moment in time, as stated in the prologue to John's gospel. For Muslims, the *Qur'ān* is quite an accurate recitation, within earthly history, of the eternal word of God: 'This surely is a glorious *Qur'ān*, preserved in a well-guarded Tablet' (Q. 85:21–2).

Muslims understand the *Qur'ān* to be revealed specifically in the Arabic language. Throughout the Islamic world, where Muslim speakers of other languages significantly outnumber speakers of Arabic, recitation of it remains in Arabic. A rendering into another language is considered an interpretation, not the *Qur'ān* itself.

The language of the *Qur'ān* came to set the standard for Arabic literary expression, and its powerful and elegant words and phrases have permeated all other Islamic languages. The words of the *Qur'ān* are recited in a child's ear at birth for a blessing. They are recited to bless and seal a marriage contract, a business deal, to celebrate a successful venture, or to express sorrow and solace in times of misfortune.

Throughout the Muslim world, the *Qur'ān* is recited on most special public occasions and daily on radio and television. Qur'anic recitation is an art of great virtuosity and hypnotic power. Through the art of calligraphy, the words of the *Qur'ān* have been a central motif in Islamic art, and are used to decorate Muslim homes, mosques, and public buildings.

For private devotional recitation in the course of a month, the *Qur'ān* has been divided into thirty parts of equal length. Particularly important is the recitation during the fasting month of Ramaḍān. A child's completion of a full recitation of the *Qur'ān* is considered an act of great merit and an occasion of celebration for the entire family.

The body of tradition coming orally from the Prophet describes the *Qur'ān* as a rope or link between heaven and earth, between God and the pious. With its words they pray to God, and its recitation accompanies them to their final resting-place. On the Day of Judgement, the *Qur'ān* is to intercede with God on behalf of those who recite it and live by its precepts in the world, and is to condemn those who neglect it. Tradition asserts that a person's station in paradise will be determined by the number of verses of the *Qur'ān* he or she has memorized in this life.

The *sunnah* of the Prophet

For the early Muslims, obedience to the Prophet's example was equal to obedience to God. This is because they understood whatever he said or did to be on behalf of God and by divine command. Muḥammad, Muslims believe, could not err, as all prophets are protected by God from sin and error. With regard to Muḥammad in particular, the *Qur'ān* asserts, 'Your companion did not go astray, nor did he err. He speaks not out of capricious desire; rather it is a revelation revealed to him' (Q. 53:2–4).

The Prophet reportedly declared, 'I was given the *Qur'ān* and its equivalent [i.e., the *sunnah*] along with it.' Hence, Muslims believe, the Prophet's actions and sayings are divinely inspired. The *Qur'ān* asserts that God has sent his Messenger with 'the Book and wisdom' (see Q. 62:2). Al-Shāfi'ī, the architect of Islamic jurisprudence and founder of one of the four Sunnī legal schools, argued that 'the Book' is the *Qur'ān* and 'the wisdom' is the *sunnah*. His view has been generally accepted by Muslims.

The Prophet's *sunnah* includes his actions and his tacit consent. His acts are reported in anecdotes of situations or events to which he reacted or in which he participated. In situations where the Prophet neither approved nor objected, his silence is taken to signify approval. Thus the *sunnah* of consent became a normative source in the development of Islamic law.

Beside the *sunnah* of action and the *sunnah* of consent, there is the *sunnah* of speech. Accounts that report the Prophet's sayings, termed *ḥadīth*, must go back to an eyewitness of the event. The *ḥadīth* literature is often called 'tradition' in English, in a quite specific sense. Islamic 'tradition' (or 'Prophetic tradition') is the body of sayings traced to the prophet Muḥammad through chains of oral

Hadith

transmission. *Ḥadīth* is the most important of the three elements of *sunnah*, since it most directly expresses the Prophet's opinions or judgements regarding the community's practice.

Compiling the *Qur'ān*

When the Prophet died in 632, ten years after the *hijrah* from Makkah to Madīnah, the *Qur'ān* was reportedly scattered in fragments and partial private collections, written on stones, bones, palm leaves, and animal parchment. Private collections varied in length, form, and contents.

There apparently existed minor but often significant variations as well in the reading of certain words or phrases. These variant readings persisted and became identified with specific *Qur'ān* readers of the first and later generations of Muslim scholars. As Islam spread outside Arabia, major disagreements in reading and actual grammatical mistakes by reciters pointed up the need for a standard or official collection to be used throughout the Islamic domains.

This task may have been initiated by Abū Bakr, the first caliph or successor of the Prophet as the head of the Muslim community. Abū Bakr is said to have feared the loss or distortion of the orally transmitted text through the death of a large number of *Qur'ān* reciters in the so-called wars of apostasy, discussed later.

The process of producing an official and universally recognized text of the *Qur'ān* was completed under the aegis of the third caliph 'Uthman b. 'Affān (r. 644–56), within twenty years of the Prophet's death. Since that time, the *Qur'ān* has remained unchanged, except for adding vowel diacritics and minor adjustments in the ordering of certain verses. It was copied in manuscript until modern times, when the Royal Egyptian edition produced in the 1930s became the most widely accepted printed text.

As an earthly book, the *Qur'ān* has been shaped by Muslim history as well as shaping it. Tradition asserts that while the verses of each individual *sūrah* were arranged by the Prophet at Gabriel's instruction, the order of the *sūrahs* in relation one to another—roughly in decreasing order of length—was fixed by the committee that 'Uthmān appointed to compile an official recension of the *Qur'ān*. The 114 *sūrahs* are separated by the invocation that precedes each, *bism-illāhi ar-raḥmān ar-raḥīm* ('in the name of God, the All-merciful, the Compassionate'). The ninth *sūrah*, which lacks this invocation, is thought by commentators to be a continuation of the eighth.

As noted, the original compilers' arrangement of the *sūrahs* of the *Qur'ān* was by length; after the first *sūrah*, the 'opening' (*al-Fātiḥah*), they generally placed the longer *sūrahs* first. This means that the shortest *sūrahs*, which were earliest but whose terse poetic form probably sustained their oral transmission and memorization, came at the end. This arrangement made it impossible to determine with certainty the chronology of the recitation of the *Qur'ān*.

In outward form and structure, the *Qur'ān* does not present a unified and coherent book with beginning, middle, and end. Rather, it reflects a gradual and often circumstantial process of accumulation. It is neither a story with a well-defined and developed plot, nor a well-argued philosophical or theological treatise. Behind this apparent disunity and incoherence, however, there is a clearly discernible unity of message, purpose, and worldview.

Commentary or *tafsīr*

The *Qur'ān*, expressing a self-consciousness about its own status, urges Muslims to ponder its verses to discern its divine authorship and inner unity (see *Q*. 4:82, 47:24, and 38:29). Through the years, the Muslim community has dedicated some of its best minds to the task of understanding and interpreting the *Qur'ān*. The rich accumulation of exegetical literature begins in the eighth century CE and continues to the present.

The term *tafsīr*, for Islamic commentary, means 'unveiling', or elucidating the meaning of a text. The primary sources for this science are the *Qur'ān* itself, Prophetic *ḥadīth* or tradition, and opinions of the Prophet's Companions and their successors. *Tafsīr*, like the *Qur'ān* and the *ḥadīth*, was an orally transmitted legacy. In theory, it was always based on the pronouncements and opinions of the first generation of Islam.

By the tenth century, interpretation of the *Qur'an* was developed into a science with a number of ancillary fields of study. These include the grammatical and general linguistic structure of the *Qur'ān*, the meaning or purport of its metaphors and parables, as well as the historical and hagiographical contexts of its stories.

In fact, every legal or theological school, religious trend, or political movement in Muslim history has sought to find in the *Qur'ān* its primary support and justification. The result has been a wide exegetical diversity reflecting the historical development of the Islamic tradition, its sects and legal schools, mystical and philosophical movements, as well as its hagiography and piety.

The *Qur'ān* served as a practical moral and legislative guide for the Prophet and his nascent community. It has in the centuries since been the community's ideal constitution, a vital and unifying force across a diversifying tradition. As the primary source of Islamic faith and morality, law and piety, 'It is indeed a noble *Qur'ān* in a treasured Book. None but the pure shall touch it' (*Q*. 56:78–9).

The Concept of God

The *Qur'ān* presents its view of God in direct and unambiguous declarations of faith in the One and only God, creator, sustainer, judge, and sovereign Lord over all his creation. The *sūrah* known as 'the *Sūrah* of Sincere Faith (*ikhlāṣ*)' or 'the

Sūrah of Divine Oneness (*tawḥīd*)' is regarded by Muslims as the clearest expression of their faith: 'Say: God, He is One [*aḥad*]. God is the eternal refuge [*ṣamad*]. He neither begets, nor was he begotten. Nor is there any one equal to him' (*Q*. 112).

This *sūrah* affirms God's absolute transcendence as one and unequalled. It affirms his dependability; *ṣamad* means solid, like an immovable rock. And it affirms his eternity and immutability by asserting that he neither begets nor was begotten; for birth implies change and multiplicity, and God as merciful creator and sustainer is above such creaturely phenomena. The *sūrah* rejects the concept of God as father of any creature; such would compromise his absolute uniqueness, transcendence, and sovereignty.

Like Judaism and Christianity, Islam affirms that God is a moral and jealous God who abhors sin and wickedness and tolerates no other gods beside himself. For Islam it is a sin, called *shirk* ('associating'), to associate any other being with God, to ascribe divinity to any but God alone.

'Allāh' is not the name of a particular deity but the Arabic word for God, 'the Lord of all beings' (*Q*. 1:2), who demands faith and worship of all his rational creatures. Moreover, the term Allāh for God is used by Arab Christians and Jews, and was also used by the pagan Arabs before Islam. It is misleading therefore to use the word Allāh to speak of God in any language other than Arabic.

Islamic theology holds that in his essence God is unknowable, inconceivable, and above all categories of time and space, form and number. Materiality and temporality cannot be attributed to him. Nor, properly speaking, can masculinity or femininity, although God is referred to in the *Qur'ān* and throughout Islamic literature by pronouns, verbs, and adjectives that are masculine in form.

God is known through attributes called in the *Qur'ān* his 'most beautiful names', often also translated 'wonderful names'. These divine attributes are manifested in the creation in power and mercy, life and knowledge, might and wisdom. The *Qur'ān* declares:

> He is God other than whom there is no god, knower of the unknown and the visible. He is the All-merciful, the Compassionate. He is God other than whom there is no god, the King, the Holy One, Peace, the Faithful, the Guardian, the Majestic, the Compeller, the Lofty One (*Q*. 59:22–3).

The three monotheistic religious traditions of Middle Eastern origin—Judaism, Christianity, and Islam—claim firm roots in history. History, as these traditions view it, begins with the creation of all things by God, and will end with the Day of Judgement. In between, on the stage of history, God and humankind act out a great drama. This drama, of good and evil, salvation and damnation, will culminate in the reward of everlasting bliss for the righteous and eternal punishment for the wicked.

The human response to God, expressed in ritual, moral, and social obligations, is both personal and communal. The community collectively, as well as each individual, is rewarded or punished for good or evil conduct in this world or the hereafter. The *Qur'ān* conceives of all orders of creation as communities similar to those of humankind: 'There is not a beast in the earth, nor a bird that flies with its two wings, but that they are communities like you' (*Q.* 6:38). Animals then, like people and *jinn* or spirits, will be assembled on the Day of Judgement, as the vivid description in *Q.* 81:1–14 implies.

FAITH AND ACTION

Righteousness as it is expressed in the *Qur'ān* (e.g., *Q.* 2:177) has several components. It includes faith in God, his angels, Books, prophets, and the last day. It includes good works: a person should give of his or her wealth, however cherished it may be, to the orphans and needy or for the ransoming of slaves and war captives. It includes patience and steadfastness in times of misfortune or hardship and war. And it includes the integrity of one's motives, requiring honesty in the fulfilment of one's covenant with others.

Because all men and women belong ultimately to one humanity, they are all equal before God, regardless of race, colour, or social status. They may excel one another as individuals and groups only in righteousness and good works. The *Qur'ān* asserts, 'Humankind, We have created you all of one male and one female and made you different peoples and tribes in order that you may know one another. Surely, the noblest of you in God's sight is he who fears God most' (*Q.* 49:13).

The *Qur'ān*, particularly in the Madīnan revelations, frequently addresses the Muslims with the words 'O you who have faith and perform good deeds'. The Arabic word *īmān* means faith, trust, and a personal sense of safety and well-being in God's providential care, mercy, and justice. On this level of inner personal commitment, *īmān* is synonymous with *islām*, meaning the total surrender of the human will and destiny to the will of God. Personal faith must be manifested in individual moral conduct and concrete civic responsibility.

The opposite of *īmān* is *kufr*, or rejection of faith. Faith is to know the truth and assent to it in the heart, profess it with the tongue, and manifest it in concrete acts of charity and almsgiving. *Kufr*, on the other hand, is to know the truth but wilfully deny or obscure it by acts of rebellion against the law of God. The word *kufr* literally means 'to cover up, deny, or obscure'.

The *Qur'ān* further makes an important distinction between Islam and faith. Outwardly, Islam is a religious, social, and legal institution, whose members constitute the worldwide Muslim *ummah* or community. *Īmān*, faith, is an inner conviction whose sincerity or insincerity God alone can judge, a commitment to a way of life in the worship of God and in moral relations with other persons.

In Prophetic traditions, Islam, as a way of life and worship, is defined as acts of worship (*ʿibādāt*) and human interrelations or transactions (*muʿāmalāt*). Thus transactions such as buying and selling or establishing any agreement or pact with others, as well as family, social, and international relations, should be legislated and conducted in accordance with the moral dictates of faith. Faith, as a comprehensive framework of worship and moral conduct, is explicitly depicted in the following answer the Prophet is said to have given to the question 'What is faith?': 'Faith is seventy-odd branches, the highest of which is to say "There is no god except God" and the lowest is to remove a harmful object from the road.'

Above Islam and *īmān* stands *iḥsān* (doing good). On the level of human interrelations, *iḥsān* is a concrete manifestation of both Islam and *īmān*. On the level of the personal relationship of the man and woman of faith with God, *iḥsān* constitutes the highest form of worship. According to the Prophetic tradition defining *īmān* just cited, '*Iḥsān* is to worship God as though you see him, for if you do not see him, he sees you.'

Not every Muslim, then, is a man or woman of faith (*mu'min*), but every person of faith is considered a Muslim. Furthermore, a Muslim who believes in all the principles of Islam may not necessarily be a righteous person or doer of good (*muḥsin*, a doer of *iḥsān*), but a truly good and righteous person is counted as both a Muslim and a true person of faith.

The Five Pillars of Islam

Individual faith and institutional Islam converge in the worship of God and service to others. As both Muslim and non-Muslim scholars have observed, Islam is more concerned with orthopraxy than orthodoxy. A well-attested Prophetic tradition characterizes Islam as built upon five 'pillars'. Except for the first, the *shahādah*, they are personal and communal rites of worship. Islam is:

- to declare, or bear witness, that there is no god except God, and that Muḥammad is the Messenger of God
- to establish regular worship
- to pay the *zakāt* alms
- to observe the fast of Ramaḍān
- to perform the *ḥajj* pilgrimage

The Five Pillars are the foundations upon which Islam as a religious system of faith and social responsibility, worship, and piety rests. All rational creatures—the angels, humankind, and *jinn*—are to worship God and serve him. Acts of worship (*'ibādāt*) are obligatory duties (*farā'iḍ*) incumbent on all Muslims. The regular performance of these obligations in sincere faith and obedience to God assures the pious of salvation and the bliss of paradise on the Day of Resurrection. Neglecting them is an act of rebellion against God and is therefore a cause for eternal perdition.

The Five Pillars of Islam are not mere obligations whose efficacy and meaning depend on mechanical observance and superficial understanding. Rather, they are to be interiorized and observed as an expression of personal faith and piety. Thus each of the Five Pillars has an outer and public obligatory dimension and an inner and private voluntary dimension.

Bearing Witness

The first of the pillars is the *shahādah*: 'I bear witness that there is no god except God, and I bear witness that Muḥammad is the messenger [*rasūl*] of God.' It consists of two declarations. The first, affirming the oneness of God, expresses the universal and primordial state of faith in which every child is born. The Prophet is said to have declared, 'Every child is born in this original state of faith [*fiṭrah*]; then his parents turn him into a Jew, Christian or Zoroastrian, and if they are Muslims, into a Muslim.'

It seems that initially only the first declaration of the *shahādah* was required of non-Muslims to be admitted into the Muslim *ummah*, or at least to be granted the legal status of a protected people: Jews, Christians, and other scriptural communities or 'People of the Book'. This conclusion is supported by another widely accepted tradition, in which the Prophet says:

> I have been commanded to wage war against people until they say 'There is no god except God.' When they say this, they protect from me their lives and their possessions, except what is required of them [as the *zakāt* alms], and their final reckoning is with God.

The second declaration, affirming the apostleship of Muḥammad, signifies a person's acceptance of the truth of Muḥammad's claim to prophethood, and hence the truth of his message. It is the assertion of a person's Islamic identity and his or her commitment to live by the law (*sharī'ah*) that Muslims believe Muḥammad brought from God.

Outwardly, the *shahādah* legally safeguards a person's rights as a member of the Muslim community. Inwardly, however, it is meaningless unless it becomes a true expression of personal faith (*īmān*) and righteous living (*iḥsān*). Without this inner dimension of the *shahādah*, Islam loses its meaning as a faith tradition.

THE ISLAMIC VIRTUE OF PATIENCE

[A ḥadīth traced by Ibn Mājah to 'Ā'ishah, quoted in the prayer manual al-Kalim al-ṭayyib *(The Good Word) by Taqī al-Dīn Abū al-'Abbās of Damascus.]*

If he saw what pleased him he said: 'Praise be to God whose grace brings all goodness to perfection.' If he saw what he disliked he said, 'Praise be to God in any case' (Padwick 1961:79).

[An account from al-Silsilah al-dhahabīyah *(The Golden Chain), by Muḥammad ibn Ḥasan Ẓāfir al-Madanī.]*

Shaqīq al-Balkhī asked Ja'far ibn Muḥammad al-Bāqir about generosity. And Ja'far said, 'What do you think it is?' He replied, 'Generosity is to give thanks when we receive gifts and to endure patiently the withholding of them.' Ja'far replied, 'Our dogs in Medina do as much as that.' Then Shaqīq said, 'O son of the daughter of the Prophet of God, what is generous behaviour with you?' He said, 'If gifts are bestowed on us we accept them and if they are withheld from us we give thanks' (Padwick 1961:79).

Prayer

The second pillar is the obligatory prayers (*ṣalāt*). These are distinguished from other devotional acts, such as meditations and personal supplicatory prayers, for while voluntary devotions may be offered at any time, *ṣalāt* must be performed five times in a day and night: at dawn, noon, mid-afternoon, sunset, and after dark. Among the rituals of Islam, the *ṣalāt* prayers were the first to be instituted.

The *ṣalāt* prayers must always be preceded by ritual washing. *Wuḍū'* ('making pure or radiant') or partial washing involves washing the face, rinsing the mouth and nostrils, washing the hands and forearms to the elbows, passing one's wet hands over the head and feet, or washing the feet to the two heels. If water is unavailable or too scarce, then clean sand may be used. *Ghusl* (meaning 'washing of the entire body') is used to remove impurities viewed as major, such as those caused by sexual relations, menstruation, or direct contact with blood or a dead body.

Five times a day, on radio and television, loudspeakers, and from high minarets (the towers that flank mosques), a *mu'adhdhin* chants in a melodious voice the call to prayer (*adhān*) inviting the faithful to pray together in a mosque or at home. But whether a Muslim prays alone or behind a prayer leader (*imām*) in congregation, he or she is always conscious of countless other men and women engaged in the same act of worship. Each phrase of the following call to prayer is repeated at least two times for greater effect and emphasis:

Taṣlīyah, the Calling Down of Divine Blessing on the Prophet Muḥammad

[The Qur'ān:*]*

Surely God and His angels shower blessings on the Prophet. O you who have faith, bless him and salute him with the great salutation of peace.

[The formula is:]

May God call down blessing on our Lord Muḥammad and on the family of our Lord Muḥammad and greet them with peace.

[A ḥadīth *reports (Muḥāmmad 'Uthmān al-Mirghanī,* Majmū' mushtamil 'ala fatḥ al-Rasūl.*]*

Ubayy b. Ka'b said, 'O Apostle of God, many a time do I call down blessings on you for love of you. How much of my prayer shall I devote to you?' He said, 'What you will.' Ubayy said, 'A quarter?' He said, 'What you will, but if you do more it will be for your good.' He said, 'Half?' The Prophet said, 'What you will, but if you do more it will be well for you.' He said, 'Two-thirds?' The Prophet said, 'What you will, but if you do more it will be for your good.' Then Ubayy said, 'I will devote my whole prayer to you.' The Prophet replied, 'Then your anxieties will be met and your sins forgiven' (Padwick 1961:143–4).

[Prayer addressed to Muḥammad as mediator and intercessor with God (in Aḥmad Ḍiyā' al-Dīn, Majmū'at al-aḥzāb.*]*

O Thou who art transfigured in radiance, have mercy on my abasement. O Thou who are exalted, set to rights my state. O Apostle of God, help! and supply of succour! O Beloved of God, on thee is reliance. O Prophet of God, be to us a mediator. Thou, by God, art an intercessor who meets with no refusal.

O my lord, O apostle of God, O my support, my refuge, my apostle, thou sufficest me. I have placed in the praise of the apostle of God my confidence, for he, when I seek for sufficiency, suffices me (Padwick 1961:143–4).

> God is most great. I bear witness that there is no god except God, and I bear witness that Muḥammad is the Messenger of God. Hasten [all of you Muslims] to the prayers! Hasten to success or prosperity!
> [Shī'ī Muslims add:] Hasten to the best action! God is most great. There is no god except God.

The *ṣalāt* prayers begin with the proclamation of consecration (*takbīrat al-iḥrām*), 'God is most great.' The proclamation signifies a person's total separation from the world and standing before God, as though in the balance for the last judgement. The prayers consist of cycles or units called *rak'ahs*, with bowing, kneeling, and prostration. The dawn prayers consist of two cycles, the noon and mid-afternoon of four each, the sunset prayer of three, and the night prayers of four cycles.

The *ṣalāt* prayers are largely liturgical. Apart from some moments of contemplation and personal supplication at the end of the prayers, the obligatory prayers are fixed formulas repeated in every *ṣalāt* worship. They consist largely of the opening *sūrah* and other passages of the *Qur'ān*.

The first or opening *sūrah* (*al-Fātiḥah*) of the *Qur'ān* plays a role in some ways similar to that of the Lord's Prayer for Christians. It is repeated in every *rak'ah*, at least seventeen times in a day and night. The *Fātiḥah* reads as follows:

> In the name of God, the All-merciful, the Compassionate:
>
> Praise be to God, the All-merciful, the Compassionate, King of the Day of Judgement. You alone do we worship, and to you alone do we turn for help. Guide us to the straight way, the way of those upon whom you have bestowed your grace, not those who have incurred your wrath, nor those who have gone astray (*Q*. 1:1–7).

Unlike Judaism and Christianity, Islam has no Sabbath specified for rest. Friday, named the day of *jum'ah* ('assembly'), is designated as a day of gathering for congregational prayers. The *Qur'ān* enjoins upon all Muslims: 'O you who have faith, when the call to prayer is raised on Friday [noon], leave off all manners of trade and hasten to the remembrance of God ... But when the prayer is accomplished, disperse in the land and seek God's bounty' (*Q*. 62:9–10). The Friday prayers consist of two short sermons, meant to substitute for the first two *rak'ahs* of the noon prayers, followed by two *rak'ahs*. Friday sermons usually deal with religious, moral, and political issues. They have often served as a platform to launch social, political, and military activities and movements, particularly in today's troubled Muslim world.

The Islamic place of worship is called *masjid* ('place of prostration in prayer') or *jāmi'* (literally, 'gatherer'). The English word 'mosque' comes from pronunciation of the Arabic word *masjid* with a hard g instead of *j*.

Other congregational prayers are those performed on the first days of the two major festivals, 'Īd al-Fiṭr and 'Īd al-Aḍḥā, at the end of Ramaḍān and the *ḥajj* pilgrimage respectively. Where possible, these prayers are held in the open, so as to allow for the largest possible number of participants.

The Prophet's birthday is another occasion when in many Muslim countries people come together for prayers in the mosque, to listen to *Qur'ān* recitations, and religious and political speeches extolling the Prophet and calling upon the Muslim community and its leaders to emulate his example.

On a journey, or in a state of fear in battle, prayers may be shortened from four to two *rak'ahs*. If a person is sick, unable to perform all the genuflections and prostrations of the *ṣalāt* prayers, he or she may pray in any position, sitting or lying down. Women in menstruation are exempt from prayers until they are cleansed. Children below the age of reason and persons suffering from mental illness, senility, or dementia are likewise excused.

The inner dimension of the obligatory five daily prayers is the extradevotional prayers called *nawāfil*. These devotional prayers are offered by pious Muslims in the quiet of the night and after the obligatory prayers as means for the individual woman and man of faith to draw near to God.

Faithful Muslims view all things, good or evil, as contingent on God's will. Hence many do not state a future commitment or prediction without prefacing it with the phrase *in-shā' Allāh*, 'if God wills'. The hope is that one's plan of action will be accepted by God and guided to completion.

Almsgiving

The close relationship between worship of God and service to the poor and needy is instituted in the third pillar of Islam, namely, paying the *zakāt* alms. The *Qur'ān* frequently couples the observance of regular worship with almsgiving (see Q. 2:43, 5:55, and 9:71). The root meaning of the word *zakāt* is 'to purify or increase'. Offering alms purifies a person from greed and attachment to material possessions. Furthermore, wealth spent in the *zakāt* alms and other voluntary gifts to the poor and needy assures the giver of blessing and increase in this world and rich rewards in the hereafter.

Zakāt is an obligatory welfare tax to be paid annually by all adult Muslims on all surplus earnings. The *zakāt* tax consists of 2.5 per cent of the value of all accumulated wealth. This includes savings earned through trade or any financial gain, livestock, agricultural produce, real estate, or any other revenues.

During the early centuries of Islam, when the community was cohesively controlled by a central authority, the *zakāt* revenues were kept in a central treasury and disbursed for public educational and civic projects, care for the orphans and needy, and the ransoming of Muslim war captives. Now that the Muslim world is divided into so many independent nation-states, most of which have adopted some form of modern Western taxation, the *zakāt* obligation has become a largely voluntary affair that many ignore and others dispense through private religious and philanthropic organizations.

The devotional aspect of the *zakāt* alms is the voluntary almsgiving (*ṣadaqah*). The *Qur'ān* calls *ṣadaqah* a loan given to God, which he will repay in manifold measure on the Day of Resurrection (Q. 57:11). Although charity must begin at home, that is, with one's nearest blood relatives, *ṣadaqah* is not bound by any considerations of race, colour, or creed. It must be given to the needy and destitute, the orphan, the beggar and wayfarer, whoever they may be. Even the *zakāt* alms, when offered voluntarily for God's good pleasure, become *ṣadaqah*, an expression of a person's true righteousness.

Fasting During Ramaḍān

The fourth pillar of Islam is the fast of the month of Ramaḍān. Fasting is recognized in the *Qur'ān* as a universal form of worship, enjoined by all scriptures. The Prophet appears to have observed a variety of voluntary fasts in Makkah, which are still honoured by many pious Muslims. In Madīnah, the Prophet saw the Jewish community observing the fast of Yom Kippur, and enjoined it upon the Muslims as well.

In the second year of the *hijrah*, and after the Battle of Badr, which took place in Ramaḍān of that year, the fast of Ramaḍān was instituted. No doubt, the victory of Badr added greatly to the prestige and holiness of this month. While prayers and almsgiving are frequently enjoined by the *Qur'ān*, fasting during Ramaḍān is mandated in a single passage, which in part reads as follows:

> O you who have faith, fasting is ordained for you as it was ordained for those before you, that you may fear God ... Ramaḍān is the month in which the *Qur'ān* was sent down as a guidance to humankind, manifestations of guidance and the Criterion. Therefore whosoever among you witnesses the moon, let him fast [the month], but whosoever is sick or on a journey, an equal number of other days (Q. 2:183, 185).

This passage accords Ramaḍān the honour of being the month in which the revelation of the *Qur'ān* took place. This may be simply a reference to the beginning of revelation on Mount Ḥirā'. Tradition, however, goes far beyond this brief reference to insist that not only the *Qur'ān* but other scriptures—the Torah, *Psalms* (*zabūr*), and the Gospel (*injīl*)—were also revealed in Ramaḍān.

Ramaḍān is a month-long fast extending each day from daybreak till sundown. It is a complete abstention from food, drink, smoking, and sexual relations. The fast is broken at sunset, at the sound of a cannon and the call to prayer. A light meal is consumed also at the end of the night, just before dawn, after which the next day's fast continues till sunset.

In the course of elaborating the rules of fasting of Ramaḍān, the *Qur'ān* declares, 'God desires ease for you, not hardship' (Q. 2:185). Hence, the sick, travellers, children, and pregnant and menstruating women are exempted from the fast altogether, or until they are able to make up the missed days.

The Arabs before Islam observed a lunar calendar wherein the year consisted of 354 days, in contrast with the 365-day solar year. Therefore, as with the lunar calendar of the Jews (and parallel to others such as the Chinese), an intercalary month was added every three years to keep festivals and sacred months in their proper seasons. The *Qur'ān* abolishes this custom, however, allowing the fast of Ramaḍān, as well as all other religious festivals, to rotate throughout the year.

When Ramaḍān occurs in the summer, particularly in the hot countries of Asia and Africa, fasting can be a real hardship. But when it comes in winter, as in the 1990s in the Northern hemisphere, it can be relatively tolerable. Nonetheless, all work activities are sharply curtailed during Ramaḍān, and those who can afford it fast and sleep most of the day, and eat, drink, and engage in religious and social activities at night.

Ramaḍān ends with a happy festival called 'Īd al-Fiṭr, a three-day celebration of breaking the fast. During these days people exchange gifts and well-wishing visits. Children receive gifts and wear new bright-coloured clothes for the occasion. People visit the graves of loved ones, where special sweet dishes are distributed to the poor. Before the first breakfast after the long fast, the head of every family must give special alms for breaking the fast, called *zakāt al-fiṭr*, on behalf of every member of his household. Moreover, those exempted for reasons of chronic illness or old age must feed a poor person for every day missed.

The fast of Ramaḍān becomes not a mere ritual but a true act of worship when a person shares God's bounty with those who have no food with which to break their fast. True fasting is not only giving up the pleasures of food and drink, but also abstaining from slandering others and any idle talk, and turning one's heart and mind to God in devotional prayers and meditations.

Pilgrimage to Makkah

The *ḥajj* pilgrimage is the fifth pillar of Islam. According to the *Qur'ān*, Abraham institutes the pilgrimage to the Ka'bah at God's command after he and his son Ishmael are ordered to build it (see Q. 22:26–9 and 2:125–7). Although tradition carries the ritual into the sacred history of scripture back to Abraham, and even to Adam, it is certain that the pilgrimage was an ancient pagan rite observed by the polytheistic Arabs long before Islam.

Islam modified and reinterpreted this rite so as to fit it into the Islamic monotheistic faith and model of prophetic history. Thus most of its ritual elements are taken to re-enact the experiences of Abraham, whom the *Qur'ān* declares to be the father of prophets and the first true Muslim.

Before the pilgrims reach the sacred precincts of Makkah, they exchange their regular clothes for two pieces of white linen, symbolic of the shrouds in which people are wrapped for burial. With this act, they enter the state of consecration (*iḥrām*). They approach Makkah with the solemn proclamation: 'Here we come in answer to your call, O God, here we come! Here we come, for you have no partner, here we come! Indeed, all praise, dominion, and grace belong to you alone, here we come!'

Once in Makkah, the pilgrims begin with the lesser *ḥajj* (*'umrah*). It is performed in the precincts of the Great Mosque and includes the ritual of counterclockwise circumambulation (*ṭawāf*) of the Ka'bah and the running between the two hills of al-Ṣafā and al-Marwā. In the traditional narrative Hagar, Abraham's handmaid and mother of his son Ishmael, runs between these two hills in search of water for her dying child. After the seventh run, water gushes out by the child's feet, which Hagar contains with sand. The place, according to Islamic tradition, is the ancient well of Zamzam, meaning 'the contained water'. The water of Zamzam is regarded by Muslims as holy water, and pilgrims often bring back containers of it as blessed gifts for family and friends.

The *ḥajj* pilgrimage proper begins on the eighth of Dhū al-Ḥijjah, the twelfth month of the Islamic calendar, when throngs of pilgrims set out for 'Arafāt, a plain located about 20 km (13 mi.) east of Makkah. In accordance with the Prophet's practice (*sunnah*), many pilgrims spend the night at Minā, while others press on to 'Arafāt. 'Arafāt is a large plain on which stands the Mount of Mercy (Jabal al-Raḥmah), which is the goal of every pilgrim. As the sun passes the noon meridian, pilgrims gather for the standing (*wuqūf*) on the Mount of Mercy in 'Arafāt.

Standing on 'Arafāt is the central rite of the *ḥajj* pilgrimage. Men and women stand in solemn prayers and supplications till sunset, as though standing on the last day before God for judgement. This rite links the present moment to the sacred time, to the time when Adam and Eve stand on that plain after their expulsion from paradise. It recalls the time when Abraham and his son Ishmael perform the rite. According to Muslim tradition, they perform the first *ḥajj* pilgrimage.

It was on the occasion of the *wuqūf* at 'Arafāt that Muḥammad gave his farewell oration, affirming the brotherhood of all Muslims. Tradition also reports that on 'Arafāt occurred the final instance of revelation of the *Qur'ān*, with the verse representing the religion as complete: 'Today have I perfected your religion for you, bestowed fully my grace upon you, and accepted Islam as a religion for you' (*Q*. 5:3).

At sundown, the sombre scene of prayers and supplications abruptly changes, as the pilgrims pour forth from 'Arafāt to Muzdalifah. This sacred spot is located a short distance on the road back to Makkah. There the pilgrims observe the combined sunset and evening prayers and gather pebbles for the ritual lapidation at Minā the next day. The pouring forth (*ifāḍah*) from 'Arafāt to Muzdalifah, where pilgrims are enjoined 'to remember God at the sacred monument (*al-mash'ar al-ḥarām*)' (*Q*. 2:198), is an ancient rite given significance by Islam.

The tenth of Dhū al-Ḥijjah is the final day of the *ḥajj* season, and the first of the four-day festival of sacrifice ('Īd al-Aḍḥā). The day is spent at Minā, where the remaining pilgrimage rites are completed.

Tradition tells that on his way from ʿArafāt to Minā, Abraham is commanded by God to sacrifice to God that which is dearest to him, his son Ishmael. Satan whispers to him three times, tempting him to disobey God's command. Abraham's response is to hurl stones at Satan to drive him away. So at the spot called al-ʿAqabah, meaning the hard or steep road, a brick pillar has been erected to represent Satan. Pilgrims gather early in the morning to throw seven stones at the pillar, in emulation of Abraham. Three other pillars in Minā representing the three temptations are also stoned.

Following the ritual of stoning, the pilgrims offer a blood sacrifice—a lamb, goat, cow, or camel—to symbolize the paradisal victim with which God ransoms Abraham's son (Q. 27:107). After this, the pilgrims end the state of consecration, ritually clipping a minimum of three hairs from their heads, or shaving the head completely. The *ḥajj* ends with a final circumambulation of the Kaʿbah and the completion of the rites of the lesser *ḥajj* (*ʿumrah*) for those who have not done so.

Often pilgrims spend the four days of the festival of sacrifice in and around Makkah. They then visit the Prophet's tomb in Madīnah, and other sites associated with important events and personalities of early Islam. When possible, pilgrims also visit Jerusalem, Islam's third holy city, in observance of the traditions of the Prophet's spiritual journey there. Shīʿī Muslims visit the shrines of the *imāms*—descendants of the Prophet through his daughter Fāṭimah and cousin ʿAlī b. Abī Ṭālib—in Madīnah, Iraq, and Iran.

The *ḥajj* experience marks a new stage in the life of a Muslim. The *ḥajj* is regarded by Muslims as a form of resurrection or rebirth. Tradition asserts that a person returns from a sincerely performed *ḥajj* free from all sins, as on the day when he or she was born. Furthermore, a pilgrim is henceforth marked out, as it were, with the title *ḥājjī* before his or her name. It is therefore imperative for a *ḥājjī* to strive to maintain the purity and freedom from attachment to material and vain pleasures which he or she has attained through this experience. The voluntary aspect of the *ḥajj* obligation is the lesser *ḥajj* (*ʿumrah*), which may be performed at any time as an act of personal devotion.

Religious obligations are meant to discipline Muslims and test their commitment to fulfilling the demands of their faith. This is why prayers or fasts missed for a legitimate reason must be made up later. The sincerity and determination of a person in his or her effort to obey God's law will determine his or her state in the life to come. Since there is no outside agency of redemption in Islam comparable to what is offered in Christianity, the only means for a person to earn his or her salvation is to live a life of sincere faith and righteous action and hope in God's mercy.

The *Qur'ān* asserts, 'God shall not charge a soul except to its capacity' (Q. 2:286). Therefore, any obligation should be within a person's capacity to fulfil it. Otherwise, it would be an act of wrongdoing on God's part, which Muslims consider an impossibility. This principle is clearly articulated in the *Qur'ān* with regard to the *ḥajj* pilgrimage: 'God has made pilgrimage to the House [i.e., the Ka'bah] a duty for humankind, those who can make their way to it' (Q. 3:97).

To sum up, Islam is a religion of continuous reform through disciplined worship. Disciplined reform is called in Islam *jihād*, or striving in the way of God. *Jihād*, too, becomes an obligation when social and religious reform is gravely hampered, or the community's integrity is threatened. It has found political and military expression over the centuries, but the greatest *jihād* is for every person to strive against his or her own carnal soul. Its goal is to attain a perfect harmony between Islam, *īmān*, and *iḥsān*. 'It is to worship God as though you see him.'

The Caliphate

Succession and Authority

When Muḥammad founded an Islamic commonwealth in Arabia, he hoped for wider expansion. This is clear because he sent expeditions to Byzantine-held Syrian territory. The first was unsuccessful, but he ordered a much larger one shortly before his death.

Muḥammad's authority, understood religiously in the society and culture of Madīnah, depended in part on his personal charisma and political wisdom, but also to a very great extent on his prophetic office. These two spheres of authority were not really separated; his political and social power was intimately linked with his prophetic authority.

Obedience to the Prophet, tantamount to obedience to God, is thus an essential component of Muslims' faith commitment. The *Qur'ān* categorically asserts: 'No, by your Lord, they will not have faith until they accept you as judge in whatever conflict may arise among them, find no blame in what you decide and submit absolutely' (Q. 4:65). Muslims, the *Qur'ān* further enjoins, should refer all matters of dispute to God and to the Messenger (see Q. 4:59). The exalted status and concomitant authority of the Prophet in the community is indicated by the *shahādah*, which couples his name with God's: 'I bear witness that there is no god except God, and I bear witness that Muḥammad is the Messenger of God.'

Within less than a century after the Prophet's death, the Muslims came to administer the largest dominion that until that time the world had ever known. But Muḥammad left no political system for a world empire, nor any clear designation of a leader to succeed him, nor any specific guidelines for choosing one. His death in 632 precipitated a major crisis that grew into a permanent ideological rift. The various sects and schools that emerged based their theological and political claims on the legitimacy, scope, and nature of postprophetic authority in the community.

That this issue was of crucial importance for the disparate tribal society of Madīnah may be seen in the urgency and decisiveness with which it was treated. While the Prophet lay still unburied, a group of the Helpers (Anṣār) of Madīnah met to elect a leader. Three of the Makkan companions of the Prophet, all men of high status in the community, rushed to the scene: Abū Bakr, 'Umar b. al-Khaṭṭāb, and Abū 'Ubaydah b. al-Jarrāḥ. The men of Madīnah were divided along tribal lines, and thus could not agree among themselves on a candidate.

Abū Bakr, the First Caliph

'Umar first argued for the right of the Quraysh as the Prophet's own people to succeed the Prophet in leadership. Then, in the commotion that followed, he offered his hand to Abū Bakr as a pledge of allegiance, and soon others followed suit. Thus Abū Bakr became the first successor (*khalīfah*) of 'the Messenger of God'.

Abū Bakr was not elected in accordance with the principle of consultation (*shūrā*), clearly enunciated in the *Qur'ān* (see Q. 42:38), nor was he chosen by the representative tribal council that customarily chose a *shaykh* or *sayyid* ('chief') of the tribe. Rather, from the beginning the election of Abū Bakr represented a deep division between the Immigrants (Muhājirūn) and Helpers (Anṣār) on the one hand, and the Hashimites and other clans of the Quraysh on the other.

The notables of the Quraysh, outside the clan of Hāshim, favoured Abū Bakr because he was one of them, a highly respected companion and father-in-law of the Prophet. The Hashimites, being the nearest relatives of Muḥammad, expected that one of them would be chosen. Many of them favoured 'Alī b. Abī Ṭālib, the cousin and son-in-law of the Prophet and the first, after Khadījah the Prophet's wife, to embrace Islam. 'Alī was at the time about thirty years old. It was therefore argued that he was too young for such an awesome office. 'Alī, most of the men of Hāshim, and many of the men of the Anṣār remained opposed to Abū Bakr's election, but in the end everyone gave the pledge of allegiance to him.

Abū Bakr's rule was brief (632–4) but highly significant for the survival of Islam and the Muslim community. He had to consolidate his own authority over the community's social and religious organization and also to fight several pretenders to the prophetic office after Muḥammad's death.

Moreover, a number of the nomadic tribes around Madīnah, considering their pact with the Muslim community to have ended with the death of its leader, refused to pay the *zakāt* alms. Sensing the danger in such fragmentation of the community, Abū Bakr insisted, 'By God, were they now to withhold from me even the rope of a camel's knee which they gave as *zakāt* to the Messenger of God, I would fight them over it.' And fight them he did.

These wars, known as the wars of apostasy, occupied most of Abū Bakr's two-and-a-half-year reign, but they laid the firm foundations of an Islamic state in an otherwise seminomadic Arabian peninsula. They also trained and disciplined a highly motivated army, which burst out of Arabia to change the shape of world history. The resulting vast conquests spread Islam far beyond its original home, brought rich revenues into the Muslim treasury, and turned the energies of the disaffected tribes of Makkah and Madīnah away from their intertribal squabbles, at least for a while.

The First Four Caliphs

The institution of the caliphate was devised by the elders of the Muslim community. It was essentially modelled on the function of a tribal *shaykh* or chief, who was first among equals. His authority was therefore of a moral and advisory nature.

A *khalīfah* is one who represents, or acts on behalf of, another. The few references to the caliphate or individual caliphs in Prophetic tradition are depictions of later conditions and views, projected back to the Prophet and his immediate companions.

The caliphate as an institution does not appear in the *Qur'ān*, but Muslims locate its rationale there. The stewardship (*khilāfah*) of Adam and the authority of David are both exercised on behalf of God (Q. 2:30 and 26:38).

Similarly, Muḥammad's political and administrative authority is believed to be bestowed upon him by God. Whoever assumes his role after him inherits his divine mandate, at least in theory. For this reason Abū Bakr was called the 'successor' or 'representative' of the Messenger of God (*khalīfat rasūl Allāh*). Abū Bakr's successor, 'Umar b. al-Khaṭṭāb, was at first called the 'successor of the successor of the Messenger of God'.

The caliphal institution had a worldly as well as a religious dimension from the beginning. As a successor of the Prophet, and later representative of God (*khalīfat Allāh*) on earth, the caliph was a religious leader. But as a chief or administrative head of the community, a caliph was an *amīr* or commander of the Muslims in times of war and peace.

Perhaps conscious of this temporal dimension of his office, 'Umar is said to have adopted the title 'commander of the faithful' (*amīr al-mu'minīn*) instead of the more cumbersome title 'successor of the successor of the Messenger of God'. This title was henceforth assumed by all caliphs as well as by revolutionary leaders claiming caliphal authority. Nevertheless, the caliph continued to function as the chief religious leader (*imām*) of the community. Where he could not actually lead the prayers, he was represented by his appointed deputy or governor, who functioned as a prayer leader on his behalf.

'Umar

Before his death, Abū Bakr appointed as his successor 'Umar b. al-Khaṭṭāb, who stood by him throughout his brief reign. 'Umar ruled for ten years, 634–44. He was the first actual administrator of an ever-expanding Muslim state. In order to handle foreign correspondence and treaties and distribute efficiently vast revenues in gifts and stipends to a rapidly growing Muslim population and army, ʻUmar instituted state registers and adopted the *hijrī* dating of Islamic history. Thereafter, the 354-day lunar years are counted from the Prophet's migration or *hijrah* to Madīnah in 1 AH, which was in 622.

During ʻUmar's reign Syria, Palestine (including Jerusalem), Egypt, modern-day Iraq, and Persia were all conquered and incorporated into the Islamic state. Soon all these provinces became important centres of Islamic learning and culture.

ʻUmar was fatally stabbed by a disgruntled Persian slave while leading the morning prayers one day at the Prophet's mosque in Madīnah. Before dying, ʻUmar appointed a consultative committee of six men to elect from among themselves a new caliph. The two candidates to emerge were ʻAlī b. Abī Ṭālib, who had already been passed over twice, and ʻUthmān b. ʻAffān, a rich scion of the influential Umayyad clan. After much wrangling, ʻUthmān was chosen over ʻAlī, and this event ushered in an era of political strife and religious dissension in an already troubled Muslim state.

ʻUthmān

ʻUthmān ruled for twelve years, 644–56. He was a pious and generous man, and a close companion of the Prophet and twice his son-in-law. ʻUthmān was, however, too prone to favouring his own Umayyad relatives. As he grew older and weaker, they freely manipulated him to their advantage. The resulting nepotism and the abuses of authority, of basic Islamic principles of justice and fairness, and of Arab custom led to the first major sedition (*fitnah*) in the Muslim community.

ʻUthmān's governor of Egypt was a close relative against whom the people brought sharp complaints, demanding his resignation. ʻUthmān was unable to deal decisively with this grave conflict, and soon matters went completely out of hand. After the caliph was besieged in his house by an angry mob of both Egyptian and local insurgents for over forty days, some men broke into the house and killed ʻUthmān.

In Arabian society kin were expected to avenge a murder. ʻUthmān's bloodstained shirt was carried to Damascus, where the governor, Muʻāwiyah b. Abī Sufyān, an Umayyad relative of ʻUthmān, used it to agitate the people to exact revenge for ʻUthmān's blood. Muʻāwiyah accused the Prophet's Companions, particularly ʻAlī, of being accomplices in the murder of the caliph, as they had failed to protect him from such mob brutality.

ʻAlī

Fearing that things might deteriorate even further, the men of Madīnah unanimously acclaimed ʻAlī as the fourth caliph. Muʻāwiyah, however, continued with even greater zeal to demand that 'Alī as the caliph punish the murderers of 'Uthmān. 'Alī (r. 656–61) refused to accept this demand as a condition for the legitimacy of his authority. This led to the division of the Muslims into two camps, the partisans of 'Uthmān and the party (*shī'ah*) of 'Alī.

The split involving 'Alī's partisans, or Shī'īs, over against the majority of Muslims, termed Sunnīs, gave rise to the Islamic community's principal division, lasting to the present day. We shall treat Shi'ism in detail later. Significantly, Islam's historic divisions began as practical conflicts over community leadership, though over time justifications for them were sought in points of theological doctrine.

Two of the notables of the Quraysh, Ṭalḥah and al-Zubayr, who were also well-regarded companions, opposed 'Alī's rise to power. They persuaded 'Ā'ishah, the Prophet's young wife, who held an old grudge against 'Alī, to go with them to lead an army against him. Near Baṣrah in southern Iraq, 'Alī's forces met those of Ṭalḥah and al-Zubayr in the first bloody battle of Muslims against brother Muslims. The battle raged around 'Ā'ishah's camel; hence it was called the War of the Camel. 'Alī's opponents were defeated, both Ṭalḥah and al-Zubayr were killed, and 'Ā'ishah was sternly reprimanded and returned to Madīnah.

Following these serious developments, 'Alī moved the capital, perhaps temporarily, from Madīnah to Kūfah, a garrison town on the edge of the desert in southern Iraq. This move was no doubt motivated by the fact that 'Alī had strong support in that region of Iraq. It was in fact in Kūfah that the Shī'ah, or party of 'Alī, began to develop as a distinct political and religious movement within the Muslim *ummah*.

'Alī was a man of high ideals. He rejected the compromises and diplomatic manoeuvres that a complex political office, such as the caliphate had become, demanded. He was therefore intent on removing 'Uthmān's favoured relatives from office and appointing instead his own ideologically motivated supporters. Mu'āwiyah, who had been appointed by 'Umar as governor of Syria many years earlier, and who ruled as a traditional monarch over a highly urbanized and loyal population, refused to abdicate.

'Alī and Mu'āwiyah met in battle in 657 at Siffīn, on the frontier between Iraq and Syria. As the protracted battle turned in 'Alī's favour, Mu'āwiyah's men lifted up copies of the *Qur'ān* on the tips of their spears and called for God to judge among the people. Fighting ceased, and two arbiters were chosen. Their negotiations in turn were inconclusive, and matters remained unresolved.

The Khārijīs

'Alī's men considered his acceptance of human arbitration as an act of unbelief (*kufr*). Their slogan was, 'No judgement but God's judgement.' As 'Alī did not accept the charge of unbelief, the men left his camp and turned against him and everyone who opposed their view. They were thus called Khawārij or Khārijīs, meaning 'seceders' or 'dissenters'.

A tradition attributed to the Prophet came into wide circulation, asserting that the *imāms* (i.e., caliphs) ought to be of the Quraysh tribe. Such had been the argument for Abū Bakr's election, and it was now invoked because of the growing religious, social, and political significance of the caliphate. The Khārijīs opposed the dictum on the grounds of the equality of all believers. They argued that anyone, even 'an Abyssinian slave', who is a pious Muslim is fit for the caliphate.

The Khārijīs further argued that any Muslim who commits a grave sin is an unbeliever whose blood it is lawful to shed and whose property, wives, and children are lawful for Muslims to seize as war booty. Theirs was not a reform plan for the civil and religious system of Muslim rule, but a radical alternative that could never be implemented. Their anarchical and highly individualistic ideology was in the end rejected by all Muslims, including the moderate wing of their own movement.

While they accepted the two elders, Abū Bakr and 'Umar, as legitimate and righteous caliphs, the Khārijīs repudiated the caliphates of 'Uthmān and 'Alī, regarding them as infidels. They likewise declared Mu'āwiyah and his collaborator 'Amr b. al-'Āṣ to be unbelievers. Having thus condemned Muslim society and its institutions in the name of what they considered to be true Islam, they took to pillaging and indiscriminately killing anyone who disagreed with them. While excessive, their zeal was rooted in piety and strict adherence to the practice of religion.

After repeated attempts to convince the Khārijīs to return to the fold, 'Alī finally inflicted on them a crushing defeat in the battle of al-Nahrawān in 658. This only increased their determination and quest for martyrdom. They called themselves *shurāt*, meaning 'those who have sold their lives to God'. This they did in answer to the Qur'anic challenge for the people of faith to exchange their lives for paradise and God's good pleasure (see Q. 9:111 and 2:86).

After their defeat at Nahrawān, the Khārijīs became an underground movement. They vowed to kill 'Alī, Mu'āwiyah, and 'Amr b. al-'Āṣ on the same day. The two men who were charged with killing 'Amr and Mu'āwiyah failed and were themselves executed. In 661, as 'Alī stood to lead morning prayers, a Khārijī assassin dealt him a fatal blow on the head with a poisoned sword. 'Alī's rule had been short and tumultuous.

'Alī was the last of the close Companions of the Prophet to assume the caliphal office. Anxious to preserve Muslim unity and minimize the effect of the Shī'ī schism, elders of the Sunnī majority regarded the period of the first four caliphs as normative and designated the four as the 'rightly guided' caliphs.

The Umayyads of Damascus

'Alī's supporters proclaimed his older son Ḥasan as caliph after him. Realizing his own weakness and Mu'āwiyah's strength, Ḥasan wisely chose to end the bloodshed and conclude a peace agreement with Mu'āwiyah. Thus Mu'āwiyah became the founder of an Umayyad dynasty, which ruled a vast Islamic empire for nearly a century.

Mu'āwiyah was a shrewd diplomat who quickly established peace and prosperity during most of his two-decade reign (661–80). He moved the capital to Damascus, Syria, where it remained till the end of Umayyad rule. This shift of the centre of power—first from Madīnah, with its simple seminomadic Arab society, and then from Kūfah, with its heterogeneous and volatile populace—to one of the oldest cities of the Middle East greatly altered both the ideal and reality of the caliphate. 'Umar, who had lived a simple and even austere life in Madīnah, is said to have reproached Mu'āwiyah as he observed the latter's great pomp and ceremony, 'Is this a Persian imperial state, O Mu'āwiyah?' Mu'āwiyah justified his style of life on the grounds that were he to live as 'Umar had done in Madīnah, no one would respect his authority.

In spite of the many problems that beset the earlier Umayyad rulers from the beginning, theirs was an epoch of remarkable cultural, administrative, and military achievements. The Dome of the Rock in Jerusalem and the Umayyad Mosque in Damascus are two of its great enduring monuments. These and other famous mosques became places of pilgrimage next in importance to the sanctuaries of Makkah and Madīnah. It was also during this period that the Arabic writing of the *Qur'ān* was standardized.

Culturally and administratively, the Umayyad caliphate was an Arab state, but it was far more than an Arabian state. The Arab settlers in Syria from the Arabian peninsula, including South Arabia, found themselves amid other, more sophisticated and cosmopolitan Arab populations. These other Arabs, in Syria, were largely Christians and had had long contacts with Byzantium and Persia. Their poets, like the famous al-Akhṭal (c. 640–710), graced the Umayyad court. Their administrators, like John of Damascus (c. 675–c. 749), helped run an efficient state machinery.

'Abd al-Malik b. Marwān (r. 685–705), the caliph under whose auspices this cultural legacy reached a high point, changed the state administration inherited from the conquered populations, Greek and Persian, into a strictly Arab administration. His Arabic coins set the standards not only for Muslim domains, but for other states as well. Even the legal, religious, and other sciences, which as we shall see flourished under the 'Abbāsids, had their beginnings during the Umayyad period.

Reportedly 'Umar, the second caliph, remarked on hearing the suggestion of building a fleet of warships, 'I will not go to any spot that I cannot reach on

On the site of the Hebrew temple in Jerusalem, which was destroyed in 70, Caliph ʻAbd al-Malik b. Marwān built the Dome of the Rock in 687. (Baruch Gian)

my camel.' Nevertheless, Muʻāwiyah built the first Muslim fleet, embarking on sea warfare. This venture led to wider conquests and soon rendered the Mediterranean an Islamic lake in both warfare and commerce. In 711, Umayyad armies sailed east to India and west to southern Spain. Seafaring Arab traders, sailing from the ports of Arabia, began to carry Islam to Africa, China, and Southeast Asia.

Shīʻī Opposition to the Umayyads

Before his death in 680, Muʻāwiyah appointed his son Yazīd as his successor. This dynastic behaviour constituted a total break with earlier Arab and Islamic tradition and a new practice in caliphal succession. The action, together with Muʻāwiyah's hostility to the sons of Alī and their followers, antagonized many of the notables of the holy cities of Makkah and Madīnah and strengthened the opposition to Yazīd. From the start, Yazīd's brief Umayyad reign (680–3) was beset with grave problems.

The most serious opposition to his appointment came from the second son of ʻAlī, Ḥasan's younger brother Ḥusayn. In contrast with the realistic Ḥasan,

Ḥusayn was a man of uncompromising idealism. When Ḥasan died during Mu‘āwiyah's reign, Ḥusayn began to prepare the ground for a revolt against Umayyad authority. He led a small band of seventy-odd fighters to Kūfah, in southern Iraq, whence he led a general uprising against Yazīd. However, Ḥusayn was intercepted by a large army dispatched against him by Yazīd's governor of Kūfah.

With his women and children and a few supporters, Ḥusayn was halted at a spot near Kūfah called Karbalā' on the banks of the Euphrates River. A brief battle between Ḥusayn and Yazīd's army ensued on the morning of the tenth of Muḥarram, the first month of the Muslim year, 61 AH/680 CE. It resulted in the massacre of Ḥusayn and his relatives and supporters. His women and the only surviving son of ‘Alī, known as Zayn al-‘Ābidīn ('the most excellent of all worshippers'), were carried as captives, along with the heads of Ḥusayn and his fellow martyrs, first to Kūfah and from there to Yazīd in Damascus.

The tragedy of Karbalā' has had far-reaching ramifications for Muslim faith, thought, and history. It provided an ethos of suffering and martyrdom characteristic particularly of Shī‘ī faith and piety, discussed later, but it has had a deep influence on general Sunnī piety as well. Ḥusayn's martyrdom drew for Muslims a clear distinction between the ideal Islamic polity and what was henceforth considered to be irreligious monarchical rule.

Ḥusayn's death directly undermined the Umayyad caliphate and in the end brought about its demise. The immediate consequence of the death was civil strife, which lasted for over a decade and had to be put down with cruel repression. It brought to power another Umayyad line, the Marwānids, who ruled generally with an iron hand for nearly three-quarters of a century. In spite of its cultural, military, and administrative achievements, Umayyad rule had little support, particularly among non-Arab Muslims.

Another result of the death of Ḥusayn and its religious and political aftermath was the rise of the first extremist Shī‘ī sects. Most, if not all, were manifestations of political and economic unrest expressed in short-lived religious movements. An important phenomenon was their denial of the death of a leader. They would declare him to be in occultation, that is, in hiding, and await his imminent messianic return. Furthermore, most of the sects looked to a descendant of the prophet Muḥammad, in a hereditary line through his daughter Fāṭimah and cousin and son-in-law ‘Alī, for guidance and ultimate salvation.

The ‘Abbāsids of Baghdad

The ‘Abbāsid revolution was so named after the descendants of al-‘Abbās, the Prophet's uncle. It was largely organized by a Persian called Abū Muslim in the province of Khorāsān, in northeastern Iran. The slogan of this revolution was, 'We accept anyone of the family of Muḥammad.' First in secret, then publicly,

'Abbāsid men assumed leadership of the revolution and turned it decisively in their favour.

In 750, this remarkable movement achieved its purpose, and the 'Abbāsid dynasty came to power. The Umayyads, who had become weak and ineffectual, were quickly vanquished, rounded up, and virtually massacred. One prince escaped. After wandering as a fugitive for nearly four years, he reached southern Spain. There, he established a new and independent Umayyad state with a brilliant culture, discussed later.

In contrast to the Syrian outlook of the Umayyads, the 'Abbāsid revolution was conceived and developed in Iraq and Persia. It was therefore natural for the new regime to move its capital to that region. Al-Manṣūr (r. 754–75), the second caliph and actual founder of the state, built a new capital, which would come to be known by the name of the small village on the site in southern Iraq: Baghdad. He observed with marked satisfaction that God had turned all previous rulers away from this site, preserving it for him.

Al-Manṣūr planned Baghdad, which he called Madīnat al-Salām ('the city of peace'), as a centre of an international empire. He viewed the capital's location as ideal, between Syria to the west, Arabia to the south, and Persia to the east. The city did indeed live up to his expectation, as it was for centuries the centre of 'Abbāsid administration and a focal point of international culture and trade.

Because the 'Abbāsids came to power on the strength of a religious ideology, they adopted messianic and highly eschatological names. Thus the first of their caliphs was called al-Saffāḥ ('the bloodletter'), the second al-Manṣūr ('the victorious'), and the third al-Mahdī ('the rightly guided messianic ruler').

Under Hārūn al-Rashīd (r. 786–809) and his son al-Ma'mūn (r. 813–33) the 'Abbāsid state reached its zenith as a world empire. Hārūn al-Rashīd is immortalized in the stories of the Arabian Nights as a legendary patron of culture who surrounded himself with poets and musicians, singing girls, and drinking companions. All this of course was a far cry from the austere life of Madīnah. The high culture of the 'Abbāsid court contrasted equally sharply with the rudimentary culture of the court in Europe of the Frankish emperor Charlemagne (r. 768–814), al-Rashīd's contemporary.

Although the 'Abbāsids rose to power on the tide of Shī'ī sympathy, they soon allied themselves with the majority Sunnī establishment and ruthlessly repressed Shī'ī movements. Early in the caliphate of al-Manṣūr, 'Abd Allāh b. al-Ḥasan, a great-grandson of Ḥasan, the son of 'Alī b. Abī Ṭālib, and his two sons Muḥammad, known as al-Mahdī, and his brother Ibrāhīm, known as *al-Nafs al-Zakīyah* ('the pure soul') led an uprising against 'Abbāsid rule. The revolt was mercilessly put down, Muḥammad and Ibrāhīm were killed, and their father with a large number of his 'Alid supporters languished in prison until they died. This repressive policy was followed by most of al-Manṣūr's successors.

The 'Abbāsids did not abandon the religious character of their claim to caliphal authority. Rather, they endeavoured to distance themselves from the very revolution that had brought them to power. They patronized the well-known jurists and other religious scholars of their time. For example, Mālik b. Anas, the founder of the Mālikī legal school, wrote for al-Manṣūr the important book *al-Muwaṭṭa'*, which is a primary source of prophetic *ḥadīth* and legal tradition. Furthermore, al-Rashīd appointed the well-known scholar of the Ḥanafī legal school Abū Yūsuf as chief judge. Only al-Ma'mūn among early 'Abbāsid caliphs clearly showed Shī'ī sympathies. Not long after him, however, al-Mutawakkil (r. 847–61) reversed this trend and turned vehemently anti-Shī'ī.

Within half a century of 'Abbāsid rule, the state began to show clear signs of disintegration. State defence and administration were gradually taken over by foreign army generals and state ministers. The real danger, however, came not so much from state administrators but from foreign warlords. Baghdad fell under the control of Turkish soldiers, who had been brought in initially by al-Mu'taṣim (r. 833–42) to defend the caliph and his capital. The political conflicts in the end broke up the 'Abbāsid state into numerous little dynasties that were often at war with one another. All these conflicts were a direct outcome of its cosmopolitan character.

Yet it was this unique character that created a universal and rich Islamic civilization, a synthesis resulting from the interaction of many cultures and religious ideas. Using Arabic as the universal language of religion, science, philosophy, and literature, Muslim, Jewish, eastern Christian, and other scholars developed a civilization that could have never been conceived within the confines of Arabia.

The framework of the synthesis was ancient Greek science and philosophy. Interest in them may have begun early in the Umayyad period. It culminated in the first official institution of higher learning, Bayt al-Ḥikmah ('the house of wisdom'), which was built by al-Ma'mūn. In this great academy, al-Ma'mūn gathered a number of scholars who translated the works of Plato, Aristotle, and their commentators into Arabic, either directly from the Greek or Syriac translations. These translations constituted the primary sources for Islamic philosophy, theology, and science.

The Fragmentation of the Caliphate

As the central authority of the 'Abbāsid state weakened and finally disappeared altogether, other cultural centres arose to rival Baghdad. It was in such centres in Persia, Central Asia, North Africa, and Spain that the humanistic and religious sciences flourished. Hence, most of the noted historians, *Qur'ān* exegetes, *ḥadīth* traditionists, philosophers, and grammarians were non-Arabs, yet they all wrote their most important works in Arabic. By the tenth century, however, Persian poetry and prose literature began to develop. This set the precedent for other

Islamic languages, which in due course eventually developed their own rich literary traditions.

In spite of its collapse as a central power, the 'Abbāsid caliphate was generally accepted as a legitimate institution by the Sunnī majority. Although the 'Abbāsids laid claim to Prophetic family relations, being the descendants of the Prophet's uncle al-'Abbās, 'Alī's descendants' claims to authority continued to have a powerful appeal among Arabs and non-Arabs alike. Shī'ī Muslims recognized the line from the Prophet, 'Alī, and Fāṭimah as the only legitimate holders of authority in the Muslim community.

Around the middle of the tenth century the Būyids, a Persian dynasty, came to rule large areas of the 'Abbāsid domains, including Baghdad. The Būyids were Shī'ī sympathizers, and thus patronized Shī'ī learning, so that their century-long rule is known as the 'Shī'ī century'. It was during the Būyid period (945–1055) that Shī'i *ḥadīth* tradition, theology, and jurisprudence were developed.

After a period of secret revolutionary ferment in North Africa, the Ismā'īlī Shī'ī Imām al-Mu'izz li-Dīn Allāh ('he who brings honour to God's religion', r. 953–75), appeared in Egypt in 953 to proclaim himself as legitimate caliph. The dynasty of which he was the fourth caliph was known as the Fāṭimid caliphate, so called after Fāṭimah, the Prophet's daughter. The Fāṭimids ruled Egypt and parts of Syria for over two centuries. Cairo, which al-Mu'izz built as the capital of his realm, is so named because it was built under the sign of the star al-Qāhir ('the conqueror'). Fāṭimid authority rested on a powerful missionary organization that operated throughout the Muslim world. On more than one occasion, the Fāṭimids of Egypt threatened the 'Abbāsid caliphate of Baghdad.

'Abd al-Raḥmān III (r. 912–61), the Umayyad ruler of Muslim Spain, also proclaimed himself caliph in 912. The Umayyad caliphate there, which he founded, ruled the Iberian Peninsula for over a century. Thus the caliphal office, which was meant to manage the affairs of the entire Muslim *ummah*, was now occupied by three competing claimants. Among these, the 'Abbāsid caliphs were by far the weakest. They in fact became ceremonial figures used to legitimize the illegitimate rules of *sulṭāns* who seated and unseated them at will.

In this state of fragmentation and disunity, the Muslim dominion could not face a powerful common enemy. Thus the Mongols of the steppes of inner Asia advanced upon the Muslim domains of Central Asia, Persia, and the Middle East like wildfire, leaving death and devastation in their wake. In 1258, the Mongol general Hulagu sacked Baghdad and killed the last 'Abbāsid caliph.

With the fall of Baghdad as a centre of Islamic spiritual and material culture, a new era of Muslim history began. Henceforth, not conquerors but traders, religious scholars, and mystical teachers assumed the role of preserving and spreading Islam as a faith and civilization throughout Asia and Africa. These new domains produced their own religio-cultural centres. And although the caliphate ceased to exist as a reality, it has remained as an ideal rule that many Muslims still long to recover.

SHI'ISM

The Shī'ī Tradition

By the tenth century, Sunnī Islam had developed a stable and generally uniform legal and theological system. The Shī'ī tradition has in contrast been a movement of change, instability, and wide diversity. 'Shi'ism', as it turns out, is a broad term covering a large number of disparate religio-political movements, sects, and ideologies. Common to most of these movements, however, is a general allegiance to 'Alī and his descendants, and their right to spiritual and temporal authority in the Muslim community after Muḥammad.

For Sunnī Muslims, the term *imām* means simply the leader of prayer at the mosque, a role the caliph sometimes performed. For Shī'īs, though, the term becomes an important title. The Imām is the one individual held to be the rightful, divinely mandated leader of the Muslim community.

The crisis of authority following the death of the Prophet created a permanent rift in the Muslim community. This rift began as a political movement or party (*shī'ah*) upholding 'Alī's right to succeed the Prophet as leader or *imām* of the community. It was therefore called, somewhat scornfully, *shī'at 'Alī* (''Alī's party').

'Alī's supporters included some notable Companions outside the merchant aristocracy of the Quraysh, many of the Anṣār of Madīnah, and the Arab tribes of Kūfah in Iraq. Generally speaking, the Shī'ah of 'Alī represented the poorer and underprivileged elements of Muslim society. It therefore very early attracted large numbers of non-Arab converts called *mawālī*, meaning clients or subordinate allies of an Arab tribe or clan, who thus had a quasi-Arab identity and status as well as protection.

The *mawālī* were conquered people who generally had a superior culture to that of their Arab conquerors. During Umayyad rule, these people were second-class members of Arab Muslim society. They thus played a major role in the 'Abbāsid revolution and its subsequent cosmopolitan administration and culture. Moreover, they exerted a great influence on Islamic, and particularly Shī'ī religious and political ideology.

Apart from a few short-lived movements that either deified the *imāms* of 'Alī's descendants, or regarded their own erstwhile leaders as incarnations of the *imāms*, Shi'ism has always signified an absolute devotion to and love for the Prophet's household. This devotion is based on a number of Qur'anic verses exalting the families of major prophets, including that of the Prophet Muḥammad. The *Qur'ān* states, 'God has chosen Adam and Noah, the family of Abraham and the family of 'Imrān [the ancestor of Moses and Aaron and Mary the mother of Jesus] over the rest of humankind' (*Q.* 3:33). To Shī'īs the high status of Muḥammad's family is indicated in the assertion, 'Surely, God wishes to take away all abomination from you, O people of the House, and purify you with a great purification' (Q. 33:33). Furthermore, Muḥammad is prompted to declare in the *Qur'ān*: 'Say, 'I wish no reward for it [i.e., conveying God's revelation] except love for [my] next of kin'" (Q. 42:23). The household (*ahl al-bayt*) and next of kin (*al-qurbā*) have generally been interpreted to be the Prophet's daughter Fāṭimah, her husband 'Alī, and their two sons, Ḥasan and Ḥusayn.

Shī'ī Muslims have based their claim of 'Alī's right to succeed the Prophet as the leader or Imām of the Muslim community on the following rather enigmatic Qur'anic verse: 'O Messenger, convey that which has been sent down to you from your Lord, for if you do not, you would not have conveyed His messages; and God will protect you from the people' (Q. 5:67). This verse is reported to have been revealed shortly before the Prophet's death in 632, when he led the Muslims in his farewell *ḥajj* pilgrimage. According to Shī'ī tradition, the command to the Prophet was: 'Convey that which was sent down to you from your Lord concerning 'Alī'.

In obedience to this divine command, we are told, on his way back from Makkah, the Prophet halted at a spot between Makkah and Madīnah called Ghadīr Khumm. Taking 'Alī by the hand, he addressed a large gathering of Muslims, saying:

> O people, hear my words, and let him who is present inform him who is absent: Anyone of whom I am the master [*mawlā*], 'Alī, too, is his master. O God, be a friend to those who befriend him and an enemy to those who show hostility to him, support those who support him and abandon those who desert him.

On the basis of this and other sayings wherein the Prophet is said to have directly or indirectly designated 'Alī as his successor, Shī'ī traditionists (that is, specialists on the corpus of Prophetic oral tradition) and theologians constructed an elaborate legal and theological system of legitimate authority based on the doctrine of *imāmah*, that is, the imamate, the office of the Imām as designated leader.

The death of the Prophet's grandson Ḥusayn at Karbalā' in 680 contrasts sharply with the otherwise triumphant success story of early Islam. The anniversary date, the Tenth of Muḥarram, has come to express Shī'ī hopes and frustrations, messianic expectations, and a highly eschatological view of history.

The day of 'Āshūrā', as the Tenth of Muḥarram eventually came to be known, continues to be commemorated throughout the Muslim world. It is a special day blending sorrow and merriment, blessing and mystery. It has inspired a rich devotional literature, providing the theme and context for numerous popular passion plays in Persian, Arabic, and other Islamic languages. Above all, it is observed by the Shī'ī community as a day of suffering and martyrdom. Its symbolism is expressed in solemn processions, public readings or enactments of the story of Ḥusayn's death, a liturgical pilgrimage to the sacred spot of Karbalā', and other devotional acts.

The theme of suffering in Shī'ī piety has instilled various attitudes in Shī'ī Muslims. It has engendered quietistic resignation in the face of injustice and wrongdoing. But it has also nourished an irredentist ideology and a revolutionary spirit that refuses to tolerate tyranny and oppression. In a modern-day manifestation of this spirit, momentum for revolution in Iran in fact began on the day of 'Āshūrā' in 1962 and culminated in fall of the Shah and the establishment of the Islamic Republic in 1979.

Early Shī'ī Sects

Following the martyrdom of Ḥusayn in 680, a group of his followers who deserted him during his fateful battle with the Umayyad army were filled with remorse, and thus were known as the 'penitents'. Wishing to expiate their sin with their own blood, they rose against Yazīd's governor of Iraq, but were quickly routed and massacred.

This revolt inspired a shrewd and enthusiastic man called al-Mukhtār (c. 622–87) to lead a more serious uprising aimed at avenging the blood of Ḥusayn and his fellow martyrs. Al-Mukhtār's revolt plunged the Muslim state into a period of chaotic civil strife, lasting twelve years. It was finally put down ruthlessly by the Marwānids, a new line of the Umayyad dynasty that lasted till the end of Umayyad rule in 750.

Kaysānīyah

Al-Mukhtār introduced a serious innovation into the nascent Shī'ī ideology by claiming Muḥammad b. al-Ḥanafīyah, the son of 'Alī by a woman other than Fāṭimah, as the rightly guided Imām (*al-mahdī*). He thus removed the condition of Fāṭimid descent for the Imām, and that soon led others to remove the condition of 'Alid descent altogether. Al-Mukhtār's idea led to the rise of the first extremist Shī'ī sect, called al-Kaysānīyah.

This new sect, which was named after 'Amrah b. Kaysān, a non-Arab follower of al-Mukhtār, introduced yet another belief that was to be adopted by many other Shī'ī sects and schools: the doctrine of the occultation or concealment (*ghaybah*) of the Imām. It thus denied Muḥammad b. al-Ḥanafīyah's death, asserting instead that he went into occultation on a mountain near Makkah called Mount Raḍwah, and that he will return to vindicate his followers and establish just rule on earth. The sect attracted a large following before it fragmented into many disparate groups and died out.

The Zaydīs

An important phenomenon common to most Shī'ī movements is that they were born out of bloody but unsuccessful revolts. Thus a pious and highly revered grandson of Ḥusayn, called Zayd, led a brief uprising in Kūfah against the Umayyad caliph Hishām b. ʻAbd al-Malik in 740. Zayd was betrayed by his fickle followers and met his grandfather's fate.

Zayd's followers established a legal school bearing his name and based on his theological and legal ideas. In contrast to most other Shīʻī schools, the Zaydīs accept the legitimacy of the caliphate of Abū Bakr and ʻUmar, although they, too, hold that ʻAlī was the rightful Imām after Muḥammad. They further hold that the Imām must be a descendant of ʻAlī and Fāṭimah, through either the Ḥasanid or Ḥusaynid line. He must, however, claim the office and support his claim by rising up with the sword against injustice and oppression.

The Zaydī school belongs to the moderate wing of Shiʻism, and possesses a rich legal and theological tradition. It predominates to this day in the Yemen along with the Shāfiʻī legal school, discussed below. The Zaydīs are now without an Imām, as their last Imām was overthrown by the Yemeni revolution of 1962.

We should note the important role of Muḥammad al-Bāqir, who was Zayd's older brother, and his son Jaʻfar al-Ṣādiq in the development of Shīʻī theology and jurisprudence. The two *imāms* lived during a tumultuous period of transition from Umayyad to ʻAbbāsid rule. A number of their followers claimed divinity for them, or for themselves, and were denounced by the *imāms* and executed with their followers by the authorities.

'Sevener' or Ismāʻīlī Shiʻism

The majority of Shīʻīs accepted the line of Ḥusaynid *imāms* down to Jaʻfar al-Ṣādiq (d. 765) as the sixth Imām. A major schism occurred when Jaʻfar's oldest son and successor, Ismāʻīl, died about ten years before him. Jaʻfar then appointed a younger son, Mūsā al-Kāẓim, as his successor.

This was regarded by many as an irregular appointment. It was therefore denied by a significant group of Jaʻfar's supporters who insisted that the imamate should continue in Ismāʻīl's line. They thus came to be known as Ismāʻīlīs or Seveners. The largest faction, called Nizārīs, carried on the line of *imāms* through Ismāʻīl's son Aḥmad and his descendants down to the present.

Basic to Ismāʻīlī faith and worldview is the doctrine of the divine mandate of the Imām and his absolute temporal and religious authority. This fundamental teaching was developed in an impressive esoteric system of prophetology by a number of famous Ismāʻīlī philosophers and theologians over the centuries. This made Ismaʻilism a secret cult that was spread widely through an active network of missionaries and agents of the *imāms* and their deputies.

The Fāṭimid caliphs of Cairo encouraged the development of an Ismāʻīlī legal tradition. The third Fāṭimid caliph al-Muʻizz li-Dīn Allāh established in Cairo al-Azhar, the first institution of religious learning, as the headquarters of his missionary activities. But before the end of Fāṭimid rule, interest in the *sharī'ah* altogether died out, and Isma'ilism has remained an antinomian (antilegal) phenomenon in Islam.

Like most other Shī'ī sects, the Ismā'īlī movement broke up into a number of often conflicting secret societies. Yet in spite of their chequered history, the Ismā'īlīs have played a very conspicuous intellectual and political role in Muslim history.

For centuries the Ismā'īlīs lived as an occult and obscure sect in the Indo-Pakistan subcontinent, East Africa, Syria, and Iran. Their leader or Imām came to be known as the Agha Khan, an Indo-Iranian title signifying nobility. The third Agha Khan (1877–1957, r. 1885–1957) initiated a process of reconciliation and reintegration of his followers into the Muslim community. This process has continued under his Harvard-educated successor Karim Agha Khan (b. 1936). In modern times Ismā'īlīs have migrated in large numbers to the West, where they live as a prosperous and well-organized community.

Druzes

During the reign of the highly idiosyncratic Fāṭimid Imām al-Ḥākim bi-Amr Allāh ('the ruler by God's command', r. 996–1021) a group of his extremist followers preached the doctrine of his divinity as the manifestation of God. The group was for a while led by a Turkish missionary called Muḥammad b. Nashtakīn al-Darazī (d. c. 1019), hence the name of the new sect al-Durūz ('the Druzes').

The Druzes are essentially a chiliastic or millenarian religious sect, holding that their leader Ḥamzah b. 'Alī, a Persian missionary who disappeared under mysterious circumstances in 1021, is the 'Master' (*walī*) of the age, that he is in occultation, and that he and al-Ḥākim, the One [god], will return at the end of time to rule the world and usher in the end of this aeon. They also believe in the reincarnation of the soul in a newborn child immediately after the death of a person. The Druzes still exist as a small occult sect in Syria, Lebanon, and Israel.

'Twelver' or Imāmī Shi'ism

According to the doctrine of *imāmah*, as elaborated by the Twelver Shī'ī tradition, the Prophet, through divine designation, appointed 'Alī as his vicegerent or legatee (*waṣī*). 'Alī in turn appointed his son Ḥasan to succeed him as Imām, and Ḥasan appointed his brother Ḥusayn. Thereafter, each Imām designated his successor, who was usually his eldest son.

The line of *imāms* of the descendants of Ḥusayn continues (through Ja'far's son Mūsā al-Kāẓim as the seventh Imām), till the twelfth Imām, Muḥammad b. Ḥasan al-'Askarī, who was Ḥusayn's ninth descendant, and who disappeared at the age of four in 874, going into occultation or hiding. Shī'īs hold that he communicated with his Shī'ah through four successive deputies until 941 and then entered into his greater occultation, which will last till the end of the world. Before the Day of Resurrection, he (as the Mahdī, 'the rightly guided one') and Jesus will return to establish universal justice and true Islam on earth. On the matter the Prophet is quoted thus:

> Even if only one day remains of the time allotted for this world, God will prolong this day until he sends a man of my progeny whose name shall be my name and whose patronym [*kunyah*] shall be my patronym, who will fill the earth with equity and justice as it has been filled with inequity and wrongdoing.

Imāmī Shī'īs agree with Sunnī Muslims on the centrality of the *Qur'ān* and *sunnah* as the primary sources of Islamic law. However, they define the *sunnah* not simply as the life-example of the Prophet Muḥammad and his generation, but as the life-example of the Prophet and what they believe to be his rightful successors, the *imāms*. Hence the *sunnah* for Twelver Shī'ī Muslims extends over a period of three centuries, till the end of the lesser occultation of the twelfth Imām in 941. We discuss Imāmī Shī'ī legal interpretation in our treatment of Islamic law later.

Because Imāmī Shi'ism is a *sharī'ah*-based legal school, it has generally been accepted by the rest of the Muslim community. With regard to the fundamentals of faith and worship, the Imāmī Shī'īs may also be regarded as Sunnīs. Moreover, Shī'ī piety, and especially Shī'ī devotion to the Prophet's family, has deeply influenced popular Sunnī piety.

Later Shī'ī Sects

As Imāmī Shi'ism spread into most areas of the Muslim world, it interacted with many currents of thought and piety. The result has been the rise of a number of antinomian (that is, law-rejecting) sects and movements on its fringes. Two major currents of extremist Shi'ism that persisted till the nineteenth century are the Mukhammisah—that is, sects that deify the five (*khamsah*) personages: Muḥammad, 'Alī, Fāṭimah, Ḥasan, and Ḥusayn—and the Mufawwiḍah ('delegationists').

Sects based on the first current generally held that the five holy persons are from eternity united in essence, but differentiated only in name. Thus they appear in history in the forms of prophets and *imāms*.

The delegationists held that God, who is unknowable in his essence, has delegated the creation of the world and its sustenance, as well as the final judgement of all of humankind to these five divine personages. The notion that the final judgement will be delegated by God to the *imāms* has had a clear influence on Imāmī Shī'ī messianic eschatology.

After the lesser occultation of the Twelfth Imām, this ideology produced the extremist sect of the Nuṣayrīs. The sect was founded by a companion of the Tenth and Eleventh *imāms* called Muḥammad b. Nuṣayr al-Namīrī. The Nuṣayrīs are also known as ʻAlawīs, those who regard ʻAlī as an incarnation of God. The Nuṣayrīs exist to this day as a fairly large and influential community in Syria.

A number of sects with a mixed popular Ṣūfī (mystical) and extremist Shīʻī piety appeared between the thirteenth and sixteenth centuries in various regions under Imāmī Shīʻī influence. In the eighteenth century, a fascinating theosophical sect (that is, a group cultivating privileged knowledge of divine wisdom) known as the Shaykhīs appeared in Arabia. The sect was named after its founder Shaykh Aḥmad Zayn al-Dīn (1753–1826), of the province of Aḥsā' in the present kingdom of Saudi Arabia. Out of the theosophical ideas of this school arose the Bābī and Bahā'ī movements in Iran in the nineteenth century.

About one-eighth of the world's Muslims today are Shīʻīs. They are strongest in Iran, where Imāmī Shiʻism became the state religion in the sixteenth century.

Islamic Law

The 'Religious Sciences'

A learned person is termed in Arabic an *ʻālim*. The plural, *ʻulamā'*, refers collectively to the religio-legal scholars, or religious intellectuals, of the Islamic world. What Muslims term the 'religious sciences' were part of a comprehensive cultural development as Islam expanded geographically far beyond the religio-political framework of its initial Arabian homeland.

The expansion far outran the capacity of the Arabian framework to rule the conquests, but cosmopolitan Islamic cultural centres like Baghdad, Córdoba, and Cairo provided a highly creative pluralistic milieu for the rise of a rich civilization. The 'religious sciences' developed mainly in these new cultural centres. Comprehensive achievement in philosophy, theology, literature, and science began in the eighth century and continued in different parts of the Muslim world well into the seventeenth century.

A major branch of the religious sciences deals with jurisprudence, the theoretical and systematic aspect of law. Islam is a religion more of action than of abstract speculation about right belief. Hence the first and most important religious science, Islamic law, aims at right living as the essence of faith. The Prophet characterizes a Muslim thus: 'Anyone who performs our prayers [i.e., observes the rituals of worship] and eats our ritually slaughtered animals [i.e., observes the proper dietary laws] is one of us.' To Muslims, inner personal submission to the will of God is God's way for all of humankind. At both the personal and the societal level, Islam as a faith and way of life is to be realized within the framework of divine law, the *sharī'ah*.

However, *sharī'ah* is not law in a strict sense but a way of life or conduct based on a set of moral imperatives. These moral imperatives, the *Qur'ān* insists, are to express a genuine commitment to strive to reform one's life and the life of one's family, immediate society, and the Islamic *ummah* or community at large. Their proper observance is ultimately measured inwardly by the sincerity of the person's intention and faith, and outwardly by his or her righteous works.

The *Qur'ān* does not legislate human relationships in a vacuum. It rather addresses itself primarily to the society and cultural and moral values of pre-Islamic Arabia and the day-to-day problems arising as that society is transformed into a normative Muslim community. Laws concerning marriage and divorce, child rearing, and inheritance are promulgated. Likewise, laws governing cases of retaliation and compensation for injury or death are instituted as a substitute for the pre-Islamic custom of vendetta. Laws of retribution for theft and highway robbery, adultery, false accusation, and other offences are legislated.

Within Arabia, the *Qur'ān* and the life-example (*sunnah*) of the Prophet Muḥammad and his generation guided Muslim life and piety. These two sources emerged as the framework for the wider Islamic society. Islamic jurisprudence developed in a reciprocal relationship with the interpretation of the *Qur'ān* and the study of *ḥadīth*, both building on these enterprises and contributing to them.

As the compilation of the *Qur'ān* was arranged mechanically according to the order of the *sūrahs*, it was important for jurists to place the various revelations in their historical context. They needed to determine whether a ruling was abrogated by a later ruling, or itself abrogated an earlier one. It was also important for historians to relate certain revelations precisely to their appropriate events in the Prophet's career in Makkah and Madīnah. The Qur'anic science developed for this purpose is known as knowledge of the 'occasions of revelation' (*asbāb al-nuzūl*) of the *sūrahs* and verses of the sacred text.

Ḥadīth traditions, reporting the words and actions of the Prophet, were informally remembered and passed on for at least a century before any attempts to record them were made. In fact, *ḥadīth* tradition was not fully codified until the tenth century for the Sunnī community and at least a century later than that for the Twelver Imāmī Shī'ī legal school.

The *Qur'ān*, and hence the *sharī'ah*, are centrally concerned with relating individuals and societies to God. Human social interrelations move from the most particular and intimate relationship between a husband and wife to that of a person to his or her parents and children. They then move further to include the extended family, then the tribe, and finally the *ummah* and the world.

The *Qur'ān* places kindness and respect towards one's parents next in importance to the worship of God. A Muslim is enjoined to care for his or her parents in old age without showing any signs of annoyance or displeasure. Rather, one should show humility and mercy to them and pray God to bestow mercy upon them (see *Q.* 17:23–4).

Qur'anic Principles for Society

Islam has no official priesthood. Every person is responsible not only for his or her own moral probity, but for the moral reform of the entire Muslim *ummah*: 'Let there be of you a community that calls to the good, enjoins honourable conduct [*ma'rūf*] and dissuades from evil conduct [*munkar*]. These are indeed prosperous people' (*Q.* 3:104).

Through the *zakāt* (welfare religious tax) and *ṣadaqah* (voluntary almsgiving) the *Qur'ān* makes care for the poor and needy a social responsibility and a meritorious act. The revenues from these two sources must be distributed among 'the poor and needy, those who collect them, those whose hearts are reconciled [i.e., non-Muslim sympathizers with the view of attracting them to the new faith], for the ransoming of captives of war, for debtors in God's cause, and the wayfarer' (*Q.* 9:60). Yet even charity must have its limits. The Prophet is said to have counselled a rich and overenthusiastic man who wanted to give all he had to the poor that he should not give everything away and leave his children to beg for charity after him. No more than a third of the wealth of a person having children or other dependants should go to charity.

The *Qur'ān* strictly forbids usury as a means of increasing one's wealth. It also forbids illicit profit based on hoarding, speculation, or the sale of unknown commodities. The ideal is not voluntary poverty or total attachment to material possessions. Rather the *Qur'ān* enjoins, 'Seek amidst that which God has given you, the last abode, but do not forget your portion of the present world' (*Q.* 28:77).

The *Qur'ān* stipulates harsh punishments for grave offences considered to be transgressions of the bounds of social conduct set by God. These include amputation of the hand for theft, amputation of the hand and foot for highway robbery, eighty lashes for adultery, and capital punishment for premeditated murder. Yet the ultimate purpose of punishment is not to compound suffering, but to protect public order and reform society. The aim of such punishment is ultimately to lead the offender to repentance and virtuous conduct.

The *Qur'ān* does not promulgate absolute laws, even where it strictly demands the severe punishment of the thief, adulterer, or murderer. It is more concerned with moral issues in actual life situations. Among its over 6,000 verses, no more than 200 are explicitly legislative.

On the whole, the *Qur'ān* points the way to a good and righteous life and leaves the details of how this goal is to be achieved to those who strive to attain proper understanding of the religion (see *Q.* 9:122). They are the jurists and *ḥadīth* specialists, who assumed this responsibility with utmost seriousness. Their efforts have shaped the moral and social life of the Muslim community.

Prophetic Tradition, or *ḥadīth*

As a source for law the Prophetic *ḥadīth* tradition in Islam is in some ways parallel to the Oral Torah in Judaism. Like the Oral Torah, Prophetic *ḥadīth*s are believed to be divinely inspired. Again like the Oral Torah, Prophetic *ḥadīth*s reflect the community's understanding of the intent of its founder. But, importantly, the role Prophetic *ḥadīth* tradition has played in the development of Islamic jurisprudence is also closely parallel to what the Oral Torah became in the development of rabbinic Jewish law.

Some scholars have asserted that the *ḥadīth* is essentially a phenomenon beginning only in the ninth century. Contrary to such a view, there is now increasing evidence indicating a beginning of interest in *ḥadīth* transmission and compilation early in the eighth century. Such interest was based on political, legal, and theological needs. But what took more than three centuries to develop was not simply interest in the Prophet's *sunnah*, but an evolving technique of *ḥadīth* criticism and the integration of *ḥadīth* into the discipline of jurisprudence.

A *ḥadīth* consists of a chain of transmission (*isnād*), beginning with the compiler or last transmitter and going back to the Prophet, followed by the text (*matn*). The aim of the study of *ḥadīth* is to ascertain the authenticity of a *ḥadīth* by establishing the completeness of the chain of its transmission and the veracity of its transmitters.

Thus a *ḥadīth* that has three or more complete chains of transmission, and all of whose authorities are well known and recognized as pious people who could not be accused of falsification, is considered a sound (*ṣaḥīḥ*) and universally accepted (*mutawātir*) tradition. A *ḥadīth* that has one complete chain of well-attested authorities going back to the Prophet through a well-known Companion is sound.

Where one or more links of the chain of authorities are missing, or one or more of its transmitters are unknown, the *ḥadīth* would be considered either good or weak, depending on the veracity of its remaining authorities. However, a *ḥadīth* most or all of whose transmitters are unknown, or known to be untrustworthy, is considered weak or fabricated. Finally, *ḥadīth*s transmitted by single authorities are doubted or altogether rejected.

Although some rules were set for *matn* criticism, they have not been applied as rigorously as those of *isnād* criticism. This is because, it was assumed, if the honesty and piety of a transmitter is beyond question, then what he or she says cannot be subject to doubt. Furthermore, generally speaking, the majority of *ḥadīth* traditions follow a set pattern of expression and subject matter. A *ḥadīth* that deviates from this pattern, but is otherwise considered to be good, is usually called strange (*gharīb*) or rare (*nādir*).

An exception to this norm is the genre known as *ḥadīth qudsī* ('divine or sacred saying'). While Prophetic *ḥadīth* generally deal with legal or moral issues or legislation, *ḥadīth qudsī* traditions consist of pious exhortations and reflections. *Ḥadīth qudsī* traditions, moreover, are held to be not the words of the Prophet but of God. Often their *isnād* beyond the Prophet goes through Gabriel and several other angels before it reaches God, who is their final authority. Thus *ḥadīth qudsī* traditions are held to be extra-Qur'anic revelations received by the Prophet either from the angel Gabriel or in dreams.

These pious divine sayings have been a rich source of solace for Muslims in times of sorrow and adversity. Ṣūfīs, the mystics of Islam, have freely augmented the *ḥadīth qudsī* literature, making it a means of human colloquy with God, and a source of affirmation of his nearness and love for his pious servants.

The Six Canonical *ḥadīth* Collections

The science of *ḥadīth* criticism was not perfected and fully implemented until the middle of the ninth century. It was actually an integral part of the science of jurisprudence, indeed its crowning achievement. The comprehensive works based on it were intended as sources, and to some extent as manuals, to be used by later jurists.

The most important Sunnī *ḥadīth* traditionists are Muḥammad b. Ismā'īl al-Bukhārī (810–70) and Muslim b. al-Ḥajjāj al-Nīsābūrī (c. 817–75). They were, as their names suggest, from the city of Bukhārā in Central Asia, and from Nishapur in the northeastern Iranian province of Khorāsān. The two men did not know each other, yet they simultaneously journeyed for many years across the Muslim world in search of *ḥadīth* traditions. The two works their long search produced are amazingly alike, a fact strongly suggestive of an already existing unified and well-established *ḥadīth* tradition.

Al-Bukhārī and Muslim are said to have collected hundreds of thousands of *ḥadīth*s, out of which they selected about 3,000, discounting repetition. Their methodology and organization became the criterion that all subsequent *ḥadīth* compilers followed. Their two collections, entitled simply *Ṣaḥīḥ al-Bukhārī* and *Ṣaḥīḥ Muslim*, soon achieved canonical status, second in authority to the *Qur'ān*. Although the *Ṣaḥīḥ* of Muslim is better organized and methodologically superior to that of al-Bukhārī, the latter has achieved first place among all *ḥadīth* collections.

Within less than half a century after Muslim and al-Bukhārī, four other collections—of Abū Dāwūd al-Sijistānī, Ibn Mājah, al-Tirmidhī, and al-Nasā'ī—were produced. It is noteworthy that, like Muslim and al-Bukhārī, these four were all from Central Asia and Iran. Their works are entitled *Sunan*, the plural of *sunnah*.

Use of the plural implies that they combine the *sunnahs* of action, consent, and speech. In contrast, the works of Muslim and al-Bukhārī are essentially collections of sound *ḥadīth*, as their titles indicate.

The six canonical collections and others modelled on them are organized topically. They are legal manuals dealing first with laws governing the rituals of worship, and then the laws regulating the social, political, and economic life of the community.

They are divided into books or sections beginning with the topic of *īmān* and Islam, physical purification before prayers, and then the rest of the pillars of Islam. In addition, they treat dietary laws, marriage and divorce, inheritance, and related matters. They also include a section on *jihād*, war, and journeying along God's way. This section includes laws dealing with the status and treatment of *dhimmīs*, that is, Jews, Christians, and other protected religious communities. Other sections include criminal laws, trade, and related matters.

The Four 'Roots of *fiqh*'

Sharī'ah and Fiqh

For Islam, God is the ultimate lawgiver. The *sharī'ah* is sacred law, or 'the law of God'. It consists of the maxims, admonitions, and legal sanctions and prohibitions enshrined in the *Qur'ān*, and explained, elaborated, and realized in the Prophetic tradition.

An important distinction must be made between *sharī'ah* and *fiqh*. *Fiqh*, or jurisprudence, is the process of human comprehension, interpretation, and codification of the *sharī'ah* or sacred law. A scholar who specializes in this exacting science is called a *faqīh* ('jurist'; plural, *fuqahā'*).

Islamic law as it was developed in the legal schools is based on four sources. Two of these, the *Qur'ān* and *sunnah* of the Prophet and his generation, are its material and primary sources. The other two are formal sources representing human endeavour and acceptance. These two are personal reasoning (*ijtihād*) of the scholars, involving analogy (*qiyās*), and the general consensus (*ijmā'*) of the community. The schools of Islamic law differed, among other things, in the degree of emphasis or acceptance that they gave to each of these.

Personal reasoning is the process of deducing from the *Qur'ān* and *sunnah* laws that provided the foundations for and diversity of the legal schools. The term *ijtihād* signifies a scholar's best effort in executing this process. It uses *qiyās*, or analogical reasoning, as its instrument.

The process of analogical reasoning consists of four methodological steps. The first is to find a text in the *Qur'ān* or *Ḥadīth* pertinent to the new case or problem facing the jurist. The second is to discern the similarities and differences of the conditions surrounding the judgement in the two cases. The third step is for the jurist to allow for such differences in making his judgement. The final step is to extend the rationale of the Qur'anic or *ḥadīth* judgement to cover the new case. Not surprisingly, the elaboration and application of these principles presented many difficulties and differences of opinion among jurists.

The principle of consensus (*ijmā'*) is meant to insure the continued authenticity and truth of the three other sources. In its widest sense, this principle embodies the community's acceptance and support of applied *sharī'ah*. More narrowly, at least during the creative period of Islamic law, it has preserved an active interchange of ideas among the scholars of the various schools. Consensus, moreover, has remained the final arbiter of truth and error, expressed in the Prophetic assertion, 'my community will not agree on an error'.

Yet even this important principle has been the subject of much debate and dissension among the scholars of the various schools. Questions such as whether the consensus of earlier generations is binding on the present one, or whether consensus implies only the scholars or implies the community at large, are only two examples of the many issues of this debate.

At the heart of the debate have been the negative consequences of consensus, for while it preserved the integrity of the *sharī'ah*, the principle of consensus has arrested the development of Islamic law at its most crucial stage. This happened by making *ijmā'* so sacrosanct that no change after the establishment of the major Sunnī legal schools was possible. The result has been that Islamic jurisprudence became a thick wall protecting the *sharī'ah*, but largely depriving it of an adaptive and dynamic moral and spiritual role in Muslim society.

Early Jurisprudence

The *Qur'ān* calls upon Muslims to choose a group from among them to dedicate themselves to the acquisition of religious knowledge, and instruct their people when they turn to them (Q. 9:122). The need to have such a group was felt from the beginning when some of the pilgrims from Madīnah accepted Islam and took with them men who had acquired religious knowledge to teach the people of Madīnah the rituals and principles of the new faith. As tribe settlements and cities in Arabia, including Makkah, became Muslim domains, governors with special religious knowledge were sent by the Prophet to administer these new domains and instruct their people in Islam.

Among these was Mu'ādh b. Jabal, a man of the Anṣār (the Prophet's 'helpers'), well known for his religious knowledge. Before sending him to the Yemen, the Prophet is said to have had the following exchange with him. The Prophet asks how in his rule Mu'ādh would deal with the People of the Book (Jews and Christians), which is what most people in Yemen were. Mu'ādh answers that he will deal with them in accordance with the Book of God and the *sunnah* of his Prophet. The Prophet asks what will happen if he does not find the answer to a problem in either of the two sources. Mu'ādh answers, 'I would then use my reason, and would spare no effort.'

This pious tale no doubt reflects much later developments. It was invoked to bestow on a developing discipline an aura of Prophetic blessing and authority. Nevertheless, the anecdote aptly describes the development of Islamic law in its early stages. Not only Mu'ādh, but other Companions as well, were known for their ability to deduce judgements from Qur'anic principles and the acts and instructions of the Prophet.

As the Muslim domains expanded through rapid conquest, the need for a uniform body of religious law became increasingly evident. For a time, it was filled by Muslims of the first and second generations (the Companions and their successors), particularly those among them who were distinguished as *Qur'ān* reciters and transmitters of the Prophet's *sunnah*. They laid the foundations for subsequent legal traditions. Until the eighth century, these traditions centred in Iraq, especially in Kūfah and Baṣrah, and in the Ḥijāz or western Arabia, particularly in Madīnah and Makkah. It was in these centres that the 'living tradition' of jurisprudence was transformed from an oral to a written science, with a rich and ever-growing body of literature.

The Legal Schools

By the middle of the eighth century, the process of establishing distinctive legal schools with independent legal systems was well under way. Three men in the eighth century and two in the ninth distinguished themselves as the jurists of their time and founders of the earliest legal schools. The three eighth-century figures all knew and respected one another.

Ja'farī (Shī'ī) Law

Ja'far al-Ṣādiq (c. 700–65), the sixth Shī'ī Imām, was especially revered as a descendant of the Prophet and heir to the lore of the Prophet's family (*ahl al-bayt*). He lived in Madīnah and was one of its leading scholars. He is regarded as the founder of the Shī'ī legal and religious system, which bears his name as the Ja'farī legal school. After the martyrdom of Ḥusayn b. 'Alī, the third Shī'ī Imām and grandson of the Prophet, his descendants shunned politics and devoted themselves to religious learning and the task of establishing a new interpretation of Islam.

Ja'far and his father, Muḥammad al-Bāqir, the fifth Imām and grandson of Ḥusayn, are venerated by the Muslims in general for their learning and piety. Yet in spite of their seminal role in the development of Shī'ī legal and theological thought and devotion, they left no written works, but a rich tradition preserved and codified centuries later.

Ḥanafī Law

Abū Ḥanīfah (699–767), the son of a Persian slave, was the most famous jurist of Iraq and founder of the Ḥanafī legal school, yet he, too, left no written sources that can be ascribed to him with certainty. However, his two disciples al-Shaybānī and Abū Yūsuf, who lived during the early and vigorous period of 'Abbāsid rule, developed their master's system into the most impressive and widespread Sunnī legal school.

Mālikī Law

Mālik b. Anas (c. 715–95), the scholar of Madīnah and founder of the Mālikī legal school, developed his system in the framework of a collection of *ḥadīth* and legal tradition. His book *al-Muwaṭṭa'* (The Levelled Path) was the earliest such collection. It thus reflects the early development of legal thought in Islam.

Unlike later jurists or traditionists, Mālik gave equal weight to the Prophet's *sunnah* and the 'practice', or living tradition, of the people of Madīnah. He also shows far greater reliance on the effort to deduce well-considered legal opinions (*ijtihād*) than later distinguished religious scholars. He was guided in this effort by the principle of common good (*maṣlaḥah*).

Abū Ḥanīfah had also shown great reliance on rational thinking and living tradition. He resorted to the two principles of analogical reasoning (*qiyās*) and rational preference (*istiḥsān*). The work of both Mālik and Abū Ḥanīfah indicates that the principle of Prophetic tradition (*sunnah*) as a material source of jurisprudence was still in the process of development. It went hand in hand with the 'living tradition' of major cities or centres of learning. Both were ultimately referred back to the Prophet or first generation of Muslims.

Shāfi'ī Law

A decisive stage in jurisprudence came in the ninth century with the crucial work of Muḥammad b. Idrīs al-Shāfi'ī (767–820), a systematizer. Although Shāfi'ī was closer to the school of Madīnah, he travelled widely and studied in different centres, but without clearly allying himself with any school. He spent his last years in Egypt, where he wrote the first systematic treatise on Islamic jurisprudence. His hitherto unsurpassed work radically changed the scope and nature of Islamic jurisprudence. Shāfi'ī advocated absolute dependence on the two primary sources of Islamic law, the *Qur'ān* and *sunnah*. He based his own system on a vast collection of *ḥadīth* and legal tradition, entitled *Kitāb al-Umm*, which he compiled for that purpose.

Shāfi'ī restricted the use of *qiyās* or analogical reasoning, and rejected both the Ḥanafī principle of *istiḥsān* and the Mālikī principle of *maṣlaḥah*. In his insistence on basing all juridical judgements on the *Qur'ān* and *sunnah*, and in opposition to the majority of jurists of his time, he preferred *ḥadīth*s transmitted on single authorities to personal opinion. His argument was that jurists should not rely on the opinions of men instead of the Book of God and the *sunnah* of his Prophet.

Although Shāfiʿī's legal system was later adopted as the basis of the school bearing his name, he himself expressly opposed the idea. He saw himself not as the founder of a new legal school, but the reformer of Islamic law.

Ḥanbalī Law

Not long after Shāfiʿī, the well-known traditionist Aḥmad b. Ḥanbal (780–855), a strict conservative, founded the Ḥanbalī legal school strictly in conformity with Shāfiʿī's dictum. He produced one of the standard *ḥadīth* collections, the *Musnad*, on which his legal system was founded. The *Musnad* of Ibn Ḥanbal was arranged not by subject as other standard collections were, but by the names of primary transmitters, usually the Prophet's Companions and other early authorities. While the *Musnad* of Ibn Ḥanbal is not the first work of this genre, it is by far the largest and most important one.

The Spread of the Sunnī Schools

After a period of often violent conflict, the four principal Sunnī legal schools gained universal acceptance as true and equally valid interpretations of the *sharīʿah*. They geographically divided the Muslim world among them.

The Ḥanafī school was for centuries accorded state patronage, first by the ʿAbbāsid caliphate and then by the Ottoman Empire. It spread in all the domains influenced by these two empires: (1) Egypt, Jordan, Lebanon, Syria, Iraq, Central Asia, and the Indian subcontinent; and (2) Turkey and the Balkans.

The Mālikī school was carried early to Egypt, the Gulf region, and North Africa and from there to Spain, West Africa, and the Sudan.

The Shāfiʿī school took root early in Egypt, where its founder lived and died. It then spread to southern Arabia, and then followed the maritime trade routes to East Africa and to Southeast Asia, where it remains the dominant legal school.

The Ḥanbalī school has had the smallest following, but also a disproportionately great influence, especially in modern times. It exists only in central Arabia, the present Saudi kingdom, with scattered adherents in other Arab countries. Its conservative ideology, however, has been championed by revolutionaries and reformers since the thirteenth century.

Other minor schools have either died out, or still exist in small and isolated communities. The Ẓāhirī legal school, which was established early by the literalist jurist Dāwūd b. Khalaf (d. 884), ceased with the end of Muslim rule in Spain. The Ibāḍī school, established during the first century of Islam by the Khārijī leader and jurist ʿAbd Allāh b. Ibāḍ, is still represented in small communities in North Africa and Oman.

The End of *ijtihād*

The Prophet is reported to have declared, 'The best generation is my generation, then the one that follows it, and then the one that follows that.' This judgement expresses well the widely held view that after the normative period of the Prophet and the first four 'rightly guided' caliphs, Muslim society grew increasingly corrupt and irreligious. There were, however, exceptions to the rule, men who modelled their lives and piety on that normative period. These were the well-known pious scholars, jurists, and traditionists of the formative period of Muslim history.

With the establishment of the major Sunnī legal schools by the tenth century, and by a sort of undeclared consensus, the 'gate of *ijtihād*' was considered to be closed. This did not mean that Islamic legal thinking ceased altogether; it simply meant that no new legal systems would henceforth be tolerated.

In fact, this process of exclusion began earlier. It depended not on religious or scholarly considerations, but on the awarding of political patronage to some schools and the denial of it to others. From this time, *ijtihād* was limited to the jurisconsult, or *muftī*, of each city or country. To this day, *muftī*s continue to issue legal opinions, called *fatwā*s, in accordance with the principles of their respective legal schools. Collections of famous *fatwā*s have been made, which serve as manuals especially for less creative or less able *muftī*s.

Imāmī Shī'ī Legal Interpretation

Twelver Imāmī Shi'ism crystallized into a legitimate legal school in the tenth and eleventh centuries under Būyid patronage. It developed largely as a reaction to earlier extremist and highly heterodox Shī'ī movements. These movements, moreover, left a noticeable mark on some of its basic beliefs and worldview. Nevertheless, along with Zaydism, Twelver Shi'ism possesses the Shī'ī legal school closest to Sunnī orthodoxy.

In contrast with Sunnī tradition, which developed first a science of jurisprudence and then a canonical *ḥadīth* tradition to buttress it, the Ja'farī or Imāmī school based its legal system on a vast *ḥadīth* tradition transmitted from the *imāms* over a period of three centuries. Beginning with al-Kulaynī, who died in 941 at the end of the lesser occultation, this tradition was collected in 'the four books of *ḥadīth*'. Al-Kulaynī compiled the first major *ḥadīth* collection, entitled *al-Kāfī* (The Sufficient), organized with books dealing first with the fundamentals of doctrine and worship and then with books on ancillary legal matters, along the lines of Sunnī *ḥadīth* collections.

An important exception is the section dealing with the imamate, entitled *Kitāb al-Ḥujjah* (Book of the Proof of God), which is included among the books dealing with the fundamentals of faith. In fact, the essential point of difference between the Shīʿī and Sunnī legal traditions is the Shīʿīs' fundamental belief in the necessity of the *imāms* as guardians of the *sharīʿah* and guides of the community to its correct interpretation and implementation. The Imām is believed to be the proof or argument (*ḥujjah*) of God over his human creatures. Hence, the earth cannot be without an Imām, be he manifest and active in the management of the affairs of the community or hidden from human sight and perception.

Following al-Kulaynī, important *ḥadīth* collections were compiled by Ibn Bābawayh (c. 923–91), of the Iranian holy city of Qom and known as al-Shaykh al-Ṣadūq ('the truthful shaykh'), and Abū Jaʿfar al-Ṭūsī (d. 1067), 'the jurist doctor of the community'.

With Ṭūsī the foundations of Imāmī Shīʿī *ḥadīth* and legal tradition were virtually fixed. In the absence of the Imām, however, scholars of the community must fulfil his role, however imperfectly, as guardians of the *sharīʿah*. This meant that *ijtihād*, or personal reasoning, must go on and consensus must be limited to the *ijmāʿ* of the scholars only.

Ijtihād was likewise narrowly defined as the scholar's rational effort not so much to formulate new laws, but to comprehend and interpret the *imāms*' rulings in ways that would apply to new situations.

For this reason the Imāmī Shīʿī legal school rejected analogical reasoning as an instrument of *ijtihād*. This does not mean that reason came to play a secondary role in the growth of Shīʿī jurisprudence. On the contrary, the primary sources of law were very early defined as the transmitted tradition (*naql*), including the *Qur'ān*, and human reason (*ʿaql*). Furthermore, where transmitted tradition and reason conflict, reason takes priority over tradition in the scholar's effort to resolve the conflict.

Ijtihād has remained in principle a primary source of law for Shīʿī jurists to the present. But also operative has been the principle of precaution (*iḥtiyāṭ*), based on the fear of error in judgement in the absence of the Imām. Precaution has tended to minimize the use of personal reasoning so much that jurists with any measure of originality are few and far between.

Taqlīd means following the *ijtihād* of a particular jurist. In Sunnī Islam, it meant following one of the founders of the recognized legal schools; hence, it implied the strict adherence to a traditional legal system, leaving no room for innovation. Shīʿīs made *taqlīd* of a living jurist, a *mujtahid*, a legal necessity in the absence of the Imām. This emphasis has had the same effect on the Shīʿī community that the closing of the gate of *ijtihād* has had on Sunnī Muslims. The need for courageous and sensitive new approaches to the interpretation and application of the *sharīʿah* is therefore imperative in both communities.

Before the Iranian revolution of 1979, genuine efforts were made at achieving a meaningful rapprochement among all Islamic legal schools. This noble goal has unfortunately fallen victim to the political turmoil of recent decades. It nonetheless remains the hope of many Muslims today.

The Scope of Islamic Law

The term *sharī'ah* originally signified the way to a source of water. Metaphorically it came to mean the way to the good in this and the next world. It is 'the straight way' that leads the faithful to paradise in the hereafter. Muslims believe the *sharī'ah* to be God's plan for the ordering of human society. It is understood not as an abstract system of ethics or moral philosophy, but as a practical way of life.

From the beginning it has been the framework of the positive law of government. In theory, Islam is a 'nomocracy'—a government of laws, not of people. Ideally, the purpose of an Islamic government is to ensure the implementation of God's law in human society.

The failure of Muslim governments to accomplish this purpose does not absolve the individual from the obligation to live his or her own life in accordance with the *sharī'ah*, and to urge others to do likewise. On the Day of Judgement, every person will be judged by the extent to which he or she has endeavoured to fulfil this purpose in this life.

Within the framework of the divine law, human actions fall between those that are absolutely obligatory and therefore will bring good rewards on the Day of Judgement, and those that are absolutely forbidden and therefore will bring harsh punishment. Actions are classified into five categories, as follows:

- lawful (*ḥalāl*), and therefore obligatory
- commendable, and therefore recommended (*mustaḥabb*)
- neutral, and therefore permitted (*mubāḥ*)
- reprehensible, and therefore disliked (*makrūh*)
- unlawful (*ḥarām*), and therefore forbidden

These categories govern all human actions. The correctness of an action and the intention that lies behind it determine its nature and consequence. This is the reason for the stress in Islam on outward moral conduct rather than definitions of orthodox belief. Right belief is expressed in right worship, which is one of the chief concerns of the *sharī'ah*.

The two domains of the *sharī'ah* are acts of worship (*'ibādāt*) and human interrelations or transactions (*mu'āmalāt*). *'Ibādāt* can be seen as the acts of ritual and duties of worship: the Five Pillars of Islam and their ancillary rules. There is a close agreement among all legal schools with regard to *'ibādāt*, which reflects the unity and coherence of the *sharī'ah* and its priority in Muslim life.

Differences among the various legal schools are for the most part due to different interpretations of the *sharī'ah* with regard to the domain of *mu'āmalāt*, human interrelations. These regulations govern personal conduct regarding food and drink, dress, and general behaviour. They also cover family and social relationships, business transactions, and international and interreligious relations.

ISLAMIC PHILOSOPHY AND THEOLOGY

The Scope and Sources of Theology

The Islamic religious sciences may be divided into two categories: the transmitted sciences (*al-'ulūm al-naqlīyah*) and the rational sciences (*al-'ulūm al-'aqlīyah*). The first category includes the sciences of the *Qur'ān*, *ḥadīth*, and jurisprudence, and their ancillary branches, treated already. The second includes principally theology and philosophy, to which we now turn.

Theology is called *'ilm al-kalām*, meaning the science of speech or discourse. It is discourse about God, his attributes, and his creation and nurture of all things. It is also concerned with human free will and predestination, moral and religious obligations, and the return to God on the Day of Resurrection for the final judgement. The *Qur'ān* defines itself as the speech (*kalām*) of God (see *Q*. 2:75 and 9:6). Thus the 'Arabic *Qur'ān*', which Muslims believe to be literally the revealed word of God, has itself been the subject of much theological debate.

Insofar as theology deals with human faith and conduct, it falls under the science of *fiqh* or jurisprudence. During their formative period, theology and law were indistinguishable. Like jurisprudence, the primary sources of theology are the *Qur'ān* and Prophetic tradition. Likewise, its formal sources are the personal effort (*ijtihād*) of the scholars and the broad consensus of the community.

But theology came to be concerned also with the rational investigation of the existence of God, creation, and theodicy, that is, the defence of God's power and goodness in view of the experience of suffering and evil. In these areas, theology is more akin to philosophy, whose principles and rationalistic methodology it employed in the formulation and argumentation of its principles.

After their consolidation into two independent fields, theology and law were again combined in comprehensive religious learning known as the knowledge or study of 'the fundamentals of the religion' (*uṣūl al-dīn*).

Christian theology was a contributing source for Muslim theological reflection. Early Muslim contacts with theologians among the Nestorian and Jacobite (Monophysite) Christians in Iraq and Syria raised new questions. These regarded God's attributes and essence, particularly his attribute of speech and its relation to the eternal or created *Qur'ān* as the divine word.

There were also contacts with certain forms of dualism associated with the teaching of the Manichaeans, followers of a third-century Iranian teacher, and other forms associated with the Zoroastrian religion. Iranian dualistic conceptions held good and evil to be personified in cosmic powers locked in eternal conflict, and played out in good and evil human behaviour. These teachings brought into sharp focus such questions as God's responsibility for human good and evil conduct, and inevitably the issue of free will and predestination.

Greek philosophy also provided an important rational framework for a rich and sophisticated Islamic theological and philosophical system. It provided the discipline of logic, a necessary tool for analytic thought. It also contributed metaphysical inquiry, that is, exploration of the nature of ultimate reality. It addressed important theological issues, such as the eternity or creation of the universe, and the relationship of reason to revelation. But in the end, although the interaction of Muslim theology with other faiths and ideologies left a mark on its development, Islamic theology rests fundamentally on the *Qur'ān* and the Prophetic *sunnah*.

Politics and the Murji'ah

The political crisis occasioned by the Prophet's death produced schisms in the community. The spectrum included the Shī'ah and the Khārijīs, discussed already. In addition, there appeared two theological schools, the Murji'ah and the Mu'tazilah. An issue on which differences emerged was the question of the appropriate judgement for a grave sinner.

A grave sinner, according to the *sharī'ah*, is one who violates 'the bounds' (*ḥudūd*) of God by committing adultery, murder, or theft, drinking intoxicating drinks, or committing an act of infidelity (*kufr*). The sin of infidelity may be committed through a wilful denial of Islam, or a grave violation of its basic norms.

All four schools arose in response to the great sedition (*fitnah*) in the community, which began during the reign of 'Uthmān (r. 644–56), the third of the four 'rightly guided' caliphs, and ended in his murder, the assassination of 'Alī four years later, and the establishment of the Umayyad dynasty by Mu'āwiyah b. Abī Sufyān (r. 661–80).

The Shī'īs considered 'Alī and his descendants to be the sole legitimate heirs of the Prophet. Thus the three previous caliphs (Abū Bakr, 'Umar, and 'Uthmān) were considered usurpers of his right, and those who came after them usurped the rights of his descendants. In the Shī'ī doctrine of the imamate, the Imām is a manifestation of divine grace, mercy, and justice in the world. As a just and merciful God, God must insure that the earth is never without an Imām. A grave sin, akin to *kufr* or rejection of faith, is therefore for one to die not knowing the Imām of his time. Such a person, the Prophet is said to have declared, 'dies the death of pre-Islamic foolishness (*jāhilīyah*)'.

The Khārijīs regarded both 'Alī and Mu'āwiyah as grave sinners, and therefore rejecters of faith. 'Alī, they said, rejected faith because he accepted human arbitration instead of God's judgement, and Mu'āwiyah rejected faith because he rebelled against the Imām of the Muslims. This extreme position and its violent political consequences raised the basic question of the status in this and the next world of a Muslim who commits a grave sin.

The term Murji'ah means 'those who postpone', in this case judgement regarding the ultimate fate of a Muslim grave sinner. In its moderate form, Murji'ism came to represent the official Sunnī position. In contradistinction to the Khārijīs, the Murji'ah held that a Muslim remains a believer in spite of his sin, and it is up to God to forgive or punish him or her on the Day of Judgement. They therefore argued that so long as a Muslim continues to profess the faith of Islam, that person should be treated both socially and legally as a Muslim.

Another school, the Mu'tazilah, dealt with the issue of the grave sinner in the context of their well-known five fundamentals. These are:

- God's oneness (*tawḥīd*)
- God's justice (*'adl*)
- God's promise (*wa'd*) of rich reward for the people of faith, and his threat (*wa'īd*) of eternal punishment for grave sinners
- That the reprobate Muslim is neither a person of faith (*mu'min*) nor a rejecter of faith (*kāfir*), but is in a state (*manzilah*) between the two
- The Qur'anic injunction of commanding the good (*ma'rūf*) and forbidding evil conduct (*munkar*)

According to the fourth of these principles, a Muslim grave sinner is destined neither for hell nor for paradise but remains in an intermediate state. One who dies as a grave sinner will in spite of faith in God be condemned, according to the third principle, to eternal punishment.

Mu'tazilī Theology

Though their movement likely had earlier antecedents, the Mu'tazilah ('separatists') are so named as representing a group that separated itself from mainline Sunnī theology as represented by al-Ḥasan al-Baṣrī (642–728). The movement addressed far broader issues than that of the grave sinner.

Mu'tazilī theology was from the beginning deeply rationalistic. It was influenced by Greek rationalism as well as Christian theology. Thus in contrast with Christian Trinitarianism, Mu'tazilī theologians argued that God's absolute oneness necessitates that his attributes be one with his essence. Otherwise, there would be God and his Word, God and his power, God and his knowledge, and so on. This would imply a multiplicity of gods, an error considered worse than the Christian doctrine of the Trinity.

For Mu'tazilīs such attributes as speaking and creating are not eternal, but rather attributes of actions that come into being only when such acts take place.

Therefore, in contrast with the general Sunnī belief that the *Qur'ān* is the eternal word of God, Mu'tazilīs held the *Qur'ān* to have been created as it was being sent down to Muḥammad by the angel Gabriel.

The Mu'tazilī view of divine oneness also meant that all anthropomorphic assertions about God in the *Qur'ān* are to be taken as symbolic. Hence, references to God's hands and face, his sitting upon the throne and coming down with the angels for the final judgement must be interpreted metaphorically. The Mu'tazilīs denied the frequent assertion in both the *Qur'ān* and Prophetic tradition that the faithful will see God in the hereafter. Seeing God, they argued, means that he is a body limited in time and space, and that is impossible.

God's justice implies that he cannot wish evil, let alone be its cause in any way. He is constrained by his justice to wish for his servants only what is best for them. This means that human beings are themselves the creators of their own acts, and hence fully responsible for their consequences. It also means that what humans recognize as good and evil God must also recognize as such.

This made God an absolutely just judge incapable of either mercy or forgiveness, subject to human reason in all his dealings with humankind. This view, moreover, goes against one of the most fundamental principles of popular Muslim piety, namely the hope of the faithful in the Prophet's intercession with God on their behalf on the Day of Judgement.

According to God's promise to the obedient of eternal bliss in paradise and threat to the rebellious of eternal chastisement in hell, human beings are not predestined by God, but freely make their own destiny. Consequently within the scope of our limited knowledge and judgement, a sinful Muslim is in only an intermediate state between faith and rejection of faith. But as such people freely plot the course of their own destiny, God will judge them on the last day. All that Muslims can and must do is to enjoin the good and dissuade from evil.

Mu'tazilī theology was vehemently opposed by mainline Sunnī *'ulamā'*, particularly the 'people of the *Ḥadīth*', as traditionists or jurists were called. During the reign of the 'Abbāsid caliph al-Ma'mūn (r. 813–33), Mu'tazilīs attempted to impose their theological beliefs on the rest of the community. They established a sort of inquisition known as the *miḥnah* ('test' or 'ordeal'), whereby traditional Sunnī scholars had to profess publicly the doctrine of the createdness of the *Qur'ān*, or suffer harsh punishment. The great traditionist and founder of the Ḥanbalī legal school, Aḥmad b. Ḥanbal, was a notable victim of the *miḥnah*. He was publicly flogged and imprisoned for insisting that the *Qur'ān* was the eternal word of God, preserved in the well-guarded heavenly tablet (according to Q. 85:21–2).

The caliph al-Mutawakkil (r. 847–61) reversed this policy, reaffirming Sunnī orthodoxy and persecuting the Mu'tazilīs. Mu'tazilism as a rationalistic school of Islamic theology gradually lost its vitality and not long thereafter died out, but its basic tenets of divine unity and justice have been preserved in Zaydī and Twelver Imāmī Shi'ism.

Ashʿarism and Sunnī Orthodoxy

Al-Ashʿarī

A major factor contributing to the decline of Muʿtazilism was the rise of Ashʿarī theology. Abū al-Ḥasan al-Ashʿarī (873–935) was for a time a prominent Muʿtazilī thinker. He abandoned Muʿtazilism and, using Muʿtazilī dialectical reasoning, set himself the task of refuting Muʿtazilī theology and establishing his own orthodox school.

Ashʿarī argued that God is One, the sole creator and sustainer of all his creation. Nothing happens except by his will and eternal decree. His attributes 'are neither He, nor are they other than He.' Hence, God is not life, knowledge, power, and so on, as the Muʿtazilī position would imply. Rather, God knows by a special knowledge that is his alone, and the same is true of all his attributes.

With regard to God's hands, face, and his sitting upon the throne, Ashʿarī argued that to deny these would amount to nullifying God's attributes. Yet if these attributes are taken literally, it would amount to anthropomorphism, to making God a body like any other body. Both positions are erroneous. Hence, Qur'anic statements on such matters must be accepted, but 'without asking how (*bilā kayf*)'.

Al-Ghazālī

According to a widely accepted Prophetic tradition, at the start of every century God is to raise a scholar to renew and strengthen the faith of the Muslim community. Such a man is known as a *mujaddid* ('renovator') of the faith. Abū Ḥāmid Muḥammad al-Ghazālī (1058–1111), of Ṭūs, near the modern Iranian city of Mashhad, has been regarded as the *mujaddid* of the sixth Islamic century. His work went far beyond theology and philosophy, to cover mysticism and all the religious sciences.

In 1091, al-Ghazālī was appointed as a professor of theology and law at the prestigious Niẓāmīyah college in Baghdad. There he tirelessly defended mainline Sunnī Islam against the innovations of the theologians and the heresies of the philosophers and occult Ismāʿīlī doctrines.

Four years later, al-Ghazālī underwent a deep psychological crisis. He gave up his teaching and embarked on a long quest for true knowledge. Certain knowledge, he came to realize, could be attained through neither the senses nor the rational sciences, but through a divine light that God casts into the heart of the person of faith.

Having gained a reason thus enlightened, al-Ghazālī produced an indispensable work, one of the most ambitious on the religious sciences. Appropriately entitled *Iḥyā' ʿulūm al-dīn* (The Revivification of the Religious Sciences), this *magnum opus* deals with all religious learning from a deeply mystical point of view.

Predestination and Free Will

We saw earlier how Muslim thinkers used Prophetic *ḥadīth* tradition to define precisely the concepts of *islām* ('submission') and *īmān* ('faith'). Included in the definition of faith is 'faith in divine decree, be it good or evil'. Through politically motivated consensus, such traditions became the basis of a broad Sunnī Muslim orthodoxy affirming God's ultimate responsibility for both good and evil in the world, and his ultimate predestination of humankind, some for paradise and others for hell.

In its extreme form, this concept left no room for human initiative, and made God look like a capricious tyrant. It was therefore challenged through an emphasis on God's justice by Mu'tazilī and Shī'ī theologians and traditionists.

Ash'arī rejected the Mu'tazilī view of divine justice, arguing instead for God's absolute freedom to will and act as he chooses, without being answerable to any one of his creatures. God is just because he wills to be just; were he to will otherwise, his actions would still be right and good.

Similarly, good and evil are what they are not in themselves. They are determined not by human reason but by God through legislation. Good and evil are not rational or even moral in essence, but legislative. Were God to stipulate in the *sharī'ah* that lying, adultery, and theft were good, they would be allowed in spite of the fact that human reason may judge them evil. God only allows human beings to discern good and evil, but not to legislate or determine them.

As extreme Mu'tazilism circumscribed God's power to will and act by insisting on absolute freedom of the will, extreme Ash'arism rendered human striving to do good or evil meaningless. In order to insure God's absolute freedom, some Ash'arīs like al-Ghazālī went so far as to deny causality altogether.

Al-Ghazālī argued a doctrine called occasionalism. According to it, each time God wills an act by a human being, both the act and its cause are created. For example, if God were to will that a person murder another, he would occasion the cause for that act by making the knife or gun to be used as an instrument of killing, and finally he would cause the murderer to walk to his victim, raise his hand, and kill him. The murderer would be doing nothing more than fulfilling what God had decreed for him from eternity.

Ash'arī himself avoided such an extreme predestinarian position by arguing that God creates all actions but also allows human beings to earn them by giving them the capacity to do so. This is known as the doctrine of *kasb* (earning good reward through meritorious deeds) and *iktisāb* (accruing evil recompense through evil acts). This doctrine is based on the Qur'anic assertion: 'God does not charge a soul except what is in its capacity. To it belongs [the good] it has earned and against it shall be [the evil] it has gained' (Q. 2:286).

The *Qur'ān* is not a systematic treatise. It affirms human free will and responsibility and at the same time divine predestination. On the tension between these the Muslim community came to be divided theologically into two distinct camps, the Qadarīyah and the Jabrīyah. The former either denied altogether or minimized the divine decree (*qadar*), and the latter affirmed it absolutely as divine predeterminism (*jabr*). The first camp included Shīʿīs, Muʿtazilīs, and philosophically inclined thinkers, and the second included the Sunnī majority.

In the end, it was the extreme predestinarian position that triumphed. To this day, Friday prayer leaders affirm from mosque pulpits around the world belief in divine decree, be it good or evil. They warn their faithful listeners with this *ḥadīth*: 'The most evil of things are novelties; for every novelty is an innovation. Every innovation is an error, and every error leads to the Fire.'

While Christians considered theology 'the queen of the sciences', Muslims came to consider it the work of Satan. This is because theology has confused the rank and file of Muslims. It has discouraged any kind of innovative thinking. It has paralyzed the intellectuals, preoccupying them with unsolvable questions.

Like the 'gate of *ijtihād*', the 'gate' of theological creativity remained virtually closed in the Sunnī community from the twelfth century onward. Towards the end of the nineteenth century, the Egyptian reformer Muḥammad ʿAbduh (1849–1905), in his treatise *Risālat al-tawḥīd* (The Message of Divine Oneness), reviewed traditional positions and judged them irrelevant. In the Shīʿī community, however, both theology and philosophy continue to flourish with occasional moments of originality.

The Transmission of Greek Philosophy

Greek philosophy was introduced to Muslim learning in the Umayyad period, early in the eighth century. Thus the two disciplines of theology and philosophy developed concurrently, but while the motivation for theology was indigenous, philosophy was an altogether foreign discipline. Furthermore, while speculative theology (*kalām*) is concerned with God's existence and attributes and human destiny, philosophy (called in Arabic *falsafah*) is concerned with rational truth, being and non-being, and the nature of things, God, and the cosmos. Nevertheless, the two disciplines have a common goal, human happiness in this and the next world.

The rapid spread of Islam out of Arabia into Syria and Mesopotamia brought Muslims into touch with Hellenized Syriac Christians, Jews, and people of other faiths and ethnic backgrounds. With the rise of the ʿAbbāsid dynasty, interest in Greek philosophy, science, and medicine increased. Translations into Arabic from either the Greek original or the Syriac began to appear. The court of al-Manṣūr (r. 754–75) attracted a large number of Muslim theologians and traditionists, as well as Christian, Jewish, and Mandean scholars. (In the *Qur'ān*, 2:62 and 5:69, the Mandeans are called Ṣabians. They represent an ancient religion of star worship, with an eclectic overlay of Jewish, Christian, and Gnostic ideas.)

This quest for knowledge reached its peak under the caliph al-Ma'mūn, whose Bayt al-Ḥikmah ('the house of wisdom') was the first institution of higher learning in the Islamic and Western world. Nestorian and Jacobite (Monophysite) Christian scholars had already translated many Greek medical, philosophical, and theological treatises into Syriac and commented on them. They were thus able to carry on their work with greater exactitude at the House of Wisdom, which housed an impressive library of Greek manuscripts. Families of translators, such as the well-known scholar Ḥunayn b. Isḥāq (d. 873), his son Isḥāq b. Ḥunayn, and other members of his family worked in teams, rendering into Arabic the ancient treasures of Hellenistic science and philosophy. Already existing centres of philosophical and medical studies in the Syrian city of Ḥarrān and the Iranian city of Jundī-Shāpūr also made their notable contributions.

The Islamic worldview as presented in the *Qur'ān* rests on the principle of the unity of truth. Muslim philosophers assumed this principle in the study of Greek philosophy, particularly that of Plato and Aristotle and their commentators. For a long time a philosophical work comprising a paraphrase of parts of the *Enneads* of the great mystical philosopher Plotinus (205–70) and a work of the well-known Alexandrian Neoplatonist Proclus (c. 410–85) on the highest good were mistakenly ascribed to Aristotle and known as 'the Theology of Aristotle'.

Thus, in spite of major differences, Plato and Aristotle were considered to have been in total harmony. This mistaken ascription gave Islamic philosophy a distinct character. It was Aristotelian in its logic, physics, and metaphysics, Platonic in its political and social aspects, and Neoplatonic in its mysticism and theology.

Muslim philosophers also studied Greek medicine, notably the works of Galen (129–c. 199); science and astronomy, including Ptolemy's *Almagest* (second century); and mathematics, including Euclid's *Elements* (c. 300 BCE).

Early Muslim Philosophers

Al-Kindī

The first major Muslim philosopher was Abū Yūsuf Ya'qūb al-Kindī (d. 870). He was a theologian-philosopher who, at least intellectually, belonged to the Mu'tazilī rationalistic school. Using philosophical principles and methods of reasoning, al-Kindī defended fundamental Islamic beliefs, such as God's existence and oneness, the temporal creation of the universe by God's command out of nothing, the necessity of prophets, and the inimitability of the *Qur'ān*. Unlike the philosopher who acquires his knowledge through rational investigation and contemplation, the prophet, argues al-Kindī, receives his knowledge instantaneously through divine revelation.

Al-Rāzī

In contrast, Abū Bakr Zakarīyah al-Rāzī (c. 865–926) was a thoroughgoing Platonist. He rejected the Qur'anic view of creation out of nothing, presenting instead a view based on Plato's theory as elaborated in the *Timaeus*. The universe has evolved, according to Rāzī, from primal matter, floating gas atoms in an absolute void. God has imposed order on this primeval chaos, and thus the universe or cosmos has come into being. Moreover, at some distant point in the future, chaos will set in again, as matter will revert to its primeval state.

Since the existence of the world, including humankind, has no moral or religious basis or purpose, there is no need for prophets, nor for religion at all. Human souls, which came down to the body from the celestial realm of the universal soul, will all in the end despise this material body and return to their original source. Salvation, or eternal happiness, may be attained through wisdom and the contemplation of higher things. But in the end, all will be saved.

Rāzī was a humanistic philosopher for whom religion has been the source of social strife and conflict. He was therefore considered a heretic by both theologians and moderate philosophers. For this reason, the works of this fascinating thinker were lost, and the little that is known about his thought is derived from extensive quotations by his detractors.

The Flowering of Islamic Philosophy

In spite of Rāzī's originality and stature, it was really al-Kindī's system of relating philosophy to faith that influenced his successors, notably al-Fārābī and Ibn Sīnā. These two encyclopedic minds dominated the philosophical scene of the tenth and eleventh centuries.

Al-Fārābī

Abū Naṣr al-Fārābī (c. 878–950) was a great philosopher, musical theorist, and accomplished instrumentalist. His Platonic philosophical system was comprehensive and universal. According to al-Fārābī, God is pure intellect and the highest good. From his self-knowledge or contemplation emanate the first intellect, which generates the heavenly spheres and the next in a succession of intellects. Each subsequent intellect generates a sphere and another intellect. The lowest, and hence least perfect, in this hierarchy of being is the active intellect (*'aql*), which governs this world and links its rational elements, the human souls, to their celestial source.

For al-Fārābī, therefore, human society could realize its full potential goodness if it is ruled by a prophet-philosopher. On this basis he constructed a universal political system embodied in a work modelled on Plato's *Republic*, entitled *The Views of the People of the Virtuous City*.

Agreeing with al-Kindī, al-Fārābī held that a prophet is gifted with a sharp intellect capable of receiving philosophical verities naturally and without any mental exertion. He then communicates these truths to the masses, who are incapable of comprehending them on the philosophical level. Religion, for al-Fārābī, is the imitation of philosophy. It is philosophy in imaginative and symbolic form. Since, moreover, the essential truth of religion and philosophy is one, all religions are one in essence. Hence, religious differences are due to the diversity of languages and cultures, not of the truth itself.

Ibn Sīnā

Al-Fārābī was called 'the second teacher', after Aristotle. He was excelled, however, by 'the great master' Ibn Sīnā (980–1037). Ibn Sīnā was a self-taught genius who at the age of ten mastered the religious sciences, and at the age of eighteen became a leading physician, philosopher, and astronomer. His encyclopedic manual of medicine, *al-Qānūn fī al-Ṭibb*, and his philosophical encyclopedia, *al-Shifā'* (The Book of Healing), were part of the curricula of European universities throughout the Middle Ages.

Ibn Sīnā built on al-Fārābī's Neoplatonic ideas a comprehensive system of mystical philosophy and theology. He accepted and developed al-Fārābī's emanationism, placing it in a more precise logical and philosophical framework. He argued that all existing things must be either necessary or possible in themselves. Yet there must be only one being whose existence is necessary in itself and who bestows existence on all other beings and things. This being is God, on whom the existence of all things is contingent. God is the first and necessary cause of all existence; otherwise, there would be infinite regress or circular causality, which is impossible. Thus God is the sole and necessary cause or creator of all things.

The process of creation—or, more precisely, emanation—of the universe begins with God's eternal self-knowledge. This necessitates the existence of a first intellect. It then undergoes a threefold act of cognition: knowledge of God, knowledge of itself as necessitated by him, and knowledge of itself as only a possible being. This act in turn produces three beings: a second intellect, a universal soul, and a body, the outermost sphere of the universe. This threefold act is repeated by each successive intellect till the active intellect, from which emanates the world of generation and corruption, is produced.

The human soul emanates from the active intellect. It is immaterial, but becomes individuated as it enters the body. Ibn Sīnā mystically compares the soul to a beautiful heavenly bird that descends into the body after great reluctance. The body is like a cage out of which the soul seeks to escape. Good souls return to their celestial abode to exist eternally in the great bliss of beholding God and contemplating him. Bad souls, on the other hand, exist in eternal misery, deprived of this beatific vision but forever seeking it.

Ibn Sīnā accepted al-Fārābī's view of religion as the imitation of philosophy. He affirmed the prophethood of Muḥammad and the revelation of the *Qur'ān*. He also affirmed the immortality of the soul, but denied both the resurrection of the body and the reward of paradise and punishment of hell, as depicted in the *Qur'ān* and Islamic tradition.

In his book *The Incoherence [or collapse] of the Philosophers*, al-Ghazālī criticized the philosophers on twenty counts. Seventeen were for errors, but three were for expressions of unbelief (*kufr*). These are: the pre-eternity of this world, Ibn Sīnā's assertion that God knows only universals and not particulars, and denial of bodily resurrection. As an Ash'arī theologian, Ghazālī rejected the philosophical view of causality and the necessity of the world for God. Thus he countered this view with his theory of occasionalism, which denies causality altogether. Al-Ghazālī's critique was itself criticized by the Andalusian Aristotelian philosopher Ibn Rushd.

Philosophy in North Africa and Spain

As philosophy began to decline in the eastern lands of Muslim rule, it experienced a veritable flowering in the West. The decline was due to several important factors. Some of these were: al-Ghazālī's scathing critique, which strengthened an already strong antirationalist reaction among the traditional *'ulamā'*; the tumultuous political, religious, and intellectual situation; and the Seljuqid patronage of Sunnī orthodoxy. Still another important factor was that Ash'arī theology had by then adapted the philosophical rationalistic method for its scholastic purpose, and thus could easily dispense with formal logic and metaphysics, the two fundamental elements of philosophy.

Islamic philosophy in Spain began as a somewhat eclectic mystical movement initiated by Ibn Masarrah (d. 931), a shadowy figure who had no appreciable influence on the development of philosophy. The first true philosopher and heir to al-Fārābī's political and metaphysical thought was Ibn Bājjah (c. 1095–1138). But the two most important philosophers of the twelfth century in Muslim Spain were Ibn Ṭufayl and Ibn Rushd.

Ibn Ṭufayl

Ibn Ṭufayl (c. 1100–1185) was a physician, philosopher, and astronomer of the Almohad court. His numerous philosophical and scientific writings are lost, except for the well-known allegorical tale of Ḥayy b. Yaqẓān. First recounted by Ibn Sīnā, this story seeks to explain the natural relation of religion to philosophy.

On a lush tropical desert island, an infant boy called Ḥayy b. Yaqẓān ('the alive, son of the awake') mysteriously comes into being. He is suckled and cared for by a female gazelle whom Ḥayy takes for his mother. As Ḥayy grows older, he discovers how to clothe and protect himself. In time the gazelle dies, and Ḥayy tries to bring her back to life by dissecting her. But finally he comes to know through his unaided reason that his true mother was a spirit, and not the gazelle.

Through ascetic and spiritual exercises, Ḥayy arrives at the knowledge of God and the highest metaphysical truths.

On a neighbouring island live two brothers called Absāl and Salāmān with a community of non-philosophical religious people. Salāmān is their religious teacher, but Absāl, who is a philosopher, tries in vain to teach them the higher truths of philosophy. Discouraged, Absāl gives up and seeks solitude on a desert island, which turns out to be Ḥayy's island.

Absāl teaches Ḥayy language, and the two live a life of contemplation and asceticism. Finally, they decide to go back and try again to teach the people of Salāmān philosophy, but again to no avail. Ḥayy then enjoins them to remain as they are, and he and his companion return to the desert island to spend the rest of their days.

The story of Ḥayy resembles in some ways the Qur'anic account of how Abraham arrives at the knowledge of God through his native rational and religious disposition (*fiṭrah*). But it is also meant to affirm the view that religion is the imitation of philosophy, as elaborated by al-Fārābī and Ibn Sīnā. In fact, the story was offered as an allegorical explanation of Ibn Sīnā's mystical philosophy.

Ibn Rushd

Ibn Rushd (1126–98) was the greatest Muslim commentator on Aristotle. He came from a long family line of Mālikī jurists, and was himself a noted scholar of Islamic law. His legal training decisively influenced his philosophy.

Ibn Rushd's critique of al-Ghazālī, entitled *The Incoherence of the Incoherence*, methodically criticizes both al-Ghazālī and Ibn Sīnā, the former for his misapprehension of philosophy and the latter for his misunderstanding of Aristotle. Ibn Rushd was the first to reject philosophically the 'theology of Aristotle', and thus construct a true Aristotelian philosophical system.

Ibn Rushd essentially shared his eastern predecessors' views of the relation of religion to philosophy. However, he elaborated this view in his famous double-truth theory, which affirmed the equality of the two approaches to truth. Still, however, religion is meant for the masses, while philosophy is meant for the intellectual élite. His views of the hereafter are ambiguous. While he affirms bodily resurrection, for example, his actual philosophy of the soul leaves little room for this and other Islamic eschatological ideas.

Ibn Rushd was the last great philosopher of Sunnī Islam. After him the thirteenth century witnessed the great philosopher-mystic Ibn 'Arabī, discussed later, and his systematic Aristotelian expositor Ibn Sab'īn (d. 1270). A more empirical philosopher was the Tunisian-born 'Abd al-Raḥmān Ibn Khaldūn (1332–1406).

Through his extensive travels and the positions he held as a jurist and political theorist, Ibn Khaldūn gained great insights into the workings of nations and political and religious institutions. This led him to write a universal history.

In the more important prolegomenon (*Muqaddimah*) to this work, he presents the first social philosophy of history in either the Islamic or the Western world.

The ninth through the twelfth centuries, from al-Kindī to Ibn Rushd, constituted a great epoch of philosophical thinking. Islamic philosophy, particularly Aristotelianism, had a lasting influence on medieval and Renaissance thought in Europe. Muslim philosophers were known to Europeans by Latinized forms of their names: Rhazes for al-Rāzī, Alpharabius or Avennasar for al-Fārābī, Avicenna for Ibn Sīnā, Algazel for al-Ghazālī, Avempace for Ibn Bājjah, Averroës for Ibn Rushd.

Hellenistic philosophy did not end with Ibn Rushd. In the Shī'ī community of Iran especially, philosophy has continued to grow and prosper. For the most part, however, Shī'ī philosophy is heir to Ibn Sīnā's mystical thought and Suhrawardī's illuminationist mystical philosophy.

Since the mid-nineteenth century, the Arab and Muslim world has been influenced philosophically by the West. Only a few Islamic thinkers during this period can be truly considered philosophers. The future does not seem to promise any real revival of this noble discipline.

ISLAMIC MYSTICISM

Sufism, the Mystical Tradition

As we have seen, the rise and rapid spread of Islam was an eminently successful story. There was, however, a darker side to this story, manifested in the power struggles and tribal intrigues and loyalties, as well as the wealth and worldliness that naturally resulted from Islam's rapid expansion. Very early, voices that came to represent important movements of protest were raised against the materialism of Muslim society and its rulers.

Origins

The term *taṣawwuf* (Sufism) is derived from the Arabic word *ṣūf*, meaning 'wool'. In emulation of Jesus, who is represented in Islamic hagiography as a model of ascetic piety, early Ṣūfīs wore a garment of coarse wool over their bare skin as a sign of ascetic poverty.

Although early ascetics sought out Christian desert hermits, from whom they learned ascetic practices and ideas, the primary sources of Islamic mysticism are the *Qur'ān* and Prophetic tradition, as well as the lives of early pious Muslims. The Qur'anic doctrine of God, which simultaneously affirms God's transcendence as the sovereign Lord, creator, and judge of the universe, and his immanence as its merciful sustainer, has been a rich source of mystical piety. God knows the

MYSTICISM

[Rābiʿah al-ʿAdawīyah (713–801), of non-Arab background, was a slave and a flute player before entering a life of religious contemplation.]

The Ṣūfis of Baṣra urged Rābiʿa to choose a husband from among them, rather than continue to live unmarried. She replied, 'Willingly,' and asked which of them was most religious. They replied that it was Ḥasan. So she said to him that if he could give her the answer to four questions, she would become his wife.

'What will the Judge of the world say when I die? That I have come forth from the world a Muslim, or an unbeliever?'

Ḥasan answered, 'This is among the hidden things known only to God ... .'

Then she said, 'When I am put in the grave and Munkar and Nakīr [the angels who question the dead] question me, shall I be able to answer them (satisfactorily) or not?' He replied, 'This is also hidden.'

When people are assembled at the Resurrection and the book are distributed, shall I be given mine in my right hand or my left?' ... 'This also is among the hidden things.'

Finally she asked, 'When mankind is summoned (at the Judgment), some to Paradise and some to Hell, in which group shall I be?' He answered, 'This too is hidden, and none knows what is hidden save God—His is the glory and the majesty.'

Then she said to him, 'Since this is so, and I have these four questions with which to concern myself, how should I need a husband, with whom to be occupied?' [She remained unmarried.] (Smith 1928:11)

[The poetry of Jalāl al-Dīn Rūmī (1207–73) *expresses Islamic mysticism's experience of*

promptings of the human soul and is nearer to every human being 'than one's own jugular vein' (Q. 50:16).

An essential aspect of mysticism is the remembrance of God. The *Qur'ān* enjoins the pious to 'remember God much' (Q. 33:41), to 'remember God in the morning and evening' (Q. 76:25), for 'in the remembrance of God hearts find peace and contentment' (Q. 13:28). The ultimate purpose of all creation is to worship God and hymn his praise (see Q. 17:44 and 51:56).

Theistic mysticism adores God's majesty as well as his beauty. The *Qur'ān* proclaims God's majesty in many verses, but one that has captivated the imagination of pious Muslims is the Throne verse, celebrating God's absolute oneness, eternal sovereignty, and all-encompassing knowledge, power, and providential care. He is the 'Lord of the throne', whose throne encompasses the heavens and the earth (Q. 2:255).

God's beauteous qualities are celebrated in another equally popular verse, the Light verse, which reads:

union with God, using various metaphors for dissolving individual identity, including ardent love and death. From Mathnavi, *III.3901, translated by Nicholson (1950:103).]*

I died as mineral and became a plant
I died as plant and rose to animal,
I died as animal and I was Man.
Why should I fear? When was I less by dying?
Yet once more I shall die as Man, to soar
With angels blest; but even from angelhood
I must pass on: *all except God doth perish* (Q. 28:88).
When I have sacrificed my angel-soul,
I shall become what no mind e'er conceived.
Oh, let me not exist! for Non-existence
Proclaims in organ tones, 'To him we shall return' (Q. 2:151).

[Farid al-Din 'Aṭṭār, who lived in Iran at the turn of the thirteenth century, echoes the phrase bilā kayf *('without asking how') that was used by the theologians of the* kalām *to express paradox, but here uses it in a poetic context to express the mystic's sense of ineffability.]*

His beauty if it thrill my heart
If thou a man of passion art
Of time and of eternity,
Of being and non-entity,
Ask not.
When thou hast passed the bases four,
Behold the sanctuary door;
And having satisfied thine eyes,
What in the sanctuary lies
Ask not. ...
When unto the sublime degree
Thou hast attained, desist to be;
But lost to self in nothingness
And, being not, of more and less
Ask not.
(Arberry 1948:32–3)

> God is the light of the heavens and the earth. The similitude of his light is like a niche in which is a lamp. The lamp is in a glass. The glass is like a radiant star, kindled from a blessed tree, an olive neither of the east nor of the west. Its oil is about to shine forth, even though no fire touches it. Light upon light, God guides to his light whomever he will; God strikes similitudes, and God is knower of all things (Q. 24:35).

The Prophet's night vigils and other devotions, alluded to in the *Qur'ān* (see Q. 73:1–8) and greatly embellished by hagiographical tradition, have served as a living example for pious Muslims across the centuries. *Ḥadīth* traditions, particularly the 'divine sayings' (*ḥadīth qudsī*), have provided a rich source of mystical piety. Most of all, the Prophet's *mi'rāj*, or heavenly journey, has been a guide for numerous mystics on their own spiritual ascent to God.

The Prophet's Companions, especially 'Alī and Abū Bakr, have provided the mystical tradition with good examples of ascetic piety and esoteric knowledge.

Like the Prophet, they renounced this world and lived in poverty. Other Companions and their successors have also been presented in Ṣūfī hagiography as great examples of mystical piety for the faithful to emulate.

Early Asceticism

In Islamic mysticism's beginnings as an ascetic movement, the early ascetics were known as *zuhhād*, meaning 'those who shun [the world and all its pleasures]'. One of the earliest champions of this movement was the well-known theologian and traditionist al-Ḥasan al-Baṣrī, who was born in Madīnah in 642 and died in Baṣrah, in southern Iraq, in 728. He thus lived through both the crises and the rise to glory of the Muslim *ummah*. In a letter addressed to the pious Umayyad caliph 'Umar b. 'Abd al-'Azīz (r. 717–20), Ḥasan likens the world to a snake, soft to the touch, but full of venom. He further holds that God hates nothing more than this world and since creating it has not even once looked upon it.

The early ascetics were also called weepers, for they wept incessantly in fear of God's punishment and yearned for his reward. In this, too, they were following a well-attested Prophetic *ḥadīth*, which says, 'Two eyes will not be touched by Hell-fire, an eye that keeps watch at night in the way of God [that is, in *jihād*] and an eye that weeps constantly in awe of God.'

Significantly, this early ascetic movement began in areas of mixed populations, where other forms of asceticism had existed for centuries. These centres were Kūfah and Baṣrah in Iraq, Khorāsān in northeastern Iran (particularly the region of Balkh in modern Afghanistan), and Egypt. Iraq had long been the home of eastern Christian asceticism. Balkh was an ancient centre of Buddhist ascetic piety. Long before Islam, Egypt was the home of Christian monasticism as well as Gnostic asceticism. However, one indication that Islam is not essentially an ascetic religion is that its ascetic movement was soon transformed into something else. It became a genuinely Islamic mystical tradition.

Divine Love and *gnōsis*

This transformation had its basis in the repudiation of monastic celibacy in both the *Qur'ān* and Prophetic tradition and their insistence on total involvement in the affairs of this world. Opposition to asceticism for its own sake was expressed by well-known scholars and representatives of early mystical piety. Among these was Ja'far al-Ṣādiq, who argued that when God bestows a favour on his servant, he wishes to see it manifested in the servant's attire and way of life. Ja'far's grandfather 'Alī Zayn al-'Ābidīn is said to have argued that God should be worshipped not out of fear of hell or desire for paradise, but in humble gratitude for his gift to the servant of the capacity to worship him.

Rābi'ah

This important development culminated in the woman mystic Rābi'ah al-'Adawīyah of Baṣrah (c. 713–801), who combined in her own life both asceticism and divine love. Because of adverse family circumstances, Rābi'ah was sold into slavery as a child. Her master was so impressed with her piety that he set her free, and she lived the rest of her life alone.

Rābi'ah loved God with no other motive but love itself. Her love was free from either desire for paradise or fear of hell. Her prayer was: 'My Lord, if I worship you in fear of the fire, burn me in hell. If I worship you in desire for paradise, deprive me of it. But if I worship you in love of you, then deprive me not of your eternal beauty.'

Mystical love is not a metaphysical principle, but an outpouring of passionate love. Mystics of all religious traditions have used the language of erotic love to express their love for God. Rābi'ah was perhaps the first to introduce this language into Islamic mysticism. She loved God with two loves, the love of passion (*hawā*) and a spiritual love worthy of him alone.

Dhū al-Nūn

The ninth to the eleventh centuries constitute the formative period of Sufism during which most of its basic principles, beliefs, and practices were developed. An important figure of the ninth century was Dhū al-Nūn al-Miṣrī (i.e., 'the Egyptian', d. 859), who was the first to distinguish between *ma'rifah*, or divine *gnōsis*, and *'ilm*, knowledge acquired through discursive reasoning. In his aphoristic sayings, Dhū al-Nūn speaks tenderly of the love of God, whom the true gnostic hears and sees in every sound and phenomenon of nature.

Dhū al-Nūn spoke of God in opposites that coincide in God alone. God is the one who gives life and causes death, the one who loves his servant and afflicts him with pain and torment. Dhū al-Nūn was also the first to elaborate the theory of the stations and states that the mystic experiences on his spiritual journey to God.

Mystical Ecstasy

The love of which Rābi'ah and Dhū al-Nūn spoke was a devotional love of the worshipful servant for his or her Lord. It did not imply an absolute union of the devotee with God. Such ideas belong to ecstatic mysticism, of which there were many well-known and controversial proponents.

Bayazīd

Bayazīd Bisṭāmī (777–848), about whose life little is known, was one of the best representatives of ecstatic Sufism. Bayazīd saw the quest of the mystic lover as the attainment of absolute union with and hence total annihilation in God. In this union only God exists, for the attributes of the mystic lover are completely annihilated in the divine attributes. In this state of annihilation (*fanā'*), it is not the lover who speaks when he speaks, but God who speaks through him.

Bayazīd couched his mystical theories in pithy theopathic utterances (statements of sympathy with the divine reached through contemplation) known as *shaṭaḥāt* ('fantastic utterances'), which shocked his uninitiated hearers. His intoxicated cries of 'Glory be to me, how great is my majesty' and 'There is none in this garb save God' were regarded as utter blasphemy by the *'ulamā'*. For the initiated mystics, however, such utterances are excusable because they are uttered in the state of mystical intoxication.

Bayazīd was a pious scholar of the religious sciences who strictly observed the rituals of worship and other requirements of the *sharī'ah*. In his mystical life, however, he represents intoxicated Sufism, in contrast with his near contemporary Abū Qāsim al-Junayd of Baghdad (c. 825–910), who typified sober devotional mysticism.

Al-Ḥallāj

Ḥusayn b. Manṣūr al-Ḥallāj (c. 858–922) was another intoxicated Ṣūfī. He was brutally executed for his theopathic utterances in 922 by the 'Abbāsid authorities. Al-Ḥallāj was initiated into Sufism early in life and travelled widely, studying with the best-known Ṣūfī masters of his time, including al-Junayd.

After some time, al-Ḥallāj broke away from his teachers and embarked on the long and dangerous quest of self-realization. It all began when he went one day to see al-Junayd, who asked who was at the door, and al-Ḥallāj answered, 'I, the absolute divine truth' (*anā al-Ḥaqq*). *Al-Ḥaqq* is one of the ninety-nine 'wonderful names' of God mentioned in the *Qur'ān*. Al-Junayd is reported to have sharply reprimanded his wayward disciple and predicted an evil end for him.

After a period of travel as far as India, where he came into contact with sages of other religious traditions, al-Ḥallāj returned to Baghdad and became an itinerant preacher with great charismatic appeal. He attracted many disciples, but also many enemies among the *'ulamā'* as well as moderate Ṣūfīs. He was suspected by the authorities of secretly allying himself with the Qarmatians, an extremist Ismā'īlī sect that posed a considerable threat to the central government of Baghdad.

While the core of al-Ḥallāj's message was moral and deeply spiritual, his at times antinomian behaviour and seemingly incarnationist theology shocked most Muslims of his time. In contrast with Bayazīd, who preached annihilation of the mystic in God, al-Ḥallāj preached total identification of the lover with the beloved. This is clearly expressed in the following ecstatic verses:

> I am He whom I love, and He whom I love is I.
> We are two spirits dwelling in one body.

If thou seest me, you see Him; and if thou seest Him, you see us both
(Nicholson 1931:210–38)

In these verses, al-Ḥallāj speaks of God as dwelling in a human body. To the *'ulamā'*, this meant incarnation. The term *ḥulūl*, which al-Ḥallāj used to mean 'dwelling', is used by Arabic-speaking Christians to signify the incarnation of Christ, the eternal *logos*, in a human body. He was therefore accused of spreading a Christian heresy.

Most probably al-Ḥallāj had no theological or metaphysical theories in mind. Rather, he spoke as one under the influence of divine intoxication. Furthermore, both he and his later defenders were well aware that the secret of love must not be divulged to the uninitiated, who would rightly be scandalized by it. But al-Ḥallāj, who remained continuously in a state of intoxication (*sukr*), could not keep his love for God a secret.

Like Jesus on the cross, al-Ḥallāj, too, forgave his executioners. He did not pray God to forgive them 'for they knew not what they do', but rather for rightly condemning him to death in defence of God's religion. After an eight-year imprisonment and much controversy, al-Ḥallāj danced in his chains to the gallows. He begged his executioners: 'Kill me, O my trusted friends, for in my death is my life, and in my life is my death.' Al-Ḥallāj lives on in the piety and imagination of many Muslims as the martyr of love who was killed for the sin of intoxication with the wine of the love of God by the sword of the *sharī'ah* of God.

The Crystallization of Sufism

Although ecstatic mysticism contributed substantially to the intellectual and spiritual maturity of Sufism, it was too esoteric for the masses and highly suspect for the religious establishment. Sober devotional Sufism, however, continued to appeal to Muslims who found the hair-splitting arguments of the jurists and theologians irrelevant to their spiritual needs.

With the spread of Ṣūfī spirituality, moreover, there was a pressing need for a body of literature that would explain Sufism and legitimize it as one of the religious sciences. To meet this need, a vast literature was produced, which included manuals, biographical dictionaries, *Qur'ān* commentaries, theosophical writings, and mystical poetry. The manuals especially were used to explain esoteric ideas and sayings of ecstatic mystics, to place Sufism in the framework of the *Qur'ān*, Prophetic tradition, and the *sharī'ah*, and to present it as a universal and non-sectarian way to God open to all Muslims. Sufism thus functions not as a sect but as a devotional spirituality cutting across all legal and theological schools.

The mystical life is in reality a spiritual journey to God. The novice who wishes to embark on such an arduous journey must be initiated and guided by a master, *shaykh*, or *pīr*. The *shaykh* of a disciple (*murīd*) is his or her spiritual parent. So intimate should the relationship be between master and disciple that the disciple must absolutely obey the master. As Sufism grew and many well-recognized masters had too many disciples to allow for a one-to-one relationship, teaching manuals became necessary to impart the ideas of great masters to eager disciples.

The crystallization of Sufism and its general acceptance as a legitimate mode of Islamic piety reached a high point in al-Ghazālī. His greatest work, *Iḥyā' 'ulūm al-dīn* (The Revivification of the Religious Sciences), deals with all religious learning from a deeply mystical point of view.

Through this work and al-Ghazālī's own combination of mysticism with his impeccable Sunnī orthodoxy, Sufism secured a place of honour in Muslim piety. Thenceforth, many jurists were also noted masters of the mystic way.

Stations and States

A Ṣūfī disciple is called a traveller (*sālik*). His or her spiritual journey consists of many stations (*maqāmāt*, plural of *maqām*) and psychospiritual states or conditions (*aḥwāl*, plural of *ḥāl*). Once attained, a station remains with the traveller, who should progress to the next. Five stations express the Ṣūfī's effort to realize the quest for God.

> The first step on this spiritual journey is the intention of the traveller to turn to God with sincere repentance (*tawbah*).
>
> The second is steadfastness or patience (*ṣabr*) in all things.
>
> The third station is gratitude (*shukr*) for whatever God decrees, be it good or ill.
>
> The fourth is absolute trust (*tawakkul*) in God.
>
> The fifth is complete acceptance of, or contentment (*riḍā*) with, whatever God decrees for the servant.

A state (*ḥāl*) is a divine gift, a momentary flash of spiritual insight or psychological condition. Mystical states are alternating psychological conditions the mystic experiences on a spiritual journey. States of extreme depression or contraction of the self (*qabḍ*) may alternate without any apparent reason with states of extreme elation or expansion (*basṭ*). In spiritual strivings, a mystic may alternate between moments of intoxication (*sukr*) and sobriety (*ṣaḥw*) but should not remain in any state permanently.

The following four states, also described as stations, are states of intimacy of the lover with the beloved culminating in a new life in God.

> The first is love (*maḥabbah*), which is a divine favour, the capacity to respond to God's love for his faithful servants. The *Qur'ān* says concerning

them, 'those whom God loves and who love him' (*Q*. 5:54).
True love impels the lover to seek nearness (*qurb*) to the beloved, which is the second state or station.
The third is happiness or bliss (*uns*) in the company of the beloved.
The fourth is annihilation or passing away (*fanā'*).

To explain the final stage of this journey to God, Ṣūfī poets have often used the simile of the moth that flutters around a lamp in a state of total absorption until it plunges into the flame and is consumed, thus becoming one with the light. The stations of love, proximity, and blissful companionship inevitably lead to the state of annihilation (*fanā'*) of the lover's self with all the self's attributes in God's attributes.

Since God is the final quest of the mystic, even *fanā'* must be renounced, so as not to stand as a veil between the lover and the beloved. Hence, the final station of the journey is the annihilation of the goal of annihilation. When, like the moth, the lover no longer exists, then God grants him or her a new life or subsistence in him. Thus transformed, the mystic lover returns to the world to show others the way.

Theosophical Sufism

The term 'theosophy' means 'divine wisdom'. In contrast with philosophy, which aims at the knowledge of God or ultimate reality through rational wisdom, theosophy seeks divine knowledge through esoteric *gnōsis* or divine illumination.

The journey to God follows different paths, depending on the spiritual and intellectual potential of the traveller. These paths are the ways of illumination and contemplation. God, the ultimate goal of the journey, is held in his essence to be beyond human conception and knowledge. A third way, the way of negation, is therefore advocated to guide the traveller along the middle course between divine immanence and transcendence, between extreme monism and pantheism. The way of negation, which speaks of God as 'not this, not that', to use a phrase from a Hindu text, insures a proper relationship between the worshipful servant and his or her Lord.

Suhrawardī

The way of illumination was elaborated by the great master of illumination (*shaykh al-ishrāq*) Shihāb al-Dīn Suhrawardī (c. 1155–91). Drawing on the Qur'anic Light verse and al-Ghazālī's interpretation of it in his famous treatise *Mishkāt al-Anwār* (The Niche of Lights), and on ancient Iranian and Neoplatonic wisdom, Suhrawardī constructed an impressive cosmos of light and darkness populated by countless luminous angelic spirits.

The source from which this divine cosmos emanates is God, who is hidden from the human soul by veils of light and darkness. The soul's ultimate quest is to penetrate these veils through the power of intellect until it returns to its original heavenly source. While in the body, the soul is in the exile of the west, the realm of darkness. The body is likened to a deep well into which the soul falls and out of which it seeks to escape and return to the east, the source of light.

Suhrawardī belongs to the ancient Gnostic tradition, which had its source in Greco-Iranian wisdom. Gnosticism, which was rejected by the ancient Church, was accepted in its Islamic form by Shīʿī theosophy as *ʿirfān* (divine *gnōsis*). Thus Suhrawardī's theosophy has had a deep and lasting influence on Shīʿī esoteric wisdom.

Ibn ʿArabī, the Great *shaykh*

By far the most important master of Islamic theosophy was Muḥyī al-Dīn Ibn ʿArabī. Ibn ʿArabī was born in 1165 in Muslim Spain, where he received his early Islamic education. He thus belonged to Spain's eclectic mystical tradition. He then travelled widely in the Middle East, finally settling in Damascus, where he died in 1240.

The core doctrine of Ibn ʿArabī's theosophy is 'the unity of being' (*waḥdat al-wujūd*), which he elaborated in numerous books and treatises. According to this doctrine, God in his essence remains from eternity in 'blind obscurity'. He manifests himself, however, in his creation through an eternal process of self-disclosure or manifestation (*tajallī*). According to Ibn ʿArabī therefore, human beings need God for their very existence, but God needs them to be known.

This means that all beings are in reality manifestations of God's attributes of either majesty or beauty. Beings that represent harmony, love, compassion, and mercy manifest God's beauteous attributes, which are supremely manifested in paradise. On the other hand, beings that represent disharmony, overwhelming power, and judgement manifest God's attributes of majesty, which are fully manifested in hell. It follows from this that if Muḥammad, as a guide to God, represents God's attribute *al-Hādī* ('he who guides aright'), then Satan, who leads into error, represents God's attribute *al-Muḍill* ('he who leads astray'). This means that there is in reality no good or evil, but God, the highest good.

Ibn ʿArabī's doctrine of the unity of being had many implications. If God alone really is, then all ways ultimately lead to him. This means that the various religions are mere names, for the reality is one. Ibn ʿArabī says:

> My heart has become capable of every form, a pasture for gazelles, a cloister for monks, a temple for idols, the votary's Kaʿbah, the tablets of the Torah, the scroll of the *Qur'ān*. It is the religion of love that I hold: wherever turns its mounts, love shall be my religion and my faith.

Between the material world of multiplicity and the divine realm of unity stands the Perfect Man whose existence is necessary for the world's existence. This Perfect Man is the prophet Muḥammad, whose light, or Muḥammadan reality, was the first to be created by God. Thus Muḥammad becomes the divine creative *logos*, for whose sake all things were created. He is the seal of the prophets, and the Perfect Man after him is the seal of the saints (*awliyā'*).

Little of Ibn 'Arabī's thought is new or original. Yet as a systematizer, he remains one of the greatest mystical geniuses of all time. In the poetry of ecstatic mystics, his idea of the unity of being led to the cry of Persian Ṣūfīs of 'All is he' (in Persian, *hama-ūst*). His idea of the Perfect Man raised Muḥammad to a divine status high above mortal man. In fact the Muḥammad of Ibn 'Arabī is more like the Christ of Christianity than the all-too-human Prophet of Islam. Ibn 'Arabī's theosophical system is arguably the most creative product of the multireligious society of Muslim Spain.

Mystical Poetry

The thirteenth century was one of the most troubled, but also the most creative, periods of Muslim history. Besides Ibn 'Arabī, great Persian and Arab poets presented the mysticism of love in a rich variety of themes and expressions. The Egyptian poet 'Umar b. al-Fāriḍ (c. 1181–1235) presents the spiritual journey to God in exquisite verses unsurpassed in Arabic poetry. Another poet, the Persian Ṣūfī Farīd al-Dīn 'Aṭṭār (c. 1142–c. 1220), presents the same journey in touching allegorical tales.

In his allegory *The Conference of the Birds*, 'Aṭṭār tells of thirty birds setting out on a long and arduous journey in search of the legendary phoenix, the king of birds. 'Aṭṭār employs an ingenious play on the two Persian words *sīmurgh*, meaning 'phoenix', and *sī murgh*, meaning 'thirty birds'. Having passed through the various mystical states and stations, they arrive at the realization that the object of their quest was in reality within them.

Rūmī

The most creative poet of the Persian language is Jalāl al-Dīn Rūmī (1207–73), who, like Ibn 'Arabī, was the product of a multireligious and multicultural environment. Rūmī was born in Balkh, but fled with his parents as a child before the advancing Mongols. At last they settled in Konya, the ancient Byzantine city Iconium, in central Anatolia (Turkey).

In 1244, Rūmī met Shams of Tabrīz, who was a wandering Ṣūfī. The two men developed a relation of closest intimacy, so that Rūmī neglected his teaching duties, as he could not be separated from his friend for a single moment. In the end Shams disappeared, and Rūmī poured out his soul in heart-rending verses expressing the love he held for the 'Sun' (Shams) of Tabrīz.

Rūmī's greatest masterpiece is his *Mathnawī* (Couplets), consisting of nearly 30,000 verses. The spirit of this vast panorama of poetry may be clearly discerned in its opening verses, which portray the haunting melodies of the *nay* (reed flute) telling its sad tale of separation from its reed-bed. In stories, couplets of lyrical beauty, and at times even coarse tales of sexual impropriety, the *Mathnawī* depicts the longing of the human soul for God.

Ṣūfī Brotherhoods

The institution of religious fraternities is an ancient and widespread phenomenon. The Ṣūfī idea of the friendship (*ṣuḥbah*) of kindred spirits provided the framework for this phenomenon in Muslim piety. The Islamic emphasis on communal life and worship was no doubt another determining factor.

The earliest Ṣūfī brotherhoods date back to the late eighth century. Small ascetic groups gathered on the island of Abadan in the Persian Gulf away from the allurements of city life. Abadan, with its harsh climate, was well suited for ascetic austerities. Two terms for Ṣūfīs are derived from words for 'poor', Arabic *faqīr* and Persian *darvīsh*.

The Būyids were succeeded in the eleventh century by the Seljuqs, a staunch Sunnī dynasty. To promote Sunnī orthodoxy, Seljuq rulers encouraged Ṣūfī brotherhoods as a counterweight to Shī'ī, and particularly Ismā'īlī, missionary activities. This patronage made Ṣūfī fraternities an important social and spiritual force in Muslim society.

By the thirteenth century, these fraternities became institutionalized in mystical paths (*ṭarīqahs*) or Ṣūfī orders. They began as teaching and devotional institutions centred in *khāngāhs* and *zāwiyahs* in Persian and Arab urban centres. A Ṣūfī order is usually founded by a famous *shaykh* or a disciple in his *shaykh*'s name. A *zāwiyah* or *khāngāh* was often a large compound consisting of a school, mosque, and humble dwellings of disciples surrounding the residence of the *shaykh* or head of the order.

Ṣūfī orders often attached themselves to craft or trade guilds in the city's main bazaar. It has been a widely accepted custom for many Muslims to belong to a Ṣūfī order. Lay associates provided the order with a good source of income and received in return the blessing (*barakah*) of the *shaykh* as they participated in the order's devotional observances.

The truth and authenticity of a *shaykh*'s claim to spiritual prominence depended on his spiritual genealogy. By the thirteenth century, Ṣūfī chains of initiation, similar to chains of *isnād* in *ḥadīth* transmission, were established. A Ṣūfī *silsilah*, or chain of initiation, begins with the *shaykh*'s immediate master who invested him with the Ṣūfī patched frock (*khirqah*) and goes back in an unbroken chain to 'Alī, one of his descendants, or to other companions of the Prophet or their successors.

It is not unusual for a famous *shaykh* to be initiated by several well-known masters, thus greatly enhancing his prestige and *barakah*. Some *shaykhs* claimed to have received their patched frock from al-Khiḍr, the mysterious green prophet who lives forever as a wandering ascetic initiating spiritual adepts into the Ṣūfī path and helping the pious who call upon him in times of danger or difficulty.

Generally speaking, two main chains of initiation came to be recognized. The first goes back to al-Junayd and typifies sober Sufism, the other to Bāyazīd Bisṭāmī and typifies intoxicated or ecstatic mysticism. From these two, hundreds of *silsilahs* evolved.

Out of the ecstatic branch of Ṣūfī *silsilahs* arose the order of the Malāmatīyah (self-blaming or self-reproaching Ṣūfīs). The Malāmatī Ṣūfīs eschewed all forms of ostentation, and thus rejected Ṣūfī initiation or the guidance of a *shaykh*, and lived in continuous self-examination. Although they were meticulous in their observance of the *sharī'ah*, the Malāmatī Ṣūfīs often brought blame and sharp reproof upon themselves through strange and unsanctioned behaviour. An extreme form of the Malāmatīyah is the wandering dervishes, who were known as Qalandarīyah. They impudently spurned all religious laws and practices.

Veneration of the Saints

The term *walī* (plural, *awliyā'*) means an intimate friend or ally. The *Qur'ān* uses the term to refer to God, who is the protecting friend or patron (*walī*) of the people of faith. The *Qur'ān* also uses the term to refer to the righteous who are the intimate friends (*awliyā'*) of God.

The epithet *walī* has been applied to Ṣūfī *shaykhs*, particularly the heads of Ṣūfī orders. Through his spiritual lineage, a Ṣūfī *shaykh* inherits the grace or *barakah* of his masters, who inherited it from the Prophet. In turn, the *shaykh* bestows his *barakah*, or healing power, on his devotees, both during his life and, with even greater efficacy, after his death.

The concept of Ṣūfī saintship (*walāyah*) developed out of the idea of the Perfect Man, as elaborated in Ibn 'Arabī's cosmic hierarchy. This doctrine was further developed by the great *shaykh*'s successors, particularly 'Abd al-Karīm al-Jīlī (1365–1424) in his famous treatise *al-Insān al-kāmil* (The Perfect Man).

The Perfect Man must exist in every age. He is the intimate (*walī*) of God and repository of his blessing. He is thus known as the great succour or refuge and the pole or axis (*quṭb*) around whom the existence of the world revolves. The Perfect Man is assisted by a large hierarchy of lesser saints, whose presence in the world preserves its stability and well-being.

As this high office came to be claimed for many *shaykhs* simultaneously, it led to great rivalry among some of the more popular Ṣūfī orders. It also led to exaggerated forms of saint veneration, manifested in pilgrimages to the tombs of famous *walī*s to whom prayers for healing, prosperity, and intercession continue to be directed.

The *shaykhs* of Ṣūfī orders are like the saints of the Catholic Church in that miracles as divine favours (*karāmāt*) are ascribed to them, but unlike Christian saints, they are recognized through popular acclaim rather than through official canonization.

Devotional Practices

Besides the acts of worship prescribed in the Five Pillars of Islam, Ṣūfīs observe additional devotional prayers, night vigils, and fasts. The purpose of such ritual practices is to draw the devotee closer to God. In a well-known *ḥadīth qudsī*, God declares:

> My servant continues to draw nearer to me through extradevotional prayers (*nawāfil*) until I love him. When I love him, I become his eye with which he sees, his ear with which he hears, his hand with which he grasps, and his foot with which he walks. Thus through me he sees, hears, grasps, and walks.

The Dhikr

The most characteristic Ṣūfī practice is the *dhikr* (remembrance) of God, which may be a public or private ritual. The congregational *dhikr* ritual is usually held before the dawn or evening prayers. It consists of the repetition of the name of God, Allāh, or the *shahādah*, 'There is no god except God' (*lā ilaha illā Allāh*). The *dhikr* is often accompanied by special bodily movements and, in some Ṣūfī orders, by elaborate breathing techniques.

Often the performance of the *dhikr* is what distinguishes the various Ṣūfī orders from one another. In some popular orders, it is a highly emotional practice intended to stir the devotee into a state of frenzy similar to charismatic ritual practices in some Pentecostal churches. In the widespread sober Naqshbandī order (founded by Bahā' al-Dīn al-Naqshbandī, d. 1388), the *dhikr* is silent, offered as an inward prayer of the heart.

True *dhikr* must progress from the audible remembrance of the tongue to the silent remembrance of the heart and finally to the recollection of the innermost being of the pious Ṣūfī. At this stage, *dhikr* becomes a constant state of the devotee, so that every breath or heartbeat is an inward utterance of God's name.

The Samā'

Another distinctly Ṣūfī devotional practice is the *samā'*, meaning 'hearing' or 'audition'. It consists of listening to often hypnotically beautiful chants of mystical poetry, accompanied by various musical instruments. As instrumental music is not legally allowed in the mosque, the *samāʿ* sessions are usually held in halls adjacent to the mosque, or at the shrine of a famous *shaykh*.

In the Mevlevi (Mawlawī) order—so called after Mawlānā ('our master') Jalāl al-Dīn Rūmī and founded by his son shortly after his death—music and dance constitute a vital element of the order's devotional life. Here the dance is a highly sophisticated art symbolizing the perfect motion of the stars, where the haunting melodies of the reed flute and large orchestra accompanying the chants of mystical poetry in praise of the Prophet and the great founder of the order echo the primordial melodies of the heavenly spheres. It is this primordial music that the soul hears on the day of the primordial covenant, 'the day of *alastu* (Am I not [your Lord])', and which it recollects in the music and dance of the Whirling Dervishes, as the Mevlevis are called.

This elevated use of music is not, however, typical of all orders. In some cases music led to wine drinking and the use of drugs to induce a state of heightened consciousness. Among popular and antinomian (i.e., anti-law) Ṣūfīs, it also led to the neglect of regular worship. Furthermore, the beautiful face of a beardless boy, which figures prominently in Ṣūfī poetry as a symbol of divine beauty, became an actual object of erotic love as such boys adorned the *samāʿ* sessions. This, of course, led to the banning of music by most jurists, or greatly restricting its use by others. Nevertheless, music remains an integral part of Ṣūfī devotions.

Ṣūfī Orders and the Decline of Sufism

The decline of Sufism in modern times can be attributed to some external, but also many internal, causes. Perhaps the most important of these is the actual growth of Ṣūfī orders from small spiritual fraternal societies to large international *ṭarīqahs*. Leadership in these orders was no longer a spiritually transmitted authority, but a hereditary office passed on from father to son with little regard to leadership qualities or spiritual attainments.

This development reached a high point by the mid-fourteenth century. Thenceforth, Ṣūfī brotherhoods generally were centres not of spiritual training, but rather of cultural adaptations of Islamic faith and piety in areas as far apart as North Africa and Southeast Asia. This in turn led to the introduction of strange shamanistic practices into the rituals of some Ṣūfī orders.

Among the major external causes are the rise of reform movements, such as the Wahhābī movement in the eighteenth century, and the strong influences of Western secularism and rationalism on Muslim thought in the nineteenth and twentieth centuries. Such political and intellectual religious movements rejected Sufism as an irrational and world-renouncing distortion of what they held to be true Islam. Of course, exaggerated practices of saint veneration have been a determining factor in this generally negative attitude towards Sufism.

Many educated Muslims claim that Sufism is an otherworldly religious movement that neglected the social, political, and military requirements of *jihād*. This claim is unfounded. From the beginning, well-known Ṣūfī ascetics died in battle. Widespread as a phenomenon in the Middle Ages and highly important were the military Ṣūfī fraternities called *ribāṭ*, a term meaning 'keeping watch in times of war for the enemy' and recalling Q. 3:200. In fact, the well-known Western military monastic orders, such as the Templars and Hospitallers, were patterned on the Ṣūfī *ribāṭ*. The motto of such fraternities is 'be monks (*ruhbān*) by night and knights (*firsān*) by day.'

Moreover, Ṣūfī orders such as the Sanūsīyah (founded by Muḥammad b. 'Alī al-Sanūsī, c. 1787–1859) in North Africa, and the Tijānīyah (founded by Abū al-'Abbās Aḥmad al-Tijānī, 1737–1815) in North and West Africa, played a primary role in the struggle of these regions against Western colonialism and in the preservation of their religion and culture.

In spite of its many ups and downs throughout Muslim history, Sufism has always shown an amazing capacity for self-reform and regeneration. It was the Ṣūfīs who preserved Islamic learning and spirituality after the fall of Baghdad in 1258. It was also the Ṣūfīs and Ṣūfī piety that carried Islam to Africa and Asia, and it is now Ṣūfī piety that is exerting the deepest spiritual influence of Islam on the West. While Sufism lacks the vitality and creativity of earlier centuries, it is experiencing a real revival in many parts of the Muslim world.

ISLAMIC ARCHITECTURE AND ART

Architecture

The function of mosques included not only prayer, implied in the Arabic *masjid* ('kneeling place'), but also other community activities, implied in Arabic *jāmi'* ('gatherer'). Early mosques functioned as treasuries, with financial records; as law courts, where the *qāḍī* or judge heard cases; and as educational centres with formal and informal classes and study circles. These other institutions in time received their own buildings, appropriate to their activities, while the function of public assembly and prayer continued to dictate the architectural form of mosques. Two other main types of buildings with religious functions developed: the *madrasah* or religious school, and the tomb or mausoleum; in their architectural execution, they drew on much the same repertory of styles that mosques did.

The essential features of a mosque are a fountain for washing hands, face, and feet upon entering, a broad area for kneeling and prostration in prayer, a pulpit (*minbar*) from which the leader of Friday noon worship may deliver the *khuṭbah* or sermon, and an imageless niche (*miḥrāb*) in the middle of the wall closest to Makkah, indicating the *qiblah* or direction of prayer. Not part of the earliest

The Mughal emperor Shah Jehan built the Taj Mahal in loving memory of his wife. Construction of the mausoleum was begun in 1632 and completed in 1643. (Suraj N. Sharma/Government of India Tourist Office)

mosques in Arabia but introduced in Umayyad Damascus and characteristic of Islam in many places is the minaret, a tower from which the voice of the *mu'adh-dhin* delivers the call to prayer five times each day.

Most mosques, beginning with the Prophet's mosque in Madīnah, located the ablution fountain in an open-air entrance courtyard, and roofed over the prayer area with a colonnade or portico-type construction. As worshippers took their place side by side in rows facing the *qiblah*, the prayer area was often wider than deep, in this sense more like a Chinese or Japanese temple than like a Christian cathedral. In the larger early Arab mosques, the roof over the prayer hall most commonly rested on an orchardlike arrangement of columns, and new rows could be added if expansion was called for.

A development in Persian architecture, influential also in India, was the *īwān*, a tall apselike or half-domed area flanking the ablution court. One for each

Worshippers use the fountain in the entrance court of the Qairiwiyin Mosque in Fès, Morocco, to wash hands, face, and feet before going in for prayer. (Willard G. Oxtoby)

side of the court, *īwāns* gave an architectural focus to the structure as well as entrance to the roofed area beyond. For symmetry, Persian mosque entrances, somewhat similar to the *īwāns*, are often flanked by a pair of minarets.

The Turks made much use of the dome, an important feature of church architecture among the Byzantines who had preceded them. A high central dome, resting on four semidome apses, enclosed the prayer space. Some major Turkish mosques enjoyed four or more minarets, marking the corners of the mosque. Central dome architecture, but often simpler and without minarets, characterizes mosques in Malaysia and Indonesia, where the rainy climate dictates that the prayer space be roofed over.

Ultimately, much in Islamic architecture is specific to geographic regions and their distinctive idioms. The keyhole arch, for instance, though it appears in the great Umayyad mosque of Damascus, is characteristic mainly of North Africa and Islamic Spain. A shallow pointed arch like the English Tudor arch emerged in Iraq, dominated in Iran, and spread to Central Asia and Mughal India. The bud- or onionlike domes of Indo-Muslim architecture have been picked up in Southeast Asia. In China, many mosques are built like Chinese temples, with tiled roofs resting on wooden columns and bracket structures. A number of Chinese minarets are built in the form of East Asian Buddhist pagodas.

Art

For many Buddhists, Hindus, and Christians, deity is represented in human form in rich and elaborate detail, and portraits and statues of holy teachers and saints abound. On first glance it would seem that Islamic art is hopelessly austere, its repertory of admissible themes severely restricted.

Muslims assemble for prayer every Friday at midday. Worshippers line up in rows for the prayers, which include a series of bows and prostrations. (C.V. McArthur)

Extended exposure to Islamic art can produce an opposite impression, however. Within the themes and limits set for it, Islamic art appears rich, elaborate, even exuberant. Three achievements stand out. Calligraphy, that is, the decorative use of script forms and units of text, has been given a sophistication that only the users of the Chinese character script in East Asia can rival. Islamic geometrical decoration, particularly the interlaced hexagonal and octagonal motifs termed arabesques by the West, knows no rival in other world art. And Islamic floral motifs, particularly in the arts of Iran, complement the other two.

If a common aesthetic binds calligraphic, geometrical, and floral decoration together, it is perhaps that each of these elements offers a means of covering surfaces decoratively but abstractly, and that each therefore must point beyond itself in a way that pictorial images are not necessarily obliged to do. Design using each of these three techniques can capture the attention of the viewer, but direct it to the larger structure being decorated, whether that be a page of an illuminated *Qur'ān*, a Turkish prayer rug, an inlaid wooden *minbar*, or the tiled entrance of a mosque. Even in secular applications of Islamic art, such as Syrian brass utensils or Persian pile carpets, the success of Islamic decoration is not detail alone, but organizational structure.

In Xi'an, China, the Great Mosque is built in the architectural style of Chinese palace and temple halls, and its minaret resembles a Chinese pagoda. (Willard G. Oxtoby)

Islamic calligraphy offers the most palpably religious content, for the texts used in mosque decoration are often passages from the *Qur'ān*, and bazaar craft items are adorned with some of the ninety-nine 'wonderful names' or attributes of God.

The characteristic understanding of Islamic art is that Islam, like Judaism before it, is an iconoclastic religion that bans the making of images on theological grounds. For Judaism this was true of the norms in rabbinic literature more than in the actual decoration of Greco-Roman synagogues. It is therefore surprising that in its normative text the *Qur'an* nowhere specifically prohibits the making of images.

Instead, Islamic iconoclasm appears not to be directly mandated but to be derivative in the *ḥadīth* tradition from the Qur'anic concern that the worshipper elevate no other being to parity or equivalency with God. A further contribution to the Islamic repudiation of images is the notion that humans should not usurp God's unique role as creator. At the folk level, this idea plays out in interesting ways. For instance, Persian carpets have been woven with deliberate minor asymmetries or flaws because, it is asserted, only God is perfect.

Besides the Jewish reluctance to make images, there was the Christian. In particular, during the Umayyad caliphate in Damascus, the Byzantines were hotly divided into pro-image and anti-image parties in Constantinople. Some scholars of Christian history think that Byzantine iconoclasm was spurred along the Umayyad-Byzantine frontier by Islamic rejection of images, while some Islamics scholars have given the Byzantines credit for encouraging such tendencies in Umayyad Syria. Perhaps both things happened. We do know that the Umayyads' coinage carried portraits of the rulers in Byzantine style for almost two decades before coin designs switched to Arabic names and mottoes. In those years, the reverses of Umayyad coins continued to use a Byzantine cross, complicating our options if we theorize about what symbolic meaning various designs had for their users.

Three-dimensional sculpture has remained absent from the art of Muslims, but outside of mosque contexts two-dimensional representation of living creatures has enjoyed important development. Some Persian carpets have animals in their garden scenes. Persian and Mughal Indian manuscripts are illustrated with miniature paintings of legendary heroes and current rulers. Among Iranian Shiʿis, portraits of ʿAlī are a focus of popular piety. While representations of the Prophet himself are avoided, the steed of his *miʿrāj* or heavenly journey, Burāq, is portrayed in popular art (such as on Afghan and Pakistani trucks and buses) as a winged horse with a human head. And calligraphy consisting of Arabic script has been used ingeniously to create the outlines of birds and animals, as well as crescents, mosques, minarets, and other forms to the present day.

The principal elements of Islamic decoration—floral, geometrical, and calligraphic—can be seen on the glazed tiles on the Dome of the Rock in Jerusalem. (Baruch Gian)

THE SPREAD OF ISLAM

Like Christianity, Islam is a universalistic and therefore a missionary religion. Muslims believe that its message of faith is intended for all humankind, to be implemented in a community transcending geographical, cultural, and linguistic borders.

The vast domains of this community are designated as *dār al-Islām*, meaning the 'house' or abode of Islam. The rest of the world constitutes the sphere of peace or truce (*ṣulḥ*), also called the sphere of war (*ḥarb*), yet the whole world is regarded by Muslims as potentially the sphere of Islam.

Islam is ideologically and historically a post-Jewish, post-Christian reli-

Figure 4.1
LANGUAGE AND CULTURE IN THE SPREAD OF ISLAM

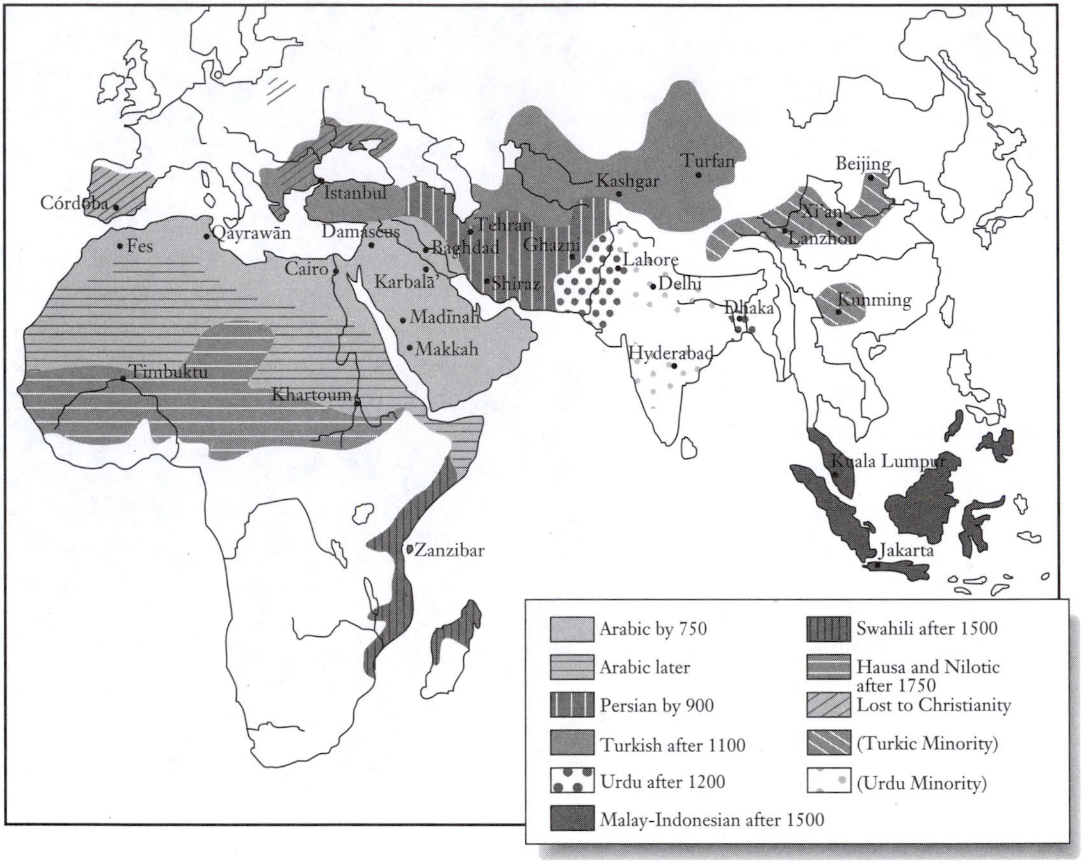

gion. Ideologically, it saw itself as one of the religions of the Book, confirming the scriptures before it, notably the Torah and the Gospel. Historically, Muslims from the beginning reacted to and interacted with the communities of other faiths, notably Christians and Jews. It was therefore necessary for Islam as a religio-political power to regulate its relations with non-Muslim subjects.

The *Qur'ān* regards Jews and Christians as People of the Book. They were promised full freedom to practise their faith in return for a poll tax called *jizyah*, which also guaranteed physical and economic protection and exemption from military service. Legally such communities came to be known as *dhimmīs*, meaning protected people. In the course of time, this designation was expanded to encompass other communities with sacred scriptures, including Zoroastrians encountered in Iran and Hindus in India.

In the first century of Islam, conquest and military occupation provided the impetus for its spread. Much of the Byzantine and Roman world and all of the Sasanian Persian domains yielded to the Arab armies and came under Umayyad rule. In subsequent centuries, especially where Arabs, Persians, and Turks ruled, politico-military regimes continued to contribute to Islam's dominance.

But over time, the piety achieved through the preaching and living examples of mystics, teachers, and traders has reached further and endured longer than the activity of caliphs and conquerors. It was principally through these that Islam spread to China, Southeast Asia, and East and West Africa. In modern times, migration and missionary activity have carried it to the Western hemisphere as well.

The original home (Arabia) and the earliest conquests (Egypt, Syria, and Iraq) remained the heartland of Arab Islam. The Arabic language replaced the Greek of the Byzantine Christians as the vernacular, and likewise replaced the Syriac (Aramaic) of Syro-Mesopotamian Christians. The interaction of Muslims with Christian and Jewish minorities and with the culture of the Greco-Roman world contributed to the outlines of medieval Arabic civilization.

But while part of the Byzantine Empire remained Byzantine, the Arabs became masters of the entire domain of the Byzantines' rivals to the east, the Sasanian Persians. From Iraq to the Central Asian frontier of India, Muslims shaped a medieval Iranian civilization in many ways the equal of the Arabs'. In this region, while Arabic was the language of worship and theological learning, it did not replace Persian as the vernacular. Iran became Muslim without ceasing to be Iranian. Its rich literature, architecture, and art made it a leader among what would be numerous non-Arab Muslim civilizations in different parts of the world.

North Africa

After the conquest of what came to be the heartland of Islam—Syria, Egypt, and Persia—North Africa was conquered in the second half of the seventh century. Before Islam, North Africa was first an important Roman province, and then an equally important home of Latin Christianity. With its indigenous Berber, Phoenician, Roman, and Byzantine population, North Africa was an area of rich cultural and religious diversity. It has therefore always maintained a distinct religious and cultural identity, reflecting its ancient heritage.

Soon after the conquest, North Africa's Berber aristocracy was adopted into the Arab tribes, assuming the names of their conquerors. Thus the famous young general Ṭāriq b. Ziyād, who crossed from Morocco into southern Spain in 711, was an Arabized Berber. Gibraltar, the small rock settlement on which his forces first landed, still bears his name, Jabal Ṭāriq ('Ṭāriq's mountain'). The complete integration of North Africa into Arab Islam, however, was a slow and often turbulent process, lasting nearly four centuries.

With the shift of the capital from Damascus to Baghdad, the main orientation of the eastern Islamic domains consequently became more Persian than Arab, more Asian than Mediterranean. Meanwhile, the centre of Arab Islamic culture shifted from Syria to the western Mediterranean: to Qayrawān, the capital of North Africa, in what is today Tunisia; and to Córdoba, Islam's western capital, in Spain, which rivalled Baghdad and Cairo in its cultural splendour. North African mystics, scholars, and philosophers were all instrumental in this remarkable achievement.

North African society under Islam was as diverse as it had been in Roman and Christian times. There were Shī'īs, or at least 'Alid sympathizers, making it possible for the Fāṭimids to launch their successful missionary and military ventures. There were also Khārijīs, whose moderate Ibāḍī legal school is still represented among some Berber tribes.

The most lasting and creative expression of this diversity has been the Ṣūfī orders and suborders known as *zāwiyahs*. Members of such orders, like the Murābiṭūn (in Spanish, Almoravids) constituted one of the dynasties that ruled Islamic Spain after the demise of the Umayyad caliphate. The *zāwiyah* piety under Almoravids, known in European languages as that of the Marabouts, has continued to influence North African Islam till the present. A Marabout is 'one who keeps watch by night' (*murābiṭ*). Originally this term referred to fighters who kept watch over the borders of the Muslim state. As many such fighters were pious Ṣūfīs, a *murābiṭ* became a legendary saint venerated by the pious, who visit his tomb for miraculous healing and other favours.

Recently, in their struggle for independence from French and Italian colonization, North African religious scholars and particularly Ṣūfī masters have played a crucial role. They helped preserve the religious and cultural identity of their people and mobilized them to resist Italian and French colonization in Libya and Algeria. In spite of the deep influence of the French language and secular culture, North African popular piety still reflects its classical heritage.

Spain

Before the appearance of Arab conquerors on the Iberian Peninsula in 711, Spain was torn by civil strife. The Jews, who had for centuries lived in Spain, were subjected to harsh restrictions by rulers recently converted to Catholic Christianity. (Prior to the sixth century, Spain had known the form of Christianity called Arianism, which had spread among the Goths.) The Jews aided the Arabs, seeing them as liberators.

With astonishing rapidity, Umayyad forces conquered the land of Andalusia, or al-Andalus, as the Arabs called southern Spain. They laid the foundations for a unique and fabulous Hispano-Arab culture. Arab men intermarried with local women, thus creating a mixed but harmonious society. The resulting culture was Arab in language and expression and Arabo-Hispanic in spirit.

Muslims, Christians, and Jews lived together in mutual tolerance for centuries before fanatical forces on both sides stifled one of the most creative experiments in interfaith living in human history.

The 900-year-long history of Arab Spain (711–1609) witnessed the usual symbiotic creativity as well as the tensions and conflicts that beset any multireligious, multicultural society ruled by a minority regime. It witnessed the great achievements and the ultimate failure of Islamic faith and civilization not only in Spain, but in Europe as well.

The Muslims of Spain adopted the conservative Mālikī legal school, introduced from North Africa, where it prevails to this day. In spite of its religious conservatism, however, Arab Spain produced some of the greatest jurists, mystics, and philosophers, such as the jurist, *littérateur*, and heresiographer Ibn Ḥazm (994–1064), the mystics Muḥyī al-Dīn b. ʻArabī (1165–1240) and Ibn Masarrah (d. 931) and his mystical-philosophical school, and the great philosophers Ibn Ṭufayl (c. 1109–85) and Ibn Rushd (Averroës, 1126–98), among others.

Arabo-Hispanic mysticism and philosophy reflected their Islamo-Christian-Jewish environment. Andalusian society was made up of three classes. There were the adopted (*muwallad*) converts, who accepted both Islam and the Arabic language. There were the Arabized (Spanish, *mozarrab*) Christians, who accepted the Arabic language and its culture, but not Islam. And there were those who remained Latin in both religion and culture. Cluniac and Benedictine monks who worked tirelessly to preserve Latin Christianity and culture in Spain had at times to resort to extreme measures to counter the appeal of the Arabic language and culture among their Christian coreligionists.

The Umayyad caliphate, which ended in 1031, was followed by a period of petty dynasties known as 'Party Kings'. These were followed by the two conservative Moroccan dynasties of al-Murābiṭūn (1056–1147) and al-Muwaḥḥidūn ('believers in the One God'; in Spanish, Almohads) (1130–1269). The latter was a messianic dynasty that, by its nature and ideology, could not tolerate the multireligious society of Umayyad Spain. Its repressive policies towards non-Muslims, and even Muslims who did not share their ideology, hastened the trend towards the Christian reconquest of Spain, which had begun already during the Umayyad period.

By 1492, when King Ferdinand of Aragon (r. 1479–1516) and Queen Isabella of Castile (r. 1474–1504) were united in marriage, and thus unified most of Spain under one Catholic crown, only the city of Granada remained in Muslim hands. The Naṣrid dynasty, the last Muslim dynasty to exercise power in Spain, ended with the surrender of Granada in that year. Also in 1492, the Jews were expelled from Spain, and those who remained suffered extreme persecution under the Inquisition established by the Catholic Church and the state authorities. Although the Muslims were officially expelled in 1609, they, too, were subject to the Inquisition. For a while they practised their religion secretly, but in the end Islam was obliterated from Spanish society and culture with blood and fire.

Under Islam, Spain was the cultural centre of Europe. Students came from as far away as Scotland to study Islamic theology, philosophy, and science in the schools of Córdoba, Toledo, and other centres of higher learning. It was in these centres that the European Renaissance was conceived, and the great universities in which it was nurtured were inspired by their Arabo-Hispanic counterparts.

In Muslim Spain, the Jews enjoyed a golden age of philosophy and science, mysticism, and general prosperity. Jewish scholars, court physicians, and administrators occupied high state offices and served as political and cultural liaisons between Islamic Spain and the rest of Europe.

Although the Muslims had been stopped in 732 by Charles Martel (c. 668–741) in the Battle of Poitiers from advancing into France and the rest of western Europe, their scientific and cultural achievements succeeded where their military might failed. Arab learning did indeed penetrate deeply into western Europe and contributed directly to the rise of the West to world prominence.

West and East Africa

Islam may have come to sub-Saharan Africa as early as the eighth or ninth century. It was first brought in by Khārijīs who settled in oasis towns north of the Sahara. The Almohads, who ruled Spain and North Africa, may have originally come from Senegal, a point that clearly indicates the close relationships between North Africa and the rest of the continent. Furthermore, through the Almoravids, the Mālikī legal school was introduced and it remains dominant to this day in sub-Saharan and West Africa.

The spread of Islam into West Africa took place in three stages. Initially, a small Muslim community began to form under non-Muslim kings. This was followed by the adoption of Islam as the court religion. As Islam gained official recognition, it gained in numbers as well through mass conversions. By the eighteenth century, Islam became a formidable social and political force in Africa. It could therefore provide the framework and the principles for social and political reform. Islamic law also increasingly came to compete with traditional legal custom.

The spread of Islam in Africa followed a pattern comparable to other places where it became the dominant religion. It was first spread by traders, then on a much larger scale by preachers. Finally jurists came to consolidate and implement the new faith as a religious and legal system. Ṣūfī orders played an important role in both the spread of Islam and its use as a motivation and framework for social and political reform.

Islam always had to compete with traditional African religion. The prayers of Islam, for example, had to be demonstrated as potent in competition with the rain-making prayers or magic of the traditional priest. Especially in times of social or family crises, African Muslims till today fall back on their ancient traditions for help. The phenomenon of adapting a new faith to earlier tradition, so common in both Christian and Muslim history, was observed among the Muslims of the Mali Empire and vividly described by the Moroccan Muslim traveller Ibn Baṭṭūṭah (1304–68).

In East Africa, Islam spread largely through maritime traffic from Arabia and the Gulf, along the African coast. Trade was in commodities, and also in slaves. From the sixteenth century onward, after Portuguese navigators rounded the southern cape of Africa, the cultural and political development of East African Islam was directly affected by European colonialism as well.

In language, the populations of East Africa did not switch to Arabic as had been the case in the initial spread of Islam in Syria, Iraq, Egypt, and North Africa. But Arabic vocabulary penetrated the local African languages, so much so that at least one-third of the Swahili lexicon is Arabic. Until recently, most of the major African languages were written in the Arabic script.

Perhaps because of the close exposure of the African languages to Arabic, many African scholars have excelled in Arabic and produced impressive works in that language in all Islamic disciplines. But while Arabic is the language of worship and the religious sciences, the medium of African popular culture and devotional life remains the vernacular languages. A vast and ongoing popular panegyric literature in praise of the Prophet and on other religious themes continues to appear in the local languages.

The arrival of the Portuguese in Africa in the sixteenth century introduced Catholic Christian missionary activity on a large scale. With the coming of the British and other European colonial powers, missionary activity was further intensified and Protestant Christianity was also introduced. Islam therefore had to compete not only with traditional African religions, but also with a variety of Christian sects and denominations.

The success of Islam in Africa has been in large measure due to its ability to accommodate itself to local culture. Islamic rituals have been overlaid with traditional myths and ritualistic practices. Likewise, legal matters, such as dietary restrictions, have often been explained on the basis not of Islamic law but of local custom. Islam in Africa today continues to vacillate between accommodation and reform, between particularism and universalism, and between quietism and political activism. This is due in part to the informality of religious affiliation in African society. People still move freely between Islam and Christianity, and between both and their traditional folk religions.

An important element of East African society has been the Khoja Ismā'īlī and Twelver Shī'ī community, reflecting the influence of Muslims from the Indian subcontinent. The Khojas immigrated from India to Africa over a century and a half ago. They have on the whole been successful business people with Western education and close relationships with Europe and North America. These relationships have been strengthened by the migration of large numbers of the Khoja community to Britain, the United States, and Canada, where they remain prosperous and well organized.

Central Asia

Central Asia, or 'the lands beyond the river Oxus', had a cosmopolitan culture before Islam. Buddhism, Zoroastrianism, Judaism, and Christianity existed side by side in mutual tolerance. The Arab conquest of this region was slow, lasting over a century. It began in 649, less than two decades after the Prophet's death, and was not completed till 752.

Under the Sāmānid dynasty, which ruled large areas of Persia and Central Asia in the ninth and tenth centuries, the region witnessed an impressive flowering of Persian culture and religious learning in the Arabic language. The best-known classical *ḥadīth* traditionists, historians, philosophers, and religious scholars flourished in that epoch. The celebrated cities of Bukhārā and Samarqand, in what today is Uzbekistan, became important Islamic centres of learning. Their great prosperity depended largely on industry and trade with India, China, and the rest of the Muslim domains. With the first notable Persian poet, Rūdakī (c. 859–940), Bukhārā became the birthplace of Persian literature.

In contrast to their contemporaries the Būyids, who patronized Shīʻī learning and public devotions in Iraq, the Sāmānids firmly established Sunnī orthodoxy in Central Asia. Many Sunnī theologians and religious scholars lived and worked in Bukhārā and Samarqand under Sāmānid patronage. Among the great minds who belonged to this epoch were the theologian al-Maturīdī (d. 944), the philosopher Ibn Sīnā (980–1037), the great scholar and historian of religion Abū Rayḥān al-Bīrūnī (973–1048), and the famous Persian poet Ferdowsī (c. 935–c. 1020).

In this intellectual environment, Islam was spread by persuasion and enticement rather than propaganda and war. There were many instances of mass conversions in the second half of the tenth century. To a large extent, the rapid spread and consolidation of Islam as a creative religious and cultural system was due to its success in remoulding the culture of the people and focusing it around one faith and worldview.

Central Asian Islam was deeply influenced by Sufism and the saint cults it engendered. This, of course, allowed for the importation of old cultic practices from Buddhism, Christianity, and Zoroastrianism. The mystical piety that developed in the Persian cultural environment of central Asia was largely pantheistic and ecstatic. It expressed itself in rich poetry, music, and dance.

Early in the eleventh century, the Sāmānids were succeeded by the Seljuq Turks in the Middle East and the Karākhānid Mongols in Persia and Central Asia.

The Mongols profoundly altered the situation in that region as they did in the Middle East a century later. The devastating consequences of the Mongol conquest of Persia and Central Asia were compounded by the loss of trade revenues. This is because sea travel to India and China replaced the traditional caravan routes. All this led to a decline in culture and prosperity from which Central Asia never recovered.

The Turks

Turkic tribal populations, moving into parts of the Middle Eastern Muslim heartland, were converted to Islam, especially through the activity of Ṣūfī missionaries. They became influential from the tenth century onward in Central Asia, Armenia, Anatolia, and Syria. Maḥmūd of Ghazna in Afghanistan (r. 998–1030), of Turkish descent, broke away from the Persian Sāmānid dynasty; his successors, the Ghaznavids, extended Muslim power in northern India. Maḥmūd was the first individual to be called *sulṭān*, until his time a word for the authority of the state.

The Seljuqs, another Turkic family, prevailed in Iran and farther west a generation after Maḥmūd. The second Seljuq *sulṭān*, Alp Arslan (r. 1063–72), inflicted a crushing defeat on the Byzantines at Manzikert, in eastern Anatolia, in 1071. Bit by bit, eastern Anatolia (today's Turkey) fell to the Seljuqs, who ruled until conquered by the Mongols in 1243.

The Ottoman Turks ruled for over six centuries, from their dynastic founder Osman I (r. 1299–1326) until 1923. They began in the fourteenth century by absorbing former Seljuq territory in eastern Anatolia and taking over western Anatolia from the Byzantines. In the sixteenth century they reached their greatest power, occupying the Balkans as far north as Vienna, the Levant (i.e., the Syro-Palestinian region), and all of northern Africa except Morocco. Consequently, Christian Europe from then until the nineteenth century perceived Islamic culture as primarily Turkish.

The Ottomans adopted the crescent as their imperial symbol. Extensive use of what had previously been an ancient and Byzantine symbol followed the Turks' capture of Constantinople (in Turkish, Istanbul), the Byzantine capital, in 1453. The croissant originated in Budapest in 1686, when bakers who were up before dawn detected Turks in tunnels under the city attempting a surprise attack. To celebrate foiling it, the bakers produced pastries in the shape of the Turkish symbol.

Conspicuous on the Turkish flag, the crescent was perceived by Europeans and eventually also by Muslims as the symbol of Islam. On independence from Ottoman rule, Algeria, Tunisia, and (until 1952) Egypt kept the crescent on their flags. Outside the Ottoman world, the crescent symbolizes Islamic identity on the flags of post-British Pakistan, post-French Mauritania, and post-Soviet

Azerbaijan, Uzbekistan, and Turkmenistan. It also flies over Malaysia and some smaller jurisdictions in the Indian Ocean region. In a number of Muslim lands, the twentieth-century organization supplying emergency medical assistance is the Red Crescent.

Turkic languages prevail in much of the region of Central Asia ruled until 1989 by the Soviet Union. From Azerbaijan to Uzbekistan and Turkmenistan, a dominant element in the population is Turkic. Such is also the case in Chinese Central Asia, in the vast region of Xinjiang.

China

The first contacts of Islam with China may have happened shortly after the Prophet's death. Literary sources dealing directly with Islam in Chinese, however, do not appear till the seventeenth century. For earlier information, we have to rely on Chinese sources that unfortunately focus on commercial activities. They therefore have little to say about the social and intellectual life of Chinese Muslims.

The extent of Muslim presence in a new area may often be gauged by the number of mosques. There seem to be no mosques in the main inland cities of China before the thirteenth and fourteenth centuries under the Ming dynasty. The minaret of the mosque in Guangzhou (Canton) on the Chinese coast, and inscriptions in the coastal cities of Fujian, however, suggest maritime trade considerably earlier, in 'Abbāsid times.

Persian and Arab merchants were from the beginning allowed to trade freely, so long as they conformed with Chinese rules. It must be that when Muslim traders began to reside in China in reasonable numbers, mosques began to appear. Thus the presence of Islam in China before the thirteenth century may have been more localized and limited.

Our ability to reconstruct the history of Islam in China is hampered by the cultural pride of Confucian literati, who to some extent looked down on foreigners and scorned their customs and religious practices. Be that as it may, under Mongol rule, the Muslims arriving overland from the West, predominantly of Central Asian origin, appear to have enjoyed many privileges. This close collaboration with a foreign regime stirred hostility and mistrust among the Chinese towards Muslims. Nevertheless, Muslims were able to maintain a life of prosperity throughout Mongol (1206–1368) and Ming (1368–1644) rule. In the thirteenth century, Muslim communities sprang up in all parts of China.

After the Mongol period, Chinese Muslims were culturally but not religiously assimilated. They kept in touch with the rest of the Muslim *ummah* through trade. Hence, the decline of trade with Central Asia in the seventeenth century had devastating effects on the Chinese Muslim community. It became virtually cut off from the rest of the world, so that after the seventeenth century, our information about Muslims in China is largely a matter of conjecture.

Unsuccessful attempts were made after the seventeenth century to assimilate Islam in China into the Confucian ethics and worldview. Not surprisingly, this led to Muslim revolts, which led to repression by the authorities. In 1784, religious leaders belonging to the Naqshbandī Ṣūfī order attempted to establish an independent Muslim state in northwestern China. The revolt was put down, and unrest continued intermittently into the twentieth century.

Persistent negative images of Muslims among the Chinese exacerbated an already tense situation. The Muslims of Xinjiang, who were mostly of Central Asian origins, made numerous futile attempts to establish a Muslim state in that province. Islam in fact was never able to establish itself in China as it did in the rest of Asia because the Chinese already had an advanced culture and a closely knit society.

Unlike Buddhism centuries earlier, Islam did not become assimilated as culturally Chinese. Muslims remained an identifiable minority in Chinese society. For many, identity was defined linguistically and regionally, as in Xinjiang, Chinese Turkestan. But even the Chinese-speaking Muslims in the principal eastern cities of 'Han' China are set apart by their diet. They avoid pork, a staple item in China's cuisine, with the result that *ḥalāl* (ritually acceptable) restaurants and butcher shops mark the presence of Muslim neighbourhoods.

The situation has not been substantially different since the mid-twentieth century in the People's Republic of China. The Muslims under communism have had their share of repression, particularly during the Cultural Revolution of 1966–76. Since its end, there has been improvement. Estimates of Muslim population in China range from a conservative figure of 15 million to over 50 million. The future for China's Muslims is uncertain, like the future of other religious communities in contemporary China, but the ethnic base of the minorities in China's Central Asian interior is not likely to disappear soon.

South Asia

Islam came to India early through traders and Arab settlers. As we have already observed, when Umayyad armies advanced west into Europe in 711 they also went east into India. The initial incursion was a reprisal for an alleged case of mistreatment of Muslim traders. Since that time, Islam has become an integral part of Indian life and culture.

The Muslim conquest of India was not a single campaign but a long process. In the second half of the tenth century, the city of Ghazni, in what is today Afghanistan, became the headquarters of the conquest and rule of India. From there the armies of the *sulṭān* Maḥmūd the Ghaznavid (r. 998–1030) and his successors advanced over the famous Khyber (Khaybar) pass into the North Indian plain. By the fourteenth century, most of India came under Muslim rule, with the exception of the far south in Tamil Nadu and Kerala.

A Traditionalist Muslim Critique of Akbar

[The Mughal emperor Akbar ruled as a Muslim over subjects, the majority of whom were Hindu, with other religious identities represented as well. His openness to the diversity in his domain is criticized by the Muslim historian 'Abd al-Qādir Badā'ūnī (1540–c. 1615) in his Muntakhab al-Tawārīkh *(Selection from History), a work that was published only after Akbar's death in 1605.]*

And later that day the emperor came to Fathpūr. There he used to spend much time in the Hall of Worship in the company of learned men and shaikhs and especially on Friday nights, when he would sit up there the whole night continually occupied in discussing questions of religion, whether fundamental or collateral. The learned men used to draw the sword of the tongue on the battlefield of mutual contradiction and opposition, and the antagonism of the sects reached such a pitch that they would call one another fools and heretics. The controversies used to pass beyond the differences of Sunni and Shī'a, of Ḥanafī and Shāfi'ī, of lawyer and divine, and they would attack the very bases of belief. And Makhdum-ul-Mulk wrote a treatise to the effect that Shaikh 'Abd-al-Nabī had unjustly killed Khizr Khān Sarwānī, who had been suspected of blaspheming the Prophet [peace be upon him!], and Mir Habsh, who had been suspected of being a Shī'a, and saying that it was not right to repeat the prayers after him, because he was undutiful toward his father, and was himself afflicted with hemorrhoids. Shaikh 'Abd-al-Nabī replied to him that he was a fool and a heretic. Then the mullās [Muslim theologians] became divided into two parties, and one party took one side and one the other, and became very Jews and Egyptians for hatred of each other. And persons of novel and whimsical opinions, in accordance with their pernicious ideas and vain doubts, coming out of ambush, decked the false in the garb of the true, and wrong in the dress of right, and cast the emperor, who was possessed of an excellent disposition, and was an earnest searcher after truth, but

The Muslim rulers of India were for the most part foreigners. Thus, maintaining and expanding Muslim power in such a vast and diverse subcontinent meant continuous warfare. Yet in spite of an often repressive Muslim rule of a large Hindu population, Indian Islam developed a unique and rich religious and intellectual culture.

Islam in India developed along two distinct lines. There was the Islamic official literary culture of the scholars. Quite different from it was the popular pietistic culture of the masses. The literary culture was enshrined in the classical languages of Islamic learning, Arabic and Persian, but these were completely foreign to the masses of India. In Bengal, for instance, conscious efforts were made

very ignorant and a mere tyro, and used to the company of infidels and base persons, into perplexity, till doubt was heaped upon doubt, and he lost all definite aim, and the straight wall of the clear law and of firm religion was broken down, so that after five or six years not a trace of Islam was left in him; and everything was turned topsy-turvy ... And at one time a Brahman, named Debi, who was one of the interpreters of the *Mahābhārata*, was pulled up the wall of the castle sitting on a bedstead till he arrived near a balcony, which the emperor had made his bed-chamber. Whilst thus suspended he instructed His Majesty in the secrets and legends of Hinduism, in the manner of worshiping idols, the fire, the sun and stars, and of revering the chief gods of these unbelievers, such as Brahma, Mahadev [Śiva], Bishn [Viṣṇu], Kishn [Kṛṣṇa], Ram, and Mahama (whose existence as sons of the human race is a supposition, but whose nonexistence is a certainty, though in their idle belief they look on some of them as gods, and some as angels). His Majesty, on hearing further how much the people of the country prized their institutions, began to look upon them with affection ...

Learned monks also from Europe, who are called *Padre*, and have an infallible head, called *Papa*, who is able to change religious ordinances as he may deem advisable for the moment, and to whose authority kings must submit, brought the Gospel, and advanced proofs for the Trinity. His Majesty firmly believed in the truth of the Christian religion, and wishing to spread the doctrines of Jesus, ordered Prince Murād to take a few lessons in Christianity under good auspices, and charged Abū'l Fazl to translate the Gospel ...

Fire worshipers also came from Nousarī in Gujarat, proclaimed the religion of Zardusht [Zarathushtra] as the true one, and declared reverence to fire to be superior to every other kind of worship ... He ordered that the sacred fire should be made over to the charge of Abū'l Fazl, and that after the manner of the kings of Persia, in whose temples blazed perpetual fires, he should take care it was never extinguished night or day, for that it is one of the signs of God, and one light from His lights ... (Ranking and Lowe 1895–1925: vol 2, 255–61).

to express Islamic devotional ideas in the vernacular language. This phenomenon was common to most Indian language groups.

Indian Muslim society was at least as diverse as elsewhere in the Islamic world. Besides the Sunnī majority, which virtually adheres to the Ḥanafī legal school, but is overlaid with a rich tapestry of Ṣūfī popular piety, there is a small but vibrant Shī'ī community. This community made notable contributions to the political and cultural life of India, particularly to Urdu and Persian literature and music.

Around the middle of the thirteenth century, and in response to the Mongol devastation of the Middle East, many well-known religious scholars

The Quṭb Minār, an Indo-Muslim minaret in New Delhi, exhibits the repeated parallel lines familiar in Hindu temples but with surface decoration in Arabic calligraphy rather than Indian representational sculpture. (Willard G. Oxtoby)

migrated to India and founded new mosques and religious schools. Such endeavours were encouraged and patronized by the Turkic *sulṭāns* of Delhi, the present capital of India. Most religious institutions, however, depended not on government patronage, or the largesse of rich landholders, but on private pious donations. This general involvement in the devotional and intellectual life of the Muslim community indicates the depth and extent to which Islam had penetrated Indian society.

Through the shared culture and social customs of Muslims with the Hindu community, a sort of caste system developed in Indian Muslim society. Thus the *'ulamā'*, or religious scholars, came to constitute a special aristocracy akin to that of the brahminical priestly class in Hinduism. This high status could also be gained through intermarriage with the *sayyid* class, a Muslim nobility claiming descent from the Prophet through his daughter Fāṭimah and his cousin 'Alī b. Abī Ṭālib.

There developed a type of Muslim gentleman who disdained even to speak

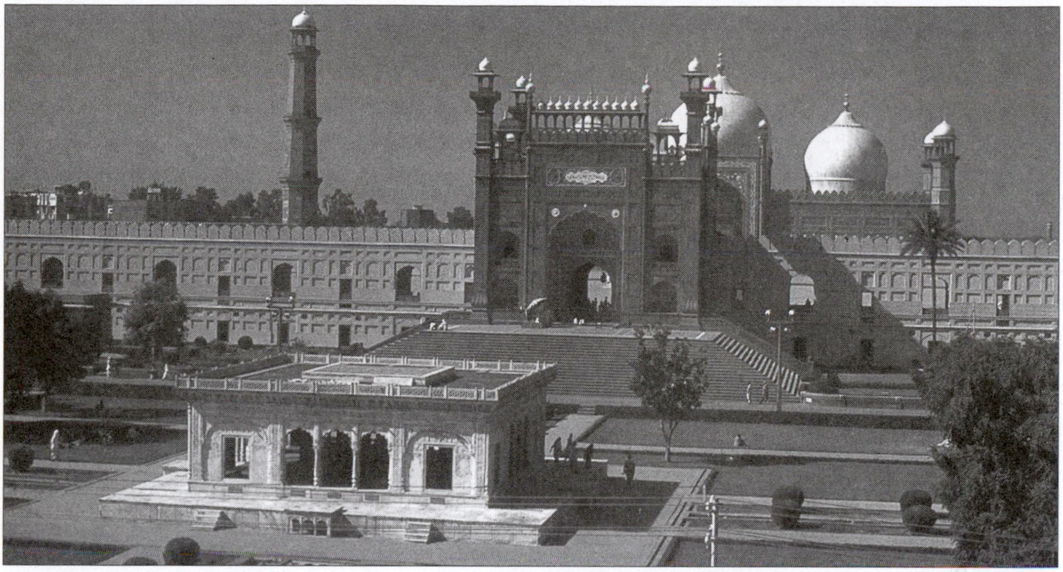

Details of sixteenth- to eighteenth-century Mughal architecture such as the entrance archway to the Great Mosque in Lahore, Pakistan, have affinities with Iranian architecture of the same period. (Willard G. Oxtoby)

about Islam in any language but establishment Arabic or Persian. These two languages, therefore, came to occupy a prestige in Indian Muslim society somewhat resembling that of Sanskrit in classical Hinduism. And the extent of Indian Muslim literary activity was such that today there are more Persian manuscipts in the libraries of India than in those of Iran.

Well into the nineteenth century, the dominant culture of northern India was the Mughal Persian culture. Arabic remained an important language of religious and literary communication. Out of the interaction of these two languages with the vernacular dialects was born an indigenous language called Urdu, comparable to Hindi, but written in the Arabic script. The Urdu language has in turn developed its own rich literary heritage. It is the language of educated Muslims in India and the official language of Pakistan.

Before the modern period, religious thought in South Asia differed little from that in other regions of the Muslim world. The uniqueness of Indian Islam lay in its popular piety; the popular Ṣūfī preachers offered a marked contrast to the religious scholars. Members of local Ṣūfī brotherhoods, such as the Chishti and wandering Qalandar *darwīshes* ('dervishes'), interacted with the ascetic sages or yogis of different schools of Hinduism. This gave Islam in India a distinct character. Popular Sufism had a wide influence, parallel to that of *bhakti* or devotional

Hinduism. It was particularly reflected in the cult of the *shaykh* or preceptor, who could be a Ṣūfī *shaykh* or Hindu-Muslim *guru*.

To be sure, influences of the Arabic and Persian literary and philosophical tradition, with its mysticism, can be clearly discerned in the development of Indian Sufism. Nevertheless, the Indian phenomenon is distinctive. From the fifteenth century onward, the Hindu idea of the divine-human *guru* led many Ṣūfī *shaykhs* to claim prophetic or messianic qualities for themselves. Thus the personality of the prophet Muḥammad, around which a rich popular cult had developed, was actually shared among local spiritual heroes.

Vernacular piety resulted in a rich common Hindu-Muslim religious culture. Kabīr, a fifteenth-century Hindu-Muslim mystic, is still venerated by Hindus and Muslims alike. The Sikh religious tradition, born in this milieu, was founded by Gurū Nānak (1469–1539), a follower of Kabīr.

In this piety, a rich eclectic culture developed under Mughal rule. The Mughals established in India a prosperous society with a high culture. It reached its zenith under the great emperor Akbar (r. 1556–1605). Akbar used to enjoy gathering Hindu, Muslim, Christian, and Zoroastrian religious scholars for open debate. Convinced of the narrowness and the divisive role of all institutionalized religions, Akbar established what he thought to be a universal religion combining the best of Indian and Middle Eastern traditions. He called this new faith Dīn-i Ilahī, meaning 'Divine Religion'.

Akbar's daring religious innovation created conflict and disunity in the Muslim community. The prince Dārā Shikōh (1615–59) attempted to carry further Akbar's interreligious work. He was unfortunately deposed and tragically executed by order of the *'ulamā'*. Quickly the empire slid into anarchy, and Mughal rule was soon replaced by British rule.

By the beginning of the nineteenth century, the British ruled all of India, including Delhi and Agra, the two centres of Mughal culture and authority. This changed radically the Muslim situation, and with it the Muslims' self-image and destiny. Before this, non-Muslims did conquer Muslim lands, but they were themselves eventually assimilated into the Muslim community. Now, however, Western imperialism and aggressive missionary activity sought to undermine traditional Islamic values and authority. Even Islamic law, which was hitherto the sacred domain of the Muslim *'ulamā'*, was controlled in its application by the British colonial authorities.

Revivalist movements arose in the nineteenth century, calling Muslims in a variety of ways to return to the *Qur'ān*, the Prophetic *ḥadīth* tradition, or both. Some called upon Muslims to rise up in armed struggle, or *jihād* against all non-Muslim elements. The British colonialists and the Sikhs, who had become bitter opponents of the Muslims in India, were especially targeted.

There were also reformers like Sayyid Aḥmad Khan (1817–98), who saw in the British rule a way for Muslims to survive and reform their own social and political system. He therefore called for cooperation with the British and the westernization of the Indian Muslim community. Others, like Muḥammad Iqbāl (1877–1938), called for a return to the spirit of classical Islam, but using Western philosophical thought to provide the modern framework for this important undertaking. As things turned out, British rule ended in 1947 with the partition of India and the creation of Pakistan, from which Bangladesh subsequently separated in 1971.

The Indian subcontinent, if one groups together India, Bangladesh, and Pakistan, has the largest Muslim population in the world. The Muslims of India alone comprise the largest population after Indonesia, numbering between 80 and 100 million, yet the Muslims of India are a minority whose future appears bleak in the face of rising Hindu nationalism. Pakistan, despite the loss of Bangladesh in the 1970s, seems to offer a more promising future.

Southeast Asia

Islam came to Southeast Asia, not to large metropolitan urban centres, but to small kingdoms and settlements possessing a wide diversity of languages and cultures. Before Islam, Southeast Asian religious cultures had been strongly influenced by the Hindu and Buddhist traditions. This influence is still evident in the ancient Hindu culture on the island of Bali and the great Buddhist stupa complex of Borobudur in Indonesia. In fact, most of Southeast Asia was Theravāda Buddhist, with Mahāyāna represented also, especially in Vietnam.

There is no evidence for the presence of Islam in Southeast Asia before the tenth century. Scattered evidence from Chinese and Portuguese travellers, as well as passing references by the Arab traveller Ibn Baṭṭūṭah, indicate that by the fifteenth century, Islam had spread widely in Southeast Asian society. By the seventeenth century, when British and Dutch trading companies arrived in the region, Islam became the dominant religion and culture of the Malay archipelago.

The spread of Islam in Southeast Asia was a slow and modest process, unlike the first great expansion in the Middle East, North Africa, and Central Asia. It is probable that Arab traders carried Islam into Southeast Asia as they did into China by the eighth century if not earlier. Yemeni traders are reported to have sailed into the islands of the Malay archipelago long before Islam. This situation would clearly indicate an early contact of Malay people with Islam.

As more Muslim merchants settled in the region, they intermarried with local women, thus beginning the process of establishing permanent native Muslim communities. These communities were as diverse as the cultures in which they grew as well as the people who initiated them. Arab and South Asian

Muslims, however, in interaction with the local people, helped shape Islamic culture and popular piety in Southeast Asia.

By the thirteenth century, socio-political Muslim communities in small states ruled by *sulṭāns* are widely reported. The earliest of these was Pasai, a small kingdom on the east coast of northern Sumatra. Other states appeared in the following centuries. Some of the states that arose in the fifteenth century gained considerable prominence. In every case, prosperity attracted Indian Muslim *'ulamā'* to these states. Many may have been of Arab ancestry, the claim of which gave them an advantage in prestige.

The *sulṭān* Iskandar Muda of Acheh (r. 1607–36) ruled the first Southeast Asian Muslim state with international relations. Iskandar Muda established alliances with European powers in his effort to expand and strengthen his realm. This state, moreover, produced noteworthy Islamic scholarship, which continues to be used in the Malay world till the present.

From the seventeenth century on, the expansion of the authority of the Dutch United East India Company ended the rise and fall of small Muslim kingdoms. The resulting stability helped to establish Islam even more firmly as an indigenous religion. Islam, particularly in Java with its ancient rural cultures, has always been mixed with native ritualistic and ancestral cults. Inspired by the Wahhābī reform movement of Arabia in the eighteenth century, local *'ulamā'* began to call vigorously for reform to purify Islam. Thus in the 1840s a civil war ensued in Java, leading to the expansion of Dutch colonialism in the region.

As elsewhere, and even to a greater extent, Ṣūfī orders played a crucial role in the Islamization of Southeast Asia. They were also prominent in later political and social struggles for reform and liberation. Modernist reform movements in the late nineteenth and early twentieth centuries in the Middle East inspired similar movements in Indonesia and other countries of the region. The institution that has had the longest and most sustained influence on the intellectual life of Southeast Asia is the Islamic university of al-Azhar in Cairo, Egypt. Al-Azhar continues to graduate the majority of the Islamic scholars from the Malay Muslim community.

At present, Islam is the majority religion in Malaysia, Indonesia, and Brunei. There are Muslim minorities in all the other countries of Southeast Asia. The Muslims of Southeast Asia mostly follow the Shāfi'ī legal school.

Islam did not attain in Southeast Asia the universal character that it achieved through the Arabic, Persian, and Turkish languages and cultures elsewhere in Asia and Africa, yet Southeast Asia can claim at least one-third of the Muslims of the world. Indonesia alone has a Muslim population of at least 130 million, making it the largest Muslim country among the political units of today's world.

Southeast Asia is far from the sectarian, demographic, ethnic, and political problems that have bedevilled the Balkans, the Middle East, and South Asia.

Perhaps the industrious and peaceful tendencies in the culture of the region can be nurtured for the benefit of many and a brighter future.

The Modern World

Islam and Modernity

Throughout Muslim history, individuals and groups have taken it upon themselves to reform the rest of the community. Sanction for this responsibility is the *ḥadīth* tradition: 'God shall raise at the head of every hundred years for this community a man who will renew for it its faith.' As this *ḥadīth* specifies no characteristics of such renovators of the faith, the field has been open for many to be considered *mujaddids* (renewers) of Muslim faith and conduct.

Active involvement in the reform of society is further specified in the oft-quoted Prophetic injunction:

> Any one of you who sees something lewd or dishonourable (*munkar*), let him change it with his hand. If he is unable, then with his tongue, and if he is still unable, then let him change it with his heart, but this is the weakest of faith.

This *ḥadīth* has been taken as a call for social and religious *jihād* for the purification of society. Heeding this call with utmost seriousness, the Khārijīs became an extreme example of reform through violent means, but by no means the only one. In fact, as we shall see, later movements resembled them in many respects.

An external impetus for reform has been Muslim interaction with and reaction to Western Christendom. The first major Western challenge to Muslim power and to Islam's great capacity to rally its people in a universal *jihād* for the defence of the integrity of its domains was the crusades. Fired by a spirit of Christian *jihād* or holy war for the liberation of Jerusalem from Muslim domination, the armies of the first crusade were able to capture the Holy City in 1099 after a great massacre of its Jewish and Muslim inhabitants. For nearly two centuries, Frankish Christian kingdoms existed side by side with Muslim states along the eastern Mediterranean shores, sometimes peacefully, but most of the time at war.

Although in the end the crusaders returned home, and those who remained were assimilated, the spirit of the crusades and the distorted images of Islam and its followers that the crusaders took back with them continued to live on. Conversely, the equally distorted images of Christianity and Western Christendom that the crusades left in Muslim lands have been reinforced and greatly embellished through Muslim reactions to Western imperialism and its aftermath.

Pre-modernist Reform Movements

We shall examine Islam in the modern era from two perspectives: internal reform and the challenge of the West.

Common to all reform movements has been the call to return to pristine *islām*, the *islām* of the Prophet's society and the normative period of his 'rightly guided' successors (*al-khulafā' al-rāshidūn*). Among those who championed this cause was the great Egyptian religious scholar Ibn Taymīyah (1263–1328). Ibn Taymīyah was a neo-Ḥanbalī jurist who fought relentlessly against Shī'ī beliefs and practices, Ṣūfī excesses of saint veneration and esoteric doctrines, blind imitation of the established legal tradition, and the reluctance to revive the practice of *ijtihād*. Ibn Taymīyah exerted a powerful and long-lasting influence on subsequent reform movements.

First to adopt Ibn Taymīyah's ideas as the basis of its reform program was the Wahhābī movement, so called after its founder Muḥammad Ibn 'Abd al-Wahhāb. Significantly, this uncompromising and influential revivalist movement began in the highlands of Arabia, the birthplace of Islam. Ibn 'Abd al-Wahhāb's long life (1703–92) allowed him to establish his movement on firm ideological and political grounds. He allied himself with Muḥammad 'Āl Sa'ūd, a local tribal prince, with the understanding that the prince would exercise political power and protect the nascent movement, which would hold religious authority. This agreement remains operative to the present, as the kingdom of Saudi Arabia is a Wahhābī state, ruled by the descendants of 'Āl Sa'ūd.

Like the Khārijīs before them, the Wahhābīs regarded all those who did not share their convictions to be either misbelievers (*kuffār*) or persons gone astray. They waged a violent campaign aimed at purging Muslim society of what they considered to be its un-Islamic beliefs and practices. They destroyed the Prophet's tomb in Madīnah and levelled the graves of his Companions. They attacked the Shī'ī sacred cities of Najaf and Karbalā', massacred their inhabitants, and demolished the shrines of 'Alī and his son Ḥusayn. They also went on a rampage in Arab cities, desecrating the tombs of Ṣūfī saints and destroying their shrines.

The Wahhābīs preached a strictly egalitarian Islam based solely on a direct relationship between the worshipper and God. They repudiated the widely cherished hope that the Prophet and other divinely favoured *walī*s would intercede with God for the pious to receive blessing and succour in this life and salvation in the next. The Wahhābīs regarded saint veneration, including veneration of the Prophet, as a form of idolatry. They even advocated the destruction of the sacred black stone of the Ka'bah, holding that it, too, stands as an idol between the faithful Muslim and one's Lord.

Again like the Khārijīs, the Wahhābīs understood Islam as an Arab heritage and limited their activities to Arab society. This helps to account for the fact that the Wahhābī movement has survived only in Arabia. There it has been the ideological framework for a regime that has become increasingly unpopular. While spiritually egalitarian, Wahhabism has been put to the service of a politically élitist Arab government.

Wahhābī ideology has not been without influence elsewhere. Its basic ideals have had wide appeal to reformist and revivalist groups and individuals. Especially significant is the Wahhābī influence on eighteenth- and nineteenth-century Ṣūfī reforms.

Nineteenth-Century Revivalism

A number of Ṣūfī *jihād* movements arose in the nineteenth century, in part as a Ṣūfī answer to Wahhābī reform and in part as a reaction to European colonial encroachment on Muslim domains. Several of these movements were able to establish short-lived states, such as those of Usman ('Uthmān) dan Fodio (1754–1817, r. 1804–15) in Nigeria, Muḥammad al-Sanūsī (1787–1859) in Libya, and Muḥammad Aḥmad al-Mahdī (1844–85, r. 1882–98) in the Sudan. Common to all these movements was an activist ideology of militant struggle against outside colonialism and internal decadence. They also strove for reform and the revival of *ijtihād*.

Because of their broad-based appeal, these Ṣūfī reform movements exerted a lasting influence on most subsequent reform programs and ideologies. In North Africa in particular, Ṣūfī *shaykhs* and religious scholars spearheaded a long and bloody struggle against French and Italian colonialism. They also helped preserve the religious, linguistic, and cultural identity of North African countries, which they led to independence. The Ṣūfī *shaykh* Abdelkader ('Abd al-Qādir, 1808–83), for example, played an important political role in the long struggle for Algeria's independence. King Muḥammad V of Morocco (r. 1927–57) was a Ṣūfī *shaykh* and a 'venerable descendant' (*sharīf*) of the Prophet. Likewise, the grandson of al-Sanūsī, Idrīs I, ruled Libya as king from independence in 1951 until he was overthrown in a revolution in 1969.

The Sanūsīyah movement spread in North and West Africa, where it worked for reform and Muslim unity. In contrast, the Mahdīyah of the Sudan was an eschatological movement. Its founder, al-Mahdī, saw himself as God's representative on earth who was to re-establish the Prophet's paradigmatic state. He thus called his own companions Anṣār, or helpers, as Muḥammad had called his supporters in Madīnah earlier. He regarded the Ottoman-Egyptian rule of the Sudan as an irreligious occupation and waged a war of *jihād* against it. In 1885, he triumphed over Egyptian forces and established an Islamic state based on a strict application of the *sharī'ah* law, which lasted till 1889.

Modernist Reformers

When Napoleon landed on Egyptian shores in 1798, he brought with him not only soldiers, but also scholars and the printing press. Through Napoleon's Oriental adventure, the Middle East discovered Europe. Furthermore, the great Ottoman Empire, which in the early decades of the sixteenth century had threatened Vienna, had by the nineteenth become 'the sick man of Europe'. With the British Empire ruling India and controlling much of the Muslim world, Muslim thinkers everywhere were awed by the West and resentful of the state of somnolence into which the Muslim *ummah* had fallen.

In spite of political Muslim inertia, however, there was an intellectual and cultural revival in many areas of the Islamic east in the nineteenth century.

Egypt, for instance, was the home of an Arab intellectual renaissance. Due to unsettled social and political conditions in the Levant, a number of Western-educated Syro-Lebanese Christians immigrated to Egypt, where they established newspapers and cultural journals, and actively participated in the recovery of the Arabo-Islamic heritage.

The Arab renaissance of the nineteenth century was largely stimulated by a Western cultural and intellectual efflorescence. With the break-up of traditional church-dominated regimes and institutions as a consequence of the Protestant Reformation and the Enlightenment, secularism and romantic nationalism largely supplanted religious faith and institutions in nineteenth-century Europe. These ideas similarly appealed to eastern Mediterrean Muslims, and in the end led to the rise of Arab nationalism. The same ideas also influenced other Muslim peoples, so that nationalistic identities came to compete with, and in some cases even supersede, Islamic identities.

These and other Western cultural and intellectual influences were strengthened by Western Christian missionary schools and institutions of higher learning, which proliferated greatly throughout the Muslim world. Islamic reform of the nineteenth and twentieth centuries in Asia, Africa, and the Middle East must be viewed in light of this extensive cultural and intellectual ferment.

Afghānī and 'Abduh

The second half of the nineteenth century was dominated by two figures, the Iranian Jamāl al-Dīn al-Afghānī (1838–97) and the Egyptian Muḥammad 'Abduh (1849–1905). Afghānī had a traditional Shī'ī philosophical and theological as well as a Western education. He was a religious humanist who cherished an ideal vision of a pan-Islamic *ummah*. It was to occupy a vast area stretching from Southeast Asia to North and West Africa.

True to his pan-Islamic vision, Afghānī adopted the epithet 'Afghānī' in order to obscure his Iranian Shī'ī identity. Like a number of other reformers of the time, he tirelessly worked for the realization of an Islamic cultural, religious, and political revival in a rejuvenated international Ottoman state. He travelled far and wide, from India through the main centres of Islamic culture in Asia and Africa to Europe, preaching his pan-Islamic ideology.

Afghānī introduced a new approach to the West, which has continued to be upheld in one way or another by reformers till the present. He admired the vigour, industry, and seriousness of Europeans, but argued that these are in fact Islamic qualities that Muslims have lost and must recover. Science is not the exclusive property of the West, but a universal field of knowledge open to all peoples, regardless of religious and cultural identity.

Islam, for Afghānī and his followers, is a rational religion in full accord with science. In contrast, Christianity is irrational, Afghānī asserts, as it is based on mysteries that people are enjoined to believe without understanding. Therefore, when Europe was most Christian, it was most backward, while the Muslim community was most advanced when it was most Muslim.

Afghānī was for some years exiled from the Middle East with his disciple Muḥammad 'Abduh. They lived in Paris, where they began an international journal entitled *al-'Urwah al-Wuthqā*, borrowed from a Qur'anic expression meaning 'the firm handle' (see Q. 2:256). In this journal they continued to urge reform, the resumption of *ijtihād*, and the adoption of Western science and technology but not Western materialistic values. They further urged all Muslims to overthrow their corrupt and despotic regimes and unite in a pan-Islamic state, capable of freeing the *ummah* from European domination.

Afghānī was, however, more of a political agitator than a thinker. His legacy of active reform provided the needed motivation for twentieth-century reform and revivalist movements. Afghānī spent the last years of his life as a prisoner in Istanbul, strictly confined to a comfortable home.

In contrast with Afghānī's public and dynamic personality, *shaykh* Muḥammad 'Abduh was a quiet, introspective, and mild character. He grew up in the small Egyptian town of Ṭanṭā, whose shrine of the popular saint Sayyid Aḥmad al-Badawī remains to this day the home of a rich tradition of Ṣūfī folk piety. 'Abduh was brought up by his uncle, who was a noted Ṣūfī. Although 'Abduh in the end repudiated both popular and theosophical Sufism, his Ṣūfī upbringing left its mark on his personality.

While sharing Afghānī's view of the superiority of Islamic faith and civilization over Christianity and Western civilization, 'Abduh was a pragmatic reformer. He was convinced that for reform to be effective, it must begin from within. He therefore began a series of reforms of religious education that transformed Cairo's al-Azhar University from a traditional into a modern institution, where both religious and secular subjects were taught. He used his office as the Grand Muftī, or jurisconsult, of Egypt to implement his educational reforms and embark upon an ambitious project of editing and publishing the primary sources of Islamic philosophy, theology, history, and jurisprudence. 'Abduh left a far greater and more lasting influence on Arab and Islamic thought in general than any reformer before or after him.

The Indian Subcontinent

The religio-political situation prevailing in India in the eighteenth and nineteenth centuries was the consequence of a unique experience. A Muslim community, while remaining a minority, ruled most of the subcontinent for a long time and gave its Hindu-Muslim society a rich Perso-Indian culture. From the tenth century there were sharp differences between the traditionists (*ahl al-ḥadīth*), who insisted on basing everything on the *Qur'ān* and *sunnah*, and the more Ṣūfī-oriented syncretistic mystics and poets, who served as a bridge between Hindu and Muslim piety. With the demise of the Mughal Empire in the seventeenth century, calls for reform on traditional lines grew more vocal. One of the strongest voices for reform was that of Aḥmad Sirhindī (1564–1624). Sirhindī called for a return to the *sharī'ah*. He condemned Ṣūfīs as deviants, and Ibn 'Arabī in particular as an infidel.

Shāh Walī Allāh of Delhi (1702–62) initiated the most important movement of Islamic reform in the Indian subcontinent in modern times. Although he was a disciple of Ibn 'Abd al-Wahhāb, unlike his mentor he was a Ṣūfī who did not reject Sufism, but sought to reform it. Shah Walī Allāh was a moderate reformer with encyclopedic learning. He rejected the legal principle of blind imitation (*taqlīd*) and called for reopening the door of *ijtihād*. He also sought to reconcile Shī'ī-Sunnī differences, which have been a source of great friction in the community, particularly in the Indian subcontinent.

Shāh Walī Allāh's grandson Aḥmad Barelwi (i.e., 'of Bareilly', 1786–1831), however, transformed his program into a *jihād* movement against British rule and the Sikhs. In 1826, he established an Islamic state based on the *sharī'ah* and adopted the old caliphal title 'commander of the faithful'. Although he was killed in battle in 1831, his movement lived on as a *jihād* movement.

For Aḥmad Barelwi, India ceased to be an Islamic domain after the end of Mughal rule. Hence, Muslims should wage a *jihād* to liberate it. If independence from infidel sovereignty was not possible, Muslims should depart in an act of religious migration (*hijrah*) to an area ruled by Muslims.

The shock that Indian Muslims suffered through the consolidation of British rule was intensified by the fact that the British tampered with Islamic law itself. The result was the interesting but short-lived code known as Anglo-Muḥammadan law. This code was a mixture of Islamic law and Western humanistic rulings.

On the spectrum of reaction to British rule, at the opposite end from *jihād* movements like Aḥmad Barelwi's were the apologetic approaches of Sayyid Aḥmad Khān and Sayyid Amīr 'Alī (1849–1928).

Like Muḥammad 'Abduh, Aḥmad Khān (1817–98) was a thorough rationalist. But while 'Abduh typified Mu'tazilī rationalism, Khān followed medieval Muslim philosophers, notably Ibn Rushd, and the deists of his own time. 'Abduh held that even where they may disagree with the laws of nature, basic principles of religion are eternal verities that cannot be questioned.

For Aḥmad Khān, on the other hand, nature follows a strict system of causality allowing for no exceptions. Revelation, or 'God's word', and nature, or 'God's work', argued Khān, cannot contradict each other. Therefore, where revelation seems to contradict science, it must be interpreted, showing the inner harmony between the two. Aḥmad Khān's rationalism was in large measure a consequence of his westernization.

Like all reformers, Khān called for modern *ijtihād* or rethinking of the Islamic heritage, but unlike most of them, he rejected *ḥadīth* tradition as a legitimate source of modern Islamic living. He founded the Aligarh Muḥammadan College (later, Aligarh Muslim University), where he attempted to implement his ideas in a Western modern program of education.

Muḥammad Iqbāl

Sayyid Aḥmad Khān's ideas and those of his fellow apologists culminated in the philosophy of Muḥammad Iqbāl (1876–1938), the greatest Muslim thinker of modern India. Central to Iqbāl's thought is the idea of an inner spirit that moves human civilization. This idea is akin to the French philosopher Henri Bergson's (1859–1941) idea of the vital urge (*élan vital*). While Iqbāl's theory of Islamic civilization drew on the dynamic Sufism of Jalāl al-Dīn Rūmī, it was actually constructed on the thought of Western philosophers. Besides Bergson, these included Friedrich Nietzsche (1844–1900) and G.W.F. Hegel (1770–1831).

Like Afghānī and 'Abduh before him, Iqbāl argued for the acquisition of Western science and philosophy, which rightfully belong to the Islamic heritage. He, however, argued for a process of integration of these fields of knowledge into a fresh *Reconstruction of Religious Thought in Islam*, which he gave as the title of his only major work in English. This call for a dynamic rethinking of Islamic faith and civilization is frequently repeated in Iqbāl's philosophical or mystical Urdu and Persian poetry.

Although Iqbāl did not wish to meddle in politics, he is regarded as the father of Pakistan. He suggested to Muḥammad 'Alī Jinnah (1876–1948), the chief founder of Pakistan, the idea of an autonomous Muslim state in northwestern India. It is doubtful whether he actually conceived of an independent Muslim country in the Indian subcontinent.

Iqbal

[Muḥammad Iqbāl (1873–1938) was a teacher and lawyer in Lahore, but is best remembered as the poet and philosopher of twentieth-century Indo-Muslim communal self-consciousness. From his Rumūz-i bīhkūdī *(The Mysteries of Selflessness), 1918.]*

Our Essence is not bound to any place;
The vigor of our wine is not contained
In any bowl; Chinese and Indian
Alike the shard that constitutes our jar,
Turkish and Syrian alike the clay
Forming our body; neither is our heart
Of India, or Syria, or Rum,
Nor any fatherland do we profess
Except Islam …
The mighty power of Rome,
Conqueror and ruler of the world entire,
Sank into small account; the golden glass
Of the Sassanians was drowned in blood;
Broken the brilliant genius of Greece;
Egypt too failed in the great sea of time,
Her bones lie buried neath the pyramids.
Throughout the earth, still the Community
Of World-Islam maintains its ancient forms.
Love is the universal law of life,
Mingling the fragmentary elements
Of a disordered world. Through our hearts' glow
Love lives, irradiated by the spark
There is no god but God.
(Arberry 1953:29, 36–7)

Twentieth-Century Secularism

Afghānī, 'Abduh, and their fellow reformers were at one and the same time liberal modernists and traditional thinkers. They are known as *salafi*s, that is, reformers who sought to emulate the example of 'the pious forebears' (*al-salaf al-ṣāliḥ*). This important ideal of equilibrium between tradition and modernity was lost by the third decade of the twentieth century. Consequently, Islamic reform was transformed into either Islamic revivalism, apologetics, or secularism.

After the Ottoman defeat in the First World War, a young army officer, Mustafa Kemal Atatürk (1881–1938), led a revolutionary movement. He abolished the caliphate in 1924, transforming the Turkish state from a traditional Islamic domain into a modern secular republic, of which he was the first president. Although for centuries the caliphate had been a shadowy office without any power, it still embodied the only hope for a viable pan-Islamic state. This action therefore had far-reaching effects on Islamic political thought.

Atatürk banned Ṣūfī orders, dissolved Islamic religious institutions, and substituted the Latin alphabet for the Arabic alphabet used until then for writing Turkish. He waged a nationwide campaign for literacy in the new script. His express aim was to westernize the Turkish republic thoroughly and cut it off com-

SAYYID QUṬB

[Sayyid Quṭb (1906–59), a leading intellectual of the Muslim Brothers in Egypt, in Ma'ālim fī al-tarīq.*]*

Islam came to elevate man and save him from the bonds of earth and soil, the bonds of flesh and blood ... There is no country for the Muslim except that where the *sharī'ah* of God is established, where human relations are bonded by their relationship to God. There is no nationality for a Muslim except his creed which makes him a member of the Islamic *ummah* in the Abode of Islam. The Muslim has no relatives except those who proceed from faith in God ... The relatives of the Muslim are not his father, mother, brother, wife or tribe unless the primary relationship is to the creator; from there it proceeds to blood relations.

This religion is a universal declaration of human liberation on earth from bondage to other men or to human desires ... To declare God's sovereignty means: the comprehensive revolution against human governance in all its perceptions, forms, systems and conditions and the total defiance against every condition on earth in which humans are sovereign, or to put it in other words in which divinity belongs to humans ... in which the source of power is human ... making some the masters of others with disregard to God. This declaration means the extraction of God's usurped sovereignty and its restoration to Him (Quṭb n.d.:185–6).

pletely from its Islamic past. His use of broad-brimmed European hats was another gesture of repudiation, for the various forms of headgear traditional throughout the Muslim world, which are without brims, permit a person at prayer to touch the forehead to the ground.

While his ideology has remained the official state policy in Turkey, his aim largely failed. The people's Islamic roots could not be easily destroyed. Islamic faith and practice remain strong among the people, and Turkey has its own powerful revivalist movements.

Twentieth-Century Islamic Revivalism

Perhaps due to the international upheavals of world wars and the break-up of the Ottoman empire, Islamic reform experienced a loss of nerve. The nineteenth-century reform movements, though diverse and idealistic, represented a dynamic and courageous spirit of reform and progress. The premature stifling of their spirit may derive partly from the lack of a coherent program of reform for post-colonialist Muslim thinkers to implement or build upon. Consequently, nine-

KHOMEINI

[*From* Sayings of the Ayatollah Khomeini.]

It is often proclaimed that religion must be separated from politics, and that the ecclesiastical world should keep out of affairs of state. It is proclaimed that high Moslem clerical authorities have no business mixing into the social and political decisions of the government. Such proclamations can come only from atheists; they are dictated and spread by imperialists. Was politics separate from religion in the time of the Prophet (God salute him, him and his faithful!)? Was there a distinction at that time between the religious and the high functionaries of the state? Were religious and temporal powers separate in the times of the Caliphs? Those are aberrations invented by the imperialists with a view to turning the clergy away from the material and social life of Moslem peoples, and thus to getting a free hand to pillage their wealth.

Since the Almighty did not designate anyone by name to form the Islamic government in the absence of the hidden Imam [the Twelfth Imam], what are we to do? But while God did not name anyone, He intended that the virtues characteristic of Islamic governments from the dawn of Islam to the reign of the Twelfth Imam be perpetuated. These virtues, these qualities, represented by perfect knowledge of law and justice, are to be found in many of the religious learned of our time. If those learned come together, they will be able to establish the authority that will bring about universal justice. If a competent man, combining in himself these supreme virtues, appears and founds a true Islamic government, it means that he has been invested by the Almighty with the same mandate as the Holy Prophet to lead the people; therefore, it is the people's absolute duty to follow him (Salemson 1980:16–17, 27).

teenth-century liberal reform ideas were transformed in the twentieth century into traditional revivalist movements.

Muḥammad 'Abduh was succeeded by his Lebanese disciple Muḥammad Rashīd Riḍā (1865–1935). Before his death, 'Abduh established *al-Manār* (The Beacon), an important religio-cultural journal that Riḍā continued throughout his lifetime. Chiefly through this journal, 'Abduh's rationalist school continued to shape Arab thought in the first half of the twentieth century, but the school, indeed the whole ideology of reform, had a diminishing role. The twentieth-century Muslim world was radically transformed by new political, social, and economic realities.

On the eve of the abolition of the caliphate in 1924, Riḍā published an important treatise on the Imamate or Supreme Caliphate. In it he argued for the establishment of an Islamic state that would be ruled by a council of jurists or religious scholars. Such a state would recognize nationalistic sentiments and aspirations, but subordinate them to the religio-political interest of the larger community. As this Islamic state idea remained theoretical and unrealized, Riḍā became increasingly nationalistic and traditional.

Riḍā's Islamic revivalism and Arab nationalism came to represent a major trend in twentieth-century revivalist thinking. Riḍā's political idea of a council of jurists was to be implemented later in the century. As the religio-legal scholar Ruhollah Khomeini's ideal of *walāyat al-faqīh*, (the guardianship or authority of the jurist), it figured in the ideological framework of the Iranian revolution of 1978–9, discussed later.

Contemporary Revivalist Movements

Although it remains the ideal of Islamic reform to establish a transnational Islamic caliphate, the reality has been the rise of local movements reflecting local needs and ideas.

Common to most revivalist movements in the second half of the twentieth century is an ideal of an all-inclusive and self-sufficient Islamic order. This ideal has its roots in the social and educational organization of the Muslim Brothers. In 1928, Ḥasan al-Bannā (1906–49), an Egyptian schoolteacher, founded the Society of Muslim Brothers (Jam'iyat al-Ikhwān al-Muslimīn). The aim of this society was to establish a social, economic, and political Islamic infrastructure through which the total Islamization of society might in time be achieved. Thus through schools, banks, cooperatives, clinics, and other social and educational facilities, the Muslim Brothers penetrated all levels of Egyptian society.

Revivalism's political and militaristic aspects also had their beginnings in the Society of Muslim Brothers, particularly after the assassination of the populist and generally peaceful founder Ḥasan al-Bannā in 1949. He was succeeded by hard-line leaders who advocated active *jihād* against the Egyptian state system, which they regarded as un-Islamic. Among the products of the Muslim Brothers' ideology were the young officers who successfully led the 1952 Egyptian socialist revolution, which abolished monarchical rule.

Nevertheless, Gamal Abdel Nasser (r. 1954–70), the leader of the revolution and charismatic proponent of Arab nationalism in the 1950s and 1960s, clashed with the Muslim Brothers. He imprisoned, exiled, or executed most of their leaders in the mid-1960s. Following the Arab defeat in the six-day Arab-Israeli war of June 1967 and the death of Nasser thereafter, the Muslim Brothers were superseded by other and more powerful revivalist movements under Anwar Sadat (r. 1970–81) and his successor Hosni Mubarak.

Although driven underground in its virtual demise in Egypt, the Brotherhood has spread into other Arab countries, where it has remained active;

but in exile, without its social infrastructure, the Brotherhood has been a largely ideological movement.

In 1941, a similar organization, the Jamā'at-i Islāmī (Islamic Society), was founded by Mawlānā Sayyid Abū al-A'lā Mawdūdī (1903–79). Like Ḥasan al-Bannā', Mawdūdī was committed to pan-Islamic unity. But also like al-Bannā', he concentrated his efforts on his own society, in this case the Muslims of India and later Pakistan. The influence of both organizations spread far beyond their original homes.

While most contemporary revivalist movements, including the two organizations mentioned, have been open to modern science and technology as well as the reform of Muslim society, they reject such social ideals as women's liberation, capitalist democracy, Western forms of entertainment and styles of dress, and the free mixing of the sexes as decadent Western values and practices. Therefore, unlike nineteenth-century reformers, who looked to the West for ideas of reform, contemporary revivalist reform movements looked for Islamic alternatives. Mawdūdī, for example, wishing to distinguish his Islamic state model from Western democracies, describes it as 'theo-democracy', based on the broad Qur'anic principle of consultation (*shūrā*) and the *sharī'ah* law.

State Islam and the Islamic Revolution

Besides the nineteenth-century Islamic states of the Mahdī of the Sudan and Aḥmad of Bareilly in India, in the second half of the twentieth century a number of attempts to create Islamic states based on the *sharī'ah* law have been made. Such attempts have in part been reactions to the secular nation-states of the Muslim world that came into being after the first and second world wars. In the majority of cases, these states adopted European law codes for all areas of social and economic life except family and personal law.

After a coup in the Sudan in 1969, Gaafar Mohamed el-Nimeiri (r. 1971–85) plunged that agriculturally rich country into deep conflict between the generally Christian south and Muslim north because he insisted on applying the *sharī'ah* as the law of the land. The tragic results continue to be famine and bloodshed under short-lived and unstable governments. Likewise, General Mohammad Zia-ul-Haq (1924–88) attempted after a coup in 1977 to transform Pakistan, for three decades constitutionally Islamic but modern, into a state governed by the *sharī'ah*. Here, too, the result has been social and political conflict.

In Egypt and Algeria, revivalist movements continue to resort to violent means in their quest for Islamic states. The results are similarly social strife and instability.

In practically every Muslim country there is at least one revivalist movement striving for some form of an Islamic state. In some cases like Malaysia and Indonesia, the governments themselves espouse Islamic national policies aimed at forestalling such attempts and silencing extremist voices calling for radical reform. Nevertheless, in most Muslim countries tensions continue to run high between Islamic movements made up of middle-class educated men and women and despotic regimes determined to hold on to power at any cost.

In such highly charged social and political conditions, religion serves as a powerful moral, social, and spiritual expression of discontent not only for Islamic activists, but for a broad spectrum of the community as well. It was upon this mass discontent that Imām Ruhollah Khomeini (1901–89) and his fellow Shīʿī mullahs (religio-legal functionaries) built the Iranian Islamic republic.

The roots of the Islamic revolution in Iran lie deep in the worldview of Twelver Imāmī Shiʿism. Its ethos responds to the cruel death of Ḥusayn b. ʿAlī in 680 with an ideal of martyrdom as a means of rectifying an errant Muslim society in the absence of the Imām. Until the Imām returns to right all wrongs, his oppressed community must struggle against all rulers, for all rulers are regarded as usurpers of his divinely instituted authority.

In view of the dichotomy between an ideal legitimate divine authority and an illegitimate human rule, a religious hierarchy of scholars and jurists came to represent the Imām's authority during his long absence. Headed by a supreme *mujtahid* or jurist regarded as a sign of God (*āyat Allāh*) in learning and religious authority, this highly organized religious hierarchy dominates the social, political, economic, and religious life of the community.

Throughout the long period of Shīʿī secular rule in Iran (1501–1979), the authority of the religious *ʿulamāʾ* operated in more or less continuous tension with the secular authorities. This tension was greatly exacerbated during the reign of the late Shah, Mohammad Reza Pahlavi (r. 1941–79), who sought to westernize the country, obscuring its Islamic identity by asserting Iran's pre-Islamic cultural past.

In 1963, during the Muḥarram observances of Ḥusayn's martyrdom, matters came to a head between the Shah and the religious establishment. The Shah's dreaded secret police, the SAVAK, ruthlessly put down mass demonstrations led by the *ʿulamāʾ* and sent Khomeini, an already prominent religious leader, into exile. A broad alliance between religious elements, student activists, and leftist groups was formed secretly to oppose the Shah's regime.

In a series of lectures to a group of religious students in one of the *madrasahs* (seminaries) of the holy city of Najaf in Iraq, Khomeini elaborated his religio-political theory of *walāyat al-faqīh* (the guardianship or authority of the jurist). The question of the role of the jurist as the Imām's representative during his absence is an old one. For most Shīʿī religious scholars even today, the jurist's authority is limited to religious and legal affairs. But on the basis of a number of *ḥadīth* traditions from the *imāms*, Khomeini argued for an all-embracing authority of the jurist in the community. Thus *walāyah* or guardianship came to mean for Khomeini the actual role of the jurist.

After a brief period of exile in France, Khomeini returned to Iran in 1979 as the head of the Iranian Islamic revolution. The Islamic republic he founded has had a turbulent history. It fought an eight-year-long war with Iraq (1980–8), out of which it emerged greatly weakened but still intact. The dramatic assassinations and other acts of sabotage that the Mujāhidīn-i Khalq opposition carried out also had their effect. But in the absence of an alternative program, and with the popular support that the religious establishment in Iran continued to enjoy, the 'authority of the jurist' remained unchallenged.

The Iranian Islamic revolution and the state it engendered are a unique and highly significant phenomenon in modern Islamic history. For the first time, an indigenous revolution succeeded, not by armed resistance but by the will of people who triumphed over guns by the sheer numbers of their unarmed bodies. While the Islamic republic has not been able to export its revolution to other Muslim countries, it has spurred groups and individuals around the world to reaffirm their confidence in the ability of Islam to transform their corporate lives.

Islam in Western Europe

Islamic presence in western Europe began early and in a variety of ways. After the establishment of Umayyad rule in southern Spain in 711, commercial, political, and cultural relations were begun with both Latin and Byzantine states, but medieval Europe did not tolerate a permanent Muslim community on its soil. The establishment of today's Muslim communities in western Europe is a more recent phenomenon.

Some Muslims migrated to Europe from its colonies as students, visitors, and merchants. Many Muslims also went as menial labourers and factory workers, especially after the Second World War. The majority of emigrants were male workers ranging from teenagers to men in their forties.

The ethnic make-up of these Muslim immigrants to Europe was largely determined by colonial ties. Emigrants from French colonies in North Africa and elsewhere went to France. Indian and later Pakistani and Bangladeshi Muslims tended to go to Britain. Turkish Muslims and Muslims from the former Soviet Turkic republics went to Germany and the Netherlands, and Bosnians went to Austria. Such emigrations began in the early decades of the twentieth century and continued in spite of many restrictions.

Muslim communities in Europe tend to form along ethnic and linguistic lines rather than sectarian affiliations. With the recent establishment of hundreds of mosques, centres, and religious and cultural organizations in European cities, Muslim communities have become a dynamic religious and intellectual force in European society. In France and Britain, where many Muslims are citizens, Muslims are no longer confined to the status of 'guest workers'. It is anticipated that in the early decades of the twenty-first century, Muslims will constitute half the population of France.

After the Islamic revolution of 1978–9, many Iranians also migrated to Europe, thus adding yet another ethnic and religious component to the already wide diversity of European Muslims. Likewise, the fifteen-year-long Lebanese civil war of 1975–90, as well as the disturbances in other Arab countries, including the Gulf War of 1991, sent many political and economic refugees to the West. Intermarriages and conversions have also infused new blood into the Muslim community in the Western world.

Since the mid-1980s, most European countries have taken legal measures to limit immigration, and some have repatriated some of their Muslim immigrants. Such actions may have been prompted by economic considerations, but perhaps equally by nationalistic fears that Muslim immigrants may alter the social and ethnic character of these countries. European-born Muslims of foreign parentage are increasingly assimilating into European society and culture. However, European discrimination against ethnic minorities and the Islamic awakening precipitated by the Islamic revolution of Iran have made Muslims more aware of their own religious and cultural identity.

Another important factor contributing to the integration of Muslims into European society is interfaith dialogue. Very useful and sophisticated discussions have been sponsored by the Roman Catholic Church, the World Council of Churches, and the Islamic Council of Europe, as well as local church and Islamic organizations. Many hope that honest and constructive dialogue between Muslims and people of other faiths and ideologies will promote a spirit of mutual respect and acceptance in an increasingly pluralistic world.

Islam in North America

When the first Muslims arrived on American shores is a matter of conjecture. Hints that Muslims from Spain and West Africa sailed to America long before Columbus should not be discounted, but are far from conclusive. It is very likely that the fall of Granada in 1492 and the harsh Inquisition that followed against Muslims and Jews led many to flee to America soon after Columbus's historic voyage. Scattered records point to the existence of Muslims in Spanish America before 1550.

In the sixteenth and seventeenth centuries, hundreds of thousands of slaves were brought mainly from West Africa to the Spanish, Portuguese, and British American colonies. At least 20 per cent of these slaves were Muslims. Among the slaves brought from the coast of Senegal, Niger, and the Sudan the majority were Muslims, and many were well educated in Arabic and the religious sciences. They were able to preserve their faith and heritage, and some tried to maintain contacts with Muslims in their home areas, but Muslims were quickly absorbed into American society, adopting their masters' religion and even family names.

Islamic customs and ideas can still be traced in the African-American community. The Islamic history of these early slaves in the United States is being reconstructed from slave narratives, oral history, and other archival materials, including observation by White travellers of some Islamic activities in the mid-nineteenth century.

Beginning in the late nineteenth century, African-Americans made conscious efforts to recover their Islamic heritage. In the early 1930s, Elijah Muhammad (born Elijah Poole, 1897–1975) became a follower of Wallace D. Fard (1877?–1934?) and founded the Nation of Islam in America. He saw Islam as the religion of the Blacks only, thus misrepresenting the universalistic and non-racial nature of Islam. However, his sons and successors, after travelling in the Muslim world and observing the international and multiracial character of the *ḥajj* pilgrimage, have drawn closer to classical Islam. African-American Muslims often refer to themselves as Bilalians, after Bilāl, an African Companion of the Prophet's time and community. Islam continues to be the fastest-growing religion in America, particularly among African-Americans.

Prior to the revival of Islam in the African-American community early in the twentieth century, Muslims mainly from Syria and Lebanon came to the United States and Canada in small numbers. These early immigrants were uneducated men who came to North America to earn money and return home. Instead, many married Canadian or American wives and were soon completely assimilated.

The first Muslim missionary in America was Muḥammad Alexander Webb (d. 1916), a jeweller, newspaper editor, and diplomat, who was converted to Islam on his travels in India. On his return, Webb founded an Islamic propaganda movement. He wrote three books on Islam and established a periodical, *The Muslim World* (not to be confused with the academic journal of the same name). He travelled widely to spread the new faith and established Islamic study circles or Muslim brotherhoods in many northeastern and midwestern American cities. When Webb died, his movement died with him.

Immigration to Canada and the United States has markedly increased during the twentieth century. Moreover, many of the new immigrants came as students who chose to stay, or well-educated professionals who came in search of better opportunities. Others came to escape persecution in their homeland on account of their religious or political activities. Interestingly, many in recent years were staunch anti-Western revivalists, but once they arrived in the United States or Canada, they forgot their previous hostilities and took up life as peaceful, responsible, and law-abiding citizens.

While these and other religiously committed Muslim immigrants may have toned down their political convictions, they retained a high degree of religious zeal, which they put to good use in the service of their own community as well as the society at large. They have played a crucial role in preserving the Islamic identity of fellow immigrants and promoting a better understanding of Islam through media activities and academic meetings.

The first mosque in the United States was built in 1915 by Albanian Muslims, and another followed in Connecticut in 1919. Other mosques were established in the 1920s and 1930s in South Dakota and Iowa. In 1928, Polish Tatar Muslims built a mosque in Brooklyn, New York, which is still in use. The first Canadian mosque was built in Edmonton, Alberta, in 1938. Muslim communities also became organized in smaller towns in Alberta.

The exact number of Muslims in the United States and Canada is a matter of debate. The United States has not had a religious census since 1936. Estimates for the 1980s ran between 2 and 8 million and even higher. More recent numbers are in dispute, ranging in the United States from 3 to 14 million and in Canada from 200,000 to 2.5 million. Whatever the numbers may be, Islam in North America is no longer an exotic rarity. Rather, it is the faith of many people's co-workers and neighbours.

Women and the Family

Before Islam, marriage in Arab society was a transaction of sale or barter between the would-be husband and the father or guardian of the bride. Once the sale was concluded, the woman became the property of her husband, to do with as he pleased. Thus a man could marry an indefinite number of women, whom he could divorce, remarry, and divorce again as often as he wished. A divorced woman, moreover, had no security or freedom of her own. If she returned to her family or tribe, her life would be one of shame and degradation.

Of course, there were exceptions based on the woman's social position and personal initiative, which could play an important mitigating role in her marital and personal status. Still, the situation of a woman in pre-Islamic Arab society was in general precarious and paradoxical. Much value was placed on the honour of the female, on which the honour of her family or tribe depended. Therefore, the protection of women from forced capture and concubinage was of paramount concern in Arab society.

To guard against such an eventuality, families sometimes buried alive one or more of their female infants. This custom may have initially been dictated by the fact that Arab society was either a trading society as in Makkah, or a hunting and pastoral society as in most of the rest of Arabia. In either case, women were not the productive members of the workforce in the way that they have been and continue to be in agrarian and urban societies. The worth of a woman's life was considered nothing in itself, but rather a burden and a liability.

Islam strictly forbade female infanticide and demanded of those who killed their daughters before Islam to make expiation for such a heinous act. On the Day of Resurrection, the *Qur'ān* states, the female buried alive will be asked, 'For what sin was she slain?' (Q. 81:8–9). This means that such women are to be vindicated and recompensed on the Day of Judgement for the wrong done them in this life.

With regard to marriage, while the *Qur'ān* retains its contractual character, it makes it a contract essentially between the husband and wife, based on mutual consent. The father or guardian, 'he in whose hand is the tie of marriage' (Q. 2:237), should act on behalf of the woman, and ideally in her interest. Divorce is likewise limited to two times only. Thereafter, the woman must marry another man, and only if he divorces her can she remarry her first husband (see Q. 2:229–30). In any case, the *Qur'ān* makes divorce a last resort to be used only after all efforts to save the marriage have been tried and have failed.

While allowing polygyny, that is, simultaneous marriage to more than one wife, the *Qur'ān* places on such marriage two significant restrictions. First, it limits it to four wives only at one time, in contrast to the unlimited number before Islam. Second, it stipulates strict justice and equality in a man's material and emotional care for all his wives. If this is not possible, the *Qur'ān* stipulates, 'then only one'. The *Qur'ān* further insists, 'You cannot act equitably among your wives however much you try' (Q. 4:3 and 129).

Even more significantly, the *Qur'ān* changes the condition for polygyny from the male's unrestricted right of sexual gratification to a social responsibility. The verses dealing with this subject open with the proviso, 'If you [men] are afraid that you would not act justly towards the orphans [in your care], then marry what seems good to you of women: two, three, or four' (Q. 4:3).

This statement may be interpreted in two ways. The verse may mean that a man could marry the widowed mothers of orphans in order to provide a family situation for them. It may also mean that a man could marry two, three, or four orphan girls after they have attained marriageable age, again to provide a home and family for them. In either case, marriage to more than one wife is allowed by the *Qur'ān* in order to deal with the problem of female orphans and widows in a traditional society beset with continuous warfare, a society wherein a woman could have the love and security she needs only in her own home.

The *Qur'ān* provides further security and personal worth for women in allowing them to own property and dispose of it as they please. Women may acquire property through bequest, inheritance, and bride dowry, called in Arabic *mahr* or *ṣadāq*. To be sure, judged by today's social and economic needs and circumstances, these rights may seem inadequate. Yet, as Muslims regularly assert, the *Qur'ān* undeniably bestows on women human dignity and a social and emotional personality that were denied until recently in many societies.

Islamic law and social custom, however, have been far less generous and forward-looking than the *Qur'ān*. In general, they have tended either to restrict these rights or to render them virtually inoperative.

There are many social and political issues currently exercising the Muslim community. Chief among these is the age-old issue of the rights of women, with all its ramifications.

The *Qur'ān* does not refer at all to the *hijāb* or veiling of women as we have it today. It only demands that women avoid wearing jewellery and dress modestly, and in the very next verse demands modesty of males. However, we can see from the *ḥadīth* that the Muslim community adopted the *hijāb* during the time of the caliphates. This was probably under the influence of eastern Christian and ancient Greek usage. An extreme manifestation of the *hijāb* has been the seclusion of women, attributable to these non-Arab influences. It became a hallmark especially of Turkish life in the *ḥarīm* system of the Ottoman aristocracy and court.

In the twentieth-century Muslim world and in the West, the *hijāb* has come to symbolize for some an affirmation of women's Islamic identity, but for many a limitation of their rights. The question at issue is whether and to what extent women can be excluded from public life. Increasingly social and economic conditions throughout the world call for equal participation and equal rights of women and men, particularly since self-sufficiency has become an important part of modern life. We can anticipate an ongoing debate on this among other issues in the worldwide Muslim community.

A major development in the history of Islam is now underway in the West. Muslim communities whose migration has taken them from lands where they were a majority to life as a minority are being spurred to articulate the priorities of their faith. Their decisions as to what to pass on to their Western-born children will shape the contours of Islam in the twenty-first century and beyond. Moreover, life in the West, with its atmosphere promoting open discussion, calls Muslims of different cultural and regional backgrounds to work out a keener and clearer sense of the shared and the distinctive features of their historically diverse heritage.

Muslims, one hopes, will find a new home for Islam in the West. Perhaps they will use their Western technology and democratic institutions to revitalize the Muslim communities in their countries of origin, as well as the rest of the Muslim *ummah*. The speed and frequency of modern travel and communication contribute to this process. Political developments may aid, too; many have hoped that the end of the forty-year cold war in 1989 and the moves towards ending more than four decades of conflict between Israelis and Palestinians might allow for better relations between the Western and Muslim worlds.

Muslims can accomplish much in the West if they promote Islamic humanism and a spirit of trust allowing collaboration with their non-Muslim neighbours for greater justice and moral consciousness. There is still a significant need to change old images and ideas if future generations of Muslims in the West are to remain active as Muslims in a society that integrates Muslims and others.

KEY TERMS

dhikr. 'Remembering' God's name. In group devotional exercises, Ṣūfis repeat it in rhythmic chant. The devotees often dance in a circle.

dhimmīs. Non-Muslim religious minorities accorded tolerated status in Islamic society. Jews and Christians as scriptural communities were termed *ahl al-kitāb*, 'People of the Book'.

fanā'. 'Passing away', a supreme stage of ecstasy in the Ṣūfī mystical tradition.

faqir. A Ṣūfī ascetic, from the Arabic word for 'poor'; the corresponding Persian word is *darvīsh*.

Fātiḥah. The short, often recited opening sūrah of the *Qur'ān*, which praises God as lord of the universe and the day of judgement and asks for divine guidance.

fatwā. A ruling issued by a traditional religio-legal authority, who is termed a *muftī*.

fiqh. Jurisprudence, the principles of law. The body of specific regulations is termed the *sharī'ah*, while *fiqh* is the more theoretical analysis of them.

ghaybah. Hiding ('occultation'), from which according to 'Twelver' or Imāmī Shī'ī expectations the Mahdī is eventually to return.

Ḥadīth. Texts containing traditional reports of Muḥammad's words and example, taken by Muslims as a foundation for conduct and doctrine. A *ḥadīth* is an individual unit of the literature, and the *Ḥadīth* is the literature considered as a corpus.

ḥajj. The annual pilgrimage to Makkah.

ḥalāl. Ritually acceptable, in the context particularly of the slaughter of animals for meat.

ḥanīf. A type of pre-Islamic Arab with monotheistic tendencies. The *ḥanīf*s are mentioned separately from the Jews of Arabia and also cannot be conclusively connected with the Christian community.

ḥarām. 'Forbidden', especially a forbidden action. A related word, pronounced differently, is *ḥaram*, 'reserved', especially a sanctuary space. Practices in other religions described by the word 'taboo' have the same pair of connotations.

hijāb. A woman's veil or head covering.

hijrah. Muḥammad's migration from Makkah to establish a community in Madīnah. With dates, the abbreviation AH stands for Latin for 'year of the *hijrah*', counting 354-day lunar years from the event in 622 CE.

'Īd al-Fiṭr. The holiday that celebrates breaking the month-long daylight fast at the end of Ramaḍān. The festival traditionally occurs following the actual sighting of the new moon.

ijmā'. The consensus of the community's religio-legal scholars, used as a principle for extending application of Islamic law. Some schools made more extensive use of it than others.

ijtihād. The process of developing legal opinions. References to 'closing the gate of *ijtihād*' imply a fixing of the legal system, restricting the scope of change.

Imāmīs. 'Twelvers', Shī'īs who recognize as legitimate heirs to the Prophet's authority a succession of twelve *imāms*, the last of whom, expected to return as the Mahdī, has been in occultation since 874.

Ismā'īlīs. 'Seveners', Shī'īs whose lineage runs through Ismā'īl as the seventh Imām and continues to the present in the Indo-Islamic leader, the Agha Khan.

isnād. The pedigree or chain naming the transmitters of a unit of *ḥadīth*, with which the individual unit begins.

Jāhilīyah. Ignorance or barbarism, a Muslim term characterizing Arabia before Islam as unredeemed prior to the preaching of the Qur'anic message.

jihād. Struggle in defence of the faith. Muslims regard military *jihāds* or 'holy war' as responses to threats to the community's security or welfare, but also speak of spiritual *jihāds* aimed at improving moral conduct in society.

jinn. Spirits or demons (the singular is *jinnī*).

jizyah. The poll tax levied on non-Muslims in the early caliphate. It promised protection and exemption from military service. It could be avoided if one converted to Islam, which many did.

kalām. Classical Islamic scholastic theology. The enterprise involved rationally investigating the status of revelation and of divine power and goodness. Theology contrasted with law, where *fiqh* investigated the actions expected of humans.

kufr. Rejection of Islam (etymologically, 'ingratitude'). The implication is that a Muslim is someone who gratefully acknowledges God's favour, and that someone who repudiates Islam denies that God is gracious.

Mahdī. The Shī'ī twelfth Imām, understood in his role as the 'rightly guided one', who will return at an unspecified future date from hiding, to restore righteousness and order to the world.

mu'adhdhin. The person whose voice from the mosque calls people to prayer. The premodern caller ascended the stairs of a minaret so that his voice could be heard; today, the call is amplified electronically.

mufti. A jurist issuing religio-legal decisions or *fatwās*.

Mu'tazilah. A rationalist early Muslim theological school that attempted to promote, even enforce, symbolic understandings of Muslim tenets. The conservative response committed Islamic theology to a strict literal reading on numerous points.

pīr. The Persian and Urdu term for a Ṣūfī master, referred to as a *shaykh* by Arabic speakers.

qiblah. The direction of Makkah, faced in prayer, marked in a mosque by a niche inside the wall nearest Makkah.

qiyās. Reasoning by analogy, a principle in development of Islamic law. Of the four Sunnī schools the Ḥanafī (first under 'Abbāsid and then under Ottoman patronage) made the most liberal use of it, while the others restricted it.

Ramaḍān. The month throughout which Muslims fast during daylight hours.

ṣalāt. The prescribed daily prayers, said five times during the day (added voluntary prayers are called *nawāfil*).

shahādah. Declaring one's faith, 'bearing witness' as a Muslim. The brief declaration formula is a twofold profession of faith: in God as the only god, and in Muḥammad as God's prophet.

sharī'ah. The specific regulations and conduct of Islamic law (jurisprudence, or theoretical discussion of the law, is *fiqh*).

shaykh. Arabic for a senior master, especially of mystical devotion. In Ṣūfī contexts in Persian and Urdu, the *shaykh* is also referred to by the corresponding term *pīr*.

Shī'is. One of the two main divisions of Muslims, a minority constituting about one-sixth of the world's Muslims today, who trace succession to the Prophet's authority through *imāms* in the lineage of 'Alī.

sunnah. The aggregate 'life-example' of Muḥammad's word and deed, constituting for Muslims a guide to proper conduct. The *Ḥadīth* literature is the principal source for its details.

Sunnīs. One of the two main divisions of Muslims, a majority constituting about five-sixths of Muslims today, who trace succession to the Prophet's authority through the institution of the caliphate, lasting until the twentieth century.

sūrah. A chapter of the *Qur'ān*. There are 114 in total, arranged in decreasing order of length apart from the first one, the *Fātiḥah*.

tafsīr. Commentary on the *Qur'ān*.

taqlīd. Following the *ijtihād* or legal opinion of a particular jurist.

ṭarīqah. The organized following or brotherhood of a Ṣūfī saint.

ummah. The Muslim community.

walī. (plural, *awliyā'*) Term for a Ṣūfī saint. It means 'friend', implying that the respected spiritual masters were intimate friends of God.

waqf. A charitable endowment, such as for the upkeep of a mosque or for community welfare purposes.

zakāt. The prescribed welfare tax of 2.5 per cent of one's accumulated wealth, collected by central imperial treasuries in earlier times but now donated to charities independently of state governments (additional voluntary almsgiving is termed *ṣadaqah*).

FURTHER READING

Abu-Lughod, L. 1986. *Veiled Sentiments: Honor and Poetry in a Bedouin Society.* Berkeley: University of California Press.

Ahmed, L. 1992. *Women and Gender in Islam: Historical Roots of a Modern Debate.* New Haven: Yale University Press.

Ayoub, M.M. 1972. *Redemptive Suffering in Islam.* The Hague: Mouton.

Coulson, N.G. 1964. *A History of Islamic Law.* Edinburgh: Edinburgh University Press.

Duncan, A. 1972. *The Noble Sanctuary: Portrait of a Holy Place in Arab Jerusalem.* London: Longmans.

Esposito, J. 1984. *Islam and Politics.* Syracuse: Syracuse University Press.

______. 1995. *The Oxford Encyclopedia of the Modern Islamic World*, 4 vols. New York: Oxford University Press.

Fernea, E.W., and B.Q. Bazirgan, eds. 1977. *Middle Eastern Muslim Women Speak.* Austin: University of Texas Press.

Grabar, O. 1973. *The Formation of Islamic Art.* New Haven: Yale University Press.

Haddad, Y.Y., and J.I. Smith, eds. 1994. *Muslim Communities in North America.* Albany: State University of New York Press.

Hooker, M.B., ed. 1983. *Islam in South-East Asia.* Leiden: Brill.

Keddie, N.R., ed. 1972. *Scholars, Saints, and Sufis: Muslim Religious Institutions in the Middle East Since 1500.* Berkeley: University of California Press.

Lewis, B., ed. 1976. *Islam and the Arab World: Faith, People, Culture.* London: Thames and Hudson; New York: Knopf.

Mernissi, F. 1991. *The Veil and the Male Elite: A Feminist Interpretation of Women's Rights in Islam.* Reading, Mass.: Addison-Wesley.

Nicholson, R.A. 1907. *A Literary History of the Arabs.* London: T. Fisher Unwin.

Padwick, C. 1961. *Muslim Devotions: A Study of Prayer-Manuals in Common Use.* London: SPCK.

Rahman, F. 1966. *Islam.* London: Weidenfeld and Nicolson; New York: Holt, Rinehart & Winston.

Rypka, J. 1968. *History of Iranian Literature*. Dordrecht: D. Reidel.

Schimmel, A. 1975. *Mystical Dimensions of Islam*. Chapel Hill: University of North Carolina Press.

Trimingham, J.S. 1968. *The Influence of Islam upon Africa*. London: Longmans; New York: Praeger.

von Grunebaum, G.E. 1951. *Muhammadan Festivals*. New York: Henry Schuman.

______. 1962. *Modern Islam: The Search for Cultural Identity*. Berkeley: University of California Press.

Watt, W.M. 1962. *Islamic Philosophy and Theology*. Edinburgh: Edinburgh University Press.

Waugh, E.H., and R.B. Qureshi, eds. 1983. *The Muslim Community of North America*. Edmonton: University of Alberta Press.

REFERENCES

Arberry, A.J. 1948. *Immortal Rose*. London: Luzac.

______. 1953. Muhammad Iqbal, *The Mysteries of Selflessness*. London: John Murray.

______, trans. 1955. *The Koran Interpreted*. London: Allen and Unwin.

______, et al., eds. 1968–91. *The Cambridge History of Iran*, 7 vols. Cambridge: Cambridge University Press.

Dawood, N.J., trans. 1990. *The Koran*, 5th ed. London: Penguin.

Glassé, C., eds. 1989. *The Concise Encyclopedia of Islam*. London: Stacey International.

Holt, P.M., et al., eds. 1970. *The Cambridge History of Islam*, 2 vols. Cambridge: Cambridge University Press.

Houtsma, M.T., et al., eds. 1913–38. *The Encyclopaedia of Islam*, 4 vols, plus supplement. Revised version edited by H.A.R. Gibb et al. Leiden: Brill.

Nicholson, R.A., 1931. 'Mysticism'. In *The Legacy of Islam*, edited by T. Arnold and A. Guillaume, 210–38. London: Oxford University Press.

______, trans. 1950. *Rumi: Poet and Mystic*. London: G. Allen and Unwin.

Peters, F.E. 1994. *A Reader on Islam*. Princeton: Princeton University Press.

Philips, C.H., ed. 1963. *Handbook of Oriental History*. London: Royal Historical Society.

Quṭb, S. n.d. *Milestones*. Cedar Rapids, Iowa: Unity Publishing Co.

Ranking, G.S.A., and W.H. Lowe, trans. 1895–1925. *Abd al-Qadir al-Bada'uni, Muntakhab al-Tawarikh*, vol. 2. Calcutta: Asiatic Society.

Roolvink, R. 1957. *Historical Atlas of the Muslim Peoples*. Amsterdam: Djambatan.

Salemson, H.J., trans. 1980. *Sayings of the Ayatollah Khomeini*, edited by J.M. Xavière. New York: Bantam Books.

Smith, M. 1928. *Rabi'a the Mystic*. Cambridge: Cambridge University Press.

Williams, J.A. 1994. *The Word of Islam*. Austin: University of Texas Press.

Chapter Five

Rivals, Survivals, Revivals

Willard G. Oxtoby

The major traditions covered in this volume—Judaism, Christianity, and Islam—share the idea that their origins constitute a sharp break with the religious practices of their neighbours, practices that they gradually supplanted. As we have noted, the repudiated predecessors have characteristically been termed pagan. The etymology of the word 'pagan' hints at a historical process. Coming from the Latin for 'rural', it alludes to the situation of Christianity's spread in the Roman Empire. While the newer religion took hold in the cities and along the trade routes, older practices and allegiances survived for a considerable time in more remote areas.

Zoroastrianism does not have a comparable concept of 'paganism'. In its case, the older religious practices of the Indo-Iranians were not pushed aside but amalgamated with the prophetic faith of Zarathushtra's *Gathas*, the Indo-Iranian deities becoming the heavenly deputies of Ahura Mazda. To dismiss alternative allegiances as pagan, one has to portray the deity as 'jealous' or exclusive, more like Yahweh than like Ahura Mazda.

In the course of this chapter we shall examine some of Judaism's, Christianity's, and Islam's 'pagan' rivals, noting in a few cases that the rivalry did not always finish in antiquity. Modern rebirths or revivals of interest in the content of these other traditions have sometimes been an indicator of dissatisfaction with the emphases or performance of Western civilization's 'mainstream' monotheistic traditions.

Rivals

The Ancient Near East

Civilization, as we have come to use the term, emerged first in the lands stretching from Egypt through Syria to Mesopotamia, today's Iraq. We identify civilization as a package of organizational and technological developments, on the basis of which life in these lands can be contrasted with what went before.

People became organized into larger social groups. One of the reasons such organization occurred earlier in Mesopotamia and Egypt than in other places must have been the development of irrigation technology. If one herds animals in hilly terrain watered by rainfall, one's tribal or clan group need not be large in order to survive; indeed, pasture size tends to place an upper limit on the animal population and therefore the human population that can be sustained in an area. But in the fertile flat plains of the Tigris, Euphrates, and Nile rivers, as larger concentrations of population developed, they designed and built canals and regulated the flow of water from these rivers. And this larger-scale organization permitted role differentiation of other sorts as well, including priesthoods and specialists in many techniques.

Writing was one of the most important of these. Spoken language itself is of course a symbol system, naming things or representing ideas by means of acoustic sounds, with different arbitrarily chosen sounds standing for a particular idea among different speech communities. Spoken language was important in the emergence and success of humans as a species much earlier in prehistoric time. Now writing operated as a second process of symbolization; it represented sounds as well as ideas through the use of graphic signs. Invented somewhere around 5,000 years ago, it permitted the preservation of individuals' names and the record of their accomplishments. Without it, we would have little evidence on which to construct history. With the emergence of writing in the Ancient Near East, history begins.

Clay, which was available in abundance, was the principal material the Mesopotamians used for writing. On a rectangular tablet the size of a computer disk but made of moist, soft, low-tech clay, the writer could make a pattern of indentations with the point of a stick or stylus. When baked, the tablet was permanent. Since the individual marks were wedge-shaped, the script has been known in modern times as cuneiform, from the Latin *cuneus*, 'wedge'. Any of various languages—Sumerian, or Akkadian and Ugaritic (languages of the Semitic family related to Hebrew and Arabic), or Hittite and Old Persian (languages of the Indo-European family related to Latin and Sanskrit)—could be written with such signs. In Egypt, a separate system of symbols was developed, often written with ink on sheets of papyrus, made from the pressed crisscrossed stalks of a grasslike plant. Hieroglyphic, meaning 'priestly writing', is the name given in modern times to one pictorially representative form of the Egyptian writing, again the form of the signs as a system rather than the spoken language that they symbolized.

These systems were at first very complex, each with a repertory of hundreds of signs for syllables. Literacy was not widespread; instead, the writing systems were the privilege and skill of a specialized palace-temple scribal bureaucracy. Writing was used much more to record what was already deemed authoritative than to create original compositions. Many records were of business transactions or temple offerings, important since the treasury of the sanctuary, placed under the god's protection, functioned in a way like our modern banks. Other records included the laws promulgated by the ruler, again under the protection of the gods and acting as the deity's representative or maintainer of order on earth. Some texts recorded the temple rituals and recounted the myths involving the deities. Although mythological texts constitute only a tiny minority of the written material surviving from Near Eastern antiquity, they have attracted perhaps the lion's share of modern interest.

The Mesopotamian epic of creation begins with the Akkadian words *Enūma eliš,* 'when on high':

> When on high the heaven had not been named,
> Firm ground below had not been called by name,
> Naught but primordial Apsu, their begetter,
> And Mummu-Tiamat, she who bore them all,
> Their waters commingling as a single body …
> Then it was that the gods were formed within them.
> (Speiser 1950:61)

Tiamat is associated with the waters of the primeval chaos, and creation consists of introducing order, establishing the world as we know it and defeating Tiamat. This is accomplished by the hero-god Marduk, armed with the flood-storm, who slays Tiamat in combat. Splitting her carcass like a shellfish into two parts, he forms and arranges the heavens from one half and the earth and the regions below from the other, and assigns the various gods their roles and functions. The narrative was widely influential in Near Eastern culture. References to chaos as watery, to division of waters, and to the primordial slaying of a monster all turn up subsequently in the Hebrew Bible, and the Hebrew word for the watery deep in the opening of *Genesis* appears to be derived from the Mesopotamian name Tiamat.

If one of the universal questions religion must answer is where we came from, the other is where we are going. What life is like beyond the grave is the question underlying Mesopotamian literature's other great epic. It is known by the name of its hero, Gilgamesh, who in a lengthy quest seeks to discover what things are like in the realm to which his slain warrior friend Enkidu has gone. To try to reach Enkidu, Gilgamesh consults Utnapishtim, the old sage, who tells how he survived a primeval flood by building a boat and taking animals aboard. Utnapishtim's narrative again reflects the Near Eastern background of biblical themes, but with its own flavour. Utnapishtim reports celebrating his return to dry land after surviving the flood:

> I poured out a libation on the top of the mountain.
> Seven and seven cult-vessels I set up.
> Upon their pot-stands I heaped cane, cedarwood, and myrtle.
> The gods smelled the savor,
> The gods smelled the sweet savor,
> The gods crowded like flies about the sacrificer.
> (Speiser 1950:95)

There were indeed many gods in Mesopotamian religion, both because of diverse heavenly functions and because power passed in the course of time from Sumerian to Akkadian to Assyrian and late Babylonian powers. A Mesopotamian pantheon is therefore a construct; indeed, lists of deities were constructed by scribes in antiquity in order to keep track of the deities. We name only a few; if two names are given, the first form is Sumerian, the second Akkadian. Anu's domain is the sky and Enlil's the storm, while Enki or Ea is the god of pools and marshes. The goddess Inanna or Ishtar has several fertility associations: the date crop, the spring season, the planet Venus, and loose sexual conduct. Marduk, the creation hero, is also the city protector of Babylon, while Ashur is the chief god and protector of Assyria's capital, which bears his name.

An important feature of Mesopotamian religion was the ritual and practice of divination. For public military success as for individual health and well-being, the deity had to be kept on side. Diviners specialized in figuring out what would promote future benefit as well as what had caused current illness or misfortune. Another type of priestly specialist was the exorcist, whose rituals or spells were engaged as therapy once the diviner had arrived at a diagnosis.

In its general functions ancient Egyptian religion was broadly similar to ancient Mesopotamia's. For the Egyptians, too, the idea of a pantheon is a construct, bringing order out of diverse regional traditions and shifts over time. Among the important deities, at least at times, were Atum, to some the oldest or a parent god; Re, a creator or sun god; Nūt, sky; Geb, earth; Osiris, the lord of the underworld; Isis, his sister and wife; and Horus, their son. Some of the Egyptian deities were represented with human bodies but animal heads: Horus as a falcon, Anubis as a dog, and Khnum as a ram. Others of the deities, however, were always in anthropomorphic form. Ptah, worshipped in Memphis, Amun of Thebes, Atum in Heliopolis, and the sexually erect Min of Koptos are examples. Scholars link the narrative of Osiris's death and rebirth with the annual agricultural renewal occurring as the rising waters of the Nile deposited rich silt in the river's flood plain.

In the eyes of many, ancient Egyptian culture was obsessively concerned with death and the hereafter. There are grounds for the view; clearly, vast effort was expended to preserve the physical remains of the deceased. Mummies (the word is from the Arabic for 'wax') are the embalmed and wrapped remains at least of the wealthy. Grave goods to accompany the deceased into the next existence included symbolic models of retinues. Famous are the pyramids built above ground in Lower or down-river Egypt to house the remains of the Fourth Dynasty (2613–2494 BCE) rulers, and likewise spectacular are the chambers hollowed in the cliffs of Upper or upstream Egypt for the burials of the Eighteenth Dynasty (1558–1303 BCE) pharaohs.

Two things need to be said to mitigate a blanket characterization of the Egyptians as obsessed with death. One of these takes the evidence as representative and interprets it: the concern with death is fact enough, but fact that affects life in the here and now. That is because the judgement of the dead, based on conduct in one's prior earthly life, is a stimulus to thisworldly morality. The classic scenario of judgement shows one's heart weighed in a balance against *ma'at*, truth or goodness, symbolized by a feather. A different argument challenges whether the evidence is representative. Might it not be that we are lured into viewing Egyptians and others as obsessed with death because the grave contents are what most commonly find their way into museums? In daily life, things are used until they break and are then discarded as trash, whereas new, whole items are included in burials. Much of the time, the collector or exhibitor will choose the tomb piece as visually the more attractive.

Egyptian civilization was never forgotten completely. Greek and biblical literature mentioned the Egyptians. The pyramids have been in full view on the Cairo horizon for 4,500 years; in fact, local Arab folklore in Petra in southern Jordan attributed the Nabatean structures there to 'Pharaoh'. But the European decipherment of Egyptian hieroglyphics and excavation of Egyptian monuments beginning at the start of the nineteenth century spurred a new response to ancient Egypt as the treasurehouse of mystery. More than almost anywhere else because of the demonstrable antiquity of its monuments, Egypt was thought to contain occult secrets that today's believer might interpret.

Ancient Near Eastern religion, as an alternative to biblical religion, has had a few modern advocates. One of the groups that became spiritually fascinated with Egypt was the Rosicrucians. They trace their identity to a German, Christian Rosencreutz (reportedly 1378–1484), whose followers at the time of the Reformation claimed his tomb contained sundry alchemical and mystical contents. Before the nineteenth century, Rosicrucians were drawing on European occult sources available for interpretation as mysteries. As Egyptian material came to notice in the nineteenth century, they incorporated it. There is a Rosicrucian museum of Egyptian materials in San Jose, California.

The Greek and Roman World

For much of the experience of ancient Greece and Rome, religion was local and shrine-oriented. If we expect an organized, doctrinally explicit portrayal of Greek religion, we invite disappointment.

What characterizes Greek and Roman religion is its status as the religion of the people. We do not find theology, but we find narrative mythology. People were told the stories of the gods in their homes and childhood upbringing. They participated in rituals that alluded to such stories, the myths serving as the rituals' metaphorical rationale. But, in mainstream Greek and Roman society, if thinkers analysed the universe in a theoretical way, they adopted a perspective different from the childhood narratives. This, we may remark, is how the word 'myth' even in antiquity gained its connotation of falsity: a *mythos* was a narrative of the gods in which one might participate ritually or with a kind of suspension of judgement, but from which one distanced oneself if one was thinking philosophically. Even in antiquity, intellectuals interpreted the myths allegorically or devised explanations of how they might have come into being.

Myths often offered etiologies, that is, explanations of why things came to be as they are. One of the best-known is the story of Daedalus and Icarus, in which the human wish to fly like a bird, in this case by fastening feathers to one's arms with wax, is frustrated. Flying too close to the sun, so that the wax melts and the feathers fall off, might be sheer carelessness, but it can also be read as *hubris* or excessive pride, illustrating the teaching that we humans are not meant to fly.

Deities in the Greek and Roman pantheons have roles related to the powers of nature or the overarching needs of human existence. Greek Zeus/Roman Jupiter is ruler of the gods, his power manifest in the storm and his symbol the thunderbolt; Romans even referred to Jupiter as Pluvius, 'the rainy one'. Hera/Juno is his consort, while the domains of love are assigned to another female deity, Aphrodite/Venus. Hermes/Mercury is the messenger of the gods, Ares/Mars the god of war, Poseidon/Neptune the god of the sea, Artemis/Diana the goddess of the hunt, Hephaistos/Vulcan the patron of blacksmiths, and Dionysos/Bacchus the god of wine and revelry. There were numerous others.

Greek philosophy contributes to our image of ancient Greece, so that we think of the Greeks as rational. However, Greek popular religion involved practices that were a world apart from philosophy. The cult of Dionysos, for instance, involved group trances and what were interpreted as possession states on the part of his followers. The mystery initiation religions at Eleusis and other initiation cults involved secret teachings and, one presumes, some cultivation of trancelike experiences.

Greek and Roman 'paganism', as a rival to Christianity, was the loser in antiquity after Constantine's gradual sponsorship of Christianity. However, its deities and myths resurfaced later not as a religion but as a cultural alternative to Christianity. If, after the European Middle Ages, one were to look for cultural values to counter those of the established institutional Church, to what would one turn? The period we refer to as the Renaissance turned to the chief literary source available: the pre-Christian content of Latin and Greek literature. The myths became Christendom's secular stories, the figures of the deities Europe's secular iconography, and the architecture of Greek and Roman temples the models for Europe's secular architecture. The humanistic tradition of the Greek philosophers, which in antiquity had little to do with the popular religiosity of the masses, was now symbolized in Europe by the details of ancient Greek and Roman religion.

Islam's Rivals

The prevalent view of Arabia before Islam is very much a theological construct, a construct that serves to heighten Islam's own sense of destiny. In the Islamic interpretation, what preceded the time of the Prophet in Arabia was *jāhilīyah*, that is, ignorance or barbarism. It was a time of polytheism and idolatry.

Non-Muslims also have stereotypical views of ancient Arabia. A prevalent view is that the typical Arabs were camel-herding Bedouin, and that their life consisted of random wanderings among the sand dunes of a trackless desert. Never mind that as pastoral nomads the Bedouin tribes have claimed their particular migration territory for generations and know it like the back of their hand, so that their movements are hardly aimless. Never mind that they eke their living more from stony than from sandy terrain, and more from the pastures and pools within it than from the stones. The real mistaken impression is that the population of Arabia was primarily nomadic. Most of the people lived in oasis towns. Arabia was remarkably urbanized, as Canada and Australia are today. The population is not in the empty spaces, but huddles together where settlement can flourish.

Moreover, Arabian society knew monotheism as well as polytheism, thanks to the presence of Jews and Christians, who were already established for several centuries prior to the time of Muḥammad. The *Qur'ān*'s message of a prophetic warning to the people of Arabia is one that builds on the presumption that God has already spoken through other prophets. Islam's rivalry with its predecessors is a differentiating rivalry: a condemnation of polytheism in the case of Arabian paganism, but an endorsement of the terms of prophetic monotheism in the case of the biblical tradition.

The pagan religion of Arabia enumerated largely two types of deities: overarching heavenly gods, and special tribal spirits and protectors. The sun and moon were the dominant celestial deities, but important also was the planet Venus, appearing sometimes as the morning and sometimes the evening star. Worship of the local deities involved pilgrimage sites and a sense of the localized presence of the deity in unusual trees or rocks. The black stone, likely a meteorite, incorporated into the Ka'bah at Makkah, is an example. While repudiating the pagan deities, Islam incorporated some of their practices, such as pilgrimage, into the worship of the one God.

The displacement of Arabian paganism by Islam appears to have been complete. Classical Islamic civilization was shaped in the interaction of Arab rule with the Greco-Christian culture of the eastern Mediterranean and with the national traditions of Iran. Neither of these civilizations in the lands of Islam's early spread perpetuated any substantial influence of the pagan gods of ancient Arabia, as Arabia had lain outside their territory.

The Bahā'ī Faith

A significant modern rival to Islam arose in nineteenth-century Iran. However, the basis of the rivalry was not over a plurality of gods, for this movement shared Islam's faith in the one God. At stake was the plurality of prophetic revelations or dispensations. We know the movement from today's perspective a century and a half later as an aspiring world religion, the Bahā'ī faith.

Bahā'ī roots are in the particular eschatology of Iranian Shi'ism. Twelver Shī'īs entertained the expectation that an individual might be the Bāb ('gateway') offering the community access to the line of *imāms*, the last of whom was thought not to have died but to have disappeared in 874 and to be in hiding. After ten centuries, most people were not holding their breath in the expectation of an imminent reappearance, but seeds of messianic expectation did germinate in the soil of political unrest.

Sayyid 'Alī Muḥammad (1819–50), from Shiraz in southwestern Iran, became caught up in eschatological teachings and in 1844 declared himself to be the Bāb, the gateway to a new prophetic revelation. His followers began a rebellion, and he was imprisoned in 1845 and transferred to northwestern Iran. Insurrection continued: the Bābīs, as his followers were called, repudiated Islamic *sharī'ah* law in 1848, and in that year, the Bāb proclaimed himself the hidden Imām. The Bāb was executed by a firing squad in the city of Tabriz in 1850, but left behind the religio-legal *Persian Bayān* (Exposition), an *Arabic Bayāṇ*, and other writings that have been considered scriptural.

Momentum passed to a follower from a leading Tehran family, Mīrzā Ḥusayn 'Alī Nūrī (1817–92), whose religious name is Bahā'u'llāh, 'Glory of God'. He had not met the Bāb personally, but became active in his movement. While imprisoned in Tehran in 1852, he had a profound experience of divine support. On release the following year, he was banished from Iran to Baghdad in Turkish-controlled Iraq, where he became a spiritual leader of Bābīs in exile. He was still near enough to Iran to be regarded as a threat, so in 1863 the Persian consul pre-

AN INTERVIEW WITH BAHĀ'U'LLĀH

[The Cambridge professor Edward G. Browne tells of paying a visit in Acre, Palestine, in 1890.]

The face of him [Bāha'u'llāh] on whom I gazed I can never forget, though I cannot describe it. Those piercing eyes seemed to read one's very soul; power and authority sat on that ample brow; while the deep lines on the forehead and face implied an age which the jet-black hair flowing down in indistinguishable luxuriance almost to the waist seemed to belie. No need to ask in whose presence I stood, as I bowed myself before one who is the object of a devotion and love which kings might envy and emperors might sigh for in vain!

A mild dignified voice bade me be seated, and then continued: 'Praise be to God that thou has attained! ... Thou hast come to see a prisoner and an exile ... We desire but the good of the world and the happiness of the nations; yet they deem us a stirrer up of strife and sedition worthy of bondage and banishment ... That all nations should become one in faith and all men as brothers; that the bonds of affection and unity between the sons of men should be strengthened; that diversity of religion should cease, and differences of race be annulled—what harm is there in this? ... Yet so it shall be; these ruinous wars shall pass away, and the "Most Great Peace" shall come ... Do not you in Europe need this also? Is not this that which Christ foretold? ... Yet do we see your kings and rulers lavishing their treasurers more freely on means for the destruction of the human race than on that which would conduce to the happiness of mankind ... These strifes and this bloodshed and discord must cease, and all men be as one kindred and one family ... Let not a man glory in this, that he loves his country; let him rather glory in this, that he loves his kind' (Browne 1891, 2:xxxix–xl).

vailed on the Turks to move him to Istanbul. Before going, he declared himself to his followers to be 'the one whom God shall manifest' as foretold by the Bāb.

This politically enforced transfer to the Mediterranean world transformed the sphere of Bahā'u'llāh's spiritual activity. The horizons were no longer Shī'ī nor Iranian. Instead, Bahā'u'llāh addressed the religious diversity of the Ottoman Turkish Empire and also invited support in letters to rulers in Europe and to Pope Pius IX. Squabbles broke out between the Bahā'īs, as Bahā'u'llāh's followers were now called, and the Azalīs, as those of his half-brother Mīrzā Yaḥyā Nūrī (Ṣubḥ-i Azal, 'Dawn of Eternity'; 1830–1912) were called. In response, the Turks in 1868 banished Ṣubh-i Azal to Cyprus, where the Azalī following dwindled, and Bahā'u'llāh to Acre in Palestine, where his following grew. Nearby Haifa, today in Israel, remains the world headquarters of the Bahā'īs.

During and after imprisonment, his first nine years in Acre, Bahā'u'llāh continued to write. His output amounts to more than 100 volumes, considered by Bahā'īs as God's inspired revelation for this age. Of them the *Kitāb-i Aqdas* (The Most Holy Book) and *Kitāb-i Īqān* (The Book of Certitude) rank high in importance.

For sixty-five years after Bahā'u'llāh's death in 1892, authority in interpreting the tradition was passed on to family heirs. Bahā'u'llāh's son 'Abbās Effendī (1844–1921) was considered an infallible interpreter of his father's writings and had the title 'Abdu'l-Bahā', 'Servant of [God's] Glory'. Infallibility was then bequeathed to 'Abbās Effendī's grandson, Shoghi Effendi Rabbani (1899–1957). Leadership was subsequently vested in an elected body of representatives called the Universal House of Justice.

Bahā'ī teachings have a strong ethical bent, with a concern for world solidarity and community. All religions are highly respected, and taken as evidence of God's continuing self-manifestation. Bahā'ī worship features readings from Bahā'ī scriptures rather than liturgical or preaching activity. The Bahā'ī calendar is distinctive, consisting of nineteen months of nineteen days each. Bahā'īs assemble once each month, marking the occasion with a feast. The last month is a Ramaḍān-like time of dawn-to-dusk fasting, coming just before the spring equinox, the traditional start of the Iranian year.

Many Bahā'īs are of Iranian descent, but many others are converts made by missionary activity throughout the world, and they can enjoy high status in the community. For instance in 1937, Shoghi Effendi Rabbani married Mary Maxwell, daughter of the Canadian architect of Bahā'ī shrine buildings in Haifa. Meanwhile, the Bahā'ī faith was taken to North America when a Syrian convert to it, Ibrahim George Kheiralla was in Chicago during the World's Parliament of Religions in 1893. A nine-sided domed temple was subsequently constructed in Wilmette, a northern suburb of Chicago.

From its very beginnings in the Bābī movement, then, the Bahā'ī faith has been at odds with Islam. Its revelation does not conclude with the *Qur'ān* but goes on to incorporate later prophets and their texts. Its notion of the ideal for society departs from the *sharī'ah*. Its calendar is its own, and it was born in conflict with Muslim state authority in nineteenth-century Iran. That its headquarters are in what became Israel did not endear it to Muslims following Israeli statehood in 1948. Particularly after Israel gained control over Jerusalem's Muslim sites in 1967, non-Arab Muslims took more of an interest in the Israeli-Arab struggle and increasingly looked on the Bahā'īs as Israeli sympathizers. However, the most serious confrontation has come since 1979, when revolution in Iran ushered in a theocratic Islamic republic. Public missionary and religious activities by Bahā'īs were banned in 1983, and the community suffered serious losses in lives and property. It is hard to imagine the terms, practical or theological, on which a reconciliation between Iran's Bahā'īs and Muslims could soon be effected, despite—or because of—what they have in common.

SURVIVALS

African Traditional Religion

Compared with the 5,000-year span of recorded history in the Middle East, Africa's past is a mystery because its cultures were without writing until the contact of Middle Eastern and European civilizations in recent times. The line dividing Africa's 'prehistory' from history is a recent one. A sketch of Africa's past is based on some oral traditions and on works of sculptural or pictorial art, but mainly on two lines of inferential reasoning: first, that features shared by different population groups are more likely original than those that are different; and second, that whatever was observed by outsiders at the time of initial contact can be supposed to have survived from time immemorial. Notice the tension between these two lines of reasoning: the first must presuppose change if differentiation is to take place, while the second presupposes the absence of change.

To generalize about all of Africa's religion is as presumptuous as to generalize about all of Asia's. The African continent is vast, with varied wet and dry climates producing jungle, grassland, and desert, with their varied fauna and flora. The historical experience of contact with outsiders and the influences they have brought is likewise diverse. Yet some universal themes of human existence shape much of African religion as they do religion elsewhere—appropriately so, because Africa is where the human species first emerged long, long ago.

One can view as universal in African religion a sense that power affects human life. This power is personified in deities manifested in the forces of nature, and in spirits that may take up residence in people, animals, and plants, or may on occasion depart from them. The spirits of the dead, now disembodied, may continue to make their force felt. Myths and legends tell how the creation of the universe and of humans came to pass; one Zulu account says that the god of the sky lowered a human, attached by an umbilical cord, down through a hole in the sky.

The individual's and the society's relationships with the world of the supernatural are maintained in a variety of rituals. People dance, sing, pray, or make sacrifices and offerings to mark special moments and give special attention to the spiritual powers. Many rituals have to do with turning-points in the agricultural year, and are performed to promote fertility. Some have to do with stages in the life of an individual, such as the initiation of an adolescent into adult responsibility. Some are devoted to specific *ad hoc* situations, such as preparation for battle.

Certain articles such as masks and amulets, and certain locations such as tree groves or hilltop shrines, are set apart from everyday use and treated as sacred, reserved for appropriate ritual contexts. In smaller family societies, the chief or a senior member of the clan may perform the rites on behalf of the group. In larger societies, role specialization generally develops, so that there are ritual specialists who prepare for their tasks through apprenticeship and training.

The practices and techniques of such specialists may entail entering a state marked by silence, speech, or movement that the society interprets as spirit possession, in which case outside observers have categorized the activity in terms of a cross-cultural conception of shamanism. The techniques may also entail ritual actions performed on the bodies of persons or images to induce benefit, especially to bring healing, in which case the cross-cultural interpretive categories are magic and medicine. Techniques are employed also to curtail the power of enemies and bring misfortune on them; we term such activity witchcraft. Shamanic activity, healing, and witchcraft are all oriented towards producing results in the present earthly lives of the human community, more than towards any future existence.

Along with prescribed ritual action goes a strong sense of social action in the community. African religion has a strong sense of right and wrong behaviour, of appropriate honour and respect—in short, an implied code of morality. Specific moral injunctions vary locally and regionally, and differ from Western values on such points as polygamy, but the idea of social custom is important across the continent.

The expression of religious life in artistic forms is one of the salient features of African culture, a 'must' for anyone seeking to understand Africa. The culture is dominantly oral, with storytelling and poetry highly refined. It is also a musical culture, with great importance given to dance and song, and a sophisticated exploration of drum rhythms. It is a pictorial culture as well, with important sculptural traditions particularly in wood-carving. The shape of tree trunks as the available material has contributed to an elongated verticality in much African sculpture.

Moving from the broad overall similarities to appreciate regional and local diversity, the student of Africa needs to distinguish the experience of major culture regions. It is easiest today to speak of East Africa, southern Africa, and West Africa.

East Africa

East Africa, from the southern Sudan through Uganda, Kenya, and Tanzania, has been influenced by Islam for some centuries. Muslims have been a presence particularly as traders along the East African coast; the regional trade language,

Swahili, is an African language, but with a large admixture of Arabic loanwords. Christianity has been a significant influence in East Africa only more recently, with the arrival of European missionaries; the long history of Monophysite Christianity in the highlands of Ethiopia was largely a history of isolation.

From the nineteenth and twentieth centuries we have information about leaders of local movements that have been responses to instability and change. These leaders have arisen as prophets, claiming divine aid and often uniting various groups to resist outside influences. Among the Nuer of the southern Sudan at the end of the nineteenth century, one such was Ngundeng, who opposed both Arab slave traders and British colonialists. Among the Lugbara of Uganda and Zaire, a prophet named Rembe distributed water that would allegedly revive cattle that had died in epidemics, make people who drank it immune from bullet wounds, and drive away foreign intruders. His movement ended with his arrest in 1917. Similarly, the followers of Kinjikitele in Tanganyika, opposing German colonial forces in 1905–7, thought that the water he gave them would immunize them from bullets; but Kinjikitele was hanged, and 250,000 of his followers died in the revolt, many from bullet wounds.

Southern Africa

Compared with East Africa, southern Africa was largely isolated from Islamic influences prior to European contact. It had a flourishing local civilization; the archaeological remains of a complex called the Great Zimbabwe, roughly 500 years old, attest to this. However, in more recent times southern Africa has been massively influenced by the Christianity of colonial administrators, and in some regions a large White settler population. When gold was discovered near Johannesburg in 1885, particularly disruptive changes were introduced into the life of the Bantu people, as the men moved away from their traditional village settings to work in the mines.

These changes were the setting for the career of Isaiah Shembe (c. 1870–1935), a Zulu prophet. His call experience was of hearing a voice telling him to climb a mountain, where he had a dream in a cave, and telling him to survey the earth, whereupon he had a vision of his own decaying corpse. Waking, he announced, 'I have seen Jehovah.' He had ties to a Zulu rebellion of 1906 and the leader of a new Baptist denomination, and then in 1911 formed his own independent church, the amaNazaretha Baptist Church, with Saturday rather than Sunday worship. After a mountain retreat the following year, in which he experienced temptations by evil spirits (resisted) and gifts of heavenly bread and wine from angels (accepted), he began to practise spiritual healing.

Shembe's church utilized traditional Zulu social patterns in its worship, grouping the worshippers by age and gender to participate in dance rituals. The hymns he composed speak from the idiom of Zulu tradition also, rather than being stiff translations of European models. At the age of forty, Shembe learned to write in order to spread these compositions. He called himself 'the Servant', seeing his role among his own people as helper and healer, comparable to Moses's and Jesus's among the Jews. In Zulu society, one does not approach a king without being introduced by one of the subordinate chiefs; Shembe as servant culturally understood his role to be to lead his people to the throne of Christ.

The anti-White thrust of Shembe's movement was not shared by all emerging southern African charismatic churches. Some, called the Ethiopian churches, were more ambivalent. They espoused the organizational forms of the Whites' Christianity. Modernity in southern Africa has meant the adoption of European education, science, and technology, but many of the Native population still view the sky and the ground, illness and social evil, in personal terms as powers to be dealt with. The techniques still include divination and witchcraft, despite the pressures of change.

West Africa

West African religion is likewise a phenomenon in transition, and has been so at least since the arrival of European Christians via the coast and Arab Muslims via the interior. In many cases, the old religion is giving way, but only slowly, and the observer can note instances of fusion and integration of traditional African ways with the newer imports. Traditional rituals following the birth of a child, for instance, have been maintained by peoples who have become Muslim, and a chief who has more than one wife may espouse Islam without loss. Christian missionaries, by contrast, have had a more rejectionist stance towards rituals regarded as pagan and towards polygamy.

Prophets have emerged in West Africa as well in response to transitional situations. Particularly remarkable is the career of William Wade Harris (c. 1865–1928). He was from Liberia and was literate thanks to a mission education. He worked as a mission schoolteacher and as a government interpreter, but was imprisoned in 1909 for flying the Union Jack when his people, the Grebo, were agitating against the American-related Liberian government. In prison he had a vision of the angel Gabriel commissioning him to spread Christianity to his people, which he did following his release in 1913. His initial efforts among the Liberians met with little response.

Harris then went to the nearby Ivory Coast, where his preaching was phenomenally successful. Traditional religion had not warded off colonial inroads, but Harris offered an alternative. He told the people to destroy their traditional masks, altars, and other religious materials and to give up worshipping the local nature spirits in favour of the universal creator god. He promised tangible benefits: sovereign freedom from colonial rule, but at the same time the enjoyment of the conquerors' technology.

Prior to Harris, Roman Catholic missionaries under French colonial sponsorship had baptized only 400 people in twenty years. Within a single year,

Harris reportedly baptized between 100,000 and 120,000. When the first European Protestant missionaries finally arrived in 1924, they were astonished to find indigenous Protestants, Harris's followers, waiting for the 'teachers with Bibles' whom Harris had led them to expect. The taste for scriptural religion, which Harris had acquired in his Protestant upbringing, had not been satisfied in the meantime by the Catholic missionaries.

Harris was an impressive, even flamboyant figure. His wife thought he had gone insane, and she reportedly died of grief. Legends about him grew, and miracles were attributed to him. Traditional African priests who opposed him died mysterious deaths. Traditional shrines were consumed by unexplained fires. The French colonial officials feared his influence and banned him from the Ivory Coast in 1914 after he had been there for little more than a year. He returned to his native Liberia, where he did not have the same impact and spent the last fifteen years of his life in comparative obscurity.

Harris claimed to be the final prophet of God. To symbolize his role, he wore a white robe with black bands and carried a Bible, a cross, a baptismal bowl, and a gourd rattle. One branch of his followers, the Church of the Twelve Apostles, made much of the gourd rattle, and actually broke with the British Apostolic Church when that group insisted on tambourines instead. Some of the churches deriving from Harris's activity added their own culturally African prohibitions to the standard Christian ones: they specifically forbade sex outdoors, and were against 'eating human flesh', by which was meant witchcraft, but which was extended to not celebrating the Christian Eucharist.

Influences between the Harris movement and the traditional African roles of the spirits are not easy to sort out. Grace Thannie in the Gold Coast had been a traditional medium and founded the Church of the Twelve Disciples. Marie Lalou (d. 1952), who founded the Deima Church, moved towards reintroducing traditional practices. She believed that European missionaries had been ineffective against local witches, that Harris had driven them out, but that they had subsequently returned. Unlike Harris, she thought the Bible was useless against malevolent powers, and preferred holy water and ashes as her means to counter witchcraft.

African Religion in the Western Hemisphere

Brazil

African slaves were taken to Brazil in the sixteenth century, but only in the nineteenth century do we begin to have much evidence of the persistence of African religion in a Western hemisphere context. The presumption is that the traditions (mainly of the Yoruba people of southwestern Nigeria) are what were transplanted to the Brazilian context, but this is based on inference. We do not have records of where the slaves came from; instead, observers note similarities between what they find in Brazil and features of Yoruba religion, such as the deity Xango (Shango).

In Brazil, communities of Blacks of African descent are found in the northeastern state of Bahia, in the vicinity of Rio de Janeiro, and in other locales. In Bahia the groups are called Candomblé, and in Rio, Macumba. The activity of these groups centres on the cultivation of spirit possession trances, with mediums as leaders. The mediums are in touch with the deities, often termed *orixās*, who take on specific manifestation characteristics in relating to particular individuals. The activity of the mediums has a social value: a feature of Afro-Brazilian religion is the *consulta* or 'consultation', when the functioning medium is available to help individuals with particular problems such as illness, job problems, poor business, or anything thought to be the result of witchcraft.

In its operation, Afro-Brazilian religion is fundamentally monotheistic. It treats the manifestations of spiritual power as varied manifestations of a supreme deity. Organized hierarchically, the *orixās* are similar to the roster of saints in Roman Catholic Christianity. Indeed, it seems that the identification of the Yoruba spirits with the Catholic saints was deliberately encouraged, in order to prevent the suppression of Afro-Brazilian religion by White Catholic slave-owners.

The Afro-Brazilian cults have from time to time been officially forbidden, suppressed, or persecuted, such as under the dictator Getúlio Vargas (r. 1937–45). They command a large number of the poorer element in the population, however, an element in search of identity and dignity. Hence politicians have courted their favour to gain votes; the Umbanda community around Rio is thought to represent one-sixth of Brazil's population.

Haiti

In the Caribbean, African religious components have developed in a distinct way in what is popularly termed 'Voodoo', the religious practice of 80 to 90 per cent of the population of Haiti. The name Voodoo is actually a designation of a particular ritual or dance pattern, and is derived from an African word in a language of Benin, formerly Dahomey, in West Africa. The names of Voodoo spirits and the practices in their worship are traceable to the African origin of Haiti's Black population, but that origin is diffuse rather than precise; it includes the Fon people of Benin, but also the Yoruba of Nigeria and the Kongo people of Zaire and Angola.

The broad outlines of Voodoo psychology and terminology reflect the ideas and vocabulary of the French Roman Catholic slave-holders and their clergy. These were adapted into the Haitian Creole language to describe African perceptions of the individual personality and the spirits. A few examples will have to suffice.

Voodoo spirits are termed *lwa* (in the Yoruba language, a term for 'mystery' or 'spirit'), but also *sint* ('saints'), *envizib* ('invisibles'), *mistè* ('mysteries'), or occasionally *zanj* ('angels'). The human personality has spiritual components that may move about independently of the body before or after death, including the *gro bonanj* ('big good angel'), which is the personality component sorcerers try to capture, and the *ti bonanj* ('little good angel'), the conscience of the living and the ghost of the dead. A person is protected by various spirits including the *mèt-tet* ('master of the head').

Cemeteries are a focus of Voodoo ritual. The first male buried in a cemetery is called the Baron. A cross located centrally or at the entrance is the *kwa Baron* ('Baron's cross'), and after household rituals, remaining candles and food offerings are deposited at the base of this cross, since the cemetery is the principal spatial contact between the realms of the living and the dead. The principal time of contact is the Christian eve of All Souls, Hallowe'en.

In the cities and villages of Haiti, as well as among Haitians living in Miami, New York, and Montréal, the ritual calendar usually associates Voodoo spirits with corresponding Roman Catholic saints' feast days. Rituals venerating the spirits characteristically involve the sacrifice of a chicken, goat, or cow. There are also initiation rituals and death rituals, and annual pilgrimages to places sacred to the spirits, which again are often matched with Catholic religious sites. Much ritual is of a magical character, to bring practical benefit such as prosperity or healing to the client. Only some ritual is the 'left-handed' sort that led to criticism of Voodoo by outsiders, where people obtain spirits by purchase, deal in *zombi* or captured souls of the dead, or use magic for social control. President François Duvalier (r. 1957–71), Haiti's dictator known as 'Papa Doc', exploited Voodoo for political purposes.

Jamaica

Jamaica's Rastafarian movement is presented as an African connection, but one may remark that Western hemisphere Blacks have created it rather than inheriting it. As participants in Christian worship, they took note of biblical references to Ethiopia, the one region of Black Africa mentioned in the Bible and also the one region to have a continuous Christian tradition. From early in the twentieth century, both in Jamaica and in the United States, writings explored such references, particularly *Psalm* 68:31, 'Let Ethiopia hasten to stretch out her hands to God'. With the accession of Haile Selassie (r. 1930–74) in Ethiopia, who was known as Ras ('prince') Tafari, the movement began to focus interest on this ancient African Christian royal lineage as the hope of the despondent among Caribbean Blacks.

In time, a millenarian and revivalist scenario developed: Jamaica is depressed but Ethiopia is practically heaven and Emperor Haile Selassie the living God. He will repatriate Western hemisphere Africans, and historical roles will be reversed with Whites serving Blacks. Rastafarians see themselves as successors of the biblical prophets. They view modern powers as exemplifying the degeneracy that biblical passages assign to Babylon: colonial Britain, industrial America, bourgeois Jamaica, and the corrupt Church. Repudiating these, one promotes 'natural' expression in diet, beards, uncombed hair, *ganja* (marijuana), and rhythmic music on which reggae is based. Haile Selassie was deposed in 1974 and died in 1975, but the poverty and despair that gave the movement its appeal continue unmitigated and still fuel Rastafarian yearnings.

Native Traditions in North America

Inuit

In their own language, Canada's Native peoples of the Arctic call themselves Inuit, meaning 'the people'. For use by others as well, the name has been replacing the older term 'Eskimo', which may have come from the Algonkian Indians to the south and which was mistaken to mean 'eater of raw meat'. To the surprise of many Canadians, their country does not have the largest Inuit population in the world, but only the third largest. Besides the 25,000 in the Canadian Arctic, there are 35,000 in Alaska and 43,000 in Greenland. No longer isolated from one another, the Inuit of the three political jurisdictions have expressed their shared identity since 1977 through representatives in the Inuit Circumpolar Conference.

Nor do the Inuit live in isolation from the technology of the modern world. Their winter dwellings made of snow, stone, or wood have given way to construction materials brought in from the south. The traditional boats—the small kayak for seal hunting and the larger umiak for whaling—are now covered not with the skins of these marine mammals but with imported materials. The storytelling that helped time to pass on long winter nights has been replaced by television. The young are educated in schools, the Inuit have become Christian except for a few in Siberia, and even they do not observe the old traditions. To describe traditional ways, one has to use the past tense.

Central to the old religion was humans' close dependency on the land and sea mammals, birds, and fish that they hunted. Inuit understood all these creatures to have souls, which the human hunter was obliged to treat respectfully. When one killed a polar bear, one placed it in a dwelling facing in the direction from which the bear had come, so that its spirit might return. When seals or whales were harpooned and brought ashore, they were offered a drink of fresh water so that their souls could re-enter the sea refreshed and prepare to be caught again. Skins of birds and animals were kept rather than being destroyed, and in the annual Alaskan Bladder festival, all the bladders of seals caught during the previous year were returned to the sea so that their souls could reproduce.

The principal religious specialist in Inuit society was the shaman, who learned the techniques of achieving ecstatic trances and experiencing spiritual journeys from apprenticeship to other shamans. Alaskan shamans had masks, and Greenland shamans used drums. Their summoning of the spirits was often sought in response to practical necessities. The shaman was thought to facilitate contact with the domains from which the animal species came. An individual's bad luck in hunting might be attributable to the violation of a taboo such as the requirement to keep game separate from human blood shed in birth, menstruation, or death. In such a case, a shaman could conduct a ritual of confession and expiation. As healers, shamans attempted to treat the location on the body where the negative spirit influence was thought to have entered, sometimes by sucking a wound to draw out the spirit.

Power in the universe was perceived in the personified form of deities. The sea, important as the source of marine mammals, was the domain of the Sea Woman, whom the Inuit of Baffin Island name Sedna, probably meaning 'the one down there'. The sun was also feminine, while the moon was masculine, and the theme of incest figures in a myth of their origins. In the narrative, a man repeatedly visits in the dark of night and makes love to a girl. To find out who he is, she puts soot on her hands and touches his face. By the light of the next day, looking at the men of the village for a mark of soot, she discovers the lover is her brother. She picks up her lamp and chases him, rising into the sky to become the sun while he becomes the moon, and they continue to chase each other across the sky.

The rituals and the narratives of the traditional Inuit, dispersed across a vast area, were never uniform nor systematic. They have receded before the pressures of modernity from elsewhere. Among the Inuit today are some leaders who seek to recover a sense of pride in their own identity and are gathering up the old traditions to preserve them. What may well emerge as the legacy of Inuit religion in the future is a cross-regional amalgam, to some extent systematized and integrated. In that configuration, surely an important and central theme will be the respect for the lives and spirits of the hunted species, with whom humans share the planet and on whom humans have depended.

The North American Indians

Different cultural patterns existed among different peoples among the Native American population prior to contact by European Whites, and the periods and circumstances of such contact have also varied widely. As a target for description, Native American religious culture is consequently a scattered one and also one that moves as we approach it. Moreover, it is elusive because some of its stories and teachings are shared as secrets only with initiated members of the tribe or band, so that full public description would be a violation of their integrity.

The Atlantic Coast of North America and the Great Lakes region were home to a culture described as Northeast Woodlands culture. The southern American states were the region of the Southeast Woodlands culture. From the Mississippi and Missouri rivers west to the Rocky Mountains is the region of the Plains Indians, while the deserts of the American southwest, the intermountain basin of Utah, Nevada, and Idaho, and the northwestern Pacific coastal regions

The Indian cliff dwellings of Mesa Verde in southwestern Colorado include cylindrical ceremonial chambers called kivas.
(Willard G. Oxtoby)

and the continent's sub-Arctic constitute other regions. Environments differing from region to region in climate, vegetation, and topography present different opportunities and challenges to the populations that live in them.

The forms of houses are only one example. In the Northeast Woodlands, the longhouse is common; found on the Plains is the cone-shaped tent, the *tipi*; and characteristic of the southwest is the adobe brick pueblo, this latter sometimes constructed under an overhanging cliff if one is available. Similarly, the basis of subsistence, whether hunting or farming, depends on what species flourish in the local climate.

However, diversity of climate, of natural species, or of material technology is not the only significant variation. The writer and curator Peter Farb (1929–80) synthesizes the results of North American ethnography and anthropology to build a cultural-evolutionary thesis regarding Native American societies. Different Native American groups at the times of the first White encounter with them can be taken to represent virtually every step along a scale of development of social organization, from the very simple to the highly complex. Some Native American societies, like the Digger Indians of Nevada, remained rudimentary hunter-gatherers, while other societies, in the Arizona–New Mexico southwest for example, had developed sophisticated agricultural techniques, with complex social structures to match. The Northeast Woodlands, at the time of White contact, already had an intertribal political confederation that regulated relations and balanced power across a wide area. Farb reminds us that, ironically, cultural development has not necessarily been conducive to cultural survival. There was little in the Digger Indians' subsistence economy and society that White contact could disrupt, whereas the delicate balance of the Iroquois confederation collapsed under outside pressure.

As with other Native societies, the world of the Native American is perceived as filled with powers in the heavens, the weather, in animals and plants, and in human ghosts and spirits. The creator spirit generally has an important role. Benefit for the living community is sought in the form of fertility brought by rain, success in the hunt and in warfare, and in the avoidance or control of illness. There is less agreement over how the spirits of the dead are to be considered. Some think of them as now distant in the heavens, observable in the Milky Way or in the northern lights. Others think of them as hovering in the immediate vicinity of their former life and intervening to cause misfortune if their interests are ignored.

A practice widespread among Woodlands and Plains Indians is the effort to gain the protection of a spirit, often one in animal form, experienced in a vision brought about after a period of retreat and fasting. Another practice is the sweat lodge ceremonial, where several males gather in the steam of a saunalike session in a domed hut made of saplings and covered with hides or blankets where water is sprinkled over heated stones. The ritual specialist is the shamanic healer or medicine man, who has a bundle containing twigs, stones, or feathers and bones with beneficial magical qualities. He has a supervisory role in initiations, sweats, and vision quests, and can also lead the entire society in ritual activity in crisises, for instance in dances to induce rain. Other rituals, especially seasonal agricultural or hunting rituals, can be routinized and performed by clans or societies without requiring shamanic activity.

Native American society was ravaged by military defeat, which wiped out some populations and displaced others to lands, often remote, termed reservations in the United States and reserves in Canada. Deprived of the means or locale of their former life and work, many Natives drifted into urban poverty and alcohol abuse. In the wake of conquest also came Christian missionary activity, which in its earlier phases repudiated the Native heritage as pagan and sponsored the confiscation or destruction of its ritual artefacts. Responses to such intervention could on occasion produce new spiritual movements.

Handsome Lake (1735–1815) was a shaman of the Seneca nation in what became western New York state, who lived during the collapse of Iroquois power and the loss of their land to the Whites. While seriously ill in 1799, he experienced dream visions, in which four angelic messengers from the Creator spirit commissioned him as a prophet. Recovering, he dedicated himself to reforms that might mitigate social breakdown and strengthen his shattered community. He attacked adultery, wife beating and desertion, abortion, child abuse, and alcoholism. He also worked to eradicate witchcraft and the use of charms. He proposed to replace the people's multifamily longhouse dwellings with individual houses like the farmhouses the Quakers had. The ideal for him was a renewal of Native society through internal harmony and rational action, not through confrontation and conflict with the Whites; but he resisted White education for Native youth, fearing it was corrosive. He presented all of his program as the Native destiny, in line with the will of the Creator. Handsome Lake continues to attract interest as a North American prophet figure, to be compared and contrasted with prophets on the African scene.

The Ghost Dance movement began in 1870 on a reservation at Walker Lake, Nevada. A Paiute Indian, Wodziwob (1844–1918?), had a trance vision that the old tribal life and hunt animals would be restored if people performed nightly dances, without fires. Wovoka (1856–1932), also known as Jack Wilson because of the White family for whom he worked as a farm hand, was the son of one of Wodziwob's followers. He experienced a trance during a solar eclipse, probably in 1889, and issued messianic predictions to his people that peace with the Whites and return of the game were at hand if people would perform the strenuous nightly dances. Indians of the Plains in the Dakotas, Montana, and Wyoming, hearing of Wovoka, sent emissaries to learn more, and interpreted what they heard as implying that the Whites were to be exterminated. Dancing spread all over the Plains in the summer of 1890 and fuelled militant expectations, provoking repression by White authorities. The Lakota Indians wore 'ghost shirts' with emblems, possibly patterned after Mormon clothing, which they thought would serve as armour against Whites' guns. Sitting Bull (c. 1837–90), the Lakota leader, was arrested and assassinated, and large numbers of Natives perished in 1890 in a massacre at Wounded Knee in South Dakota.

From the beginning of the twentieth century, the Native American Church gained in popularity especially among the Plains Indians all the way from northern Mexico and Texas to Canada. Central is its use of peyote, which contains the hallucinogen mescaline, as its sacred plant. In its overnight ritual on a Saturday night, the congregation sits in a circle around a fire altar in a traditional cone-shaped canvas *tipi*, set up especially for the ceremony. There are regular prayer meetings and also special ceremonies such as birthdays, funerals, and send-offs or return welcomes for travelling members of the community.

In the ceremony, led by the 'roadman' or ceremonial chief, cigarettes of tobacco rolled in corn husks are smoked, and then each member in turn around the circle consumes some 'buttons' of peyote and sings songs to the accompaniment of a drum and a gourd rattle. The effort and rhythm of the singing in the

Totem poles are a feature of Northwest Coast Indian culture. These poles were formerly grouped in a park on the University of British Columbia campus in Vancouver.
(Willard G. Oxtoby)

context of group support heighten the hallucinatory effect of the peyote. At midnight and again at dawn, a container of water is brought in, some is splashed on the participants, and then each takes a drink. A communal breakfast concludes the ritual. Despite missionaries' disapproval of the 'peyote Church', congregations reflect Christian influence to lesser or greater degrees, some of them placing a Bible in front of the altar, singing and praying to Jesus Christ, and interpreting the consumption of peyote as a eucharistic ritual. As the twentieth century progressed, the Native American Church gained some acceptance outside Native circles, as well as some non-Native adherents.

By the late twentieth century, the practical life and day-to-day technology affecting Native Americans was thoroughly modernized. In transportation, communication, food production, entertainment, and recreation, Natives became hardly distinguishable from the Whites of the continent. Most Natives were Christian. While lost as a practical way of life, however, the Native heritage underwent a revival as a symbolic value. In the context of a growing Native political self-awareness and with sympathetic support from interfaith-minded Church circles, Native spirituality was explored and valued anew. Its sense of dependence on the bounty of nature was welcome at a time of increasing ecological concern

Figure 5.1

NATIVE CULTURE GROUPS AND MISSIONARY ACTIVITY IN NORTH AMERICA

in the society at large. Realistically or unrealistically, the Native way of life was celebrated and promoted as having been the ecologically correct way all along. As interest in Native tradition grew, historic cultural differences from one part of the continent to another were swept aside in a synthesizing corporate self-consciousness, a kind of pan-Indian 'ecumenical' spirit. The vision quest and sweat lodge of the Plains Indians became the heritage of the entire Native peoples, as did the calumet or pipe, the symbolic use of feathers, and the totem symbolism of the Northwest Coast. The Native heritage as it is celebrated today is a relatively new construct, with a future still to unfold.

Religion in Mexico

We piece together our knowledge of preconquest Mesoamerica (the region of Mexico, Guatemala, and Honduras) from its archaeological sites and stone sculptures, from anthropological investigation of the languages and folklore of the surviving Mayan population, and from the extensive literary record of the Spanish conquest that began under Hernán Cortés (1485–1547) in 1519. That record includes the important description of New Spain by Bernardino de Sahagún (c. 1490–1590). The earliest wave of Europeans in Mexico did not reach Sahagún's level of sophistication, however. When Spanish scouts from Cuba landed on the flat eastern peninsula of Mexico in about 1510, they asked the indigenous people on the beach the name of the place. They perpetuated as a name (Yucatán) the response they received, 'Uic athan', which in the local Mayan dialect means 'We don't understand what you're saying.'

The civilization of Mexico goes back to a people whose traces we know from sites along the southern shore of the Gulf 2,000 years before the Spanish conquest, whom modern archaeologists call Olmecs from the name of an elusive local population mentioned by Sahagún. The Olmecs had a high degree of social organization and specialization. They developed calendars and a hieroglyphic writing system, had ceremonial sites, and must have advanced the cultivation of maize, domesticated previously from grain whose cobs archaeology shows to have been only one-fifth the length of a corn cob today. Olmec religion had a jaguar deity, and the Olmecs' chubby human figurines of jade, with half-jaguar, half-human facial features seem to be the prototype for jaguar masks of rain spirits in later cultures. A robed human with a duck bill was carved about 2,000 years ago. Later cultures represented other animal figures: a plumed serpent, an eagle, and the bird with a serpent perpetuated in the Mexican coat of arms.

Olmec culture was passed on to the peoples who overthrew them, giving rise to classic civilizations. The most important among these was Mayan culture, dominant in the lowland tropical rain forest of the Yucatán and northern Guatemala, and extending also into the southern Guatemalan highlands. Mayan civilization reached its apex between about 600 and 900. The Mayan sites reflect a vast expenditure of energy to maintain clearings in the jungle and to build not so much permanent cities as ceremonial complexes, each having a pyramid with stairways up the four sides. The pyramid at Tikal in Guatemala is as high as a twenty-storey building, and the city site could house 100,000 people at the time of a major festival. The Mayans were assiduous astronomers and mathematicians, and worked out a calendar of eighteen twenty-day months, with five extra days. The greatest Mayan centre, Chichen Itza in the Yucatán, was conquered by peoples from the west, possibly Toltecs, in the tenth century, and decline set in long before the arrival of the Spaniards as the Mayan ceremonial sites fell into disuse.

Mayan religion had rain deities called Chacs, who were seen as sprinkling the earth with water from gourds when they were pleased but dumping their contents to produce floods and throwing stone axes (thunderbolts) when angry. There were solar and astral deities and also the four Itzamna, twin-headed dragon serpents ruling the compass directions and represented by the colours yellow, red, black, and white. Also important was the god of maize. Much of what we know of Mayan religion comes from traditions recorded at the time of the Spanish conquest: the *Books of Chilam Balam* and, from the highland Quiché Indians in Guatemala, the *Book of Books of Popol Vuh*. Important observations were made by Diego de Landa (1524–79), a Franciscan missionary and the first Roman Catholic bishop of Yucatán, in his *Relación de las cosas de Yucatán* of 1556.

The other classic cultural focus was the upland valley of Mexico, at an altitude of nearly 2,300 m (over 7,500 ft) above sea level. The successors of the Olmecs built one of the Western hemisphere's first real cities at Teotihuacán, 70 km (45 mi.) northeast of today's Mexico City, with extensive complexes of temples and pyramids. The deities of the Mexican pantheon appear: rain god, feathered serpent, sun god, moon goddess, and the spirit of annual agricultural renewal, Xipe Totec. Remains of the dead after cremation were buried. A Náhuatl song indicates traditional views about the hereafter:

> And they called it Teotihuacán because it was the place where
> the lords were buried.
> Thus they said, 'When we die, truly we die not, because we
> will live, we will rise, we will continue living, we will
> awaken. This will make us happy.'
> Thus the dead one was directed, when he died: 'Awaken,
> already the sky is rosy, already dawn has come, already
> sing the flame-coloured guans, the fire-coloured swallows,
> already the butterflies fly.'
> Thus the old ones said that who has died has become a god,
> they said: 'He that has been made a god there,' meaning,
> 'He has died' (Coe 1962:111).

Toltec invaders had a unifying effect in the tenth century, but of the various rulers in the history of the upland valley our impressions are formed by the Aztecs, who came to power in the fourteenth century and were encountered there by the Spanish. The Aztecs were ruthless conquerors themselves, earning a brutal reputation. In his lightning raids against rivals, Moctezuma I (r. 1440–59) burned their temples, imposed heavy tribute, and sacrificed to his god Huitzilopochtli, who became elevated from a tribal god to sun god and creator. Aztec religion sees Huitzilopochtli as the sun locked in a struggle with the jaguars of darkness, and regards the duty of humans to be to sustain him with the nectar of the gods, human blood.

The Aztec capital, Tenochtitlán, was built on a swampy island in Lake Texcoco where Mexico City now is (the landlocked valley of Mexico, lacking external river drainage, had shallow lakes). The temple in the midst of the capital was dedicated to Huitzilopochtli and Tlaloc, its twin parallel stairways drenched with the blood of victims. With every Aztec success in war with their neighbours, captives became the victims in the Aztecs' gory human sacrifices. In these, the victim was stretched out on the temple platform, where the officiating priest cut open the victim's chest, removed the heart, and placed it on the fire. The body was flayed and the priest or a penitent wore the victim's skin to impersonate or represent the god Xipe, 'the flayed one', for twenty days. In front of the temple platform stood the 'skull rack' with tens of thousands of skewered human heads. And in Aztec art, the fearsomely portrayed Coatlicue, mother of the gods, wears a necklace of sacrificed hands, hearts, and skulls.

Religion in Peru

Two thousand years before the Spanish conquest, the Peruvian Chavín culture flourished at the site of Chavín de Huantár, in the mountains north of Lima. The Chavín site has an extensive temple complex, and human figures with feline details such as tusks and claws suggest animal deities. By 1,000 years before the conquest, the Moche culture succeeded Chavín in northern Peru. It, too, had fanged feline creatures, and its pictorial representations shows humans being sacrificed to these creatures. In southern Peru, contemporary with the Moche, was the Nazca culture, which also depicted a catlike deity. On the surface of the Nazca desert near the coast southeast of Lima are some geometrical designs several kilometres long, made by removing the darkly weathered stones from the surface to reveal a fresher, yellowish layer beneath. Informed scholarly speculation suggests that the designs, actually more readily visible from the air than from ground level, had a function relating to the agricultural calendar.

The Incas of Peru began as conquerors around the twelfth century, taking over the skills of their neighbours, and by the time of the Spanish conquest in the early sixteenth century had put together a realm stretching from Ecuador to central Chile, integrated by a remarkable network of roads and a sophisticated system of government to match. The supreme god of the Incas was a celestial ruler, Viracocha. He is creator of the sun, moon, spirits, humans, and animals, distant and enthroned much like an earthly ruler but ruling through his subordinate powers. In some creation narratives he is displeased with the humans he has created his first time around, so turns them to stone, sends a flood, and then starts over. He gives humans their customs, languages, and songs, and then, to see whether humans are obeying his instructions, he goes around incognito as an old man with a staff. Stoned as an unwelcome stranger, he explodes in a burst of fire, accounting for the volcanic 'burned hill' of Tinta between Cuzco and Lake Titicaca in the Andes.

The sun and moon figure in narratives that similarly appear to have an explanatory function. Eclipses of the moon are caused by a puma or snake attempting to devour it. To ward off the attacking animal, people make as much noise as possible during an eclipse, a practice still surviving among the people of Cuzco in Peru. The power of deities other than the celestial ones is localized in places or objects termed *huacas*. Many of these have to do with the promotion of agricultural fertility and management of the food supply.

Inca temples were not places of congregational worship but rather accommodated the priests and their ritual paraphernalia. Inca sacrifices were primarily of llamas or guinea pigs, but human sacrifices of captives or youths appear to have been made in times of particular crisis. Before engaging in any action, one undertook divination, one technique of which was to count grains, pebbles, or pellets of llama dung to see whether they came out odd or even. Sorcery was practised, and animal cries in the night could be taken as omens of death. On death, virtuous people and all nobility regardless of virtue proceed to an upper world. The wicked go a lower world to suffer from cold and hunger, with only stones for food.

REVIVALS

Religion in Pre-Christian Europe

Northern and eastern European pre-Christian religion is known through a combination of archaeology, descriptions by Christians upon contact, and folkloric survivals. It has undergone a renaissance of interest in recent years because of Goddess associations and connections.

European Prehistory

From many thousands of years ago, evidence of human activity survives in Europe in the form of chipped flint implements, burials, and cave paintings. We can only speculate about prehistoric people's concerns and motives, but from the burials it is clear that significant effort went into covering the bodies of the dead with heavy stones in some cases and in breaking the bones of the corpses in others. Both practices lead us to the inference that the living feared the return of the dead and the possible activity of their spirits to settle unresolved grievances with the community still living. As for the cave paintings, the dependence of hunting societies on the hunted animals is obvious, and there are hints that animal skins were used in early rituals parallel to shamans' usage observed among the Lapps and Siberian peoples in our own day.

Neolithic stone circles in Europe excite considerable fascination. The largest one in Britain is Stonehenge, on the upland plain northwest of Salisbury, in southern England. Its early phases of construction go back 5,000 years or more and make it older than the pyramids of Egypt. Stonehenge consists of two concentric circles of large, erect stones with lintel stones placed across the top. Some of the stones weigh over 50 tons, and construction must have required the efforts of more than 1,000 people for a season. There are burials associated with some of the stones, and the whole site may have been a burial mound, but the alignment of the stones suggests an astronomical orientation that may have had to do with eclipse prediction or with seasonal rituals, possibly agricultural rituals. The very fact that Stonehenge's significance cannot be conclusively established has made it possible for all manner of groups and movements to read meaning into it. Especially on solstices and equinoxes, it has been a gathering place for throngs of excitable visitors, to the extent that the authorities have had to protect the stones from their devotees by restricting access.

The alignment of the prehistoric circle of Stonehenge suggests prehistoric use in solar observation and ritual. (British Tourist Authority)

Agricultural technology in Europe gradually spread westward and northward from the Balkan and Black Sea region during a period extending roughly 9,000 to 5,500 years ago. Neolithic culture in Europe is seen in its implements and pottery, including a widespread practice of making clay female figurines with ample busts and hips. Evidence of these figurines led to the virtually inescapable conclusion that agriculturalists had an earth mother goddess, associated with agricultural as well as human fertility. Moreover, once written traditions appear in

Mesopotamia and the Greek world, we find narratives of a female figure descending to the underworld and returning to this one, associated with the cycle of the agricultural seasons. The interpretive question to be asked, therefore, is how a central role of the goddess came to be suppressed in the ancient patriarchal societies that we know of in Ancient Near Eastern and Mediterranean literature. One theory would be that state organization began to give more power to warriors than to agriculturalists, but the question still remains very much open to discussion.

Scandinavian Religion

Scandinavian burials and the grave goods included in them reflect a belief that spirits live on after the death of the body, and Scandinavian rock carvings from more than 3,000 years ago show humans, animals, and sun symbols, suggesting seasonal fertility rituals in a region where the contrast between the length of summer and winter days is great because of the high northern latitude. By all odds, however, the most significant evidence for Scandinavian religion is the preservation of its mythic narratives in the *Edda*s, compositions produced when political refugees went from Norway to Iceland after 874.

Tradition credits the *Verse Edda* to Saemundir the Wise (1056–1133), but it is more likely a composite work by many authors from the ninth to thirteenth centuries. It narrates the stories of the gods and heroes in a miscellaneous but sincere fashion, inviting participation and belief. Meanwhile, the *Prose Edda* of Snorri Sturluson (1179–1241), an Icelandic historian, offers a more constructed and systematic view of the same material, but with the distance of scepticism and wit.

In the pantheon that Norse mythology shares with German mythology, three masculine gods stand out. Odin is the father and king of the gods and ruler of Valhalla, the hall of reward for dead warriors. Thor is the god of war and thunder. Frey is a god of fertility, ruling over growing plants, the sun, and the rain. The principal feminine deity is Freya, Frey's sister, who has affinities with the older European Goddess worship, and is absent during winter. She mates somewhat indiscriminately with other deities in the pantheon, and is also associated along with Odin in governing the fate of the dead; Snorri says that when she rides with Odin in battle, she divides them half and half with him. Other deities include Balder, a handsome son of Odin, associated with mistletoe and the dying-rising vegetation cycle; and Loki, the trickster or scourge of the gods, the source of treachery.

Celtic Religion

Early descriptions of religion in France and Britain come from outsiders, so the student of its ancient Celtic peoples has to probe behind the outsiders' evaluations to form a picture of them. The Roman ruler Julius Caesar (r. 59 BCE as consul–44 BCE as dictator) wrote about his campaigns in Gaul (France) and Britain, describing Celtic priests, the Druids, as an élite group who kept their teachings and training to themselves and resisted recording them in writing. Christian writers later disapprovingly described the indigenous peoples as pagans.

The Celts may have stored ritual objects in huts, but seem to have conducted their services in the open air. The locations deemed appropriate for their cult were features of the natural world believed to be connected with their gods: hills, groves of trees, caves, islands, and sources of water such as springs and wells. The spirits of the dead proceeded to the spirit realm through such locations. Humans might communicate with the spirit world by attendance at such places, particularly on the last night of October, the festival Samuin or Samhain, which ended the summer half of the year that began at Beltane, the first of May. May Day and Hallowe'en festivities are folkloric survivals of the Celtic calendar.

The Druid priests conducted sacrifices of animals and also of humans, usually criminals. Since the ancient Romans no longer practised human sacrifice, their opposition to it was the pretext for a campaign to wipe out the Druid priests; the historian Tacitus (55?–117?) gives a vivid description of a raid on a Druid grove in northern Wales in 62, complete with priests, pools of blood, and women robed in black. Celtic ritual survived after Roman times; according to an eleventh-century source, a newly enthroned king in northern Ireland had to mate ritually with a white mare embodying the fertility goddess, following which the animal was slaughtered and cooked and the new king bathed in the broth, lapped up some of it as an animal would, and partook of the meat.

The deities, whose names vary evidently with tribal identity, were sometimes symbolized as severed heads without bodies. The head symbolically was the locus of the soul and of wisdom. It could speak independently, and offer desirable things such as music and hospitality and especially fertility. The role of heads and masks in folk tradition is strong. Deity was also represented in the form of animals, as the gods could change their forms or shapes and appear as stags, horses, dogs, or birds. In Irish legends, characters have animal or bird ancestors or have animal horns or features. The natural world and the supernatural world converge, each serving as the threshold of the other.

The Witchcraft Revival

We remarked in the chapter on Christianity that in the late Middle Ages in northern Europe, the Church opposed witchcraft practices as pagan. The Church campaigned extensively to suppress witchcraft, and accusations of witchcraft were frequent well through the eighteenth century. By the early twentieth century, in industrialized countries witchcraft was a matter largely of historical and literary curiosity, while the curiosity about surviving witchcraft practices in African society was anthropological.

The nineteenth century produced archaeological and historical discoveries supplying a cultural context for the Bible, but also many teachings for which privileged information, spiritual communication, or secret transmission were claimed but not confimed by historians. These made much of Egypt and India, but surprisingly little of pagan Europe. Until well into the twentieth century, we find little documentation of any attempt to claim northern European paganism as a participant tradition. The German nationalist mystique of the Hitler era was interested in the heroic side of Germanic mythology and in the operas of Richard Wagner (1813–83) that dramatized it, but not in Anglo-Saxon or Celtic witchcraft. The British witchcraft movement comes into view only around the time of the Second World War. As with other renewal movements, its adherents claim that it was passed along through the centuries in unbroken transmission. The *Oxford English Dictionary* lists an Old English etymology for the word 'witch', but gives no indication that anyone before the twentieth century ever used 'Wicca' as the name for a continuing tradition.

The movement began in 1939 on the south coast of England, taking medieval witchcraft as described historically in the writings of Margaret A. Murray (1863–1963) and refashioning it for contemporary practice. After the Second World War, a retired civil servant, Gerald B. Gardner (1884–1964), led the movement, and his writings became standard. Another figure linked with the British witchcraft revival was Aleister Crowley (1875–1947). Some women were involved too, but both Gardner and Crowley were males. Women's interest increased after 1948, when Robert Graves (1895–1985) published *The White Goddess*, a work on myth that posited a mother goddess in European prehistory. In 1953, Doreen Valiente was initiated into the movement and wrote *The Book of Shadows*, the nearest thing to a liturgical handbook for witchcraft.

From the 1960s the influence of the movement spread and diversified in North America as well as in Britain, and increasing numbers of publications appeared. Soon anyone who wished to organize a coven (an assembly of witches) could do so, and only a fraction of the witchcraft circles could trace a clear lineage from Gardner. Soon, too, people outside the movement were becoming aware of the name Wicca as a designation of the movement. It is difficult to estimate its current size, but based on publications sales, claims of coven attendance, and other clues, there are likely at least 85,000 adherents in North America, and perhaps four times as many, or a third of a million. The nearest aspirant to a pan-Craft organization is the Covenant of the Goddess, organized in California in 1975 along local-autonomy lines patterned after the Congregationalist government of the United Church of Christ, but it enlists at most only one coven out of every twenty in the United States.

Along with many other new religious movements, members of the Covenant of the Goddess took part in the 1993 centennial World's Parliament of Religions in Chicago. In an age of interfaith acceptance, Wiccan priestesses sought recognition of their role as institutional chaplains, in hospitals, prisons, universities, and military units. As they could not point to formal documentation of clerical training, some Wiccan priestesses turned to Unitarian theological seminaries to obtain credentials in religion. The term 'witch' began to be used within the Craft as the designation of a clergy leader of a group, as distinct from lay adherents.

Open-air sites have been acquired or used for the re-enactment of ancient rituals. These can involve gathering around a circle in which a star or other design has been inscribed and invoking spiritual power, sometimes as a 'cone' of power. Kindling a small fire on the ground and leaping over it is another witchcraft practice. Publications about British witchcraft make something of ritual nudity, but the wearing of robes is widespread. The principal urban activity of the Craft is in temples, churchlike buildings with worship at stated times. The officiating witch performs ceremonies at an altar, some of them symbolically sacrificial in parallel to or parody of the Christian Eucharist. Some covens declare their services open to all, but others still expect that an individual will be introduced by a trusted friend to a ritual announced only by word of mouth.

Among recent spokespersons for witchcraft in North America is Margot Adler (b. 1946), who traces her involvement to an experience when as a broadcast journalist she was listening to a tape sent by a witchcraft circle in Wales. Despite the scepticism of her secular childhood upbringing, she says, she had a feeling of power. Her investigation of others' involvement in the Craft indicates that the visionary or aesthetic side is important, as are the mysteries of birth and growth, a concern for the natural environment, and particularly a sense of feminist empowerment. Feminism, along with an overt sexuality, is central also in the reflections of Miriam Simos (b. 1951), who uses the name Starhawk. Starhawk sees the religion of the Goddess as the pulsating rhythm of life, and sees human sexuality as a reflection of the fundamentally sexual nature of the earth itself. At a lake high in the Sierra Nevada mountains of California, she writes,

> Up here, it seems clear that earth is truly Her flesh and was formed by a sexual process: Her shakes and shudders and moans of pleasure, the orgasmic release of molten rock spewing forth in fiery eruptions, the slow caress of glaciers, like white hands gently smoothing all that has been left jagged (Starhawk 1982:136).

Neopagan witchcraft is, it seems, a mixture of quest and rejection. It entails a quest for the tangible and physical in experience, a return to primal nature. However, it also entails an angry repudiation, a repudiation of classical Christianity or Judaism. We may look on the growth of the Bilalian or Black Muslim movement as fuelled in part by rejection of Christendom for its record of slavery. Similarly, the appeal of Wicca today is in very significant part a women's critique of the Western monotheistic traditions for their patriarchal record.

New Age Spirituality

The expression 'New Age' has varied connotations. There are biblical notions of eschatological renewal that hope for divine intervention to restructure society, to reward the righteous, and in some scenarios also to bash the wicked with long-overdue punishment. The nineteenth century saw a number of eschatological and millenarian movements, some seeking fulfilment of a literal reading of the biblical books *Daniel* and *Revelation*. On the whole, we should observe, these expectations were for a reconstitution of society.

The 'consciousness revolution' of the 1960s ushered in an expectation of a different sort of novelty. In a mutational frenzy of symbol and metaphor, individuals claimed that they had found keys to an expanded personal or individual religious experience. Popular songs proclaimed the dawning of the Age of Aquarius. To some this meant the drug culture or the culture of rock music, or some combination thereof as occurred on a summer weekend in 1969 when about 300,000 to 500,000 congregated in a farmer's fields in the Catskill Mountains at Woodstock, New York, north of Manhattan. To others, however, the new spirit was hardly superficial, but rather a serious exploration of the meditational resources and therapeutic disciplines of the spiritual traditions of the East.

The term 'New Age' gained popular currency after the 1987 airing of a television miniseries based on the autobiographical *Out on a Limb* (1983) by the actress Shirley MacLaine (b. 1934). It serves as a shorthand term for a cluster of emphases illustrated in her book: a quest for spiritual insight to be experienced individually, an expectation of personal transformation, an optimistic expectation of success, an emphasis on physical healing and psychological peace through discipline and self-help, and a reliance on astrology and psychic powers.

Characteristically, New Age activity seeks transformation on an individual basis. Its proponents give testimonial accounts of how they have reoriented their own lives. The movement's stability and visibility are a publishing phenomenon, as a steady stream of books appears and New Age bookstores (the principal ongoing gathering places of the movement) build up steady clienteles. It is also a seminar or workshop phenomenon, as resident or visiting speakers promote particular insights, disciplines, regimes, and cures. Part of the picture is the promotion of holistic medicine and vegetarian or health-food diets, and the use of soothing music or recordings of the ocean surf for relaxation. Disavowed by some in the movement are television's entrepreneurial phone-in late-night psychics, but the commercial viability of such broadcasting is evidence of a strong public market. If the New Age movement is a worshipping or celebrating community to any great extent, it is not as a permanent or boundaried group but as a sequence of *ad hoc* events promoted through informal advertising. A group phenomenon occurred on 16 August 1987 as thousands of New Agers experienced a 'harmonic convergence' of forces that were to rescue the earth and society from disaster.

Even this, however, was diffuse, as the 'power centres' where they gathered were scattered around the world.

Scholars look for historical roots of the New Age. They mention Emanuel Swedenborg (1688–1772), a Swedish mystic who wrote about the evolution of the human soul in terms of a mechanistic universe. They mention the American Ralph Waldo Emerson (1803–82) and the ideas of New England Transcendentalism associated with him. They mention the New Thought movement of Christian Science's Emma Curtis Hopkins, and the spiritual-healing churches that grew from it and spread internationally, such as the Unity Church, Homes of Truth, and Divine Science. They mention the Theosophical movement, founded in New York in 1875 by Helena P. Blavatsky (1831–91), which claims to discover the wisdom of the ages in Asian teachings, particularly in Hindu Vedānta. Scholars locate contact with spirits, which New Agers term 'channelling', in the 1882 book *Oahspe*, by John Ballou Newbrough (1828–91). They point to the place given to gems and crystals by the medium and writer Edgar Cayce (b. 1918). Scholars do not claim that any of these earlier developments constitute the New Age, but rather that they fertilized the spiritual soil of the English-speaking world so that from the 1970s onward the New Age fascination with the exotic, the occult, the experiential, the curative, and the futuristic could take root and spread rapidly.

Wicca, the witchcraft tradition discussed already, responds to some of the same concerns as New Age spirituality, but differs sharply on others. The New Age declines to speak of magic or witchcraft; in New Age bookstores, magic is shelved with 'spiritual discipline' and witchcraft often with 'women's studies'. New Agers treat all religious traditions as teaching an essential fundamental truth, while Wiccans reject traditional Judaism and Christianity. New Agers generally share South Asian religions' views of spiritual achievement as a release from the burden of rebirths, whereas Wiccans think of rebirth as a positive reward for their spirituality. New Agers idealize the future, while Wiccans idealize the pagan world of the past. Finally, the Wiccan neopagans regard their teaching as something that should be offered free of charge, and scorn what they consider as the crass entrepreneurship of New Age writers, teachers, and psychics.

Nonetheless New Age religion offers something in common with the witchcraft tradition: a feminist spirituality. It encourages women to find power in religious structures not currently dominated by males. In meditation, in astrology, in diet and self-help therapy, it allows women their own initiative, and many have responded. For a true feminist agenda, however, one problem remains: if New Age spirituality is individualistic, how can dedication to it resolve in any practical way the problem of male patriarchy entrenched in society's group structures? Only time will tell, and it may be some time until an ideal age of that sort becomes implemented in society.

Further Reading

Bastide, R. 1978. *The African Religions of Brazil: Toward a Sociology of the Interpenetration of Civilizations*. Baltimore: Johns Hopkins University Press.

Černý, J. 1952. *Ancient Egyptian Religion*. London: Hutchinson.

Ellis Davidson, H.R. 1964. *Gods and Myths of Northern Europe*. Harmondsworth: Penguin.

Farb, P. 1968. *Man's Rise to Civilization as Shown by the Indians of North America from Primeval Times to the Coming of the Industrial State*. New York: Dutton.

Frankfort, H., et al. 1946. *The Intellectual Adventure of Ancient Man: An Essay on Speculative Thought in the Ancient Near East*. Chicago: University of Chicago Press. (Partially reprinted as *Before Philosophy*.)

Gimbutas, M. 1991. *The Civilization of the Goddess*. San Francisco: Harper SanFrancisco.

Hooke, S.H. 1953. *Babylonian and Assyrian Religion*. London: Hutchinson.

Jonas, H. 1958. *The Gnostic Religion: The Message of the Alien God and the Beginnings of Christianity*. New York: Beacon.

Klimkeit, H.J. 1993. *Gnosis on the Silk Road: Gnostic Texts from Central Asia*. San Francisco: HarperSanFrancisco.

Kramer, S.N., ed. 1961. *Mythologies of the Ancient World*. Garden City, NY: Doubleday.

Krickerberg, W., et al. 1968. *Pre-Columbian American Religions*. London: Weidenfeld and Nicolson.

Lawson, E.T. 1984. *Religions of Africa: Traditions in Transformation*. San Francisco: Harper & Row.

Lieu, S.N.C. 1985. *Manichaeism in the Later Roman Empire and Medieval China: A Historical Survey*. Manchester: Manchester University Press.

MacCulloch, J.A. 1948. *The Celtic and Scandinavian Religions*. London: Hutchinson.

Maringer, J. 1960. *The Gods of Prehistoric Man*. London: Weidenfeld and Nicolson.

Martin, L.H. 1987. *Hellenistic Religions: An Introduction*. New York: Oxford University Press.

Mbiti, J.S. 1975. *Introduction to African Religion*. London: Heinemann.

Métraux, A. 1959. *Voodoo in Haiti*. London: A. Deutsch.

Nilsson, M.P. 1959. *A History of Greek Religion*. Oxford: Clarendon Press.

Pritchard, J.B., ed. 1950. *Ancient Near Eastern Texts Relating to the Old Testament.* Princeton: Princeton University Press.

Ray, B.C. 1976. *African Religions: Symbol, Ritual, and Community.* Englewood Cliffs: Prentice-Hall.

Rose, H.J. 1946. *Ancient Greek Religion.* London: Hutchinson.

______. 1948. *Ancient Roman Religion.* London: Hutchinson.

Rudolph, K. 1983. *Gnosis: The Nature and History of Gnosticism.* San Francisco: Harper & Row.

Seznec, J. 1953. *The Survival of the Pagan Gods: The Mythological Tradition and Its Place in Renaissance Humanism.* New York: Pantheon.

Turville-Petre, E.O.G. 1964. *Myth and Religion of the North: The Religions of Ancient Scandinavia.* London: Weidenfeld and Nicolson.

REFERENCES

Browne, E.G., ed. 1891. *A Traveller's Narrative Written to Illustrate the Episode of the Bab,* 2 vols. Cambridge: Cambridge University Press.

Coe, M.D. 1962. *Mexico.* London: Thames & Hudson; New York: Frederick A. Praeger.

Speiser, E., trans. 1950. 'Akkadian Myths and Epics'. In *Ancient Near Eastern Texts Relating to the Old Testament*, edited by J.B. Pritchard, 60–119. Princeton: Princeton University Press.

Starhawk. 1982. *Dreaming the Dark.* Boston: Beacon Press.

אנכי יי
לא יהיה
לא תשא
זכור את
כבד את
לא תרצח
לא תנאף
לא תגנב
לא תענה
לא תחמד
שויתי יי לנגדי תמיד

Chapter Six

Traditions in Contact

Willard G. Oxtoby

Suppose someone asks: 'The religions are all pretty much the same, aren't they?' The question appears simple enough at first. It looks like an effort to sum up the description of diverse religions, treating as essential certain points in which they resemble one another, while dismissing differences in detail as secondary.

To answer responsibly, one might start by unpacking the question itself. The questioner might be asserting that the religions accomplish some common result in their practice or share some essential core in their teachings. We take up the descriptive problem of what a central core might consist of, in concluding the treatment of the Eastern group of religions in another volume. In the paragraphs that follow here, we shall read the question as an evaluation of religious diversity. Let us presume that our questioner holds the religions to be equally valuable, to deserve equal acceptance or equal status. Indeed, evaluation floods in when one compares religions, especially when people include others' alongside their own in the comparison.

Who Is God?

The diversity of religion is nowhere more evident than in the diversity of representations of supernatural power. Localized in tangible objects, or claimed to be beyond all forms whatever, the deities and spirits of the world's religions defy simple classification and description. One can marvel not only at the divine itself but at the bewildering array of its manifestations. Still, some groupings emerge when one tries to make sense of diversity by sorting its content into classifications.

Monotheism

The terms 'monotheism' (from Greek for worship of only one god) and 'polytheism' (from Greek for worship of many) appear in European writing about religion in the seventeenth century, a time when the authority structure of traditional Christianity was undergoing challenges both intellectually and institutionally. At the time, the word was sometimes used with an intra-Christian agenda, by Protestants calling Roman Catholic saint-veneration polytheistic, but then as now, the terms took as their model the contrast between Hebraic exclusive devotion to one god and Hellenic devotion to many. Then as now, monotheism implies making a judgement about diversity.

Western civilization owes to the faith of ancient Israel the idea that there is only one god. Well before the seventeenth century and the word 'monotheism', the idea was a distinctive characteristic of the principal trio of religions in this volume: Judaism, Christianity, and Islam. The Sikh tradition, which emerged in a partly Islamic milieu, is monotheistic as well.

The Zoroastrians also think of themselves as monotheists, especially as their tradition was maintained under Islamic rule in Iran and under Christian rule in British India, yet Zoroastrian worship reveres a host of divine entities, some of them corresponding to the gods of the Hindu *Vedas*. Zoroastrian monotheism is a monotheism of inclusion, co-opting these spirits as agents and deputies of the Wise Lord, Ahura Mazda.

Jewish, Christian, and Muslim monotheism, by contrast, is exclusive. It declares that the faithful should worship only the one God, that the worship of any other deity is an abomination to God, and that no other gods even exist. The deity's exclusive status is matched by an exclusivity in the communities of followers, with efforts to delineate clear boundaries between the tradition's adherents and outsiders. Moreover, when coming into contact with Eastern traditions whose communities are less clearly demarcated, Christians and Muslims have tended to encourage the intellectual or institutional attempt to pin down those other traditions as belief systems and boundaried communities, along lines already familiar in the West.

Christians and Muslims have little doubt about where their monotheistic faith came from. They readily acknowledge their indebtedness to the tradition of the Hebrew scriptures. Christian and Muslim roots in the Jewish tradition extend also to a shared view that this one God speaks to human beings from time to time through prophets, that he created the universe, and that he will one day review it in a final judgement. Westerners in modern times have taken this 'Judaeo-Christian' (but also Islamic) heritage as a kind of standard to which all religion should measure up.

A subtler question is where and how the Jewish tradition originally obtained its monotheistic faith. The issues are open to dispute between traditionalists' and historians' interpretations. Some historians have considered the Egyptian pharaoh Akhenaten (r. 1363–1347 BCE) the world's first monotheist and a contributor to Hebrew monotheism. A revolutionary in several ways, this pharaoh suppressed the priesthood and worship of the deity Amun, replacing it with the worship of the old sun god, symbolized by a disk. He may well have had genuine religious motives for so doing, but he must also have wanted to curtail the institutional influence of the Amun priesthood. He eradicated Amun's name from inscriptions, but was apparently not antagonistic towards the traces of worship of other deities. His reforms, which were reversed soon after his death, were probably influential principally in the circles of his up-river court and were unlikely to have percolated to Hebrew crews labouring downstream in the Nile Delta in the following century. Akhenaten's religion, if a thoroughgoing monotheism, is hardly a source for the faith of Moses, if Moses's was a thoroughgoing monotheism. Moreover, argues the American Egyptologist John A. Wilson (1899–1976), any monotheism on the part of Akhenaten can only have been his own personal faith, since to his subjects the pharaoh was also presented as a god.

Many devout Jews and Christians understand biblical monotheism as instituted by divine command or revelation. God addresses Abraham in *Genesis* 17, 'I am God Almighty [in Hebrew, *El Shaddai*]; walk before me, and be blameless.' The first of the Ten Commandments in *Exodus* 20 is that one have no other gods besides Yahweh. And Moses declares to the Israelite people in the well-known *Shema* of *Deuteronomy* 6, 'Hear, O Israel: Yahweh alone is our God.' Conservative tradition through the centuries has taken Hebrew monotheism to have been delivered whole to Moses if not already to Abraham.

Yet these passages, along with many other details in the experience of the Hebrew kingdoms from the tenth to the sixth centuries BCE, do not explicitly say that Yahweh is the only god who exists. What they do say is that Yahweh is the only god the Hebrews ought to worship. During much of the ancient Israelite experience, Yahweh underwent promotion from status as a clan or ancestral protector spirit to that of a national god, but other nations had other gods. Scholars sometimes use the terms 'henotheism' to describe this form of religion, the worship of only one god without the denial of the existence of others.

There is ample evidence for this picture in the period of the Hebrew kingdoms. Solomon (r. c. 973–922 BCE) built the first Yahweh temple, but in marriage alliances with foreign princesses he also accommodated their identities by setting up sundry altars around Jerusalem to their deities. The later editor of *1 Kings* condemns this, even making it the grounds for divine intervention to divide Solomon's kingdom, but by the standards of the tenth century BCE Solomon's behaviour was politically correct. Yahweh was the Hebrews' god, but at that time other deities were appropriate for other peoples.

A century later, the northern Israelite king Ahab (r. 875–853 BCE) married a Phoenician princess and sponsored the worship of her deity, the Canaanite god

Ba'al. The Hebrew prophet Elijah led the opposition to this foreign influence in Yahweh's territory. Matters come to a climax in his encounter with the prophets of Ba'al, narrated in *1 Kings* 18. With the land suffering a drought, the two sides set up altars for animal sacrifice on Mount Carmel, the ridge overlooking today's Haifa. The dancing rituals of the Ba'al prophets prove ineffective either to ignite the sacrificial fire or bring rain, but Elijah's prayers accomplish both, and Yahweh triumphs. Is Ba'al powerless because he doesn't exist, or merely because Mount Carmel is outside his territory? In the choice between these two interpretations, both plausible, a historian who leans towards tracing gradual development in the scope of Yahweh's power will opt for the second of them.

The prophetical movement, with a rewards-and-punishments theology of national morality, was influential in expanding the scope of power claimed for Yahweh. Prophets looked for signs of the times, for God's purpose in the unfolding of history. Catastrophe came in 722 BCE when the Assyrians conquered and dispersed the ten northern Israelite tribes, and in 586 BCE when the Babylonians conquered the two remaining southern tribes and exiled their leadership. Interpreting the news of the day in terms of the covenant relationship, the prophets read these calamities as divine punishment for the people's defaulting on the moral or ritual obligations of their covenant with God. Significantly, the logic of this interpretation meant that Yahweh was using the Assyrians (and subsequently, the Babylonians) as 'the rod of his anger', the instrument by which he could settle scores with a wayward Israel. Not only did God's power now extend to other nations, but in the course of time a genre of prophetic denunciations of the foreign nations emerges, castigating them for overstepping their punitive mandate and therefore incurring Yahweh's punishment themselves.

The monotheization of Hebrew religion culminates in the sixth century BCE when events could hardly have gone worse for those who put their trust in Yahweh. The Babylonians laid siege to Jerusalem, destroyed the temple, terminated the rule of the dynasty descended from David, and deported a significant leadership element to Mesopotamia, yet the logic of exile meant that Yahweh's worship was no longer tied to city, temple, and dynasty. One could indeed sing the Lord's song in a foreign land. He was lord not only on Zion, the ridge in Jerusalem where the temple stood, but indeed in the whole earth. The anonymous author whose writing has been incorporated into *Isaiah* as chapters 40–55 puts it in words to the exiles that speak to humanity across the ages:

> Did you not know,
> had you not heard?
> Was it not told you from the beginning?...
> He lives above the circle of the earth ...
> Lift up your eyes and look,
> Who made these stars

if not he who drills them like an army,
calling each one by name?...
Did you not kow?
Had you not heard?
Yahweh is an everlasting God,
he created the boundaries of the earth.
(*Isaiah* 40:21–2, 26, 28)

In the sixth century BCE, just when the Hebrews lost their worldly kingdom, their god appears to have consolidated his unchallenged dominion of the universe. Now he is not just the protector of the fortunes of the Israelites but the one sole power over earth. For Judaism, born of Hebrew religion in the changes wrought by exile, God is now the power who in six days fashions the entire world and on the seventh inaugurates the weekly rest of the Sabbath into the cosmic rhythm.

In the Mediterranean classical era that followed, Jewish and Christian devotion to the one God contrasted sharply with Greek and Roman civic and popular worship of many gods. As things developed, however, biblical monotheism proved more closely compatible with some of the currents of Greek and Roman philosophy. Various philosophers, speculating on the nature of the universe, were looking for a unifying principle behind the diversity manifested in local shrines and rituals and their associated narrative myths. Behind or beyond the many, might there not be the One?

Philosophically speaking, as a creator of the cosmos and guarantor of order and morality, the God of the philosophers was not all that different from the cosmic Creator that the Jews (and their offshoot, the Christians) had come to understand Yahweh to be. In late antiquity and well through the Middle Ages, numerous Jewish and Christian religious thinkers found that the philosophical tradition inherited from Greece could be pressed into service to confirm the content of what their ancestors had received by prophecy or revelation. Western philosophy came to refer to belief in a God as 'theism', especially in the context of whether such a belief can be justified by philosophical argumentation. 'Monotheism' is a term more descriptive of a religious exclusion or denial of other gods. For all practical purposes, what philosophers mean by 'theism' is what religious people mean by 'monotheism': belief in a single power as ultimate.

European civilization's voyages of discovery and trade after the 1490s led not only to a new dominance in the world but to a virtual explosion of historical information. By the nineteenth century, 'history' had emerged as much more than a collection of data; it now included the concept of process, change, and development—and, in the views of some, continuous progress. In this context, monotheism, as a form of religion, was viewed as the culmination and pinnacle of human development. What Christians and Jews had long understood as a divine gift or command was now seen by many in the West as a cultural achievement. So, whether on theological or cultural grounds, monotheism enjoyed favoured status as the highest form of religion.

Development is central, for instance, in the thought of the influential German philosopher G.W.F. Hegel (1770–1831), who saw monotheism specifically in its Christian form as the culmination of religion. However, for Christian developmental interpreters of religion, Islam posed a problem. Coming later than Christianity, did it not constitute an evolutionary advance over Christianity? For much of the nineteenth century, European Christians were sufficiently ill-informed about Islam that they could get away with dismissing it as an aberration or devolution from an overall sequential ascent of religions. In the twentieth century, strictly evolutionary theories tended to fade.

If monotheism is the essence of religion, must it necessarily be a late arrival on the historical scene? Most nineteenth-century discussion of religion in tribal societies described the worship of multiple spirits and divine powers, and concluded that human prehistory must have been similar. However, a different theory of religious origins was elaborated by the German Roman Catholic priest Wilhelm Schmidt (1868–1954), a member of the Divine Word missionary society who was particularly interested in anthropological investigation in Australia and the southwestern Pacific. His multivolume study *Der Ursprung der Gottesidee* (The Origin of the Idea of God, 6 vols., 1912–35) maintains that people in various culture regions started with the idea of a single high god or Supreme Being. If Schmidt is right, humans were monotheists long before the author of *Isaiah* 40, but critics of Schmidt's work think that it projects a more cosmic monotheism onto the worldviews of the tribal populations than the data warrant.

Dualism

By 'dualism' religion scholars mean a conception of the universe that postulates two ultimate principles opposed to each other and more or less evenly matched. Personified, these principles are usually a good God and a devil figure.

Serious students of religion may be surprised at how elusive the devil is in doctrinal formulations of Judaism, Islam, and particularly Christianity. He is mentioned in late antiquity, as Satan in the late strata of the Hebrew Bible, as *diabolos* in Greek, and as Iblīs in the *Qur'ān*. He is a visible presence in the narratives and art of the Middle Ages. In folklore and popular piety today, the devil continues to figure significantly, but philosophical theologians who want to affirm God in terms of purpose and power in any modern sense are reluctant to make room for a second locus of ultimate power. The God of the philosophers, who symbolizes order and purpose and sometimes also caring concern and goodness, leaves little conceptual room for a rival symbolization of chaos and evil. Instead, the demonic is viewed by some modern interpreters as a personification of human rather than cosmic wickedness. The demonic, in modern thought, is something for which not God but human beings are to be held accountable.

Surprisingly, too, the devil does not figure significantly in the early layers of biblical narrative. Mention of Satan as an adversary of Yahweh appears to make its appearance only at about the same time as the elevation of Yahweh to cosmic creatorship and rulership. Was this a logical outgrowth of monotheistic ideas internal to the development of Hebrew religion? Did a God now held responsible for everything that happens need an adversary to whom people could assign the blame for what goes wrong? An opponent to God offers a solution to the principal experiential problem that confronts monotheistic faith, namely how it is that an all-good and all-powerful god would allow suffering and evil. If there is an arch-fiend, God's rival, one can clear God of the blame.

It follows from such thinking that the scope of God's power is in principle limited by whatever the demonic adversary can control. In antiquity and the European Middle Ages, the world of Mediterranean and Middle Eastern monotheistic religion provided fertile ground for explorations that were largely narrative in form. Judaism, Christianity, and Islam structured their own thinking about existence in this world in a linear trajectory from creation to a final judgement and transformation. If God is both physical creator and moral sovereign, then the religious narrative must offer answers to two questions regarding the force of evil. First, how was it that the creator's power became compromised in the first place, to permit the introduction of evil? Second, despite the present force of evil, how may we be assured that good will triumph in the end?

An influential narrative response to these questions came in the movement we call Gnosticism. It spread in Jewish and Christian circles, particularly in the first three centuries of the Common Era, in each community suggesting that the primal entrapment of the cosmos in sinful existence was to be overcome by a divine redemption and rescue. Inasmuch as pure spirit was seen to have fallen into material existence, the task of the faithful was to renounce physical satisfactions and achieve an ascetic's release from entrapment in matter.

In the third century, Mani (216–c. 274) organized his own new religion, Manichaeism, on a largely Christian Gnostic base. It spread westward across the Mediterranean, with its narratives of a conflict between good and evil lingering into the Middle Ages in the Balkans and in southern France. It also spread across Central Asia to China, again lasting for centuries before dying out. In its Central Asian spread, it came into Buddhist territory, where both its emphasis on a saving message and its program of asceticism appear to have landed on fertile soil. However, Manichaeism's Mediterranean and Middle Eastern answer to monotheism's problem of suffering and evil was not an answer to a characteristically Buddhist question. Buddhism treats suffering as a fact to be dealt with, not as a reason to question divine power. The Westerner asks why a good God allows suffering, but a Mahāyāna Buddhist credits the celestial powers with goodness for their aid in the path to gain release from it.

Mani lived in Iran, where the Zoroastrian tradition was rooted, and in the time just after Mani, Zoroastrianism became the established religion of Iran's Sasanian dynasty (r. 226–651). The Sasanian Zoroastrians sketched a scenario of the universe from creation to final judgement and renewal drawing on earlier Iranian ideas that may underlie the biblical and Gnostic-Manichaean narrative as well. In one crucial respect, however, Zoroastrian and Manichaean interpretations of the struggle between good and evil differ. For Gnostics and Manichaeans, spirit is good, while material existence is inherently evil. For Zoroastrians, on the other hand, good and evil are moral forces, operating in a material world that is in itself morally neutral. Only at certain times in its history, principally in the Sasanian era, has the Zoroastrian tradition seriously explored the philosophical idea that the ultimate power of Ahura Mazda, the Wise Lord, is in any substantial way compromised by the activity of the evil spirit.

Both the ethical struggle of the Zoroastrians and the spirit-matter opposition of the Gnostics and Manichaeans have been termed dualistic. The word 'dualism' was coined in 1700 by the Englishman Thomas Hyde (1636–1703), writing on Zoroastrianism, to refer to a system of thought in which an evil being is set over against the being who is the source of good. For Hyde at first, then, the spirit-matter contrast that we find in the Gnostic tradition was not a defining characteristic of dualism. However, within a generation, connotations were blurred through the term's use in other contexts. The German philosopher Christian Wolff (1679–1754) applied it to the contrast between mind and matter in the philosophy of René Descartes (1596–1650). In the years since, the term has been applied to such a wide variety of dualities that it has almost lost useful meaning. To call Taoism dualistic, as some have done on account of its opposition between *yin* and *yang*, is hardly instructive, since Taoists, while privileging *yin* in conduct, speak of goodness in the universe as inhering in an ideal dynamic balance of the two. But if by 'dualism' one explicitly means a struggle between good and evil as ultimate powers, then one does have an alternative to monotheism, which may have flourished out of frustration with one of monotheism's main difficulties.

Polytheism

If dualism is a philosophical alternative to monotheism, polytheism is an anthropological one. Schmidt's theories notwithstanding, it would appear that most societies in the world have been polytheistic—that is, that they have supported the worship of a plurality of gods and spirits. The development of exclusive monotheism in the biblical tradition appears as an exception worldwide rather than as the norm.

Before continuing, we should take note of the negative connotations that can adhere to the term 'polytheism' as a description of people's faith and practice. Theologically, many Christians, Jews, and Muslims have condemned polytheism as the elevation of alien deities to the status they reserve for their one God. In practically the same breath, they have also termed it idolatry, regarding the images of these deities to be false. In the West, it may not be easy to set aside these pejorative connotations, but we should attempt a somewhat more detached description.

One may offer various reasons why most human societies have been polytheistic. One explanation is that power is perceived in nature in diverse tangible manifestations, such as the sun, the weather, the seasons, and the sea. Humans, dwarfed by them and dependent on them, feel their own powerlessness by comparison. Most nature deities are conceived of as ambivalent, capable of bestowing benefit on humans, but also of bringing calamity. In the narrative myths of many peoples, they are portrayed anthropomorphically, able like their earthly devotees to undergo mood swings from anger to delight, from passion to caprice. The deities are unchallenged especially in the realms that humans do not inhabit: the heavens above the earth, the sea, and beneath the surface of the earth. They are also credited with power in human existence, for example as bringers of health or disease.

Most polytheistic cultures have sun deities, which is no surprise since the sun appears practically the same worldwide. In the case of other nature deities, the form of nature that is experienced may affect the conception of the deity. For instance, the religion of the Polynesian islands in the Pacific, in the huge triangle from New Zealand to Hawaii to Tahiti, has a repertory of deities in common, with their names in common as well; but only Hawaii knows Pele, the volcano goddess, because (apart from New Zealand) only Hawaii has active volcanoes.

It can be argued that people turn to more than one deity because they have more than one specific need. The deities, after all, are associated with particular aspects of nature and human life. A fisherman strives to be on good terms with the god of the sea, a soldier with the god of war, and so on. Someone eager for success in love seeks the aid of the love goddess, while women bearing and raising children often petition the assistance of a mother goddess. The 'yellow pages' of polytheistic religion are not unlike the lists a modern homeowner maintains of appliance repairers, plumbers, electricians, and other household contractors.

Moreover, petitions for the special benefits expected from different deities are often offered in separate locations. In ancient Greece, for instance, one temple might be dedicated to Athena, another to Zeus, and so forth. The ritual specialists at a particular temple serve its particular deity, and the worshippers often pray to that deity in that place, but to other deities elsewhere. In India, temples are often dedicated to Viṣṇu in one of his manifestations, or to Śiva, but seldom to both simultaneously. Polytheism can be viewed as a kind of sequential monotheism, in which for the moment of devotion and for the purpose at hand, one particular deity is the focus of devotion and may even be praised in flattering hymns as the most important or most powerful.

In addition to the deities with large domains, there are specialized ancestral spirits. In many societies it is an obligation of the living to keep the spirits of the dead happy. Sometimes elaborate goods entombed with the body of the deceased are thought to accomplish this, and later on, fruit and flower offerings are placed at an altar or the grave, especially on anniversary dates of the death. Some cultures believe that all the clan's spirits return to particular places or on particular nights and haunt the living, while other cultures believe that the harassing ghosts are principally the angry or hungry ones for whom proper respect and food offerings have not been given.

Ancestral spirits are not universal in the same sense that nature deities are. The clan spirits' specific identity actually reinforces the distinction between one human group and another. But while one tribe is unlikely to revere another's ancestors, even tribal societies readily recognize the importance of ancestor veneration as a common denominator of their experience. A secular parallel in modern society is an awareness of how people's old family photographs can be treasured possessions, although different families treasure different photographs.

Polytheism as an organizing concept enters not for individual devotional purposes but in order to maintain a sense of order among the various spiritual allegiances of a human social group. Within a particular society or territory, as the various gods' roles were demarcated, the relationship among the deities was modelled on human family and group relationships. Creation narratives treat different gods as parents and offspring. In tribes and ancient city-states, the gods sit in a council not unlike councils familiar on earth. The well-known story of the war between the Greeks and the Trojans treats the conflict as mirroring a squabble among the gods.

People generally worshipped only one deity at a particular time or place, but it would be overstating our case to claim that they always did so. Within a sanctuary to a particular deity one may find side altars to others. There have even been, as in ancient Rome, buildings dedicated to the entire pantheon, that is, to all the gods collectively. Sometimes prayer formulas address more than one deity. One is more likely to encounter such multiple dedication in civic cults, where the ruling establishment is eager to bridge the allegiances of various elements of the population, than in shrines maintained by communities that recruit their membership on a deliberate and voluntary basis. Multiple dedication is also found in royal inscriptions, whose public rhetoric is often inclusivist. The Achaemenian Persian king Artaxerxes II (r. 404–358 BCE) asks in his inscriptions for the protection not just of Ahura Mazda as his predecessors had but of Ahura Mazda, Anahita, and Mithra.

The specific rosters of deities worshipped could develop or change through the contact, conquest, and amalgamation of human social groups. Sometimes victors acquired religious motifs from those they conquered. When the ancient Babylonians conquered the Sumerians, for instance, the Babylonian deity Marduk took over many of the functions of the Sumerian deity Enlil, in effect assuming his role while displacing him. Sometimes victors introduced new religious motifs with their conquest. An example is the spread of the deities of the *Vedas* in India following the Aryan invasion of the subcontinent.

In cases of cultural contact and cross-cultural description, the portfolio nature of polytheism lent itself readily to the functional equation of one people's deity with another's. Familiar to generations whose education included the Greek and Latin classics is the parallel roster of Greek gods and their Roman equivalents: Zeus identified with Jupiter, Hera with Juno, and all the rest. Less familiar but equally significant is the experience of the Greeks as travellers, traders, and eventually conquerors in the eastern Mediterranean. The gods of the Levant, the Syro-Palestinian coast, were likewise equated with those of Olympus: Ba'al, the storm god, with Zeus; Astarte, the goddess of love and fertility, with Aphrodite; the virile and youthful Adonis with Apollo. A continent away and centuries later, Ryōbu Shintō entailed the identification of individual Buddhist deity figures with the local Japanese deities or *kami*.

The biblical tradition overtly and consciously disapproves of equating Yahweh with any rival deity, even at the same time as it engages in borrowing, appropriating for the worship of Yahweh such elements as the Ba'al imagery of *Psalm* 29. Islam took over the shrine of the Ka'bah and its associated pilgrimage practices from pre-Islamic pagan usage. Jews, Christians, and Muslims have consciously striven to hold their traditions aloof from the polytheistic cultures that preceded them: biblical Israel from its Canaanite neighbours, the early Church from rival initiation-based cults in the Roman Empire, and the early Muslim community from the astral and tribal deities of ancient Arabia. The 'pagans', that is, the predecessors whose religion survives in the countryside after the conversion of the towns, are dismissed with a rhetoric of differentiation.

Given a theology of difference, it is understandable that Christians might disapprove of borrowing, whether conscious or unconscious. Historians and anthropologists who observe borrowing or fusion between traditions frequently term it 'syncretism' without intending any negative judgement, but when the term is used by theologians, it drips with opprobrium. In a biblical view, the mixture of religions amounts to the pollution of pristine, normative religion with borrowed contaminants. To the historically minded, it is clear that in times of vitality and confidence, religions borrow without hesitation or qualms whatever they find to be useful and compatible with their central values.

BEARING WITNESS

Missionaries' activity presumes a difference among religions—a difference so consequential that one must not keep silent about it, but spread the word. To missionaries' credit, let it be said that motives for propagating the message are often profoundly altruistic. A missionary may devote long years serving in remote territory, living a frugal life and possibly a dangerous one, for the purpose of helping others—of bringing people a message that will save their souls. Any acquisition of worldly fame or otherworldly merit through such dedicated service is generally secondary.

Missionary Religions

No one can say with any accuracy how many religions there have been in the world. The boundaries distinguishing some religions are fluid or arbitrary at best, and new religions are launched all the time, but a mere three religions account for half the world's population, thanks to their worldwide diffusion. Buddhism, Christianity, and Islam have succeeded as missionary religions.

In their spread far beyond the lands of their origin, these three traditions are readily labelled 'universal' rather than 'ethnic'. That is, they present their message as appropriate to all human experience rather than addressed specifically to a group defined by heredity or descent.

When Buddhism began in an Indian context, a sense of Indian geographical nationhood in contrast to other regions may not have been very firmly established, but Indian society was already stratified into four broad social classes, a result of the conquest of the indigenous Dravidians by Aryan invaders. One may debate whether in India these distinctions continued to have any real ethnic connotation, but in any case Buddhism set them aside as irrelevant to the achievement of liberation.

Christianity began as a sect of Judaism, a religion that emphasized special national destiny, privilege, and responsibility even while in antiquity it engaged in some proselytizing activity. An early decision that steered Christianity on its missionary course was that one did not need to become a Jew first in order to become a Christian. Hand in hand with this went a Christian rhetoric taking over the traditional divine promises to Israel and claiming them in the name of an ethnically inclusive Church as the new Israel. Early Christian preaching promoted a universal spiritual and moral interpretation of the ideas of community and kingship received from Hellenistic Judaism. Paul's repudiation of the difference between Jew and Greek, in *Galatians* 3 and *Romans* 10, reverberates through the centuries in the Christian community's consciousness.

The *Qur'ān* takes clear note of the differences among peoples, addressed by God through different prophets and messengers. The *Qur'ān* describes its own message of divine sovereignty as clear, reasonable, even self-evident. Being explicitly and self-consciously in Arabic, it is addressed to the population of Arabia, and it invites the comparison of its message with other revelations. However, the purpose of the comparison is evidently not so much to show them false as to incorporate them and sum them up. The words that God has been sending to particular communities are seen as parts of an overall word to humanity at large. It is not ethnic identity but devout obedience that will render humans acceptable in the sight of God. In principle, the community inaugurated among the Arabian followers of Muḥammad was capable of expansion beyond Arabia. Within a century, that expansion became a practical reality all the way from Spain to India.

Important to the missionary spread of religions is the idea of free choice between one tradition and another. People virtually everywhere have the choice to be willing followers or rebellious deviants from their own society's prescribed path of conduct, but by no means everywhere have societies offered a choice among religions as alternative paths. Indeed, one might argue that such a choice was a historical novelty about 2,500 years ago.

Recorded history in the Middle East goes back 5,000 years to the introduction of writing, at about 3000 BCE. For the first half of that span, down to the sixth century BCE, we may characterize the religions of the Mesopotamians, the Egyptians, and their neighbours as theocratic. The king was a representative of the gods, the temple bureaucracy was linked with the palace bureaucracy, and one participated in the practices of one's locale. One did not choose one's religion.

Developments in the sixth century BCE began to loosen the ties between government and religion. At least in the non-Iranian territories that they conquered, Cyrus (r. 550–530 BCE) and his successors in the Achaemenian Persian dynasty apparently did not impose Persian religious institutions. Instead, they seem to have posed as the sponsors or fulfillers of local traditions and hopes. 'Church' and 'state' became distinguishable, since the Persian state permitted local variety in worship. The religion of Israel, now operating in Judea under Persian rule, was part of this variety.

Persian rule was followed by Greek and then Roman, and the variety of religious options grew. While the Hellenistic and Roman states had their civic deities and rituals, much of the religious development of the period took place in movements based on voluntary membership. One was not born into such a movement nor adopted into it as an infant, but joined it when one was old enough to know what one was doing. Ritual initiation into whatever privileges or secrets the movement offered would come only after a course of instruction or apprenticeship. Part of the success of such movements in the Roman Empire, scholars have argued, is that membership offered intimate and supportive social relationships to many who might otherwise feel adrift in a world of large scale political and economic forces over which the average individual had little control.

In its first three centuries, Christianity was an affinity-based movement of that sort. So also, in the third century, was Manichaeism. However, as the third century neared its close, the Zoroastrians succeeded in curbing the influence of Manichaeism in Iran and in establishing Zoroastrianism as the official religion of the Sasanian Empire. And as the fourth century opened, Constantine (r. 306–37) gradually conferred imperial favour on Christianity. Christianity, which had been a missionary religion, now also became a state religion. The era of wide-open religious diversity initiated by Cyrus in the sixth century BCE gave way eight centuries later to the entrenchment of Zoroastrianism in the Persian Empire and Christianity in the Roman Empire. Zoroastrianism's hegemony was comparatively short-lived; it gave way to the Islamic conquest of Iran after three centuries.

Islam and Christianity paralleled each other as state religions for a millennium, but also as missionary religions. A comparison of the national spread of each is instructive.

Christianity frequently looked for the conversion of an entire population through the conversion of its ruler. If missions to the Slavs or to the Chinese could result in the ruler's favour to Christianity, an entire nation could be incorporated into the Christian fold. The effort was successful in the Slavic case and among some peoples of northern Europe, but Christianity did not succeed on a national basis later among either the Japanese or the Chinese.

In its earlier centuries, Islam likewise achieved significant national conversions. It offered an improved juridical status, including especially tax exemption, to those who became Muslims. The Mediterranean from Iraq to Gibraltar became Muslim and adopted the Arabic language. Iran and Central Asia became Muslim, but retained Persian as their language. The third great wholesale conversion was of the Turkish people, who continued to speak Turkish. A mark of Islamic identity among both the Persians and the Turks, however, is that they adopted the Arabic script for writing their languages.

Christianity's spread after the 1490s was connected with European military and cultural expansion. Priests accompanied soldiers in Mexico and Peru, and the sponsoring Spanish and Portuguese regimes took it as their responsibility to save the souls of the Native peoples at the same time as they enslaved their bodies. The cultural-religious imperialism of Catholic countries in the sixteenth century was matched by that of Protestants in the nineteenth as England extended its influence in Africa.

Muslim rule in northern India, with the establishment of the Delhi sultanate in the thirteenth century, represents the first time that Islam did not successfully convert whole populations in the lands to which it spread. The Muslims in India were minority rulers of a subcontinent that remained dominantly Hindu. Only in the Indus Valley, Bengal, and the mid-southern interior did Muslims become the majority.

In the later centuries of its expansion, Islam grew not through military conquest but through trade and the missionary activity of its Ṣūfī circles. The devotional life of the Ṣūfīs resonated with the Hindu and Buddhist meditational piety already present in Southeast Asia and provided Islam with an entrée to that region in which it became dominant. Similarly, in Africa south of the Sahara, traders and Ṣūfīs were the principal means for the spread of Islam.

In general, missionary efforts by the major religions have been more successful in recruiting converts from the religions of small-scale tribal societies than they have been in dislodging adherents of the other major religions. This may not have occurred for solely religious reasons; the material culture and technology of the major civilizations has conferred a powerful advantage on those who possessed it. Writing systems and literatures are an important part of that technological advantage, as the major traditions with their scriptural literatures have impressed primarily oral cultures and have been able to shape the target societies' values with the content of the written documents they have introduced.

To Aśoka goes the credit for the early missionary spread of Theravāda Buddhism. We do not know enough about the indigenous traditions in the lands to which Aśoka's missionaries went to form a judgement about why their teaching was effective. In the case of the spread of Buddhism to China, primarily Mahāyāna, we have a clearer idea. It appears that magical and healing techniques were something that interested the Chinese. Taoist fascination with what the Buddhists had to offer provided the Buddhists with their initial foothold in China.

Can we evaluate missionary activity in general? At times, missionaries have been intrusive and invasive, blind or insensitive to the inner dynamics of the target culture. Some have often imposed alien customs and cultural values from their own homeland, values not necessarily integral to the core message of the tradition they were preaching. Some missionaries were pawns of the geopolitical interests of the sending countries, but other missionaries have been ardent advocates of the interests of their host peoples, working for their defence in the face of colonial or entrepreneurial exploitation. Moreover, missionary activity has produced some of the ablest linguistic, ethnographic, and historical study of indigenous traditions, especially since missionaries with theological training often had a scholarly bent. The missionary record was definitely a mixed one.

In the twentieth century, some Christian denominations reassessed and began to curtail their missionary activity. Part of this stems from an increasing respect for other communities and traditions, a theme to which we shall return. But part of the retreat entails the evaluation that no matter how much one might want to make converts, the returns are too small in relation to the resources invested. Generations of European missionary effort in the eastern Mediterranean resulted in hardly any conversions from Islam, but rather principally in recruits from eastern Christian bodies.

After the middle of the twentieth century, much of Africa gained independence from European colonial rule. European Christian missionaries suffered from identification with colonial interests, particularly in West African lands, where the Christianity of the coast was in competition with Islam spread mainly by traders in the interior south of the Sahara. Europeans had a reputation as slave traders in West Africa, while Arab Muslims in the Gulf had that reputation in East Africa. Missionary efforts in Africa were replaced by an emerging generation of indigenous church leadership.

Missionaries were often more welcome for the social contributions they made than for the theology they brought. Some countries that now denied visas to Westerners for evangelistic missionary activity continued to grant them for agricultural development, education, and medical work. The schools and hospitals operated by Christians were an important influence in many parts of Asia, but that influence declined as government-sponsored educational and medical institutions came to be funded on a much larger scale.

Interreligious Competition

Religious literature reflects centuries of competitive zeal. We term 'apologetic' the works that through the centuries have sought to make a positive case for their tradition. Works that seek to score points off the competition by preying on its weaknesses are referred to as polemics. The two genres go hand in hand. Given today's standards of informed and sympathetic description, much premodern literature smacks of deliberate distortion. To understand the spirit of earlier ages, however, we should perhaps approach their output by entertaining the possibility that some of its views were at least sincere, even if grossly misinformed.

We can see earlier prejudices illustrated by looking at the first translation of the *Qur'ān* into English, which came out in 1649. The title page describes the work as 'newly Englished, for the satisfaction of all that desire to look into the Turkish vanities'. Appended to the translation is a fifteen-page discourse by Alexander Ross (1591–1654), 'A needfull Caveat or Admonition, for them who desire to know what use may be made of, or if there be danger in reading the *Alcoran*'. Ross begins:

> Good Reader, the great Arabian Imposter now at last after a thousand years, is by the way of France arrived in England, and his *Alcoran*, or Gallimaufry of Errors (a brat as deformed as the Parent, and as full of heresies as his scald-head was of scurffe) hath learned to speak English. I suppose this piece is exposed by the Translators to the publike view, no otherwise than some

> Monster brought out of Africa, for people to gaze, not to dote upon; and as the sight of a Monster, or misshapen creature should induce the beholder to praise God, who has not made him such; so should the reading of this Alcoran excite us both to blesse Gods goodnesse towards us in this land, who injoy the glorious light of the Gospell, and behold the truth in the beauty of holinesse; as also to admire Gods judgements, who suffers so many Countreyes to be blinded and inslaved with this misshapen issue of Mahomets braine (Ross 1649:406).

Reading the *Qur'ān* might be dangerous to 'such as like reeds are shaken, and like empty clouds carried about with every wind of doctrine', Ross argues, but to 'staid and solid Christians' the reading of Muḥammad's 'heresies' should be no more dangerous than reading in the Bible about ancient Israel's rivals, or reading about early Christian heresies. Besides, he says,

> If there were any lovelinesse, beauty, excellency, or any thing else in the *Alcoran* that might win the mind, and draw the affection after it, I should hold the reading of it dangerous, but whereas it is such a misshapen and deformed piece, I think the reading of it will confirm us in the truth, and cause us love the Scripture so much the more (Ross 1649:407).

Ross's prose speaks for itself, telling us more about the mentality even of liberal minds in seventeenth-century England than about the magnificence of the *Qur'ān*. Whoever is frustrated by the slow pace of progress in interreligious understanding today may draw comfort from observing that standards have indeed changed in the past three-and-a-half centuries.

In late antiquity, early Christian apologists were already wrestling with the faith of others as a theological problem. What did God intend for the Roman pagans if indeed he intended the salvation of all humanity? What was the status, significance, or value of their religion? Particularly problematical was any similarity between pagan religion, taken as false, and Christianity, held to be the truth. One Christian theological view was that the other religions were a preparation for the gospel. Another was that the seeming similarities between other teachings and the Christian message were diabolical imitations of Christianity, traps set by the devil to test the faithful.

By no means was it only the Christians who engaged in polemic. Medieval Jewish literature contains numerous defences of Jewish practice and scriptural interpretation, contrasting them favourably with Christianity. Judaism's problem in handling other religions was not to explain their existence, since Israel had always known non-Israelite neighbours, but to explain their success in competition with the people of God's covenant. Medieval Jewish polemics were composed to bolster the pride of European Jews in the reasonableness of their tradition and strengthen their resolve not to capitulate to the pressure to become Christian. On the Christian side, polemics demonized the Jews, accusing them socially of all sorts of reprehensible behaviour and theologically for a stubborn refusal to go along with Christian claims about the role of Jesus as messiah and saviour.

Another threatened minority was the community that continued as Zoroastrian in Iran after that land's conquest by Islam. From the ninth-century Zoroastrian author Mardan-Farrokh comes a delightful work, *Shikand-Gumānīk-Vichār* (The Decisive Resolution of Doubts). The first half of this is an apologetic presentation of the Zoroastrian teaching as reasonable. Mardan-Farrokh then engages in a critique of competing religions, one after another. Of the Hebrew biblical account of creation, for instance, he asks how creation could consist of days prior to the fourth day, when the sun is created.

Of the Christian account of the virgin birth of Jesus, Mardan-Farrokh has Mary reporting that she has been told by the angel Gabriel, 'You are pregnant by the pure wind [holy spirit].' He complains that there is nobody else present to corroborate Mary's testimony as truthful: 'You should also observe that the origin of their religion has all come forth from this testimony of a woman, which was given by her about her own condition.' Like many polemicists, Mardan-Farrokh has read his own tradition liberally and symbolically, but has tried to nail the opposition on a strict literal reading of its statements.

The history of religion is replete with such examples of disputation and competitiveness. Often people criticize the competition for the failures in its achievement or the flaws of its logic, while overlooking the shortcomings of one's own tradition. If we are to compare and evaluate religions, a cardinal rule is to compare like with like: achievements with achievements, ideals with ideals. Fairness demands it.

DIALOGUE IN A PLURALISTIC AGE

We use the term 'pluralism' readily today to denote a combination of two things: the fact of diversity, and the evaluation of that diversity as desirable. Today's pluralism, which has come into clear view since the middle of the twentieth century, reflects a convergence of developments and trends.

The factual situation has been shaped by increasingly intimate intercultural contact. Within the lifetimes of people still alive today, transportation and communication have been intensified and transformed almost beyond recognition. As late as 1950, very few Europeans or North Americans had been to East Asia, and if one did have the opportunity, it might be only once in a lifetime and the sea voyage would require weeks. Today, tens of thousands of passengers cross the Pacific or the entire Asian land mass by jet aircraft every day, in a day. And without travelling one can be in touch by electronic communication instantly.

Besides travel, migration has increased significantly. Since the end of the Second World War, the demographic profile of European and North American cities has been visibly transformed by the arrival of South Asian and East Asian populations, who have brought their Muslim, Hindu, Buddhist, and other faiths with them. As neighbours, they now contribute a rich repertory of cultural and religious traditions to the societies in which they have settled. Apprehensive at first, the host societies have progressed a few steps towards being better informed about and appreciative of the new neighbours' heritages.

Change in the evaluation of diversity is reflected in many details of contemporary life, large and small. Sometimes institutions remain, but new rationales are given for them. For instance, Sunday, the Christian day of religious observance, remains the day of reduced business activity in a now more secular context. But over the past two generations, the main arguments for preserving Sunday store closing through legislation have shifted from religious reasons to family and recreational ones.

We should distinguish pluralism from the secularism just mentioned. Secularism is the exclusion in principle of all religious groups, institutions, and identities from public support or from a role in public decision making. Pluralism, on the other hand, is according equal support, acceptance, or decision-making roles to more than one religious group. Whereas recreational arguments for Sunday closing are secularist, arguments for school holidays on the Jewish New Year and on Passover, or on the Muslim festival ending the Ramaḍān fast, are pluralist in character. Up to a point, secularism and pluralism go hand in hand because in the West, both propose to place limits on Christianity as society's standard, but secularism and pluralism differ over what they would propose to replace it with.

Pluralism places a parallel and a positive value on the faith and practice of different communities. It often does so on the assumption that religion itself, religion in general—whatever that religion—is beneficial to society. It can also presume that the act of accepting one's neighbour's religion—whatever that religion—is an act beneficial to society. Essentially, pluralism downplays the differences engendered by particular religions' distinct and specific commitments, concentrating on shared values. In its scale of priorities, it subordinates religions' differences to the value of harmony in the total society.

Dialogue

The word 'dialogue' is from the Greek, meaning to argue, reason, or contend. Presumably in order to establish credentials as firm maintainers of their own tradition, some Christian writers on interreligious dialogue have started by citing the Bible as a precedent for dialogue. They point to Paul in Ephesus in *Acts* 19:8–9 'arguing and pleading about the kingdom of God'. On a daily basis, Paul is putting the Christian case to a Jewish audience in the local synagogue and to another audience in the Greek philosophical school of Tyrannus. Paul is a missionary, and enjoys considerable success in Asia Minor among both Jews and non-Jews. But if that is the defining context for the word 'dialogue', we are talking about missionary apologetic. History is replete with examples of missionary argumentation. In the modern era, however, dialogue has come to mean something different: an openness to the opposite party's point of view.

Dialogue is also a literary form. Literary dialogues are presented as reports of exchanges of argument. A few may reflect actual conversations, but most are imaginative compositions, designed to advance the author's point of view. In effect, literary dialogues are position papers, not tape-recorded transcripts. A master of the dialogue form was the Greek philosopher Plato (427?–347 BCE), who set out his own views and those of his mentor, Socrates, in dialogue form. The questioners and objectors are like 'straight men' in modern comedy: whether profound or naïve, they provide a demonstration that not their own but Plato's and Socrates's ideas possess an invincible logic.

Likewise, the Hindu *Upaniṣad*s are in dialogue form. Their outcome is not open-ended, however; they are composed to advance an argument. The early Christian writer Justin Martyr (c. 100–165) in his dialogues with the Jew Trypho, the Buddhist Nāgasena who answers the questions of the Greco-Indian king Milinda (Menander), and the Khazar king in the *Kuzari* of Yehuda Ha-Levi (1075–1141)—all these likewise have questioners whose questions are like puppets manipulated by the logic and strategy of the author's prior commitment to a position.

Closer to our own times, the French Enlightenment philosopher Nicolas Malebranche (1638–1715) wrote a dialogue, *Entretien d'un philosophe chrétien et un philosophe chinois* (Dialogue of a Christian and a Chinese Philosopher), in which a Christian debates with a Confucian. The Christian wins the debate, principally because what Malebranche has him present as Christianity is what matches Malebranche's rationalist preferences. Malebranche shows the Confucian as sometimes faintly, sometimes clearly reflecting Christian ideas. 'I see', he has the Christian say, 'your idea of *li* [cosmic principle] comes close to our idea of God'.

A true openness to alternative points of view is a rare thing in premodern literature from any of the traditions, but we do find instances of it. Highly significant as an example is the awareness of diversity and the response to it that we find in the Mughal Indian emperor Akbar (r. 1556–1605). As a Muslim ruler of a dominantly Hindu population, Akbar could have taken a tolerant stance towards Hindu spirituality on purely pragmatic public-relations grounds. Akbar went far beyond that. He was a genuine seeker of religious insight, and summoned to his court a series of representatives and spokespersons of the various religious communities within his domain. Pursuing conversations late into the night, Akbar proclaimed his own Dīn-i Ilahī, an eclectic 'Divine Faith'. Much like

Akhenaten's religious reform, it did not spread far beyond his court nor long outlast him. But unlike Akhenaten's alleged monotheism, Akbar's Divine Faith could address a remarkable phenomenon in his society: a widespread perception that despite their communal boundaries, Hindus and Muslims had a devotional spirituality in common.

The more committed conservative Muslims—and often it is the more conservative in any community that appear the more demonstrably committed—disapproved of Akbar and thought he had succumbed to feeble-mindedness in being so open to heretical views. This is nothing new. For traditional religions, disputation is encouraged when one is secure in advance about the outcome. But Akbar's explorations were open-ended. A dialogue that treats participants of both sides as equals is something over which orthodoxy no longer has control. To those committed to a fixed position, such dialogue implies a threat.

The World's Parliament of Religions in Chicago in 1893 accompanied the exposition celebrating the 400th anniversary of the 'discovery' of the New World by Columbus. Conceived by a Presbyterian clergyman, John H. Barrows (1847–1902), the Parliament was an adventure in dialogue. It brought together representatives of many of the world's faiths—Islam, however, was absent—to present their religious goals and understandings. It reflected the religious scene, but was also affected it, by affording Vedānta a platform to present itself as the definitive form of Hinduism, Zen to claim to represent Buddhism, and the Bahā'ī faith to appear as an overarching synthesis of religion. (As a follow-up, the centennial anniversary Parliament in 1993 provided a forum to a bewildering variety of new religious movements, to the consternation of some of the old ones.)

Akbar spoke for himself only, not the Muslim establishment. Barrows and the Parliament represented widespread liberal sentiment, but Barrows did not speak for his own denomination regarding exclusive and final claims to truth. The novelty after the middle of the twentieth century was that conversations between religious communities increasingly took place involving community representatives with the communities' official sponsorship and endorsement.

It is easy enough for an individual to be open to others. It is much harder for a group representing a community to be open because no one individual within the group wants to let the others down. There are also problems if a religious community is not organized with a central authority structure to validate the ideas of a particular spokesperson as those of the community rather than simply his or her own private musings. Interfaith dialogue between communities in the second half of the twentieth century proceeded like the proverbial two porcupines making love—that is, gingerly—to arrive at joint statements on matters of mutual concern.

Some of the strongest interfaith links in North America from mid-century onward were forged along practical lines. In urban areas from Montréal to New York and Washington, and westward to Toronto, Chicago, and the Pacific Coast,

Christians and Jews increasingly knew each other as fellow students, fellow employees, and neighbours. They were often able to work for shared civic goals long before they could arrive at any awareness of how differently they interpreted the Prophets and the Pharisees, heroes or villains in the 'Judaeo-Christian' heritage many rather naïvely claimed as common. Clergy and rabbis' desire to safeguard the status of religious personnel in military, hospital, and educational chaplaincies was also a factor; it might be self-interest, but it was a common interest. Importantly, personal links were being forged, and family and neighbourhood links. One saw one's neighbour from a different community not as a pagan or heretic but as a fellow human being, often one struggling with the same kind of intellectual and social difficulties living an ancient tradition in a modern world that one experienced oneself.

For Christians, interfaith dialogue is not the same as Christian ecumenism, but it springs from parallel roots and follows a similar logic. Protestants from 1910 onward increasingly subordinated their denominational differences to a common cause in the overseas mission field, in university chaplaincies, and in efforts to improve social welfare. By mid-century the World Council of Churches was formed, and in the 1960s the Roman Catholic Church became an important ecumenical participant. The logic that applied to intra-Christian ecumenism was extrapolated to interreligious dialogue particularly through the articulate voices of Christians who lived as minorities in lands like India. A conference of the World Council of Churches involving representatives of other faiths was held for the first time in 1970. Staff positions responsible for dialogue were created in the World Council as well as in national councils and in particular individual denominations.

Participants in dialogue emphasized that it involves setting aside one's claims to exclusivity, in order to understand the other for the other's own sake and on his or her own terms. One avoids the premodern polemical move of distorting the other's view in order to score points. To distort the other's view for the sake of advantage would be to violate one of the Ten Commandments, the commandment not to bear false witness against one's neighbour. One must also be open to the possibility of change in one's own views, revising them in the light of what one learns in an encounter. This is easier said in the abstract than done in practice, for many well-intentioned participants in dialogue try to read their own view into the other's. The influential Roman Catholic theologian Karl Rahner (1904–84) spoke of others as 'anonymous Christians', that is, as being Christian without their knowing it; by this token, could Rahner just as well have been an anonymous Buddhist?

Dialogue has 'understanding' as its goal, but 'understanding' religion is a slippery term in more than one context. The academic student of religion understands religion in general, as well as particular religions, by explaining them, that is, by describing as accurately and perceptively as possible what they require of their adherents and how they have developed to be what they are. For such a person, understanding may be informed by sympathy, but it is different from participation or identification. Similarly, the participant in dialogue understands the dialogue partner by *identifying* the partner's commitments, but that is a different task than *identifying with* those commitments. Particularly in the Jewish-Christian-Muslim dialogue area, there have been calls for complete solidarity on complex and hotly debated issues, characterized by one critic as 'ecumenical blackmail'. Does true understanding of Judaism require, as some have claimed, an uncritical endorsement of Israel's policies towards the Palestinians? If one truly 'understands' Islam, must one agree with Iran's handling of its Bahā'ī minority? Or with the death sentence imposed on the Indo-British novelist Salman Rushdie (b. 1947) for the blasphemous remarks of his fictional characters? No; real understanding is no limp acquiescence but a quest for a patient and appreciative relationship that can persist despite disagreement.

In Search of a Criterion

In recent years, the 1978 tragedy of the Peoples Temple movement has stood as a challenge to any open-minded acceptance of religious diversity. In Jonestown, an agricultural commune that they established in Guyana in 1972, 914 people died in a mass suicide by taking a fruit drink spiked with cyanide. They were Americans, about 70 per cent Black and 30 per cent White, followers of the Reverend Jim Jones (1931–78), who took his own life with them. For the study of religion the task is twofold: to understand how and why the Jonestown community came to act so drastically, and to decide the grounds on which one is to accept or condemn such an action.

Jim Jones was a charismatic leader, a messiah to his followers. He began the Peoples Temple in Indianapolis, Indiana, in the 1950s, and moved with some of his group in the mid-1960s to establish a rural settlement in Redwood Valley, near Ukiah, California. In time they also established an urban following in San Francisco. One of the Peoples Temple objectives was to improve the living standards of the poor who were attracted to the movement, and they attempted to take organized advantage of United States government social programs extended during the presidency of Lyndon Johnson (r. 1963–9).

Jones's eschatological goals, a vision of an overhaul of the existing world order, were compatible with a reformist and utopian strand in Protestant (and also in Marxist) thought, but he also sought from his followers an uncritical dedication to his personal leadership that frightened many. Still, his denomination spoke in his defence when a journalist criticized him as a cult leader. When the political climate in the United States shifted to the right in the early seventies, Jones apparently gave up on the hope of achieving reform in American society and chose withdrawal, taking several hundred of his followers to rural Guyana and setting up the commune there in 1972. The mass suicide followed six years later, after investigations including the visit of an American congressman (whom the Jonestown group killed on the airfield in Guyana) convinced Jones and his followers that the forces they saw as evil were closing in on them and that the only honourable escape was death.

History repeats itself. The call to a group to commit suicide, to preserve its perceived integrity against overwhelming opposition, is part of the rhetoric reported from the Jewish Zealot garrison at Masada surrounded by Roman troops in 73. Suicide and the psychology of martyrdom have been linked at various times by Christian groups, and in other traditions as well. Acceptance of martyrdom is one interpretation of the conduct of the Adventist sectarian Branch Davidians, followers of David Koresh (1959–93), eighty-five of whom perished with him rather than escaping from the flames of their heavily armed religious commune outside Waco, Texas when it was stormed with tanks and tear gas by United States law enforcement forces for firearms violations in 1993. To approve of Masada's defenders while condemning the Branch Davidians at Waco implies distinguishing among suicides by deciding what constitutes a genuine provocation worth resisting to the death.

Jim Jones and David Koresh were both leaders of proselytizing movements, movements that attempted to recruit and retain converts. That in itself is not unusual in missionary religions through the ages; Buddhism, Christianity, and Islam are recognized and established examples. Since the late 1960s, numerous new religious movements, some of Asian origin but others new Western movements, have marketed their wares. If modern pluralistic society proclaims the freedom to preach or follow religion without state intervention, fairness demands that such freedom be extended to all.

But my freedom to practise a religion, or to invite others to follow it, is limited by the freedom of others to know openly what I am offering and to refuse it if they so choose. Religious groups forfeit their right to acceptance in a pluralistic society if they engage in illegal activities (such as narcotics abuse, firearms abuse, or fiscal fraud) or maintain themselves through psychological or physical coercion. Critics of new religious movements that have flourished since the 1960s, terming them 'cults', have often implied that these movements are fraudulent, coercive, or both. People who in this context use the word 'cult', originally meaning worship, are using it disparagingly, implying that the movements' leaders are demanding an excessive personal dedication, total and uncritical, from their following. Critics find it particularly alarming when the recruit is told by the movement to sever all ties with family, although there have been parallels to such demands in the early Christian movement and in the operation of some religious orders.

The new religious movements spurred an anti-'cult' reaction. As numbers of young people left family or friends to live with and serve the Unification

Church ('Moonies') or International Society for Krishna Consciousness (Hare Krishna movement), or pay expensive fees to the Church of Scientology, parents and relatives attempted to retrieve them with a coercion that matched or even outdid the coercion they accused the movements of. A young person kidnapped from the movement by parents might be subjected to intense one-on-one interrogation sessions known as 'deprogramming', justified on the assumption that one could use fire to fight fire, in this case psychological influence to fight psychological influence. In the same years, sociological and psychological researchers investigated the reasons why such movements appealed so strongly to the children of economically privileged families. One answer appeared to be that to young people whose parents gave them practically everything they wanted, the new religions offered precisely what the parents had not given: a strict and demanding discipline, with structured goals to be achieved.

In the last decades of the twentieth century, some of the new religions achieved a degree of institutional maturity and public acceptance. Their function as religions was more likely to be seen as compatible with mainstream denominations. One criterion for acceptance that was conducive to this in some circles was theological: that one's own tradition mandated love and acceptance of one's neighbour, including that neighbour's identity as adherent of a different tradition. A secular criterion for acceptance was the value of harmony and benefit in society. New groups could be hailed as helping their members to cope with their lives, and making them good citizens in a pluralistic society.

Religions are not all the same, but many are humanly acceptable. The test of acceptability is whether they in fact bring benefit to human beings. The result-oriented words of Jesus in the Sermon on the Mount, 'you shall know them by their fruits' (*Matthew* 7:16), are an appropriate test. Various religions have on occasion lived up to their ideals and passed it. Those same religions on other occasions have fallen short of their ideals and have failed. Humankind is the common denominator of the religions, as they all in one way or another address the human predicament. And human benefit is a fair test of the performance of each.

Characteristically, however, religious traditions see their distinguishing and distinct features as eminently valuable. If all religions were of equal worth, why should one adhere to one rather than another? If there is no fundamentally important distinction among religions, why should one sacrifice one's resources or energy to engage in missionary activity? Surely a Christian, for instance, will want to assert how salvation through Jesus Christ is different from a Hindu or Buddhist achievement of liberation. Pluralism, while socially desirable, poses a serious theological challenge. Does it really require one to modify one's ritual or devotional conduct and alter one's doctrinal claims?

I personally am convinced that it does. Modern philosophy of religion and theology has shifted the force of religious statements away from being physical descriptions of the material universe and stenographic reports of past events.

Thinkers in several traditions now present their heritage as a symbolic outlook on the physical world and a metaphorical narrative of the past. What is more, they now contend that such is the way the traditions should have always been viewed, and that literalism through the centuries has been a mistake.

One would be less than honest to claim that pluralism, and the other challenges of the modern world, do not require religious traditions to modify, change, and develop. Our task here is not to state what that modification will be. Religious communities in the third millennium, whose society is bound to be far more interconnected than human societies have been hitherto, will be facing that challenge. They will be doing so with a clearer view of one another's activities, in more open dialogue with one another, than in past ages. The observer of religion will want to be alert to the new forms and formulations that emerge.

REFERENCE

Ross, A. 1649. 'A Needfull Caveat or Admonition'. In *The Alcoran of Mahomet*, 406–20. London.

APPENDIX

ISLAMIC TERMS AND NAMES FROM ARABIC

Arabic is the classical language of the Islamic tradition. It is a Semitic language that is closely related to Hebrew, Aramaic, Akkadian (a language of ancient Mesopotamia), and Ethiopic.

The consonants of Arabic are written, as in other Semitic languages, in a script reading from right to left. Vowels can be left unwritten, since speakers of the language can generally infer the vowel patterns from the context. When written, as in copies of the *Qur'ān*, they are indicated by diacritical marks above and below the consonantal text.

Arabic vowels belong to three classes—*a, i,* and *u*—and can be either short or long:

Short *a* is like the *a* in 'pattern'.
Long *ā* has the same vowel quality but is sustained longer, like the *a* in 'grand'. (In the context of the rear-of-the mouth consonants *ḍ*, *ṣ*, *ṭ*, and *ẓ*, however, and the l in 'Allāh', it is pronounced like the *a* in 'father'.)
Short *i* is like the *i* in 'hit'.
Long *ī* is like the *i* in 'machine'.
Short *u* is like the *u* in 'put'.
Long *ū* is like the *u* in 'true'.

Thus in Arabic the name of the religion, Islām, rhymes with the English words 'this lamb'. (Muslims from lands east of the Arab world will pronounce 'Islam' differently. Speakers of Persian, for instance, will use the vowels in 'yes dawn', and to Urdu speakers from Pakistan and India the name will rhyme with 'this calm'.)

Among the consonants, Arabic *kh* is pronounced like the *ch* in German *ach* or Scottish *loch*. (Indian and Pakistani pronunciation for this sequence, however, is as in the English word 'blockhead'.)

- Arabic *gh* is like *kh* but with vibration of the vocal cords.
- Arabic *th* is as in English 'thin'.
- Arabic *dh* is as in English 'this'.
- Arabic *ḥ* is a deep but frictionless 'h', reminiscent of an espresso machine or of blowing on a pair of eyeglasses to fog them for cleaning.
- The ' as an Arabic consonant is a constriction at the rear of the tongue, roughly resembling the quality of the 'a' vowel that you pronounce when a physician depresses your tongue with a stick and asks you to say 'ah'.
- The ' is also a consonant in Arabic. It is the closure of the breath passage that English speakers produce at the sudden onset of a vowel, as for instance between the two *o*'s in the English expression 'oh-oh'.

Arabic associates lexical meanings with abstract sequences of three consonants, termed roots. In actual use, these are combined with sequence patterns of vowels and affixes that manipulate the meanings. For example, *ḥamd* means 'praise', and the name Muḥammad means 'highly praised'. A *kātib* is a scribe, *kitāb* a book, and *maktabah* a library. The name Islām means 'submission' (i.e., to God), and a Muslim is 'a submitter'. 'Islam' is thus always a noun, never an adjective.

Arabic nouns that are masculine in form take plurals in *-ūn* when they are the subject of action in a sentence, and in *-īn* when their relationship to the preceding noun is expressed in English by the preposition 'of'. Arabic nouns that are feminine in form end in *-ah* when singular and *-āt* when plural.

In Arabic names, *ibn,* meaning 'son of', is abbreviated as 'b'.

Acknowledgements

P. ALEXANDER. Extracts from *Textual Sources for the Study of Judaism*, translated by Philip S. Alexander (Manchester: Manchester University Press, 1984).

R.H. BAINTON. Extract from *Encyclopaedia Britannica*, William Benton, publisher (Chicago: Encyclopaedia Britannica Inc., 1974).

H. BETTENSON. Extracts from *Documents of the Christian Church* by H. Bettenson (London: Oxford University Press, 1977). Reprinted by permission of Oxford University Press.

FIONA BOWIE and OLIVER DAVIES. Extract from *Scivias*, translated by Robert Carver in *Hildegard of Bingen: Mystical Writings*, edited by Fiona Bowie and Oliver Davies (New York: The Crossroad Publishing Co. Inc., 1990).

E. BRADFORD. Extract from *The Great Betrayal: Constantinople 1204* by E. Bradford (London: Hodder & Stoughton, 1967).

R.C. BUSH et al. Adaptation of the map 'Religions of the World' in *The Religious World*, edited by R.C. Bush et al. (New York: Macmillan; London: Collier Macmillan, 1988).

CAMBRIDGE UNIVERSITY PRESS. Extracts from the *New English Bible* © Oxford University Press and Cambridge University Press 1961, 1970.

MICHAEL D. COE. Extracts from *Mexico* by Michael D. Coe (London: Thames & Hudson, 1962). Copyright © 1962, 1977, 1984, 1994 Michael D. Coe. Reprinted by permission of Thames & Hudson Ltd.

DARTON LONGMAN AND TODD LTD and DOUBLEDAY CO. INC. Extracts taken from the *Jerusalem Bible*, published and copyright 1966, 1967, and 1968 by Darton Longman and Todd Ltd and Doubleday & Co. Inc., and used by permission of the publishers.

R. FABER. Extract from *The Vision and the Need: Late Victorian Imperialist Arms* by R. Faber (London: Faber and Faber Ltd, 1966). Reprinted by permission of Faber and Faber Ltd.

I.R. al FĀRŪQĪ and D.E. SOPHER. Adaptation of the map 'Expulsion and Migration of Jews from European Cities and Regions, Eleventh to Fifteenth Centuries CE' in

Historical Atlas of the Religions of the World, edited by I.R. al Fārūqī and D.E. Sopher (New York: Macmillan, 1974). Reprinted by permission.

W.H.C. FREND. Extract from *The Early Church* by W.H.C. Frend (Oxford: Basil Blackwell Ltd, 1965). Reprinted by permission of Blackwell Publishers.

F.C. HAPPOLD. Extract from *Mysticism* by F.C. Happold reprinted by permission of D.C.D. Happold.

JOHN W. HARVEY. Extract from *The Idea of the Holy* by Rudolf Otto, translated by John W. Harvey (London: Oxford University Press, 1923). Reprinted by permission of Oxford University Press.

J. HASTINGS. Extract from 'Demons and Spirits' in *Encyclopaedia of Religion and Ethics*, James Hastings, Editor (New York: Charles Scribner's Sons, 1908–26).

JEWISH PUBLICATION SOCIETY. Extracts from *The Tanakh: The New JPS Translation According to the Traditional Hebrew Text*. Copyright 1985 by the Jewish Publication Society. Used by permission.

MARTIN LUTHER KING, Jr. Extract from *Why We Can't Wait* by Martin Luther King, Jr. Reprinted by arrangement with The Heirs to the Estate of Martin Luther King, Jr, c/o Joan Daves Agency as agent for the proprietor. Copyright 1963, 1964 by Martin Luther King, Jr, copyright renewed 1991, 1992 by Coretta Scott King.

J. McMANNERS. Extract from *The Oxford Illustrated History of Christianity*, edited by J. McManners. Reprinted by permission of Oxford University Press.

C.G. MONTEFIORE AND H. LOEWE. Extracts from *A Rabbinic Anthology*, edited by C.G. Montefiore and H. Loewe (New York: Schocken, 1974).

NATIONAL COUNCIL OF CHURCHES OF CHRIST IN THE UNITED STATES OF AMERICA. Extracts from the *Revised Standard Version Bible*. Scripture quotations are from the Revised Standard Version of the Bible, copyright 1946, 1952, and 1971 by the Division of Christian Education of the National Council of the Churches of Christ in the United States of America. Used by permission.

ELMER O'BRIEN. Extract from *Varieties of Mystic Experience* by Elmer O'Brien (New York: Henry Holt & Co. Inc./The New American Library of World Literature, 1964).

R. OLIVER. Extract from *Sir Harry Johnston and the Scramble for Africa* by R. Oliver (London: Chatto & Windus, 1957). Reprinted by permission of Chatto & Windus Ltd.

A. OUTLER. Extract from *Augustine: Confessions and Enchiridion*, Volume VII, translated by A. Outler (London and Philadelphia: SCM Press and Westminster Press/John Knox Press, 1955).

BETTY RADICE. Extract from *Collected Works of Erasmus*, translated by Betty Radice (Toronto: University of Toronto Press, 1986). Reprinted by permission of the University of Toronto Press.

G.G. SCHOLEM. Extract from *Zohar: The Book of Splendor* by G.G. Scholem (New York: Schocken, 1949).

E. SPEISER. Extracts from *Ancient Near Eastern Texts Relating to the Old Testament*, translated by E. Speiser (Princeton: Princeton University Press, 1950). Reprinted by permission of Princeton University Press.

STARHAWK. Extract from *Dreaming the Dark* by Starhawk (Boston: Beacon Press, 1982). Reprinted by permission of Beacon Press.

J. STEVENSON. Extract from *A New Eusebius*, edited by J. Stevenson (London: Society for Promoting Christian Knowledge, 1957).

FRANCIS G. STOKES. Extract from *Epistolae obscurorum virorum (Letters of Obscure Men)*, translated by Francis G. Stokes (London: Chatto & Windus, 1909). Reprinted by permission of Chatto & Windus Ltd.

H. ST J. THACKERAY. Extracts from *Josephus in Nine Volumes*, reprinted by permission of the publishers and the Loeb Classical Library from *Josephus in Nine Volumes*, translated by H. St J. Thackeray, Cambridge, Mass.: Harvard University Press, 1927.

C. WEISSLER. Extract from *Four Centuries of Jewish Women's Spirituality: A Sourcebook*, translated by C. Weissler, Beacon Press, 1992.

ALFRED NORTH WHITEHEAD. Extract from *Process and Reality* by Alfred North Whitehead (Cambridge: Macmillan Publishing Company, 1929).

JOHN A. WILSON. Extract from 'Egyptian Hymns and Prayers' in *Ancient Near Eastern Texts Relating to the Old Testament*, edited by J.B. Pritchard (Princeton: Princeton University Press, 1950).

Index

Page numbers in **boldface** indicate an illustration.
Page numbers in *italics* indicate a map.

Abadan, Ṣūfis in, 440
'Abbās Effendī, 502
al-'Abbās, 394
'Abbāsid rule, 394–6, 412, 420; and the Ḥanafī school, 413; and the *mawālī*, 398
'Abd al-Malik b. Marwān, 392
'Abd al-Muṭṭalib, 357
'Abd al-Qādir, 469
'Abd al-Raḥmān III, 397
'Abd Allāh b. al-Ḥasan, 395
'Abd Allāh b. Ibāḍ, 413
Abdelkader, 469
'Abduh, Muḥammad, 423, 470–2, 476
abortion, Jewish law on, 74–5
Abraham, 16, 21–6, 33; covenant with, 79; and divine law, 32; and Hebrew monotheism, 533; and Islam, 354–5; and the One God, 369; pilgrimage, 383; prophet of power, 364–5; temptation of, 385
Abraham-Isaac-Jacob lineage, 26
Abū Bakr, 359, 372, 387–8, 391, 431
Abū Dāwūd al-Sijistānī, 408
Abū Ḥanīfah, 412
Abū Lahab, 359
Abū Muslim, 394
Abū Ṭālib, 357, 359
Abū 'Ubaydah b. al-Jarrāḥ, 387
Abū Yūsuf, 396, 412
Achaemenian era, 159, 162, 166–9, 185, 543
acquisition (*kinyan*), 143
Active Intellect, 92
Act of Supremacy (England), 285
Acts of the Apostles (New Testament), 212
Acts of the Religion (*Denkart*), 174
acts of worship (*'ibādāt*), 376–7, 416
'Ād (tribe), 364
Adam: and divine law, 32; and Eve, 20; as living soul, 54; in the *Qur'ān*, 363
adam ha-kadmon (primeval man), 96
Adar Sheni (second Adar), 112
adhān (call to prayer), 378
'adl (God's justice), 419
Adler, Margot, 525
adultery: in Hebrew law, 35; metaphor of, 37–8
Advent, 221
Adventists, 316, 554
al-Afghānī, Jamāl al-Dīn, 470–1
Africa: and colonialism, 546; deities in Brazil, 307, 508; and Islam, 454–5; Jews in, 81–3; Christian missions in, 319–20; traditional religion in, 503–7
African-American community, and Islamic customs, 482
Afrikaner population, South Africa, 331
Afro-Brazilian religion, syncretism, 508
afterlife: ancient Egyptian culture, 497; Arabs before Islam, 356; Inca, 520; and Judaism, 25, 53–5; and Sadducees, 48; Zoroastrian, 183–4
agada (anecdotal narrative), 70, 100
Against Apion (Josephus), 44
Age of Aquarius, 526
aggiornamento (updating), 328
Agha Khan, 402
agiari (fire temple), 180–1, 190; architecture of, 185
agricultural laws, *Zera'im* (Seeds), 104
agricultural settlements, *kibbutzim*, 134
AH (year of the *hijrah*), 359
Ahab (king), 533
Ahad Ha-'am, 135
Aharonim (the later) commentators, 121
Ahaz (king), 208
ahl al-bayt, 411
ahl al-ḥadīth (traditionists), 472
ahl al-kitāb. See People of the Book
Aḥmad, 401
Aḥmad Khān, Sayyid, 464–5, 473
Aḥmad Zayn al-Dīn, Shaykh, 404
Ahriman, 162
Ahura Mazda, 153, 155–6, 159, 162, 175, 493; and Achaemenian era, 168; and the evil spirit, 538

aḥwāl (states), 436
Aiguptioi (Egyptians), 237
'Ā'ishah, 390
Akbar, 460–1, 464, 550–1
Akhenaten, 533, 551
al-Akhṭal, 392
Alaskan Bladder festival, 510
'Alawīs, 404
Albertus Magnus, 271
Albigensians, 254
Alexander II (czar), 137
Alexander III (czar), 137
Alexander VI (pope), 306
Alexander the Great, 163, 166
Alexandria: patriarchs of, 217; synagogues of, 61; theologians of, 233–5
Algazel. *See* al-Ghazālī
Algeria, 469, 478
'Alī b. Abī Ṭālib, 359, 385, 387, 389–91, 395, 399, 418, 431
Aligarh Muslim University, 473
'ālim (learned person), 404
'Alī Muḥammad (the Bāb), 500
aliyah (going up), 118
'Alī Zayn al-'Ābidīn, 394, 432
Allāh (God), 355, 374
allegory, Philo's use of, 50
Almagest (Ptolemy), 424
Almohads, 427, 453–4
almsgiving: *ṣadaqah*, 356, 381–2, 406; zakāt, 376–7, 381–2, 406
Alp Arslan, 457
Alpharabius. *See* al-Fārābī
Also sprach Zarathustra (Thus Zoroaster Spoke) (Nietzsche), 155
al'ulūm al-'aqlīyah (rational sciences), 417
al-'ulūm al-naqlīyah (transmitted sciences), 417
'Am 'Olam (Eternal People), 134
Amazing Grace, 314
St Ambrose, beehive symbol, 263
American University of Beirut, 320–1
Amesha Spentas, 178–9, 182
al-Amīn (Muḥammad), 357
amīr al-mu'minīn (commander of the faithful), 388
Amīr 'Alī, Sayyid, 473
Amish farmers, 289
Amorites. *See* Canaanites
Amos, 37
'Amr b. al-'Āṣ, 391
'Amrah b. Kaysān, 400
Amun, 533
Anabaptists, 282, 288–9
analogy (*qiyās*), 409, 412, 415
Anan ben David, 71
ancestor veneration, 303
ancestral spirits, 540
Ancient Near Eastern cultures, 22, 154; spirit possession, 36
angel (messenger), and end-time, 55–6
angel Gabriel, and the *Qur'ān*, 367
angels, 267–8; *zanj*, 509
Anglicans, 285–7; and ecumenism, 330; high church, 286, 293
Angra Mainyu, 162; evil spirit, 175
animal sacrifice, 24, 385; Druid, 523; Inca, 520; Samaritan, 46, 58; Temple Mount, 23
anjuman (community organization), 190–2
annihilation, spiritual (*fanā'*), 434, 437
Annunciation, 264
anointing, Hebrew inauguration ritual, 56
anonymous Christians, 552
Anquetil du Perron, A.H., 165
Anṣār (helpers), 360
Anselm, 270–1
anti-Semitism: Hellenistic period, 44; modern, 134–5, 137, 339
Antichrist. *See* Satan
antinomian, 99; sects, 403; Ṣūfīs, 443
Antioch, patriarchs of, 217
Antiochene Christology, 234–5, 237; in Syria, 237
Antiochus III the Great, 44
Antiochus IV Epiphanes, 44–5
Antitheses (Marcion), 215
Antony, 218, 237
apartheid (apartness), 331–2
Apion, 44
apocalypticism, 38, 53, 55–7, 57, 95, 316–17, 326
apologetic writings, 546–7
Apostles' Creed, 217, 231, 295
apostleship, of Muḥammad, 377
apostolic succession, 217
al-'Aqabah (stoning of pillar), 385
'aql (human reason), 415
Aquinas, Thomas, 93, 254, 272–3, 328
Arab-Israeli war (1967), 135, 334, 477
arabesques, in Islamic art, 447
Arabia: ancient, 499; Jews and Christians in, 356; nationalism, 477; pre-Islamic history, 355–7; prophets in Islamic tradition, 364; values in, 356; and Wahhabism, 469
Arabic language, 162; in India, 463; and Muslims, 544;

names from, 557–8; and the *Qur'ān*, 370; translations of ancient works, 396; and Turkey, 474
Arabic script: for African languages, 455; for Persian, 162; and spread of Islam, 544
'Arafāt (Makkah), 384
Aramaic language, 38, 69, 72, 110, 162
Arba'a Turim (Four Rows) (Jacob ben Asher), 73
archaeology, and biblical history, 18, 22, 323
architecture: of churches, 227–9; early Christian, 223–4; Islamic, 444–6; medieval Christian, 259–62; Protestant, 295; of synagogues, 61; Zoroastrian, 185
Ardashir, 172
Arda Viraf Namak, 174
Arianism, 233–4
Aristophanes (in *Symposium*), 66
Aristotelianism, 90–3, 271, 424, 428–9
Aristotle, 271, 310, 426
Arius, dispute with Athanasius, 233
ark, in synagogue, 61–2
Ark of the Covenant, 27
Armenians, 237–8, 246
Arminius, Jacobus, 290
Arsaces I, 170
art: and African religion, 504; Byzantine, 240–1; Central Asian Buddhist, 172; decorative in synagogues, 63–4; early Christian, 223–4; in early Protestant churches, 295; Islamic, 446–9; Persian, 240; Zoroastrian, 184–5
Artaxerxes, 172
Artaxerxes II, 168, 540
Aryans, 160–2
asbāb al-nuzūl (occasions of revelation), 405
asceticism, 217–19, 432–3; biblical prophets, 95; and Christian spirituality, 274; Gnostic in Egypt, 432; in Judaism, 99
asha (righteousness), 179, 183
al-Ash'arī, Abū al-Ḥasan, 421–2
Ash'arism, and Sunnī orthodoxy, 421
Ashem Vohu, 179
Ashkenazim, 80–1
'Ashūrā', 399–400
Ash Wednesday, 222
Asia: Catholic missions in, 301–4; Jews in, 81–3; Nestorians in, 235; spread of Islam in, 456–66
Aśoka, and spread of Theravāda Buddhism, 545
assassination, of Yitzhak Rabin, 143
assassinations, by the Mujāhidīn-i Khalq, 480
assimilation: in American culture, 136, 139–40; and Judean Hellenizers, 45–6; versus rejection in missionary activity, 301
associationism (*shittuf*), 79
Assumption, of Mary, 264
Astruc, Jean, 30
asura (demon), 162
Atatürk, Mustafa Kamal, 474
atesh adaran, atesh Behram, atesh dadgah (Zoroastrian fires), 181
Athanasius, 218, 233–4
atheism, of Marx, 336
atonement theory, 271, 287
'Aṭṭār, Farīd al-Dīn, 439
St Augustine, 216, 221, 248–50, 270
authority: of the Bible, 281, 322–5; and Constantinople, 246; Hebrew scripture and Matthew, 207; of the institutional church, 327; in the Muslim community, 386–7, 398
Auto-Emanzipation (Self-Emancipation) (Pinsker), 134
Avempace. *See* Ibn Bājjah
Avennasar. *See* al-Fārābī
Averroës. *See* Ibn Rushd
Avesta, 156, 158–9, 161, 163
Avestan: hymns, 158, 164–5; language of Zoroastrian prayers, 180; prayers in, 179; scriptures, 155–6, 162–6, 173
Avestan script, 163; lack of capitalization, 178
Avicenna. *See* Ibn Sīnā
Awake!, 317
awliyā' (saints), 439, 441
Aws tribe, 360
AY, year of Yazdegerd, 174
Azalīs, 501
al-Azhar University, 401, 471
Aztecs, 304–5, 518–19

Ba'al, 28, 37, 534
Ba'al-zabul (mighty lord), 268
Baal Shem Tov (master of the Good Name), 99–100
Bāb (gateway), 500
Bābīs, 404, 500–1
Babylonian conquest, 28–9, 38–9

Babylonian Jewish community, 40, 69
Babylonian Talmud, 68–9
al-Badawī, Sayyid Aḥmad, shrine of, 471
Baghdad, 82, 395, 397, 404
Bahā'ī faith, 187, 404, 500–3
Bahā'u'llāh. *See* Nūrī, Mīrzā Ḥusayn 'Alī
Bahia, 508
Balder, Scandinavian deity, 522
'Ballad of East and West' (Kipling), 7
Baltimore, Lord George Calvert, 308
ban (*herem*) on polygamy, 84
al-Bannā, Ḥasan, 477
baptism: of adults, 288–9; by Harris in Western Africa, 507; by immersion, 246, 292; Christian, 58, 217, 220–2; for the dead, 319; rite of, 123
Baptists, 292
Baradae. *See* Jacob
barakah (blessing), 440–1
Bar Cochba revolt, 57, 59, 68, 106
Barelwi, Aḥmad, 472
Barlaam the Calabrian, 242
Bar Mitzvah, 13–15, 110–11, 121
Baron's cross (*kwa Baron*), 509
Barrows, John H., 551
Barth, Karl, 337–8, 342
Bartholomew, 238
Basil (bishop of Caesarea), 219
basilica: Christian architecture, 229; synagogue buildings, 61
basṭ (elation), 436
Bat Mitzvah, 13, 121
Battle of Badr, 361, 382
Battle of al-Nahrawān, 391
Battle of Poitiers, 454
Battle of the Trench, 361–2
Bayan (Bābī exposition), 500
Bayazīd Bisṭāmī, 433–4, 441
Bayazid II (Sultan), 95
Bayt al-Ḥikmah (House of Wisdom), 396, 424
BCE (before the Common Era), 9, 17
The Beacon (*al-Manār*), 476
bearing witness, 542–8; *shahādah*, 377
beauty (Tiferet), 97
Bede, 263
Bedouin tribes, 499
Bellarmine, Robert, 300, 310
bēma (rostrum), 62
Benedict, 251, 270
Benedictine monasteries, 251
Bene Israel (Jews in India), 82
Bengal, 460
Benjamin of Nehavand, 82
Ben Yehudah, Eliezer, 134
Ber of Mezeritz, 100
Bergson, Henri, 473
berith. See covenant
Bernard, abbot of Clairvaux, 263, 275
Berthold, 254
Besht. *See* Baal Shem Tov
bet din, 123
Bethlehem, 206
Bet Yosef (House of Joseph) (Karo), 73
Biandrata, Giorgio, 289
Bible: contextualizing, 322–4; *King James* version, 159; language of, 279; *New Revised Standard Version*, 341; rabbinic interpretation, 66; *Revised Standard Version*, 341; translation of, 43. *See also* authority
biblical figures, as Islamic prophets, 363
biblical monotheism, 533
Biddle, John, 290
bigamy, in Israel, 86–7
bilā kayf (without asking how), 421
Bilalian movement, 482, 525
Bina (insight), 101
biological creationism, 321
birth: and Hebrew Bible, 34; and Jewish rituals, 117–18
birth control, Roman Catholic Church, 329, 341
al-Bīrūnī, Abū Rayḥān, 456
bishop (*episkopos*, supervisor), 217
Bisutun inscription, 185
Black community: Baptist, 292; US, 331
Black Death, 269
Black Friars, 254
Black Muslim movement, 482, 525
Blavatsky, Helena P., 527
blessing: of Judaism, 107; *barakah* of Sufism, 440
blood, significance of, 54; of Christ, 220
body and soul, in ancient Hebrew thought, 53
Boethius, 270
Boleyn, Anne, 285
Bombay, 82, 181, 189
Bonaventure, 275
Boniface VIII (pope), 256
Book of Common Prayer (Cranmer), 285
Book of the Covenant (in *Exodus*), 30
Book of Mormon, 318–19

Book of Mysteries (*Sefer ha-Razzim*), 102
Book of the Proof of God (*Kitāb al-Ḥujjah*), 414
book of the Torah (scroll), 70
Book of Beliefs and Opinions (Saadia), 87
The Book of Certitude (Bahā'u'llāh), 502
The Book of Healing (Ibn Sīnā), 426
The Book of Shadows (Valiente), 524
Booth, William, 331
Bora, Katherina von, 282
born again, 325
Borobudur (Indonesia), 465
boundary: *eruv*, 109; *havdalah*, 108
bounds (*ḥudūd*) of God, 418
Branch Davidians, 554
Brazil, African religion in, 507–8
bridal canopy (*huppah*), 143
Bridge of the Separator (Chinvat Bridge), 183
Britain: Franciscans in, 254; and Parsis, 189–91; Protestant denominations in, 290–3, 313–14, 331; Reformation in, 285–7; witchcraft movement, 524; and world Anglicanism, 286
British Apostolic Church, 507
British East India Company, 320
British rule: of India, 464–5; and Islamic law, 472
Bronze Age, covenanting in, 24
brotherhoods: Muslim Brothers, 477; Ṣūfī, 440
Browne, Edward G., 501
Bruno, 253
Bryan, William Jennings, 325
Buber, Martin, 131–2
Bucer, Martin, 287
Buddhism: art, 240; and asceticism, 218; as missionary religion, 542; in Southeast Asia, 465; and suffering, 537–8
al-Bukhārī, Muḥammad b. Ismā'īl, 408
Bundahishn (Original Creation), 173, 175–6
Bunyan, John, 290
Burāq, 449
burial, in modern Judaism, 119; in modern Zoroastrianism, 184
Būyids, 397, 440
Byzantine Empire, 229, 239

Caesar, Julius, 522–3
caesaropapism, 239
Cairo, 397, 404, 471; al-Azhar in, 401, 471
calendar: Christian, 221–3; Mayan, 518; of western Europe, 247; Zoroastrian, 174, 182
California, Franciscans in, 308
caliphate, 388, 396–7
calligraphy: in Islamic art, 447–9; and the *Qur'ān*, 370
Calvin, John, 264, 287, 294
Campbell, Alexander and Thomas, 316
Canaan: migration into, 25–8; sexual rituals, 52
Canaanite religion, 28
candlestick (*menorah*), 62–3
candomblés (Afro-Brazilian), 307, 508
Canisius, Peter, 300
canon: *ḥadīth* collection, 408–9; law, 327; Hebrew scripture, 65; New Testament, 203, 215
Canterbury, **265**
Canterbury Tales (Chaucer), 266
cantors (*hazanin*), 110
capital punishment, 35
Capuchins, 254
cardinals, selection of popes, 255
Carême, 222
Caribbean peoples, and Christianity, 304
Carmelites, 254–5
Carnival, 222
Carthusian order, 253
Cartier, Jacques, 308
catacombs, 224
catechism, 220
Catherine of Aragon, 285
Catherine of Siena, 277
cave paintings, 521
Cayce, Edgar, 527
CE (Common Era), 9, 17
celibacy: modern Roman Catholicism, 329; in religious traditions, 255, 293
Cellarius, Martin, 289
Celtic cross, 230
Celtic religion, 522–3
cenobites, 219
Central Asia: migration of Aryans from, 160; and spread of Islam, 456–7
Central Conference of American Rabbis, 125
Chabad (Ḥ-B-D), 101
chain of initiation (*silsilah*), 440
chain of transmission (*ḥadīth*), 407
Chaldean Christians of Iraq, 246
Champlain, Samuel de, 308
channelling, 527
Channing, William Ellery, 290

chanting: in early Christianity, 242–3; Jewish traditions, 110; Zoroastrian, 180
chapters (*sūrahs*), of the *Qur'ān*, 367
charismatic activity, 315; influence of Jesus, 58
charity, Qur'anic principles, 406
Charlemagne (Charles the Great), 255, 395
Charles I, 306
Charles V, 281
Chartreuse abbey, 253
Chaucer, Geoffrey, 266
Chavín culture, 519
Chavín de Huantár, 519
Chichen Itza, 518
chief (*shaykh* or *sayyid*), 387
Chilam Balam, Books of, 518
Children of Israel (Bene Israel), in India, 82
children's crusade, 257
child sacrifice, 28, 37, 41. *See also* human sacrifice
China: and Christianity, 302–4; and Islam, 458–9; Jews in, 83; spread of Buddhism to, 545
Chinese Rites controversy, 303
Chinvat Bridge (the Bridge of the Separator), 183
Chishti, 463
chosenness, of Judaism, 52
Christ: messiah, 211; and the *Qur'ān*, 370
Christian Century, 316
Christian Church (denomination), 316
Christian Democratic parties, 309
Christian Science, 317–18
Christian Science Journal, 318; *Monitor*, 318; *Sentinel*, 318
Christianity: compared with Islam, 544; early, 216; and the Hebrew scriptures, 215; interfaith dialogue, 552; and Judaism, 52, 57–8, 210; major branches of, 201–2; as missionary religion, 542; monotheism, 532; and Noachic commandments, 79; Paul's letters, 213; People of the Book, 450; and pluralism, 342; polemics, 548; population estimates, 200–2; in Southern Africa, 506; spheres of influence, *284*; as a state religion, 238. *See also* theology
Christians of St John, 216
Christians of St Thomas, 301
Christmas, 199–200, 221–2
Christology, Alexandrian school, 236
St Christopher, 263
christos (anointed), 56
christotokos (bearer of Christ), 235
Church: in Germany, 283–4; and the state, 250
Churches of Christ, 316
Church of Christ, Scientist, 317–18
Church of England. *See* Anglicans
Church of God, 315
Church of the Holy Sepulchre (Jerusalem), 227, **227**, 243 burning of, 256–7
Church of Jesus Christ of Latter-Day Saints, 319
Church of the Nativity, 227
Church of the Nazarene, 315
Church of Scotland, 286, 288
Church of South India, 330
church and state, 200, 250, 255, 289; sixth century BCE, 543
Church of the Twelve Disciples (West Africa), 507
circumcision, 117, **118**; debate in early Christianity, 212–13; and Greek culture, 45; Jewish (*milah*), 122–3
Cistercians of the Strict Observance, 253
The City of God (Augustine), 250
civil-rights movement, 331
civil war, in Java, 466
Civil War, US (1861–5), 331
Clara of Assisi, 254
classical Greek civilization, 167
clay: material for writing, 494; neolithic figurines, 521
Clement VII (pope), 285
clothing: friars' habits, 254; of Jews in prayer, 105–6; Zoroastrian rituals, 182–3
Cluny, Fathers of, 252
Co-operative Commonwealth Federation, 334
Cochin, Jews of, 82
codes, of Jewish law, 72
coinage: Christian symbols on, 226; Umayyad, 448–9
collective unconscious, 339
colonialism: in Africa, 505–7, 546; and East African Islam, 455; in Latin America, 306–7; missionary, 320; and North Africa, 452; and Ṣūfī orders, 444, 469
Columbus, Christopher, 304
commander of the faithful (*amīr al-mu'minīn*), 388
commandments: and conversion, 122; for Jews and

Gentiles, 78; traditional 613, 139
commentary: *midrash* on scripture, 65–6; *pesher,* 47; on the *Qur'an,* 373; on the *Talmud,* 72
Common Era (CE), 169
communalism, of early Christianity, 58; in Mughal India, 550–1
communion, 220, 294; Zoroastrian *jashan* as, 182
Communism, Orthodox Christianity under, 245
Communist Manifesto (Marx and Engels), 335
community, Islamic, 362, 375
Companions of the Prophet, 391, 411, 431–2
concentration-camp survivors, 137
Concerning Married Life (Luther), 282
The Concise Encyclopedia of Living Faiths (Zaehner), 6
The Condition of the Working Class in England (Engels), 335
The Conference of the Birds ('Aṭṭār), 439
confession: Catholic, 269; Protestant creeds, 291, 295; in Protestant worship, 326; and repentance in Judaism, 77–8
Confessions (Augustine), 249
confirmation, Christian, 217
Congregationalism, 290–2, 330
conscientious objectors. *See* pacifism
consciousness revolution (1960s), 526
consensus (*ijmā'*), 409–10
Conservative Judaism, 108, 126–8; American, 127; synagogues, 17
The Consolation of Philosophy (Boethius), 270
Constantine, 225–7, 544
Constantinople, 225, 239; conflict with Persia, 238; patriarchs of, 217; and Rome, 246–7
contemplation, way of, 437
contentment (*riḍā*), 436
convent, for women, 251
conversion: of Augustine, 249; Christian from Hinduism, 301; and evangelical preachers, 326; to Catholicism, 301; to Islam, 354; to Judaism, 41–2, 80, 122–3; Zoroastrian, 192
conversos (New Christians), 94
converts: (*mawālī*), 398; (*muwallad*), 453
cooking *eruv* (*eruv tavshilin*), 109
Cook's Creek Ukrainian Catholic church (Winnipeg), **245**
Copernicus, Nicolaus, 310
Copts of Egypt, 237, 246
Córdoba, 404, 452
Cortés, Hernán, 304–5, 517
Council of Chalcedon, 236, 238–9
Council of Constance, 256
Council of Constantinople, 233
Council of Ephesus, 235–6
Council of Nicaea, 231; second, 265
Council of Trent, 297–9, 328; and Luther, 280
Counter-Reformation, 297
covenant: with Abraham, 23–5, 79, 365; at Mount Sinai, 13; and the exile, 38–41; with God, 60; and Israel, 30, 51; of Madīnah, 360; with Noah, 17, 79; Ten Commandments, 27
Covenant of the Goddess, 524–5
covens, 524–5
Cowdery, Oliver, 318
Cranmer, Thomas, 285
creation: 32, 50; and evolution, 321–2; *fiṭrah*, 354 in *Genesis*, 18–21; of the gods, 540; Inca, 520; Mesopotamian, 495; Native American, 513; in *Yasna*, 169
creeds: Christian, 231–4, 343; Judaic, 51
crescent, symbol of Islam, 457–8
Cromwell, Oliver, 291
cross, as symbol, 229–30, 309
crossing (architectural), 259
Crowley, Aleister, 524
Crown of Thorns, relics, 266
crucifix, 296
crusades, 256–9, 467
cults: in ancient Greece, 498; contemporary, 554; Indo-Iranian deities, 168; Isma'ilism, 401; in Latin America, 307
cultural contact, and polytheism, 541
Cultural Revolution (1966–76), 459
cuneiform script, 162, 494
Curaçao, Jews in, 136
custom (*minhag*), 84
Cyril (d. 444), 234–5
Cyril (826–69), 244
Cyrillic alphabet, 244

Cyrus (Persian king), 39–40, 56, 168–9, 543–4

D source, 31
Da'at (knowledge), 101
Dadistan-e Dinik (Religious Judgements) (Manushchihr), 174
daivas (demons), 162, 168
dakhma (tower of silence), 184
Damascus, 392–3; museum, 63; and Paul, 213; siege of, 257
dance, Mevlevi (Mawlawī), 443
The Dangers of Updating Judaism (Hirsch), 127
Daniel: excerpt, 35; and mystical tradition, 95; and resurrection, 54–5
dār al-ḥarb, 81
dār al-Islām (house of Islam), 449
Dārā Shikōh, 464
al-Darazī, Muḥammad b. Nashtakīn, 402
Darius (king), 168, 185, 188
darkness and light, in *Isaiah*, 19; and Zoroastrianism, 169
Darrow, Clarence, 325
darvīsh (poor), 440
Darwin, Charles, 321–2, 325
dastur (priest), 180
dates: Christmas and Easter, 222–3; of Zoroaster, 159–60, 174
David, 28–9, 33–4, 208
Davidic line, 41, 56
Dāwūd b. Khalaf, 413
Day of Atonement. *See* Yom Kippur
Day of Judgement, 354, 367–8, 371, 375, 416
Day of Resurrection, 403
De Nobili, Robert, 301
deacon, in the early church, 217
dead: exposure of, 184; prehistoric practices, 520–1; Scandinavian practices, 522; soul, 54; spirits of and Native Americans, 513; spirits of in polytheism, 540; washing of, 378
Dead Sea Scrolls, 47
death: and ancient Egyptian culture, 497; of Jesus, 204–5, 207; and Jews, 119; and medieval Christian world, 269; and time, 356; and Zoroastrian ritual, 154, 182
death penalties, in the Bible, 78
Deborah, prophetess, 33–4, 37
debt, and slavery, 35–6
decisions for Christ, 326
The Decisive Resolution of Doubts (*Shikand–Gumānīk-Vichār*) (Mardan-Farrokh), 174, 548
Decius, 225
Deima Church, 507
Deism, 311
deities: Mayan, 518; Olmecs, 517; *orixās*, 508. *See* gods
delegationist sect, 403
Demiurge, 214
demons (*daivas*), 162; possession, 268–9
Denkart (Acts of the Religion), 174
denominations, new American, 315–19; Reformation, 283–93
Derekh Eretz (European life), 129
dervishes, Qalandar, 463
Descartes, René, 538
The Descent of Man (Darwin), 322
desert: fathers, 219; monks and Arabs, 356; as region for contemplation, 217
destiny, of the individual: Arabian, 355; Zoroastrian, 183–4. *See also* afterlife
Deuteronomy, 27, 31; *Sifre*, 66
deva (god), 162
devil, 267–8; and dualism, 536
devotion: in medieval Byzantine theology, 242; of the monasteries, 252; in Mughal India, 464
devotional prayers (*nawāfil*), 381
dhikr (remembrance of God), 442
dhimmīs, 450
Dhū al-Nūn al-Miṣrī, 433
dialogue, 549–53
Dialogue (Catherine of Siena), 277
Dialogue of a Christian and a Chinese Philosopher, 550
Diaspora, 43; Armenian, 238; attitudes in, 50; role of synagogues, 60–1; Zoroastrian, 191–2
Diaz, Bartolomeu, 278
Diego, Juan, 307
dietary laws, and Noah, 365
Digger Indians (of Nevada), 512
Dilthey, Wilhelm, 131
Dīn-i Ilahī (Divine Faith), 464, 550
Diocletian, 225
Dionysius, 274
disciples, of Jesus, 204–5, 212
Disciples of Christ, 316
divination, rituals, 496
divine *gnōsis*: *'irfān*, 438; *ma'rifah*, 433
divine grace, in rabbinic Judaism, 77–8

divine name, 26
divine nature, of Jesus Christ, 236, 248
Divine Religion (Dīn-i Ilahī), 464
divine sayings (*ḥadith qudsī*), 408, 431
Divine Science, 527
Divine Word missionary society, 536
divorce: Islamic, 405, 484; in Judaism, 84–7, 119, 130; Pharisaic tradition, 67
docetism, 216
doctrine: and Christianity, 199; of the end-time, 55–6; of *imāmah* (imamate), 399, 418; of *kasb* and *iktisāb* (good and evil), 422; of occasionalism, 422, 427; of original sin, 213; of resurrection, 53–5; of transubstantiation, 298, 328; of the Trinity, 211, 232, 317; unity of being, 438; of virgin birth, 208; Zurvan (Time), 174
Doctrine and Covenants (Smith), 318
Documentary Hypothesis (Wellhausen), 30–2
dogma, and Mary, 264–5
dome architecture, 446
Dome of the Rock (Jerusalem), 82, 229, 392, **393**, **449**
Dominic, 254
Dominicans, 254, 264
Dönmeh (returners), 99
Dormition, 264
Do's and Don'ts (*Shayast Ne-Shayast*), 174
double-truth theory, 428
Dravidians, of India, 160
dress. *See* clothing
Dreyfus, Alfred, 134
drug or *druj* (Lie), 183
drugs: Native American Church, 514–15; and Ṣūfīs, 443
Druids, 523
drums, Greenland shamans, 510
Druzes, 402
dualism, 417–18, 536–8 of Zoroastrianism, 52, 173, 175
Dura-Europos (Syria), 63, 223–4
Dutch East India Company, and Muslim kingdoms, 466
Duvalier, François (Papa Doc), 509

E (Elohist source), 31
earth mother goddess, 521
East Africa, 320; and Islam, 454–6, 504–5
Easter, 199, 221, 223, 243
Eastern Orthodoxy, 220, 244, 246, 264, 340
Ecclesiastical History (Eusebius), 226
Echmiadzin, 238
Eckhart, Johannes (Meister), 274
ecological concern, 330, 510–11, 516
economics: and Christians, 332–4; and relics, 266
ecstasy, 36; and mysticism, 273–4, 433, 435, 441
ecumenism, 329–31, 552
Eddas, 522
Eddy, Mary Baker, 317
Eden, 20–1, 31, 50
Edessa, 235, 257
education, for Jews, 120–2
educational institutions, and Asian culture, 320
Edward VI, 285
Edwards, Jonathan, 314, 317
effulgence (*shefa*), 97
Egypt, 22; Christian monasticism, 432; Christians and Chalcedon formula, 236; civilization in, 323, 496–7; Copts (*Qubṭ*), 237; and the Exodus, 27; Gnostic asceticism, 432; religion, 496; revivalist movements in, 478
Ehud, 33
élan vital (vital urge), 473
Eleazar ben Yair, 50–1
elements, (bread, wine), 220
Elements (Euclid), 424
Elijah, 36
Elisha, 36
Elizabeth I, 285–6
Elohim, 30; divine name, 26; E, 31
emanationism: of Ibn Sīnā, 426; of Kabbalah, 96
Emerson, Ralph Waldo, 527
Emmanuel, 208
Encomium moriae (The Praise of Folly) (Erasmus), 278
Encyclopedia of Religion (Eliade), 8
endogamy, 41
energia, 239
Engels, Friedrich, 335
Enlightenment, 309–13; Haskalah, 137
En Sof (without end), 96
Enneads (Plotinus), 424
Entretien d'un philosophe chrétien et un philosophe chinois (Dialogue of a Christian and a Chinese Philosopher) (Malebranche), 550

envizib (invisibles), 508
Eostre (pagan goddess), 223
Epiphany (manifestation), 221–2
Episcopalians, 286. *See also* Anglicans
Erasmus, Desiderius, 278–9
Erigena, John Scotus, 270
erotic love, of boys in Sufism, 443
eruvs, 109
ervad priests, 180
eschatology: and goals of Jim Jones, 553; in Jewish literature, 53; Zoroastrian, 154
Eskimo. *See* Inuit
The Essence of Christianity (Feuerbach), 336
Essenes, 47–8, 57–8, 217
eternal lamp (*ner tamid*), 62
Eternal People (*'Am 'Olam*), 134
eternity of Israel (*nezaḥ Yisrael*), 89
ethical monotheism, 79
ethicization of prayer, 104
ethics: rabbinic Judaism, 73; and ritual, 209; of Zoroastrians, 154, 158
Ethiopia: Christian influence in, 237, 506; Easter service, 243; Jews in, 81–2; Rastafarians, 509
Ethiopic language, 237
Eucharist, 199, 220; interpretation of, 282; Protestants, 293–4; Uniate churches, 246
Europe: prehistory, 520–2
Eusebius (bishop of Caesarea), 226
Eutyches, 236
Evangelical Church (Lutheran), 283
Evangelicalism, 324–7
evil, 267–9; force of in religion, 537; and suffering, 312–13; and Zoroastrian tradition, 154. *See also* good and evil
evil conduct (*munkar*), 419
evil spirit (Angra Mainyu), 175
evolution: and creation, 321–2; teaching of, 325
exclusivity, 532, 552
exilarch, 70
exile, 38–40; *galut*, 98; of Khomeini, 479–80
existentialism, 131, 312, 337
Exodus, 25–7; *Mekhilta*, 66
Exodus from Egypt, 208
exorcism, Mesopotamian, 496
exposure, of dead, 184
expulsion: of Jews from Spain, 93–5, *94*; of Muslims from Spain, 453
Ezekiel, 39
Ezra, 41

Fackenheim, Emil, 139
faith: *īmān*, 375, 422; and works, 280
The Faith of Catholic Israel (Schechter), 128
Falasha (Ethiopian) migrants, 81, **83**
falsafah (philosophy), 423
family and Islam, 405–6, 483–5
family purity, in Orthodox Judaism, 76
fanā' (annihilation of the self), 434, 437
faqīh (jurist), 409
faqīr (poor), 440
al-Fārābī, Abū Naṣr, 425–6
farā'iḍ (obligatory duties), 377
Farb, Peter, 512–13
Fard, Wallace D., 482
farohar, 185
Fars (province), 166
Farsi (language), 162
fast: of Ramaḍān, 360, 371, 376, 382–3; Yom Kippur, 360, 382
al-Fātiḥah (opening), 372, 380
Fāṭimah, 385, 399
Fāṭimid caliphate, 397
fatwās (legal opinions), 414
Feast of Weeks, 223
Federal Council of Churches, 330
female infanticide, in Arab society, 483–4
feminism, 340–1, 525, 527; and Marian theology, 265
Ferdinand II (Hapsburg), 300
Ferdinand of Aragon, 93, 453
Ferdowsī, 189, 456
fertility rituals, 37, 503, 522
festivals: Christian, 221–3; Jewish, 41, 63, 71, 111–16; Muslim, 380–5; Samuin (Samhain), 523
Feuerbach, Ludwig, 336
filioque (and from the son), 246
Final Solution (*Entlösung*), 138
fiqh (jurisprudence), 409
fire: at Easter vigil service, 243; Zoroastrian, 162, 180–2
fire of fires (*atesh adaran*), 181
fire temple (*agiari*), 173, 180, 190; architecture of, 185; Zoroastrianism, 179–80
fish, as Christian symbol, 224
fitnah (sedition), 418; in the Muslim community, 389
fiṭrah (creation), 354
five fundamentals, 419
five *gahs*, 180
Five Pillars of Islam, 376–7, 416

flags, European, 230; Islamic, 458
flesh, life of in Christian theology, 214
flood narrative, 323; Inca culture, 520; Mesopotamian, 495–6; Old Testament, 21
flying buttresses, 259
folk songs, in Protestant worship, 295
food: and American Reform Judaism, 127; and Chinese Muslims, 459; Parsi, 192; and the Sabbath, 108–9; taboos, 75; Zoroastrian marriage ceremony, 183
foreskin, as relic, 266
forgiveness: concept of, 76–8; teachings of Jesus, 202
fountain: in a mosque, 444; of the Qairiwiyin Mosque, **446**
Fountain of Wisdom (*Pēgē gnōseōs*), 242
Four Rows (Asher), 73
Fox, George, 292
France, and Judaism, 125–7
Franciscans, 254, 264
Francis of Assisi, 254
Frank, Jacob, 57, 99
Frankel, Zecharias, 127
Frankfurt-am-Main, 129
fravashi (spirit), 183
Frederick II, of Hohenstaufen, 257
Frederick (prince), 279, 281
free will, 91, 422–3. *See also* predestination
French Revolution, 124, 309
Freud, Sigmund, 338–9
Frey, Scandinavian god, 522
Freya, Scandinavian goddess, 522
friars, 254
Friday prayers, Muslim, 380
Friends, Society of, 292–3
Fuller, Charles E., 326
fundamentalism, 324–7; in Iran, 82; modern Roman Catholicism, 329
The Fundamentals, 325
funeral practices: in Jewish home, 119; Zoroastrian, 184
funerary art, 224, 497

gabars (polytheists), 186, 188
Gabriel (Jibrīl), 358; *ḥadīth qudsī* traditions, 408; and the *Qur'ān*, 367, 420
gahambars, 181–2
gahs, 180; prayers, 164
Galen, 424
Galilee, 204; early synagogue buildings in, 63
Galileo Galilei, 310–11
galut (exile), 98
Gama, Vasco da, 278
Gandhi, Mohandas K., 190
Garden of Eden, 20–1, 31, 50
Gardner, Gerald B., 524
gate of *ijtihād*, 423
gateway (Bāb), 500
Gatha Days, 182
Gathas, 155–60, 163, 493; faith of Zoroaster, 168
Gayamaretan (Gayomart), 176
Geiger, Abraham, 127
Gelasius (pope), 255
Gemarah, 68–9
gender, and God, 340
genealogical research, in Utah, 319
Genesis, 18–21; interpretation of, 66; and the Sabbath, 107
Geneva, of Calvin, 287
geonim, 70–1
Germany, and Judaism, 125–7, 136
Gershom, Rabbenu, 85
get (divorce), 84
Ghadīr Khumm, 399
ghaybah (occultation) of the Imām, 400
al-Ghazālī, Abū Ḥāmid, 421–2, 427–8, 436
ghettos, 124
Ghost Dance movement, 514
ghusl (washing), 378
Gibraltar, 451
Gilgamesh, 323, 495
Ginés de Sepúlveda, Juan, 306
Ginsberg, Asher, 135
Gladden, Washington, 334
glory of God (*kavod*), 95
glossolalia, 315
Glueckl of Hamelin, 86
Gnosticism, 172, 177, 215–16, 537–8; Suhrawardī, 438
God: Allāh, 355; for Calvin, 287; and control, 34; as the First Cause, 312; Hebrew name of, 30; in Islamic tradition, 354, 363, 373–5; Jewish concept of, 17, 51–3; Marcion's concept of, 214–15; and Moses, 26; Mu'tazilī view of, 420; one God of the Israelites, 22; presence as Shekhinah, 97
God's Friday, 223
God's oneness (*tawḥīd*), 419
God's promise (*wa'd*), 419
God's threat (*wa'īd*), 419
God's will, and Muslims, 381
goddess, in neolithic culture, 521
gods: Brazilian, 508; *devas*, 162; and diversity, 532; Mexican, 517–18; in popular Israelite

religion, 52. *See also* polytheism.
going up (*aliyah*), 118
golden rule, 65
Gonzaga, Aloysius, 300
good (*asha*), 183
good (*ma'rūf*), 419
good and evil, 76, 175, 249; and Ash'arī, 422; and fundamentalism, 326; and Gnosticism, 215–16; and God's power, 537; in *Isaiah*, 19; *kasb* and *iktisāb*, 422; Mu'tazilī view of, 420; as universal concept, 170; in the Zoroastrian tradition, 155
Good Friday, 223
good news, 325
Good Samaritan, 206
good works, and Islam, 375
Gospel (*injīl*), and Ramaḍān, 382
Gospel of Thomas, 216
gospels: and Hebrew biblical passages, 207; and Jesus, 202–5
Gothic arch, 259
Goths' sack of Rome, 250
Graham, Billy, 326
Grant, George M., 334
gratitude (*shukr*), 436
Graves, Robert, 524
Great Awakening, 292, 314, 317
Great Mosque (Xi'an, China), **448**
Great Persecution, of the Christians, 225
Great Schism, 256
Great Zimbabwe, 505
Greco-Roman world, and Paul's agenda, 213. *See also* Hellenistic period
Greek Christianity, 239, 246; celibacy and, 255; and Chalcedon formula, 236; marriage of clergy, 250; mysticism in, 274; orthodoxy in, 238–9
Greek cross, 230
Greek gods: representations of, 63; and Roman gods, 541
Greek philosophy: and Islamic theology, 418; in Muslim learning, 423–4; universe in, 52
Greek traditions, and Jewish traditions, 44
Gregorian chant, 247
Gregory I 'the Great' (pope), 247, 263, 269
Gregory VII (pope), 255
Gregory XIII (pope), 247
Gregory the Illuminator, 238
Gregory of Nazianzus (the Theologian), 242
Gregory of Nyssa, 274
Gregory Palamas, 242, 271
Grey, Lady Jane, 286
Grey Friars, 254
gro bonanj (big good angel), 509
Guangzhou (Canton), 458
guardian angel, 267
guardianship of the jurist (*walāyat al-faqīh*), 477, 479
Guide for the Perplexed (Maimonides), 89, 91
guilt, sense of, 249
Gujarat: fires in, 181; Zoroastrians in, 187–8
Gujarati, household dialect, 189
Gulf War (1991), migration after, 481
Gutenberg, Johann, 281
Gutiérrez, Gustavo, 336
Guyard, Marie (Marie de l'Incarnation), 276, 300, 340

Ha-Levi, Yehuda, 88–9, 133, 550
ha-Shem (the Name), 26
Ḥabad (Ḥ-B-D), 101
habits (religious dress), 254
Hadhokht Nask, 164
ḥadīth qudsī (divine saying), 408, 431
ḥadīth tradition, 405, 412, 414, 431; and chain of transmission, 407; literature, 371–2; and reform, 467; rejection of by Aḥmad Khān, 473
Hagar, 355, 384
Haggadah narrative, 115
Hagia Sophia, 243
Haile Selassie, 509–10
Haiti, religion in, 508
ḥajj pilgrimage, 376, 380, 383–6; Prophet's farewell, 399
al-Ḥākim bi-Amr Allāh, 257, 402
ḥāl (mystical state), 436
halakha (prescription for conduct), 69, 70
ḥalāl: lawful, 416; restaurants in China, 459
ḥalizah (unbinding), 86–7
al-Ḥallāj, Ḥusayn b. Manṣūr, 434
halloth, 108
halo, in Persian art, 240
Hammurabi, 24
Ḥamzah b. 'Alī, Persian missionary, 402
Ḥanafī law, 396, 412–13, 461
Ḥanbalī school, 413, 420
Handsome Lake, 513–14

ḥanīfs (pious ones), Makkan Arabs, 356
Ḥanukkah, 44–6, 71, 113, 342
haoma/soma (sacred intoxicant), 162
al-Ḥaqq, 434
ḥaram (sacred place), 355
ḥarām (unlawful), 416
ḥaredim (tremblers), 141; at the Western Wall in Jerusalem, **142**
Hare Krishna movement, 555
ḥarīm system, 485
Harmon, Ellen Gould, 316
Ḥarrān, 424
Harris, Barbara, 340
Harris, William Wade, 506–7
Hartshorne, Charles, 338
Hārūn al-Rashīd, 395–6
Harvard University, 291
Ḥasan b. 'Alī, 392–4, 399, 402
al-Ḥasan al-Baṣri, 419, 432
Hasdai b. Shaprut, 88
Hashimites, 387
Hasidei Ashkenaz, 96
Ḥasidim (pious ones), 100
Hasidism, 99–101, 123
Haskalah (Enlightenment), 137
Hasler, August, 329
Hasmonean dynasty, 46, 113
ḥatzi tallith (half *tallith*), 105
Haug, Martin, 158
Havdalah (boundary), 108
havuroth (brotherhoods), 49
Ḥayy b.Yaqẓān, allegorical tale of, 427–8
hazanin (cantors), 110
health cures, 316
Healthy Body (*Tan Dorosti*), 179
hearing (*samā*ʿ), 442
heathen, 227
heaven, 55. *See also* afterlife
heavenly ascents, 95
heavenly journey (*mi'rāj*), 431
Heavenly Wisdom (*Menok-e Khrat*), 174
Hebrew language, 17, 35, 38, 42–3; of the *Mishnah*, 68–9; and Zionism, 133–4
Hecataeus of Abdera, 44
Hegel, G.W.F., 473, 536
Hekhaloth texts, 95
Helena, mother of Constantine, 227
heliocentric theory, 310
hell, realm of, 268
Hellenistic period, 42–58, 62
Helpers (Anṣār) of Madīnah, 387
Henning, Walter B., 159
henotheism, 533
Henry III (German emperor), 255
Henry VIII (English king), 285
hereditary priesthood, 180
herem (ban), 84
heresy, 233
Hermippus, 158
hermits, 218; of Mount Carmel, 254; of St Augustine (Austin Friars), 255
Herod, 50, 207
Herzfeld, Ernst, 159
Herzl, Theodor, 129, 134–5
ḥesed (lovingkindness), 97, 100
Hess, Moses, 134
hesychasm, 242
Hidetada, *shōgun*, 302
hierarchy: Church, 217, 247–8; of creation, 19; Ibn 'Arabī's cosmic, 441; religious of the Imām, 479
hieroglyphic writing, 494, 517
hijāb (veiling of women), 485
hijrah (migration), 359, 382
hijrī dating, of Islamic history, 389
Hildegard of Bingen, 275, 277
Hillel, 65, 67, 74
ḥilm, 355
Hinduism: and asceticism, 218; and Bene Israel, 82; Christian conversions from, 301; and Islam, 464; in Southeast Asia, 465; and Sufism in India, 463; *Upaniṣads*, 550; Vedānta, 527
Hippo (North Africa), 248
Hirsch, Samson R., 127, 129
Hishām b. 'Abd al-Malik, 401
Historia de las cosas de Nueva España (History of Matters in New Spain) (Sahagún), 305
Historia de las Indias (History of the Indies) (Las Casas), 306
historical criticism, of the Bible, 322–4, 327
history: nineteenth-century concepts, 535–6; as prophetic history, 363; social philosophy of, 429
Hitler, Adolf, 125, 137–9
hocus-pocus, 298
Ḥokhma (wisdom), 101
holiness churches, 314–15
holistic medicine, 526
Holocaust, 137–9; and Martin Buber, 132
Holy Communion, 220
Holy Sepulchre, 227, **227**, 243, 256–7
holy rollers, 315
Holy Spirit, 246, 315; and the disciples, 212; feast of, 223; Protestant denominations, 294. *See also filioque*, Trinity

holy war: crusaders, 258; *jihād*, 467
Holy Week, 222
Homes of Truth, 527
Hooker, Richard, 290
Hopkins, Emma Curtis, 527
Horeb, 30
hosanna (O save now), 222
Hosea (Hebrew prophet), 37, 208
Hospitallers, and Ṣūfī *ribāṭ*, 444
House of Joseph (*Bet Yosef*) (Karo), 73
House of Wisdom, 424
houses, of North American Indians, 512
How the Pope Became Infallible (Hasler), 329
Hubal (rain god), 355
Hūd, 364
Ḥudaybīyah, truce of, 362
ḥudūd (bounds of God), 418
Huitzilopochtli, 519
ḥujjah (proof), 415
Hulagu, 235, 397
Humanae Vitae (On Human Life) (Paul VI), 329
humanism, 279; of Greek philosophers, 499
humankind, Adam as father of, 363
human sacrifice, 523; of the Aztecs, 519; of the Canaanites, 23; Inca, 520. *See also* child sacrifice
human sexuality, and Christianity, 340–1. *See also* sexual intercourse
human sinfulness, and divine redemption, 248
Ḥumash, 70
humata, hukhta, huvarshta, 175
Hume, David, 312
humour, rabbinic, 114–15
hunter-gatherers, 512–13
huppah (bridal canopy), 143, **144**
Hus, John, 279
Ḥusayn b. 'Alī, 393–4, 399–402, 411, 479
Hutten, Ulrich von, 279–80
Huxley, Thomas, 322
Hyde, Thomas, 538
hymns, Protestant, 295–6
I and Thou (Buber), I-Thou experiences, 132
'ibādāt (acts of worship), 376–7, 416
Ibāḍī law, 413, 452
Iblīs, 536
Ibn 'Abd al-Wahhāb, Muḥammad, 468, 472
Ibn 'Arabī, Muḥyī al-Dīn, 428, 438–9
Ibn Bābawayh, 415
Ibn Bājjah, 427
Ibn Baṭṭūṭah, 455, 465
ibn Ezra, Abraham, 121
Ibn Ḥazm, 453
Ibn Isḥāq, Ḥunayn, 424
Ibn Khaldūn, 'Abd al-Raḥmān, 428–9
Ibn Mājah, 408
Ibn Masarrah, 427, 453
Ibn Rushd, 427–9, 453
Ibn Sab'īn, 428
Ibn Sīnā 426–7, 456
Ibn Taymīyah, 468
Ibn Tibbon, 89
Ibn Ṭufayl, 427, 453
Ibrāhīm, 395
iconoclasm: Greek church, 240–2; Islamic, 448
iconostasis (place for icons), 240
icons, 240–1
'Īd al-Aḍḥā, 380, 384
'Īd al-Fiṭr, 380, 383
Idea of the Holy (Otto), 3
Idea of the Jewish State (Herzl), 129
idolatry: and adultery, 38; Hellenistic period, 62–3; Judaism, 27; and Muḥammad, 357; and prayer, 101–2
Idrīs I, 469
Ignatius Loyola, 299–300
ignorance (*jāhilīyah*), 499
iḥrām (state of consecration), 383
IHS (Jesus), 230
iḥsān (doing good), 376–7
iḥtiyāṭ (principle of precaution), 415
Iḥyā' 'ulūm al-dīn (The Revivification of the Religious Sciences) (al-Ghazālī), 421, 436
ijmā' (consensus), 409–10, 415
ijtihād, 423, 472; closing the gate of, 414–15; legal opinions, 412; personal reasoning, 409, 415
ikhlās (*Sūrah* of Sincere Faith), 373
iktisāb (evil), 422
Iliad, 44
illumination, way of, 437
'ilm (knowledge), 355
images: and Islamic art, 448; and Protestantism, 296
imām, 391; and religious hierarchy, 479; religious leader, 378, 388; for Shī'īs, 398, 415; shrines of, 385; for Sunnī Muslims, 398
imāmah (imamate): doctrine of, 399, 418; treatise on, 476–7

Imāmī Shi'ism. *See* Twelver Shi'ism
īmān (faith), 375–7, 422
Immaculate Conception, 264
Immigrants (Muhājirūn), 360, 387
immigration: Muslim to North America, 482; and pluralism, 342. *See also* migration
incarceration, as punishment, 35
incarnationist theology, 434
Incas, 305, 519
incest, and Inuit myth, 511
inclusive language, 341
Incoherence of the Incoherence (Ibn Rushd), 428
Incoherence [or collapse] of the Philosophers (al-Ghazālī), 427
independence, Indian and Israeli, 82
Index of Prohibited Books, 298; Copernicus on, 310
India: Catholic missions in, 301; culture in, 460; Jews in, 82; and missionaries, 320; Muslims in, 472–3, 544–5; Zoroastrians in, 154, 187–91
Indian National Congress, 190
Indians, of North America, 511–17
indigenization, 307
individual destiny, 183–4. *See also* afterlife
Indo–Iranians. *See* Aryans
Indonesia, and Islam, 466
indulgences, sale of, 279, 297
inerrancy of the Bible, 325
infallibility, 327
Infallible? An Inquiry (Küng), 329
infant sacrifice, 52. *See also* child sacrifice
information age, and Zoroastrian tradition, 193
initiation: Ṣūfī, 440–1; Zoroastrian rituals, 182
injīl (Gospel), and Ramaḍān, 382
Innocent IV (pope), 268
Inquisition, 94, 298, 454; Galileo, 311
inquisition, Mu'tazilī, 420
al-Insān al-kāmil (The Perfect Man) (al-Jīlī), 441
Institutes of the Christian Religion (Calvin), 287
interfaith dialogue, 551
intermarriage: in Judaism, 45, 140; Zoroastrian, 190, 192
International Missionary Council, 329
International Society of Krishna Consciousness (Hare Krishna movement), 555
interpretation: gospel accounts as, 210; of the *Qur'ān*, 373
interreligious competition, 546–8
intoxicated mysticism, 434–6, 441
Inuit, 510–11
investiture controversy, 255
invisibles (*envizib*), 508
Iqbāl, Muḥammad, 465, 473–4
Iran: and Bahā'ī faith, 502; homeland of the Aryans, 161; Islamic context, 185–7; and Judaism, 82, 169–70; migration of Aryans from, 160; Nowrūz, 178; revolution (1978–9), 186–7, 400, 477–80; Salman Rushdie, 553; Zoroastrian emigrants from, 192; Zoroastrianism in, 153–4, 158–9, 186, 548
Iraq: and eastern Christian asceticism, 432; and war with Iran, 480
'irfān (divine *gnōsis*), 438
Irish legends, 523
Iroquois confederation, and White contact, 513
irrigation technology, and social groups, 494
Irving, Edward, 315
Isaac, 23, 365
Isabella of Castile, 93, 453
Isaiah, 19, 40, 208; and Zoroaster, 169
Isḥāq b. Ḥunayn, 424
Ishmael (Ismā'īl), 355, 365, 383, 385
Iskandar Muda, 466
Islām (name), 353
islām (submission), 422
Islam: and Bahā'ī faith, 502; capture of Jerusalem, 256; compared with Christianity, 544; and faith, 375–6; interpreters of religion, 536; in Iran, *see* Iran; and Judaeo-Christian tradition, 355; medieval and Jews, 81; as missionary religion, 542; monotheism, 532; and Noachic commandments, 79; religious sciences, 404–6, 417; spread of, 449–67, *450*; and Zoroastrianism, 185
Islamic Council of Europe, interfaith dialogue, 481
Islamic revivalism, 469, 475–80
Islamic Society (Jamā'at-i Islāmī), 478
Islamic state, idea of, 477–8
Islamic terms, 557–8
Ismā'īl (Ishmael), 355, 401

Ismā'īlī Shi'ism, 401–2
isnād (chain of transmission), 407
Israel, 17; Judaism in, 129, 141; of northern tribes, 29; and Palestinian conflict, 82, 139, 143; and the Sabbath, 141; Sephardim and Ashkenazim in, 81
Israel ben Eliezer, 99
Istanbul, 239
istiḥsān (rational preference in law), 412
Ivory Coast, Harris in, 506
īwān, 445–6

J (Yahwist) source, 31, 226
Jabal al-Raḥmah (Mount of Mercy), 384
Jabal Ṭāriq (Ṭāriq's mountain), 451
jabr (divine predeterminism), 423
Jabrīyah, 423
Jacob ben Asher, 73
Jacobites, 237
Jadi Rana, 188–9
Jael, 34
Ja'far al-Ṣādiq, 401–2, 411, 432
Ja'farī (Shī'ī) law, 411, 414
Jäger, Johann, 279
jāhilīyah, 355; ignorance, 499; pre-Islamic, 418
Jamā'at-i Islāmī (Islamic Society), 478
Jamaica, 509–10
Jamasp, 175
James, 50, 212
jāmi' (mosque), 380, 444
Jam'iyat al-Ikhwān al-Muslimīn (Muslim Brothers), 477
Jamnia, 59, 65
Japan, Catholic missions in, 301–2
jashan (thanksgiving) ceremony, 181–2, 191
Jason, 44
Java, and Islam, 466
JE epic, 19, 31
Jehovah, 26
Jehovah's Witnesses, 317
Jephthah, 34
Jerusalem, 23, 28; fall of in 70, 58, 250; Muslims and the Crusades, 256; patriarchs of, 217
Jerusalem (Mendelssohn), 124
Jerusalem Talmud, 68–9
Jesuits, 299–301; cultural-assimilationist strategies of, 303; and Native American peoples, 308
Jesus: birth of, 199–200, 206; double nature of, 52; early depictions of, 224; historical life of, 203; Marcion's concept of, 214–15; as messiah, 206; pictorial representations of, 240; in the *Qur'ān*, 364, 366; as ruler of creation, 240; and Torah, 58
Jesus movement, and private property, 58
Jesus Prayer, 242
Jethro (Shu'ayb), 364
Jewish-Christian-Muslim dialogue, 553
Jewish communities: Alexandria, 43; in early Arabia, 356
Jewish law, versus gospel, 210
Jewish polemics, 547
Jewish School (*Das jüdisches Lehrhaus*), 131
Jewish Zealot garrison (Masada), 554
Jews: expulsion from Madīnah, 361; as God's chosen people, 17; in India, 82; of Madīnah, 360; as People of the Book, 450
Jibrīl (Gabriel), 358
jihād, 258, 386; against the British, 464; against the Egyptians, 477; and Aḥmad Barelwi, 472; holy war, 467; and Sufism, 444
al-Jīlī, 'Abd al-Karīm, 441
Jinnah, Muḥammad Alī, 473
jizyah (poll tax), 186, 450
John, 210–11
John II Sigismund Zápolya, 289
John III of Portugal, 301
John XXII (pope), 328
John XXIII (pope), 328, 330
John the Baptist, 58, 204, 206, 217
St John of the Cross, 275
John of Damascus, 241, 392
John of Gischala, 51
John of Monte Corvino, 302
John Paul II (pope), 265
Johnston, Harry, 320
Jolliet, Louis, 308
Jonah, prophetic mission of, 364
Jones, Jim, 553–4
Jonestown (Guyana), 553
Joseph (Khazar king), 88
Josephus, Flavius, 44, 47, 49, 50–1
Josiah (king), 31
Journey of the Mind to God (Bonaventure), 275
Judaeo-Christian heritage, and Marxism, 336
Judah, 'Maccabee' (hammer), 45
Judah, Rabbi, 67–8, 72
Judah, southern tribes, 29
Judaism, 15–18; chosenness of,

52; Christianity as a sect of, 542; and Christianity, 131; and Hellenization, 47; and monotheism, 532–5; twentieth-century theology, 130–3
Judas, 205
Judas of Galilee, 50
Judea, 40, 43; and Hellenism, 45
Judean dynasty, David, 29
judges, and Israelite tribal confederation, 28
Jüdische Wissenschaft (Science of Judaism) movement, 126–8
Das jüdisches Lehrhaus (The Jewish School), 131
Julian (emperor), 227
Julian calendar, 247
Julian of Norwich, 277, 340
jum'ah (Friday assembly), 380
al-Junayd, Abū Qāsim, 434, 441
Jundī-Shāpūr, 424
Jung, Carl Gustav, 339
jurisprudence: *fiqh*, 409; *ḥadīth*, 407; of Islam, 404, 410–11; and Prophetic *ḥadīth* tradition, 407
jurist (*faqīh*), 409; authority of, 479; *muftī, 414;* and the *Qur'ān*, 405
Justin II (emperor), 236
Justinian (emperor), 236, 243, 270

Ka'bah (shrine), pilgrimage to, 355–7
Kabbalah (received tradition), 96–8
kabbalat 'ol ha-mitzvoth, 122
Kabīr, 464
Kaddish prayer, 120
al-Kāfī (The Sufficient), 414
kāfir (rejecter of faith), 419, 468
kāhin (soothsayer), 358
Kaifeng Jews (China), 83
kalām: speculative theology, 423; speech of God, 417
Kant, Immanuel, 271, 312
Kaplan, Mordecai, 132
Karaites (scripturalists), 71
Karbalā', tragedy of, 394
Karo, Joseph, 73
Kartēr, 173
kasb (good) and *iktisāb*, 422
Kavad (king), 175
kavod (glory of God), 95
kavvanah, 101, 105; in United States, 141
Kaysānīyah, 400
Keble, John, 286
Kermanshah, Iran, 185
Ketuvim, 65
Khadījah, 357–9
khalīfat rasūl Allāh (successor of the Messenger of God), 388
Khan, Sayyid Aḥmad, 464–5, 473
khāngāhs, 440
Khārijīs, 390–1, 418, 452, 467
Khazars, legend of, 88–9
Khazraj tribe, 360
Kheiralla, Ibrahim George, 502
khilāfah (stewardship), 388
khirqah (patched frock), 440–1
Khoja Ismā'īlī community, 455–6
Khomeini, Imām Ruhollah, 476–7, 479
Khorda Avesta, 164, 189
Khosrow Anoshirvan ('immortal soul'), 175
khuṭbah (sermon), 444
kibbutz, **112**
kibbutzim, agricultural collectives, 134
Kierkegaard, Søren, 312
Kiev, 244
al-Kindī, Abū Yūsuf Ya'qūb, 424
King, Martin Luther, Jr, 331–3
king, as messiah, 56
King James version of the Bible, 159
Kingdom Halls, 317
kingship: Israelite, 27–9; Malkut, 97
Kingsley, Charles, 334
Kinjikitele, 505
kinyan (acquisition), 143
Kipling, Rudyard, 7; on missionaries, 320
kippah (cap), 105–6
Kitāb al-Ḥujjah (Book of the Proof of God), 414
Kitāb al-Umm (al-Shāfi'ī), 412
Kitāb-i Aqdas (The Most Holy Book) (Bahā'u'llāh), 502
Kitāb-i Īqān (The Book of Certitude) (Bahā'u'llāh), 502
knights (*firsān*), 444
Knights Hospitaller, 257
Knights of St John, 253
Knights Templar, 253, 257
knowledge: Da'at, 101; *gnōsis*, 215; *mandā*, 216
koinobios (community life), 219
Korea, Presbyterianism in, 288
Koresh, David, 554
kosher laws, 114–15
Kraemer, Heinrich, 268
Kūfah, 390, 394; Muslim capital, 392
kufr: infidelity, 418; misbelief, 468; rejection of faith, 375; unbelief, 390
al-Kulaynī, 414–15
Küng, Hans, 329
Kurdistan, Nestorians in, 236
kustis, 182–4
Kuzari (Ha-Levi), 88, 550

kwa Baron (Baron's cross), 509

labarum, 230
ladder to heaven (*mi'rāj*), 367
laity, as preachers, 293
Lakota Indians, 514
Lalou, Marie, 507
Lamentations, 39
Landa, Diego de, 518
language: Arabic, 396, 423–4; Aramaic, 38, 69, 72, 110, 162; Armenian, 238; Aryan roots, 161; Coptic, 237; and Eastern Orthodoxy, 244; Ethiopic, 237; and flood myth, 21; Greek, 42–3; Hebrew, 38, 68–9, 133; inclusive, 341; of the mass, 328; of Muslims, *450*, 451; of the *Qur'ān*, 370; Swahili, 505; symbol system, 494; in synagogues, 15; Syriac, 235; Turkic, 458; vernacular in Bengal, 461; and Zionism, 133; and Zoroastrianism, 158, 161
Las Casas, Bartolomé de, 305–6
Al-Lāt, 355
Latin: cross, 230; mass and music, 298–9; sites in Holy Land, 254; and vernacular, 279, 328; world, 239
Latin alphabet: eastern Orthodoxy, 244; and Turkey, 474
Latin America: church and society in, 306–7; Muslims in, 481; secularism in, 309
Latin American Council of Bishops, 336
Latter-Day Saints (Mormons), 218–19
Laud, William, 290
law: codes, 30, 72; and the covenant, 60; divine origin of, 24; and gospel, 210, 214; Islamic, 404–17, 464; Jewish, 71–3; and religion, 227; of retaliation (*lex talionis*), 73; *sharī'ah*, 377; Ten Commandments, 27;
Law: scripture, 64; Torah, 65
lawful (*ḥalāl*), 416
laws of nature, 311, 322
leadership: and Muslim divisions, 390; Southern US, 331
Lebanese civil war (1975–90), 481
lectionaries, Protestant, 294
legal interpretation: Imamī Shī'ī, 414–15; Pharisees, 49; rabbinic, 70–5
legal opinions: *fatwās*, 414; *ijtihād*, 412
legal schools, Muslim, 411–13
Lent, 222
Leo III (pope), 255
Leo XIII (pope), 273, 328
lesser *ḥajj* (*'umrah*), 384
Lessing, Gotthold, 124
Letter from Birmingham Jail (King), 332–3
Letters of Obscure Men (von Hutten and Rubianus), 279–81
Levant, and Greek gods, 541
The Levelled Path (*al-Muwaṭṭa'*) (Mālik), 412
levirate marriage (*yibum*), 85
Leviticus, *Sifra*, 66
Levy, Cerf, 86
lex talionis (law of retaliation), 73
Liberal Judaism, 126
liberation theology, 336
Libya, and Ṣūfī reform movement, 469
Lie (*drug* or *druj*), 183
life after death. *See* afterlife
Life of Constantine (Eusebius), 226
life-cycle rituals. *See* rites of passage
life-example (*sunnah*), 366
Light verse, 430–1
Lindsey, Theophilus, 290
literary criticism, of the Bible, 324
liturgy, Conservative synagogue, 128; eastern Christian, 220; Zoroastrian, 179
Livingstone, David, 320
logos (Word), 52, 210, 234
Loki, Scandinavian deity, 522
Lonergan, Bernard, 337
longhouse, 512, 514
loose constructionists, Pharisees as, 49
Lord's Prayer, 219
Lord's Supper, 220
Los Angeles, Parsi community in, 191
Louis IX, 267
love: *maḥabbah*, 436; rabbinic emphasis on, 84
love, passionate (*hawā*), 433
lovingkindness (*ḥesed*), 60, 97
Loyola, Ignatius, 299–300
Lubavitcher Ḥasidim, 101
Lucifer, 268
Luke, 206–7; on Pentecost, 212
lunar calendar, 111, 222; Muslim, 359, 382–3, 389
Luria, Isaac, 98–9
Luther, Martin, 255, 264, 278–83, 295
Luther Bible, 281
Lutheranism, 283–5, 330,

lwa (mystery), 508

Ma'ālim fī al-tarīq (Quṭb), 475
ma'at (truth), 497
Maccabean revolt, and Ḥanukkah, 44–6
MacLaine, Shirley, 526
Macumba, 508
Madīnah (the city), 359–60, 392; law in, 412
Madīnat al-Salām, 395
madrasah (religious school), 444
Magen David (shield of David), 62
Maggid (preacher), 100
magi, 159, 168; priests, 206; visitors to Jesus, 169, 221–2
magical spells, 95
magisterium, 327
maḥabbah (love), 436
Mahāyāna Buddhism, spread of, 172
Mahdī, the, 403
al-Mahdī, Muḥammad Aḥmad, 395, 469
Mahdīyah, of the Sudan, 469
Maḥmūd the Ghaznavid, 457, 459
Maigrot, Charles, 304
Maillard de Tournon, Charles Thomas, 304
Maimonides, Moses, 73, 89–93
Maitreya, 172
Makkah (Mecca), 355–6, 361–2; pilgrimage to, 383–6; *sūrahs* in, 368
makrūh (reprehensible), 416
Malabar Coast, Christians, 235, 237, 247
Malāmatī Ṣūfīs, 441
Malebranche, Nicolas, 550
Mali Empire, 455
Mālik b. Anas, 396, 412
Mālikī school, 412–13, 453–4
Malkut (kingship), 97
Malleus Maleficorum (Witches' Hammer) (Kraemer and Sprenger), 268
Maltese cross, 230
Malthus, Thomas, 321
al-Ma'mūn, 395–6, 420, 424
al-Manār (The Beacon), 476
Manāt (goddess), 355
mandā (knowledge), 216
Mandeans, 216
Manekji Limji Hataria, 186
Mani, 172–3, 216, 537–8
Manichaeism, 216, 537–8; and Augustine, 248; dualism, 177; and Muslims, 417; third century, 544
Manṣūr, Abū al-Qāsem (Ferdowsī), 186
al-Manṣūr: founder of Baghdad, 395; and scholars, 423
manthra (chant formula), 180
manuscripts: Essene, 47; Gnostic, 216
Manushchihr, 174
manzilah, 419
maqāmāt (mystic stations), 436
Marabouts, 452
Marathi, 189
Marathon, 167
Marcion, 214–15
Mardan-Farrokh, 548
Mardi Gras, 222
Marduk (Babylonian deity), 39, 168, 495
Marian devotion, 263–4
Marie de l'Incarnation. *See* Guyard, Marie
ma'rifah (divine *gnōsis*), 433
Maritain, Jacques, 337
Mark, 202–5, 237, 263
Maronites of Lebanon, 246
Marquette, Jacques, 308
Marranos (pigs), 94
marriage: among Hebrews, 32; in Arab society, 483; Greek Church clergy, 250; and Islamic law, 405; in Israel, 130; and Judaism, 84–7, 119, 143–4; law and Noah, 365; Pharisaic tradition, 67; Zoroastrian rituals, 182–3. *See also* divorce
married clergy, 246; in Protestantism, 282
Martel, Charles, 454
Mar Thoma (St Thomas) Church, 237–8
martyrdom, 225; asceticism as alternative to, 218; of Ḥusayn, 394, 400; ideal of, 479; and Judaism, 54, 139
ma'rūf (good), 419
Marwānids, 394
Marx, Karl, 335–6
Marxism, 335–8; and Kaifeng community, 83
Mary: and Eastern Orthodox Christianity, 264; figure of, 263–5; in Protestantism, 295; relics from, 266–7; status of, 234–5
Mary Tudor, 285
Masada, 51, 61, 554
Masani, Rustom, 193
mashiah (anointed one), 56
masjid (mosque), 380, 444
masks: Alaskan shamans, 510; in folk tradition, 523
maṣlaḥah (common good), 412
Masoretes, 110
mass, 199, 220
Massachusetts Metaphysical College, 318
massacre: at Wounded Knee,

514; of Jews (*pogrom*), 134–5, 137
master of the Good Name (Baal Shem Tov), 99
master of the head (*mèt-tet*), 509
Mathnawī (Couplets) (Rūmī), 440
matn (text of *ḥadīth*), 407
Matthew, 204, 206–10
al-Maturīdī, 456
Maundy Thursday, 222
Maurice, Frederick Denison, 334
mausoleum, 444
mawālī (converts), 398
Mawdūdī, Abū al-A'lā, 478
Maxwell, Mary, 502
Mayan culture, 304–5, 517–18
Mazda worshippers, 153
Mazdak, 175
Mecca. *See* Makkah
mechanistic theory, 311–13
media: and evangelism, 326; and the *Qur'ān*, 370
medical missionaries, 316; and Asia, 320
medical treatment, and Jehovah's Witnesses, 317
medicine, Greek, 424
medieval Christianity, 247–77 and death, 269
medieval Judaism, 80–101
Mehmet II the Conqueror (Sultan), 94
Mehta, Pherozeshah, 190
Mekhilta for *Exodus*, 66
melting-pot, American, 140
Memoirs of Glueckl of Hamelin (Glueckl), 86
Menahem, 50
Menander (Milinda), 550
Mendelssohn, Felix, 126
Mendelssohn, Moses, 124–6
mendicant orders, 253–5
Menelaus, 44
Mennonites, 289
Menok-e Khrat (Heavenly Wisdom), 174
menorah (candlestick), 62–3, 113
menstruation: and washing, 378; in Zoroastrianism, 177, 193
Mer-ne-Ptah (pharaoh), 18
Mercier, Désiré-Joseph, 330
mergers, denominational, 330
Merici, Angela, 300
Merkabah mysticism, 95–6
Merton, Thomas, 253
Mesa Verde cliff dwellings, **512**
Mesoamerica, 517
Mesopotamia, 22, 323; Aramaic alphabet, 162; early civilization, 494; empires, 29; law in, 35
Mesrop Mashtots, 238
Message of Divine Oneness (*Risālat al-tawḥīd*), 423
messenger (*rasūl*), 364
messiah, 55–7; as future king, 41; Jesus as, 207, 210–11; Sabbatai Zvi as, 99; and suffering, 57
messianism, 38, 57; Imāmī Shī'ī, 403
mèt-tet (master of the head), 509
metaphor: and the prophets, 37; of resurrection, 54
Methodists, 313–14, 330, 334
Methodius, 244
Mevlevi (Mawlawī) order, 443
Mexico: religion in, 517–19; revolution, 309; Spanish conquest of, 304–6
mezuzah (scroll on door frame), 106
Micaiah ben Imlah, 36
Midian, 364
midrash (commentary), 65–6, 96-7
Midrash as *agada*, 70
migration: early Zoroastrian, 188; and European Catholicism, 308; *hijrah*, 359; of Ismā'īlīs, 402; of Jews, 81, *94*, 136–7; of the Khoja community, 456; and Mennonites, 289; Muslim, 462, 480–1; Parsi, 191–3; and pluralism, 549; and spread of Islam, 451
miḥnah (test), 420
miḥrāb (niche), 444
mikveh (ritual bathhouse), 76, 123
milah (circumcision for men), 122
Milinda (Menander), 550
military chaplaincy, 335
military Ṣūfī fraternities (*ribāṭ*), 444
Miller, William, 316
Milton, John, 290
Minā, 384–5
minaret, 445, 458
minbar (pulpit), 444
Ming dynasty, 458
minhag (custom), 84
minister, clergy, 293
minyan (quorum for group prayer), 13, 101
miracles: of Jesus, 366; of Moses, 366
mi'rāj: heavenly journey, 431; ladder, 367
Miriam (prophetess), 34, 37
Miryam, 219
misbelievers (*kuffār*), 468
Mishkāt al-Anwār (The Niche of

Lights), 437
Mishnah, 67–9, 72
Mishneh Torah (Maimonides), 72, 89
missionaries, 545–6; and colonialism, 320; medical, 316; Mormon, 319; and Native Americans, 513; in North America, *516*; Presbyterian and Bene Israel, 82; Roman Catholic, 244; Seventh-Day Adventist, 316; to the New World, 308; and spread of Islam, 451
missionary religions, 202, 449, 542–6
mistè (mysteries), 508
Mithraism, 162, 170–2
Mithridates I, 170–1
Mitnagdim (opponents), 100
mitzvoth, 79, 139
Mizrah (east), 61
mobed priests, 180
Moche culture, 519
Moctezuma I, 519
Moctezuma II (Montezuma), 305
modernity: and the Christian tradition, 343; North America versus Israel, 140–3
Mohammedan (term), 353
mohel, 117
monarchical role of pope, 328
monasticism, 218–19, 250–2; Christian in Egypt, 432; and Copts, 237; orders, 252–3
Mongols, 397, 458; in Central Asia, 457; Nestorian missions, 235
Monica, mother of Augustine, 248
monks (*ruhbān*), 444. *See also* monasticism
Monophysites, 236–9, 417, 424, 505
monotheism, 532–6; Afro-Brazilian religion, 508; in ancient Arabia, 499; Hebrew, 44; Islamic, 79, 374; of Makkan Arabs, 356; of modern Zoroastrians, 176
Monothelites, 239
Monte Cassino, 251
Montezuma, 305
Moonies (Unification Church), 554–5
morality: in Arabian society, 356; and humanity, 21; and Judaic law, 51, 73; Noachic commandments, 79; and the *Qur'ān*, 405–6; and Zoroastrianism, 154, 175
Moriah, 23
Mormons, 318–19, and Blacks, 331
mortal sins, 269
Moses, 208; biblical narrative, 19–20; in *Deuteronomy*, 31; editing the five books of, 29–30; and the Exodus, 25–7; and Hebrew monotheism, 533; mission in *Qur'ān*, 365; Muslim tradition, 364–6
Moses ben Maimon. *See* Maimonides, Moses
Moses ben Shemtov, 96
Moslem (term), 353
mosques: function of, 444; in North America, 483; Turkish, 446
mother of God, Mary as, 264
Mount Athos, 244
Mount Gerizim, and Samaritans, 46
Mount Ḥirā', 357–8, 382
Mount of Mercy (Jabal al-Raḥmah), 384
Mount Raḍwah, 400
Mount Zion, 133
mozarrab (Arabized) Christians, 453
Mu'ādh b. Jabal, 410
mu'adhdhin, 378
mu'āmalāt (human interrelations), 376, 416
Mu'āwiyah, 389–93, 418–19
mubāḥ (neutral action), 416
Mubarak, Hosni, 477
muftī (jurisconsult), 414
Mughal rule in India, 463–4
Muhājirūn (immigrants), 360
Muḥammad, 81, 158; birthday celebration of, 380; life of, 357–9; as messenger of God, 354; Perfect Man, 439; Prophet of the end of time, 366; prophet of power, 364–5; and Shī'īs, 398-9
Muhammad, Elijah, 482
Muḥammad, Sayyid 'Alī (the Bāb), 500
Muḥammad V (king), 469
Muḥammad al-Bāqir, 401, 411
Muḥammad b. al-Ḥanafīyah, 400
Muḥammad b. Ḥasan al-'Askarī, 402
Muḥammad b. Nuṣayr al-Namīrī, 404
Muḥammad (al-Mahdī), 395
muhapas, 188
muḥsin (righteous person), 376
al-Mu'izz li-Dīn Allāh, 397, 401
mujaddid (renovator), 421, 467
mujtahid, 415
Mukhammisah, 403
al-Mukhtār, 400; and revolt, 400
muktad (released souls) 180, 182

mu'min (person of faith), 376, 419
Mumbai. *See* Bombay
mummies, ancient Egyptian, 497
munkar (evil conduct), 419
Müntzer, Thomas, 282
murābiṭ (one who keeps watch at night), 452
al-Murābiṭūn, 453
murder: and capital punishment, 77–8; in Hebrew law, 35; of 'Uthmān, 389
murīd (disciple), 435–6
Murji'ah (those who postpone), 418–19
Murray, Margaret A., 524
Mūsā al-Kāẓim, 401–2
music: Byzantine era, 243; in Christian worship, 220; and Christmas, 200; Gregory I, 'the Great', 247; and Latin mass, 298–9; and prayer, 104–5; in Protestantism, 295–7; in Sufism, 442–3; in synagogues, 109–11
Muslim (term), 353
Muslim b. al-Ḥajjāj al-Nīsābūrī, 408
Muslim Brothers (Jam'īyat al-Ikhwān al-Muslimīn), 477
Muslims: and crusaders, 259; earliest community, 359–61; in Europe, 480–1; in Indian society, 462; and marriage, 84; at prayer, **447**. *See also* Islam
The Muslim World (periodical), 482
Musnad, 413
mustaḥabb (commendable), 416
musulmān (term), 353
al-Mu'taṣim, 396
al-Mutawakkil, 396, 420
mutawātir (accepted), 407
Mu'tazilah (separatists), 419–21
al-Muwaḥḥidūn, 453
muwallad (converts), 453
al-Muwaṭṭa (The Levelled Path) (Mālik), 396, 412
Muzdalifah, 384
Mysteries of Selflessness (*Rumūz-i bīhkūdī*) (Iqbāl), 474
mysticism: Arabo-Hispanic, 453; Christian, 340; Islamic, 408, 421, 427, 429–44; Jewish, 55, 93–6; of love, 439; and Martin Buber, 132; medieval, 242, 273–7
myths: Greek and Roman, 498–9; and Israel, 21–2; Scandinavian, 522

nabī (prophet), 358, 364
Nablus (town), 46
nādir (rare), 408
al-Nafs al-Zakīyah (the pure soul), 395
Nāgasena, 550
Nag Hammadi, Gnostic manuscripts, 216
nahath, 119
al-Nahrawān, battle of, 391
naiskos, 61
Nānak (Gurū), 464
Naoroji, Dadabhai, 189
Napoleon, 124–5, 323, 470
naql (transmitted tradition), 415
Naqshbandī order, 442, 459
narrative: anecdotal, 70, 100; mythology, 498; Passover Haggadah, 115
al-Nasā'ī, 408
nasi (prince), descendant of David, 41; title of Rabbi Judah, 67–8
Naṣrid dynasty, 453
Nasser, Gamal Abdel, 477
Nathan of Gaza, 99
Nathan the Wise (Lessing), 124
Nation of Islam, 482
national identity: Canadian concept of, 140; and language, 133
National Party (South Africa), 331
nationality, Judaism as, 141
Native American Church, 514–15
natural selection, 321
Natural Theology (Paley), 311
nature gods: Ancient Near East, 22; in polytheism, 539
navjote (new birth), 182
nawāfil (devotional prayers), 381
amaNazaretha Baptist Church, 505
Nazca culture, 519
Nazis, 137–9
nefesh (soul/person), 53–4
negation, way of, 437
Nehemiah, 41
nekudot, 110
neolithic stone circles, 521
neopagan witchcraft, 525
Neoplatonism, 90, 248, 274, 424
Nero (emperor), 214
ner tamid (eternal lamp), 62
Nestorians, 234–6; in China, 302; and Monophysites, 239; in Syria, 237
Nestorius, 235
Nevi'im, 65
New Age spirituality, 526–7
new birth (*navjote*), 182
Newbrough, John Ballou, 527

New Christians (*conversos*), 94
New Democratic Party, 334
Newman, John Henry, 286–7
New Testament: *Acts of the Apostles*, 212; image of Jews in, 138; Pharisees in, 48
New Theologian, Simeon, 242
New Thought movement, 527
Newton, Isaac, 311–12
New World, Jewish settlement in, 80
New Year, Jewish, 113
neẓaḥ Yisrael (the eternity of Israel), 89
Ngundeng, 505
Nicene Creed, 231–2, 246, 295
niche (*miḥrāb*), 444
Niche of Lights (*Mishkāt al-Anwār*), 437
St Nicholas of Myra, 200
Nicholas II (pope), 255
Nicolaus IV (pope), 235
Nicomedia, 225
Nietzsche, Friedrich, 135, 155, 473
Nigeria, and Ṣūfī reform movement, 469
Night (Wiesel), 139
nimbus, 240
el-Nimeiri, Gaafar Mohamed, 478
Ninth of Ab, 116
Niẓāmīyah college (Baghdad), 421
Nizārīs, 401
Noachic commandments, 79; in Muslim tradition, 365
Noah: covenant with, 79; and divine law, 32; and his ark, 323; prophet of power, 364–5
nomads: Bedouin, 499; and sedentary populations, 159
nomocracy, Islam as, 416
North Africa, Islamic conquest of, 451–2
North America: Ashkenazic Jews, 81; Bahā'ī faith in, 502; Catholicism in, 307; Islam in, 481; Judaism, 130; Native traditions in, 510–17; witchcraft revival, 524; and Zionism, 135
Northeast Woodlands, 513; culture, 511
Nowrūz, 178
Numbers, Sifre, 66
nuns, and Luther, 282
Nūrī, Mīrzā Ḥusayn 'Alī (Bahā'u'llāh), 500–2; interview with, 501
Nūrī, Mīrzā Yaḥyā (Ṣubḥ-i Azal), 501
Nuṣayrīs, 404
Nyaish prayers, 164
Nyberg, Henrik S., 159

Oahspe (Newbrough), 527
occasionalism, 422, 427
occasions of revelation (*asbāb al-nuzūl*), 405
occult: in ancient Egypt, 497; and New Age, 526–7; Rosicrucians, 497
occultation (*ghaybah*) of the Imām, 400, 402–3
Odenathus (king), 173
Odin, Scandinavian god, 522
Odyssey, 44
Ohrmazd. *See* Ahura Mazda
Old Catholics, 328
Old-Fashioned Revival Hour, 326
Old Order Amish farmers, 289
Olivi, Peter John, 328
Olmecs, 517
ontological argument (Anselm), 270
Oral Torah, 67; and *Ḥadīth*s, 407
oral tradition: Avestan literature, 163; and Muḥammad, 355, 371–2; Zoroaster, 158
ordination: Christian, 217; of women, 340
Origen, of Alexandria, 232
original sin, doctrine of, 213, 268
Origin of Species (Darwin), 321–2
orixās (deities, Brazil), 508
Orthodox Church, 239–41
Orthodox Jews, 128–30; dress of, 105–6; and education, 121–2; and family purity, 76; and Hasidism, and Israel, 135; and law at Sinai, 30; in North America, 141; and Sabbath restrictions, 109
Osirus, 496
Osman I, 457
Otto, Rudolf, 3–4, 312
Ottoman Turks, 94, 130, 457; and Ḥanafī law, 413
Our Father, prayer, 219
Out on a Limb (MacLaine), 526
Oxford English Dictionary, witch, 524
Oxford movement, 286

P, Pentateuchal source, 32
Pachomius, 219
pacifism, 334–5
paganism: Arabian, 499–500; and Christianity in Latin America, 307; concept of, 493; Greek and Roman, 498–9; and Judaism, 44;

and pilgrimage, 383; under Constantine, 226
Pahlavi, Reza, Shah, 186, 479
Pahlavi: literature, 173; script, 162, 165
Pakistan: idea of, 473; and *sharī'ah* law, 478
Palamas, Gregory, 242, 271
Palestine, 28; partition of, 139, 143
Palestinian Talmud, 68–9
Paley, William, 311
Palm Sunday, 222
Palmyra, 173, 233
pan-Islamic ideology, 470–2
pantheons. *See* gods, polytheism
Pantheon (Rome), architectual influence, 227
pantokrator (ruler of all), 240
Papacy: 247–8; infallibility, 328; power, 297
Papa Doc, 509
parables, Christian, 206–11
paradise, in Hebrew thought, 54
Parham, Charles Fox, 315
Paris: exile of Afghānī in, 471; of Khomeini in, 480
Parsis (Zoroastrians), 154, 187–91
Parthenon (Athens), architectural influence, 229
Parthian era, 162, 170–2
partition: of India, 465; of Palestine, 139
Pasai, 466
Passion, 209
Passover, 27, 75, 114–16, **116**, 220; Haggadah, 104; and Samaritans, 46
pastor, clergy, 293
Pater noster, prayer, 219
patience (*ṣabr*), 375, 378, 436
patriarchal societies, role of the goddess, 522
patriarchs, Hebrew, 22–3
Paul, 49, 72, 211, 213–14
Paul III (pope), 300
Paul VI (pope), 265, 329
Paul of Samosata, 233
Pazand (Pahlavi as Avestan), 165
p.b.o.h. (peace be on him), 367
peace: *salām*, 353. *See also* pacifism
Pearl of Great Price (Smith), 318
Pēgē gnōseōs (Fountain of Wisdom), 242
Pelagius, 249
Pele (volcano goddess), 539
penance, by monks, 252
penitents, 400
Penn, William, 292
Pennsylvania Dutch, 289
Pentateuch, 30, 226
Pentecost (Shavuoth), 116, 121, 223
Pentecostalism, 315
People's Republic of China, 459
People of the Book, 186, 368, 410, 450
Peoples Temple movement, 553
Perfect Man, 441; Muḥammad, 439
Perfect Man (*al-Insān al-kāmil*) (al-Jīlī), 441
Peroz (king), 235
persecution: of Christians in Japan, 302; of early Christians, 224–5; of Jews, 81; of Muḥammad, 359
Persepolis, 159, 163, 166, 185; Achaemenian ruins, 185; celebration 1971, 186
Persia: conflict with Constantinople, 238; empire, 41, 52, 166, 544; Mongol conquest of, 457; and Sāmānid dynasty, 456
Persian language, 186; in India, 463; and Muslims, 544; script forms, 162
Persian literature, 396–7
personal reasoning (*ijtihād*), 409, 415
Peru, religion in, 519–20
pesher, commentary, 47
Peter, 212; and bishops of Rome, 247; keys, 263
peyote, as sacred plant, 514
Pharaoh, and Moses, 365
Pharisaism, 48–50, 59, 76; and biblical exegesis, 67; and early *midrashim*, 66
Philistines, 28
Philo, 47, 50, 52, 61; on the messiah, 56
philosophy: Anglo-American empiricism, 337; and biblical monotheism, 535; *falsafah*, 423; Greek, 498–9; Islamic, 424–9; in the Middle Ages, 87–101; in North Africa, 427–9; of religion, 312–13; scholastic, 269; in Spain, 427–9
Photius, 246
phusis (nature), 236
phylacteries, 106
Pietism, 313
Pilate (governor), 205, 207
Pilgrim's Progress (Bunyan), 290
pilgrimage, 265–7, 355; *ḥajj*, 376, 380, 383–6, 399; and pagan religion, 499–500; Ṣūfī, 441–2; to the Holy Land, 256; to Makkah, 355, 362, 383–6; to Udvada, 181
Pinsker, Leo, 134–5
pious ones (*ḥanīfs*), Arabs, 356

pīr, 435
Pīr-e Sabz, shrine of, **187**
Pirke Aboth, 64
Pius V (pope), 272
Pius IX (pope), 264, 327
Pius XI (pope), 300
Pius XII (pope), 265
Pizarro, Francisco, 304
plague, 269
Plains Indians, 511
plainsong, medieval, 298
Plato, 66; dialogues, 550
Platonism, 90–1, 424–5
Pliny, 158
Plotinus, 248, 424
pluralism, 200, 341–3, 548–9; theological challenge of, 555–6
poetry, mystical, 439–40, 442–3
pogrom (massacre of Jews), 134–5, 137
pole-sitters, 218
polemic works, 546
politics: in India, 190; in Israel, 129–30; Jesus movement, 58; of Khomeini, 479; and Luther, 279; and the Murji'ites, 418–19; and Prophet's death, 418; and race, 331; and religious right, 334; Shi'ism, 398; and theological issues, 232–4, 238
poll tax: *jizyah*, 450; on non-Muslims, 186
pollution: substances as, 75–6; Zoroastrian, 176–7
polygamy, 85; and Jews, 84; Mormons and, 319
polygyny, and Islam, 484
Polynesian islands, deities in, 539
polyphony, Renaissance, 298
polytheism, 532, 538–41; in ancient Arabia, 499; in Vedic and Avestan rituals, 161–2; Zoroastrianism, 163, 186
Poole, Elijah, 482
poor: *darvīsh*, 440; *faqīr*, 440
Poor Clares, 254
popes: authority of, 327; *papa*, father, 247; and princes, 255–6
Popol Vuh, 518
popular religion: Greek, 498–9; Israelite, 52
population: Christian, 200–2; of Inuit, 510; Muslim, 465–6; Muslim in North America, 483; world of Jews, 16; of Zoroastrians, 153–4, 190
power: possession by spirits, 508; in African religion, 503; of God, 537; of the Hebrew god, 534–5; Inca deities, 520; and Inuit religion, 511; and nature deities, 539
power centres, New Age, 527
Praise of Folly (*Encomium moriae*) (Erasmus), 278
prayer: Christian, 219; direction of (*qiblah*), 444; exemption from, 381; items worn in, 105–6; in Judaism, 101–7; Kaddish, 120; Muslim, 378–81, **447**; in Protestant denominations, 294; for women, 86; Zoroastrian, 179
prayer leader (*imām*), 378
prayer shawl (*tallith*), 14, **14**, 105
pre-Islamic foolishness (*jāhilīyah*), 418
predestination, 249, 290, 417–18, 422–3
prejudice, in religious translation, 546
Presbyterians, 82, 288, 330; and US Civil War, 331
presence (*shekhinah*), 95
priesthood: and Luther, 282; modern Roman Catholicism, 329; and Parsis, 190
priestly law code, *Leviticus*, 30
priests: in early Judaism, 42; Jews as, 52–3; role of in Zoroastrianism, 179–80; status of, 293
primal couple, 20–1
primal man, 96, 176
principle: of common good (*maṣlaḥah*), 412; of consensus (*ijmā'*), 410; of consultation (*shūrā*), 387; of precaution (*iḥtiyāṭ*), 415
printing: Latin Bible, 281; *Qur'ān*, 372
private property: Jesus movement, 58; Mazdak, 175
process theology, 338
Proclus, 424
profession of faith (*shahādah*), 354
progeny, importance of, 53
prologue, *John*, 210
property, and Muslim women, 484
prophecy, from God, 92
prophetic revelation, and Bahā'ī, 500
prophetic tradition, 36; *ḥadīth*, 396, 407; *sunnah*, 412
Prophet's Companions, 373, 389
Prophets, 64–5
prophets, 36–8, 358, 514; Islamic, 364–7; in West

Africa, 506; Zoroaster, 157–8
prophets of power (*ulū al-ʿazm*), 364–5
Prose Edda (Snorri), 522
Proslogion (Anselm), 270
Protestant Ethic and the Spirit of Capitalism (Weber), 290–1
Protestant Reformation, 277–97
Protestants: and ecumenism, 330; and Islam in Africa, 455; missions of, 319–21; post-Tridentine era, 298; reformers, 264; versus Catholic in worship, 293
Psalm 22, and death of Jesus, 209
Psalm 100, 296–7
Psalms, 65; excerpt, 35
Psalms (*zabūr*), and Ramaḍān, 382
psalter, 296
Pseudo-Dionysius, 274
psychology, and religion, 338–9
Ptolemy, 310, 424
Ptolemy V (Egypt), 44
pulpit (*minbar*), 444
Pumbeditha, rabbinic academies in, 70
punchayet, 190
punishments: physical to fiscal, 73; under the *Qur'ān*, 406
Purification, 264; Zoroastrian fires, 181
Purim, 113
Puritanism, 290–2
purity: and community, 75–6; Pharisaic tradition, 67; rules and Christianity, 58, 76; Zoroastrian, 176–7
pyramids: Egyptian, 497; Mayan, 517
Q (gospel source), 206–11
qabḍ (depression), 436
qadar (divine decree), 423
Qadarīyah, 423
al-Qāhir (the conqueror), 397
Qairiwiyīn Mosque, fountain, **446**
Qalandar *darwīshes* (dervishes), 441, 463
al-Qānūn fī al-Ṭibb (Ibn Sīnā), 426
Qarmatians, 434
Qayrawān, and Arab-Islamic culture, 452
qiblah (direction of prayer), 360, 444
Qisseh-e Sanjan (Story of Sanjan), 188–9
qiyās (analogy), 409, 412, 415
Quakers, 292–3
Quetzalcoatl, 305
Quimby, Phinehas, 317
Qumran sect, 47
quorum (*minyan*), 13, 101
quotas, of Jewish immigration, 137
Qur'ān, 353, 367–73; differences among peoples, 543; Jesus in, 366; and Madinan Jews, 360; as revelation, 369–70; standardized, 392; translations, 43, 546
Quraysh tribe, 357, 360–1, 391
qurb (nearness), 437
quṭb (axis), 441
Quṭb, Sayyid, 475
Quṭb Minār (New Delhi), **462**
Rabbani, Shoghi Effendi, 502
rabbi, meaning of, 59
rabbinic Judaism, 58–80; conversion, 122
rabbinic law, and God's actions, 78
Rābiʿah al-ʿAdawīyah, 430, 433
Rabin, Yitzhak, 143
race, and politics, 331
radio: call to prayer (*adhān*), 378; and preaching, 326
Rahner, Karl, 337–8, 342, 552
rakʿahs (cycles), 380
ram's horn (*shofar*), 113
Ramaḍān, 380; fast of, 360, 382–3; Muḥammad during, 357
Rambam (R-M-B-M). *See* Maimonides, Moses
Rashi (R-Sh-Y), 72
al-Rashīd, 396
Rastafarian movement, 509
rasūl Allāh (the Messenger of God), 362
rational preference (*istiḥsān*), 412
rational sciences (*al-ʿulūm al-ʿaqlīyah*), 417
rationalism: Greek, 419; Hasidism, 100; and Khān, 473; Maimonides, 90–3; Muʿtazilī, 419–20, 424; opposition of ʿulamāʾ to, 427; and Sufism, 443
Rauschenbusch, Walter, 334
al-Rāzī, 425
Reagan, Ronald, 334
reason: and the Enlightenment, 309; and faith, Christianity, 272–3; and Islam, 92–3; and revelation, Judaism, 87–91
Rebbe (Yiddish), 100
rebirth, New Agers and Wiccans, 527
received tradition (Kabbalah), 96
recitation, *Qur'ān*, 367
Reconquista, 93

Reconstructionism, 107, 132–3
Reconstruction of Religious Thought in Islam (Iqbāl), 473
reducciones (reductions), 306
reform, of society, 331–5, 467
Reform Judaism, 17, 107–8, 110, 124–6; American, 127; and dress, 105–6; and education, 121; rabbis meeting (Pittsburgh 1885), 126; and Zionism, 135
reform movements: Muslim modernist, 470–2; Muslim pre-modernist, 468–9; Protestant, 285; of Roman Catholicism, 297–9, 329; Sufism, 443
Reformation, Protestant, 287–8
Reformed Churches, 287–8; in South Africa, 332
reincarnation, Druzes, 402
rejecter of faith (*kāfir*), 419
Relación de las cosas de Yucatán (Landa), 518
relics, 265–7; and indulgences, 279
religion: in African society, 455; Canaanite, 28; Greek, 498–9; Mesopotamian, 496; and pluralism, 342
religious, a, 251; clergy, 250
religious fraternities, 440
Religious Judgements (*Dadistan-e Dinik*) (Manushchihr), 174
religious literature: and competitive zeal, 546; Jewish, 65
religious scholars. *See* *'ulamā'*
religious school (*madrasah*), 444
Religious Society of Friends, 292
reliquaries. *See* relics
Rembe, 505
remediation (*takkanah*), 74, 84–5
remembrance of God, mysticism, 430
renewers (*mujaddids*), 467
Reorganized Church of Latter-Day Saints, 319
repentance (*tawbah*), 76–8, 436
repression, of Chinese Muslims, 459
requiem mass, choral, 299
responsa: literature, 72; of Maimonides, 89
Restoration of Charles II, 291
resurrection: Christianity, *see* Easter; Judaism, 53–5
retaliation, and Islamic law, 405
returners (Dönmeh), 99
Reuchlin, Johann, 289
revāyet literature, 186
revelation, *Qur'ān* as, 366–7, 369–70
revivalism: Christian, 326; Islamic, 469, 475–80; phenomenon of, 314; Wahhābī, 468–9
Revivification of the Religious Sciences (*Iḥyā' 'ulūm al-dīn*) (al-Ghazālī), 421, 436
revolt, against Rome, 51, 250
revolution: Islamic in Iran, 186–7, 400, 477–80; secular in Turkey, 474
rewards-and-punishments theology, 31, 534
Reza Shah, 186
Rhazes. *See* al-Rāzī
ribāṭ (military Ṣūfī fraternity), 444
Ricci, Matteo, 302–3
Richard I (Lion-hearted), 257
Riḍā, Muḥammad Rashīd, 476
riḍā (contentment), 436
righteous, and resurrection, 53–5
righteousness, and the *Qur'ān*, 375
righteous person: *muḥsin*, 376; *tsaddik*, 100
Righteous Teacher (Essenes), 47
right living, Islamic law, 404
rights of women, 485
Rio de Janeiro, 508
Risālat al-tawḥīd (The Message of Divine Oneness), 423
Rishonim (the earlier) commentators, 121
rites: of atonement, 76–7; of baptism, 123; of worship, 355
rites of passage, 117–20; Bar Mitzvah, 13–15; Zoroastrian, 182–3
ritual bathhouse (*mikveh*), 76
ritual life: Israelite, 27; Jewish, 69
ritual prostitution, 28
rituals, 115; in African religion, 503–7; ancestor worship, 303; Avestan and Vedic sacrifices, 161–2; baptism, 220; of Christian worship, 219; of counter- clockwise circumambulation (*ṭawāf*), 384–5; dance of death, 269; divination, 496; of the Druids, 523; Eucharist, 199, 220; of the *ḥajj* pilgrimage, 383–5; honouring Confucius, 303; immersion (*tevilah*), 122– 3; of Native Americans, 513; Passover, 115; of stoning, 385; Ṣūfi, 442; in the synagogue, 109–10; Voodoo, 509; washing, 378; Zoroastrian, 154, 181–3, 192
Robber Synod, 236

Robert of Molesmes, 253
rock carvings, 522
Rom und Jerusalem (Rome and Jerusalem) (Hess), 134
Roman Catholic Church, 221, 234, 246; birth control, 329, 341; celibacy and, 255; and Chalcedon formula, 236; and ecumenism, 330; interfaith dialogue, 481; in Latin America, 307; and Luther, 280; mass, 220; in North America, 307; Protestant break with, 293–7; and Voodoo, 509; and women, 340
Roman centurion, 205, 207
Roman Empire: Christianity in, 69, 544; and Jews, 59; religious options in, 543
Roman gods, and Greek gods, 541
Rome: bishop of, 247–8; and Constantinople, 246–7; patriarchs of, 217; versus Parthia, 170
Roncalli, Angelo Giuseppe (Pope John XXIII), 328
rosary, 264
Rosencreutz, Christian, 497
Rosenstock-Huessy, Eugen, 130
Rosenzweig, Franz, 130–1
Rosh Hashanah (New Year), 112
Rosicrucians, 497
Ross, Alexander, 546–7
rostrum (*bēma*), 62
Rubianus, Crotus, 279–80
Rūdakī, 456
ruhbān (monks), 444
Rule of St Augustine, 253–4
Rule of St Basil, 219, 250
Rule of St Benedict, 250–1
rules of purity, Pharisees, 49, 60
Rūmī, Jalāl al-Dīn, 439–41, 443, 473
Rumūz-i bīhkūdī (The Mysteries of Selflessness) (Iqbāl), 474
Rushdie, Salman, 553
Russell, Charles Taze, 317
Russian Orthodoxy, 244
Russian settlers, in North America, 308
Ruth, and conversion, 41–2
Ruysbroeck, Jan van, 274

Saadia, 87
Sabbatai Zvi, 57, 86, 99; Sabbatianism, 123
Sabbath, 18–19, 32; for Jews, 13, 15, 107–9; law, 67; regulations and Israelis, 141
Sabbath Blessings, for Reading the Torah Scroll, 102
sabbatical year, and money transactions, 74
ṣabr (patience), 375, 378, 436
sacrament, concept of, 221
sacred place (*ḥaram*), 355
sacrifice. *See* animal sacrifice; child sacrifice; human sacrifice
ṣadaqah (almsgiving), 381, 406
Sadat, Anwar, 477
Sadducees, 48
Saemundir the Wise, 522
Safed, 98
al-Saffāḥ (the bloodletter), 395
Sahagún, Bernardino de, 305, 517
Sahak, 238
ṣaḥīḥ (sound), 407
Ṣaḥīh al-Bukhārī, 408
Ṣaḥīḥ Muslim, 408
ṣaḥw (sobriety), 436
St Paul's cathedral (London, England), **228**
St Peter's basilica (Rome), **248**, 279
la Sainte Chappelle, 267
la Sainte Chemise, 266
le Saint Prépuce, 266
saints, 262–3; *awliyā'*, 439; *sint*, 508; title, 217
salafīs, 474
Salāḥ al-Dīn (Saladin), 89, 257
salām (peace), 353
Salamis, 167
ṣalāt prayers, 378–80
Salem, Massachusetts, 269
Ṣāliḥ, 364
sālik (traveller), 436
Salmān the Persian, 361
salvation: in Islam, 385; John's agenda, 211; through faith, 213
Salvation Army, 331
samā' (hearing), 442–3
ṣamad, 374
Sāmānid dynasty, 456
Samaria, 29, 206
Samaritans, 46–7
Samarqand, 456
Samhain (Samuin) festival, 523
sanctuaries, 229
Sanhedrin, 48, 125
Sanjan (Gujarat), Zoroastrians, 188
Santa Claus, 200
al-Sanūsī, Muḥammad b. 'Alī, 444, 469
Saoshyant, 176
Sarah, 33
Sasanian era, 153, 162, 172–5; Persians, 235; and Zoroastrianism, 544
Satan, 267–8; and dualism, 536
'Āl Sa'ūd, Muḥammad, 468

Saudi Arabia, Wahhābī state, 468
Saul, 28
Sault Ste Marie, 308
sayyid (chief), 387; class, 462
Scandinavia: Lutheran, 284; pagan, 522
Schall von Bell, Adam, 303
Schechter, Solomon, 128
Schleiermacher, Friedrich, 312
Schmidt, Wilhelm, 536
Schneerson, Menachem (Rabbi), 101
Scholastica, 251
scholasticism, 269–71
schools, Jewish day, 121
science: and Islam, 471; and religion, 93, 310–11
Science and Health (Eddy), 317
Science of Judaism (*Jüdische Wissenschaft*) movement, 126–8
Scivias (Hildegard of Bingen), 277
Scopes, John T., 325
scribes of revelation, 368
scripturalists (Karaites), 71
scripture: Jewish, 645; Matthew and, 208–9. *See also Avesta*, Bible, canon, *Qur'ān*
Sea Woman, 511
second commonwealth, 40–2
Second World War: Jewish deaths in, 138
Secretariat for the Promotion of Christian Unity, 330
secret knowledge, and Gnostics, 215
secret societies, Ismā'īlī movement, 402
sectarianism, 46–51; and rabbinic Judaism, 59–60
sects: antinomian, 403; delegationist, 403; Druzes, 402; Shī'ī, 394, 400–2
secular clergy, 250
secularism, 309–10, 549; and Christmas, 200; and Sufism, 443; twentieth-century Islamic, 474–5
seder, 115, **117**
sedition (*fitnah*), 389, 418
Sedna, 511
sees, in the Roman Empire, 217
Sefer Emunoth veDeoth (*The Book of Beliefs and Opinions*) (Saadia), 87
Sefer ha-Razzim (Book of Mysteries), 102
sefer Torah (book of the Torah), 70
Segundo, Juan Luis, 336
Seleucia-Ctesiphon, 235
Seleucid dynasty, 44
Seljuqs, 440, 456, 457
Seneca nation, 513
Separatists, of Plymouth, 291
separatists (Mu'tazilah), 419
Sephardim, 80–1
Septuagint Bible, 43, 65
sermon (*khuṭbah*), 444
Sermon on the Mount, 204–6
seven, idea of: Amesha Spentas, 178. *See also* Sabbath
Seven Deadly Sins, 269
Sevener Shi'ism, 401–2
Seventh-Day Adventists, 316
sexual intercourse: and mysticism, 97; and purity laws, 76; and washing, 378
sexual rituals: Canaan, 52; fertility, 37
Seymour, William J., 315
al-Shāfi'ī, Muḥammad b. Idrīs, 371, 412
Shāfi'ī law, 401, 412–13, 466
Shahādah, 377
shahādah (profession of faith), 354, 376–7
Shāh Nāmeh (Book of Kings) (Ferdowsī), 186, 189
shamanism: in Africa, 504; Inuit, 510–11; Native American, 513; Siberian, 159; and Ṣūfī orders, 443
Shamash (god of wisdom), 24
Shammai, 67
Shams of Tabriz, 439
Shango (Xango), 508
Shapur I, 173
sharī'ah: approaches to, 415; divine law, 405; interpretations of, 403, 413; law, 377, 469, 478; meaning of, 416; sacred law, 364–5, 409
shaṭaḥāt (fantastic utterances), 434
Shavuoth (Pentecost), 116, 121, 212, 223
Shayast Ne-Shayast (Do's and Don'ts), 174
al-Shaybānī, 412
shaykh al-ishrāq (master of illumination), 437
al-Shaykh al-Ṣadūq (the truthful *shaykh*), 415
Shaykhīs (Arabia), 404
shaykhs: chief, 387; head of the order, 440; master, 435; of Ṣūfī orders, 441–2
Sheba, queen of, 29, 82
shefa (effulgence), 97
shekhinah (presence), 95, 97–8
Shema, creed of Judaism, 51, 106
Shembe, Isaiah, 505–6
Sheol, 53
Sheshbazzar. *See* Sin-Ab-Usuru
Shī'ī theosophy, 438

shield of David (*Magen David*), 62
al-Shifā' (The Book of Healing) (Ibn Sīnā), 426
Shi'ism, 390, 398–404 doctrine of the imamate, 418; in India, 461; Ja'farī law, 414–15; line from the Prophet, 397; mullahs, 479; in North Africa, 452; opposition to the Umayyads, 393; pilgrimages, 385; schism in, 391; secularism in Iran, 479
Shikand-Gumānīk-Vichār (The Decisive Resolution of Doubts) (Mardan- Farrokh), 174, 548
shirk (associating), 374
shittuf (associationism), 79
Shiur Koma literature, 95
Shiva (sitting), 120
Shlomo ben Yitzhak, Rabbi. *See* Rashi
shofar (ram's horn), 110, 113
shofetim (judges), 28
shrines, of the *imāms*, 385
Shrove Tuesday, 222
shtetl (little town), 136
Shu'ayb (Jethro), 364
shukr (gratitude), 436
Shulhan Arukh (Spread Table) (Karo), 73
shūrā (principle of consultation), 387
Siberia, native peoples of, 245
Sifra, *Leviticus*, 66
Sifre, *Numbers* and *Deuteronomy*, 66
Sikh tradition, 464; monotheism, 532
silence, practice of, 253
silsilah (chain of initiation), 440–1
Simeon, and infant Jesus, 207
Simeon, the Stylite, 218
Simeon bar Yohai (Rabbi), 96
Simmel, Georg, 131
Simon, 50
Simons, Menno, 289
Simos, Miriam (Starhawk), 525
sin: and Adam, 363; and God, 374; Latin Christianity, 269; and redemption, 280; and repentance, 77–8
Sin-Ab-Usuru (Sheshbazzar), 41
Sinai, law at, 30
sinfulness, 290; Paul, 211
sint (saints), 508
Sirhindī, Aḥmad, 472
Sirozah, 164
Sitting Bull, 514
Six-Day War (1967), 135, 334, 477
Sixteen Revelations of Divine Love (Julian of Norwich), 277
skullcap, 105–6
sky burial, in Tibet, 184
slave traders: in Africa, 455, 505–7; and missionary activity, 546
slavery: in the American South, 313; in ancient society, 35; in Brazil, 507; and Britain, 320; Muslim, 481–2; in the US, 331
Slavic Christianity, 244–7; in the Balkans, 245
Smith, Joseph, Jr, 318
Smith, Wilfred Cantwell, 343
Smolenskin, Peretz, 134
Snorri Sturluson, 522
social classes of Judea, 43
social contract, covenant as, 30
social custom: and the Makkans, 358–9; medieval Jewish, 84–7
social gospel movement, 334
socialism, in Europe, 334; of Mazdak, 174–5
social justice, 330
society: Israelite, 32–6; Qur'anic principles for, 406–7; reform of, 331–5; and religion, 200
Society of Jesus, 299
Socinianism, 289
Socrates, 550
solar calendar, 222; Zoroastrian, 182
Solomon, 28–9, 82, 533; temple of, 38
soma/haoma (sacred intoxicant), 162
Son of Man, 95
soothsayer (*kāhin*), 358
sorcery, Inca culture, 520
soul (*urvan*), 183
souls, of hunted creatures, 510
South Africa, 331–2
South Asia, spread of Islam, 459–65
Southeast Asia, spread of Islam, 465–7
Southeast Woodlands culture, 511
Southern Christian Leadership Conference, 331
Sozzini, Fausto, 289
Spain: conquest of Mesoamerica, 517; Islamic conquest of, 452–4; Jews in, 80, 82, 93; mystical tradition, 438; Umayyad caliphate, 397
Spanish Inquisition. *See* Inquisition
speaking in tongues, 315
speculative theology (*kalām*), 423
speech (*kalām*) of God, *Qur'ān* as, 417

Spener, Philipp Jakob, 313
spherot (emanations), 96; feminine gender of, 97
Spinoza, Baruch, 123
spirit (*fravashi*), 183
spirit and matter, 249; and Gnosticism, 215–16
spirits, and Inuit shamans, 510–11
Spiritual Exercises (Ignatius), 300
spirituality, Christian, 274
Spread Table (*Shulhan Arukh*) (Karo), 73
Sprenger, Johann, 268
spring equinox, 182
Sraosha, 178
stability, in monastic communities, 250, 254
stained-glass windows, 259–62
Starhawk (Miriam Simos), 525
Star of David, 62
Star of Redemption (*Der Stern der Erlösung*) (Rosenzweig), 130–1
state: Church of England, 286; and Jehovah's Witnesses, 317; Lutheran Christianity, 283; as officially Christian, 227; under Abd al-Malik b. Marwān, 392
statehood: Jewish, 134; Pakistan, 473
state religion: Christianity in fourth century, 544; Imāmī Shi'ism in Iran, 404
states, mystical, 433, 436–7
stations of the cross, 261
Stephen (apostle), 214
Der Stern der Erlösung (The Star of Redemption) (Rosenzweig), 130–1
stewardship (*khilāfah*) of Adam, 388
Stewart, William and Milton, 325
Stone, Barton, 316
Stonehenge, 521, **521**
strict constructionists, Sadducees as, 48
struggle. *See jihād*
Struggle with evil (*Bundahishn*), 176–7
Student Christian Movement, 330
Student Volunteer Movement, 321
study, in the Jewish tradition, 122
stylites, 218
Ṣubḥ-i Azal. *See* Nūrī, Mīrzā Yaḥyā
submission (*islām*), 422
succession, and death of Muḥammad, 386–7
Sudan: conflict in, 478; and Mahdīyah, 469
sudreh, 183, 184
ṣūf (wool), 429
The Sufficient (*al-Kāfi*), 414
Ṣūfī: brotherhoods, 440, 463; *ḥadīth qudsī* literature, 408; *jihād* movements, 469; orders (*ṭarīqahs*), 440, 443, 452, 466
Sufism, 96, 429–32 and 'Abduh, 471; crystallization of, 435–6; decline of, 443–4; in India, 461, 464; and spread of Islam, 545
ṣuḥbah (friendship), 440
Suhrawardī, Shihāb al-Dīn, 437–8
suicide, and the psychology of martyrdom, 554
sukkah, 112
Sukkoth festival, 41, 63, 113
sukr (intoxication), 435–6
ṣulḥ (sphere of peace), 449
sulṭāns, 457; in Southeast Asia, 466
Summa Theologiae (Summation of Theology) (Thomas Aquinas), 272–3
sun: in art, 172; as halo, 240; worship under Constantine, 226
Sunan, 408
sunnah (life-example), 360, 366; Prophetic tradition, 371–2, 412; for Twelver Shī'ī Muslims, 403
Sunnī tradition, 390–1, 395, 397, 398; *ḥadīth* tradition, 405, 408; Ibn Rushd, 428; schools, 371, 412–13
supernatural, in African religion, 503–7
Supreme Caliphate, treatise on, 476–7
Sura, rabbinic academies in, 70
Sūrah of Divine Oneness (*tawḥīd*), 374
Sūrah of Sincere Faith (*ikhlāṣ*), 373
sūrahs (chapters), of the *Qur'ān*, 367, 372–4
Susa, 166
Swahili: and Arabic vocabulary, 455; language, 505
sweat lodge ceremony, 513, 517
Swedenborg, Emanuel, 527
Swiss Reformation, 287
symbolism: in apocalyptic literature, 53; religious, 339
symbols: Christian, 226, 229–30; and saints, 263; Zoroastrian, 184–5
Symposium (Plato), 66
synagogues, 38, 60–4; Bar

Mitzvah celebrations, 15; in Dublin, **111**; groupings of, 17; and music, 109–11
syncretism, 541; in Latin America, 307
synoptic gospels, 210; Passover supper in, 220
Syria, Aramaic alphabet, 162
Syriac language, 235
Syrian Orthodox Church, 237, 301

taboos, 75; incest, 511
tabulae rasae (empty slates), 92
Tacitus, 523
tafsīr (commentary), 373
tajallī (manifestation), 438
Taj Mahal, **445**
takkanah (remediation), 74, 84–5
Ṭalḥah, 390
tallith (prayer shawl), 14, **14**, 105–6
Talmud, 68–71; in education, 121; as *halakha*, 70; writing of, 40
Talmudic reasoning, contemporary, 72
tan dorosti (be well), 179
Tan Dorosti (prayer), 179
Tanakh (T-N-K), 65, 70
Tania (As It Is Taught) (Zalman), 101
Tannaim, 68, 72
Tansar, 173
Taq-e Bostan, 171, 185
taqlīd (imitation), 415, 472
Targum, 110
Ṭāriq b. Ziyād, 451
tarīqahs (Ṣūfī orders), 440
taṣawwuf (Sufism), 429
Tauler, Johann, 268
ṭawāf (circumambulation), 384–5
tawakkul (trust), 436
tawbah (repentance), 436
tawḥīd: God's oneness, 374, 419
tax revenues, church in Germany, 283
Teacher of Righteousness (Essenes), 47
techina (devotional prayer) for women, 86
technology, and Inuit, 510. *See also* printing, radio, television
tefillin, 106
televangelists, 326
television, call to prayer (*adhān*), 378
temperance movements, Protestant, 334
Templars, and Ṣūfī *ribāṭ*, 444
temples, and congregational life, 38; Reform Jews, 126
Ten Commandments, 27, 30, 33, 79
ten lost tribes of Israel, 82
Tenochtitlán, 519
Tenth of Muḥarram, 399–400
Teotihuacán, 518
Teresa of Ávila, 276–7, 340
Tertullian, 225, 337
teshuvah (repentance), 72, 76
Tetzel, Johann, 279
Teutonic order, 253
tevilah (ritual immersion), 122
Texas Christian University, 316
Thaddeus, 238
Thamūd tribe, 364
thanksgiving: eucharist, 220; *jashan* ceremonies, 191
Thannie, Grace, 507
theism, 535
theistic mysticism, 430
theocracy, 359, 478, 543
theodicy, 313
Theodore of Mopsuestia, 234
Theodore of Studios, 250
Theodoric, 270
Theodosius I, 227, 233
Theodosius II, 69, 235–6
the Theologian, Gregory of Nazianzus, 242
theology: Byzantine, 241–2; Christians and Islam, 417; commitment-based, 312–13; of difference, 541; early Christian, 210, 214–16; *'ilm al-kalām*, 417; Islamic, 374, 417–18, 423; in the Latin Church, 247–50; and study of religion, 4; twentieth-century, 130–3, 337–8
theopathic utterances, 434
Theophrastus, 44
theory: of emanationism, 426; of evolution, 321; of Islamic civilization, 473; of occasionalism, 422, 427; of stations and states, 433, 436–7; of two swords, 255
Theosophical movement, 527
theosophy: Shaykhīs, 404; Sufism, 437–8
theotokos (bearer of God), 234, 264
Thermopylae, 167
theurgic journey, 95
Third World peoples, Adventist, 316
Thirty Years' War, 300
Thomas, 238
Thomas Aquinas, 93, 254, 272–3, 328
Thor, Scandinavian god, 522
Throne verse, 430

Thus Zoroaster Spoke (Nietzche), 155
Tiamat, 495
Tibet, sky burial in, 184
ti bonanj (little good angel), 509
Tiferet (beauty), 97
al-Tijānī, Abū al-'Abbās Aḥmad, 444
Tikal (Guatemala), pyramid, 517
tikkun (rectification), 98
Tillich, Paul, 337–8
Time (Zurvan), 174
Timur (Tamerlane), 235
Tiridates III, 238
al-Tirmidhī, 408
tithing: obligations, 75; Pharisaic tradition, 49, 67
Tokugawa government, 302
Toltecs, 518
Tonantzin, 307
tongue speaking, 315
Torah, 14–15, 17, 70–1 classic rabbinic interpretation of, 79; and the Gospel of Jesus, 364; oral, 70; and *pesher*, 47; and Ramaḍān, 382; writing of, 42
Torah scrolls, 61; Cape Town, **71**
Toronto, Parsis in, 191–2
Tosafot (additions), 72, 121
Tosefta (addition), 68, 72
Totem poles, **515**
tourism, pilgrimage as, 266
tower of silence (*dakhma*), 184, 190
towns, religious orders in, 253
Toyotomi, Hideyoshi, 302
trade, 357; Arabian, 356–7, 393; and Chinese Muslim community, 458; Sasanians, 172; and spread of Islam, 455; Yemeni into Malay region, 465
traditionists (*ahl al-ḥadīth*), 472
trance, spirit possession, 508
Transcendentalism, 527
transept, 229
transubstantiation, doctrine of, 298, 328
Trappists, 253
traveller (*sālik*), 436
Tree of the Knowledge of Good and Evil, 20
tribal council, and successor to Muḥammad, 387–8
tribal societies: ancestor veneration, 540; and missionary efforts, 545; polytheism in, 536; solidarity in, 356–7
Tridentine formulations, 297
Trinity, 231–4; doctrine of, 211, 232, 317, 419; Mu'tazilism, 419; and Unitarianism, 289
Trojan War, 158
truce, of Ḥudaybīyah, 362
True Cross, relics from, 266
trup (tropes), 110
truth: 'I am the', 434; of myth, 22, 498–9
Trypho, 550
tsaddik (righteous person), 100
tsimtsum, 98
Turkey: and spread of Islam, 457–8; westernization of, 474–5
al-Ṭūsī, Abū Ja'far, 415
Twelfth Fundamental Principle of Faith (Maimonides), 90
Twelver Shi'ism, 402–3, 414, 455; and Bahā'ī, 500; and divine unity and justice, 420; in Iran, 479; legal school, 405, 414–15
Übermensch (superior being), 135
Udvada, fire in, 181
Uḥud, Muslim defeat at, 361
'ulamā' (religio-legal scholars), 404, 427, 462; and al-Ḥallāj, 434–5; and secular authorities, 479; Sunnī theology, 420
Ulfilas, 234
ulū al-'azm (prophets of power), 364
al-'ulūm al-'aqlīyah (rational sciences), 417
al-'ulūm al-naqlīyah (transmitted sciences), 417
'Umar b. 'Abd al-'Azīz, 432
'Umar b. al-Fāriḍ, 439
'Umar b. al-Khaṭṭāb, 359, 387–92
Umayyad: armies, 459; caliphate, 432, 453; dynasty, 392–3, 418; end of, 395; Mosque (Damascus), 392
Umbanda community (Rio de Janeiro), 508
ummah (community), 362, 368, 375, 471; and non-Muslims, 377
'umrah (lesser *ḥajj*), 384
unbelief (*kufr*), 390
understanding, goal of dialogue, 552–3
Uniate churches, 246–7
Unification Church (Moonies), 554–5
Union of Brest-Litovsk, 246
Union Oil Company of California, 325
Unitarianism, 289–90
United Brethren, 330
United Church of Canada, 330, 343

United Church of Christ, 330
United Reformed Church, 330
United States, Jews in, 136
Uniting Church, 330
unity of being (*waḥdat al-wujūd*), 438
Unity Church, 527
Universal House of Justice, 502
universalism, 78–80
Universalists, 290
universal salvation, 342
unlawful (*ḥarām*), 416
uns (happiness), 437
Urban II (pope), 257
Urdu language, 463
Urschel (Teutonic moon goddess), 263
Der Ursprung der Gottesidee (The Origin of the Idea of God) (Schmidt), 536
St Ursula, 263
Ursulines, 300
urvan (soul), 183
al-'Urwah al-Wuthqā, 471
Usman ('Uthmān) dan Fodio, 469
uṣūl al-dīn (fundamentals of the religion), 417
usury, and the *Qur'ān*, 406
Utah, Mormons in, 319
'Uthmān b. 'Affān, 359, 372, 389, 391, 418
Utnapishtim, 323
al-'Uzzah, 355

Valerian (emperor), 173, 225
Valhalla, 522
Valiente, Doreen, 524
Valignano, Alessandro, 302
Vargas, Getúlio, 508
Vatican Council I, 327–8
Vatican Council II, 265, 328–9, 331
Vedas, 154, 161
vegetarian diets, 526
veiling of women (*hijāb*), 485
Vendidad, 163–4
veneration: of icons, 240–2; of Mary, 234–5; of Ṣūfī saints, 441
venial sins, 269
Venice, crusades and trade, 257–8
Verbiest, Ferdinand, 303
Verse Edda (Saemundir), 522
via negativa (negative way), 271
vicegerent (*waṣī*), 402
Videvdat (law against the demons), 163
Views of the People of the Virtuous City (al-Fārābī), 425
vigil after death, 183
Vilna edition, *Talmud*, 69
violence, of the Wahhābīs, 468
Viracocha, Inca god, 519–20
Viraf, journeys, 174
virgin birth, doctrine, 208
Virgin of Guadalupe, 307
vision quest, 513, 517
Visparad, 164
vital urge (*élan vital*), 473
Vladimir, 244
volcano goddess (Pele), 539
Voodoo, 508

wa'd (God's promise), 419
wa'īd (God's threat), 419
Wacha, Dinsha, 190
waḥdat al-wujūd (unity of being), 438
Wahhābī movement, 466, 468; and Sufism, 443
walāyah (saintship), 441
walāyat al-faqīh (guardianship of the jurist), 477, 479
walī (Master), 402, 441
Walī Allāh, Shāh, 472
Walker Lake, Nevada, 514
walking, on the Sabbath, 109
wandering dervishes, 441
war, and American Christians, 335
War of the Camel, 390
war, Jewish (66–73), 59
Waraqah b. Nawfal, 358
Warren, Max, 321
wars of apostasy, 372, 387–8
warships, 392–3
washing, Muslim ritual, 378
waṣī (vicegerent), 402
Watchtower, 317
Watts, Isaac, 296
wealth: of monastic institutions, 252; patronage, 61
Webb, Muḥammad Alexander, 482
Weber, Max, 290–1
weddings, Jewish, 143–4; Zoroastrian, 182–3
welfare tax, *zakāt* as, 381, 406
Wellhausen, Julius, 30, 32
well of Zamzam, 384
Wells cathedral, 259; double arch, **261**
Wesley, John and Charles, 313–14
West Africa: religion in, 506–7; and spread of Islam, 454–6
West Bank, Samaritans in, 46
Western Christendom, Muslim interaction with, 464, 467, 480–1, 485
Westminster Abbey, **258**
Westminster Confession, 291
Whirling Dervishes, 443
White, Ellen, 316
White, James, 316
Whitefield, George, 313–14
White Friars, 255

White Goddess (Graves), 524
Whitehead, Alfred North, 338
Whitsunday, 223
Wicca, 524–5, 527
Wiesel, Elie, 138–9
will: *thelēma*, 239. *See also* Augustine, free will
William the Pious (Duke of Aquitaine), 252
Williams, Roger, 292
Wilson, Jack, 514
Wilson, John A., 533
Wilson, Lois, 340
wine drinking, and Ṣūfīs, 443
wisdom: Ḥokhma, 101; *Qur'ān* as, 369
witchcraft, 268–9; in Africa, 504; and the Deima Church, 507; revival of, 523–5; trials, 269
without asking how (*bilā kayf*), 421
without end (En Sof), 96
Wodziwob (Paiute Indian), 514
Wolff, Christian, 538
women: in biblical period, 32–4; devotional prayer for, 86; in early Christianity, 217; and Eastern Orthodox Christianity, 340; in Hellenistic world, 43–4; and Islam, 483–5; in Judaism, 41, 61, 84, 86–7, 106; as Lutheran priests, 283; in menstruation, 381; modern roles for, 339–41; mystics, 275–7, 433; and New Age religion, 527; rights of, 485; in Roman Catholicism, 254, 300; in Zoroastrianism, 177, 193. *See also* feminism
Woodstock, 526
Woodsworth, James S., 334
Word of God, 370
Word (*logos*), 234; significance of, 210
work, and Sabbath restrictions, 108–9
works, and faith, 280
World Council of Churches, 330, 340 conference (1970), 552; interfaith dialogue, 481
World's Parliament of Religions: (Chicago 1893), 502, 551; (Centennial, 1993), 524, 551
Worms, diet at, 279–81
worship: early Christian, 219–21; in the Greek church, 242–4; Islamic, 376–7; Protestant, 293–7; *Yasna*, 163
worshipful beings (*yazatas*), 168
Wounded Knee (South Dakota), massacre at, 514
Wovoka, 514
writing: ancient, 323; as symbol system, 494
Writings, in Hebrew canon, 65
Wuḍū' (making pure or radiant), 378
wuqūf (standing), 384
Wyclif, John, 279

Xango (Shango), 508
Xavier, Francis, 300–1
Xerxes, 168
Xi'an, 235
Xinjiang, Muslims of, 459

Yahb-allaha, 235
Yahweh, 22, 26, 30, 533–5
Yahwist (J), 31
Yale University, 224, 292
yarmulke (cap), 105
Yashts: hymns, 163; religion of the Magians, 168
Yasna (worship), 155–6, 163–4
Yatha ahu vairyo, 179
Yathrib, tribes in, 359
Yavneh, 59, 65
yazatas (worshipful beings), 168, 170, 178
Yazd, *atesh Behram*, 181
Yazdegerd III, 174, 188
Yazīd (caliph), 393
year: of the *hijrah* (AH), 359; Jewish, 112; of Yazdegerd, 174
yehudi (a Judean), 41
Yemen, 410; Zaydī school, 401
Yemenite chant, 110
Yemenite rabbi, **103**
Yenhe Hatam, 179
yeshiva, 59, 121
yesod (foundation), 97
YHWH (divine name), 26
yibum (levirate marriage), 85
Yiddish, 100
Yisroel Mensch (humane member of Israel), 129
Yochanan ben Zakkai, 59, 109
Yom Kippur (Day of Atonement), 41, 77, 113, 360; fast of, 382; war on, 135
York Minster (York, England), **260**, **262**
Yoruba people, 507–8
Young, Brigham, 319
Younger Avesta, 158
Yucatan, 517

zabūr (*Psalms*), and Ramaḍān, 382
Zaehner, R.C., 6
Ẓāhirī school, 413

zakāt alms, 376–7, 381–2, 406
nomadic tribes, 387
Zalman, Shneur, 100–1
Zamzam, well of, 384
Zand (commentary on Avestan texts), 174
zanj (angels), 509
Zarathushtra, 153, 155–60, 493
Zartoshtis, 153, 186, 192
zāwiyahs, 440, 452
Zayd b. Ḥārithah, 359
Zaydīs, 400–1 and divine unity and justice, 420
Zayn al-ʿĀbidīn, 394
Zealots, 50–1, 212, 554
Zechariah, visions in, 53
Zend-Avesta, 165
Zen *koan*, 100
Zeno (emperor), 236
Zenobia (queen), 233
Zeraʿim (Seeds), agricultural laws, 104
Zerubbabel, 41
Zia-ul-Haq, Muḥammad, 478
Zinzendorf und Pottendorf, Nikolaus Ludwig von, 313
Zion, 28
Zion's Watch Tower and Herald of Christ's Presence, 317
Zionism, 133–6; Martin Buber, 132
Zohar, 96–8
Zoroaster, 153; in Greek and Latin writers, 169; legends of, 160
Zoroaster: Politician or Witch Doctor? (Henning), 159
Zoroastrianism, 493; apologetic works, 548; dualism of, 52; and Islam, 187, 417; monotheistic, 532; and morality, 175; Sasanian dynasty, 538, 544; spheres of influence, *171*; state religion, 173
al-Zubayr, 390
zuhhād, 432
Zulu tradition, 505–6
Zunz, Leopold, 127
Zurvan (Time), controversy, 174
Zwingli, Huldrych (Ulrich), 282–3, 287–8; and Eucharist, 294